Best Chinese Stories
(1949 - 1989)

Panda Books

Panda Books
First Edition 1989
Copyright 1989 by CHINESE LITERATURE PRESS
ISBN 0-8351-2066-X
ISBN 7-5071-0041-3/I.35

Published by CHINESE LITERATURE PRESS, Beijing (37), China
Distributed by China International Book Trading Corporation
(GUOJI SHUDIAN), P.O. Box 399, Beijing, China
Printed in the People's Republic of China

CONTENTS

Preface — *Li Ziyun* — 1
Recollections of the Hill Country — *Sun Li* — 9
The Girl from Mengbie — *Yang Zhao* and *Bai Honghu* — 15
The Election — *Li Guowen* — 24
The Family on the Other Side of the Mountain — *Zhou Libo* — 37
Lilies — *Ru Zhijuan* — 44
Seven Matches — *Wang Yuanjian* — 51
My First Superior — *Ma Feng* — 55
Temper Yourself — *Zhao Shuli* — 68
The Story of Old Xing and His Dog — *Zhang Xianliang* — 88
The General and the Small Town — *Chen Shixu* — 107
The Man from a Pedlars' Family — *Lu Wenfu* — 119
A Corner Forsaken by Love — *Zhang Xuan* — 133
Kite Streamers — *Wang Meng* — 150
Chen Huansheng's Adventure in Town — *Gao Xiaosheng* — 168
Pages from a Factory Secretary's Diary — *Jiang Zilong* — 176
Lulu — *Zong Pu* — 193
The Story of a Living Buddha — *Malqinhu* — 206
The Log Cabin Overgrown with Creepers — *Gu Hua* — 215
Daft Second Uncle — *Su Shuyang* — 238
A Tale of Big Nur — *Wang Zengqi* — 244
The Destination — *Wang Anyi* — 257
Eight Hundred Metres Below — *Sun Shaoshan* — 276
The Seven-Tined Stag — *Wure'ertu* — 288
Black Walls — *Liu Xinwu* — 298
The Tall Woman and Her Short Husband — *Feng Jicai* — 306
Ah, Fragrant Snow — *Tie Ning* — 315
A Land of Wonder and Mystery — *Liang Xiaosheng* — 325
Han the Forger — *Deng Youmei* — 346

My Faraway Qingpingwan — *Shi Tiesheng*	356
An Encounter in Green Vine Lane — *Liu Shaotang*	370
The Last Angler — *Li Hangyu*	389
Nobby's Run of Luck — *Zhang Jie*	400
The Tavern — *Zheng Wanlong*	407
A Soul in Bondage — *Tashi Dawa*	415
Return — *Han Shaogong*	432
The Mountain Cabin — *Can Xue*	445
Touch Paper — *Jia Pingwa*	449
Hong Taitai — *Cheng Naishan*	472
Marriage of the Dead — *Li Rui*	480
Ten Years Deducted — *Shen Rong*	487

Preface

●

—— LI ZIYUN ——

THIS is an anthology of short fiction created during the first forty years of the People's Republic of China. The observant reader will notice that only eight works, or five percent of this collection, were written during the first thirty years of that period. The greater portion of the volume was created during the last decade. This disproportionate distribution is a reflection of the tragedy that befell modern Chinese literature.

Re-reading Chinese fiction created between 1949 and 1976 one finds little of true artistic worth; works that do not bear witness to some page of history or ism are all too scarce. The reason behind this phenomenon is the fact that for a long period prior to 1976, Chinese literature was given a mission for which it was not intended. After the previous regime was toppled, building a new society became the order of the day. Many strategists of the time, with only a superficial understanding of the nature of literature, recognized its power to persuade. Furthermore, they were convinced that this power of persuasion was its only function, and therefore it must become a tool for revolutionary propaganda and serve politics directly. Its artistic value was often ignored.

The problem went much deeper. The value of literature was measured against the principles and standards set by the various levels of leadership, which, in time, became policy and even law. Those who dared contradict these guidelines were severely criticized. Thus from 1949, more accurately from 1942 onwards, literature became a tool first to wrest power and then to consolidate it. The policy was that revolution must be the theme of all literature. That is, it was to sing the praises of workers, peasants and soldiers; to glorify their noble sacrifices in their struggle against those who would destroy or endanger the new political power. Naturally, the flaws of these characters could not be portrayed. The characters which appeared in the fiction of that period were either black or white. There was never any doubt as to their political affiliation. There were no grey areas, and characters which might be ambiguous could not be central to the plot.

Intellectuals were considered unreliable and ostracized. Writers who did not conform to these dictums were punished in varying degrees. The acceptable themes for literature had become very narrow. The writer's reaction to certain social conditions and people could not be freely portrayed according to his observation, understanding and judgement. The result was that works were stereotyped, and lifeless.

In 1956 there was a brief thaw. Some young writers published poetry and fiction in which they expressed real emotion. Inevitably there was some expression of their dissatisfaction with certain policies. This indirectly led to the well-known anti-rightist movement. No writer who had expressed these sentiments was spared the "rightist" label. Thereafter, they were forbidden to write. From then on seldom was anything published that did not deal with the struggle against the phantom enemies of class struggle. Therefore, the "cultural revolution" that began in 1966 was not an isolated or spontaneous happening. It was the result of a carefully choreographed policy of thought control based on the principle of class struggle. It has been universally recognised that literature was devastated by the "cultural revolution".

The eight works written before 1976 in this anthology were created under those adverse conditions. Nevertheless, they represent a variety of forms. For instance, Zhao Shuli's "Temper Yourself" was an approved work of the time. Zhao Shuli spent much of his life in a rural area, and wrote about rural life. What distinguishes his writing from the run-of-the-mill works of the time are his characters. There are few heroes. Most of his characters are what were considered "middle characters" or even backward people. Although he was mentioned peripherally in critiques of the "middle characters", his work was never censored. This was due to the writer's treatment of his subject. His clever satirization of certain practices was construed as a criticism of backwardness among the rural population. Thus it was seen to support current government policy.

The fate of Li Guowen's "The Election" was quite different. It was immediately branded as a "poisonous weed" after publication, and the writer was labelled a rightist. Although the work lacks artistic finesse, it is nevertheless fiction that takes a long hard look at certain social conditions. It is not a hymn to current policy, but an attack on corrupt practices that allow the unscrupulous to climb the ladder of authority under a mask of democracy. Of particular interest is the term "exemplar", meaning to fabricate untruthful achievements in order to please the higher-ups, which first appeared in this work and later became a part of the vernacular. Here the writer demonstrated his prescience for things to come. This work was not re-issued until 1978.

The rest belong to the "exceptional part" of the fiction written between 1949 and 1966. While they did not directly reflect any particular policy, they did express the thoughts and feelings of ordinary people caught up in the great social upheaval. They are very lyric. Although these works were considered to be outside the main stream at the time of their original publication, they managed to escape oblivion.

During the seventeen years between 1949 and 1966 a few enduring works did appear. Wang Meng's "The Young Newcomer in the Organization Department", Zong Pu's "Red Beans", and Liu Binyan's "This Agency's Report" portrayed the anxiety of young people towards certain unhealthy social phenomena, and their fear and anguish at the suppression of human emotions. Due to the length of these works, they have not been included in the present collection.

From 1976 onward Chinese literature saw many changes. These changes did not happen at once. Literature still served policies, but the nature of the politics it served showed signs of change. But changes in people's understanding of the nature and function of literature was still a few years off.

In 1976 the political life of China took a dramatic turn. The ten years of "cultural revolution" and the tyranny of the "gang of four" were over. The roots of that tragedy such as guiding ideology, political line and so forth had yet to be examined. Actually the new direction that policy would take did not begin until 1978. It is interesting to note that literature which had been subservient to those in power for so long did not play the role of guardian of the old order but became the avant-garde of change.

In April 1976, on the eve of the fall of the "gang of four", a great many poems appeared at Tiananmen Square. This was a spontaneous eruption of curses, criticisms and rebellion against the rule of the "gang of four". It was as though after a long silence, the people had finally discovered who their enemies were, and raised a cry of protest. The first weapon they had was literature. Admittedly, most of the poetry that appeared at Tiananmen Square was crude, no better than slogans, and could hardly be considered as art. But they were the voice of the people. Their effect was still propaganda, and that phenomenon continued till about 1978.

After the fall of the "gang of four" in October 1976 there was a tremendous resurgence of literary activity that was not limited to poetry, but included drama and fiction as well. The practitioners too were not only nameless poets, but well-known authors as well as new writers. However, their works as a whole were a continuation of the poetry of Tiananmen Square. They sought to condemn the "gang of four" in literary terms and to probe for the reasons behind the historic catastrophe. Their value lay in the fact that they provided grist for the politicians' mill. But as literature they were still shackled and would remain thus till 1978.

After 1978 Chinese literature began to take on new directions. Writers began to study the law of literature existing quite apart from its relations with politics. They began to expand its boundaries, search for new techniques of expression and effects. It is worth noting that at the same time literary critics expressed views along the same lines. An article entitled "In Defence of Literature" under the by-line of "our commentator" appeared in the fourth issue of *Shanghai Literature* magazine in 1978. The article pointed out that literature should not be a tool for class struggle and subservient to politics. Starting from then on, literary creation in China had taken a tentative step away from the bonds of politics, and toward the road of multi-expressionism.

Of course change cannot take place all at once. It must be attended by certain external factors, and there must be an orderly progression. As the political climate improved and writers had more freedom to create, new subjects, themes and techniques were explored. After China's long isolation, there was a tremendous influx of Western literature. This also influenced Chinese literature's rush toward multi-expressionism.

Meanwhile, some works that exposed the tyranny of the "gang of four", the so-called "Wound Literature", also tackled other issues. They expounded problems in the economy, the general condition of morality and education. An example is Liu Xinwu's "Class Teacher". This is an outstanding portrayal of the faults of an education system that has created a generation of ignorant young people unused to thinking for themselves. As the writer's horizons widened, authors turned their attention to the poor economy, and the stultifying influence of old morality on people's lives. The tragedy of the young peasant girl in Zhang Xian's "A Corner Forsaken by Love" has nothing to do with politics. Zhang Jie's "Love Must Not Be Forgotten" deals with the repressive influence of old morality. These works have gone beyond the bounds of politics.

There also appeared some works that abandoned narrative and conflict to probe the workings of the human psyche. Zong Pu's "Who Am I?" examines the final thoughts of a woman professor driven to suicide during the early years of the "cultural revolution". Wang Meng's "The Dream of the Sea" describes the confusion of an intellectual when his name is cleared after having been wronged for twenty years. Neither of these works has a recognizable plot. In them politics and social conditions serve only as a back-drop. The writer's object was to expose the inner workings of the mind. With works like these, Chinese literature finally threw off its political shackles.

At the same time half a century of Western literature began to rush in. These works with widely differing historic, social and cultural backgrounds, expressed in a variety of techniques, and artistic values, also pushed Chinese literature toward multi-expressionism.

Multi-expressionism, which began in 1980 and reached its climax in 1985, can be described as follows:

A number of middle-aged writers still clung to realism in dealing with life and society, although they expanded the boundaries of subject matter, searched for new ways of expression, and polished their style. However, their realism was no longer the "revolutionary realism" dictated by certain political figures. Their realism dealt with our changing society, and the lives and mentalities of ordinary people. Their works examined current issues and the conflicts created by social change, or expressed the feelings and desires of people from different classes or circles. Because the themes they tackled were new and complex, new techniques of expression evolved. Today's realism is much more effective than its 19th-century predecessor. However, as social critique, in enhancing humanism, in striving for a truthful portrayal of the society, and in preserving the writer's integrity, this new realism is a direct descendant of the old. Under its banner are a number of famous authors whose works have a large following. Among them are Liu Binyan, Lu Wenfu, Li Guowen, Liu Xinwu, Shen Rong, Jiang Zilong, Gao Xiaosheng, Lu Yanzhou and Deng Youmei. The work of these authors occupies an important niche in Chinese literature today. Literature does not hold all the answers for a country in the midst of historic change, where the economy is in urgent need of development, where democracy needs to be perfected, where morality and a sense of values need to be reassessed, and where progress is always only made against great odds. However writers with a social conscience cannot ignore these issues.

Another group of middle-aged writers took a different tack. They did not set limits to their sphere of expression. Their technique and style were constantly changing to suit the subject. The representatives of this group are Wang Meng and Zong Pu, who were the first to break away from the rigidity of realism. They absorbed the principles of the stream of consciousness, the Kafka-esque fantasy, absurdism and surrealism. Although their works still possess the spirit of realism, they have realized that the depiction of the sharply changing society and the growingly complicated conflicts of people's minds requires techniques that are more vital. Thus their methods of portrayal vary with their subjects. They show concern not just for society as a whole, but for the individual too. Their works also reflect the writer's unending search for ways of presenting the world to the reader according to the writers' understanding of it.

Moving in the same current were a large group of writers who had suffered through the "cultural revolution". These were the "educated youths" who had survived years of hardship as farmers and shepherds in remote rural areas and border regions. They had witnessed the life and death struggles of the lowest strata of rural society, and their personal experiences gave them insights into the causes of these conditions. In delving through history, they sought to discover the weakness in the human psyche which allowed it to be twisted in so hideous a manner. In this they were deeply influenced by the Soviet author, Aitmatov, Latin American writers such as Rosza and his structural realism, and the surrealism of Marques. Literary content and the methods of expression had undergone great changes. The focal point of literature was no longer society and politics but humanity and its variation, and the causes of the variation. A group of writers, studying the human psyche, stressed the search of the influences of traditional culture on people's psychological make up. This group called themselves "the roots schools". (Actually their quest was not for the roots of national culture; rather, it was for the influence of cultural tradition in shaping national character.) They exposed the defects of traditional culture which fostered passivism, compromise, and the mindless habit of turning the other cheek in adversity. They reached into the sub-conscious, and expressed it in exaggeration, fantasy, allegory and symbolism. The works of this group caused a great stir in literary circles between 1984 and 1985. Some outstanding works were produced which not only focussed on the weakness of traditional culture but also offered much food for thought. These included the works of Ah Cheng, Han Shaogong, Li Hangyu and Jia Pingwa. There were also works that exaggerated the stupidity of people living in isolated areas, their primitive habits and psychology, which caused a great deal of controversy. "The roots school" freed literature from political bondage, and gave it new life.

A group of still younger writers appeared at the same time as "the roots school", intent on grafting western literary thought to Chinese literature. These writers were heavily influenced not only by Western styles but Western moral values too. Their slavish imitation of Western literature was partly due to the fact that their formative years had been taken up by the "cultural revolution", with injustice and chaos all around them. Their youth was spent in a time of change, when the new was replacing the old in ways that they only half understood. Many were discouraged by the apparent confusion and lack of direction in the world around them and they shunned politics and favoured individualism. They ignored the writer's responsibility to society. They viewed certain social phenomena and things that were once considered of value with either bitter cynicism, or angry satire. They glamourised the ugly aspects of life. This restlessness of youth is perhaps understandable. However, in their attempt to destroy old values, they are seeking a new moral order. The universe does not allow a vacuum. The works of these writers are strongly influenced by Sartre and Salinger but mere imitation cannot endure. Present-day China is a society that is attempting to shake off poverty and improve its standard of living. Although these writers are singing the praises of the have-nots, they are scrambling for a better niche for themselves at the same time. In the industrialised society of the future, youth may have the right to feelings of ennui. But for the present generation these feelings smack of insincerity. Nevertheless, these young writers are a part of modern Chinese literature, though the artistic value of their output is questionable.

It is difficult to explore the forty tempestuous years in the development of modern Chinese literature in just a few pages. It is hoped that the foregoing statement will be of assistance to the reader's enjoyment of this volume.

Finally, due to the limitation of space only one work per author is included in this volume. Thus some equally representative works by the writers have had to be omitted.

Translated by David Kwan

Recollections of the Hill Country

●

—— SUN LI ——

Sun Li was born in Hebei in 1913. After graduation from senior middle school he became a clerk in Beijing but returned home in 1936 to teach in a primary school. After the Anti-Japanese War broke out in 1937 he worked as a correspondent and editor. In 1939 he began to write stories. His works include the novel Stormy Years, *the novelette "The Blacksmith and the Carpenter" and many short stories and essays.*

A peasant delegate from Fuping came to see the Tianjin Industrial Exhibition. We were old friends meeting after nearly ten years. Going round the exhibition with him, I noticed his interest in the textiles and improved farm tools. I wanted to give him a present before he left, and decided to buy some cloth.

Why cloth specially? Because he was still wearing a light blue suit of homespun dyed with the local indigo. I don't know what to call this blue but it has countless associations for me, bringing back those three years of fighting among the barren hills and swift streams of Fuping, reminding me of many people. So to me this colour is "Fuping blue" or "hill blue".

That colour looked conspicuous in Tianjin, quite countrified. Yet in Fuping to get cloth woven and dyed was so hard that a suit like that struck you as fresh and handsome. Fuping is full of hills and they are nothing but black rock. Land is scarce and heavy rain keeps washing down soil to the Hebei plain — my home. The Fuping peasants have never seen big tracts of land but own plots the size of a *kang* or kitchen range. They take endless pains over these tiny pockets of land which may be in the old shape of lozenges, half moons or ladders. They shore them up with stone, surround them with mud, and plant date trees round the edges and maize in the middle.

It's cold up in those hills, where the sun seldom shines. No cotton grows there and when first I arrived the old women were busy twisting hemp yarn, which they use in place of cotton thread. Even the soles of socks are sewn with this.

It was all on account of socks that I got to know this family and we became friends. It was winter, the winter of 1941, and our partisan unit had fought its way to this village. Things had eased up enough for us to have a short rest there.

I went to the river every day to wash my face, squatting down on an icy rock. I made a hole in the ice, dipped my towel in the water, and by the time I'd wiped my face the towel was frozen stiff. One cold windy morning a few pale rays of sunlight were gilding the hills on the opposite bank as I squatted on my usual stone. I broke the ice and was about to wash when someone downstream shouted:

"Can't you see I'm washing greens here? Go further down if you want to wash your face!"

This sharp protest put my back up. What business was it of anybody else if I wanted to wash my face on such a cold day? I retorted angrily:

"I'm too far away to dirty your greens!"

A gust of wind carried my objection over. The other took offence in turn and shouted:

"We've to eat these greens! You wash your face and bottom up there — is that hygienic?"

"Who are you cursing?" I stood up and turned to see a girl of sixteen or seventeen. The wind had whipped a red like frosted persimmon leaves into her cheeks. Her chapped hands were like frozen red radishes. She was thinly clad in shabby pants and jacket of the local blue.

There she stood in the biting wind on the cold river bank by the village the Japanese had burned down more than once. She was holding a basket of willow leaves — probably their whole morning meal.

Something made me calm down.

"My fault," I said. "I won't wash. Come up here and rinse your greens."

She stared at me scornfully before replying:

"Wash greens where you've just been washing?"

I chuckled.

"You're not easy to please. Up here you say I'm fouling the water, though the grime from my face could never reach your greens! When I offer to change places with you, you won't. What's to be done?"

"What's to be done? I'll have to go further up."

She whirled round and walked up the shore to a jagged boulder. There she squatted down to steep her basket in the water. Tucking her hands under her tunic for warmth, she looked at me and smiled.

Not knowing whether to laugh or fume, I said:

"You're mad on hygiene."

"We believe in hygiene — you people only pretend to! You keep jeering that we hill-folk are unhygienic. Living in our homes, eating our rice, you have to rinse your mouths and wash your teeth — are you afraid our food will dirty your mouths? Why not wash your stomachs too!" Giggling, she bent over her basket.

I was tickled. When she laughed I'd seen her teeth flash white.

"Right!" I said. "You're clean, we're dirty."

"It's true! You use the same basin for rice, greens, washing your face and feet or drinking. Call that hygienic?" Smiling, she dabbled her hands in the icy water.

"Beggars can't be choosers! Wait till we beat the Japanese invaders and take back Beiping. We'll have special pots for food and special jugs for water — the whole caboodle!"

"How long will that take?" She threw me a searching glance. "They've burnt our house down three times!"

"Maybe three years, maybe five or ten. We'll keep right on fighting no matter how long it takes. We'll never give up!" Talking to her like this cheered me up too.

"Keep on fighting barefoot?" Her eyes swept my feet before she bent over her basket again.

Puzzled, I asked:

"What do you mean?"

"What's that?" She pretended not to have heard. "Why don't you wear socks? Aren't your feet cold? Call that hygienic?"

"Hygienic?" I chuckled. "I can't help it. Since September we've been beating back this last Japanese 'mopping-up campaign', and our Eighth Route Army doesn't issue socks till the end of October. Busy fighting, who's time to worry about socks?"

"Can't you buy a pair?" she asked softly.

"Where? In one of these pint-sized villages? We haven't passed any towns."

"Get someone to make you a pair."

"Where's the cloth? And if there were any, who'd make them?"

"I would!" She stood up, her willow leaves washed. "We live over there." She pointed at a slope. "If you've no cloth, we've got a bit left, enough for a pair of socks."

She went off with her leaves while I finished washing my face. I looked at my feet, frozen black in their old patched shoes. I felt for a moment that I never wanted to leave these hills, this stream and this bank.

After cleaning up I went back to my unit to eat, then made my way to the girl's house. She was tending the stove and welcomed me with these words:

"Trust you to show up!"

With some idea of her temper now, I just grinned and stepped inside. The room was full of smoke. It took me a minute to see a man of forty or so and his wife seated on the *kang* by a brazier. Behind them was an old woman with white hair. Smiling, they invited me to take a seat.

"Don't wash at the river tomorrow," said the girl. "Come over here. We can easily manage one extra ladle of water."

The man said:

"Our girl was laughing at you just now."

The white-haired granny puckered her lips in a smile.

"You mustn't mind her, comrade! That's her way."

"Suits me!" I said. "Main thing is she has a warm heart. When she saw my bare feet she was sorry for the Eighth Route Army."

The girl's mother picked up a piece of coarse white cloth from one corner of the *kang*.

"She earned this by half a year's spinning. Made me a pair of padded pants, and meant to make her dad socks with what was left. She'll make you a pair first."

"No, keep it for him!" I put in hastily. "Or let me pay for it."

"There you go again!" The girl looked up from the stove. "You got any money?"

Her mother said:

"In our family, when we make a promise we keep it. She can do more spinning to get socks for her dad. We didn't know how to spin till this spring when one of your women comrades stayed with us and taught her. She's promised to teach her to weave next time she comes. Can your folks spin?"

"Sure. But where I come from we wear machine-made cloth. Once we've beaten the enemy, aunty...."

"Once we've taken Beiping we'll have fine cloth, the whole caboodle!" put in the girl mockingly.

As it happened, things were quiet for some time after that. So we didn't have to move on. Every morning I went to the girl's house for a wash. The next day she cut out the socks, and the day after that she was sewing on the soles with fine strands of hemp.

"Do folk in your parts use hemp like this?" she asked.

"No, cotton," I fingered the soles. "Where I come from, even shoe-soles aren't so thick!"

"They're stronger this way. They'll last you three years. Is that long enough to beat the Japanese?"

"Should be," I said.

In five days I was wearing my new socks.

I had found a home from home. They were a healthy family, cheerful and lively. The girl's mother looked even sturdier than her old man. Even the ninety-year-old granny was so fit there was nothing wrong with her hearing. She seldom butted in, but listened with obvious enjoyment to our conversation.

The man was a good farmer but having nothing to do on the land just now he decided to take some dates to Quyang to sell, and asked me to lend a hand. Our army knew that the people's trading and transport work were important and agreed to my helping him. For several days we set out at the crack of dawn, each with a load of over one hundred catties, and took the hilly, riverside track to Quyang. The girl got up before it was light and sat up late to get our meals for us. We ate well, and one day her father said:

"I've you to thank for this, mate!"

"What do you mean?"

"When I carried dates into town alone before, she never fed me half so well!"

I laughed. She said:

"What are you thanking him for? He's wearing our socks, he owes us something, doesn't he?"

Then she asked:

"You've been at it two weeks now. How much have you made?"

"Hear that! She's checking our accounts now!" her father said. "Well, it's time we figured it out." He opened a small bundle stuffed under the quilts. "Whatever we've made or lost, it's all in here."

We counted the notes and they came to over 5,000. The girl said:

"That's enough."

"Enough for what?" he asked.

"To buy a loom! Won't you bring me back a loom from Quyang today?"

Fair enough. Neither her granny, her parents nor I had any objection. After selling our dates in Quyang that day, we went to buy a loom. Her father wanted a good one, even if it cost a bit more, and ended up by spending all he had. We took turns lugging the thing back, and arrived in a lather of sweat.

The whole family was delighted. It must have been the happiest day in the girl's life. She behaved as if she'd been given several mu of land, a new ox or a splendid dowry.

And it didn't take her long to learn to weave.

The day that she finished her first length of cloth, my unit set out again. After that, trudging north and south over hills and plains, I wore those socks for three years without wearing them out. In 1945, coming back from Yan'an after the defeat of Japan, I jumped into the Yellow River for a bath at Qikou and was careless enough to let the rushing water sweep away all my clothes, including this pair of socks. Then the waves of the Yellow River swirled with my memories of those years in the enemy's rear, swirled with my recollections of the girl.

The day of the founding of the People's Republic of China, I took her father to the department store and we bought some cloth: two lengths of good blue cotton for him and his wife, a length of red for their daughter. He'd never seen such bright red cotton, and said:
"Let's have a few feet more of that. Some yellow too."
"What for?" I asked.
"There's a new flag hanging from every door here in town — they won't have that yet back home! Give me a drawing of the red flag with five gold stars and I'll get my girl to make one. Then at meetings or at New Year, we'll hang it up!"
He told me that his daughter, though she had two children now, was just the same as before, interested in anything new and able to pick up new skills in no time.

1949

Translated by Gladys Yang

The Girl from Mengbie

●

—— YANG ZHAO AND BAI HONGHU ——

Yang Zhao, born in 1928 in Jiangxi, began to write while still young. He has worked as an editor in Yunnan where his wife, Bai Honghu, was born and raised. Bai Honghu began to write in 1940. "The Girl from Mengbie" is taken from her collection of short stories Miangui Drenched in Spring Rain.

1

AIJUAD'S and Hansuai's rooms faced each other on either side of the garden, in which lay a pond encircled with banyan and fruit-laden papaya trees. From time to time Aijuad would interrupt his studies to stare out of his window across at Hansuai. Through her window, he saw her erect figure by the lamp, as she concentrated on writing down the figures with one hand, while calculating with the abacus with the other.

Hansuai always studied diligently and was one of the top students in her class. At first, Aijuad had found calculating with an abacus difficult, though he could recite mathematical tables fluently, but Hansuai had never laughed at him.

"Just use this and don't be afraid," she said, pointing to her head to encourage him. "The more you use your brains the sharper they become."

Whenever Aijuad looked at Hansuai's lighted window, he was encouraged.

One afternoon, the students were going to see a film. Aijuad had never seen Hansuai go out or see a film. When he met her he asked, "Are you going to the film, Hansuai?"

"Me? I — haven't made up my mind yet."

"Why not?"

She was silent.

"You should go. I was going to do some washing, but Comrade Aifuang said the film is a very good one. Studying isn't the only way to learn. Films can teach you something too."

"O.K., I'll go then."

On reaching the cinema, Aijuad searched everywhere for Hansuai, but could not find her. Why hadn't she come, when she said she would?

Before the film ended, he left the cinema and hurried to Hansuai's room. No one was there. Through the window he looked into the garden and spotted Hansuai squatting by the pond, washing a man's headdress in a basin. Aijuad wondered to whom it belonged. Then, as she lathered it, he noticed a sky-blue stain on it. It was his. He had carelessly spilt ink on it the previous day.

Eagerly, he ran out of the room and, turning a corner, rushed to Hansuai shouting, "Hansuai! Hansuai!"

With her head bent over her washing, she was startled to see Aijuad. Raising her eyes, she asked, "Has the film finished already?"

"Why didn't you go to the film? Why stay here and wash my clothes instead?"

"Look, silly! I was doing my own washing, so I thought I'd do yours too. You're so busy with your studies. I can wash faster than you."

Aijuad found there were many clothes in the basin, not just his but those of other friends too. Rolling up his sleeves, he squatted down beside her. "Let's do them together." So saying, he took some clothes and began scrubbing one of them, a skirt of Hansuai's.

Embarrassed, she tried to snatch it back. "Put it down! Put it down!"

Looking at the skirt in his hand, Aijuad smiled, not minding a bit. "Calm down! If you can wash our clothes, why can't we wash yours?" He glanced at her affectionately.

Their eyes met, so that she turned hastily away. Her manner suddenly grew cool and she fixed her eyes on the ground as if preoccupied with some problem. After a while, she picked up her basin and went away without a word.

Looking at her retreating figure, Aijuad was puzzled. She was as beautiful as a flower, yet as cold as stone. Back in his room, he was in emotional turmoil. When the other students returned from the film, laughing and talking, he went to see Aifuang, the dean of the Nationalities' Cadre School and secretary of the Youth League branch of the accountants' training class. Aijuad told him abruptly, "Hansuai is so good. She doesn't just help us in our studies, but also in our daily lives. She was washing our clothes today. I think we should admit her into the Youth League."

Whatever the problem, Aifuang was never at a loss. But now he frowned and was silent for a long time, before sighing.

"What's the matter? Have I said something wrong?" Aijuad asked.

"Of course not! That's a good suggestion. We should try to help her, but it will take time. Now, how are you getting on in your studies? Any difficulties?" he said, changing the subject.

Since Aijuad had not come to talk about this, he soon left.

After that, Aijuad began to watch Hansuai's behaviour more closely. She was a strange contradiction of modesty and friendliness and unreasonable stubbornness. She would gaily chat in class and then snub everyone afterwards.

One fine Sunday morning, the students were up early and hurrying to go home or out. Aijuad watched while Hansuai took her time having breakfast. As always, she clearly was not going anywhere. He walked over and said, "Won't you go home today?"

"No."

"Where do you live?"

"Oh, far away," she replied.

"Then come to my home instead and meet my family."

"No, thank you."

"Come on! My family live in Manliu Village near the town. There's no need to be so formal."

When he tried to take her arm, she dodged away with a curious look, declining his invitation in a proud and bitter tone. As she ran away, he noticed there were tears in her eyes. Since he was now in no mood to go home, he went to see Aifuang again. He began, "Hansuai seems to have some problems."

"How do you know that?" the dean asked in astonishment, his composure shaken.

"I feel it."

With a deep frown, Aifuang sighed.

"Really, Comrade Aifuang! Whenever I mention Hansuai, you just sigh!"

As if he had not heard him, Aifuang moved nearer to Aijuad and stared at him. "Isn't your home in Manliu Village?" he asked.

"Yes."

"And how many are in your family?"

"Only two. My mother and I."

"What's your mother like?"

"She works very hard."

The dean nodded. "Are there many superstitious people in your village?" he continued after a pause.

"Of course. Too many!" Not quite understanding the line of questioning, Aijuad added, "A lot of them believe that illness is caused by ghost people. Once when I was sick, my mother pricked my chest with a tiger's fang and muttered to herself, 'Which village are you from, you evil ghost? What's your name? Tell me or I'll stab you with this tiger's fang.' Then she pricked me until I bled."

"Have you ever seen any ghost people?"

"Yes. It was the year before Liberation, and I was just over fifteen then. I saw a male living ghost driven out of a village near ours. He brought his wife and two children with him. On the orders of the chief, he sacrificed a cock to the gods at the crossroads. Kneeling on the ground, he made a pledge that he and his family would live far away and never return, even when they became real ghosts at their deaths...."

Aifuang's expression was furious. Cutting Aijuad short, he demanded, "Is that man a human being or a ghost person?"

"A human being of course!"

"Then you've never seen any ghosts?"

"Never! Who could see a ghost?"

"Are there any ghosts?"

"No, of course not!"

Back in his room Aijuad realized that he was still in a dilemma over Hansuai. Why had Aifuang talked to him about living ghosts? Was it possible that...? He dared not think any longer. His heart pounded. Such thoughts were ridiculous!

2

Filled with suspicion, Aijuad tried to find out where Hansuai lived, but she seldom chatted after class, especially with him. Whenever he approached she would avoid him.

It was early in April that the accountants' training class ended. The day after the graduation ceremony, the students would return home, so Aijuad was very anxious to have a talk with Hansuai. It had not been easy for them to study, since both came from poor families. But for Liberation this would not have been possible. Even if they were not to be close friends, he hoped they could at least keep in touch. That afternoon he saw her packing alone in her room. Going over, he said:

"How time flies! Half a year has passed in a flash."

Like a deer, Hansuai was flustered to see him. Controlling herself a little, she murmured, "Yes."

Sitting down Aijuad watched her packing. "We've studied and learnt how to calculate with an abacus."

"And how to develop these border areas."

"Exactly! Back home in our villages we must do all we can."

"We'll work for better harvests too."

Hansuai was rather reserved at first, but the more they talked, the more ardent and intimate they became. The afternoon passed until it was almost time for supper. Aijuad went on in high spirits:

"I'm so happy for the future of us Dais."

"And I'm so happy for the people of my village."

"Aren't your people Dais?" Aijuad asked puzzled.

"No. They — they aren't!" she retorted, her voice rising.

"Where is your village then?" he pressed, hoping to solve the mystery.

"Here on earth, in the world of men! It's a fascinating place, better than anywhere else." Although she praised her village, there was no happiness in her tone. It was as if she was arguing a case.

"So where is this paradise?" Aijuad tried to ascertain.

"Oh, it's getting late. Come on! Let's go to the office. There's so much to be done before we leave tomorrow."

She changed the subject, her face grave. Turning round, she walked away before Aijuad could say anything more, leaving her clothes scattered on her bed.

The next morning, the graduates were about to set off for home, scurrying about bidding each other farewell. Aijuad knew Hansuai would neither come to say goodbye to him nor expect him to say it to her. Walking to a huge banyan tree outside the gate, he stood hoping to see her once more before they parted. She appeared carrying two bamboo crates on a shoulder-pole. She walked slowly, her head down, her eyes misty. As she passed him her pace quickened, but at the bend of the road by a cocoanut palm she turned round to glance at him. Looking after her, Aijuad forgot that he too must leave for home. After she had disappeared into the distance, he went to see the dean once more.

With tears in his eyes, he asked where Hansuai lived. Instead of answering, the dean asked him why he wanted to know her address. Aijuad urged him to tell, but the dean just replied, "Now let things be. You run off home immediately."

"No, I won't!" declared Aijuad.

"Why not?"

"She's so mysterious. There's something troubling her. I want to find out the truth or I'll never have any peace of mind."

"Young men should be light-hearted, not so heavy."

"Comrade Aifuang, you kept her secret while she was still a student. But why won't you tell me the truth now that she has left? Must I be kept in the dark all my life?"

His sad face reminded Aifuang of another's, which had appeared six months previously, on the last day of registration for the accountants' training class.

A slender girl had entered, wearing a light green top and bright blue skirt. Pretty and intelligent-looking, she glanced around uneasily, her eyes sparkling. When the clerk asked from which village she came, she blushed and answered, "From Mengjang district."

"Yes, but which village?"

"From Mengjang district!" she insisted, as if defending herself.

Overhearing her arguing, Aifuang invited her into a vacant office and asked, "Is your name Hansuai?"

"Yes," she answered, raising her head puzzled.

"You can tell him the name of your village."

"No, I won't." She lowered her head again, biting her lips.

"Why not?"

"Because I won't tell anyone except a Communist Party member."

"Who do you think I am?"

The girl raised her head again. In spite of his cadre's uniform, one could tell he was a Dai from his face, even without hearing his pure Dai dialect. She scrutinized him, while she nervously fingered her skirt.

"As a Dai and a Party member, I understand your dilemma. But we've been liberated and those terrible dark days have gone for ever. You must believe that things have changed. Others won't judge you as before and you should not expect the worst from others."

Although he talked with her for a long time, she kept her head down and said stubbornly, "I've nothing more to say. I'm here to study for my people, that's all!"

He talked with her often about her studies, and she would beam with joy and talk animatedly. But the moment he touched on her personal life, she would stubbornly clam up, "I've nothing more to say!"

She seldom left the school grounds.

Recalling this, Aifuang paced the room in agitation, stopping at last in front of Aijuad. Patting him on the shoulder he sighed, "She's very unfortunate. No need to increase her pain."

"Please tell me the truth."

"She — she's from Mengbie Village...."

Aijuad felt a shiver go down his spine. Mengbie Village? That's where the living ghosts lived before Liberation. Only after Liberation, it had got a name.

"I can't believe it. She — she's a good girl...." His voice trembled so that he could not continue. No, it wasn't true! Hansuai from Mengbie Village! The fond dream he had hoped a moment ago would come true of Hansuai and he marrying and working together in the same co-operative suddenly turned into a nightmare. He visualized his friendly relatives and neighbours cursing and sneering at Hansuai, his mother refusing to agree to their marriage. Aijuad was deeply upset.

As if he had read his mind, Aifuang said, "Hansuai is a good girl and all the Mengbie villagers are good too." Then he added, "Have you ever seen a village headman being accused of being a living ghost? No, all accused were peasants!"

Aijuad began to understand what Aifuang was saying, and so staring at the dean, he listened carefully filled with grief and indignation.

"There is no such thing as a ghost," Aifuang emphasized. "For example, take Hansuai's mother. About thirty years ago, when she was a beautiful teenager, she lived with her parents in Mangbang Village, which had been their home for generations. The headman was a known womanizer and wanted to seduce her. At dusk one day, when she was on her way to husk rice, he jumped out from his hiding-place in a bamboo grove near the river and tried to embrace her. Although she looked frail, she was strong and slapped his face so hard that he staggered back. After that he hated her and planned his revenge. Later that summer, a woman transplanting rice seedlings fell ill with malaria. The headman started the rumour that Hansuai's mother had gone to the sick woman's home to borrow a bamboo crate and that her ghost had caused the illness. On the orders of the wicked headman, their hut was burnt and they were driven out of the village."

Aijuad cried out, "Why doesn't the government issue a law stating that there are no living ghosts and that it is against the law to brand a person as one?"

Shaking his head, Aifuang explained, "That wouldn't do. People must get rid of these ideas themselves. You asked me twice about Hansuai's past, but I didn't tell you because I was afraid you'd look down on her and discriminate against her."

Aijuad hung his head in shame. Although he did not believe in ghosts, he hadn't known the reasons why people were branded as such. If only he had known earlier, he could have helped Hansuai. How childish and ignorant he had been!

3

After leaving the dean's room, Aijuad set off for Mengbie Village, walking quickly hoping to catch up with Hansuai.

Mengbie Village was far away in a valley at the foot of a mountain. On the way, Aijuad passed many villages, fields, ridges and streams. The further he went the fewer the villages and the more rugged the path. The area, formerly a wild forest, was the haunt of tigers and leopards. As more and more living ghosts were banished there, they set up their village, clearing the forest. As Aijuad walked along the rough mountain path, he thought of those wretched people who had dragged themselves along that same way such as Hansuai's mother and her grandmother, who must have suffered deeply. But for the Communist Party and Liberation, they would have endured those injustices for ever, leading the life of outcasts from generation to generation, while more and more victims were driven there.

He lost all sense of time. Suddenly the path broadened with neat rows of banyan trees lining it like bright trellises. Among the luscious green grass, colourful wild flowers ran riot. The surface of the pools mirrored the blue sky and the white geese. Golden wheat grew in abundance. There was beauty and tranquillity wherever one looked. Aijuad's eyes drank in the beauty. Expecting to arrive at Mengbie Village soon, he wondered what it would be like and how the people were.

Suddenly he spotted a girl emerging from a wheat field. It was Hansuai! Her eyes sparkled with joy at the good harvest. Aijuad rushed towards her, taking her hand and saying, "Hello, Hansuai! I followed you here!"

Hansuai was delighted to see him, but she was uncertain what he meant. Why had he followed her?

While she had been a student, Aijuad had often been in her thoughts. He was warm-hearted and honest, an idealistic young man. She had become very fond of him and sensed he was in love with her. But whenever she thought about their future, her joy was overshadowed by her past.

As a child, she had not known there was such discrimination. When selling eggs at the fairs, the boys had buzzed around her like bees round a honey-pot, singing love songs and competing with one another for her attentions. She ignored them all. One day when she went to the market, the boys began to swarm around her as always, singing until their throats ached. Hansuai smiled. Suddenly a voice rang out, "She's from Mengbie Village! A living ghost!" The boys' faces registered horror as they fled in panic.

Heart-broken, Hansuai sobbed out her story in her mother's arms when she reached home.

Indignantly her mother said, "Ignore them, Hansuai. We live in Mengbie Village. Let the rest of the world go by!"

From that time, Hansuai's heart was heavy and she swore never to leave the village again. After Liberation, however, there were movements to give the land back to the peasants and set up co-operatives. She was chosen by the district administration to learn accounting, but she refused, afraid of persecution. "I won't go," she protested. "We can run the co-operative well without any accountants."

The Party secretary of the district committee had at last persuaded her and so she had entered the nationalities' cadre school. There she seldom went out in case someone recognized her, and kept her distance from her classmates in case they discovered about her past. She was afraid they would sneer at her if they knew the truth. As for Aijuad, he was a sincere friend, but she was sure that if he knew, he would abandon her and break her heart. Whenever she thought of this she trembled.

Now Aijuad had come to her! Had the Communist Party really destroyed superstition? Had she misjudged Aijuad?

Seeing her bewildered expression, Aijuad tried to reassure her, "This new society has given us Dai people a new life!"

Touched, she replied, "How did you find me?"

"Comrade Aifuang told me everything so I decided to come after you."

Hansuai was deeply grateful to Aifuang, who had told her many times not to expect the worst from others. Yet she still was uncertain if Aijuad was really as determined as he declared.

"How could you love such an unfortunate girl as me?"

"The past is past. Now we have a new life, a new beginning, a new way of thinking," Aijuad said, hugging Hansuai.

A pair of swans rose from the pool, flapping their wings and soaring into the blue sky.

1953

The Election

●

—— LI GUOWEN ——

Li Guowen, born in 1930, studied in the Nanjing Drama School when he was young. After graduation he joined the Tianjin Railway Drama Troupe and in 1954 was transferred to work as an editor in the China Railway Trade Union. "The Election", published in 1957, was unjustly criticized in political campaigns. His novel Spring in the Winter *won the Mao Dun Literary Award and his short story "Lunar Eclipse" won the 1980 national short story award.*

ACCORDING to the trade union's constitution, the present committee's term of office was nearly over. Unless an ammendment were made to the constitution, and elections held, then the present committee would drag on in office without the union members having a chance to approve them. Knowing this, the committee roused itself into action. The chairman began to draft a report of the previous year's work and, in order to make it a little more lively and interesting and to stop the listeners dropping off to sleep or trying to slink out of the meeting, he set out some conditions to be met by the committee: "two procedures, one exemplar".

"The material you provide will form the basis of my report. The first procedure is to make a concise report of the overall work situation. The second procedure is to make correct numerical accounts of our achievements. What is more important is the exemplar."

It may not be clear what an "exemplar" means in this case. It was a fashionable word used among union cadres at the time, meaning almost the same as a "good example". Why did people start to use it? I once asked Old Hao who had worked there for over forty years. He knit his brows and said in a disgruntled voice, "Who knows where that rubbish comes from. It probably just sounds important but doesn't mean anything."

The committee members all got busy on the "two procedures, one exemplar". The dreary factory union was like the pendulum of a clock that had not moved in a long time. No one knew who had knocked it, but it had suddenly tick-tocked into life again, and become a hive of rarely seen activity. People passing by the union windows could not stop themselves from poking their heads in and having a look, afraid that something untoward had happened. The "two procedures" were simple enough, it was the "exemplar" that was causing the problem. The committee members were not very discerning, nor was it as simple as it had been to go to the personnel department, wages department, and director's office to copy figures and other information. The chairman was like a pregnant woman who, before her baby was even born, was already imagining the sound of its voice and smiling face. It was as if he could already see the impact his report would have after it had been read at the meeting. The committe would be welcomed and trusted by every member of the union, and they would agree unanimously that it should continue in office.

The chairman called a meeting of the committee members asking them to report their "two procedures, one exemplar" to him. They all had long faces. Even the communications officer had a worried frown. He stared at a stack of stained, unused tea-cups, wondering how they could be washed clean in minutes. Then the chairman spoke up: "Gather round everyone. Where's Old Hao? No where to be seen as usual."

The communications officer hurriedly answered: "I told him about the meeting. He's gone to pay his last respects and says he'll be along right after." He was hoping that the chairman would send him to fetch Old Hao so that he could take off and forget the dirty tea-cups.

"Last respects? Who died?"

"Old Wu from the riveting workshop. Old Hao took care of the coffin and funeral arrangements. The funeral is taking place right now. Shall I go and find him?"

Although the chairman was not worried about offending the dead man who was hardly in a position to complain, he had to consider whether it was a good idea, especially at election time, to offend the crowd of mourners by removing the leader of the funeral procession and master of ceremonies. The communications officer lowered his head and went to wash the cups.

"Comrades, it is imperative to have an 'exemplar'." He was not happy with the material the committee members had reported to him. "If you don't provide me with figures I can still make do. What my report urgently needs is an exemplar. Is it possible that we've been working for a whole year yet can not find a single exemplar?" The chairman spoke fervently and in his agitation he banged his hands on the table and created a great cloud of dust which made the committee members sneeze.

Immediately everyone fell silent.

"They had plenty of planks, good ones, but the sods wouldn't let me have them." Luckily for Old Hao he was in the funeral procession when he uttered these words, otherwise the exemplar mad chairman would have grabbed him and not let him off the hook.

Old Hao walked at the head of the funeral procession, leaning on a walking stick. The dead man's wife, young son and workmates of some thirty or forty years walked by his side. With shiny bald heads, their sluggish steps and solemn manner put the onlookers in a sombre mood. Following behind was a group of sixteen pall-bearers and twenty or more grave-diggers. Although young in Old Hao's eyes, their faces were already lined with exhaustion from years of hard work. They had had their fill of life's hardships and were now not easily roused. Their footsteps were heavy. The crowd of mourners stretched out behind. There were no streamers on the bier, no floral wreaths, no banners or music. There could be no funeral more suitable for a plain, old worker.

Old Hao looked to his left and right then whispered, "I gave them a good talking to in the timber plant. Old Wu had been making rivets all his life. Even the shelves in your factory are held together with his sweat and blood. He, of all people, deserved the best wood for his coffin? But they just wouldn't let me have any. It was hard enough to get hold of this cypress wood."

By the time they got to the graveyard the trench had already been dug. Shouting in unison they untied the coffin and gently lowered it in. The first few shovelfuls of earth were thrown by relatives of the dead man, Old Hao and other workmates. Then came a surge of young people, swinging their shoulders which were more accustomed to starting up machines or wielding hammers. In the twinkling of an eye a high burial mound rose from the flat ground. According to custom, Old Hao said a few words to draw the funeral to a conclusion. He never prepared his funeral speeches but always managed to make them moving. He did not even have to try to remember the details of the dead man's life or appearance; they had been together for half a lifetime, so Old Hao was familiar with every line on the man's hands. Nearing the end of his speech, Old Hao cleared his throat and said with great feeling, "Another good craftsman gone. Old Wu's hands were invaluable! When he picked up a drill he was even more delicate than a girl with an embroidery needle. His rivets will last for thousands of years with no sign of wear. Some young people are too ambitious nowadays. Yesterday they were still in split trousers; today they have barely served out their apprenticeships and think they can piss on others." He swept his eyes over the young people standing just outside the circle. They did not dare look him in the eye but turned their faces away. "You should learn from this old man who's now gone to his grave! He lived a long time and studied all his life. You mark my words."

Old Hao saw the dead man's wife and son home. When they arrived, he pointed and probed with his walking stick, asking a string of questions: "How much rice and flour do you have left? What about coal and firewood? Does your roof leak? How much does it cost for the child to go to school? How is he getting on with his studies?..."

The wife replied in sobs but the child remained calm, trying to console his mother.

At last Old Hao said, "Right! In the future the child must come to the factory as an apprentice so his father's craft will be passed on. You've done enough crying for now. People grow old and then they die. Neither you nor I can escape it. But at the moment you are still living and so you're got to make plans for your life. Bring your son up well and your husband's spirit will rest in peace."

The wife, who had just stopped crying, became choked with sobs again.

As he was going out of the door, Old Hao turned and said, "Your coal won't last the winter, I'll get someone to bring some over tomorrow."

Every time he saw an old friend off, his legs would seize up for a couple of minutes. As he crossed the level-crossing he felt so tired he could hardly move on. He remembered that the trade union wanted him to attend a meeting and recalled the headache of the "two procedures, one exemplar". "I'll be late anyway. They'll be lenient on an old man." He thought he might as well sit on the side of the road and rest his feet. Coming up the road was a small child who was obviously just learning to walk. He was staggering along like a rheumatic old man. He went and snatched up the child. The child struggled and shouted but Old Hao never loosened his grip. He swore angrily: "Good God, whose child is this? If he were crushed by the train you'd be the first to go off to the union to kick up a fuss!"

A woman heard the clamour and rushed up, saying, "Who's being rough with my precious baby?"

"Me. It's me!" He angrily plopped the child down on the ground, where he immediately started wailing.

If it was anyone else the woman would have flared up in anger, but seeing it was Old Hao she broke into a smile. "I'm sorry to trouble you. Thank you for looking out for my child."

"Hmph!" He waved his walking stick. "What sort of a mother are you, letting your child run wild? I'm a weak, old man. If I were any stronger I would beat you with this. That would teach you how to look after children."

The woman stuck her tongue out at him behind his back, then picked up the child and went away.

By the time Old Hao arrived at the union, the meeting was long over. Only the chairman was left, engrossed in writing his masterpiece. He was concentrating so hard his face had turned completely red. Not daring to disturb him, Old Hao sat down at the side to wait. He always had great admiration for anyone who could pick up a pen and think carefully about an article. Even when his granddaughter bent over her books to study at night, he liked sitting quietly by her side, watching her and sharing her troubles and joys. Writing the chairman's report was a really hard task. He seemed to be torturing himself: he scratched his head and twisted his nose, chewed his pen-lid and banged his head so that all his veins stuck out. Finally he threw down his pen and groaned: "Oh! An exemplar, an exemplar. If I don't find an exemplar then it's all over!"

Old Hao sighed in sympathy. The chairman turned, his eyes sticking out on stalks in his surprise. "Old Hao, what's the matter with you? Every time there's a union meeting there's always some hitch. If you don't arrive late then you have to leave early. First it's 'X' looking for you, then it's 'Y'. Are you a union committee member or a public servant?"

Old Hao answered timidly: "I'm here now, aren't I?"

"Good! Then give me your report. 'Two procedures, one exemplar'. The most important is the exemplar!"

Old Hao nervously opened his bag and took out a filthy notebook. He flipped backwards and forwards through it but could not find the "two procedures, one exemplar" he had prepared. He was so anxious that his cheeks quivered. The shiny paper slipped through his fingers, as though it was purposely not doing as he wanted.

"Well?" The chairman glanced sideways at him.

"Here ... here ... I...."

The chairman seethed with anger. He felt like all the committee members were deliberately trying to upset him. No one had given him any suitable material. Old Hao was even more exasperating; he could not string a single sentence together. Angrily the chairman said, "Old Hao, what do you want me to report to the union members? How many funerals you've been to this year?"

"Everyone knows what I've been doing. It's clear at a glance, but if you ask me to put it into words I get all muddled. I asked someone to write it out in this notebook, but they messed it all up...."

How is it that a man who could head a large funeral procession and be so awe-inspiring, could become so weak, old, decrepit and pitiful before someone young enough to be his son? It had taken more than this one instance to deprive Old Hao of his full force. Although he was just a small union cadre he had been strongly affected by the various political campaigns that had swept through the union in recent years.

At first he had been the union chairman. He had a kind heart and treated people well, so was affectionately known as "Old Mr. Good", or jokingly called "Goody". If things had carried on as they were then everything would have been fine, but some unpleasant events occured.

....

He stood on the platform reading haltingly from a piece of paper, encouraging those workers who had been involved with secret societies to own up to their activities. The speech had been written by the present chairman who at the time had been a union clerk. Even forms and formulas for official documents or model letters, would have been more expressive and had richer content than this speech. Old Hao, who had not received much education, was completely confused by this long list of words and phrases loosely strung together. He did not have time to take in the last sentence properly and so the words escaped from his lips before he had time to take them back: "Comrades! Hmmm ... Together we must all enroll in secret societies...."

The whole room burst into laughter. Standing in front of the buzzing crowd of people, Old Hao totally lost his presence of mind. Hurriedly he added the sentence: "Uh, um, we must all enroll in the Yiguandao* secret society." The hullabaloo grew louder, taking a long time to subside.

The young men and women laughed the loudest; the union cadres sitting up on the platform covered their mouths, laughing discreetly.

"Damn! I meant to say 'oppose' both times. I'm useless at reading from a script." Old Hao was so worked up there were tears in his eyes.

"It's not good enough. You'll have to make a self-criticism. It's a question of your political principles and your standpoint."

Soon after, Old Hao was demoted to vice-chairman.

"There's nothing wrong with being vice-chairman. I'm a Party member anyway, and I'll do any job the Party asks me to. One can't pick and choose." Life went on just as before. Apart from a few naughty apprentices who nick-named him "Dianchuanshi**", the gossip slowly disappeared like dewdrops in the shade.

As chance would have it, that spring the rains lingered on for ages. The housing for the workers had been neglected for years and leaked terribly. If there was just the slightest hint of sunlight then damp quilts and bedding would be hung out to air in every available space, dazzling the eyes like a myriad of variously patterned flags.

At the same time, in accordance with the plan drawn up by the factory the housing department was carrying out minor repairs on the factory director's and department chiefs' houses. No consideration was giving to the plight of their fellow workers who could not sleep at night for having to constantly put out bowls and jars to catch the rainwater. In the mornings they were red-eyed, and had no energy to work.

"What about Old Hao? How come he's not here to help?"

"He can't dodge the issue. If he doesn't deal with it, no one else will."

In fact Old Hao was not in hiding at all. At that very moment he was discussing the matter with the head of the housing department. He was

---

*Yiguandao: reactionary and superstitious religious secret society banned in 1952.
**A notable preacher in the Yiguandao society.

sitting there, angry and covered in mud, waiting for the department chief to solve the problem. The department chief lounged in his armchair: "Look, you're a union cadre. You know what planning is. Plans are like laws and even factory directors cannot break them. You can't stand a little leaking water? How did you manage before Liberation? Everyone's houses collapsed and rotted then, but we made do!"

"You're a Party member! How can you talk like that?" Old Hao stormed out leaving a trail of mud behind him. He walked and walked, trying to think what to do. In the end there was nothing for it but open his umbrella and go to stand barefooted on the factory director's doorstep to try and make him see reason. By this time he was shaking with anger.

"If it were anyone else dragging their feet over this then I wouldn't be so angry, but you're the factory director! You shouldn't be treating us like this! All you ever do is hold meetings, research and investigate! How long are we going to have to wait?"

The factory director stood in the porch sheltered from the wind and rain. "Old Hao, come in and we'll talk it over."

"No, no. You can procrastinate all you like, but I'm not going in, or leaving until you've given me an answer. It's not just me, there are many other families living in the same conditions." But neither soft persuasion nor harsh words did the trick. The only solution was to order the construction workers to stop work and go straight to the workers' houses to stop the leaks.

Although Old Hao was criticized by the Party for his behaviour towards leaders, and although he was soaked and his rheumatism started again, when he saw so many smiling faces, he cared neither about the pain in his legs nor the criticism. His legs slowly improved and he was soon as busy as a beaver again.

A campaign against extravagance was brewing, putting the factory's small mill in a precarious position. Old Hao began to feel nervous about it. Every morning before work the workers would spend a few coppers on soya-bean milk so their wives and children would not have to worry about preparing food early in the morning. This was an idea that Old Hao had thought over for a long time. It happened that a small mill near the factory had shut down. He had proposed that the factory should buy it and spend a little money to do it up a bit. "Was that an extravagance? No one raised any objections at the time." Old Hao could not work it out but kept his worries to himself.

When the mill first opened for business everyone was very pleased to drink the steaming hot soya-bean milk. The workers welcomed it, the cadres were happy and even the leaders spoke highly of it. Naturally, the trade union wrote a report on the merits of establishing the mill. The Youth League wrote one too. The administration thought it its duty to follow suit and report to its higher body. Each report gave an exaggerated description but not one mentioned Old Hao's name. He had found the building materials, bought the mule to work the grinder, hired the stonemasons and organized all other aspects, but no one remembered to give him the credit. Old Hao did not mind. He laughed it off. As long as there was soya-bean milk for everyone, that was all that mattered.

But then the campaign started.

"Who's responsible for this extravagance?" People started making enquiries in the mill. Someone who previously made a report on the mill, praising it to the skies, wiped the skin of the milk from his lips and said, "Old Hao from the union is totally responsible. He arranged everything. I realized a long time ago that it was not right. A small mill today, a large flour mill tomorrow and then even a vegetable garden." He was so smug showing off his "political awareness". Workers all around looked at him in horror, worried that the mill would be closed. In the end it was not shut because it was not only the workers who liked to drink the milk, but also those "wise after the event" leaders. At the time the present chairman was committee member for propoganda. He wrote out a self-criticism on Old Hao's behalf and handed it in without Old Hao ever having put his name to it. Old Hao was then dismissed from the post of vice-chairman and made committee member in charge of workers' welfare. He was happy and content. "The mill hasn't been closed down and that's the main thing. I always try my best even if it's the death of me."

In his new post his first task was to build a rest home. He forgot the unpleasant things that had happened to him. Everyday he got up early and worked late. He bought materials, surveyed land, and although he was extremely busy, he was very happy. He looked like a builder, covered in dust from head to toe. He picked a spot in the woods, not far from the factory. Before Liberation there had been plans to build a western style house there for the factory director and so foundations had already been laid. Passers-by would stop and ask: "Old Hao, what are you doing?"

"Building a rest home so that everyone can live happily."

"Old Hao, you really do have a heart of gold!" They walked away full of admiration for him. Old Hao was overwhelmed. He felt that by doing a good deed for other people he was helping to bring the period of pure communism a little closer. Feeling very content, he happily put his back into wielding his pickaxe with great strength. From a distance he looked just like a robust young man.

By this time the present chairman was already vice-chairman. He was in the prime of his life with a healthy body and a quick mind. During a meeting, a factory leader said that building the rest home in the woods was not as good as building it in Sunny Ravine: "I went there once. The scenery really is beautiful; the air is fresh. It's as pretty as a picture...." The chairman was very good at watching a person's mood and expression and interpreting the ideas of the leaders. He immediately went and told

Old Hao to stop working and sent him to Sunny Ravine to find a new spot for the rest home.

Old Hao already knew that there was something amiss because as the workers were cutting down the undergrowth people stopped coming by to ask what they were doing. But he still flatly refused the proposal to build the rest home in Sunny Ravine. "No, I've thought about it, but it's over ten kilometres away in the mountains. Far too inconvenient."

"He's right about the difficulties involved in implementing the leader's idea" the chairman thought to himself, but said, "Every summer groups of young men go and enjoy themselves there which shows it must be good. There are persimmon, date and pear trees covering the mountainside, as well as grass lands. It's great for swimming in Sunny Ravine too."

"No, there are wolves there." Old Hao still would not agree to the proposal.

"Hey! Is the proletariat afraid of wolves? What a joke!" the chairman did not want to prolong the conversation with this obstinate old man. "This is the leaders' decision; you just implement it!"

Once the rest home had been completed the cadres went there first for a special rest. Within three days they realized how difficult it was to get provisions into the mountains. Cars could not go into the mountains so mules had to be used. They had planned to swim in the lake, but the local people did not allow them, saying that the water was for drinking and cooking and should not be used for other purposes. Most terrifying was the howling of the wolves in the middle of the night which prevented anyone from getting any sleep. Some people said they had made a full recovery and, as there was no need for them to occupy a precious bed, they applied to leave early. There were a few who were not afraid of wolves and so stayed on. These were mainly army cadres who had not used their guns for a long time and so took the opportunity to do some target practice.

After a while anyone who returned from the rest home was treated as if he had just escaped from the jaws of death. Everyone would gather round laughing and joking: "Congratulations! You made it back alive!"

When the campaign protesting that the union concentrated only on production without caring for workers' welfare began, people linked Old Hao with the rest home: "Why did he build the rest home in the mountains?"

"To turn us into monks?"

"To feed us to the wolves?"

Even the cadres blamed him: "You're the committee member in charge of workers' welfare. Why didn't you do a better job of supervising the plans?" Everyone talked so much Old Hao did not have a chance to defend himself. The more excited they got the harder it became for him to say anything. And so he became the "exemplar" for how to turn something from good to bad. Elections soon came round and Old Hao got just enough votes, as the full details had come out and no one really thought Old Hao was capable of doing anything wicked. But he was just made a nominal committee member, and not given any concrete work to do. This really upset Old Hao for: "The more I do, the more I'm disappointed." Nonetheless, he found a place in people's hearts and they grew to respect him more and more, felt closer to him and trusted him. To many workers Old Hao was the union, and the union was Old Hao. If they had a problem they would go and find him. He became "minister for everything". He was even busier than before and was seldom seen in the union.

This bumpy road had aged him. His shoulders hunched forward and his waist twisted. The few hairs left on his head were silvery white silken threads, but his heart had not weakened; he was still as intensely emotional as before. No one really knew why, but when he met those who had pointed responsibility at him he became taciturn, overcautious and even frightened.

The chairman was still waiting for an answer without the least sign of showing leniency. Old Hao pleaded softly: "Tomorrow's not too late! If I don't sleep tonight I'll be able to find your 'two procedures, one exemplar'."

The chairman muttered to himself, then nodded his head: "Alright!" Old Hao was like a criminal hearing his orders to be released. He jumped up quickly with the aid of his walking stick and got ready to go home, for his granddaughter had been waiting at the table for a long time for him to help with her homework. Just as he was stepping out of the door, the chairman called to him again: "Comrade Hao, wait a minute. Let's go together, there's something I want to talk to you about." This was the first time anything like this had happened. He studied the chairman cautiously with a nasty feeling that a bomb was about to drop.

"Comrade Hao, I was going to wait until tomorrow to mention this but...I know you're a Party member and we've worked together for so many years. I understand you. You like to be frank...."

"Well, what is it?"

"Our union needs to keep up with progress. Comrade Hao, you are an old worker...."

Losing his patience, Old Hao cut him short: "Whatever is on your mind, feel free to say it; there's no point in beating about the bush!" This tone of voice was reminiscent of when Old Hao was the union chairman and the present chairman was just a clerk. Perhaps it was this tone that angered him. He said coldly, "When we selected nominees for the election, we had a discussion about you and decided not to include you on the list. How do you feel about it?"

"You're dismissing me?"

Old Hao could tell from the look on his face what the unspoken words were: "You're old and useless. You ought to retire! Don't stand in the way of others. Show your understanding of the times. Don't make your exit harder than it need be." His legs would not respond to him; it was as if they were not his own. Somehow he struggled home. He opened the door and stood stiffly, weakly puffing on the doorstep. His granddaughter called out in fright: "Grandpa! Grandpa!" He fainted.

The next day he did not have the energy to go into the factory. The siren calling the start of the day howled for what seemed an eternity. He felt a little regretful. It was the first day he had missed since Liberation. Even when the rain had brought on his rheumatism he had continued to go to work. He became very dispirited thinking about the path that everyone eventually has to pass along. He asked his wife for a stiff drink which, red-faced, he slowly sipped. He put down the drink: "What's the matter with you? Do you want to die? No! No!" He struggled to his feet and walked to the factory leaning on his walking stick on one side, and his granddaughter on the other.

"Grandpa, what age will you live to?"

"At least a hundred, my dear! The longer the better!" They went into the factory meeting hall. He picked up the girl, sat down in the corner by the door, and listened to the chairman vividly expounding his brilliant ideas. Perhaps it was because the chairman was speaking too quickly, that he just left the sound "exemplar ... exemplar" ringing in everyone's ears. The treasurer and auditor followed with their reports. The string of figures they read out seemed to be for the sole benefit of the microphone. Not one person at the meeting paid any attention to whether they were saying one thousand or ten thousand. But the audience was polite. Anyone standing on the platform would be allowed to finish his speech without being booed off.

The sacred election began.

The chairman asked if there were any comments on the list of nominees. For a while silence reigned in the hall which was not a good sign. "When this list was preliminarily discussed in groups it was not convincing enough. It looks like it'll be difficult to get it approved." the chairman thought to himself.

"Comrades, do you have any comments?"

The air in the hall was so thick it was suffocating.

"If there are no comments then we'll pass it on a show of hands!"

"Wait a minute!" A thin and withered old worker stood up. "Why isn't Old Hao on the list this time?"

Old Hao, sitting at the back, was startled.

The chairman hurriedly explained: "As we progress...."

Another rude voice cut him off: "Get to the point! What mistake has Old Hao made? Some say the damned rest home was built by Old Hao, but that lousy idea was not his — I swear to it. He wanted to build it in the woods."

On the platform the chairman whispered in the others' ears.

The little granddaughter felt her grandpa tremble but the intense scene interested her so much that she paid no attention.

The chairman walked to the front of the platform and spoke in a loud voice. The whole hall was like a pile of dry grass on fire. "Comrades! Comrades! Everyone's opinion can...." A worker raised his hand high. The chairman let him speak.

"When our roofs were leaking who was it who got them to come and do repairs? Who works hard for the workers all year round? When we are in trouble, who always stretches out a helping hand? Who? Is this person not good enough to be a union cadre?" Indignantly he sat down, scraping his chair.

Then another worker stood up: "When Old Wu died, did you go to the funeral? And you're the chairman!" These harsh accusations really put the chairman on the spot.

The chairman called an immediate committee meeting on the platform. The hall was like a pot of boiling water, fiercely bubbling. Someone opened a window and a cold, spring breeze blew through.

The granddaughter felt her grandfather stop trembling but he held her even tighter, so she could not turn her head and see his face.

The chairman walked to the front of the stage and raised his hand to quiet everyone. He called loudly: "Comrades! We won't vote on this list of nominees. I want each workshop to send a representative to select a ballot paper. The papers had been pre-printed. So if you want to select Comrade Hao Kuishan or any other comrade, just cross a name off the list and fill in your own choice."

Once again the meeting hall was in confusion. The red ballot box was placed in the centre of the hall.

"The character for 'Hao' is written with a *chi* plus an ear radical; 'Kui' is a ghost radical plus the character *dou*; 'Shan' is the character meaning mountain...." The megaphone was of little use. Never had a meeting been as heated as it was today. No one wanted to leave before finding out the results.

Selecting vote counters and ballot guards created another hullabaloo. They were pushed forward to the ballot box by the electors and set to work.

There were three thousand, four hundred and twenty-three votes possible. An abacus from the accounting department clicked away. A record played over the loud speakers but no one could hear the words.

The granddaughter had already lost interest. People formed groups and moved apart again. Unnoticed by anyone, she went to sleep in her grandfather's arms in the gloomy corner by the door.

With all this going on, in addition to the noise of the jumping abacus beads, it really was mass confusion. Hao Kuishan's tally increased — two thousand, nine hundred; three thousand, one hundred; three thousand, three hundred ... three thousand, four hundred and five. Check it again. The calculator and the abacus gave exactly the same result. The news did not need to be announced over the megaphone. In a blink of an eye it had been passed to every corner of the hall.

The chairman announced the results of the vote: "In first place Hao Kuishan with three thousand, four hundred and five votes. In second place...." Before he had finished speaking his voice was drowned in thunderous applause.

"Quiet! Quiet!" cried the chairman.

No one listened to him. The applause took up a rhythm. It was not clear if Old Hao at the back of the hall was happy or upset. He let his head drop.

"Where's Old Hao? Speech! Speech!"

"Quiet! Quiet!" The chairman tapped on the microphone. "Quiet down, comrades! Today's meeting has been most successful! Please quiet down. This is exemplary democracy...."

"Where's Old Hao? Old Hao! Old Hao! Has he come?"

Everyone looked round for him. The granddaughter woke up and nudged him in the ribs. He was absolutely still as if in a deep sleep.

"Grandpa! Grandpa!" She removed his stiff arms from around her, turned her head and saw his wooden, staring eyes. His stiffening lips dribbled saliva. She cried out in terror.

Old Hao was dead!

He had quietly died midst the sound of the crowd. The whole hall went quiet. Even the rustling of the curtains could be heard clearly. The cool wind brought the flavour of spring with it. Everyone breathed in deeply. Remembering hardworking Old Hao, great shock waves pounded through their brains. Their eyes filled with tears. Although they tried to restrain their emotions, they missed him and felt greatly indebted to him, so few could refrain from sobbing. Even those who had shamed him felt uneasy.

In accordance with the union rules a re-election was held with more than a two-thirds taking part. This time the election was successful. The new committee got down to business.

1957

Translated by Alice Childs

The Family on the Other Side of the Mountain

●

—— ZHOU LIBO ——

Zhou Libo (1908-79), a native of Hunan, joined the China Federation of Left-Wing Writers in 1934. After the Anti-Japanese War broke out he went to take part in the resistance work serving as an editor of a magazine and newspaper. He also served as a war correspondent, translator, and teacher at Lu Xun Arts Institute in Yan'an. After Liberation in 1949 he continued to write. His works include the novels Hurricane, The Flowing Molten Iron *and* Great Change in a Mountain Village *and many short stories and essays.*

TREADING on the shadows of the trees cast on the slope by the moon, we were on our way to a wedding on the other side of the mountain.

Why should we go to a wedding? If anyone should ask, this is our answer: sometimes people like to go to weddings to watch the happiness of others and to increase one's own joy.

A group of girls were walking in front of us. Once girls gather in groups, they laugh all the time. These now laughed ceaselessly. One of them even had to halt by the roadside to rub her aching sides. She scolded the one who provoked such laughter while she kept on giggling. Why were they laughing? I had no idea. Generally, I do not understand much about girls. But I have consulted an expert who has a profound understanding of girls. What he said was "they laugh because they want to laugh".... I thought that was very clever. But someone else told me that "although you can't tell exactly what makes them laugh, generally speaking, youth, health, the carefree life in the co-op, the fertile green fields where they labour, being paid on the same basis as the men, the misty moonlight, the light fragrance of flowers, a vague or real feeling of love ... all these are sources of their joy."

I thought there was a lot of sense in what he said too.

When we had climbed over the mountain we could see the home of the bridegroom — two little rooms in a big brick house. A little ancient red lantern was hung at the door. The girls rushed inside like a swarm of bees. According to local tradition, they have this privilege when families celebrate this happy event. In the past, unmarried girls used to eavesdrop the first night of a friend's marriage under the window or outside the bridal chamber. When they heard such questions as "Uh ... are you sleepy?" they would run away and laugh heartily. They would laugh again and again the next day too. But there were times when they could hear nothing. Experienced eavesdroppers would keep entirely silent on their own first night of bliss and make the girls outside the window walk away in disappointment.

The group of girls ahead of us had crowded into the door. Had they come to eavesdrop too?

I had picked several camellias to present to the bride and groom. When I reached the door I saw it was flanked with a pair of couplets written on red paper. By the light of a red lantern one could make out the squarely written words:

Songs wing through the streets,
Joy fills the room.

As we entered, a young man who was all smiles walked up to welcome us. He was the bridegroom, Zou Maiqiu, the storekeeper of the co-op. He was short and sturdy with nice features. Some said he was a simple, honest man but others insisted he wasn't so simple, because he found himself a beautiful bride. It is said that beautiful girls do not love simple men. Who knows? Let's take a look at the bride first.

After presenting the camellias to the bridegroom, we walked towards the bridal chamber. The wooden lattice of the window was pasted with fresh paper and decorated in the centre with the character "happiness", cut out of red paper. In the four corners were charming paper-cuts of carps, orchids and two beautiful vases with two fat pigs at the side.

We walked into the room. The girls were there already, tittering softly and whispering. When we were seated they left the room in a flock. Laughter rang outside the door.

Then we scrutinized the room. Many people were seated there. The bride and her matron, who was her sister-in-law, sat on the edge of the bed. The sister-in-law had brought her three-year-old boy along and was teaching him to sing:

In his red baby shoes a child of three,
Toddles off to school just like his big brother.
Don't spank me, teacher, right back I shall be
After going home for a swig of milk from mother.

I stole a glance at the bride, Pu Cuilian. She was not strikingly beautiful, but she wasn't bad looking either. Her features and figure were quite all right. So we reached the conclusion that the bridegroom was a simple and yet not too simple man. Though everyone in the room had his eyes on the bride, she remained composed and was not a bit shy. She took her nephew over from her sister-in-law, tickled him to make him laugh and then took him out to play for a while in the courtyard. As she walked past, she trailed behind a light fragrance.

A kerosene lamp was lit. Its yellowish flame lit up the things in the room. The bed was an old one, the mosquito-net was not new either and its embroidered red brocade fringes were only half new. The only thing new were the two pillows.

On the red lacquer desk by the window were two pewter candlestands and two small rectangular mirrors. Then there were china bowls and a teapot decorated with "happiness" cut out of red paper. Most outstanding of all the bric-a-brac presents were two half-naked porcelain monks, with enormous pot bellies, laughing heartily. Why did they laugh? Since they were monks they should have considered such merry-making as frivolous and empty. Why had they come to the wedding then? And they looked so happy too. They must have learned to take a more enlightened view of life, I suppose.

Among the people chatting and laughing were the township head, the chairman of the co-op, the veterinarian and his wife. The township head was a serious man. He never laughed at the jokes others cracked. Even when he joked himself, he kept a straight face. He was a busy man, he hadn't intended to come to the wedding. But since Zou was on the co-op's administrative staff and also his neighbour, he had to show up. As soon as he stepped into the door, the bridegroom's mother came up to him and said:

"You have come just at the right moment. We need a responsible person to see to things." She meant that she wanted him to officiate.

So he had to stay. He smoked and chatted, waiting for the ceremony to begin.

The head of the co-op was a busy person too. He usually had serious talks. He also had to work in the fields and was often scolded by his wife for coming home too late at night. He worked hard and never complained. Indeed he was a busy man, but he had to come to congratulate the union of these two young people however busy he was. Zou Maiqiu was one of his best assistants. He had come to express his goodwill and to offer his help.

Of all the guests, the veterinarian talked the most. Talking on all subjects, he finally came to the marriage system.

"There are some merits to arranged marriages too. You don't have to take all the trouble of looking for a wife yourself," said he, for he had obtained his beautiful wife through an old-fashioned arbitrarily arranged marriage, and he was extremely satisfied. With his drink-mottled pock-marked face, he would never have been able to get such a beautiful wife by himself.

"I advocate free choice in marriage," said the chairman. His wife, who married him also in the old-fashioned way, often scolded him, and this made him detest the arbitrary marriage system.

"I agree with you." The township head sided with the co-op chairman. "There is a folk song about the sorrows caused by the old marriage system."

"Recite it to us," urged the co-op chairman.

> "The old marriage system promises no freedom.
> The woman cries and the man grieves.
> She cries till the Yangtse River overflows,
> And he grieves till the green mountain is crested white."

"Is it as bad as that?" laughed the co-op chairman.

"We neither cry nor grieve," said the veterinarian proudly, looking at his wife.

"You are just a blind dog who happened on a good meal by accident," said the township head. "Talking about crying reminds me of the custom in Jinshi." He paused to light his pipe.

"What kind of custom?" asked the chairman.

"The family who is marrying off a daughter must hire many people to cry. Rich families sometimes hire several dozen."

"What if the people they hire don't know how to cry?" asked the veterinarian.

"The purpose is to hire those who do. There are people in Jinshi who are professional criers and specialists in this trade. Their crying is as rhythmic as singing, very pleasing to the ear."

Peals of laughter burst forth outside the window. The girls, who had been away for some time, evidently were practising eavesdropping already. All the people in the bridal chamber, including the bride, laughed with them. The only people who did not laugh were the township head and the veterinarian's beautiful wife who knitted her brows.

"Anything wrong with you?" the veterinarian asked softly.

"I feel a little dizzy and there's a sick feeling in my stomach."

"Perhaps you're pregnant?" suggested the township head.

"Have you seen a doctor?" the bride's sister-in-law asked.

"She's in bed with a doctor every night! She doesn't have to look for one," laughed the chairman.

"How can you say such things at your age!" said the veterinarian's beautiful wife. "And you a chairman of the co-op!"

"Everything is ready," someone called. "Come to the hall please." All crowded into the hall. With her little boy in her arms, the bride's sister-in-law followed behind the bride. The girls also came in. They leaned against the wall, shoulder to shoulder and holding hands. They looked at the bride, whispered into each other's ears and giggled again.

On one side of the hall were barrows, baskets and bamboo mats which belonged to the co-op. On the table in the centre, two red candles were lit, shining on two vases of camellias.

The ceremony began. The township head took his place. He read the marriage lines, talked a little and withdrew to sit beside the co-op chairman. The girl who acted as the conductor of ceremonies announced that the next speaker was to be one of the guests. Whoever arranged the programme had put the most interesting item, the bride's turn to speak, at the very end. So everyone waited eagerly for the guests to finish their chatter.

The first one called upon was the co-op chairman. But he said:

"Let the bride speak. I have been married for more then twenty years and have quite forgotten what it is like to be a newly-wed. What can I say?"

All laughed and clapped. However the person who walked up to speak was not the bride but the veterinarian with his drink-mottled pock-marked face. He spoke slowly, like an actor. Starting from the situation in our country before and after Liberation and using a lot of special terms, he went on to the international situation.

"I have an appointment. I must leave early," said the township head softly to the co-op chairman. "You stay to officiate."

"I should be leaving too."

"No, you can't. We shouldn't both leave," said the township head. He nodded to the bridegroom's mother apologetically and left. The co-op chairman had to stay. Bored by the talk, he said to the person sitting beside him:

"What on earth is the relation between the wedding and the situation at home and abroad?"

"This is his usual routine. He has only touched on two points, so far. There are still a lot yet."

"We should invent some kind of device that makes empty talkers itch all over so that they have to scratch and cannot go on speaking," said the chairman.

After half an hour or so, the guests clapped hands again. The veterinarian had ended his speech at last. This time the bride took the floor. Her plaits tied up with red wool, she was blushing crimson in spite of her poise. She said:

"Comrades and fellow villagers, I am very happy this evening, very, very happy."

The girls giggled. But the bride who was saying that she was very, very happy didn't even smile. On the contrary, she was very nervous. She continued:

"We were married a year ago."

The guests were shocked, and then they laughed. After a while they realized that she had said married instead of engaged because she was so nervous.

"We are being married today. I'm very happy." She paused and glanced at the guests before continuing. "Please don't misunderstand me when I say I'm happy. That doesn't mean I shall enjoy my happiness by sitting idly at home. I do not intend to be merely dependent on my husband. I shall do my share of work. I'll do my work well in the co-op and compete with him."

"Hurrah! And beat Zhou down too." A young man applauded.

"That's all I have to say." The bride, blushing scarlet, escaped from the floor.

"Is that all?" Someone wanted to hear more.

"She has spoken too little." Another was not satisfied.

"The bride's relative's turn now," said the girl conductor of ceremony.

Holding her boy of three the bride's sister-in-law stood up.

"I have not studied and I don't know how to talk." She sat down blushing scarlet too.

"Let the bridegroom say whether he accepts the bride's challenge," someone suggested.

"Where is the bridegroom?"

"He's not here," someone discovered.

"He's run away!" another decided.

"Run away? Why?"

"Where has he run to?"

"This is terrible. What kind of a bridegroom is he?"

"He must be frightened by the bride's challenge to compete."

"Look for him immediately. It's unbelievable! The bride's relative is still here," said the co-op chairman.

With torches and flashlights people hurried out. They looked for him in the mountains, by the brooks and pools and everywhere. The co-op chairman and several men, about to join in the hunt, noticed a light in the sweet potato cellar.

"So you are here. You are the limit, you...." A young man felt like cursing him.

"Why have you run away? Are you afraid of the challenge?" asked the chairman.

Zhou Maiqiu climbed out of the cellar with a lantern. Brushing the dust from his clothes he raised his eyebrows and said calmly in a low voice:

"Rather than sit there listening to the veterinarian's empty talk, I thought I might as well come to see whether our sweet potatoes are in good condition."

"You are a good storekeeper, but certainly a poor bridegroom. Aren't you afraid your bride'll be offended?" said the chairman half reproachfully and half encouragingly.

After escorting the bridegroom back, we took our leave. Again treading on the tree shadows cast by the moonlight, which by now was slanting to the west, we went home. The group of girls who had come with us remained behind.

In the early winter night the breeze, fragrant with the scent of camellias, brought to our ears the peals of happy open laughter from the girls. They must have begun their eavesdropping. Had they heard something interesting already?

November, 1957

Translated by Yu Fanqin

Lilies

●

—— RU ZHIJUAN ——

One of China's most popular authors, Ru Zhijuan is best known for her short stories. She was sent to an orphanage when she was a child. In 1943 she became a primary school teacher and later joined a theatrical troupe. She published her first short story in 1950 but it was her short story "Lilies" that shot her to fame in 1958. Her first collection of short stories The Tall Poplar *came out in 1959 and her second collection* The Quiet Maternity Home *appeared in 1962. Her recent works include "The Path Through the Grassland" and "A Badly Edited Story", two national prize-winning stories.*

MID-AUTUMN 1946.

When our coastal command decided to launch a general offensive against the Kuomintang forces, some of us in the concert group were sent by the commander of the leading regiment to lend a hand in different combat companies. Probably because I was a woman, the commander kept me till one of the very last before finally assigning me to a first-aid post near the front. I put on my rucksack and followed the messenger sent to show me the way.

It had rained that morning, and though the weather had cleared the road was still slippery, and the crops on either side sparkled fresh and green in the sunlight. There was a moist freshness in the air. If not for the sporadic booming of the enemy artillery which was firing at random, you could have imagined you were on your way to a fair.

The messenger strode along in front of me. Straight off, he put a distance of about a dozen yards between us. Because my feet were blistered and the road was slippery, try as I might I could not catch up with him. If I called to him to wait, he might think me a coward; but I couldn't hope to find the post alone. He began to annoy me.

The funny thing was that he seemed to have eyes in the back of his head, for presently he stopped of his own accord. He didn't look at me, though, just stared ahead. When I had nearly struggled up to him, he strode off again, promptly leaving me a dozen yards behind. Too exhausted to catch up, I plodded slowly along. But it was all right. he neither let me fall too far behind nor get too close to him, keeping at a distance of a dozen yards. When I quickened my step, he swung along with big strides; when I slowed down, he started sauntering too. Oddly enough, I never caught him looking back at me. I began to feel curious about this messenger.

I had barely glanced at him at regimental headquarters. Now I saw he was a tall young fellow, but pretty strong judging by his strapping shoulders. He was wearing a faded yellow uniform and puttees. The twigs in the barrel of his rifle seemed put there more for ornament than camouflage.

Though I couldn't overtake him, my feet were swollen and smarting. I called out, suggesting that we stop to rest, and sat down on a boundary stone. He sat on another stone further on, his gun across his knees and his back to me, ignoring my existence completely. I knew from experience that this was because I was a girl. Girls always had trouble like this with bashful young fellows. Feeling rather disgruntled, I went over and sat down defiantly opposite him. With his young, ingenuous round face, he looked no more than eighteen at the most. My closeness flustered him. He didn't know what to do. He hardly liked to turn his back on me, but it embarrassed him to look at me and he couldn't very well get up either. Trying hard to keep a straight face, I asked where he was from. Flushing up to his ears, he cleared his throat and told me:

"Tianmushan."

So we were from the same district!

"What did you do at home?"

"Helped haul bamboo."

I glanced at his broad shoulders, and through my mind flashed a picture of a sea of vivid green bamboo, with a narrow stone path winding up and up. A broad-shouldered lad with a square of blue cloth over his shoulders was hauling young bamboos whose long tips rattled on the stones behind.... That was a familiar sight in my home village. At once I felt drawn to my young fellow countryman.

"How old are you?" I asked.

"Nineteen."

"When did you join the army?"

"Last year."

"Why did you join?" I couldn't help asking the questions, though I realized this sounded more like a cross-examination than a conversation.

"When the army passed through my village, I came along with it."

"What family do you have?"

"Mum, dad, a younger brother and sisters, an aunt who lives with us."

"Are you married?"

"...." He flushed and fumbled with his belt, looking more sheepish than ever. With his eyes on the ground, he laughed awkwardly and briskly shook his head. It was on the tip of my tongue to ask if he had a fiancee, but I bit the question back.

After we had sat there, tongue-tied, for a while, he looked at the sky and then at me, as if to say: "Time to move on!"

It was two in the afternoon by the time we reached the first-aid post. This was set up in a primary school three li from the front. Six buildings of different sizes were grouped roughly in a triangular formation, and the weeds in the yard between showed that classes had stopped for some time. We arrived to find several orderlies there preparing dressings, and the rooms filled with doors taken off their hinges and laid across bricks to serve as beds.

Presently a cadre from the local government came in, his eyes bloodshot from working late at night. To shade his eyes from the light, he had stuck a cardboard visor under his old felt hat. He had a gun over one shoulder, a scale over the other, and was carrying a basket of eggs and a large pan. He walked in, panting, put down these things, and between sips of water and bites at a ball of cooked rice produced from his pocket apologized for the state things were in. I was so fascinated by the speed with which he did all this that I hardly heard what he was saying, simply catching something about bedding which we would have to borrow. I found out from the orderlies that as the army quilts had not arrived but casualties who had lost blood were extremely susceptible to the cold, we had better borrow quilts from the villagers. Just one or two dozen mattresses would be better than nothing. Anxious to be of some use, I volunteered for the job, and because it was urgent, asked my young fellow countryman to help me before he left. After a second's hesitation he agreed.

We went to a nearby village, where he turned east, I west. Before long I had handed out three receipts for two mattresses and one quilt. Heavily laden as I was, my heart was light, and I had decided to deliver these and come back for more when the messenger walked over empty-handed.

"What happened?" The people here were so solidly behind our army and so hospitable that I couldn't understand why they had refused to lend him bedding.

"You go and ask them, sister.... These feudal-minded women!"

"Which house? Take me there." He must have said the wrong thing and annoyed someone. Getting one quilt less didn't matter, but offending the local people would have serious consequences. He stood there as if nailed to the ground till I reminded him quietly how important it was not to offend the masses and what a bad effect this was likely to have. At once he led the way.

No one was stirring in the hall of the house we entered. A blue curtain with a red border on top hung over the door of the inner room, and on both sides were pasted in bright red characters: "Happiness". Standing there, I called several times; but no one answered though we heard movements inside. Presently the curtain was raised and a young woman appeared. She was very pretty with fine features, arched eyebrows and a fluffy fringe. Her clothes were homespun, but new. Since she had done her hair like a married woman, I addressed her as elder sister-in-law, apologizing if the messenger had said anything to annoy her. She listened with a slightly averted face, biting her lips and smiling. When I had finished, she simply hung her head and went on biting her lips as if to keep from laughing. I scarcely knew how to bring out my request. But the messenger was watching me intently, as if I were a company commander about to demonstrate some new drill. Putting on a bold front, I asked bluntly for a quilt, explaining that our soldiers were fighting for the common folk. She listened to this without smiling, glancing from time to time back into her room. Then she looked first at me and next at the messenger, as if to weigh my words. The next moment she went in to fetch a quilt.

The messenger seized this chance to protest:

"Well, I never! I told her the same thing just now, but she wouldn't listen."

I threw him a warning glance, but it was too late. She was already at the door with the quilt. At last I understood why she hadn't wanted to lend it. It was a flowered quilt, completely new. The cover was of imitation brocade, with countless white lilies on a rich red ground. As if to provoke the messenger, she held the quilt out to me, saying:

"Here you are!"

Since my hands were full, I nodded to the lad. He pretended not to see. When I called him he pulled a long face, and with downcast eyes took the bedding and turned to rush off. There was a ripping sound — his jacket had caught on the door and torn at the shoulder. Quite a large rent it was. With a smile, the young woman went in to fetch needle and thread, but he wouldn't hear of her mending it. He went off with the quilt.

We hadn't gone far when someone told us that the young woman was a bride of three days' standing, and this quilt was all the dowry she had. That upset me, and the messenger looked unhappy too as he stared in silence at the quilt in his arms. He must have felt as I did, for he muttered to me as we walked:

"How could we know we were borrowing her wedding quilt? It's too bad...."

To tease him, I said solemnly: "Yes. To buy a quilt like this, ever since she was a girl she must have got up at dawn and gone to bed late, doing all sorts of extra jobs to make a little money. Think how much sleep she may have lost over it! Yet I heard someone call her feudal-minded...."

He halted suddenly.

"Well, let's take it back!"

"You'd only hurt her feelings, now that she's lent it." I was amused and touched by the earnest, unhappy look on his face. There was something extraordinarily lovable about this simple young countryman of mine.

He thought that over and evidently decided I was right, for he answered:

"All right. Let it go. We'll wash it well when we've done with it." Having settled this in his mind, he took all the quilts I was carrying, slung them over his shoulders and strode quickly off.

Back at the first-aid post, I told him to rejoin regimental headquarters. He brightened up immediately, saluted me and ran off. After a few steps he remembered something, and fumbled in his satchel for two buns. He held these up for me to see, after which he put them on a stone by the road, calling:

"Dinner's served!" Then he flew off. As I walked over to pick up the two stale buns, I noticed that a wild chrysanthemum had appeared in his rifle barrel to sway with the other twigs behind his ear.

He was some distance now, but I could still see his torn jacket flapping in the wind. I was very sorry I hadn't mended it for him. Now his shoulder would be bare all evening at least.

There were not many of us in the first-aid post. The man from the local government found some village women to help us draw water, cook and do odd jobs. Among them was the bride, still smiling with closed lips. She glanced at me from time to time, and kept looking round as if in search of someone. At last she asked:

"Where has that comrade gone?"

When I told her he had gone to the front, she smiled shyly and said, "Just now when he came to borrow bedding, I treated him rather badly." Then smiling she set to work, neatly spreading the mattresses and quilts we had borrowed on the improvised beds made of door-boards and tables (two tables put together is one bed). She put her own quilt on a door-board under one corner of the eaves outside.

In the evening a full moon rose. Our offensive still hadn't started. As usual the enemy was so afraid of the dark that they lit a host of fires and started bombarding at random, while the flares that went up one after the other to hang like paraffin lamps beneath the moon made everything below as bright as day. To attack under these conditions would be very hard and would surely entail heavy losses. I resented even that round, silver moon.

The man from the local government brought us food and some home-made moon cakes. Apparently it was the Moon Festival!

That made me think of home. At home now, for the festival, there would be a small bamboo table outside each gate, with incense and candles burning beside a few dishes of sunflower seeds, fruit and moon cakes. The children would be waiting impatiently for the incense to burn out so that they could share the good things prepared for the goddess of the moon. Skipping round the table, they would sing: "The moon is so bright; we beat gongs and buy sweets...." or "Mother moon, please shine on me...." My thoughts flew to the lad from Tianmushan who had hauled bamboos. A few years ago he had probably sung the same songs.... I tasted a delicious home-made cake, and imagined the messenger lying in a dugout, or perhaps at regimental headquarters, or walking through the winding communication trenches....

Soon after that our guns roared out and red tracer bullets shot across the sky. The offensive had begun. Before long, casualties started trickling in, and the atmosphere grew tense in the first-aid post.

I registered the names and units of the wounded. The lighter cases could tell me who they were, but when they were heavily wounded I had to turn back their insignia or the lapels of their jackets. My heart missed a beat when under the insignia of one badly injured man I read: "Messenger". But I found he was a battalion messenger. My young friend worked in regimental head-quarters. I resisted a foolish impulse to ask if casualties ever got left on the field, and what messengers did during combat apart from delivering dispatches.

For an hour or so after the offensive started, everything went swimmingly. The wounded men, as they came in, reported that we had broken through the first stockade, then the barbed wire entanglement, occupied the first fortifications, and started fighting in the streets. But at that point the news stopped. In answer to our questions, incoming casualties just told us briefly: "They're still fighting...." "Fighting in the streets." But from the mud which covered them, their utter exhaustion and the stretchers which looked as if dug out of the mire, we could imagine the fierceness of the battle.

Soon we ran out of stretchers, so that not all the heavily wounded could be sent straight to the hospital in the rear. There was nothing I could do to alleviate the men's pain, except get the village women to wash their hands and faces, give a little broth to those able to eat, or change the clothes of those who had their packs with them. In some cases we had to take off their clothes to wash away the blood and filth in which they were covered.

I was used to work like this, but the village women were shy and afraid to attempt it. They all wanted to cook instead. I had to persuade the young bride for a long time before, blushing furiously, she would consent. She only consented, though, to be my assistant.

The firing at the front was spasmodic now. I thought it must soon be dawn, but actually it was only the middle of the night. The moon was very bright and seemed higher than usual. When the next serious casualty was brought in, all the beds inside were occupied and I had him put under the eaves outside. After the stretcher-bearers laid him there, they gathered around and wouldn't go. One old fellow, taking me for a doctor, caught hold of my arm and said earnestly: "Doctor, you've got to think of a way to cure him! If you save him our stretcher-bearers' squad will give you a red flag!" The other bearers were watching me, wide-eyed, as if I had only to nod to cure the soldier. Before there was time to explain, the bride came up with water, and gave a smothered cry. I pushed through the bearers to have a look, and saw a young, round ingenuous face which had been ruddy but now was deathly pale. His eyes were peacefully closed, and the torn flap in the shoulder of his uniform was still hanging loose.

"He did it for us," said the old stretcher-bearer remorsefully. "Over ten of us were waiting in a lane to go forward, and he was just behind us when the bastards threw a hand-grenade down from a roof. The grenade was smoking and whizzing about between us. He shouted to us to drop flat, and threw himself on the thing...."

The bride drew in her breath sharply. I held back my tears while I said a few words to the bearers and sent them off. When I turned back again, the bride had quietly fetched an oil lamp and undone the messenger's jacket. Gone was all her previous embarrassment, as she earnestly gave him a gentle rub down. The tall young messenger lay there without a sound.... I pulled myself together and raced off to find the doctor. When we got back to give him an injection, the bride was sitting at his side.

Bending over her work, stitch by stitch she was mending the tear in his uniform. The doctor made a stethoscope examination, then straightened up gravely to say: "There's nothing we can do." I stepped up and felt the lad's hand — it was icy cold. The bride seemed to have seen and heard nothing. She went on sewing neatly and skilfully. I couldn't bear to watch her.

"Don't do that!" I whispered.

She flashed me a glance of surprise, then lowered her head to go on sewing, stitch by stitch. I longed to take her away, to scatter this atmosphere of gloom, to see him sit up and laugh shyly. At that moment I felt something in my pocket — the two stale buns the messenger had given me.

The orderlies brought a coffin, and removed the quilt. The bride suddenly turned pale. Snatching up the quilt, she spread half of it on the bottom of the coffin, leaving half to cover him.

"That quilt belongs to one of the villagers," an orderly said.

"It's mine!" She turned away. Her eyes were bright with unshed tears in the moonlight. I watched as they covered the face of that ordinary country lad, who had hauled bamboo, with this red quilt dotted with white lilies — flowers of true purity of heart and love.

March 1958

Translated by Gladys Yang

Seven Matches

●

── WANG YUANJIAN ──

Born in 1929 in Shandong, Wang Yuanjian joined the Chinese Communist Party's Eighth Route Army in 1945 as a cultural worker. In 1952 he became an editor of the Liberation Army Literature *magazine and took part in compiling* A Single Spark Can Start a Prairie Fire. *He began to write in 1954 and has published several collections of short stories, including* Party Membership Dues, The Descendants *and* An Ordinary Labourer. *In addition to short stories, he also writes film scenarios.*

AT dawn the rain stopped. The weather was peculiar in the marshy grasslands.*

A moment ago it had been a clear, moonlit night. But suddenly a cold wind had risen, and heavy clouds, which seemed to spring up out of the ground, covered the sky. Then rain had come pouring down, mixed with hailstones as big as chestnuts.

Red Army soldier Lu Jinyong poked his head out of the grove of trees and looked around. The grasslands were covered by a dense pall of rain and fog. The wild grass, beaten down by the storm, lay flat and glistening in the mud, neatly, as if it had been gone over by some giant comb. Even the path was hard to see. The sky was still overcast. From time to time, scattered hailstones fell, kicking up little geysers in the muddy green puddles.

Lu expelled an exasperated breath. The wound in the calf of his leg had become inflamed, and he had fallen behind. For two days now, travelling day and night, he had been trying to catch up. Originally he had thought he could do it today, but that wretched storm had delayed him

---

*Determined to resist the Japanese invaders, the Communist-led Red Army, after breaking out of the encirclement by reactionary Kuomintang crack forces, moved north in an arduous 8,000-mile trek that became known as the Long March. At one point the March passed through vast uninhabited grasslands in the extreme west of China.

half the night.

Cursing the weather, he emerged from the grove and stretched mightily. A chill gust of wind made him shiver. It was then he realized that his clothing was soaking wet.

Wringing the edge of his tunic, he watched the water trickle down his trouser-leg. If I had a nice fire to dry myself ... he thought. But he knew that was an idle dream. The day before yesterday, when he was still marching with his company, they had been forced to eat their flour ration raw because they had no matches left, in fact most of their limited supplies were almost gone.

Still, he automatically groped in his trouser pocket. His hand came in contact with a sticky substance. Delighted, he turned the pocket inside out. The remains of some barley flour had been converted by the rain into a small glutinous mass. He scraped it carefully together till it formed a ball as big as a chicken egg. Avidly, he kneaded it with his fingers, pulling it into a long thin strip, compressing it back into a ball again.

How lucky I didn't discover this yesterday! He congratulated himself.

He had eaten nothing for more than twenty-four hours. Now, seeing this food, he felt a hunger that was almost unendurable. So that he wouldn't finish it all in one gulp, he again pulled the dough into a long strip. Just as he was about to take his first bite, he heard a voice call softly:

"Comrade...."

The voice was so weak, so low, it seemed to float up from beneath the ground. After a surprised pause, he hobbled over in the direction from which the sound had come.

Limping across two ditches, Lu neared a small tree. The man who had hailed him was seated in a half-lying position, propped against the fork of the tree. The lower half of his body was completely immersed in the mire. It was plain that he had been unable to move for some time. He was shockingly pale. Rain had plastered his hair against his forehead like a piece of black felt. Water ran from his head down his cheeks and dripped to the ground. His deeply sunken eyes were shut tight. Only his Adam's apple and his dry split lips moved:

"Comrade ... comrade...."

At the sound of Lu's footsteps, the man opened his eyes with an effort. He struggled to sit up, but did not succeed.

Lu's eyes smarted. In the two days since he had dropped out of the ranks this was the third fallen comrade he had met.

He must be starving! Lu thought. Taking a quick step forward, he supported the man around the shoulders, and brought the bit of barley flour to his lips. "Eat, comrade, eat!"

The man stared at Lu with lacklustre eyes, then pushed his hand away. Again the man's lips trembled. The words were forced out between his teeth:

"No. It's no ... use."

Lu's hand paused in mid-air. He didn't know what to do. He looked at that face, blue with icy wind and cold rain, and dripping wet. If we only had a fire, just a cup of hot water, maybe he could live, Lu thought miserably. Raising his head, Lu peered off into the hazy distance. Then he pulled the man by the wrist and said:

"Let's walk. I'll support you."

The man closed his eyes and shook his head. He seemed to be mustering his strength. After a long while, he opened his eyes. Pointing with his right hand to his left armpit, he said agitatedly: "Here ... here!"

Perturbed, Lu put his hand inside the man's drenched shirt. His chest and garment were equally icy. Beneath his arm, Lu found a hard little packet wrapped in paper. Lu placed it in his hand.

With shaking fingers, the man undid the packet. It contained a Communist Party membership book. Inside the book was a little bundle of matches. Dry matches. The red tips of the matches were pressed against the vermilion seal on the Party card like a leaping flame.

"Comrade, here, look..." the man beckoned to Lu. He waited for Lu to come closer, then, with palsied fingers, he carefully counted each match. His voice was weak: "One, two, three, four...."

It took him a long time to count the seven matches. When he had finished, he gazed at Lu questioningly, as if to ask: "Do you understand?"

"Yes! I understand!" Lu happily nodded his head. This won't be hard, he thought. He could picture a bright red fire. They were both sitting beside it. He was holding the comrade in his arms.

At that moment, he noticed that the man's face was softening. A cheerful gleam replaced the drab look in the man's eyes. Ceremoniously, carefully, as if proffering a brimming bowl of water with both hands, he presented Lu with his Party card and his little bundle of matches. He gripped them and Lu's hand together in a tight clasp. His eyes were fixed on Lu's face.

"Remember, these ... these belong to all the comrades!" The man suddenly drew back his hands, took a deep breath and, with all his strength, raised his arm and pointed north. "Good ... good comrade, give them ... give them to...."

The words ended here. Lu felt the weight in his arms sink heavily! His eyes blurred. The distant trees, the nearby grass, the wet clothing, the tightly shut eyes ... all were misty, hazy, like the grasslands. Only that arm, still raised high, was clear, pointing like a road sign, straight as an arrow in the direction in which the Long March was heading....

Lu finished the rest of the journey quickly. He caught up with the rear-guard before dark.

Then, in the limitless dark night, a flame was kindled. The fighters who had spent their last few days in wind and rain and mud gathered around the merry blaze, talking, laughing. Steam rose from their damp garments. Warm cooked wild herbs rustled in their eating bowls....

Quietly, Lu walked up to the political instructor of the rear-guard company. Reflected firelight danced on his trembling hands as he delivered the Party card and the remaining six matches. In a strained voice, Lu counted:

"One, two, three, four...."

January 20, 1958

Translated by Sidney Shapiro

My First Superior

●

—— **MA FENG** ——

Ma Feng, born in Shanxi in 1922, joined the Chinese Communist Party's Eighth Route Army at the age of sixteen and got involved in propaganda work. In 1942 he published his first story "First Reconnaissance" and in 1944 he coauthored with Xi Rong the successful novel Heroes of Luliang. *Since 1949 he has published many fine works including the collections of short stories* My First Superior *and* Vendetta, *the biographical novel* Liu Hulan *and the screenplay* The Youth of Our Village. *"The 'On-the-Spot' Wedding" won a national short story award.*

SOON after I graduated from the provincial Water Conservancy School last summer I was assigned to work in this county. I was in quite a state at the time — I don't know whether it was from excitement or tension. Probably all students feel the same way when they go to their first job.

With my luggage strapped to my bicycle, I rode off to "take office". I didn't travel by bus because I wanted to start training immediately for long trips by bike. I imagined I would need that ability, working in the countryside.

I set out before daybreak and it was nearly noon by the time I reached the county seat. No sooner had I entered town than I had an accident. The streets were rather narrow and as I pedalled along I saw an old man coming towards me. He looked like an oddball. Although it was the hottest part of summer, he wore a lined jacket and black cotton-padded trousers tied at the cuffs. His head was covered by a big straw hat. Was he avoiding the heat, or was he afraid of being cold?

Head down, back bent, hands clasped behind him, he advanced with a stately gait, his toes pointing outwards. I rang my bell loudly, but he didn't even raise his head. He just kept ambling along at the same deliberate pace. When we were only a few feet apart, he suddenly looked up and moved two steps to the right.

But it was too late. When I thought that he wasn't giving way, I cut right to pass him just as he was stepping in the same direction to avoid me and knocked him down. I fell too. Tired and hungry, I had been irritated by his hogging the road. Now my tumble made me furious. I crawled to my feet and picked up the bike.

"Are you deaf or something!" I shouted. "Didn't you hear my bell?"

I felt ashamed as soon as the words left my mouth. He hadn't refused to get out of the way; he had only been a little slow. What's more, I had run him down. Of course, he must have been pretty annoyed. I was sure he wasn't going to let me get away with it; I was probably in for a row.

He picked up his hat and rose slowly. Much to my surprise he said calmly, "Don't lose your temper and I won't either. We've both had a fall, now let's go our separate ways."

This time I got a good look at him. He wasn't an old man at all. He couldn't have been more than forty. His square face was pale, his hair cropped short. He stood up, glanced at me, and brushed the dust from his clothes. Then, head down, clasping his hands behind his back, he walked off with his peculiar skating gait as if nothing had happened.

Dumbfounded, I stared after him until he turned off into a side street. Only then did I mount my bicycle and ride on. He certainly is odd, I thought.

My work was decided upon as soon as I arrived at the organization section of the county Party committee. I was assigned temporarily to Flood Control Headquarters.

Its office was in a large house on the southern side of the compound. I was received by a young fellow about the same age as me.

"My name is Qin Yongchang. Just call me Old Qin ... or Young Qin, if you like. It's up to you." Pointing around the room, he said, "This is our office. It's also our reception room and our dormitory. Maximum use of resources, you might say!"

Young Qin was a cheerful sort, and quite warm-hearted. As he talked, he helped me lay out my bedding and unpack my belongings. Then he brought me warm water to wash my face and offered half of a big water-melon. In less than an hour, we were old friends.

After a midday nap, Young Qin gave me a brief rundown on our work. Flood Control Headquarters was a temporary organization under the first secretary of the county Party committee. The actual day-to-day leadership was exercised by his second-in-command, Vice-director Tian of the Rural Construction Bureau.

"Come on," said Qin. "I'll introduce you."

The Rural Construction Bureau was diagonally across the road in a simple square compound of one-storey buildings. Tian's office was in the east wing. When we entered, he was seated writing at a desk.

Young Qin said, "The organization section has assigned us a new man,

Old Tian."

"Good!" said Tian, without looking up.

"This is Comrade Peng Jie," Qin said hastily. "He's just graduated from the water conservancy school."

Only then did Tian put down his pen and raise his head. I nearly jumped when I saw his face. What a coincidence! My immediate superior was the man I'd knocked down on the street that morning. Recalling my rudeness to him, I felt terribly embarrassed.

Like a gracious host, Qin brought forward a chair and poured me a drink of hot water from the thermos flask, then arranged the books and newspapers that were strewn over the desk into neat piles.

Old Tian didn't move. My first job, he said, was to familiarize myself with all the rivers and streams in the county; after that, there were several key villages he wanted me to visit. He spoke in a low voice, very slowly, as if he hadn't had a decent meal in a long time. When he finished telling me about my work, he suddenly said:

"You look kind of familiar. Haven't we met before? Ah, that's right. We've met."

"Where?" inquired Qin curiously.

Absolutely speechless, I went bright red. Luckily, someone came in just then with a document for Tian and I was saved any further embarrassment.

As we were returning to the flood control office, Qin pressed me to tell him how I had met Tian. I had no choice but to relate what had happened that morning.

"It's all right," Qin assured me. "He won't hold it against you. Don't worry about it."

"I was a little sore at the time," I said. "I kept ringing my bell, but he didn't even look up."

He laughed. "What good's a bell? An easygoing fellow like him; he wouldn't hear you if you fired a cannon!"

During that first week I saw little of Old Tian. He came to our office only twice and Qin and I went to his place once to report on our work. From these few contacts I got the impression that he was a very lethargic person indeed. His abstracted air when he walked, his listless way of talking, his casual approach to problems — nothing seemed to arouse him. It was just my luck to get a wash-out like that for a superior. But whatever duties he gave me I performed to the best of my ability.

My main task then was to familiarize myself with the work. At the same time I helped Qin push flood control preparations in various townships. I studied the maps of the county's waterways and went through a lot of reference material. The county had three rivers, all flowing from the mountains in the west to the plain in the east.

These so-called rivers in fact were mostly dry beds. There had been a big flood in August of 1954, but the years that followed were uneventful. I didn't see much likelihood of anything happening this year. The season for floods was just about over, and there wasn't any sign of rain.

On the night of the ninth day after my arrival however, we were hit by a cloud-burst.

The sky had been clear all day but, towards evening, clouds began to pile up in the west. It was about 10 p.m. and Young Qin had already climbed into bed. I was sitting beside the table lamp reading aloud to him from a novel when the telephone rang. The Water Commission of Zhang Family Gully reported that mountain torrents were pouring into the Yongan River and they estimated that its flow exceeded 100 cubic metres per second.

I was shocked. According to the reports I'd read, the Yongan hadn't moved that fast even in 1954. I hung up and told Qin. Just as each of us seized separate phones and started to notify the villages lower down the river, a call came in from Anle Village. Their report nearly scared the life out of me. I threw down the phone and shouted:

"Anle has a breach in the dike!"

I dashed out of the room and ran to inform Tian. I got to his office in practically one breath, pushed open the door and plunged in. He had already gone to bed, though his lamp was still lit.

"Get up, Old Tian!" I shouted. "The Yongan River is flooding! There's a breach in the dike at Anle!"

He propped himself up and asked, "Where in Anle is the breach?"

I told him it was east of the highway and already over forty feet wide. I thought he would jump right out of bed and hurry with me to headquarters. Still lying in bed, he said in a matter-of-fact way, "It's not that important. Some of the villages downstream will get a little less water for irrigation, that's all."

"Didn't you hear me?" I demanded angrily. "Anle has a break in the dike!"

"So what?" he said. "Anyhow, we can't stop it. Just let it flow."

I wanted to haul him out of bed and belt him one. How did he ever get to be leader of Flood Control Headquarters? I'd never met anyone so spineless!

Just then, Qin flew in through the door, crying, "Sancha River is rising too!"

Tian sat up, electrified. "What's the flow?" he asked urgently.

Qin said the secretary of Sancha Township had phoned. He hadn't been too sure of the rate of flow, but had said that the water was up to the rear of the Dragon King Temple.

"That means at least ninety cubic metres per second," said Old Tia. Throwing on his clothes, he instructed us: "Notify Haimen and Tianjia Villages to get everyone out on the dike, fast!"

Qin and I turned and ran.

By the time I reached the office, several people had arrived: Comrade Hao, the new secretary of the county Party committee; Comrade Wang, head of the committee's general office; Director Niu of the military service bureau; and a number of cadres of the rural work department. Obviously, Young Qin had let them know.

Some were phoning. Others were discussing the situation around a map of the county's watercourses. Everyone looked grim and the atmosphere in the room was tense. When they saw the two of us enter they asked anxiously, "Where's Old Tian?"

"He's on his way," said Qin.

I hurriedly put through a call to the village of Haimen. By the time I finished, Tian had already arrived, a walking-stick in one hand, his raincoat in the other. Although he was dressed the same as before, his appearance had completely changed. He was full of energy, serious but cool. Striding into the room, he threw his things on to the bed, then walked over to the director of the military service bureau.

"Round up all the standing militia and lead them to the south dike. You take charge personally!"

"Yes, sir!" Director Niu replied smartly, like a soldier acknowledging an order from his general. He turned on his heel and left.

To Comrade Wang, head of the county Party committee's general office, Old Tian said, "Get a car and have it waiting at the door." Then he picked up the telephone and began calling the different villages.

Everyone watched him silently. He shouted into the receiver: "Central, get me Du Village, Shangshe and Gucheng.... Du Village? Who's speaking? ... This is Old Tian. Listen, open one sluice-gate of the third branch ditch.... What? You've opened three of them all already? I was afraid of that. You'd better close two right away. We built that sluice channel only last winter. It can't take that much water all at once. Stand by your dam. There's another big crest coming after midnight!"

Tian put down the phone and picked up another. He gave detailed instructions to Shangshe and Gucheng ... what section of which dike should be watched, which channel gate should be opened, which should be closed, which emergency reservoir should be filled first, which second.... I quickly got the map of the county's water network and placed it on the table in front of him, but he didn't even glance at it. He seemed to know every ditch and its branches in the irrigation system.

Finishing his calls, Tian wiped the sweat off his brow. To the head of the general office he said, "Old Wang, you and Young Qin stay here and handle the phones. Secretary Hao, you and the others go back to bed. He turned to me. "You and I are going to Haimen. I'm afraid their south dike is in for trouble."

"The south dike is strong," I said. "It's their north dike that isn't so good." I had been to Haimen only the day before. This was one point I felt sure of.

"The gale's from the northeast," said Old Tian.

I had never noticed the wind direction.

"Your health is poor," Comrade Wang said to Old Tian. "Let me go. You look after things here."

"You couldn't manage," retorted Old Tian. He took his staff and raincoat and went out. I grabbed a padded jacket and followed.

A jeep was standing at the door for us. Old Tian said to the driver: "Haimen. Step on it."

I hadn't dreamed Tian could be so authoritative and confident. But why had he been so unconcerned about the breach in the dike at Anle, and so upset over the rate of flow of the Sancha River? It was only 90 cubic metres per second. I knew that the Sancha used to cause lots of trouble, but in the past five years many flood control projects had been built along it. Only the previous winter several emergency reservoirs had been constructed to take its overflow. Its lower reaches were very broad, and were capable of carrying a flow of up to 200 cubic metres per second. Surely 90 wasn't anything to get excited about?... Also, Tian had said there'd be another crest after midnight. How did he know?

In the car, I told him what was on my mind.

"Yongan River has a steep gradient, and its basin is small," Old Tian explained. "Its waters move fast, but in four hours at most the river is dry again. Could you plug the breach in four hours? Besides, a break there can't do much damage. All the fields east of the highway have long-stemmed crops. The water won't swamp them. From there the fields drain into the Bumper Harvest Canal, which leads north of the village to fields that seldom get enough water."

"What makes you say the Sancha River will have a flood crest after midnight?"

"No doubt about it. That 90 flow is just the water from the central branch. The mountain basins of the northern and southern branches have better retention; the water from those slopes won't come down till at least three hours later. That's after midnight, isn't it?"

Tian paused, then continued, "The Sancha gradient starts levelling out after it leaves the mountains. When it reaches the sand flats in Haimen gorge it's nearly flat. All that water piling up, and no place to drain off. It could be disastrous!"

Worried about Haimen, he lapsed into silence. I didn't say anything either. I remembered Qin telling me that Tian was the county's "home-made" flood conservancy expert. At the time I thought he was kidding but now I realized it was no joke. Listening to his analysis of the situation, I could tell he knew what he was talking about.

Haimen was about eleven kilometres from the county seat. A mile from Haimen, Old Tian told the driver to stop the jeep. "There's water in the second branch by now," he said. "You go on back." He got out and started walking. I followed.

It was a dark night with few stars and a northeast wind was blowing against us. Holding his walking-stick, Tian led the way. I trailed close behind. He was moving so fast I almost had to run to keep up. When we reached the river-bed of the second branch, sure enough, there was water in it. We waded across, but instead of entering the village of Haimen we followed a path leading directly to the southern dike.

Emerging from a field of tall sorghum, we could see lanterns moving on the dike in the distance and we could hear faint shouts and the roar of water. Tian quickened his pace. I trotted panting behind him. When we had climbed the dike, we found that the water was only one or two metres from the top. The dike was piled with straw mats, logs, sandbags.... People were bringing in material, carrying earth to make the dike higher, endless lines coming and going, calling, shouting.

We cut our way through and travelled east along the dike until we reached the command post — a little shack surrounded by heaps of flood-fighting material. The small room was jammed. Secretary Zhai of the township Party committee, the Party secretaries of the villages of Haimen and Tianjia, the chairmen of the local people's communes had all turned up. Everyone looked glum. Tobacco smoke hung so thick you could hardly breathe.

"Hey, Old Tian!" someone cried joyfully as we entered the room.

Startled, everyone stood up. They all started speaking at once:

"Is that you, Old Tian?"

"I knew you'd come!"

"You're here at last!"

The men's expressions brightened. Their voices were full of emotion. Obviously, everyone had great confidence in Tian. It was as if now that he had arrived they weren't afraid of the flood waters no matter how big they might grow.

Tian asked what material had been prepared, how many men had been organized for an emergency squad, how fast the river was rising.

"The bed was only half filled an hour ago. You've seen where it is now," the township Party secretary responded.

Tian thought a moment. "The water from the north branch is starting to come down. It'll get worse before long. Set those mat breakwaters up along the dike in a hurry. The wind's not showing any signs of dying."

Several men ran out to execute his orders.

Old Tian's eyes swept the room. "Why isn't Old Man Jiang here?" he asked.

"It didn't seem that serious," Jin, the Haimen Party secretary, responded. "So we didn't call him."

"We can't afford to take any chances," Tian snapped, reaching for the telephone. Jin said the line was broken. Somebody was out repairing it now. Pushing the phone aside, Tian said, "Go back to the village and ask him to come." Turning his head, he said to me, "You go with him. Phone Director Niu from the village and tell him to put mat breakwaters up on the dike at the county seat right away. Tell him to pay special attention to the section at Wangjia Slope."

Everyone was busy putting up mat breakwaters as we walked along the dike. I overheard a couple of men talking.

"Now that Old Tian's here, we don't have to worry," said one.

"Not worry?" retorted the other. "If there wasn't any danger he wouldn't have come!"

"It can't be too bad," said the first man. "Old Man Jiang still hasn't shown up!"

In a low voice I asked Jin about Old Man Jiang.

"Breach repair expert," said Jin. "Sending for him means we're really in for trouble." He sighed. "If this dike really goes, seven villages south of here will be under water!"

I felt very depressed. If this had been the following year, there would have been no problem. In the autumn a big reservoir was going to be built on the river's upper reaches. I had seen the plan in the county office.

We hurried down the channel and soon reached Haimen Village. While I made my phone call, Jin went for Jiang and before long returned, supporting a white-bearded old man. He appeared to be at least seventy and was so shaky when he walked, I was afraid he was going to fall. But he still refused to let Jin get him a donkey.

"You go on first," he said. "I'll get there a little later. If there's trouble, it won't be till after midnight anyway."

"Go ahead, Old Jin," I urged. "I'll look after old uncle."

Jin hurried off towards the dike. The old man and I slowly followed, with me supporting him on my arm.

"How's Old Tian's ailment?" the old man asked me. "Better?"

"What ailment?" I countered.

"You mean you don't know? His legs were so bad last winter, he couldn't get out of bed. He's got what-do-you-call-it? Ah, that's right — rheumatism!"

No wonder Tian always moved so slowly and wore padded trousers even in the hottest weather. I suddenly remembered how quickly he'd walked when we got out of the jeep. It must have been awfully painful!

Old Man Jiang liked to talk. "Old Tian got his rheumatism in 1954. We'd had a lot of rain that autumn. The whole region was flooded. Old Tian was out in that weather, wading from village to village, for seven days and seven nights, leading the flood-fighting. By the time the water receded, both his legs were badly swollen." The old man heaved a sigh. "He certainly gets things done! Even better than his father did!" He went on to tell me about Tian's background:

Tian came from Tianjia Village, a kilometre away from Haimen. His father had been good friends with Jiang, and was a famous swimmer. Whenever there was a breach in the dike, these two, and a few others, took charge of repairs. There was a commission set up by the county government in those days to control the river, but its officials were only interested in embezzling the large sums of money contributed by the local people for harnessing the river and the dike was always in disrepair. It crumbled at least twice a year whenever there was even a hint of flooding. When that happened the officials invariably disappeared. They certainly never showed their faces at the dike.

In his early teens, Tian was already helping his father and Jiang with dike work. The boy was courageous, thorough and energetic. By the age of twenty he'd built up a considerable reputation in the region.

After Liberation, the county government appointed him as a water conservancy technician. Tian was everywhere — deepening the rivers, digging irrigation canals.... Later he took courses for several months in a special school run by the regional government. Many of the water control projects in the county had been designed by him.

We had already reached the southern dike. Old Man Jiang didn't want to go up it, but insisted that we walk along through the fields in the rear and only mount the dike at the command post. When I asked him why, he laughed.

"If people see me, they'll think it's a bad sign."

When we arrived at the command post the room was quiet. Only Tian and a young woman doctor were there. Tian was saying to her, "You stay here and take phone calls. Don't leave even if the sky collapses!"

Evidently the phone had been repaired. When Tian caught sight of us, he rushed up to shake hands warmly.

"How does it look?" the old man asked him. "Is the dike going to last the night?"

Tian frowned. "The wind's too strong. It's dangerous. Uncle, rest here on the *kang*. We'll call you when we need you. I'm going to take a look at the east end."

I followed him out.

The water was much more turbid than when I had left for the village. Although it was still a metre from the top of the dike, the wind whipped it into huge waves flinging up the froth. Were it not for the mat breakwaters, the dike would never have been able to bear up under the pounding. Tian and I hadn't gone very far before our shoes and socks were soaked by flying spray.

Suddenly there was a tremendous crash, followed by the urgent beating of a big gong. The alarm signal. That could mean only one thing

— a section of the dike had collapsed.

Without waiting for Tian's order I turned and raced to the command headquarters to get Jiang. The emergency squad was running towards the break, carrying supplies and pressure lamps. At the door of the command post I met Jiang coming out.

"Where is it?" he shouted. "Where is it?"

I pointed east. He started off and I hurried to help him, but he pushed my arm aside and strode off. I was baffled. How had his old legs suddenly become so agile?

At the danger spot, the lamps were burning brightly. People shouted and ran back and forth, delivering sandbags. When they saw Jiang, the crowd quickly divided to let him through. We reached the break. It was over seven metres wide and tumbling muddy water was roaring through it.

Tian was directing the placing of sandbags. He had his back to us but from his gestures and the tone of his voice it was plain that he wasn't frightened in the least. On the contrary, he seemed cooler and steadier than before.

The sandbags were useless and were swept away by surging water. The breach was growing wider as the edges of the break continued to crumble. Secretary Zhai and Old Jin and their men on the other side were also trying to fill in sandbags but their efforts were in vain.

Jiang silently inspected the scene. Finally, he shouted, "Stop!"

Tian turned around and saw the old man. "What now? Shall we drive in stakes?"

"Yes, but we've got to strengthen the ends of the break first."

"You give the orders!" said Tian. Turning to me, he said, "Telephone the county to warn them.... But tell them we definitely will plug the breach! Definitely!" His voice was firm, confident.

Weaving my way through the noisy crowd, I hurried back to the small shack.

By the time I had made my call and returned, things were much more orderly. People were lined up in two rows on top of the dike. They were steadily passing along stakes, mats, sandbags.... I walked around them to the edge of the break. Five stakes had already been planted, starting at the edge and advancing towards the middle, with sandbags piled in front of them. This section was already up to the water level. Jiang stood by, chanting cadence for the men driving in the sixth stake. Tian and some others continued to pile sandbags.

On the opposite side of the break, Secretary Zhai was supervising men driving another row of stakes in our direction. The hammering of the stakes, the chanted cadence, the roar of the water, the howling of the wind ... created a tense, ominous atmosphere.

The work proceeded smoothly. Slowly the gap narrowed. Some time after three in the morning, a breach of only four metres or so remained. It looked as if we'd close it soon but then, a powerful rush of water swept away the stakes half driven in, taking Jiang and several young pile-drivers with them. Their safety ropes kept them from being washed very far and a dozen helping hands hauled them back to the dike.

Jiang was dripping wet. His face was ashen and he trembled violently. "We can't plug this one!" he panted to Tian, as he crawled to his feet. "It's too much for me!"

Hearing this, the men standing around were quite alarmed.

"Let the people go home while there's still time," the old man pleaded. "They ought to start working on the village dikes. Otherwise the villages will be finished too!"

His listeners became even more panicky. There were excited discussions. Several men turned to run.

"Don't move, any of you!" glowered Old Tian. His eyes were fierce.

Everyone froze and for a moment there was absolute silence. Old Tian turned on Old Man Jiang like a tiger.

"That breach must be filled!"

To the other side of the break, he shouted: "Old Zhai, organize your men immediately. We're going into the water!"

At once, we could hear Secretary Zhai calling through his megaphone, "All Party members and Youth Leaguers who know how to swim, step forward. Get ready to go in!"

While shouting to the men in the rear to hurry with sandbags and stakes, Tian was removing his notebook and fountain pen from his pocket. He was obviously going in too.

"Old Tian, you can't," I urged him. "You've got rheumatism!"

He glared at me and thrust his belongings into my hands. Turning to the crowd, he yelled: "Those who can swim, come with me!"

There was a hasty exchange among the men.

"Old Tian's going in!"

"What are we waiting for?"

Five or six young fellows ran up, then more, and more.... Arm in arm, they formed a long chain. Tian jumped in first. The water was up to their waists, then up to their chests. The raging river knocked them staggering, but they continued to drive across. A human chain led by Secretary Zhai struggled towards them from the opposite side. Three times Zhai and Tian almost touched hands, but each time huge waves smashed them apart.

Squatting on the dike, Jiang rose abruptly to his feet. To the men around him, he cried, "Bring a long telephone pole, quick!" When the pole was brought, he instructed them to throw it across the breach, then he called to the men in the water, "Grab it! Grab the pole!"

Tian and Secretary Hao dragged themselves along it until they could clasp hands. A solid human chain was formed from one end of the break to the other, with the people leaning against the pole. At this, other men, shouting, jumped into the water hand in hand to make a second and third row directly behind them. The river could never break this barrier.

Wave after wave broke on the heads of the human barricade. When a wave struck, the men vanished. Only when it receded did they appear — choking on the muddy water, gasping for breath, getting ready for the next wave....

We on the dike were also very busy. Jiang counted cadence and directed the men driving the stakes. I and others were rapidly piling sandbags into the breach that were passed to us by the rows of people along the dike. The wind and waves pushed in relentlessly, but the men in the water stood firm.

An hour passed. The line of driven stakes stretched across the breach, forming the backing for growing piles of sandbags. Gradually, the break narrowed as the sandbags mounted higher and higher....

It was darker now and much colder. Though I was standing on the dry dike dressed in a padded jacket, I was still shivering. I could see the men in the icy water clenching their teeth against the wind and the waves and the cold. Tian stood like a rock. He kept shouting:

"Hold on! Hold on and we'll win!"

He seemed to be exhorting not only the others but himself as well.

By dawn the breach was closed at last and the flood waters were locked in the river-bed. When Jiang cried, "She's closed!" everyone cheered. Shouting for joy, men crawled out of the water on to the dike. They were trembling with cold and plastered with mud from head to foot, but on each man's face was a happy grin. They crowded around bonfires which had been prepared in advance, and dried out.

Only Tian remained in the water, his eyes closed, his teeth clenched. Hands clutching the telephone pole, he lay motionless on top of a sandbag.

Frightened, I yelled, "Save him! Save Old Tian!"

Secretary Zhai, Jiang and a few others hurried over and dragged him on to the dike. He was unconscious. Both legs were drawn up in a tight cramp and his breath was very faint.

We rushed him to the command post shack. Secretary Zhai ordered some men to prepare a stretcher, then called the county and told them to send a car immediately. We removed Tian's soaked garments. Jiang, tears in his eyes, took off his own gown and gently covered Tian with it. I stripped off my padded jacket and laid it on Tian's legs. From outside the shack, men passed their own dry clothes inside. People crowded in the doorway, anxiously wanting to know how Old Tian was.

The young woman doctor quickly gave him two injections and rubbed his legs with turpentine. His knees were red and swollen and the veins in his calves stood out in bumpy knots.

The stretcher was ready. Someone had run into the village and brought back two thick quilts. When we laid Tian on the stretcher everyone wanted to carry it. As we left the shack and came out on the dike, the sun had already risen from behind the mountains and the wind had died. The river was flowing quietly. The men on the dike gazed at the stretcher, very moved. When we crossed the second branch, a car was waiting. We placed Tian in it and went directly to the county hospital.

Two months later, Old Tian was out. Once again it was on the street that I saw him. He was still the same — shoulders hunched, head down, hands behind his back, his walk slow and stately.

Watching him approach, I was greatly moved. He didn't seem at all odd now. He was my first superior on my first job; an unassuming, hard-working man, rightly respected by everyone.

April, 1959

Translated by Yin Yishi

Temper Yourself

●

—— ZHAO SHULI ——

Zhao Shuli (1906-70) was one of the most famous contemporary writers in China. Born into a poor peasant family in Shanxi, he enjoyed folk literature, drama and music when he was young. Influenced by folk arts he grew into a versatile writer. Xiao Erhei's Marriage *and* Rhymes of Li Youcai *are his best known works in China. His other works include the novels* Changes in Li's Village *and* Sanliwan *and collections of short stories.*

ZHENGXIAN Co-operative has vast lands but scarce labour,
The mobilization of the female workforce just isn't up to scratch.
Some women just want something for nothing,
If there's nothing easy to be had you'll never see them out —
One pleads a pain in the calf, she just won't get out of bed,
She even keeps back daughter-in-law to put out the night soil;
Another one has tons of food, but she's just never full.
Her husband toils in the fields and she just scoffs noodles.
If you see them in the fields the work points must be good —
When the easy work's done the old illness returns.
They don't turn up to cut wheat, but they're up early to glean:
They dare to steal and filch; they're just completely shameless.
They rarely go to meetings and they never attend night school,
If you talk about state affairs they just don't know a thing.
The moment anyone criticizes them they get a right earful,
They never admit they're wrong and argue till the cows come home.
These old problems need something to be done about them fast,
Quick, get a man of words to read out this big-character poster!

Written by Yang Xiaosi

This is a big-character poster that appeared during the Zhengxian

Co-operative rectification campaign of late autumn 1957. At dinnertime one day, as everyone went, foodbowls in hand, to read the big-character posters stuck on the wall by the co-operative office's door, Yang Xiaosi took advantage of the bustle to stick up the poster he had written, making everyone drop everything else and rush to look at it. They looked and looked and then there was a great roar of laughter. The reason it drew everyone's attention wasn't because Yang Xiaosi was deputy director, nor was it due to its being well-written; what really made people take note was that the two targets of his criticism were two important figures in Zhengxian Co-operative — one of whom was nicknamed "Pain-in-the-calf" and the other, "Never full".

Pain-in-the-calf was a woman in her fifties whose family consisted of a son, a daughter-in-law and a grandson. If she had looked after her grandchild and made the food, her daughter-in-law would have been able to work. But she didn't; she wanted to make her daughter-in-law wait on her just as she had waited upon her mother-in-law: fill her wash basin, empty her night pot, sweep the floor, do the dusting, cook the food, serve the food.... However, if there was some easy work to be done in the fields she never let the opportunity slip by. For example, when the wheat was being gathered in she would go out to the fields, but the moment it was all harvested she would stop. Her outlook was: "When you're gleaning you've got to rely on what you can steal — there's no future in just relying on your gleaning ability." When the co-operative rumbled this secret of hers, they ordered her to return all the wheat to the co-operative and she was put on piece work — but then she wouldn't work at all. Another example was cotton picking time: when the cotton buds were in full bloom and she could pick double the daily quota, she would work many days on end. Needless to say, as soon as she could only pick enough to just fulfil the quota, she stopped working — if she could exceed the quota by only thirty percent she wouldn't go either. When she was young she had a string of sores on her calf, but these had healed over twenty years ago. When she had the sores her husband had waited on her; after they healed, she maintained that the root of the pain was still there so that she could boss around her husband easier. Only she could perceive this "pain". She said that others couldn't prove or disprove the reality of her "pain", but for all that, her "pain" did have some unusual features: when she was happy it was absent, but when she was unhappy it would appear; going for a stroll, watching a play or visiting friends she would be fine — the "pain" only starting when she had to work; when her husband died with her son still small, there was no "pain" for many years, but it started again when she found a wife for her son; after joining the co-operative, there was never any "pain" when she could easily exceed the quota, but when she couldn't overfill it, or filled it only by a small margin, her calf would start hurting. Although the village medical station was pretty good, there was nothing they could do about this sort of leg-ache.

Never-full's real name was Li Baozhu and she was much younger than Pain-in-the-calf. She was only in her thirties and was one of the two best-looking people in Zhengxian Co-operative but sadly, this advantage turned into a burden for her. Her husband, named Zhang Xin, had married her quite freely; he was both clever and quick-witted, but he lacked ambition. The conditions that Li Baozhu established during the courtship period made it perfectly clear that after their marriage she would not work in the fields: these were conditions that no one could agree to in the post-Liberation countryside, but Zhang Xin agreed to them. In Li Baozhu's eyes, her husband was by no means ideal; according to her, he was "not the best, but better than the worst," for he wasn't a cadre. Consequently, she only thought of him as a "transitional" husband; when she found her ideal man she would divorce him. For a while after her marriage, Li Baozhu had considered that deputy director, Yang Xiaosi, who had written the poster about her. However, when she discovered that her nickname "Never-full" had originally been thought up by him, that idea was knocked on the head. Since she only thought of Zhang Xin as her "transitional" husband, she naturally couldn't exactly treat him as an equal, and so she developed a series of "policies" for dealing with him. Policy number one was to grasp full fiscal control: all debts in Zhang Xin's name in the co-operative were to be brought to her for settlement; all expenses in the home were to be arranged by her; any additional income Zhang Xin might have was to be handed over in full; when money was to be spent it had to be ratified by her first. Policy number two was that apart from cooking and sewing, all other work — including fetching water, making coal briquets, turning the grindstone, turning the millstone, sweeping the floor, putting out the ashes and all other odd-jobs — was Zhang Xin's responsibility. Policy number three was that the standard of food and clothing was to be fixed by her. With food, she could eat whatever she liked and Zhang Xin could have whatever she prepared for him. Similarly, with clothing, she bought whatever she wanted to wear and Zhang Xin wore whatever she bought him. This set of "policies" she secretly formulated and put into practice. After full implementation, Zhang Xin turned into her long-term hired labourer. After the state put its countryside grain monopoly into practice, she often moaned that she wasn't full. Her method was to cook some noodles for herself, eat them while Zhang Xin was in the fields, then put a few grains of rice in the water used to boil the noodles and boil up a couple of bowls of gruel for Zhang Xin to eat. Moreover, she would bake wheat cakes, lock them in a box and eat them whenever she felt like it while Zhang Xin was out. When the brigade mobilized her to take part in labour, she would say, "We haven't enough to eat — I just get to scrape the pot after Zhang Xin has finished eating — I really can't work." People who often lie always give themselves away. Zhang Xin often discovered cake crumbs on the bed and was continually finding one or two noodles that hadn't been scooped out of his gruel. However, whenever he mentioned it she got angry, and whenever she got angry she would start talking "divorce", so he didn't dare say anything; he just turned a blind eye, put up with the hardship and hunger and left it at that. Once Zhang Xin took his bowl of food outside to eat with the others and Zhang Taihe, the leader of his brigade, caught sight of a noodle in his bowl. This brigade leader was a young man who was fond of teasing people and he asked Zhang Xin: "Where did 'Never-full' learn to cook just one noodle?" From then on, every time Zhang Xin took his gruel to eat outside, people who enjoyed teasing him would snatch his chopsticks and search his bowl for noodles — they were most often not disappointed, usually managing to find a scrap. One time, Zhang Taihe said to him, "I reckon 'Never-full' wouldn't be a bad name for *you*, seeing as how you only ever get one noodle to eat." In regard to participating in production, Never-full shared exactly the same attitude as Pain-in-the-calf. Holding the purse strings, she wanted to amass some savings for after the "transitional period", and therefore, whenever there was an opportunity for a quick killing in production, she disregarded the restrictions of policy number two. When the easy work was over she would go back to pleading: "I haven't had enough to eat, so I can't work."

A short while after Yang Xiaosi had stuck up his big-character poster, Never-full heard a row outside the co-operative office door and ran over to find out what was going on. Zhang Taihe saw her coming and decided to volunteer to read the poster for her, saying, "Everyone keep quiet; I'll read it through again for everybody!" They all saw Never-full coming across and guessed what Zhang Taihe was up to, and so they all quietened down and listened to him. Zhang Taihe read the poster with great skill. He beat time with his hands, made occasional gestures and read the poster through fluently. His reading won everyone's applause and praise. Never-full slipped away as everyone applauded enthusiastically.

However, she didn't go home; she headed straight to Pain-in-the-calf's house. She and Pain-in-the-calf didn't really get on too well, but she sometimes made use of Pain-in-the-calf's prestige. Pain-in-the-calf was older than she was, had seen more of life and was the sister-in-law of Director Wang Juhai, local Party secretary Wang Zhenhai, and leader of number one brigade Wang Yinghai. She also dared kick up a racket in the co-operative office, regardless of whether she was right or wrong, and so her prestige was greater than Never-full's. Hearing Zhang Taihe read the big-character poster made Never-full tremble with rage, and her first thought had been to kick up a fuss there and then; but seeing so many people, not one of whom would stick up for her, she hadn't dared open her mouth and had just slipped off quietly to Pain-in-the-calf's house. As soon as she got in she started: "They've been sticking up posters having a go at us two!" It was the first time Pain-in-the-calf had heard that anyone had dared to attack her. She asked incredulously: "Who told you all this?" "Who told me? With all that lot making a row outside the co-operative office, did I need anyone to tell me?" "Who wrote it?" "That bastard Yang Xiaosi." "What did the bastard actually write?" "Oh, plenty! He said that you faked your leg-ache, that you kept your daughter-in-law in to put out the night soil, that you steal wheat, that you're totally unreasonable and you're always argumentative." She also stirred things up a little further by adding a few things that weren't on the poster. In no time, she made Pain-in-the-calf's leg stop hurting and got her to march stiffly to the co-operative office to find Yang Xiaosi.

At that moment, Director Wang Juhai, Deputy Director Yang Xiaosi and Party Secretary Wang Zhenhai were eating together and having a brief meeting to study the rectification movement and the problem of coordinating current production. As soon as Pain-in-the-calf came in, she disrupted their meeting. Seeing that something was up from the manner of Pain-in-the-calf's arrival, several people who had been outside reading the poster followed her in to have a look. Pain-in-the-calf didn't say a word as she entered; she just stretched out her arms and attacked Yang Xiaosi. Yang Xiaosi jumped up from his chair and dodged to one side, while Director Wang Juhai held Pain-in-the-calf back by force. Yang Xiaosi was certain this was all because of the poster and said to Pain-in-the-calf, "You want to fight? There's a law: no fighting. Fighting's illegal. If you're not worried about a fine or going to prison, then start fighting. If you dare raise a finger, I'll take you to court!" Then he said to Wang Juhai, "Don't hold her back! Let her fight!" As soon as Pain-in-the-calf heard talk of fines and going to prison, her arms dropped limply. However, her mouth didn't weaken: "I don't want to fight you! I want to ask you if there's a law that makes you swear at people." "When have I ever sworn at you?" "It's all on the wall in black and white; you can't hide it." Wang Juhai butted in: "Listen to her! Have you been mentioned by name?" Pain-in-the-calf immediately came back at him: "Oh, so if there's no name it's alright to swear at people, eh? If it's alright to swear I'll do it everyday!" Yang Xiaosi replied:"Whether your name's been mentioned or not isn't the point. What needs clearing up is whether you've been sworn at or not! If there's one sentence I've written that isn't true, then I've sworn at you! Pick one out then! If I made a mistake, it's that I didn't mention you by name. I did to start with, but the director suggested that I cut out that bit. If you're annoyed that I didn't spell it out completely, I'll add your names on now — how's that?" "You're still not satisfied eh? Add them then! You're the deputy director and you can write. How is a poor, illiterate commoner like me to go on living?"

The Party secretary Wang Zhenhai stood up."My dear sister-in-law, be reasonable, will you? Wait until the debate and then get someone to read out the poster sentence by sentence. If there's a bit that you thin. isn't true, you can challenge him! You can't just go around blaming other people! Who's stopping you from living?" "You bureaucrats always stick together; how can I reason with you? I'm going to swear! May whichever person wrote that poster die sonless! May wolves gobble the bastard up, blood and all! May...." The Party secretary interrupted solemnly: "Chairman Mao wants big-character posters put up. If you're really going to be unreasonable and act rabid, then a big co-operative like this has got ways of dealing with you!" He turned back and addressed the others: "Two vounteers step forward to take her before the township government!" Several of the onlookers were already at the end of their tether and, hearing the Party secretary, they jumped forward and surrounded her. Two of them grabbed her arms and were about to go when Wang Juhai stopped them: "Hold on a minute! Is it really worth bothering the township government over such a small matter?" Everyone had been wanting to teach Pain-in-the-calf a lesson for a long time and hearing Wang Juhai's order to stop they all felt frustrated; but he was the director, so they had to do as he said. Realizing they really meant to take her away had scared Pain-in-the-calf, but when the director held them back, she relaxed again. She pulled herself together and, seeing things had calmed down, she braced herself speaking as though she was making an honourable last stand: "Don't stop them! Let them take me! The township government can't rip out my tongue!"

Wang Juhai thought it was about time they wound things up and so he very deliberately said to Pain-in-the-calf, "Sister-in-law, why don't you go home? This is nothing we can't handle. We've got to make arrangements for tomorrow's production work now; we'll explain all this in two days' time." "Explain it? I want it all cleared up!" "Alright, alright, alright! We'll clear it all up for you!" Yang Xiaosi said, "What are you saying? Someone comes to our meeting, raises hell and then we have to apologize — is that it?" Pain-in-the-calf was worried that Yang Xiaosi and the local Party secretary Wang Zhenhai would make Wang Juhai change his mind so that she couldn't beat her retreat. When there was a pause in the conversation she said hastily to Wang Juhai, "I'm going! You deal with all this, will you? Don't let them get away with it scot-free!" When she'd finished, she turned round and walked out, only realizing when she was out the door that she had forgotten to limp.

Director Wang Juhai came from an old, middle peasant background and was settling disputes long before the Anti-Japanese War. It was often said that he was good at smoothing things over. After the arrival of the Eighth Route Army during the Anti-Japanese War, he became a village leader and showed initiative in all sorts of mobilization work. During the Land Reform period, landlords had attempted to bribe him on several occasions, but they were all refused. When the village Party secretary noted his resolve in the struggle, he recruited him into the Party. After Zhengxian Co-operative was established, he was selected to be co-operative director, and for many years, owing to the consideration given to his seniority, he had been repeatedly reappointed. Wang Juhai was a great one for studying people's characters and advocating the use of people according to what sort of characters they had. Unfortunately, he didn't realize that some bad-natured people just had to be reformed. He would settle disputes for people, advocating "settling the problem without coming down on either side." He only asked that the thing got out of the way. He believed that anyone who understood this philosophy could become a cadre, whereas those who couldn't follow his example in dealing with matters just needed to "temper themselves". For instance, in 1955, people both inside and outside the Party suggested that Yang Xiaosi should be picked as deputy director, but Wang Juhai objected, "No, no, no! He needs to temper himself for a few years more yet." Even up until the re-elections this year he was still unrelenting; but the majority of the people believed that Yang Xiaosi was better than he was, and the result of the election was that Yang Xiaosi received just as many votes as he did. After Yang Xiaosi became deputy director, he hadn't trusted him with anything and often said, "That youngster! Let him temper himself in the administrative committee and then we'll see!" To take another example, the co-operative constitution said that there should be a woman deputy director, but he thought this unnecessary, saying, "Letting women kick up a fuss is okay, but as for letting them handle problems ... well, they just haven't got a clue!" However, as all the other co-operatives had female deputy directors he couldn't stick to his position, and at the elections Gao Xiulan, from the number three brigade, was elected. There were differences in his attitude to Gao Xiulan and Yang Xiaosi: whereas he thought Yang Xiaosi could "temper himself", Gao Xiulan wasn't even capable of that. Therefore, apart from when he followed the namelist and notified Gao Xiulan of meetings of the full administrative committee, he totally forgot that such a person as Gao Xiulan existed for the gatherings of the top cadres. However, Gao Xiulan hadn't forgotten him. At the start of the rectification campaign, Gao Xiulan stuck up a big-character poster about him:

> *It's hard to strive to be first at Zhengxian Co-operative,*
> *The director's just too self-reliant,*
> *He believes only in himself; others are told to "temper themselves".*
> *He deals with every problem, big or small,*
> *No one else ever gets a look-in;*
> *He's busy from dawn to dusk, but nothing much ever gets done.*
> *Whenever there's a dispute between co-operative members*
> *He's always there with his grinning face,*
> *He just tries to keep everybody happy,*
> *He never judges who's right or wrong.*

Some undeserving folk do well, thanks to the director's help;
Reasonable people suffer, and just have to swallow the bitterness.
Good hits a brick wall; evil has its own way;
There's nowhere for people to use their strength,
So how can they strive to be first?
Let's just hope Director Wang has a big change of heart;
Rely on the collective to sort out problems,
Distinguish who's right or wrong;
Listen to the voice of the people,
Avoid being a shepherd with no flock.

Reading this poster gave Wang Juhai a bit of a surprise. However, he had a bit of style, unlike Pain-in-the-calf who would immediately have started jabbering and kicking up a fuss. He collected his thoughts, put on a wise voice and said, "I really hadn't realized that Xiulan was still ambitious. If she tempers herself well, she might be able to do a few little jobs for the co-operative in the future." That's the sort of person Wang Juhai was.

When Yang Xiaosi wrote the poster about Pain-in-the-calf and Never-full, he went to ask Wang Juhai's opinion of the rough draft. Wang Juhai was determined not to commit himself: "The medicine must fit the illness — those two have to be treated gently, not roughly. If you put out a big-character poster like this about them, I guarantee they'll give you hell; if you're set on sticking it up, you'd better leave out their names." Yang Xiaosi also asked Party Secretary Wang Zhenhai what he thought, adding what the director had said. The secretary answered: "If you're scared of trouble, don't launch a rectification campaign. As for names, it doesn't matter if they're there or not — as soon as you stick it up, everyone'll know who it's about!" In deference to Wang Juhai's seniority, Yang Xiaosi altered two sentences, removing the two people's names, but not changing the contents in the slightest. Then he stuck it up.

When Pain-in-the-calf came to the co-operative office to attack Yang Xiaosi, Wang Juhai held her back and at the same time grumbled to himself about Xiaosi: "See this trouble you've caused? It's all thanks to your not listening to me!" When everyone wanted to drag Pain-in-the-calf to the township government and he stopped them with a few bland words, convincing Pain-in-the-calf to go home, he once again secretly praised his own skill: "Now who's best at sorting things out? If it wasn't for me, things would have got really out of hand!" He hadn't imagined that after the departure of Pain-in-the-calf and all the spectators he would be criticized by the Party secretary: "Juhai! How can you stay so wishy-washy after being criticized by so many people? If we don't deal with these incorrigible people, how can the rectification campaign proceed?" These few sentences of criticism really upset Wang Juhai. He thought: "You can't settle the problems that you stir up yourselves, and when I sort them out for you,

you still say I've done badly." However, he could tell that the secretary's character was "objective rather than subjective, not scared of trouble", so instead of saying what he was really thinking, he just acknowledged grudgingly: "Alright, alright! It's all my fault! Let's hurry up and sort out the production work for tomorrow and the day after tomorrow!"

As soon as the production work was mentioned, the Party secretary started up again: "Production and rectification are indivisible. It'll be getting cold soon; most of the women aren't working in the fields, so the cotton is not getting picked and the stalks are not being uprooted; the livestock's just standing around and the ground is not yet ploughed — if we don't do some rectifying, how can we change the situation?" Director Wang replied: "Rectification is a slow business. You can't just turn things round in one or two days. The best thing to do is to stick to our experience from last year and cut down the quotas — if we reduce the amount of cotton to be picked in one working day from eight catties to six, we'll be able to mobilize the majority straight off tomorrow." "The trouble is, last year's experience was bad. We could pick ten catties a day at the moment, but ever since you made that reform last year, all those selfish people have been waiting at home for another opportuninty like that. We can't tolerate that sort of selfishness! We changed it to six catties last year so this year they'll be demanding five catties — next year it'll be four!" Yang Xiaosi added: "It's unfair to the harder working women, too! If you cut down the quotas for tomorrow, how are you going to calculate the workpoints for the last few days? A month ago the quota was set at twenty catties when forty catties could have been picked. What happened? All the lazy-bones rushed out to pick the cotton and all the hard workers had to go and cut millet — so they've already been treated unfairly once. Now they're doing the third picking and the quota's been set at eight catties for ten days or so. If you set the quota lower and get that lazy bunch back to work, what sort of behaviour's that?" Wang Juhai replied: "Leaving the quota as it is would be fine too. We'd just have to mobilize people individually. If you do mobilizing well everyone, no matter who, can be mobilized. Unfortunately no one's 'tempered themselves' in mobilization work. I've only got one mouth, so it can't be done...." He cited many examples, saying which woman was fond of hearing that she was deft of hand, which woman liked hearing she was neat and tidy — as long as you could grasp a woman's character, a few sentences would be all it would take to get her to listen to you willingly. As he chatted away giving further examples, the Party secretary interrupted him: "Alright, alright! If we could overcome capitalistic thinking, we could mobilize anyone, no matter what their character!"

They'd just got to this point when a notice arrived from the township government ordering the director and Party secretary to collect a two days' supply of food and convene immediately at the township government. They were to visit a co-operative in the suburbs and take part in a debate on rectification. The two men read the notice and then the director said, "What are we going to do?" "Go!" "What about production?" "Hand it over to the deputy!" The director looked at Yang Xiaosi and said sarcastically, "Xiaosi, I'm passing production over to you. The Party secretary says that 'production and rectification are indivisible' — sorting it out's all up to you." "What about Gao Xiulan?" "Let them talk it over together!"

After the director and the Party secretary left, Yang Xiaosi looked for Gao Xiulan and the deputy Party secretary. The three of them talked it over for a while and then called a meeting for co-operative members that evening.

When almost everyone had arrived, Pain-in-the-calf and Never-full, who had never attended a meeting before, turned up too. When they got near the crowd, Never-full prodded Pain-in-the-calf in the back and said, "Go on, quick! Before they open their mouths!" She pushed Pain-in-the-calf to the fore, but sat on the outside of the circle herself. The head of number one brigade, Wang Yinghai, thought there was something fishy about those two turning up. Seeing that Pain-in-the-calf was making straight for the rostrum, he bounded forward a couple of paces and held her back: "What are you up to now?" "What am I up to? You must know what happened at midday! First, we've got to sort out Xiaosi swearing at me, otherwise this meeting'll go nowhere!" As mentioned previously, Wang Yinghai was also one of Pain-in-the-calf's younger brothers-in-law, but when he spoke to her, he was much more biting than Wang Juhai or Wang Zhenhai. When Wang Yinghai became a brigade leader, Pain-in-the-calf had abused this family connection to get away with murder, but she was still a little scared of him. Hearing that what she was saying was completely unreasonable, and worried that she would disrupt the meeting, Wang Yinghai launched a verbal assault at her: "Haven't you had enough yet? What did he say to wrong you? Does your leg really hurt?" "Whether it hurts or not's none of your business!" "If you're part of my team it is! If it really hurts, how is it that whenever there's any trouble you run faster than anyone else? If it doesn't hurt, why can't you even cook food? You just hold your daughter-in-law back so she can't work in the fields! Someone writes a poster about you and it's like you've been stung by a scorpion, yelling your head off! Go on then, yell! The more you yell, the more they'll write. If you don't change, your front door'll be totally covered with big-character posters too!" As expected, this attack was successful. Pain-in-the-calf shut up and withdrew slowly to go and sit with Never-full. Seeing Pain-in-the-calf's ferocity extinguished, Yang Xiaosi whispered to Gao Xiulan: "It looks like our director's appraisal of her character wasn't too accurate. He said that Pain-in-the-calf responded to the soft approach, not the tough approach. I reckon that brigade number one leader's 'tough' is a bit more effective than our director's 'soft'."

The meeting was declared open. The deputy Party secretary had a few words first: "The Party secretary and the director left very hurriedly today and they didn't leave detailed arrangements regarding the rectification work. This afternoon, the two deputy directors and I discussed the matter, and we decided that we won't hold a rectification meeting for the time being, but we'll make arrangements for tomorrow's production work. Tomorrow evening we'll carry on the rectification work and have a self-criticism meeting in groups. The details of the self-criticisms will be specified tomorrow. I've got nothing else to say, so would the deputy director please come and discuss production!" After making this simple speech the deputy Party secretary sat down. Someone made a suggestion: "It would be better to announce who and what is going to be criticized first so we can all prepare!" The deputy Party secretary stood up again: "We haven't finished discussing that yet, so we'd better just wait until tomorrow."

Next Yang Xiaosi came to speak: "Everyone sees our present production problems very clearly. The cotton isn't getting picked, the cotton plants aren't getting pulled up, the livestock's just standing idle and the ploughing isn't getting done. In a few more days it'll freeze and then it'll be too late for the autumn seeding. It's unavoidable that there'll still be some cotton left on the stalks after the harvest, and it would be a shame to leave it there to be turned into fertilizer along with the stalks. Therefore, we're going to have free picking. As there are also still quite a few plants that haven't been picked a third time, there may be a few sticky-fingered people who'll steal off them. We talked about that this afternoon and decided that for tomorrow and the day after, we'll have the women deputy leaders from each brigade leading the women for free picking in an organized way. The leaders from each team will lead the male labour force to uproot the plants which have been gleaned. Once an area is cleared, we'll get the livestock to plough it and then move on to pick in another area that hasn't been harvested a third time. To prevent stealing, here are a few new rules: number one, early tomorrow morning, the deputy leaders of each team will lead their members to convene at that bit of land that's already been ploughed down by the pond at the south side of the village, and then you'll all be told which area you're assigned to; number two, the women in each team are only allowed to pick in the specified areas — no wandering about; number three, the cotton picked by anyone who doesn't gather at the pond, or who doesn't go to their assigned area will be counted as stolen — and as specified in the original co-operative regulations, five working days will be deducted for each catty discovered, with anyone refusing to pay being sent to court for reform. Okay, that's it! Meeting dismissed!"

The meeting was over after barely ten minutes. Afterwards, everyone was talking about it. Some were saying, "These youngsters just haven't any experience. They can draw up all the rules they like, but those who want to steal will still go ahead and do it!" Others said, "What's the use of team leaders? When we had free picking last year, even some of the women team leaders were pinching stuff." "Those youngsters have got guts! If they really punish a few people, no one'll dare steal!" "But they're only standing in for two days. No matter how sincerely they talk, the minute Wang Juhai gets back things'll just go back to normal!" Meanwhile, the women who were preparing to steal cotton held a powwow: "He thinks he's got it all figurred out. As soon as the team splits up, we'll scatter — who's going to interfere?" "If we get allocated a good area we'll go there, but if it's useless, we'll just refuse to follow the team leader!" "He can drag one of us off with one hand, two of us with both hands, but he can't grab the lot of us!" "Our team leader's not so honest himself!"

"When a new official takes his post, no one knows what to expect." For all the complaining, everyone still had to turn up at the ploughed area by the pond next morning.

All the people who were going to come arrived and sat down in the field which had been ploughed and harrowed flat; no one else was going to arrive now. Xiaosi, Xiulan and the deputy Party secretary had a look and noted that more or less all the women who normally pretended to be too ill, too busy or too hungry had turned up. However, that infamous pair, Pain-in-the-calf and Never-full, had not come. The three looked at each other and Xiulan remarked: "That big-character poster must have really stirred them up!" Everyone waited a moment and then Xiaosi said, "We're not waitng for them; let's stick to our original plan!" He walked to the front and addressed the crowd: "Each team check the number of people present and see how many have turned up altogether. Count women and men separately." The team leaders checked the number of people and then reported to Xiaosi, who then said, "Will all the team leaders come to the front? We want to have a little talk first." The brigade leaders gathered in front of the three of them. Xiaosi whispered a few words to them and the team leaders all laughed. When they had stopped laughing, they all sat down on one side as instructed by Xiaosi.

Xiaosi started to speak: "I'm really pleased everyone has turned out so smartly. These last few days, the team leaders have been mobilizing people every day to pick the cotton, but what with one thing or another, only a few people have been turning up. The ones who haven't been coming have all had their reasons: some have been saying they're ill, some that their children are ill or that they're so busy at home that they couldn't possibly come out ... any excuse not to work. But today, the minute they heard there was going to be free picking, no one had anything to do. That's clearly just selfishness up to its old tricks, isn't it? At the first picking, when it was possible to double the quota, everyone *but everyone* turned up like this too. Think about it: you get other people to do the normal work, and then when there's something easy, you grab at the chance. How much have the people who work in the fields all year round had to put up with because of you lot? You really want to 'pick' the leftover cotton? You couldn't even each pick one catty of it a day — that's only worth twenty or thirty cents, so you wouldn't get a full working day's workpoints in five — no one's that dumb! To be blunt, those who want to pick that cotton really just want to steal it! This year's not going to be like last year with the majority working the land and the minority stealing! You're not to pick the tiny bits of cotton left on the stalks. Just pull up the stalks, pile them by the side of the road, and the primary school students can strip them when they come home from school each day. When they've finished picking them we can turn the stalks into fertilizer. No one who's come today is allowed to go home! The women's teams can each go to their fields to do the third picking; the quota's staying the same: eight catties for one working day. The men who were carrying dung to the wheat fields can carry on doing that, and the others can go to the fields that have been picked clean to pull up cotton stalks. That's all I've got to say, but the deputy Party secretary wants a few words." A woman stood up: "Deputy director, this is gospel: I can't stay today! My kid's ill. If you don't believe me, go and take a look!" Xiaosi cut her off: "I'm not looking! If your child wasn't better, why did you come?" "Originally I couldn't come. Because...." "Because you heard there would be free picking! If you couldn't come, how come you're here? The deputy Party secretary is going to speak about all this presently." The woman had nothing else to say and seeing her thus rebuked, the others who had also been thinking up excuses to get let off didn't dare open their mouths. They thought of sneaking off quietly, too, but sitting in a ploughed field outside the village with the team leaders sitting on the road leading to the village, any movement would be seen and so there was no chance of escape.

The deputy secretary got up to speak: "What I have to say is very simple. Yesterday evening some people wanted me to make arrangements for tonight's self-criticism meeting and tell everyone who and what was going to be criticized. Now I can tell everyone: the people to do self-criticisms will be those who don't turn up normally but are here today. The theme of their self-criticisms will be 'Why I only think of myself and not of the co-operative'. Would the workpoint recorders of each team please now make a list of those people?"

The list was soon completed and Xiaosi said, "No one's allowed back to the village! If anyone sneaks off on the way or doesn't show up this afternoon, then write a big-character poster about her and present it to the township government!" Xiulan butted in: "The third team's land is to the north of the village, how can we get there without going back to the village?" Xiaosi spoke to the third team's leader, Zhang Taihe: "Taihe, take the team through the village with you and your deputy. When you get to the north road, check the number again. No one's allowed home. Each team to their work. Meeting dismissed."

As the meeting was falling out, little discussions took place again: "Xiaosi's got better ideas than Juhai." "He thinks and then he acts." "Xiaosi's really sorted out that bunch of lazy bags." "It's not just Xiaosi. All three of them have got it taped!" "Juhai only learned about internal surgery; these youngsters can actually operate." "Juhai's surgery's no good — it just doesn't cure the disease!" "It's a shame Pain-in-the-calf and Never-full didn't show up!" ... They went their separate ways, chatting as they walked.

The third team crossed the village. When they got to the north road, the team leader did a head count. They came to a field to the north of the village where, on top of a twenty foot high mound of earth there was an apricot tree. Surrounding the mound on its southern, eastern and western sides was about twenty mu of land that had been joined into one strip when the co-operative was established. Cotton was being grown there this year and the plants on the southern and eastern sides, getting the most sun, were already stripped clean; only the plants on the northern side still hadn't been picked a third time. They walked to the patch of land, keeping the men, Gao Xiulan and the other more robust women at the southern end to pull up the plant stalks, and sending the woman team leader with the weaker women to the northern end to pick cotton.

As the women skirted round the southern and eastern sides and were about to turn north, they caught sight of four women who had been picking cotton there for some time already, two of whom were recognized as Pain-in-the-calf and Never-full. They all stopped still. The woman team leader wanted to yell but another woman waved to her and whispered, "Don't shout at them. The minute you shout they'll stop picking! Let's pretend we're doing some free picking and work our way over there slowly. When we get there, we'll pick our area and they'll pick theirs. The more we let them pick, the heavier their punishment will be!" The woman team leader replied: "I was wondering why they hadn't come! They came early after all!" Another woman who didn't often work in the fields offered: "Last night after the meeting was over Never-full came and told me not to go to the meeting down by the south pond, but to come straight here. I didn't dare do as she said." Everyone wanted to play a joke on Pain-in-the-calf and the other three, so they pretended to be picking cotton, plucking leftover buds from stalks that had already been picked clean, and making their way northwards.

At the meeting the night before, when Pain-in-the-calf had not kicked up a fuss, she had gone to sit at the back with Never-full. When they heard that they were going to do some free picking the next day, Never-full whispered in Pain-in-the-calf's ear: "We won't take any notice of their rules tomorrow. We'll get a few others and set out before light, and by the time the rest of them arrive, we'll have bagged quite a few catties already! They'll go to the meeting down by the south pond and we'll go to the apricot tree field to the north of the village — that way we won't run into anyone. When they get to the apricot tree field we'll pick with them. When you pick like that no one can resist stealing, and the minute they steal anything, they won't dare denounce us!" "That's what I've been thinking," said Pain-in-the-calf. "Rules, eh? We've broken enough of 'em! Who's ever been punished? It'll be great if just us two go! Don't get anyone else!" "We'd better get in a couple of accomplices in case we get caught. Not too many though — otherwise, there won't be much for each person!" In the end they asked five people, but three of these wouldn't dare. So, only two turned up and accompanied them to the apricot tree field. They were stealing merrily from a patch of land five or six mu large which hadn't been picked a third time when they heard the voices. They looked up and saw that the women of team number three had arrived, so they sauntered over to an area which had already been picked. When they saw the women move to an area which hadn't been picked, they returned to their original field. Everyone in team number three started laughing. "What are you lot laughing at?" demanded Pain-in-the-calf. "You can steal, why can't we?" Someone replied: "How have you picked so much?" "What stopped you from coming early, too?" The women from team number three were all picking in rows, but Pain-in-the-calf and the other three were rushing around all over the field to pick the best bits. One of the women from team number three remarked: "If you must steal, at least steal from just one area!" Pain-in-the-calf replied: "It's free picking, how I do my picking's none of your business. If you're going to call it stealing, aren't you all stealing too?" No one argued seriously with her about it; they only laughed every now and then.

The woman team leader had a quiet word with one of her members: "Dragging the joke on like this isn't so good either. I'm worried that they'll cause trouble if I go. So would you run over to the southern end and let the team leader and the deputy director know, please? Ask them what they think we ought to do." The member left.

Team leader Zhang Taihe was a real jester. As soon as he heard that the infamous Pain-in-the-calf and Never-full had come, he seemed to gloat a little: "It figures. I knew that if they got an opportunity like this they wouldn't be able to resist! You go back and pick; I'll be along in a minute!" Then he said to Gao Xiulan, "Deputy director, you stay out of sight for the time being and when I've sorted them out I'll call you in. Really lay it on thick with your high position." However, Gao Xiulan didn't agree to doing things this way: "We've only just been taught what to do; we'd better do it properly. We'll go together." They walked over to the north end and when the team members saw that the deputy director and team leader had both come, they hooted with laughter again. Zhang Taihe stuck to Gao Xiulan's suggestion and said sternly, "No one's to laugh! And you lot — stop rushing all over the field!" Pain-in-the-calf acted tough again: "It's free picking. So it's none of your business." "Okay, let's call it free picking then! You're swiping my third team's cotton, so it is my business! Hand those baskets over to me!" Never-full replied: "I'm in number three team. If you're letting others steal the cotton, you've got to let me too. If we hand over our baskets, then everyone hands over theirs too!" "Everyone'll hand theirs over." As Zhang Taihe spoke, he snatched their four baskets. Next he asked them: "Why didn't you go to the south pond for the meeting?" Never-full snapped back: "Never mind that! Didn't you just say 'everyone'll hand theirs over'? Why haven't you taken theirs?" "They're picking for the co-operative." "So are we!" "Who told you to pick?" "Who told them to pick?" "Okay, we'll clear up who told them to pick first." He then described the events of the south pond meeting to the four of them. When they heard, they all sagged. Pain-in-the-calf said, "Never mind whether we were told to pick or not. Why didn't you tell us earlier?" "If we didn't want to tell you, why did we say to go for a meeting by the south pond? If we told you and you didn't go and listen, what else could we do?" "So we've wasted a whole morning picking," said Pain-in-the-calf. "Tip the cotton out, give us our baskets back and we'll go!"

At this point, Gao Xiulan started up: "It's not as simple as that. The rules were announced beforehand so that no one would break them. If they've been broken, the matter can't just end like that! This cotton is obviously stolen. Comrade Taihe, take this cotton to the co-operative, weigh it, and tell the storekeeper to stick a note on each basket clearly marking their names and the weight of the cotton. Then, keep the baskets together until there's a meeting of co-operative members, and then we'll get everyone to discuss a punishment!" As Zhang Taihe gathered the four baskets and walked off, Pain-in-the-calf spoke: "Xiulan, you can't say we were stealing. We honestly didn't know you'd gone back on your words this morning!" "We didn't go back on our words at all. Comrade Yang Xiaosi spelt it all out quite clearly to everyone yesterday evening: 'If anyone doesn't go to the meeting by the south pond tomorrow, the cotton they pick will be counted as stolen.' What's more, you've been snatching the stuff in broad daylight from an unpicked field. That's harming the interests of the co-operative so we can't just decide on it ourselves; the masses will have to discuss the punishment! If you've got anything to say you can say it at the meeting."

By breakfast, the news of Pain-in-the-calf and Never-full stealing the cotton had spread throughout the whole village. In the morning, the matter was discussed in each of the teams as they worked. Almost everyone demanded that the self-criticism meeting be put back a day so that they could have a meeting that evening to deal with the cotton stealing problem. The majority wanted to get things settled before Wang Juhai returned to prevent him just glossing over the problem. The two deputy directors accepted everyone's demands, consulted with the deputy Party secretary about delaying the meeting by a day and then called a co-operative members' meeting for that evening to deal with the cotton stealing.

The meeting opened. The agenda was for Gao Xiulan to first make a report on the capture of the cotton thieves, then the four would make a confession, and then their punishment would be discussed.

Due to the fact that their baskets were still held by the co-operative, and the director's absence, they all confessed pretty frankly with the exception of Pain-in-the-calf who was still trying to make quibbling excuses. The two accomplices confessed first. One said that she hadn't attended the meeting the night before and when Pain-in-the-calf had talked to her, she had agreed to go. When they got to the apricot tree field, they saw there was no one else around. They didn't go to the area that had been picked clean at all; the four of them went straight to the unpicked area at the north end. What the other woman said more or less corresponded with the first, but it was Never-full who had arranged it in her case. After these two confessed, three others in the crowd added that Pain-in-the-calf and Never-full had approached them too, but that they hadn't dared go. Next Never-full was called to confess. Her defences were already down and she recounted her discussion with Pain-in-the-calf frankly and in detail. Some people questioned her closely as to the logic of getting in accomplices. She explained that according to the director's usual way of dealing with problems, the more people broke the rules, the lighter the punishment — sometimes there was no punishment at all. However, the more accomplices there were, the less each person would be able to steal, so it was best just to rope in a few; then they wouldn't be on their own but they'd still each keep a fair amount. It was evident that she'd really made an accurate gauge of the director's character.

Finally it was Pain-in-the-calf's turn to confess. The reason Yang Xiaosi had put her last was because she always took advantage of her advanced age to argue with people; by getting the others to confess first, he was reducing her opportunities for argument. But the old woman was remarkable; whether she was right or wrong she always wanted to come out on top. Putting on a wronged expression, she said, "What do you want me to say? Isn't it enough that you suppose I've stolen?" Someone asked: "What's all this 'suppose' you've stolen? Did you steal or didn't you?" "I stole! And it was the deputy director who made me!" Yang Xiaosi asked: "Which deputy director made you steal?" "You! Yesterday evening you said everyone would be picking cotton. Why did it change overnight? Or were you just talking bull?" The instant she started swearing, half the crowd jumped in: "You're going to cause trouble, eh?" "You're supposed to be confessing; what are you doing swearing at people?" Third team leader Zhang Taihe spoke: "I've got an idea: don't let her confess even if she wants to — just send her to court!" Everyone agreed loudly. Pain-in-the-calf got scared and turned back and forth, looking around desperately. Seeing that she was going to be taken to court, her son and her daughter-in-law were frightened too. Her son begged her: "Hurry up and confess, mum!" Xiaosi addressed the crowd: "Everyone quieten down please!" He turned to Pain-in-the-calf: "I'll ask you one last time: are you going to confess? Reply now or you're getting sent! No more Mister Nice Guy!" "Wh-wh-wh-what do you want me to confess?" "As you like! Start swearing again if you feel like it!" "N-n-n-no. Th-that was a mistake! I'll confess!" Xiaosi asked everyone: "How about it? Do we let her confess?" "Alright!" Everyone agreed and sat down again. Pain-in-the-calf gulped several times and then said, "I've got nothing to say. Anyway, I was wrong! It's more or less like Baozhu said. After the meeting last night Baozhu said to me: 'Let's not stick to their rules tomorrow! Let's get a few people along!...' "

At this point, there was a sudden interruption. The rectification campaign meeting had finished half a day early and the Party secretary and the director had walked back several kilometres in the dark. When they saw there was a light on at the threshing ground they guessed there must be a meeting on, and so they went there rather than heading home. In the distance, the director could see Pain-in-the-calf first saying something to Yang Xiaosi, and then turning round to the crowd. He assumed the argument must still be about the big-character poster and so he hurried forward and entered the meeting place. He didn't listen to what it was Pain-in-the-calf was saying, he just stopped her: "Go home, sister-in-law! Is it really worth getting so worked up over such a little thing? In a few days we'll get it all explained and that'll be an end to it...." When everyone saw him come into the meeting place they initially felt frustrated, but when they heard him say this, they realized he didn't have a clue what was going on, and there was a rumble of laughter. One of the older men said, "Director, sit down and have a rest! If you don't know what's going on, you've no right to speak!" The Party secretary pulled him aside and said, "Let's listen first and then speak, eh? We've been away over a day, you don't know how the work's been arranged." Feeling very embarrassed, the director sat down next to the Party secretary.

As soon as Pain-in-the-calf saw that Director Wang Juhai had returned, she immediately perked up. She moved from where she'd been standing over to in front of Wang Juhai and said, "Brother-in-law, you've only been away one day, and your poor sister-in-law's nearly been persecuted to death!" When she said this, the crowd all stood up again: "Don't lie!" "You've broken the law and no one can save you!" The director got up, walked over to Xiaosi's side and said, "Everyone sit down, please! I've got something to say to you all! There's nothing that can't be sorted out...."

Someone said, "You sit down! We didn't choose you to be chairman today!" "We can sort all this out!" The Party secretary got anxious and once again pulled the director back: "Why are you so keen to stop all this? Let's hear what happened first, okay? Let's let them hold their meeting, we can go and rest in the co-operative office!" Then he said to the deputy Party secretary, "If you've got a minute, come over to the office and tell us what's been going on these last two days!" "Fine. How about now?"

The three of them left the meeting place and went into the co-operative office. The deputy Party secretary told them how Yang Xiaosi and Gao Xiulan had managed to get all the women who were always on the lookout for a free handout and who never wanted to work down to the south pond; how they had criticized them; how they had divided up the work force to pick the cotton or pull up the stalks; how they had discovered Pain-in-the-calf and the others stealing the cotton.... He described it all in detail and then said, "The cotton plants can all be picked tomorrow, the ploughing livestock have all been brought out this afternoon — uprooting the stalks can keep pace with the ploughing. The spare male workforce has been transporting dung to the fields in preparation for the winter irrigation." When he finished his report, he returned to the meeting.

When the deputy Party secretary left, the Party secretary pondered a moment and then said, "These youngsters know what it's about! Their methods may be a bit jokey, but they get the problems solved!" The director replied: "Well, I don't think that style of mobilization is very dependable. If you don't get a good gauge of everyone's character, and just force them out onto the fields, how much work's going to get done?" "Don't you dare think you can gauge somebody's character ever again! Those young comrades are really good at sizing up people's character. Those women who refuse to be mobilized have all got the same characteristics: they're bone-idle and they like something for nothing. The only reason they managed to get them out was because they understand those characteristics. Not only have they 'grasped' those characteristics of theirs, they do something about reforming them too. Think about it: after an 'exhibition of thoughts' like this one where all their evil ways of thinking have been dragged out, are they likely to go back to their old ways? You say that when those comrades mobilize there'll be no work done, but it's thanks to them that the cotton's getting picked. With their methods, the cotton can get picked in two days. If we still used your methods of 'character gauging', it probably wouldn't be picked in ten — the longer the picking went on, the fewer people there'd be. As for the rectification aspect, those comrades root out the two ringleaders of all the selfishness and not only do you not help, you even act as an apologist for them! Don't you realize you don't lead even half the women in this co-operative? The others are all led by Pain-in-the-calf and Li Baozhu! My dear old brother, it seems to me you ought to be 'tempering yourself' together with the younger comrades!" The director had nothing to say. The Party secretary pulled him along: "Let's go and see how they deal with the problem."

When they walked back to the meeting place, Pain-in-the-calf was asking Xiaosi for forgiveness: "Deputy director, please let me confess!" Originally, after she'd said that everyone had 'persecuted' her, no one would let her make her confession and they just discussed the punishments for the other three. She was being saved for the courts. Someone saw that the director had arrived and was deliberately sarcastic to Pain-in-the-calf: "Don't ask to confess! Look! The director's come back!" The director replied: "Don't talk about me. Act as you would whether I'm here or not! A minute ago you blamed me for being too subjective and for talking without understanding the situation!" Pain-in-the-calf interjected: "As long as everybody lets me confess, I'll confess no matter who comes along." She looked at the crowd but the crowd said nothing; she looked at the deputy Party secretary and the two deputy directors, but those three said nothing either. The crowd looked at the director, but the director said nothing; they looked at the Party secretary and he also said nothing. After everything had quietened down, Pain-in-the-calf's son stood up and spoke: "Chairman, I'd like to plead leniency on behalf of my mother. Please let her confess." Xiaosi looked at the youth and then turned to the crowd: "How about it? You speak up!" One old man spoke: "I suggest we let her confess, for the sake of the child." Someone else picked up the cry: "Okay, let her speak!" "Make her talk and let's see!" Hearing everyone and terrified of going to court, Pain-in-the-calf itched to speak of all the things she'd done against the collective; therefore, she made a very comprehensive confession. When she had finished, everyone decided to punish her to the tune of five working days per catty of cotton. The conditions for her were the same as those for Never-full: the work must be done by herself and she was not to use her children as substitutes.

After the meeting, the Party secretary spoke with the director as they walked along: "You reckoned those two responded to 'soft treatment, not rough'. It looks like you didn't get a proper fix on their characters, doesn't it? If your assessment hadn't encouraged them, they wouldn't have dared get so out of hand! You really should go and 'temper *yourself*!'"

July 14, 1958

Translated by Christopher Smith

The Story of Old Xing and His Dog

●

—— ZHANG XIANLIANG ——

Zhang Xianliang, born in Nanjing in 1936, began to write while he was still in junior middle school. As a result of the poem he wrote in 1957, "The Big Wind Song", he was persecuted and detained for over ten years. Following his rehabilitation in 1979, he became an editor of a literary magazine. In 1981 he became a professional writer. "The Story of Old Xing and His Dog", "Body and Soul", "Bitter Spring" and "Mimosa" were all national prize winners. Many of his works have been translated into foreign languages.

Preface

AT Han Meilin's exhibition of animal paintings I was stopped in my tracks by a water colour of a dog. One could say it was the lifelike style emphasizing its eyes that I admired so much: soft, bright but with a hint of wickedness, expressing docility and clever liveliness, but it would be more true to say that it was the title the artist gave the painting which I found so touching. It was called "A Tested Friend". I do not think the artist was being deliberately obscure, nor merely personifying an animal image but was preserving the memory of what really had been a close canine friend. Sure enough I later heard that during hard times the artist really did have this friend by his side, but that it was beaten to death by follwers of the "gang of four".

"A Tested Friend"! I think when a person is unable to find care and friendship amongst his own kind, but has to pour his love onto a four-legged animal, it is certainly because he has gone through painful times and is now experiencing unbearable loneliness. Some great writers such as Turgenev and Maupassant have written pieces using the friendship between dogs and lonely people as subject matter. The natural scientist Buffon also once wrote an excellent description of a dog. According to him, dogs were man's first friend. He also said that dogs had exactly the same emotions and moral concepts as man. Perhaps this is a slight exaggeration, but if someone were to ask me what my favourite animal was, I would definitely reply: dogs! Because I have seen with my own eyes the close friendship established between a dog and a lonely old man.

1

The dog was exactly the same as thousands of others in the countryside. It had no distinguishing features, nor was it a dog with a famous pedigree. It was a sandy coloured, untrained stray dog. Perhaps its fur was slightly glossier than other dogs, its body slightly more robust, but it had never performed any heroic deeds to write books about. What about his owner? The same as millions of other peasants in the countryside. If I had not worked in the production team in his area, if the special relationship between him and his dog had not attracted my attention, then I would not have paid any particular attention to this ordinary old man from the countryside. He was a lonely old man, getting on for sixty, of average height with a slightly hunched back. When he walked along his hands would be slightly raised in front or clasped behind his back. There was always an air of haste and solemnity about him. When he was not busy he would squat on his own against the wall or, crossing his legs, he would sit on the *kang*, lost in thought. Holding a long pipe in his mouth, he would pull on it time and time again. His dark purple face was drawn with lines, but these wrinkles opened up along the paths of his facial muscles, unlike the finely woven wrinkles on the faces of old intellectuals. His eyes were not large, the pupils slightly murky but sometimes they sparkled a little with the wisdom of old people who have seen much in their lives. His hair and beard were white of course, but he had not gone bald. In short, one would only have to look at him to realize that although he had the gloomy, despondent expression of a lonely old man, he still had a clear and clever mind, and a healthy body. He was a very able and versatile member of the production team. Sometimes he would plant vegetables, sometimes he would drive the cart, sometimes he would feed the work animals. He would do whatever he was ordered to do by the producton team, and never dispute the award of work points. He lived on his own in a poky, sun-dried mud-brick house, situated in the western part of the villge. In the doorway there was a single white poplar. In his home there was just a *kang* and two wooden trunks, so old that they had turned black, but everything was kept clean and tidy. Apart from his poverty, the old man also suffered hardship as a result of being single. "Going out lock the door, going in light the fire." This summarized his life. However, he always seemed to be full of vitality and immune from illness. As far as I know he had never had a serious illness, nor had he missed a single day's work.

Peasants' dogs do not have names. No matter how loved they are by their owners, the dogs are still called "dog". The peasants are seldom called by their first name. Adults, children, cadres and commune members always called this peasant "Old Xing". As time passed the old man's first name disappeared from people's memories. Old Xing and his dog were inseparable companions. When he drove the cart on business trips he would take the dog along with him. The man would sit on the shafts and the dog would run along in front or behind. If it saw something of interest it would dash to the front, sniff the air, sneeze and then hurriedly run up to the cart. If Old Xing was working near the village, at the end of the day the dog would rush out of the village with a group of children. The children would happily go to greet their parents, putting their shovels or hoes on their shoulders to carry home. When the dog saw Old Xing it would immediatly jump up at him, licking his face and hands, with its ears pricked back, and wagging its tail so hard that its whole back shook.

The dog's feelings for its owner were very sincere. Old Xing had only two or three hundred catties of coarse grain a year, with a few vegetables. It was barely enough to feed himself with nothing extra for his dog. When the old man lit the fire to cook his food, the dog was always close by his side, waiting until Old Xing had finished eating, locked the door and gone back to work again, before running outside to find some scraps to eat. It seemed to sense that its master had nothing to feed it and so never whimperingly begged for charity. It sat by him, watched him eat his meals, truly reluctant to be parted from him because commune members were only home for a brief period at meal times. In the evening, rest time was longer of course. After Old Xing had eaten his supper, with his pipe in his mouth he would pet the dog, wanting to chat awhile.

"Where did you go today? Let me see, are you full? My, my, you've eaten so much your belly is as round as a barrel."

Sometimes he would point fingers at the dog to frighten it, and say, "Dog, if you bite the kids, I'll give you a good hiding. If they tease you, just run off somewhere else, it's a big enough place. But don't you dare bite the kids...." In fact he had never once beaten the dog. It did not really need this kind of instruction as it was so tame the children would often take rides on its back.

At Spring Festival time, the production team would slaughter one or two sheep to give the commune members. Old Xing would say to his dog: "There are to be sheep slaughtered in the pen tomorrow. If you get yourself over there you may get some blood. There may even be some innards left behind...." Although it was not often that commune members had the chance to eat meat, unlike the others who would strip all the meat off the bone until it was shining clean, when Old Xing had some meat he would smash open the bones that still had some scraps of meat on them, and give each piece to his dog to eat. "Slow down, slow down, there's lots of meat on it. Your teeth aren't bad, but mine are not so good...." The old man did not have much to say to the villagers, but with his dog he was positively garrulous.

Only when the solitary old man was with his dog was his loneliness dispelled. In his eyes it was not a mere dog but a loved one who was by his side. In the summer evenings when he was sent to guard the vegetables, only his dog accompanied him, guarding until daybreak in those fields swarming with mosquitos and other insects. In winter, when he was feeding the draught animals, it was only his dog who endured the long cold nights with him. When the sun rose, the dog's back, tip of its tail and even its whiskers would be covered in a layer of white frost. Although the dog could not put its feelings for the old man into words, nor could it catch mosquitos for him, nor gather a fire for him to warm himself by, like a trusted soldier it always protected him. This was enough to stir the emotions of this old man numbed by poverty and overwork. On many a night the old man and the dog embraced to gain warmth from each other. In the silent dead of night it seemed there was only him and his dog left in the whole world.

In fact Old Xing once had a home and a wife. In order to properly understand the mutual reliance which existed between the old man and his dog, it is necessary to go back to his past.

2

Before liberation Old Xing had laboured on the land for ten years, never having the means to find himself a wife. After liberation he was allotted a sandy patch of land by the river. He was just thirty years old. Due to his hard work and farming skills he produced bountiful crops from his small plot of land against all the odds. He was full of confidence for the future and his life improved from year to year. When he was forty, a woman was introduced to him. Of course none of the best girls were willing to marry a forty-year-old man. His wife was always ill and sickly. After living together for just eight months she died. During those eight months, he used up several years of savings. That year there was a big drive to organize co-operatives. Old Xing's experiences made him realize that working as an individual he had no way to resist natural or man-made disasters, so he threw his land, his donkey and himself in with the co-operative. In the first couple of years his life really did improve. His ambition was to once again make good in a staunch collective. Just as he was getting the means to marry again, along came the "Great Leap Forward". He was organized into a steel-smelting contingent and taken into the mountains for "large-scale iron and steel smelting". The widow who he was about to marry did not wait for him to complete his duties but found herself another man.

Due to the organization of co-operatives and the division of labour in the production team, and due also to the amount of hard work put into working the land, together with the introduction of chemical fertilizer and simple mechanical farm equipment produce from the land increased. However, with some of the grain being handed over to the state, and surplus grain being sold, at reduced prices to the state or being left aside in case of war, outgoings always amounted to more than the increase. For several years the quotas set from above for grain contributions could only be fulfilled if the peasants went hungry. So it was best if Old Xing remained a bachelor.

But the world can change. Life is full of ups and downs. This simple philosophy was manifest in the life of this old man.

In 1972 the neighbouring province suffered a disastrous drought. In the spring of the second year groups of suffering people poured into the plain. Some came in groups of between three and five people, others brought their whole families and there were also individual travellers, all come to beg. Each of them carried a filthy cloth bag on his back preparing to beg for a little grain to take back to loved ones left at home. The city restaurants, the streets, the train carriages were all crawling with suffering people. After being driven out of the city by the militia, they went deep into the poverty-stricken countryside.

One noon, just as Old Xing was preparing his lunch, he heard someone with an accent from a different county calling, "Old man, you are a good man, spare a little!" The pitiful begging voice deeply moved him. He opened the door and saw outside an unkempt woman in her thirties. He asked her in and told her to sit on the *kang*, then busied himself cooking for two. After a while, when the woman saw what a clumsy cook the old man was, she said in a low voice: "If it doesn't offend you I'll cook this meal." Old Xing happily agreed. He filled himself a pipe and bending his waist sat on the *kang*. The woman washed her hands and started to cook. She worked quickly and cleanly. It was the same flour, the same seasoning, but Old Xing thought it the best meal he had ever eaten in all of his fifty odd years. The two of them ate two large bowls of soupy noodles. But still it was not enough for the old man and it seemed that the hungry woman could still eat more, so he asked her to make some more noodles.

Just as she was cooking for the second time, Old Wei from the east of the village pushed open the door and came in.

"Huh, I was wondering why you hadn't come to harness the plough yet. I see you've got company."

"But...." Old Xing did not know why but his face reddened. Slowly he said, "Just a beggar cooking some food. She'll be off when she's finished...."

Old Wei was the production team leader's third uncle, and the head of the team's poor peasant association.

"Ah, how dreadful. Women having to leave their homes and go begging for food." He squatted on the doorstep and took out a cigarette. "They're always saying if the old order were restored we would have to suffer again. As far as I can see this must be it. We peasants are suffering now. Are you from northern Shaanxi? How many others are there in your family?"

"Yes. I have two children as well as my parents-in-law." The woman lowered her head and replied bashfully.

"Don't be ashamed. It's not your fault. In the eighteenth year of the Republic I also begged for food. So did my wife. We had a year of great famine. What about the rest of your family?"

"Our commune gives each person half a catty of grain a day. With me gone, there's one less mouth to feed. They can eat my share."

The water in the pan was boiling so the woman busily put the noodles in the pan. Old Wei saw that she had cut the noodles long and thin just like the ones made by machine in the city.

"Well, well, excellent!" Old Wei suddenly jumped with an inspiration and said brightly, "I've an idea. Begging for food in all weathers is a dreadful thing to have to do. It's not like in the past. Nowadays no one has much grain, let alone any to spare. What's the point in begging here and there? Just stay here, cook for Old Xing, do some odd jobs around the place. Old Xing will see you're alright. He's a good man. I know."

The woman, with her back to him, made no answer but used her chopsticks to stir the pot. Old Wei turned to Old Xing and said, "Go and harness the plough first, Tiangui is looking for you. Those lads can't get near that young mule. Once it's harnessed, come back and eat." Tiangui was his nephew, the team leader.

Old Xing clipped his pipe to his waist and went out to the stable. In the time it takes to smoke two pipes, Old Wei arrived. Laughing, he clapped Old Xing on the shoulder and said, "Well, well, you ought to thank me! She's willing to stay and spend her days with you. At the moment it's still not one hundred percent certain that she will stay, You be good to her. Give her some more children and then her heart will be tied to this place. Have you got any money? If not, write a note, I'll speak to Tiangui and borrow some from the team. Go and buy her some clothes."

Old Xing grinned and laughed. All the wrinkles on his face grouped together. In the evening when he finished work, he went home and was greeted by a friendly face who quietly gave him a bowl of "oily soup and spicy water" noodles. She herself sat on the earth bricks beneath the *kang* and ate. She had washed and tidied herself up a bit and so did not look like a beggar anymore. After supper Old Xing put his pipe in his mouth wanting to chat a while. The woman was washing the dishes. Only then did he notice that the cooker and chopping board were now shining, the bottles of oil, and the salt pot were all neatly arranged.

"Old Xing, congratulations!" At that moment tall Team Leader Wei pushed open the door and came in. His eyes swept round the room and with a broad smile he said, "That's more like it. Looks much more like home. Just like crickets, a person needs a mate! Oh — here's ten yuan. The team has given you the day off tomorrow. Take your wife to the supply and marketing co-operative and buy some things."

Old Xing quickly got down from the *kang*. He filled a pipe and passed it over to the team leader, greeting his guest at the same time: "Take a seat, take a seat!"

Team Leader Wei did not sit down. He took out his cigarettes and gave one to Old Xing. Laughing he said to the woman, "You're from northern Shaanxi? You really got hit hard over there. It's so dry. There are others from those parts in villages around here. They also came to escape famine. Now all of them have married into the villages. Did you plant crops at home? Do you know how to sift?" Sifting counted as a skilled job, only women with dextrous fingers could do it.

"Yes, I do." The woman replied in a soft voice.

"That's good. You can start work the day after tomorrow. We're selecting seeds at the moment and there aren't many who know how to sift. You'll get the same work points as the others. We don't mistreat people from other areas here. And Old Xing is a good man. These last few years he has worked hard for the team. Don't you worry about being with him! Try your best. No matter what happens you'll have food to eat."

Old Xing would never have imagined that in the space of half a day he could be remarried. This was not a "match made in heaven", for as team leader Wei said, in nearby villages there were seveal marriages like this. In the countryside during the "cultural revolution" the concept of law was very scanty. A man with no wife, a woman with no husband, only had to be willing to live together and others treated them as a "married couple" with no seeming need for approval by law. This marriage was even arranged by the production team leader and poor peasant association leader.

3

Women really are innately different from men. Within a few days the woman had transformed Old Xing's house both inside and out. There had always been a band of alkali covering the bricks at the base of the mud-brick wall, eroding away a layer of mud. Now the room was clean, warm and dry. Even the bleak walls brightened up. Every midday and evening when the old couple came home from work, Old Xing would chop wood and light a fire, his wife would knead dough and chop vegetables. At these times Old Xing would feel every second was of great import. On days when he went out on the cart, he would rush back to eat and when from the outskirts of the village he caught sight of smoke curling up from the roof of his house, he would feel so happy that his legs would swing up and down on the shafts.

The Chinese have our own way of loving. Love for the Chinese working people is formed under conditions of hardship and suffering. On the rugged and bumpy road of life they support each other, encourage each other, shelter from the wind and rain and bear pressure from material and spiritual burdens on their backs; between them there need be no exaggerated, false words. No need for romantic expression. Caring for each other at times when work never ends and in times of hunger, the throb of love silently passes through them. This sort of love is both meaningful and creative. Although this woman was as quiet as a mouse, she understood Old Xing's feelings. Not only did she not reject his tenderness, she showed loving care in return. A poor lonely old man from the countryside only wanted sufficient spiritual comfort and order. He needed nothing more than a bowl of hot noodles made by his wife or a patch sewn on his clothes and her warm breath by his side at night. In the following few months Old Xing seemed to grow ten years younger. He walked with a spring in his step. A seventy-year-old man in the village who had been educated in the old way said, "The ancients weren't far wrong when they said 'a man without a wife is without a home'. Look at Old Xing, he's growing stout before our eyes. There is a light in his face, it's alight with luck."

As time passed, a shadow gradually slipped into Old Xing's dreamlike existence.

When weddings were held in the village there would always be plenty of women around to help out. The evening when Old Xing married, his poky house was completely surrounded by women. Before their openly critical eyes, the beggar woman was as terrified as a stray dog. She pulled at her hair and continuously tugged at the creases in her clothes. In time she used her modest, meek and unargumentative attitude and her excellent work to win the universal sympathy of the village women. They began to want to get close to her. Some brought cloth for shoes to her and asked her to cut out a pattern. Others came over to chat with her, while they were sewing shoe soles. But she still seemed to have a heavy heart. Although her thin, pallid face gradually broadened out, and she meticulously patched all the holes in her clothes so she no longer looked "threadworn" as they said in these parts, she still had a timid, wary expression as if she was always vulnerable. On the road to and from work she always walked alone, her tools in one hand and under the other arm, if it was not firewood that she was carrying, it would be some wild vegetables. When it was time to rest in the fields she sat on her own away from the others, never joining in their chattering. Not one of the women could find out about her past life or her present thoughts from her own lips.

If you have ever lived in the countryside, then you know that it is impossible for an outsider, especially a woman, not to raise comment among the village women. Soon gossip about this aloof beggar woman began to spread round the village. The women used their carefully thought out logic to reason that she still had a husband in her old home.

One day Old Xing was driving the cart, transporting some dung. Team Leader Wei went with him, sitting on the shafts at the front. Seeing Old Xing raise his whip looking so cheerful and contented, he felt great pity for him. He tentatively said, "Old Xing, don't be lax. You ought to tell your wife to transfer her residence card here. Otherwise you have no assurances."

In fact this was already a weight in Old Xing's heart. He had heard some of the village gossip although he did not believe it. But he also knew that if her residence was not transferred, and she had no more children, sooner or later the woman would have to return to her old home. It is hard to leave one's native land and people. He once discussed it with his wife, asking her to write the details of her previous address down and move her residence and her children over, but she lowered her head and said simply, "That can never be...." He did not dare contradict her and so asked no further.

"Don't be blind to the facts," Team Leader Wei said. "If you have her address I can go to the commune and write her out a transfer permit. If at home she still has a..., that's harder to sort out."

That evening Old Xing unloaded the cart and went home to eat. He saw his wife sitting on the doorstep as usual, using the little light from the setting sun to sew and mend. A group of children came to play under the poplar tree outside their house. Only then did she put down her work to watch them. She rested her head against the door frame, staring into the hazy distance. Old Xing knew she was thinking of her children but could not find the right words to console her. He simply wrapped a coat round her shoulders, "Don't get cold...." He sat down beside her, pondering how best to broach the subject of her residence.

The beggar woman was a very sensitive person. She could tell from Old Xing's slight nervousness and thoughtful expression, that there was something he wanted to say to her. After the sun had completely disappeared behind the mountains she gathered up her needle and thread, went into the room, swept the *kang* then knelt on it with her head lowered. Her two hands fell between her knees, like a criminal in an interrogation room.

Old Xing bent over and sat on the *kang* puffing on his pipe. The small room was enveloped in dark smoke and an uneasy calm. He smoked until he almost burnt his lips then finally plucked up his courage: "My dear, why don't you write the address? Let Team Leader Wei go to the commune and get a transfer permit. Once we've got that we'll go and fetch your children."

The woman still kept her head down, making no reply.

"Well" Old Xing let out a long sigh. "If ... if you still have a husband at home, then I won't hold it against you." By now Old Xing was breathing hard. In fact he himself did not know how he could possibly not hold it against her.

"No!" Although the woman spoke softly she stated categorically, "I have not!"

"Then —" Old Xing's eyes brightened. "Then what is it?"

After a moment the woman began sobbing gently. Her tears dripped onto the old mat on the *kang*. Old Xing was very flustered. He quickly got up and moved in front of the *kang*.

"Is it because I don't treat you well?"

"No." The woman used the back of her hand to wipe away her tears. "I've been wanting to tell you but was afraid you may throw me out?"

"Tell me! Who's going to throw you out? It's a blessing you don't want to be rid of me."

"My ... my family are rich peasants."

"Ahh...." The weight in Old Xing's heart dropped to the ground. He banged his pipe twice, knocking the ash from his pipe onto the soles of his shoes. "What's so dreadful about that? Nowadays if you work, you eat, whether you're a rich peasant or not!"

"No, you don't know the facts. My old village doesn't let rich peasants leave in search of food. I couldn't watch my children suffer, so I came away secretly. I couldn't even get a permit to escape starvation, let alone transfer my residence. I don't know if my parents-in-law are still being criticized for it."

Once she got started the woman continued talking. She blew her nose and wiped her hand along the edge of the *kang*. "I can see that you are a good man. Next spring give me a little grain, for I must return. When spring arrives things will be even tougher at home." She knelt on the *kang* facing Old Xing and respectfully kowtowed.

"Hey, hey, what are you doing?" Old Xing quickly sat on the *kang* and helped her into a sitting position. "We're not strangers now. Aren't the things in this room yours as well as mine? We'll think of a way to transfer your residence. What's the point in going back? Life out there is far too harsh. Even blind sparrows don't starve to death. There's always a way!"

That night the woman sobbed for a long time not really knowing why she felt such despair. Old Xing was such a kind man, he sat by her side comforting her half the night.

4

The next day Old Xing was still driving the cart, transporting dung. Team Leader Wei went with the cart as before. Old Xing told him what the couple had discussed the night before in great detail. Team leader Wei rolled a cigarette. He propped his arms up on his legs, rocking back and forth with the movement of the cart. For a long time he said nothing.

Then he spat: "This is even harder to deal with than if she had a husband at home."

"Why is it such a problem?" He urged the animals inside. "She's so poor she's begun begging, why is she still a rich peasant?"

Team leader Wei looked sidelong at him but knew there was no way of explaining to this old man. Old Xing had never attended any classes or meetings. When the campaigns came he was sent to a key post to work alone while someone else took his place in the campaign. Old Xing was the commune member with the least "political consciousness".

"It's hard, hard." Team Leader Wei took off his cap and scratched his head. "It's because if we write a transfer permit but they won't let her go, we're just asking for trouble. I reckon you should just live with her, with or without a residence permit. At present our team can squeeze enough grain for one more person. If there is enough to eat then that's alright, but you mustn't tell anyone else. Act as if nothing has happened but keep a tight hold on her heart. Wait until next spring then we'll see. Take it one step at a time. Who knows what changes there will be next year."

That year when the team's final accounts were worked out, the work points for the two of them amounted to five hundred catties of grain and one hundred and twenty yuan in cash. After they had taken their money and grain home it so happened that the team was sending a large cart to the town, spending three days shifting grit on a construction site to make a bit of extra money. Old Xing put some buns his wife had baked into his satchel, got on the cart and went into town.

It was on this occasion in town that he happened to see the sandy coloured dog. It was still just a pup, wild born and bred. It had never been fed by anyone. When Old Xing parked the cart on the construction site to eat his food, the dog stared a him with its head cocked on one side. Old Xing tore off a couple of pieces of the bun and gave them to it. After that it followed everywhere behind Old Xing's cart. On the morning of the fourth day when Old Xing was setting off for home, the dog ran out of town still following behind the cart. Old Xing felt sorry for it and in a moment of weakness picked it up and put it on the cart.

At midday the cart arrived back at the village. While still on the outskirts Old Xing realized that, unlike the other houses, there was no smoke pouring from his chimney. An unpleasant feeling came over him! In the stable he hurriedly unhitched the animals. Then Old Wei's wife came and found him.

"Old Xing, yesterday afternoon your wife said she was going to the supply and marketing co-operative and gave your keys to me, but she didn't come back last night. Why do you think that was?"

Old Xing took the key and quickly went home, opening the door with trembling hands. The room was cleaner than usual. The quilts, mattress and Old Xing's padded coat were all stripped and washed and piled neatly on the *kang*. There was a row of four new pairs of shoes on the pillow but no sign of the woman.

There was soon a crowd gathered round the house. Some urged Old Xing to go to the supply and marketing co-operative to look for her. This was a pretty ridiculous suggestion. Everyone knew what had happened. Old Xing dispiritedly bent over and sat on the edge of the *kang* without hearing anything the others were saying. He just repeated over and over: "She's gone, gone! She went without waiting for next year!"

Old Wei parted the people and came in saying, "Old Xing, don't just sit there like an idiot. Why don't you have a look to see what she took with her?"

Everyone clumsily helped him look around. Apart from the worn out clothes on her back and her new "wedding" gown she had taken one hundred and twenty catties of grain and fifty yuan. She had not taken the half ration or half of the money that she was entitled to.

"What a good woman." Everyone praised her admiringly. This added to the pain in Old Xing's heart. He was still sitting on the edge of the *kang* like a wooden statue.

When it was nearly time to go back to work Team Leader Wei came hurriedly into the room and said to Old Xing, "The commune's tractor has to go into town to collect some fertilizer. Go into town quickly and look for her at the bus and train stations. A woman with a hundred catties of grain isn't going to move very quickly. I've asked around. Yesterday afternoon she got on the third team's cabbage cart in to town. They didn't get there until after dark." Team Leader Wei was afraid something might happen to him and so sent a young lad to go with him.

Old Xing went to town in a daze. It was like looking for a needle in a haystack. They asked workers at the bus and train stations but all of them said they had not noticed a woman of her description. The young lad said, "She would go the way she came. She wouldn't spend money on a ticket! She would have taken a goods wagon." They went to the empty train carriages and goods vans to look again. She was not there.

The next day they got on a cart and went back home again. On the way Old Xing thought of a thread of hope that his wife had left him. "She is a kind woman, perhaps she will return." The lad also consoled him: "It's just that she missed her children and wanted to go back to see them. Perhaps next time she'll bring them with her." In a mood that alternated from despair to hope Old Xing returned to the village. Just as he was taking out his key to open the door, something hairy began to bark under his feet. It was that same small, sandy dog. In a day and a half it hadn't left the front door of this man it now recognized as its master. Old Xing picked it up and took it into his now cold, empty house.

Old Xing went back to his old way of life with just a beautiful memory to cherish, as well as a strong hope and a small sandy dog extra.

For a year, Old Xing kept up the hope that she might return. He always kept the room clean with everything exactly the way it was when she lived there. Every minute of every day when he was at home he would be expecting her to suddenly push open the door and come in. But as the days passed the patches she had sewn on for him wore through again. The clothes she had sewn had new holes, the shoes she had made for him had nearly all worn out, but still she didn't return. Slowly Old Xing's longing and hopes became buried in the depths of his heart, covered over by despair and disappointment.

During the following months only the dog consoled him in his loneliness. At times of rest, and at night when he was lost in a trance, with a pipe in his mouth, the dog would snuggle up to him giving the impression that there was a body full of warmth close to him. The dog would often lick his hand with his moist, soft tongue which would give him a lovely mellow feeling, making him think of the times he had spent with the beggar woman.

The dog's eyes, more black than white, docile and sincere, could rouse his confused memories of her and transport him into a hazy dream because her eyes had been equally sincere and docile. This sandy dog, now grown big, had become a living link between him and her. Because the day it arrived was the day that she had left, he even began to think that the dog was something left by her to remember her by, after her sudden departure.

But in the end even this link was wrenched away.

5

After the campaign to study the theory of dictatorship by the proletariat began, work teams from the county were sent to the production teams including Old Xing's. The peasants worked the fields by day and attended meetings at night. They seemed to have no time left to themselves. One evening there was an important meeting. At the end of the meeting the work team leader announced a notice which baffled the peasants. The notice was that all dogs in the countryside had to be "exterminated" within the next three days. The team leader said, "If you work it out that a dog eats half a catty of grain a day, that's fifteen catties a month or one hundred and eighty catties a year. If you don't think about it you don't realize, but once you work it out it's a frightening thought. It's almost half a person's ration. Nowadays we have to support the livelihood of everyone in the country, how can we also support all the dogs. Within three days all the dogs must be put down. Anyone who does not kill their dog will be treated as if they are hiding a class enemy. After three days small bands of the people's militia from the commune will come and kill it for them."

At first Old Xing did not think this notice very important. He used his peasant's simple reasoning: "I've never heard of anyone going without for the sake of their dog, nor have I ever heard of a country blaming its poverty on dogs. In the past even beggars kept dogs." But within a few days all the peasants who kept dogs did in fact kill them. Even Old Wei strung his big black dog that he had had for five years from a tree and poured water down it. Dogs were a way of making money. When people in the towns heard that dogs were being killed, one by one they rode their bicycles to the countryside to buy dog meat. A good dog could be sold for two or three yuan. If a peasant took it to town to sell himself he could get four or five jiao a catty.

Ten days later the only dog left in the villages round about was Old Xing's big, sandy dog. The militia spotted the dog, and circled the village twice.

That day there were four old men winnowing in the square. When the wind fell they sat together to chat. They discussed Old Xing's dog. Old Xing said with a touch of anger in his voice, "If I were even poorer than I am, I still wouldn't blame it on my dog. Who in this village feeds their dog? They all scavenge at the riverside. I'm keeping my dog and that's it."

One old man said, "Whether you feed it or not, even if you give it a little of your own food, the state will still interfere! I've heard that some people train their dogs to fetch ears of corn to their house."

Everyone laughed. Old Wei said, "If our dogs could do that then there would be no need for us to sow grain, we'd just send the dogs out to do their tricks."

An old man who used to like listening to storytelling said, "One evening I went home and thought about it for a while. In fact it's not a question of feeding grain to the dogs, it's as Old Xing said: who actually feeds their dog in this village? I've been thinking, it has to do with the campaign to criticize Confucius."

Apart from Old Xing who was still frowning, the old men all laughed.

"Confucius taught the virtues of loyalty, filial piety and integrity. What are loyalty, filial piety and integrity? Loyalty, he said, is a horse. Everyone knows that a horse is most loyal to man. If its master dies the horse refuses to eat. He said filial piety is a sheep. The minute it is born, a lamb kowtows to its mother. Integrity, he said, is a tiger. The mother tiger gives birth to a cub and feels such great pain that she won't let a male tiger near her again. Dogs have all of these virtues. We're meant to criticize Confucius' thoughts on loyalty, filial piety and integrity and so I think the authorities mean to start with dogs. Otherwise how can they say that a dog is a class enemy?"

When the old men heard this, they made jokes in derisive tones and smiled knowingly at each other. Then Old Wei sighed and said, "As I see it, the authorities just think the dogs eat grain. Now they need more grain but can't produce it from the land in a moment so they've thought out a way to get it. Later when the need is even stronger they will even reduce the food for the work animals." He turned his head to Old Xing and said, "It's alright talking and joking about it, but the sooner your dog is put down the better. Otherwise that group of militia will do it for you and they are all reckless young men. The day before yesterday they tied up a melon seeds seller and yesterday they put a carpenter out of business. They frighten people so much they scream, but they don't care. They'll just shoot your dog dead and won't even leave you a good pelt."

After supper Old Xing squatted on the edge of the *kang*, puffing on his pipe. The dog lay on the floor, raising its head and wrinkling up its nose, breathing out and sniffing the smell of tobacco he knew so well. Old Xing pondered for a while and thought out a plan to get official protection for his dog. He put on his shoes, locked the dog in the room and went to the team leader's house.

Luckily Team Leader Wei had no other visitors. He was lying on the *kang* while his wife sat under the light sewing the soles of a pair of shoes. Old Xing seldom visited other people, so when Team Leader Wei heard that he had come he quickly turned over and sat up. His wife brought them drinks.

As soon as Old Xing had sat down he stammeringly announced his intention not to kill his dog.

"I didn't realize it was such a big deal." Team Leader Wei laughed. "It's just a dog. The directive has come from above. Put it down and have done."

"Have done?" Old Xing indignantly said. "He's been with me for so many years I just don't have the heart to kill him. I swear I will never ask for grain from the team, so that's alright. My dog will only eat my own grain."

Team Leader Wei casually replied: "It's not in fact a question of the grain, it's a fact that dogs destroy crops."

"Good God, you're from this village. When have you ever seen my dog destroy crops? Dogs aren't working animals, nor are they poultry. Did they say that day that it's permitted to keep chickens but not to keep dogs?"

Because of a sympathy peculiar to women, the team leader's wife understood Old Xing's feelings and she said softly, "Old Xing has no family. His dog relieves some of the sadness."

This served to enflame Old Xing's feelings for his dog. He said earnestly, "I swear to God. If my dog is to be killed then you must kill me first."

The three people's hearts all sank. Team Leader Wei's smiling face became serious. His hands continually ran through his hair. He began to understand the close relationship between Old Xing and his dog and realized that convincing him would not be a quick or easy task. At the same time a strong feeling for this man who had lived in the same village as him for tens of years rose in him. Years of accumulated misery rolled along behind him. He could not help sighing, "Old Xing, you have your troubles, I know, but I also have mine and who can I tell them to? This evening as we aren't busy, let's talk them out.

"You watched me grow up in this village. The year I kept donkeys on the riverside, you were working for Wang Hai's family. After liberation we formed mutual aid teams and organized co-operatives. Again we were working together. At the time I was young and full of energy. I led everyone along the road to prosperity whole-heartedly. In the years afterwards I've risen and fallen three times. You know all this. During that campaign everyone had to criticize me. I never went with prostitutes, nor was I corrupt, so why was I criticized? Wasn't it because I spoke up on behalf of everyone but was accused of being a rightist. After that I realized the truth that the anthorities are never happy with a cadre who is popular with the people, and to please the authorities everyone has to suffer a little. In the last few years I have also learnt how to shoulder my burdens on a pole. If the two sides are unbalanced then you're pulled down by one end of the pole. There are some things which I think are unreasonable, but I am a Party member — just low-level — but can I do things which are not in accordance with the authorities? During the 'cultural revolution' I went with a county visiting group to Dazhai. They'd worked things out well there, I have to admit, but I reckoned it out. With the amount of corn and millet that they had, it would have been impossible for Dazhai to buy so many machines and build so many large engineering works. It was the state who footed the bill. Now we're told to learn from Dazhai but the state doesn't give us any money. We have to rely on our own efforts and make money through sideline production. Who knows when this year's campaign starts whether I'll be selected for criticism again. They accused me of having put too much emphasis on sideline production and looked down on agriculture. They say that that's promoting capitalism. You also know that our team's carpenters, bricklayers, cobblers and blacksmiths have been recalled, and that two huge carts are left unused. On the one hand they call for mechanization, on the other hand they give no money. Nor are people allowed to go and make money, nor are machines given for free. How are we meant to mechanize? We won't get as many work points as before this year to say nothing about mechanization. You are single and can eat your fill, so you can make do. But me, all three hundred people in the brigade are stretching open thair beaks to be fed and stretching their hands out for clothing. If I don't give out some cash this year then no one will have to work hard next year. You're worried about a dog, I'm worried about over three hundred people."

In his agitaion Team Leader Wei squatted up on the *kang*: "Look! We can make do this year, but when next spring arrives there will be a host of things to be done. If the villagers don't go to work in the fields, can I beat them to make them work? We're all poor or middle peasants from the same village. But I've noticed the campaigns always come in waves. Once this wave has passed over we can start doing sideline production again, otherwise we will be poverty-stricken and never able to mechanize. But we mustn't get in front of the wave. For our main goals to be achieved smoothly we have to be careful not to cross the authorities over a trifling matter. That is to say as regards killing the dogs, it's a question of keeping them occupied with small matters to steer them clear of the more important affairs. I also think it's unreasonable but the authorities have already set out the programme saying if you don't kill the dogs it is the same as harbouring counter-revolutionaries. The leader of our work team is also a member of our county committee. That day he totted it all up. There were ten dogs in our brigade, we've killed just nine. The work team said that our advanced brigade can't even implement the killing of dogs so how can we criticize capitalism? Old Xing, if the sky has fallen in because of your wife, I, Wei Tiangui, will prop it up for you, even if it means they remove me from my post as a brigade leader. As for the dog, you just put it down and that will be the end of the matter. Keep the leader happy and things will be easier for our brigade in future. Once he has gone you can get another dog. How about it?"

At first Old Xing didn't want to listen, then the more he listened, the clearer it became. When at the end he mentioned his wife all sorts of feelings ran through Old Xing's heart. He knew that Tiangui had always helped him in the past. How could he give Tiangui so much trouble over a dog? He lowered his head and clapped his hands down hard on it twice. With a wounded but resolved heart he said, "Tiangui, I don't want to give you any trouble. Everything you have said is true. Tell someone to come and put the dog down for me tomorrow. I can't do it myself."

That night he did not sleep but woodenly sat smoking on the bricks beneath the *kang*. The dog did not have the least inkling that it was its last night but placed its head in Old Xing's lap. Old Xing stroked its back while thinking back on his more than half a century of stormy experience. He had once heard that cadres, teachers, workers and actors in the cities had also suffered in the campaigns of the last few years. With his own eyes he had seen Wei Tiangui, this small county cadre, being criticized, but had never thought that in the end ordinary peasants like him, who had worked long and hard for many years would get caught up in it. Firstly his family's happiness had been ruined over a question of status, and in the end he was even to be deprived of his little bit of consolation. He didn't know why this was. He just heard in secret that this was what was called "politics" and "class struggle". He shook his head slightly and sighed. He found this sort of "politics" and "class struggle" frightening. He felt that with these sorts of "politics" and "class struggle" life had become meaningless.

Softly he patted his dog as if patting a child. In the face of unavoidable disaster Chinese peasants are always calm and restrained. Old Xing displayed this characteristic. Since he had realized his life became meaningless, what would be the use of keeping his dog? This dog's life was unexpectedly connected with the future livelihood of the whole brigade. He said in a low voice, "You go first, I'll follow on behind."

He raised his head and looked around his small room hoping to find a few traces of his wife. There was just the room. From top to bottom, every square centimetre had been cleaned by her, everything in the room had been washed by her, but she had gone. All this was as gloomy and depressing as death. But he did not blame her for leaving him in such a hurry. He realized that a good, kind woman would always have had to go back. Her not saying goodbye still left him a thread of hope, and had given him the strength to go on living for the last two years. So he felt grateful to her.

The next morning he fed the dog until it was full and then let it out. Before midday when he was standing in the square he suddenly heard the clear, sharp sound of a gun coming from the stable. He knew it was aimed at his dog. His heart was suddenly filled with guilt and remorse. When he ran into the stable, the executioner had already stalked off, leaving a group of children surrounding his dog. The dog was spread out on its side on the ground. A trickle of fresh blood flowed from beneath its neck. One wide-open eye, exactly like his wife's, had a terrified expression, as it looked sideways at the dark blue sky. Old Xing dropped his head and stood by the side of the dog's body. Trembling all over he wept loudly.

6

Soon after the work team completed its work and was withdrawn. Small businesses secretly started up again and in nearby villages the bark of dogs could be heard once more. But Old Xing's dog could not come back to life again. Old Xing grew older by the day. After a few months he lost his ability to take care of himself, relying on a neighbour to bring food over for him.

On the coldest day of the winter that year the neighbour thought it strange that by noon Old Xing still had not opened his door. When he pried open the lonely house, he discovered that Old Xing was already stiff on the *kang*.

Some said he had had heart failure, others said it was just old age, still more said "cancer". Only Old Wei grievingly said:

"If politics aren't progressing then they start criticizing Confucius! If production doesn't improve then they kill the dogs! It's not enough for just people to suffer, animals have to suffer too. If Old Xing's dog were still around he would have barked and sounded the alarm...."

Epilogue

Three years later, Young Yang, the commune's postman, had a letter from Northern Shaanxi addressed to "The fifth production team, Old Xing". Young Yang did not think much of it but just stamped it "already dead, return to sender" and returned it. Later in a break during a commune meeting a group of people were chatting together. Young Yang reported this piece of news to everyone. Wei Tiangui, now the brigade Party secretary, heard this and hitting Young Yang hard on the back swore at him: "Bloody idiot, why didn't you open the letter and read it? It must have been from that beggar woman. Now we don't know how she is getting on. Old Xing left two trunks. They're now being kept in the fifth team's storeroom."

October 1979, on Nanliang farm

Translated by Alice Childs

The General and the Small Town

●

—— CHEN SHIXU ——

Chen Shixu, from Nanchang, Jiangxi, was sent to work in the countryside for eight years after graduation from junior middle school. He began writing in 1981 and went to study in the Chinese Department of Wuhan University in 1985. Upon graduation in 1987, he started doing literary research. He is now an associated fellow in the Jiangxi Literary Research Institute. "The General and the Small Town" and "The Angry Waves" both won national short-story awards. He has published three collections of short stories: Shells Bearing Sea Breeze, Beside the Swan Lake *and* The General and the Small Town.

IN a small town like ours, miles from anywhere, the slightest change attracted great attention.

"Hey! Does anyone know why they're putting up a new house near the prison at the foot of Ringworm Hill? Who does it belong to? Are they enlarging the jail again?"

Ringworm Hill, about two li from the town centre, was actually a large rocky mound.

"You're all so dim!" The owner of this mocking tone popped his head out from behind the door of a shop. He was the barber. He was bald on top, though his few remaining hairs on the sides of his scalp were carefully oiled and combed.

Known as a newsmonger, he was an important figure in the small town. Though confined to his shop, he seemed to have his fingers on the pulse of the town and was the first to know of any new development. When passing on news, people often started with, "According to the barber...." The barber liked to add a touch of drama to the news. If he heard something important, he never announced it in his small shop. He would, like now, step out and go to the crossroads where there were all kinds of stalls.

"I bet you've no idea. The house is for a general who will soon come here to live."

"What? A general? Come to live with us?"

The news caused quite a stir. In a backwater like ours, the coming of a general was sensational news. It was indeed a great honour bestowed on us.

The barber cleared his throat and warned, damping their enthusiasm, "But don't raise your hopes! In fact, it's nothing special." The listeners craned forward, their curiosity aroused, asking why.

"Why? Humph! Listen, but this is for your ears only. Don't let on. Strictly confidential! The general's been dismissed! He's been exiled here!"

"Exiled! Why?"

"He was a renegade."

People gaped in astonishment. Like a bolt from the blue it struck at their vanity. They were disappointed and downcast.

"In name he's a retired officer." An ingenious propagandist, the barber regained the listeners' waning attention. "He still keeps his rank of general."

Then he continued in a low voice, "He was allowed to keep either his army rank or his Party membership. I may as well tell you all about it. People like us are just ordinary citizens, that's all. But he was an officer and a Party member. Now why do you think he chose to remain in the army?" He stopped abruptly, letting them ponder over this question. Holding their breath, they looked at one another, not knowing what to say.

Then a young porter from the transportation team, having put aside his barrow and elbowed into the crowd, broke the silence. "In my view, he should have kept his Party membership. It's an honour!" Quite a few people seconded him.

The barber pursed his lips disapprovingly.

"No, it's better to remain in the army," an old tailor observed prudently. "A man has to eat. Where can he get money from if he is demobbed? What can he live on if he's no income? He's probably no skills and you can't expect an old man like him to till the land, can you?"

"Right, you've got a good financial brain," remarked the barber, patting him hard on his shoulder. Excited, the tailor grew red, feeling greatly flattered.

"That's just what the higher-ups thought too, so they pensioned him off, allowing him to wear his army uniform." He paused to glance at the young porter and went on, "Don't you know, as a high-ranking officer he gets a fat pay?"

People exclaimed in admiration. But talking of money reminded the barber that he hadn't started work yet and he hurried back to his shop.

But someone caught his coat tail, asking, "Tell us, when will he come?"

"Haven't you anything in that thick head of yours?" He was obviously impatient. "Don't you see that house? When it's completed, he'll certainly move in there."

Reluctantly, people scattered, murmuring their guesses and predictions or sighing over the ill-fated general, taking the news to all the corners of the town.

Now, with the listeners departing, let's have a look at this lovely little town.

The town had two streets only wide enough to allow the passage of one jeep. Six hundred metres long altogether, they crossed at the centre of the town. The streets were paved with flagstones here and there, while paint peeled from the jutting-out buildings. All these showed its antiquity.

A stream, only ankle-deep, meandered around the town. Unfortunately, on its banks were heaped piles of rubbish and debris.

It was really surprising! People gaped when they first set eyes on the general. Everybody thought the same, "No wonder he was dismissed. An old duffer like him doesn't deserve to be called a general!"

What should a general look like then? Though we'd never met one before, he didn't fool us. A general should have grey hair, straight eyebrows, and perhaps a paunch. He must be tall and strong, looking impressive and awe-inspiring like in the films. But this man was small, wizened and wrinkled. Moreover, he was slightly hunched and lame in one leg.

Far from being broken by his unlucky circumstances, he paid great attention to his appearance as if to make up for his poor physique. Whenever he walked in the streets, his uniform was always well ironed without any creases, and he held himself straight like a soldier. The red star on his cap and his two red collar insignia stood out brightly. No matter how stifling the weather, he kept his jacket collar buttoned. Though lame in one leg from an old war wound, he walked steadily. However, all this unfortunately reminded us of his disgrace.

We often watched him, not in awe or contempt, but out of curiosity. He didn't seem to mind at all. On the contrary, he walked about, though with some difficulty, the second day after his arrival.

Leaning on his shining wooden stick, he limped from one end of the street to the other. Or sometimes, he strolled along the dry stream bed strewn with litter. Someone said, tongue in cheek, that the old man kept moving habitually because he had walked all over China!

After a short period, he began to make some unfavourable comments about our small town, in which we had lived happily for a long time. He asked, for instance, "Why don't you spend some money on putting a tarmac surface on the two streets?" or "Why don't you dig a large pit on the other side of the stream for your rubbish so that it can be made into compost?" Our sophisticated and clever local cadres would excuse themselves saying, "Where can we get the money for it? Our salaries are pretty low!" or "We're simply too busy!" Their listeners would chuckle, catching the dig at the general.

Our feelings towards this queer general were rather mixed. Though disgraced, he still got a decent pay. We all felt his criticisms and suggestions were well meant, yet no one was willing to befriend him.

Apparently, he soon noticed our mood, for he stopped making any more embarrassing criticisms. Instead, he found himself a place at the crossroads. There under an old camphor tree, whose top had once been struck by lightning, just opposite the barber's shop, he stood upright sometimes for hours, supported by his stick. Blinking his bleary eyes, he stood musing silently. No one knew what was in his mind.

His posture was really amusing. Vendors nearby raised their heads to glance at him from time to time, and even passers-by lingered to look at him before continuing on their way. Behind the glass windows of his shop, the barber gazed at him standing in the dusty street and joked cheerfully, "What do you think he looks like?"

"A sentry," someone said.

The barber shook his head.

"A traffic policeman then," said another.

He shook his head again. After some further exchanges, the barber said matter-of-factly, "Have you ever been to Hankou? At one end of Sanmin Road, there's a bronze statue of a figure standing erect and holding a walking stick. Just like him. Exactly!"

Gradually, people got used to seeing the general standing there, like a bronze statue. He became like the coppersmiths, cobblers and tinkers at the corners of the crossroads. If you didn't see one of them for a couple of days, you would feel there was something missing.

But he was not a statue, he was a man, and one with a shrewd mind moreover. And one day people would discover that he was also possessed of a hot temper.

One Sunday, there was a great commotion in front of the butcher's, as some young rascals with baskets on their backs fooled around, enjoying making a racket.

The general stood as usual viewing the scene, while his hand holding the stick trembled slightly and the veins in his temples swelled in anger. Suddenly he limped across, raised his stick and tapped a soldier on the back. Wet with sweat, he was squeezing his way through the crowds and shouting boisterously. Turning his head abruptly, he met the old man's blood-shot gaze. He withdrew from the throng at once and asked, "Anything I can do for you, sir?" Though a new recruit, he decided that the old man must be a high-ranking officer.

"Tidy yourself up before speaking to me!"

Darting a timid, worried glance at the general, the cherubic-faced soldier quickly righted his cap, did up his collar buttons, rolled down his sleeves, and finally lowered his head, staring down at his shoes.

"Which unit are you from? What's your job?"

"I'm a cook in the mess of the garrison stationed here."

A few brief seconds of silence followed.

"Attention!" the general suddenly shouted. This professional harsh order immediately silenced the noisy crowd. Heads turned to look at the two soldiers, who seemed oblivious of everything around them.

Panting, the old man gave a second order, "Turn left! At the double! Quick march!"

Still holding himself erect, the general breathed heavily, gazing at the retreating figure.

All was very quiet now at the crossroads. As though checked by some strange power, the jostling, noisy crowd automatically fell into line. At that moment, they felt the might of the old man, who had once commanded thousands of troops.

Not long after, another incident shocked the small town, making those who were inclined to side with the weak realize that something was wrong with their present situation.

It was inevitable that the old general, who had been through hard times, had had his health impaired. Apart from the care of his wife, once a head nurse in a large hospital, the general was permitted regular check-ups in an army hospital some fifty li away. A sign of charity perhaps. He could also go to the town's hospital in an emergency.

One day, he became pale and ill, breaking out in a cold sweat. As he was entering the local hospital, supported by his wife, a country woman who had been sitting on a bench by the consulting room suddenly tugged at his coat, begging, "Please save my child! I hurried over thirty li to get here before dawn, hoping to see the doctor as soon as possible, but...."

Inside it was so dim that they could hardly see each other. The general felt the boy's forehead, then started. "Hurry up!" he shouted. "Take him to the doctor at once!" Then he tore into the consulting room and said to the doctor seated at a desk, "Doctor! Here's an urgent case!"

Sitting behind the desk was the doctor, the wife of the town mayor and head of the hospital. Her occupation, social position and the way she carried herself served to demonstrate that she was the most important woman in the town. At that moment, she was listening to the heart of one of her distant relatives and chatting with the patient about her daughter's dowry. She was so engrossed that she forgot to remove the stethoscope. Interrupted by the general's cry, she glared at him and said, "Register first." Then she turned back to her relative, all smiles.

"He registered ages ago!"

"Then you'll have to wait.... Yet, it's worth having a daughter."

"But he was registered first."

She turned abruptly and asked, "Little Wang, did you call number one?"

"Of course!" replied a young nurse bent over giving an injection.

"See," said the doctor and, turning to the peasant woman, she added, "you weren't here when your number was called. You'll have to join the queue again."

"But I was here! Our village doctor told me that my boy was suffering from acute pneumonia...." The woman, carrying her child in her arms, broke off, out of either nervousness or disappointment.

"She probably didn't hear you clearly," said the general.

"Then she can learn a thing or two about our regulations. A country has its laws and a hospital its rules. If we don't stick to the rules, there'll be chaos, won't there?" Throwing her stethoscope on the desk, she shot the general a reproachful glance.

"But this is an urgent case! You can't be so rigid! Now, what number was this patient?" asked the old man, pointing to the relative.

"H'm! So you've come to make trouble today, eh? Are you the kid's father or grandfather?"

"You should be ashamed of yourself!"

"What? Ashamed? You old fool! Why should I be ashamed? Am I anti-Party or a renegade?"

The general raised his stick.

The cocky woman screamed, protecting her head with her arms.

It was so quiet that you could hear a pin drop in the room. Her relative was flabbergasted. Nobody came out to grab the general's stick. It remained quivering in mid-air. People hoped it would strike the doctor's snub nose.

But the stick did not fall. Instead, the old man stretched to grab the other end and snapped it in two.

Turning with difficulty, he asked his wife, "Is there any medicine at home?"

She nodded, knowing that he meant medicine for pneumonia.

In a trembling voice, he asked the peasant woman, "Do you trust me? Then follow us!"

The news of this incident soon got around. Now even timid people dared to show their dissatisfaction.

It was true that we were rather cut off from the world and, as a result, we were rather easily cowed. But it was precisely this that made us rely on our own judgements. If a "renegade" helped others in difficulty while a "Communist" bullied the people, shouldn't their titles be exchanged?

For a couple of days, there was no sign of the general under the camphor tree. People began to anxiously whisper about him. It was said that his condition had taken a turn for the worse. And since the incident in the consulting room, he had been deprived of the right to use the town government jeep to go to the military hospital.

Late one night, some fine young men led by the porter came to the general's house. They put the old man on a stretcher and hurried him off to the military hospital.

1976 began terribly. It was bitterly cold. Overhead the clouds were hanging thick and heavy, while the ground was muddy and slippery. Our little town looked more desolate than ever.

As if favoured by fate, despite the bad weather, the people in the town had the monotony broken by some encouraging news.

Just after the New Year, the barber came to the crossroads with an air of importance. No doubt, he had something vital to announce. People gathered around him at once. Having cleared his throat, he began, "You know what, the general's no longer a renegade! His case has been cleared!"

"Are you sure? How do you know?"

"You don't believe me?" chided the barber, glowering at the questioner. He never tolerated any doubts about his information. However, he went on, "If you don't believe me, ask him."

"I told him," admitted the porter, elbowing his way forward. Not used to speaking in public, he blushed. "When we were in the hospital, two men from the general's original army came and said that the general's record before he joined the Red Army had been cleared. He never betrayed the revolution."

"Humph! Ridiculous to have wronged a veteran revolutionary for such a long time," the barber butted in with his comment. "I said long ago that the general was every inch a damn good man! Indeed...."

"Indeed, sufferings test a man." People sighed, sympathizing with the general.

"Then he'll soon leave us, won't he?" the tailor raised his question hesitatingly.

A far-sighted man! When the inevitability of this was forced into their minds, the townsfolk again became depressed.

"Well," the barber said after a sigh, scratching his bald head. "It's only natural. Ours is a small town. How can a little temple house a big Buddha?"

People felt sad. It was always the same: you realized a thing's worth only when you had to part with it.

"What a mean lot you are!" the porter snapped in anger. "The Party and the State need him badly. You always wished him good luck. Now it's come, you're miserable. Isn't that selfish?"

Yes, it was. The general had his work to do, which was of vital importance. After all, we couldn't ask him to be our mayor, could we? So his leaving would be something worth celebrating.

People looked expectantly in the direction of the hill, hoping that the general would come and stand under the camphor tree as before. They longed to see him, and if possible, have a chat with him.

The desire to see the general grew stronger. Then someone suggested that everyone should go to call on him, since he had come back the previous day and was still unable to walk about.

Why not? So the crowds headed for Ringworm Hill.

The desolate, rocky hill became a lively spot. Normally people steered clear of it if they could. There was neither wood to collect nor grass to graze cattle. Moreover, for centuries, it was where those executed had been buried. If you had to pass this ominous hill, you'd certainly give it a wide berth.

But now, the house beside the prison was like a sacred place for pilgrims.

As they were swarming around the door, they saw the general inside, hunched over and looking thinner. They halted, not daring to cross the threshold, filled with shyness and awe. Even a wag like the barber was lost for words. Only when people nudged him did he mutter in a fluster, "General!" But it was inaudible, even to himself.

For some time, the general did not know what to say either, his eyes wide open in surprise. But when he soon realized their intention, tears brimmed over and streamed down his lined face.

Although Ringworm Hill was not far from the town, this was the first time that people had seen it joyfully. They were also astonished to find rows of pits for planting trees on the slope behind the general's house.

"Are you going to plant so many trees, general?"

"Yes. I hope to change the colour of this mound before meeting Marx in the nether world. It's a pity that fruit trees won't grow here. Still, we'll make do with pine trees."

"Do you mean to live here as a hermit?"

"Hermit?"

"Yes."

"What an idea! Ha! Ha!..." The general laughed heartily until he was seized by a fit of coughing. Then he went on, "My aim is to safeguard the small trees until they've grown big enough. When you've some time, we'll divert the stream too, build some irrigation canals and a reservoir. This will help your fields. The hills will be green and the stream will retain water all year round. If we plant some flowers, and keep some birds and animals, we'll have a fine park. I'd like to be the park keeper. And you, young man," he patted the porter on his shoulder, "can bring your beautiful wife there and have fun. I assure you I won't close the gate ahead of time!"

"Then promise not to hit them with your stick if you catch them kissing each other behind your house," the barber teased, as the people roared with laughter.

"How shall we say goodbye to him? What shall we give him as a keepsake? How can we keep in touch with him?" Those were the questions everyone in the town thought and discussed. Some even quarrelled over the order of inviting the general to dinner.

But all of a sudden, the town was overshadowed by the death of Premier Zhou. He died at a time when he was most needed. The morning that his death was announced, the general, supported by his wife, suddenly appeared under the camphor tree at the crossroads.

The sun was up, pale and dull. It was extremely cold. The small town looked more bleak and gloomy, silent as death, as if frozen numb by cold and sorrow.

The general, standing in the cutting wind, looked very pale and sallow, his deep-set eyes circled by dark shadows, his face grim. He stood erect, as solid as a bronze statue.

"Comrades...." he shouted in his hoarse voice. It sounded so unfamiliar that many stopped to listen to him. The old man bent down and unzipped his bag with an effort, revealing black mourning arm-bands. Raising his head, he uttered, swallowing hard, "Please...."

There was no need to say any more. People, one by one, took the bands and put them on their arms.

"Whose idea was this?" A hand, its fingers brown from too much smoking, suddenly touched the shoulder of the general. It was the mayor.

The general was silent.

"We've already told you that no one is going to hold any mourning ceremony. What are you up to?"

The general did not even raise his eyes.

Turning round, the furious mayor bellowed at the crowd, "Don't move, any of you! Take off your arm-bands!"

But no one complied.

"Disobeying, eh? Old tailor, you take it off first!"

The tailor was stunned. Looking at the mourning arm-band and then at the mayor's angry face, he trembled for a second. Before dawn, the general had knocked at his door and given him a roll of black cloth. The bad news had upset him dreadfully, but he had realized at once what his visitor wanted him to do. Together, they sat down to work, grief-stricken.

Now this indignant petty official was trying to force him to throw his band on the ground in shame. But it was not merely a matter of an arm-band, but of a heart loyal to the late premier. Could anything be more insulting? Clever, scrupulous and law-abiding, he never did anything harmful to others. Though he had bitter memories of being insulted and humiliated, none was worse than this. He would not swallow it.

He looked up and met the general's burning eyes, which scorched his heart. With quivering lips, he said slowly, "Is it against the law to mourn Premier Zhou? Do what you like to me. I'm a tailor. I won't die of hunger wherever I go. Sorry, I won't take the arm-band off."

"To mourn Premier Zhou isn't against the law!"

"We won't take our arm-bands off!"

Those docile, unambitious people had gone mad! They stood united in rebellion! The sense of justice, buried in their hearts, had been aroused by a general in exile, shattering their traditional timidity and humility.

Nonplussed, the mayor turned to the general.

But the old man did not even glance at him. Calm and concentrating, he seemed to be commanding a battle.

Only his wife knew the mental and physical pain racking his frail body. Despite his strained nerves and aching muscles, he stood erect. She dared not say anything, though her heart was torn.

"You'll pay for this!" snarled the mayor, his face distorted by rage. Then he took to his heels and disappeared round a corner.

Suddenly, the general gasped, short of breath, and collapsed.

A few days later, the barber heard the shocking news that the general would live in the town for the rest of his life as an "honorary" general, because of his new "mistake". This was the first time that the barber kept a piece of news to himself. He had no heart to pass it on.

Just like the changeable weather in early spring, the people became depressed once more after their few days of happiness.

Ringworm Hill was again silent. Crowds came to see the general every day, their faces showing no trace of joy.

The general never again left his bed after his collapse. In and out of a coma, he sometimes ran a high temperature, staring at the ceiling with glazed eyes, raving deliriously or muttering away.

One day, suddenly his mind cleared. Scanning each anxious face, which showed momentary delight and surprise, he said with difficulty yet distinctly, "I ... I will not leave you. I'll look after the park and ... you must plant trees ... repair the roads ... dig a canal. You won't drive me away, will you? Good...."

The general died. But his noble character had left an indelible impression on the people.

Then came an order from the authorities: the body of the general was to be cremated on the spot. No notice was to be given to his relatives or friends and there was to be no obituary, no mourning ceremony. It was a stupid decision, but they wanted to have everything under their control. In fact, no one complied with it.

The people were calm, yet stubborn, and did it their way. A mourning committee was elected, and it decided at once to hold a traditional, grand funeral. Quickly, the townsfolk went into action.

The oldest citizen contributed his cypress coffin, the only one still remaining in the town; the tailor made the shroud that night; the barber spent a long time giving the general a face-lift. When the corpse was put into the coffin, incense and an oil lamp were lit. The boy, whose life the general had saved, and his parents had tramped thirty li to join the funeral. Dressed in mourning, he served as a filial son. People not only from the town but also from the surrounding villages came to present their wreaths and mourning streamers. The huge wreath sent by the nearby garrison, whose cook had once been scolded by the general, was particularly eye-catching.

The dawn sky was overcast on the day the funeral took place. Heavy clouds hung low over the town and open country. According to his will, the deceased wanted his ashes to be scattered over the hillside. However, the long funeral procession first headed for the town. With the bier at the head, carried by sixteen stalwart young men, people marched through both short streets, which nevertheless took them the whole morning. Finally they stopped under the camphor tree, and many people made memorial speeches expressing their grief, regrets and vows.

But two people were strongly against such a funeral. One was the general's wife. She argued that her husband had been a Communist and a revolutionary soldier and had asked in his will to be cremated. Before she could finish, people pleaded with tears in their eyes, "The general would understand. He wouldn't complain. We've no objection to his being cremated later. But please let us have our way for the time being." She closed her eyes with an effort, fighting back her tears. The other was the mayor, but he could do nothing except peep through his screened window. Furiously, he vowed through clenched teeth, "Wait till I deal with you!"

One year later, the "gang of four" fell. It was not the barber or the old tailor, but the mayor and his followers, who were disgraced at last.

When the people began to modernize their small town, they first put the general's wishes into practice.

In the last three months of that year, pits for tree-planting were dug all over Ringworm Hill and some other hills near by; the rubbish dump by the stream was removed; and the two streets were given a tarmac surface. Diverting the stream was already included in the town's water conservancy plan, and the first phase of the project worked on by several thousand people was completed before the Spring Festival.

Everything went well and smoothly but, of course, there were occasional quarrels too. Once, however, there was a bitter one which shook the whole town.

It was about whether or not they should build a monument in memory of the general under the camphor tree. The porter and his mates were all for it, while the barber was in two minds. As people argued heatedly, the tailor picked his way into the crowd. Raising his hand, he pointed to the tree and said in choked voice, "Look here, what's better than this tree in memory of him? It's old and its bark has peeled, but its roots are still alive. Look at the new twigs and the lush leaves...." He faltered, swallowing hard.

Suddenly the townsfolk felt as if the tree had turned into the general wearing his green uniform buttoned at the collar, with a bright red star on his cap and red insignia on his collar. Leaning on his stick, he stood erect and blinked his eyes from time to time, silently watching the changes in the small town.

Imagining this, they forgot all about their disagreement.

1979

The Man from a Pedlars' Family

●

—— LU WENFU ——

Lu Wenfu was born and brought up in beautiful, ancient Suzhou, where he finished middle school, worked as a journalist and started creative writing. Suzhou's traditional culture and social customs had a very profound influence on him. He writes about the life and people of the city in a local style. "Devotion" (1978), "The Man from a Pedlars' Family" (1980), "The Boundary Wall" (1983) and "The Gourmet" (1984) were all national prize-winning stories.

TO speak of pedlars and well-born families in the same breath is a little unusual. Perhaps we're being a little too literal here. Let's just say that there is a certain Zhu Yuanda whose family from generation to generation has been engaged in peddling. During which dynasty did his family begin to peddle? It has never been ascertained. What things did they peddle? This too can't be said for certain. All I remember is that, thirty-two years ago, the day after I moved to this lane, just after dusk, I heard the sound of a bamboo clapper approaching from the distance. The rhythm was very marked, "Duo duo duo, duo duo, di di di duo, duo duo, di di duo." Although there were only two notes, there were many variations in modulation and in the strength of the tapping. Under the cover of night it seemed as though someone were calling or relating something.

I opened the long window facing the street, and looking down I spotted a light at the end of the alley. The light wavered on the white chalk walls, whizzing along like a spirit on night patrol. Gradually it became more distinct. It was a brightly lacquered won ton carrying pole. Steam was rising above the pole, while sticks of firewood burned in a stove. The pole carrier was Zhu Yuanda. At that time he was perhaps seventeen or eighteen, tall and thin. Beside him shuffled an old grey-haired fellow — his father. His carrying days were over. He'd very recently passed the carrying on to his son. Now he went on ahead striking the bamboo clapper, leading his son along the bumpy road he'd followed in his life that had enabled him to sell enough won ton.

In those days I was out of work. I relied entirely on helping several overworked Chinese language teachers, correcting students' composition exercise notebooks, getting a share of "classroom chalk dust" so as to make ends meet. This was not easy work and every night I was burning the midnight oil!

The "di di, duo duo" sound of that clapper passed nightly beneath my window. It would always depart at dusk and eventually return, most often just as the Beijing opera-goers were leaving the theatre.

Whoever works through the long winter nights dressed only in a thin shirt becomes frozen stiff with only his shrunken heart continuing to beat. Inside the room there is no stove, while outside the north wind cuts through the window lattice like a sharp knife. The swirling night rain is turned into ice crystals which dance on the roof tiles. After midnight the whole world becomes an icehouse. At that hour a steaming hot bowl of won ton dumplings for five cents with extra helpings of soup and hot sauce is a powerful temptation and a delightful pleasure!

Almost from the first day I became Zhu Yuanda's main customer. Later it became my habit that at the last sound of the Beijing opera gong, I would lift my eyes from the students' exercise books and wait to hear the warming sound of the clapper.

Zhu Yuanda's clapping was better than his father's. It was livelier and seemed at once both joyful and mischievous. Before long the clapper would be sounding beneath my window. "Eat, eat, come quickly and eat," it seemed to be calling. If I was a little slow, Zhu Yuanda would put down his pole and call up to me,

"Mr Gao, come down and warm yourself."

I would hurry downstairs to stand by his carrying pole, watching him fan the fire in the small oven and put the won ton in the pot while I listened to Zhu talk of the evening's business. He was very talkative; the words would flow in a stream, so that while you waited for your won ton you didn't feel the least lonely or anxious.

"Tonight's business was very good," he would invariably begin, as though sales never went poorly. "When the opera ended at least twenty people gathered around my carrying pole. And would you believe it, there wasn't enough meat stuffing. I'm not kidding you. The last few bowls had dumplings which were only half-stuffed.... Oh! Yours I set aside specially. They're stuffed with meat." He used a brass spoon to stir the won ton in the pot so as to prove this to me. "See, each one is bulging with meat."

I laughed as I said, "I don't care whether they're stuffed or not, just add a few more hot peppers!"

Zhu Yuanda didn't miss his chance to add, "It's so cold. Would you like another bowl?"

"Okay. But you're sold out of meat stuffing."

Zhu laughed heartily, his eyes winking slyly. "It would be throwing away your capital if you were to sell won ton! When you're doing business, you've got to say that there's a limited supply of your product. Then people will snap it up. If you tell them that there's no meat filling left, then the customers will want even the pastry sheets!" Saying this he withdrew from a little cupboard an earthenware bowl of meat which he thrust before me. "See if this isn't enough for you!" He laughed, thoroughly pleased with himself.

I began to laugh myself. It was just like watching a magician gaily and deliberately giving away the tricks of his trade.

At that time I didn't think that Zhu Yuanda was doing anything dishonest or that he was putting his profits ahead of everything else. I felt that the reason I wanted to correct more exercise books and he wanted to sell more won ton was because our lives were so difficult. Every night he brought me a little warmth. If I was able to buy for his sake one more bowl of won ton we would be helping each other out like two fish in a drying pond trying to spew foam on one another.

After Liberation I got a job as a cadre in an education department. Although I was still busy, I didn't have to stay up half the night. Although my salary wasn't much, I felt it was beneath me to have won ton dumplings for five cents a bowl. If I was returning home late from a Beijing opera, I would rather have noodles and shredded pork for fifteen cents to say nothing of sitting ostentatiously in a restaurant than to be eating tiny won ton dumplings standing with hunched shoulders by the seller's stall.

Although the sound of the clapper would still pass nightly beneath my window, with the passage of time, it lost its sense of mischief and joy, though it still seemed to be calling, relating something. I rarely ran into Zhu Yuanda. When he'd return home late at night striking his clapper, I would be sound asleep. If I did by chance catch that "duo, duo" sound, it would still bring a feeling of warmth in my somnolence, though it would be very faint and far away.

It was probably sometime after 1958 when, being obliged to queue up at a noodle shop, I suddenly recalled what I hadn't heard for a long time — the sound of that clapper in the dead of night. It seemed a shame, as though I was missing something. But ever since the anti-Rightists movement, I could hardly dare to keep up my old attachments. I had not only to convince myself of this but also others. Socialism required a certain uniformity. It wasn't proper to have capitalist pedlars roaming the streets late at night. I was happy for Zhu Yuanda. He'd already broken free of his shackles and leapt into the torrent of the Big Leap Forward.

But things turned out differently. Zhu was no longer beating his clapper but carrying willow wicker baskets through the streets and lanes sneakily and in a flurry. In the spring he sold red bayberries; in the autumn water chestnuts and lotus roots; in the summer it was watermelon. In the winter he would set up his stall beneath the eaves of a house and sell roasted sweet potatoes. Sometimes he would sell cabbage, soya-bean sprouts, live chickens, fish or shrimp. You could never know for certain what he would be selling. If someone in the courtyard had an unexpected guest, you'd always hear the housewife quietly ordering her husband to "run down to Zhu Yuanda and see what he's selling". I never bought anything from him and I wouldn't allow my wife or children to go. I believed that buying his things was aiding the spontaneous rise of capitalism.

I recall that during the mid-autumn festival one year the anti-Rightist inclination campaign became particularly heated in my department. I had just been engaged in a war of words with someone with a Rightist inclination. When I reached home, the moon had already passed its zenith. The scent of osmanthus flowers was floating everywhere in the city. The moonlight was like water. It felt very strange — the struggle was so intense while all around one everything was so delicately beautiful. It was as though the world was out of joint.

As I was crossing a little stone bridge, I suddenly noticed Zhu Yuanda at the other end of the bridge setting up shop. One basket contained cherry-red water chestnuts, the other, tender white lotus roots. I stopped immediately. I really wanted to buy a few to take back with me. These are the traditional delicacies of the mid-autumn festival. I hadn't seen them for years. But I hesitated because before me wasn't a state-run fruit store but a black market stall.

Zhu Yuanda came forward. "Comrade Gao, why don't you buy a few to take away with you? See, they're very fresh. You can't get these at the state-run stores. They've a few but they can't compare with mine. You could hardly call theirs *red* water chestnuts. They'd break your teeth. They're all shrivelled up and they stink!" He gave his basket of chestnuts a shake to show that his merchandise was as good as his word. He was as talkative as ever, still looking for ways to get his customers to buy.

But the moment I began to listen, something seemed wrong. His patter was exactly like that of the Rightists in my department. It was slandering socialism! I didn't want to be engaged in a "struggle" with Zhu Yuanda. But I had to say a few words to help better the man.

"You should watch what you say in the future. You'd be wise to get out of these little business activities as soon as possible. They're the roots of capitalism and they're all to be swept away very shortly!"

He was startled. "What! They even want to arrest us pedlars!"

"They won't arrest you, but sooner or later everything that smacks of capitalism will be abolished."

He began to laugh. "Relax. It can't be destroyed. There are people who want to buy and those who want to sell. If the state-run stores won't sell things, can you say capitalism will be abolished?"

"How can it be abolished! Chiang Kai-shek's armies of millions were swept away. They would think nothing of little shops and stalls like yours!" I had often used this gambit at struggle meetings. No one could resist its devastating logic.

Zhu Yuanda made a sweeping bow. "Of course, Comrade Gao, I'm an ignorant man. I know nothing of the ways of the world. I'll take you as my guide from now on." Saying this, he quickly shouldered his baskets and left as though he feared I would arrest him.

As I watched him stagger away from me, I felt a little regret. There was a taste of ashes in my mouth. Those years ago standing by his carrying pole eating won ton, how could I have thought that he would be swept away? We had formed a genuine affection. As Zhu Yuanda slowly disappeared, I simply couldn't understand how this great distance between us had come about.

I longed to run into Zhu again, to smile and nod my head at him, to say a few pleasant words to him to show that our friendship was still alive. Unexpectedly, it was he who came to see me. He carefully seated himself in my rattan chair and eyed the furniture approvingly.

"Comrade Gao, you're doing all right now. I can remember that year when you were sick and you asked me to bring up a bowl of won ton for you. All you had then was a plank bed and a broken-down desk. It was pitiful!"

I remembered this not without some grateful laughter. But I was thinking to myself, "Why has he come to see me?" To tell the truth, ever since the anti-Rightist movement, I had become afraid of keeping up intimate relationships with almost everyone, lest I stir up trouble where I would have difficulty defending myself.

But Zhu was very good at guessing your meaning from your face, so he quickly explained his reason for coming.

"Comrade Gao, I had no other choice. You're the only one I know who has a way with words. I've come to ask you to write something for me."

"Write something!" I was even more afraid of putting something in writing.

"A self-criticism."

That was better. I could do that for him. "What are you accused of?"

"Profiteering. What else could it be?" He said this very easily as though it meant nothing to ¹

I sighed. "And selling bitant prices too!"

"Actually you could ..ly call them exorbitant. I buy my shrimps at forty cents a catty and sell them at sixty. Take into account I'm up half the night running around for sixty li and all I earn is two or three yuan. I know you won't like to hear this, but you earn more than I do and all you do is sit around and shoot the breeze."

This made me very uncomfortable. "How can you make a comparison like that? We serve the people. You just earn money for yourself!"

He wasn't convinced. "I don't serve the people? If I don't serve them, how is that they have shrimps to fry?"

My goodness! This strange reasoning had to be refuted. I stood up and jabbing my finger at him said, "You serve the people when you sell at the proper price. It's profiteering when you sell at high prices. This is a very serious matter!"

Zhu suddenly woke up to the situation he'd gotten himself into. He was like a balloon with all the air gone out of it.

"Sure, comrade. But you don't understand business. You don't understand prices. If you're talking about quality goods at fair prices, well, the vegetable market doesn't have any. Those list prices they hang up there are just to fool you. They're lies!"

"How dare you!..." I had learned my lesson from our last encounter so I did my best to keep myself under control but in spite of myself I lunged forward blustering.

Zhu Yuanda immediately clasped his hands in the traditional manner of submission.

"Okay, okay. I won't say another word. Just please write the self-criticism for me."

For a moment I had him. "If you've done nothing wrong, what's there to criticize? I refuse to do it!"

Zhu grasped my sleeve; then from a pocket he pulled out a wrinkled sheet of paper.

"Don't be angry. I was mistaken. I'm a capitalist! Write what you like; dress it up a little! I've known you, old friend, since I was in my teens."

This softened me. I sat down at my desk and took up my pen. But I couldn't help asking him, "Can you guarantee that you won't break the law again?"

"I ... I promise. I promise you I'll be a little smarter next time." He winked at me as slyly as he did in his youth.

I was compelled to put down my pen and say to him earnestly, "Look, you're very intelligent. You're a very capable worker and you can put up with a lot. Why don't you become a labourer or a shop assistant? Isn't that respectable work? Why do you have to slither about like a rat?"

His face darkened. He sat dumbly in the rattan chair, his arms folded across his chest. It was a while before he spit out, "I ... I can't."

"Why can't you?" I drew my chair over towards him and began my analysis.

"Selfish thinking is the main cause of all trouble. It's the root of all evil. Capitalism rests on that. You have to be determined to reform. Naturally, it isn't easy to switch from doing everything for your own profit to looking after the common good. It will be a painful transition. Take us intellectuals for example; our reform is particularly painful."

He was startled. "You suffer too?"

"Painfully."

"No, no. Don't be polite. You and your wife are both cadres. You draw a hundred yuan a month. You don't have to worry about the weather. You get your salary the tenth of every month. If I could only exchange your sufferings for mine I'd be in seventh heaven!"

"Why ... why ... why don't you get a job? Workers.... Cadres...." I was unprepared for his attack. I was babbling like an idiot.

"Get a job? Without knowing any of the tricks of the trade, how much money do you think I would earn in a month?"

"You'd earn about ... about ... about thirty or forty yuan."

Zhu jumped to his feet. "Comrade Gao, I have four children. And then there's my father and mother. Eight mouths to feed in all. What could I do with thirty or forty yuan? I'm not a despicable man, shamelessly thinking only of money, am I? You don't see my children crying from hunger. The old woman, her eyes full of tears. It cuts into your heart more painfully than a sharp knife. I'm ... I'm ashamed of myself...." He choked back a sob and wiped away the tears running down his cheeks.

I felt as though cold water had been thrown in my face. It was as though I had been standing at the top of a high building looking up at the wide and beautiful universe when suddenly I noticed beneath me a dark mire, destroying my lofty feelings and dirtying my beautiful picture. I didn't dare say anything further. All I could do was to erect a barrier in my mind: this was an individual and temporary problem. There was no way I could find a way out for this temporary individual Zhu Yuanda. Nothing I could add by way of consolation. I was obliged to write a hurried and confused self-criticism and stuff it in his hands.

From then on I released my wife and children from their ban, allowing them to buy things from Zhu Yuanda. I felt that Zhu couldn't become a capitalist. If I could be counted a member of the proletariat, then how could he, being poorer and more wretched than I, be considered a capitalist? During the difficult periods when the free markets were permitted, I rejoiced for Zhu Yuanda. At that moment I knew for certain that he couldn't be a capitalist. But right afterwards there was a movement to adhere to the principles of class struggle. Then I was confused. He really was a capitalist! I was in a terrible muddle. Then a thunderclap split the earth. The bugles of the "cultural revolution" were sounded, announcing the end of all capitalism!

It was altogether unjust. Now it was my turn to be publicly criticized and denounced because I believed that one should work hard for one's monthly salary, not always be spouting jargon, and that each person must make up his own mind. This had become pushing an extremely reactionary capitalist line. I was angry. Fine. From now on I would be indistinguishable from the masses. I would be like everyone else.

I mingled with the crowds. I read the big character posters, watched the search and seizures, the public denunciations and the parading through the streets of the accused. When I had seen a lot of this I grew alarmed — this was no way to live. I was better in the small lanes where it was a little more peaceful. There life flowed on like a river. So every day I avoided the big streets and chose instead the laneways.

Little by little the big character posters began to appear there too. But they weren't very striking. The paper was rather small and the characters were all higgledy-piggledy. It took so much effort to read these posters that one paid little attention to them. Later when I did look at them more closely I realized how strange their contents were. There wasn't anything like "reactionary capitalist line", "horrifying massacre of the oppressed" or "cruel suppression". They were all down to earth. Who had beaten whom? Who had thrown dirty water into so-and-so's courtyard? Who had had a child out of wedlock and with whom? Who was having a love affair with whom? They employed the most awful language. And they used terms like "ruthless" and "shameful".... My heart sank after I read them. It was as though I had been watching countless people pulling at one another's hair and thrashing one another. And it was all for nothing. Sooner or later there would be a verdict on the political questions, but how could all this feuding ever be settled? I had no appetite to continue reading. I turned and started east, passing in front of Zhu Yuanda's door.

It was wide open. There wasn't a rear window, so the interior of the main room was dimly lit. I was suddenly given a terrible start. Standing on a bench in the poorly lit room was Zhu Yuanda, his arms hanging at his sides, his head lowered as though he were suspended there from something. His head was half shaved, his left cheek a dark purple, his eye above swollen to the size of a walnut. Next to the door had been stuck up a sheet of white paper on which was written, "Evil Den of Capitalism — Zhu Yuanda must bow his head and admit to his crimes! He has twenty-four hours to turn over the offending tools!"

He didn't notice me. I didn't dare watch him any longer because I didn't know to whom he was obliged to confess his crimes. Was it to me? Although I hadn't the skill to mend the heavens, I felt a twinge of conscience.

I skipped quickly past Zhu's house. I looked about again and noticed the white sheets of paper next to the doorways of the flatbread pedlar, the hot water hawker, the itinerant barber and the cobbler. The contents of the texts were the same and they all bore the signature, "Combat Unit to Smash Dens of Evil". I felt that something terrible was in the air — that Zhu Yuanda had landed himself in a dreadful fix. The "cultural revolution" was bent on digging up all the bad soil of capitalism. If it didn't uproot Zhu Yuanda, then who would it?

And so it happened. Twenty-four hours later along came a gang of the "evil den smashers". Some were carrying iron clubs. Others, in imitation of the wandering knights of old, had great shining knives at their waists with a piece of red silk tied at the handle. The children of the lane followed closely at their heels shouting, "House search. Come and watch the house search!"

I hesitated a long while upstairs. Should I go and watch or not? According to the self-protective "principles" of the times it was best not to get involved in such questions of right and wrong. But I had to take a look. They were going to a poor pedlar's house; what could they confiscate there?

By the time I arrived the combat unit had already gone into action. This wasn't like the search and seizure of a cadre's home nor like that of an intellectual's. When they searched those places the emphasis would be on the "four olds", documents, letters, diaries, manuscripts and things like that. Those whose homes were being searched would stand silently to one side, sadly and indignantly watching the work of a lifetime, precious keepsakes, the wisdom of mankind all go up in smoke. As the incarnation of evil did its work, it did so draped in a solemn cloak.

But the search and seizure at Zhu Yuanda's house was altogether different. That scene was absolutely terrifying. Even from a distance you could hear the crying and the wailing, the sound of things being smashed and torn and the shouting of the morale boosting slogans.

Zhu's house had become a battle ground. Inside, the din was deafening. Clouds of dust were being blown outside. The willow wicker basket was tossed outside and hacked to pieces by the great knives. This was because it had been an instrument of crime. It had been used to sell chestnuts and lotus roots. Neither did the vegetable basket escape. It had been used to carry fish and shrimps. One after another pots and basins flew out the door and were smashed on the stones of the street. These things had all been used in making bean sprouts. For some unknown crime a tin bucket was battered by an iron club. Zhu's wife and children would shriek everytime an item was snatched up. The wicker basket that the children clung to so desperately was something that had kept them alive. Zhu's wife hugged the earthenware bowl. Inside were green beens she had been keeping to sell. There was a great cacophony of sound as they fought, bleeding and rolling around on the ground. I couldn't believe my eyes. How could such a noble theory produce such piracy as this!

Finally the won ton carrying pole was dragged out. Zhu Yuanda was pursuing it like a madman. "Help! Spare that thing!"

How well I knew that won ton carrying pole. It had always provided warmth and a full stomach and it had never committed a single crime. On the contrary, it was a thing of exquisite workmanship. It was a miniature portable kitchen complete with cupboards, water tanks, wood shed, water canisters kept hot by surplus heat and storage compartments for salt, oil and spices. One could study it to design a galley for an airplane. I actually thought of walking straight over there and rescuing the priceless artifact. But I didn't have the courage. All I could do was stand and watch as the bamboo splinters flew under the blows of the great knives and the iron clubs.

Once the capitalist den was no more, it was all over. No one came and pestered Zhu Yuanda about a self-criticism. The storm passed quickly, but no one knew how he was going to make a living.

After dusk about three days later, I saw Zhu's wife leading along their four children. There was a length of string in each of their hands. At dawn the five of them returned one after the other. Each had a great bundle of waste paper tied to his or her back. Those large character posters that had been pasted up all over the place had been quickly blown to the four winds and were being trampled into waste paper. By picking up enough of it, you could earn four or five yuan a day. So it's true — Heaven does allow a way out! Who would have thought that those posters that had driven men insane and others to suicide could have rescued Zhu Yuanda from the flames? Life is truly a mystery!

While Zhu was nursing his wounds at home, I went to see him. He was as talkative as ever. He spoke a lot about the past. "Comrade Gao, I'm truly sorry. I should have listened to you in those days. During the Big Leap Forward, my wife and I should have managed to get into factory work. You wouldn't have to worry about looking after the little ones, you just drag them to the union office and beg for help. The Communist Party isn't going to let you starve to death. Hell no! Why should I care about losing a little face? The skin off this face can hardly compare with money. Ai! I believed in myself too much. I always believed in bringing up my children by my own efforts. Things are fine now! My old woman and the children are out picking up garbage in the streets...." Zhu's words poured out of him. It was as though he was giving me a summary of half his life.

There was nothing I could do but give him encouragement. "Calm down. First, look after yourself. Later ... oh yes, the won ton carrying pole was destroyed. That's a shame."

At that time the newspapers were carrying the resounding slogan, "We have two good hands. Let's not loaf about in the city!" The rumour was that it was thought up by a city dweller. I paid no heed to a slogan invented by some city resident. But I watched carefully if cadres were to be sent with their families down to the countryside. I couldn't allow myself to be found on such lists. So I was scurrying about looking for army representatives and workers' propaganda teams. This silent struggle was absolutely terrifying!

Very fortunately, I wasn't sent down. Zhu Yuanda came to say goodbye, his eyes filled with tears. His entire family had been sent down to the most wretched place. It was then that I understood the meaning of "We have two good hands. Let's not loaf about in the city!" Who was it that was loafing about in the city? Of course those with no jobs. Zhu Yuanda could not be counted as having a job; he must then be in the loafing category. It was useless to try to turn to someone for help.

The two of us sat in silence. He regarded me with envy, I him with shame. I couldn't see in what respect I was stronger than he. I could avoid every disturbance. But for him, there was no escape. Even if I couldn't avoid being sent down, my salary would remain the same.

Just before we parted, Zhu took something out of his bag and gave it to me. "Yesterday when I was cleaning up the mess I found this in a corner. It would be a shame if it were chopped up for firewood. I want to give it to you as a memento." As he said this he placed the bamboo clapper before me.

I received it in both hands. I studied it carefully. It was a semi-circular bamboo clapper about eight inches long. It held no secrets. What wonderful sounds it had produced in Zhu Yuanda's palms! It had been caressed by generations of hands. The sweat and oil had penetrated the wood so that it now had a deep black sheen like a bronze mirror. Zhu gave it to me perhaps because he wanted me to remember that he had lived here and that he had done a little something for others.

Zhu and his family disappeared from the lane. Their departure was very noisy. There was a great beating of gongs as the banner "Glorious Household" was pasted up at their door. How could an "Evil Den" be transformed into a "Glorious Household"? In the twinkling of an eye, an old chicken had been turned into a duck.

Four other families in the lane disappeared at the same time. One was the cadre's while the others were the hot water hawker's, the itinerant barber's and the cobbler's. These were all in the loafing category. From then on you had to walk a mile to get hot water; it took twenty days to get your shoes mended. The old men had to queue up in the streets for a haircut. The old women would start cursing then, "Damn those who said they were loafing in the city. Now they've gone off to the countryside to loaf. You can forget about getting hot water to drink. Old man, don't bother about getting your haircut; just keep it in a pigtail!"

I heard no news of Zhu Yuanda for eight years. It wasn't until this spring that I heard that his two sons had been called back for work and had both been assigned to a certain factory. Later I heard that Zhu had returned. He sent a message through someone explaining he wanted to ask something from me. The moment I heard this I knew it had to be the clapper he was after. After all at this time everyone was talking about "social service" and the "commercial network", "hot water vendors", "won ton carrying poles" and what have you. Zhu Yuanda had returned, so of course he'd be returning to his old line of work. I got the clapper out and wiped it clean. I held it in my hands. In the deep gleam of the wood it was as though I could see the kindling burning in the red earthenware stove. I thought I could hear the "duo duo" sound reverberating at the end of the alley in the dead of night. Then it seemed to pause before a lamp-lit window. Inside perhaps there was a university student, or a young worker devoted to his studies, or perhaps a weather-beaten old man. They all feel keenly how much time they've lost and how little knowledge they have stored up in them. Their efforts are not for themselves alone. Their lives too demand that there be others bringing them warmth and convenience. It's taken me more than twenty years to learn this elementary principle.

It was dusk once again when Zhu Yuanda knocked at my door. My wife and he talked spiritedly as they climbed the stairs. The sound of their voices and of their footsteps were as joyful and as playful as the sound of his clapper in his younger days. Youth itself cannot last for ever, but its spirit can be recovered.

"*Aiya*! Comrade Gao, I've been back now for over a month. I've been busy finding a home and applying for a residence permit so I haven't had any time to come by and see you. And we couldn't be enjoying this day if we hadn't gotten rid of the 'gang of four'!" His resounding voice and exuberant expression were completely out of keeping with his former self.

I was very happy. I felt that he really had managed to free himself from his awful burdens. "Sit down," I said quickly.

He took a seat in the rattan chair and took out a pack of good cigarettes. Each of us lit one up. He inhaled deeply, then poured out the story of his eight years in the countryside. I knew this story full well. It had been no picnic. But as Zhu told it, it all came off sounding like a victory for him. Even though he'd sold off all the broken furniture, he'd got a good price for it. When he was finished, he cast an appraising eye over my place. He shook his head disapprovingly. "It's all the same. Why don't you make some changes?" There was a tone of contempt in his voice as he eyed my furnishings.

I laughed. "Things haven't changed but the man has."

"Sure, that's obvious! If you don't change then how can life go on?" Zhu straightened his new clothes. "Look. Haven't things really turned out well for me? My two sons are back. They're in state-run units. The two girls are in the county now, in collectively-owned units. Then there's my youngest — the fifth; I want to see him go to the university. Four iron rice bowls and one golden one. Everything's just right. And that iron club can't smash them!" Zhu laughed heartily. He was thoroughly at ease and pleased with himself.

I quickly put the bamboo clapper in front of him. "You'll be taking up your pole again. Congratulations on the reopening of your business!"

Zhu rolled his eyes as though he didn't get my meaning. Then his face reddened a little. He put the clapper I'd given him aside. "You ... you ... you're kidding me!" He was very embarrassed as if he was a sort of crude millionaire whose shady origins had just been exposed.

I added brightly, "No, not at all. It's permitted to go into business for yourself, now. You're needed. The people in the lane have been asking after you."

Zhu raised his head. "They still expect me to work my carrying pole?"

I thought to myself: Of course that precious work of art had been destroyed long ago. You couldn't fashion a new one overnight. "Okay, then sell sweet potatoes. The old folks love that sort of thing. You can't get them nowadays."

Zhu Yuanda grinned and gave me a sly wink. "To tell the truth, the labour unit also approached me about going back to my old line. I humoured them a little. I'm already working in a factory although I'm a little unhappy with the job. Originally I'd thought of being the doorman. But they sent me to the workshop to sweep iron filings. I do a little sweeping and I get by. It's far less trouble and worry than baking sweet potatoes." Telling me his little joke was just like the time he thrust that earthenware bowl of meat in my face.

I didn't feel the least amused. I just sighed. "Why? If you don't take up your carrying pole then your son won't either. That would be a shame."

"A shame? Where's the shame in that?" He got up and straightened himself. "From now on I'm not taking a backseat to anyone."

"But you never did. You were serving the people."

"Still 'Serving the People'! That was petty capitalism! It was to be abolished! I nearly gave my life for that 'den of evil'!" He'd become very excited all of a sudden. His voice was trembling. He shook as he took out the pack of good cigarettes. "Come, let's have another smoke. Let's not talk about all those awful things. I came here today to ask you for some review materials to help my son, the fifth one, to prepare for the university entrance exams."

I was certainly not opposed to someone going to university. I got together some mimeographed materials and put them in Zhu Yuanda's hands.

He thanked me effusively, and then said he had to be going. He asked me over to his place sometime. "Come on. Don't worry that you'll eat me out of house and home. The five iron rice bowls are refilled every month!"

The door below creaked as it closed. Unconsciously I opened the large window facing the street. It was as though I was looking for some won ton pedlar coming along with his steaming won ton. It was as though I wanted to hear that "duo duo duo" sound sweeping along.... But there was nothing. There was just Zhu Yuanda with the mimeographs tucked under his arm slowly disappearing into the night. I had been a little disappointed. But I hadn't dared say so in front of him. In these past years I and others had hurt him. We had attacked so much initiative. In the end all anyone wants to do is to hold that iron rice bowl in his cupped hands and avoid trouble and worry. By the end of the month that iron rice bowl can never be very full, and the rice in the pot will never be enough to go around.

October 13, 1979

Translated by Ralph Lake

A Corner Forsaken by Love

●

—— ZHANG XUAN ——

Zhang Xuan discontinued his studies after the breakout of the Anti-Japanese War and worked as an apprentice in Shanghai. In 1951 he entered Qinghua University to study iron and steel technology. In 1956, while working in the Beijing Iron and Steel Design Institute, he began to write in his spare time. He has published a collection of short stories under the title The Unbreakable Silk Thread *and his short stories "An Unforgettable Memory" and "A Corner Forsaken by Love" both won prizes in the national short story contests of 1979 and 1980. Zhang Xuan is also a screenwriter.*

1

ALTHOUGH it was already the last year of the seventies of this century, yet to the youths of Tiantang Commune, the word "love" was still unfamiliar, mysterious and unspoken. Hence, when the new League committee secretary delivered a report at a mass meeting opposing "mercenary marriages" and spoke out this word loudly, his audience was rather surprised. The young men winked roguishly at each other and laughed outright, while the girls hurriedly bent down their heads, their faces flushed, giggling and exchanging bashful glances.

There was only one person who did not smile — a pretty girl sitting near a window in a corner of the hall. Named Shen Huangmei, she was the Youth League group leader of the ninth team of Tiantang Brigade. Her face was pale, and her large melancholy eyes stared perplexedly out of the window. She seemed to have heard nothing, as if the speech did not concern her. Yet suddenly her eyelashes blinked, and she forced herself to shake off the tears that moistened them. "Love", this word which she failed to understand, was now violently disturbing the youthful heart of this nineteen-year-old girl. She felt ashamed, sad and terribly afraid. She remembered her elder sister Cunni, the sister whom she always blamed and always thought about. Alas! If only Xiaobaozi had not entered her life, if that event had not happened, how wonderful everything would have been! Her sister would now be sitting beside her laughing unreservedly like the boys. Then, after the meeting, her sister would go arm-in-arm with her to buy some skeins of orange-red silk thread from the store to embroider their new pillowcases....

Among the five sisters, Cunni was the luckiest one. She was born in 1955 at the time of a bumper harvest. When she was one month old, her parents had no difficulty in preparing a dinner for their guests. Her young father, Shen Shanwang, holding in his hand his little treasure wrapped up in flowery quilt, said excitedly, "After I had taken Linhua to the midwife I went and put my savings into the credit co-op. When I returned the baby was already born. No one imagined that a first child could be born so easily. Somebody said that we should name her Shunni, but I thought that as this was the first time since the beginning of the world that a poor peasant like me could put money into the bank I should name her Cunni. When she grows up, she'll have a wonderful life."

His jubilance affected everyone who came to congratulate him. At that time he was the deputy head of Kaoshanzhuang Producers' Cooperative. He was optimistic, capable and full of courage and strength. The pear orchard that he grafted on a slope produced a good yield with its first crop. The wheat and corn he harvested were more than enough for his family after paying the agricultural tax. In the small village of some twenty families, everyone was as happy as he, confidently looking forward to a bright future.

But five years later, when Huangmei came into the world, conditions had changed. Kaoshanzhuang Producers' Cooperative had been converted into the ninth brigade of Tiantang Commune. The auspicious name of the commune, "Tiantang",* was chosen by the county Party committee secretary himself, taken from the saying: "Communism is our heaven, and the people's commune is the bridge leading to it." At that time, all the commune members, including Shen Shanwang, the brigade leader, were convinced that it would take only one step for them to walk into paradise. Unselfishly they had all felled their collective pear trees and the gingko and chestnut trees around their houses and sent the timber to the steel smelting factory. They believed that once the brilliant molten metal flowed out of the red hot crude furnace, they could softly cross the bridge to the communist heaven. But the only result was a pile of shapeless pig iron that had cost them ten thousand loads of firewood. This huge dump had no use aside from securely occupying a piece of farm land. That year, on account of drought, no seeds were obtained from the wheat and corn

---

*Tiantang means "heaven".

crops. The sweet potatoes sown in place of the pear trees yielded tiny potatoes only as big as Cunni's fingers. Linhua, her mother, big with child, had returned home after begging for help in a distant place. Shen Shanwang had been dismissed from his post for "attacking the movement to produce steel". He looked at his newly born, undernourished, second daughter and, with a forced smile on his puffy face, said, "Who asked you to be born in a famine year? You certainly are a Huangmei."*

Due probably to sufficient nourishment in the womb and her mother's milk, Cunni, however, grew lustily. She put on weight even if fed with grass, and seemed to gain strength by drinking cold water. Still not quite sixteen, she was a strong, well-developed girl. She took over the carrying-pole from her sickly mother (who in the meantime had given birth to three more younger sisters) to help her father shoulder the heavy burden of supporting the family. The toughest job was carrying the state forest's pine branches downhill, and the workpoints she obtained for this ranked the third among those of her own sex. Every day she went to the fields before daybreak and returned home after dark. She gulped down a bowl of sweet potatoes or corn gruel and fell asleep as soon as her head touched the pillow. At the annual distribution of profits, the overdraft of her family increased year after year, and she could not get even one cent for herself. But she was always bubbling with joy and never depressed. When she was most happy, she would even cradle her weak younger sister to her full breast and softly sing a few folk songs sung by her mother in her younger days.

Xiaobaozi, the only son of Uncle Jiagui, lived in the eastern part of the village. His real name was Xiaobao, and he was the same age as Cunni. A strong boy, he had enormous energy when working. Once, when Aunt Jiagui slipped and fell down in a winter rainstorm when they were transporting pine branches, Xiaobao helped his mother up, put the two loads together and carried them both downhill. When the load was weighed, it was found to be over three hundred catties. All the people exclaimed, "Xiaobaozi's amazing, a real leopard cub!" The nickname stuck.

In the early spring of 1974, the brigade cadres had gone at daybreak to the commune office to criticize "Confucius".** All the young labourers were sent to work at the site of the reservoir being constructed. Uncle Xiang, the storekeeper, asked Cunni to stay behind and help him tidy up the storeroom. As the old man told the girl to do this and that, he complained, "The cadres appeared and had a look around, then pointed at something. Then we were kept busy for a whole year blasting the mountains and breaking rocks. When the mountain flood came, everything was

---

*Huangmei means "a girl born in a famine time."
**At that time there was a political campaign against Confucius stirred up by the "gang of four".

quickly washed away. The next year, the cadres came again and pointed at something else. The same thing happened. What do they know about farming?"

"But aren't we supposed to learn from 'the foolish old man who moved mountains'?"* Cunni asked unconcernedly.

"If we could fill our bellies by removing mountains, that would be fine!... Come here, sift this heap first. Slowly! Don't scatter the grain!..." Then he grumbled about the corn seeds, "Look at this corn. It was grown in the soil where the pear tree roots still remain. The seeds are so small, perhaps they won't even sprout!"

"But aren't we supposed to 'take grain production as the key link'?" Cunni again replied offhandedly. She thought that although working with this old man was easy, she'd prefer carrying earth together with her chums at the construction site.

Then, the shape of a strong young man appeared on the doorstep of the storeroom. "Give me some work to do, Uncle Xiang!" he said.

"Xiaobaozi!" Cunni exclaimed joyfully. "How's your sprained ankle?"

"Go home and take a rest!" said Uncle Xiang.

"I feel bad resting," Xiaobaozi said with a naive smile. "As long as I don't carry heavy loads, I can do some light work." So saying, he picked up a wooden shovel and helped Cunni sift the corn.

Uncle Xiang squatted down beside them, smoking a cigarette. Then he remembered that he had to ask the carpenter to repair the plough. After giving the two youngsters more instructions, he went away. In the hands of these two nifty nineteen-year-olds, the work of tidying up the storeroom and sifting the corn was effortless. In no time the seeds were in the gunny sacks and the sweet potato slices were outside drying in the yard. "Let's rest a while," said Xiaobaozi, and he placed his cotton-padded jacket on a gunny sack and lay down.

Cunni wiped off the sweat from her face and sat down on the bags opposite him. She had also taken off her padded jacket, and was wearing a yellow-green woollen sweater, which had been her mother's dowry. Although it had been darned with different coloured wool and was already too small for her, it was nevertheless considered a great luxury by the young girls of the ninth brigade.

Xiaobaozi gazed at Cunni's face, which appeared unusually flushed in the bright sunshine, and at her full round breasts. A peculiar tickling sensation he had never experienced before rose in his heart, exciting him, yet making him afraid. He searched for a topic of conversation.

"You didn't go to Wuzhuang the day before yesterday to see the film show?" he asked.

"It's so far away, I couldn't be bothered," she replied, lowering her

---

*A well-known old Chinese fable advocating perseverance in doing one's work.

head to avoid meeting his scorching glance, while at the same time tearing off a dangling thread from the cuff of her sweater.

Wuzhuang was a brigade in a neighbouring county. One had to climb over two mountain ranges to reach there. Even for such a young man as Xiaobaozi, the trip would take more than an hour. It was not a rich brigade; last year the pay for each workday was only thirty-eight fen. But even that small sum was the envy of the members of Tiantang Commune. Less than thirty li along the road west of Wuzhuang, there was a railway which the young people found particularly fascinating. During the Spring Festival the previous year, Xiaobaozi had gone there with several companions to have a look at a train. They spent half a day getting there and back, waited two hours at the station and were finally rewarded with the sight of a grass-green passenger train speeding past. Almost all of the members of the ninth brigade had never had the luck to see one. As for travelling in one, only the accountant Xu, nicknamed Blindman Xu, had had such an opportunity.

Xiaobaozi straightened his back languidly and sighed, "I didn't want to go either! Films like *Tunnel Warfare* and *Land Mine Warfare* I've seen umpteen times and can recite almost every line. But it's so boring to stay behind. Our pack of playing cards is practically in shreds. We asked someone to buy a new pack for us from the store, but so far we haven't yet got it."

Besides going to see films and playing cards, the youths in this village had nothing else to do in their leisure time. The brigade subscribed to a newspaper published locally in the province, but it was only for the use of Blindman Xu at meetings. He always misread the characters *kongzi yue* (Confucius said) as *kongzi ri* (Confucius' sun), but, of course, no one dared correct the only intellectual in the whole brigade. Formerly they also used to sing folk songs, but now these were considered indecent and had been banned.

Suddenly, Xiaobaozi sat up and said, "I say, Blindman Xu told me he had seen some foreign films that were very interesting!" Then, with his mouth partly closed and smirking, he added, "In those films there are some scenes of...."

"Of what?" asked Cunni, catching the nuance in his voice.

"Oooh.... I won't tell you." Xiaobaozi, blushing, grinned to himself.

"Of what? Tell me."

"Then don't blame me if I do."

"Out with it."

"There are...." He again sniggered, doubled over. Suspecting that he was going to say something improper, Cunni stretched out her hand and grabbed a handful of sand. As she expected, Xiaobaozi plucked up his courage and exclaimed, "There are scenes of men and women embracing and kissing each other!"

"Yuck! That's dirty!" Cunni's face grew red immediately and she chucked the sand at him.

Xiaobaozi dodged, saying, "It's true. Blindman Xu said so."

"It's shameful!" Another handful. The sand mixed with the corn husks fell on to his neck and shoulders. He retaliated, and threw a handful of sand accurately at Cunni's open neck. The girl looked angry and cried, "Damn it! You ass...."

Xiaobaozi smiled awkwardly. Baring his back he wiped his hard chest muscles with his shirt. Pouting, Cunni began to take off her jumper and shake off the sand clinging to her. All of a sudden, Xiaobaozi was dazed, as if he had received an electric shock. He stared, his breath stopped and a gush of hot blood rushed to his head. While removing her sweater, Cunni had raised her blouse and exposed half of her white, full, soft breasts.

Like a wild leopard coming out of a ravine, Xiaobaozi pounced on her and clasped her tightly in his arms. The girl was terrified, lifting her arms to resist. But when his hot trembling lips touched her own moist ones, she felt a mysterious fit of giddiness. She closed her eyes, and her arms hung limply. All attempts at resistance were at once dispersed like clouds of smoke. Primitive passion raged in the blood of these two poor, uneducated, but very healthy youths. Traditional ethics, the dignity of reason, the danger of breaking the law and a girl's sense of shame were all burned to ashes.

2

After the first hoeing following the sprouting of the corn, Huangmei began to realize that her elder sister had changed. She was no longer carefree and she seldom laughed. When anyone spoke to her, she seemed deaf. Sometimes she wiped away tears from her pale face, while at other times she smiled to herself, her face glowing.... What was stranger still was that one night when Huangmei woke up, she found that her elder sister's bed was empty. The next morning, when questioned, she flushed and declared that Huangmei was dreaming.

During those few days, their mother had a relapse of her kidney disease, and their father hurried to borrow some money for a doctor from an uncle in Wuzhuang. The whole family was in confusion, and no one had time to take notice of the change in Cunni. Huangmei alone had an idea that some calamity was about to strike her elder sister.

Inevitably it came, more terrible than anything Huangmei could have imagined.

It was at the time when the corn had grown waist-high. After supper, the tired commune members gathered in the brigade office to listen to Blindman Xu reading out the news by oil lamp. Huangmei left before the meeting was over, and returned home to put her three younger sisters to bed. Then she herself went to sleep. Shortly after, she was awakened by an uproar of crying and cursing mixed with the barking of dogs echoing from the hills. Never had there been such a turmoil. Huangmei lit the lamp in surprise. The dreadful din came nearer and nearer, until it approached the door of her home. Suddenly Cunni rushed indoors, her clothes in disarray, her hair dishevelled, and threw herself on the bed weeping hysterically. Then a bare-chested Xiaobaozi, his hands tied behind his back, was escorted into the house by the militia commander. From the glare of several torches, Huangmei saw that he had been beaten with switches and was covered in blood. He was kneeling upright, very ashamed, while his furious father slapped him. His mother sat paralyzed on a stool sobbing, her face covered by her hands. Outside the door, a dense crowd of almost all the adults and children in the village had gathered. They hurled abuse and ridicule at him. Huangmei, terrified and trembling, was finally made aware that her elder sister had committed the most heinous crime in the world! She suddenly cried bitterly. Her dearest elder sister had brought catastrophe to the whole family and herself. The tender feelings of feminine self-respect, which had not yet taken root in her young heart, were especially sensitive and easily bruised. She sobbed loudly, sad tears pouring from her eyes. At the same time she mumbled words which were indistinct even to herself: "Shameless! Disgrace to the whole family! Disgusting! Disgrace to the whole brigade! Shameless! Shameless!"

The turmoil did not abate until midnight.

Then Huangmei fell half asleep again. Drowsily, she heard the brigade leader dispersing the crowd, heard the voices of Uncle and Aunt Jiagui expressing their deep regret to her father and mother, and that of Uncle Xiang comforting and cautioning them not to be too hard on Cunni and warning them to be careful in case she did something foolish to herself. Her mother's grief gradually changed into soft words of consolation. Huangmei finally fell asleep on her wet pillow, but her sleep was frequently interrupted by violent nightmares. In the last terrible dream, she suddenly heard two urgent cries coming from afar, "Help! Help...."

Huangmei hurriedly sprang up from her bed. It was already broad daylight. Cunni was not in her bed, nor was her mother who was sleeping with her. Huangmei leapt up, rushed outside in her bare feet and followed the crowd to Sanmu Pond at the edge of the village. Alas, Cunni had already been retrieved from the water and was lying stiffly on the ground. She had ended her life so quickly, so easily.

Huangmei's mother, hugging Cunni's body, was weeping hysterically and madly calling out her name. She was pulled away by her neighbours many times, but quickly she threw herself back on the ground. Her father sat quietly by the side of the pond, staring dazedly at the calm water. He was so still that people could have mistaken him for a tree stump.

The morning clouds shed light on Cunni's wet face and restored some ruddiness to her ashen complexion. She looked unusually quiet, unusually calm, without the slightest appearance of pain, protest or complaint against injustice. She had paid the highest price for her own blind impulse, and had cleansed herself of shame and culpability. Of course, her death was a terrible waste. But, to her, what remained in life worth caring about? Before jumping down into the valley of death, the only thing she could think of was to remove her old yellow-green woollen jumper and hang it on a tree. She bequeathed the only wealth life had bestowed on her, together with the warmth and fragrance of her young body, as a legacy to her younger sister....

But that was not the end of the affair. About half a month later, a mournful wailing was heard coming from Uncle Jiagui's home. Two policemen were taking Xiaobaozi away. The whole village suffered a second shock, as people came running from the fields to stand at the roadsides and silently gaze at the pair of shining handcuffs on Xiaobaozi's wrists. Only Uncle and Aunt Jiagui, with tear-stained faces, followed their son.

"Comrades, Comrades!" Shen Shanwang dropped his hoe and came up. Although the death of his daughter had aged him ten years and made him more indifferent to life, his sense of duty stirred him. He therefore said to the policemen, "Comrades, we didn't file any charge against him!"

The policemen stared at him and answered contemptuously, "Get away. Move on. We're arresting a rapist who was responsible for a girl's death. What does it matter whether a charge has been filed or not...."

Xiaobaozi, however, was quite composed. He held his head up, looking blankly around. All of a sudden, he stopped a minute and then ran quickly towards the desolate slope opposite him.

"Stop. Where are you going?" The policemen shouted chasing after him.

Xiaobaozi ran on, his frantic steps crushing the wild grass and brambles. Finally, he threw himself upon Cunni's new grave, sobbing bitterly and clawing the damp yellow earth with both hands. The policemen came up and shouted at him. Only then did he stop his tears, and, kneeling down before the grave, kowtow respectfully three times.

3

At the conclusion of the meeting, Huangmei left the hall with a heavy heart. Tiantang Commune was in a corner of the county, and the ninth brigade was in a corner of that corner. She looked once at the setting sun hung low above the pine grove in the west. Fearing that she might be unable to reach home before dark, she abandoned her plan of going to the store and half ran along the uphill footpath directly from the back street through the wheat fields.

"Shen Huangmei, wait a minute. Let's go together." She heard the voice of the Youth League secretary Xu Rongshu behind her. His home was in the eighth brigade, which was separated from the ninth only by Sanmu Pond. Huangmei, of course, was glad to have someone accompany her. In winter evenings, it was quite desolate. But she hadn't thought of walking together with a young man, especially Xu Rongshu. After a slight hesitation, she quickened her steps. When Rongshu caught up with her at the end of the wheat field, she moved away from him cautiously, keeping a distance of over four paces between them.

The death of her sister Cunni had left in her heart indelible shame and fear. She had taken over her elder sister's mulberry carrying-pole at too early an age. The burden of supporting her family was too heavy for her slender body. The spiritual burden was also too much for her young, tender heart. Fearing and hating all young men, she never talked with them when she chanced to meet them, but held herself aloof. She looked down upon her girlfriends who did not fear or hate boys. She had turned into a strained, unapproachable young woman.

But maturity inevitably came to her. The yellowish dryness disappeared from her face, giving place to a shiny, soft glow. Her eyebrows became thick while her once dull eyes were bright, clear and limpid. She felt her breasts swelling, as her shoulders and back grew fuller, and the yellow-green woollen sweater left by her elder sister became much too tight for her. In her heart there frequently rose a new, secret and strange feeling of happiness. On seeing some newly opened blossoms, she could not help plucking one and wearing it in her hair. On hearing birds' twitter, she found their songs so pleasing that she could not help standing still and listening to them for a while. Everything was so beautiful and good: the leaves on the trees, the crops, the wild flowers and the dew drops on them.... All things around her excited her. She often secretly looked at herself in her mother's broken mirror. When carrying water from the pond, she even cast a smile of satisfaction at the reflection of her own slender body. She began to chat with her companions. At New Year's Eve and other festivals, she also went with them hand-in-hand to the commune's store. Although she was still wary of young men, she gradually found them less abhorrent... At this juncture, Xu Rongshu entered her life.

She had known Rongshu since her first year in the primary school of the eighth brigade. Some boys bullied her. A boy in a higher class about the same age as Cunni came up and defended her. That was Rongshu. Later when her mother gave birth to her youngest sister, she had to quit school before she had finished her second year. When she was cutting green fodder for the pigs near Sanmu Pond with her youngest sister on her back, Rongshu often secretly left his companions, took the sickle from her hand and quickly cut a large bunch and threw it into her basket. Just as quickly he left. Not long after, a burst of gonging and drumming was heard in the eighth brigade. Huangmei went to have a look with her younger sisters. She saw Rongshu in a new army uniform, which was too large for him, a large red flower on his breast, marching along the footpath beside Sanmu Pond. He was going to join the People's Liberation Army.

At a Youth League meeting the previous year, she had seen Rongshu again. He had been demobilized some days before. On entering the meeting room, he glanced at the gathering shyly and, just like Huangmei and the other girls who had recently joined the League, sat down quietly in a corner of the room. Then several active members, who knew him well, came over, urging him to say something about his life in the army. He felt embarrassed, and, blushing, refused. "I served in peacetime. I didn't fight any battles. What have I to say?" He had none of the confidence supposedly characteristic of a revolutionary soldier. But for some reason this won the goodwill of Huangmei. When the election of a League committee member was put to the vote and the name of Xu Rongshu was read out, she boldly held up her hand to express her true regard for him.

At the next Youth League gathering, Rongshu, the newly elected secretary, expressed an opinion at variance with the others and thus annoyed the deputy Party secretary, a former militia commander.

In the past, the activities of the League members of Tiantang Commune consisted only of one kind apart from holding meetings. This was heavy manual labour, such as collecting manure or carrying stones. After a meeting, the League members had to do this gratuitously until late at night in order to "set an example as Communist League members". Rongshu, however, opposed this. He said, "Youngsters have their own ideas. I propose that we see a film tonight." On hearing this, everyone laughed and clapped their hands. He was so thoughtful that he had already ordered some tickets beforehand from a factory in the neighbourhood of Tiantang Commune. After a short meeting, he led them all there. On the way the boys and girls joked and talked excitedly. Some of them even went so far as to sing folk songs. It was just as if they were celebrating a festival. Huangmei, for the first time in her life, sat comfortably in a soft chair and enjoyed the show. That night, also for the first time in her life, a young man appeared in her sweet dream. He resembled a little the hero of the film who led the youths to build a reservoir, but he was even more like her Youth League secretary. He laughed honestly and said something to her when she was near to him. On awakening, the moon was shining by her bed, soft and clear. For the first time in her life, a sweet, tender sensation arose in her heart. But instantly she felt ashamed and afraid. "What was it all about?" she wondered miserably. "Oh, dear! Thank goodness it was only a dream!"

After she became a Youth League group leader, Rongshu often called on her. Huangmei's attitude towards him was just as before, cold and serious. She never asked him into her home. They discussed only official matters such as calling a meeting or distributing work. Rongshu would stand outside the door, while Huangmei remained inside maintaining a distance of more than four feet, the one asking questions and the other replying. As soon as their conversation finished, Rongshu left. Huangmei, however, pretending to have something to do, often went out of doors and stealthily watched him depart. How she wished he would enter her house and sit and chat with her about some other subjects. With their increased contact, her ambiguous moods grew stronger. One day, Huangmei returned home somewhat later than usual. Her eleven-year-old sister told her, "Rongshu called!"

Her mother, who had also just returned home, asked, "What did he come here again for?"

"He called on me to ask about grafting pear trees," replied Father. "He wanted to know how many years it takes a newly grafted tree to bear fruit, and how much one mu of mountain land can produce? I asked if that wasn't following the capitalist road. He said, no, it wasn't capitalism, and then he read me a newspaper article. That boy...."

Father shook his head as if disagreeing with Rongshu, but Huangmei could see that he had a good opinion of him. She was therefore secretly glad. Her mother, however, looked most displeased. She frowned and said, "He, he's always breaking the rules."

Huangmei had already heard about Rongshu's quarrel with his uncle, the leader of the eighth brigade, over the question of not allowing commune members to rear chickens. People said that he was rash disobeying his leaders. Huangmei had ignored this. On hearing her mother, however, she felt angry and thought of defending him. Then, seeing her mother's inquisitive eyes boring into her, she lowered her head and ate in silence. After supper, her mother remained whispering something to her father in her room. Huangmei heard through a chink in the door these words: "There is already some gossip about her. We must guard against her going the same way as Cunni...."

Huangmei felt as if a knife had been thrust into her heart, and she collapsed weeping on her bed. She blamed her elder sister for having committed such a dreadful sin that even death could not expiate; she blamed herself for having been attracted to a young man. "Revolting! Falling in love with a man! Shameful!" She hated herself, burying her head deep in her quilt to prevent her weeping from being heard.

She made up her mind not to talk to Rongshu starting from the next morning. Should there be a need to discuss something, let him go to the assistant group leader. Wouldn't he feel strange, feel hurt? Let him! Why was he a man?

Soon after, she began to hate Rongshu. She overheard Blindman Xu saying in the brigade headquarters, "That boy, Rongshu, doesn't know how high the sky is and how thick the earth is. He's quarrelled again with the brigade deputy Party secretary!" Someone asked, "Over what?"

"Hell! He says he wants to right the wrong done to Xiaobaozi!" replied Blindman Xu.

What? Huangmei was greatly agitated. She almost cried out aloud. Xiaobaozi's being penalized was entirely his own fault; the punishment meted out to him was quite just. It was not wrong or unjust, or based on false evidence. He deserved no remission. This was practically the consensus of all the villagers. Huangmei did not differ. The death of her elder sister only made her resent Xiaobaozi more. Yet, how could Rongshu, a member of the Chinese Communist Party and a Youth League secretary respected by her, plead on behalf of such a bad lot as Xiaobaozi? How could he sympathize with him? Had Rongshu got some favour from Uncle and Aunt Jiagui? Huangmei trembled with anger. She considered confronting Rongshu directly, but when she saw him coming towards her with an honest smile on his face along the side of Sanmu Pond, her resolve weakened. How could she speak about such a matter to him? She therefore turned round, pretending to go in some other direction, and returned home by a lengthy roundabout way. Afterwards, she regretted her action.

She felt furious with him, hated him, ignored him, feared him, and yet unwillingly thought about him.... These contradictory moods seized her alternately. Such was the mental state of this nineteen-year-old country girl.

If this can be described as "love", boys and girls living in other places will find it hard to understand. But Huangmei was living in the corner of the county, in the ninth brigade of Tiantang Commune. Most of the girls there, at about Huangmei's age, had similar experiences of a secret passion, contradictions and anguish like Huangmei and Rongshu. Yet, after a while, the turmoil completely subsided, and everything became quiet and peaceful again. A relative or some other person would show up, offering a present of a yellow-green or rose-red wollen jumper and after similar rounds of bargaining, would reach an agreement. Then, on a certain day, this relative or some other person would bring a young man, and would accompany the boy and girl, who dared not look each other in the face, to have a photograph taken in Wuzhuang or some other place. On a fixed day, the girl would then leave her father and mother, leave this corner....

This was the customary way, generally acknowledged as the correct one by the villagers. Yet this was described as a "mercenary marriage" by the Youth League secretary, who made a report at the mass meeting. He also spoke about "love". What had occurred between Cunni and Xiaobaozi? Could that be called "love"? No, no. That was a disgusting and unlawful deed. Then, was there another way? Huangmei felt it was all far beyond her comprehension. She could not help thinking about Rongshu, who was now behind her and silently accompanying her. Her companions, who came to the meeting with her, had all gone to the store. On the quiet mountain path there were only the two of them. She could hear her heart thumping loudly....

Suddenly, Rongshu stood still, looked round and in a sonorous voice sang:

> *I love this blue ocean,*
> *How long is the coast of our motherland....*

Huangmei was alarmed. Then, after hearing him sing for a while, she was touched by the warmth of his song and could not stop herself from turning round to smile approvingly.

"Seeing this pine forest on the mountain, I remembered the ocean. I thought of the days when I served on a battleship...." Rongshu said smiling as if to himself, "It broadens your vision. If all our neighbours could have a look at the ocean, how wonderful that would be!"

"Huangmei, have you been to the main street? Don't you know that no one now will drive away peasants selling eggs and vegetables at the market? The Party's agricultural policy will soon be changed! We'll plant these slopes and hills with pear trees again. Uncle Shanwang, who's such a clever farmer, will again be called on to use his skills. As a first step, plant saplings in your family's private plot...." He spoke freely and eagerly. "Aunt Shanwang's health isn't too good. She can cut branches and weave baskets at home to get some pocket money. Your third sister can begin regular work next year. The two younger ones can tend some sheep. I have an army friend who is now a cadre in our commune. He told me that the Party Central Committee will soon issue a document to encourage us peasants to become wealthier. It's true. Don't you believe it?"

His eyes shone with hope. His voice was as musical as the babbling stream water and very appealing. Huangmei didn't believe what he said. As for getting richer, she had neither hoped nor even thought about it. Ever since she had begun to understand the world, the idea of getting rich had always been criticized as capitalist. What touched her was Rongshu's knowing so much about her family's problems and being so concerned about them. This was how he answered her coldness, wariness and hatred of him! She felt regret, her face burning.

"Yes. If we don't get wealthier but remain poor all our lives, there's no use in talking about anything." He shook his head feelingly. "Take Xiaobaozi for an example. Should we blame him alone? What about poverty, backwardness, ignorance, foolishness? Plus feudalism! And so an honest young man was clapped in jail. And your elder sister, she suffered an even greater injustice!"

Hearing him say this, Huangmei at once felt insulted. She glared at him angrily and shouted, "I won't allow you to speak about that. I won't allow you to say anything about my elder sister!"

She tried to control the tears that had begun to fall. She rushed towards the top of the hill and then raced down. Rongshu was baffled.

4

Nearing home Huangmei gradually calmed down. It was already dark. Her youngest sister greeted her from afar and rushed towards her. Soon, her mother also came out to meet her, her face wreathed in smiles. This made Huangmei suspicious. Her poor, overworked, ill mother had grown old and feeble before her time. Since the death of Cunni her face registered, apart from anxiety, only a blank, distracted expression. What had happened to make her feel so happy?

"Quick, hurry and look at what's on your bed!" she told her daughter.

There on the bed was a brand-new sky-blue woollen sweater, soft and with a captivating sheen under the feeble light of the oil lamp.

Huangmei picked it up in her hands, and before she had felt its softness and warmth, threw it away as if she had been stung. She cried out in surprise, "Whose is it?"

"Yours!" said her mother, with an elated glance at her daughter, while she was scooping out a bowlful of hot corn gruel from the pot. "Your aunt brought it here."

"My aunt?" Huangmei shuddered, her legs trembled and she sat down on her bed stupefied. Her aunt had visited her home not long ago. She had talked in whispers with her mother for a full half day, while steadily eyeing Huangmei. At that time Huangmei had guessed the mysterious intention in her look. Just as she had suspected, her aunt had now brought her this woollen sweater.

Her mother sat down beside her, and with an unusually tender voice explained, "The young man is in Second Uncle's third brigade at Wuzhuang. He's three years older than you. His elder brother is a worker at Beiguan Railway Station with a monthly salary of over fifty yuan."

Huangmei felt a stream of cold sweat trickling slowly down her back. Her whole body shook, her ears buzzed, and she could not hear anything clearly.

"I don't want him!" she screamed.

She threw the woollen sweater at her mother, who, however, still smiled and held her hand saying, "They aren't asking you to go over to their home just now. He'll come to meet you at the Dragon Boat Festival and bring you your clothes. Sixteen suits. After the engagement, they'll give us five hundred yuan in cash."

"No! No! No!" The realization she was being insulted suddenly flashed into Huangmei's mind. She experienced a choking terror. She didn't know what to do and could only let her tears fall quietly. Then, she went to run outside.

Near the door stood her miserable father and her three younger sisters staring blankly at her. Huangmei rushed out, covering her face with her hands. She stopped in the courtyard, leaned against the half-demolished earthen wall of the pigsty and sobbed loudly.

"What's the matter?" asked her mother, who had quickly followed her out of doors and who took her hand in hers. "Huangmei, you're a sensible child. Look at us. My health is poor. Your three younger sisters go hungry. We haven't any swill for the pigs. After rearing them more than half a year, we couldn't even get back the money we spent on them. If I take the eggs we've saved to sell in the street, I risk being driven from one place to another. I'll feel as scared as if I were stealing. Last year, when the distribution was made, we again had an overdraft and didn't receive one cent. I thought of buying a pair of socks for you, but...."

Her mother also began to weep, while she continued complaining, "Your elder sister failed to live up to our expectations. Who else is there to depend on? We won't be able to live in our house if it isn't repaired next year. We're in debt. Where's the money for that? Your aunt said that when we got the five hundred yuan, we could...."

"Money, money!" yelled the girl vehemently. "You're selling your daughter like some merchandise."

Her mother at once became speechless. She felt she had no more strength, and holding on to the low earthen wall, she sat down slowly on the ground. "Selling your daughter like some merchandise." These words that had deeply wounded her were, nevertheless, familiar to her. Who was it who at around Huangmei's age, and with the same outraged vehemence had uttered those very words? Who was it? Who? None other than herself.

It was one winter when the land reform team had come to Wuzhuang. One night, when Linhua went to see the opera *The White-haired Girl*, she became acquainted with a good-natured, good-looking young farmhand called Shen Shanwang. From that moment, she suddenly understood the meaning of the word "love" as it was sung in the folk songs. Nineteen-year-old Linhua not only bravely participated in the mass meetings to struggle against the landlords, but also went courageously to the corn field to meet her lover at night. But her parents had already arranged her engagement to the young proprietor of a store in Beiguan Village. On hearing the gossip about Linhua, her fiancé's parents sent fifty silver dollars to her parents, demanding that the marriage take place that year. Linhua wept and raised hell, and was quite beside herself. She openly acknowledged that she had fallen in love with a poor young man from Kaoshanzhuang Cooperative, declaring that she would follow him and suffer with him in the mountains rather than return to her feudal home. Her parents were enraged. They cursed and beat her in a closed room. She wept, shouted, rolled on the ground and threw the silver dollars all about her. She angrily yelled, "You, want to sell your daughter like some merchandise!"

That was a time when the anti-feudalist blaze had burnt "the orders of parents and the contracts made by go-betweens" together with the title deeds and loan receipts held by landlords. Pictures advocating the new marriage laws were pasted on the wall outside the gate of the village government. The heroine Liu Qiao'er in the play and the child brides in her village were both clear examples for Linhua. The good-natured, good-looking Shen Shanwang held in his hand the promise of the splendid future awaiting her. Linhua had more than enough courage to break out of the fetters of feudalism!

"They want to sell their daughter like some merchandise!" The next day, in the newly whitewashed village public affairs office, acting upon this charge from Linhua, the land reform team with encouraging smiles issued to her and Shanwang a marriage certificate bearing a portrait of Chairman Mao....

She had never imagined that today her own daughter would use the same words to accuse her as she had used thirty years ago.

"Why is it like this? Can time go backwards?" She was shocked and puzzled. Lifting her head slowly, she gazed at the late winter night sky. Some cold stars shed their gloomy, dim light upon her, as if winking sarcastically. She seemed suddenly to have received some revelation that disturbed her, for she beat her breast and stamped her feet, and began to weep bitterly. At the same time she whispered to herself, "Retribution, retribution! This is what is called retribution!"

From her mother's eyes, which had long been dry, tears flowed, saturated with the sullen hatred she felt in the depths of her heart. She hated Huangmei, hated Cunni and hated their father. She hated her own unlucky fate, hated the land to which she had come in her youth dreaming of a joyful future, and which had given her nothing but sadness and worry in return for the arduous labour she had expended on it for most of her life....

Huangmei, in contrast, became more composed. She comforted her mother, saying, "Mama, now no one will drive away people selling eggs and vegetables at the market. You can cut some branches and weave baskets to sell. My younger sisters can tend sheep. The slopes can be reconstructed and planted with fruit trees. Dad's a skilled farmer. Rongshu told me, our Party Central Committee has issued a document. It urges us peasants to get rich...."

"Document, document. One document today, another tomorrow. I've had my fill of them. Aren't we still as poor as before? Huangmei, I'm not willing to let you waste your life as I did." Still tearful she began to calm down. "My child, you're a sensible girl. I know that Rongshu is fond of you, as you are of him. But you should think it over. What will you do if you're starving?"

The storm had blown over. Her mother's feeble body leaned against Huangmei. Mother and daughter sat motionless and in silence, each immersed in her own thoughts.

"Mama, you must go in." Huangmei urged in a low voice. Her eyes gazed at a cluster of houses of the eighth brigade, trying to locate one of them. "I have something to do...."

Then, she stubbornly walked in the direction of Sanmu Pond. The events that had just happened had suddenly made her wiser; she was now more mature. All her prejudices, including her opposition to the idea of redressing the wrong done to Xiaobaozi, were now found to be unwarranted. She was confident that Rongshu had good reason for whatever he suggested. He knew a lot; he had even seen the world. How could Huangmei still doubt the document encouraging peasants to get rich? He might also give her some good ideas, tell her what she should do.

A soft warm breeze, the harbinger of spring in this remote area, wafted over the surface of Sanmu Pond. It silently caressed the withered grass at the edge of the pond, silently wiped away the tears of the girl who had hurried there. Had it finally come at last to this corner forsaken by love?

Translated by Hu Zhihui

Kite Streamers

●

—— WANG MENG ——

Wang Meng, one of China's major contemporary writers, rose to prominence when he was still a youth. He published the story "The Young Newcomer in the Organization Department" in 1956, which shook the literary world and became the subject of an intense criticism campaign in 1957. As a result of the campaign he was labelled a "Rightist" and sent to work in the countryside for many years. He re-emerged during the mid-1970s and in the years between 1979 and 1986, before he was appointed Minister of Culture, he published more than seventy short stories and over one hundred articles. His novels include Long Live Youth *and* Movable Parts.

BESIDE the white-on-red slogan "Long Live the Great People's Republic of China!", its exclamation mark squeezed tightly against it, towered a two-storey high advertisement for Triangle brand spoons, forks and knives. Together with its neighbours — advertising Xinghai brand pianos, Great Wall travelling cases, Snow Lily cashmere sweaters, Goldfish pencils — it received the meek kisses bestowed by the loyal lights and revealed a glossy, covetous smile. Lean and unyielding willows and two friendly cypresses, one large, the other small, used their random, elegant shadows to console a lawn robbed of its freshness by the west wind. Between the loud billboards and the solitary lawn Fan Susu stood in a relentless early winter night wind. She wore a trim apricot coat, well-ironed grey polyester pants and pert, low-heeled black leather shoes. Around her neck her snow-white gauze scarf resembled the down of a swallow and complimented eyes and hair which were blacker than the night.

"Let's meet by those upstarts," she had said to Jiayuan on the phone. She always referred to this row of billboards as "upstarts", endearing as well as enviable new idols which had all of a sudden sprung into being.

"The more you look, the more you think you too could have a piano,"

Jiayuan had said.

"Sure, and if you keep on saying, 'kill or be killed', often enough, you become an animal yourself," she answered.

Twenty minutes had gone by, but Jiayuan had still not turned up. He was always late. Fool, have you been blackmailed again? Early one winter morning he had been cycling to the library. On his way he had seen an old woman groaning by the side of the road. Whoever had knocked her down had run away long before she knew what had happened. He had gone over and helped her up, asked her where she lived, locked his bicycle, left it by the roadside and taken her home. As a result, the old woman's family and neighbours had all come out and surrounded him, thinking he was the culprit. And that dim-sighted old woman, egged on and bombarded with questions, had insisted that it was Jiayuan who had run her down. Was it the confusion of old age? Was she driven by some negative intuition that regards all strangers as enemies? When he told the whole story, explaining that all he had done was to offer his help, a woman had shouted in a creaking voice, "Are you trying to tell us that you are a 'Lei Feng' sort of person?"* A guffaw burst from the crowd. That had happened in 1975, when everyone had studied Xunzi and believed that human nature was fundamentally bad.**

He was always late, and always so busy he didn't even have time to clean the stains and dirt on his glasses. Before she met him Susu had never been busy. If a button on her coat was loose she didn't bother to fix it, but left it dangling instead. With the exception of her grandmother's warmth, everything about this city was cold and unwelcoming. When the city had thrown her out, she had only been sixteen. To say "thrown out" is not exactly fair. Salvoes of firecrackers had been set off, and brass bugles sounded to summon her to the vast countryside. In addition, there were red flags, red books, red armbands, red hearts and red oceans, a red world to be built. All the nine hundred million people in this world, from eight to eighty, formed a circle and recited quotations from Chairman Mao in unison shouting, "Kill to the left! Kill to the right! Kill! Kill! Kill!" Her longing for this kind of world had been stronger even than her earlier desire for a kite with two bells. However, she never saw this red world, she saw a green one instead: grass, crops. She had acclaimed this green world. Afterwards it became a yellow world: dead leaves, dirt, the bare land of winter. She became homesick. Then came a black world. That was when her eye-sight was affected by a vitamin deficiency after seeing her companions pull strings to leave the countryside.

Her dream of a bright red world had been lost in the changing of green

---

*Lei Feng was a young soldier who was singled out in the early 1960s as a model for people to emulate.

**Xunzi was a 3rd century BC philosopher known principally for his theory that human nature in its original state is evil.

to yellow and then to black. She began to lose her appetite, started having stomach trouble and became emaciated. Aside from the red dream, there had been lots of other dreams of different colours which she had lost or discarded, which had been snatched away in uproar and chaos, or stolen stealthily. The white dream had been about a navy uniform and sea spray; a professor of medicine and a machinist; about Snow White. Why is every snowflake uniformly hexagonal and yet always changing? Doesn't Nature also have the character of an artist? The blue dream was about the sky, the bottom of the sea, starlight, steel, a champion fencer and parachute jumping; about chemistry flasks and spirit lamps. Oh, yes, and there had been an orange dream, a dream of love! Where was he? Tall, handsome, intelligent, kind-hearted, always smiling good-naturedly.... "Here I am!" she once shouted to the Echoing Wall at the Temple of Heaven.

Dad and mum had tried every means possible and asked as many people as they could to help get her back to the city which had bestowed, generously, so many dreams upon her. Her father had finally realized that it was unavoidable. The story of what he had gone through to get her back was another dream, strange and absurd. She no longer cared for that sort of dream, nor did she care for that kind of life or the title "Gallant Shepherd Girl". She seldom, if ever, brought up that name and those differently-coloured sides of her life.

She returned having lost many colours but having gained strength, and added a number of odours: oil, mashed garlic, fried golden spring onion; drinkers' hiccups, steam, sheep's-head meat sliced thinner than paper. She now worked as a waitress in a Muslim canteen, though she was not a Muslim. Presenting flowers, congratulations, straight A grades, extraordinary good news, trains, cars, parades, tears of joy, Red Guards brandishing leather belts against class enemies, recitations of "the highest instructions", green and maroon horses, the look on the production team leader's face.... Was all this aimed at a plate containing three ounces of fried dough? One day she found a picture of herself which had been taken when she was seven. It was National Day, 1959. She was wearing plaits with two big butterfly bows which flew with her up to the sky. Along with her teacher she flew up to the rostrum in Tian An Men Square and presented flowers to Chairman Mao. Chairman Mao shook hands with her. She was small and had never shaken hands with anybody before. Chairman Mao's hand was big, thick, warm and strong. Chairman Mao seemed to say something but she didn't catch it. Afterwards she recalled vaguely that it was something like "little child". How lucky she was. She was Chairman Mao's "little child" and she would be happy for ever and ever.

But afterwards she was not sure whether it really was a picture of her. Had it actually happened? She couldn't recognize herself. Neither when she came back to the city in 1975 could she recognize Chairman Mao. In the past Chairman Mao used to stand straight and his movements were energetic. But now when she saw him on the newsreel's "News in Brief", it seemed that he had difficulty moving his feet, that he opened his mouth and was unable to shut it again for a long time. But all day the newspapers and radio kept publicizing noisily his ambiguous "latest instructions". She felt sad and wanted to go and see Chairman Mao and prepare a bowl of yam soup for him. When grandma fell ill, she had made her soup with white, velvety, finely cut chunks of yam, sweet hot, and tasty. It was a tonic for a weak old person. No, she didn't want to tell Chairman Mao about her anxieties and grievances, mustn't bother him. If she started crying in his presence, she would have to turn her face away.

But this was all impossible. Was she no longer fortunate? Had her luck run out at the age of seven? What had she come back to the city for? For mother? Ridiculous! For grandmother! No, that wasn't why. The papers said that everything you did was for Chairman Mao, but she couldn't see him! So Susu stopped dreaming. Nevertheless, she kept talking, tossing, sighing, grinding her teeth in her sleep. "Susu wake up!" said her mother. She woke up, lost, unable to remember her dream and felt only a cold sweat on her forehead and an ache all over, as though she had just been carried out of a contagious diseases ward.

She happened to be at the roadside the day the foolish Jiayuan was falsely accused for his kindness to the old woman, saw him surrounded and attacked. Jiayuan was not tall or good-looking, and always wore a naive smile which she seemed to have known long ago.

Afterwards a policeman came to the scene. This policeman was as clever as King Solomon. "Get two witnesses to testify that you didn't knock down the old woman," he said. "Otherwise you did." "Can you get two people to testify that you're not a KGB agent? If not, then you will be executed," Susu thought to herself although she didn't, in fact, utter a sound. All she was doing was watching an interesting scene before going to work. There was row upon row of watchers because it was free and more novel than the theatre and cinema, where all you heard was "soaring to the heavens", "soaring to the empyrean" or "conquer the heavens", "shooting through the clouds and sky".* They could write of nothing but annoying the "sky".

"What do you want? Should I be punished just because I did her a good turn?" The naive smile became wide, agonized eyes. Susu felt a thorn pricking at her heart and wanted to vomit. She stumbled away, hoping that King Solomon was not chasing after her.

It so happened that that evening the young fool came to the canteen to have fried dough chips. He was all smiles again. He only ordered two ounces.

"Is two ounces enough for you?" Susu intuitively changed her practice

---

*Expressions popular during the "cultural revolution".

of not chatting with customers.

"Well, I'll have two ounces to start with," said the young fool apologetically. He crooked the second finger of his right hand to push up his glasses which, in fact, did not seem to be slipping down his nose.

"If you haven't got enough money or grain coupons," she said without realizing why, "it doesn't matter. Eat now and pay for the rest tomorrow."

"What about the canteen regulations?"

"I'll pay for you. It's nothing to do with the regulations."

"Thank you. In that case I'll have some more. I didn't have enough to eat for lunch."

"Do you want a jin and a half?"

"Oh, no, six ounces will do."

"Okay." She got him four ounces more. When the chef found out Susu knew the customer, he ladled out an extra portion of diced mutton. Each piece of dough had been freshly fried and they glittered on the plate like gold beans. The light from the gold beans shone on the young man's face and his smile became even more attractive. For the first time Susu understood that fried dough chips were a great and powerful treasure.

"They said that I knocked her down while cycling and took away all my money and grain coupons."

"But you didn't, did you?"

"Of course not."

"Why did you give them the money? You shouldn't have given them a penny! What an insult!"

"Look, that old woman needed money and grain coupons badly. Besides, I didn't want to waste my time getting angry." Customers across the room were calling. "Coming!" she shouted, and left, cloth in hand.

After she got home that night, she thought of telling her grandmother about that fool. But grandma had had an angina attack. Her father and mother couldn't decide whether or not they should send her to hospital immediately. "The emergency room of that hospital is stinking, unbearable. If anyone survives after lying there for five hours, it proves that their internal organs are made of iron," said Susu. Her father glared at her reproachfully for being so heartless about grandma. She turned and left for her room, a makeshift extra room.

That night Susu had a dream. It was a dream she'd often had years ago — about flying a kite. But each time it had been different. She hadn't had that kind of dream since 1966, and she had not had any dreams at all for the six years since 1970. Water filled the long-dried river bed. The long-blocked roads reopened to traffic, the dreams reappeared. But this time it was not from the lawn or the playground, but from horse-back that the kite was being flown. And it wasn't Susu flying it but the young man who had eaten six ounces of fried dough chips. The kite was simply made, shabby enough to make you cry! Long and rectangular, it was known locally as a "botty curtain". It flew up, higher even than the new wing of the Dongfeng Hotel, the pine trees on the hill and the eagles over the grassland. It flew higher too than the balloon saying "Long Live the Great Proletarian Cultural Revolution!" It flew and flew over mountains, rivers, rows of pines, groups of Red Guards, herds of horses and plates of fried dough chips. How wonderful! She too began to fly along after that "botty curtain", and became a long streamer trailing behind it.

She awoke from the dream. Dawn had not yet broken. She shone a torch looking for the photograph of that happiest of times. At the tenth anniversary of the founding of the People's Republic of China she had presented flowers to Chairman Mao. She thought herself a fortunate person. Humming the song "All Commune Members Are Sunflowers", she repaired the button which she had left loose and dangling for so long. Then she spontaneously wished Chairman Mao good health. She made some yam soup for her grandmother. The soup would have an almost magical effect. Her grandmother would feel better as soon as she drank it. By now it was getting brighter. Her family and neighbours were all up. She began to brush her teeth and wash with great delight, all the while making noises as if a train were rumbling through their courtyard. Her washing sounded like the legendary Nezha storming the ocean. She ate some leftover steamed bread together with hot pickled vegetables. Only when she drank a bowl of boiled water did she feel she was re-entering the real world from the "botty curtain" and in the moment doubted whether the article "Boiled Water is the Best Drink" had really been attacking the "three red banners".* She tied her shoelaces and walked with a thumping sound as though iron nails had been driven into her heels or a peg was being hammered into a board to make a Czechoslovakian-style cabinet.

"What are you so happy about, Susu?" asked her father.

"I'm going to be promoted to director," Susu answered.

Her father was overjoyed. When, at the age of six, she had been selected as group leader in the kindergarten, her father had been so happy he kept telling everybody he met about it. When at nine, she was serving as a captain in the Young Pioneers he was in heaven.... When the steam whistle of the train tooted, he had suddenly burst into tears, his face convulsed, ghastly. All the children except Susu had cried too. Susu took it much more in her stride than her father. She seemed determined to find an outlet for her talent and resolved to become a great success.

"Hello! You're back. What would you like today?"

"First, let me settle my account. Here's four ounces worth of grain coupons and the money, twenty-eight fen."

"You take it so seriously."

"I guess I'll have four ounces of fried dough chips again."

---

*An article in the Beijing Evening News which was criticized for attacking the "three red banners", namely, "the General Line, the Great Leap Forward and People's Commune".

"Why don't you have something else for a change? We've got ravioli, seven to the ounce for fifteen fen; dumplings, two per ounce, eighteen fen; beancurd jelly with sesame cakes, only thirty fen for four ounces."

"I'll have whatever's quickest."

"Just a second. There's another customer.... I'll get you some dumplings then. Do you want six ounces again? ... Here they are. Why are you so busy? Are you a student?"

"Do you think I'm capable of being that?"

"Then maybe you're a technician, an accordionist, or a new guy promoted to a top job."

"Is that what I look like?"

"Well, what do you do...?"

"I don't have a job."

"Hold on a minute, here comes another customer.... If you don't have a job why are you so busy?"

"A jobless person is also a human being with a life to lead, youth, lots of things to do."

"What keeps you so busy then?"

"Reading."

"Reading? Reading what?"

"Optimization, palaeontology, foreign languages."

"Are you going to take a university entrance exam?"

"Do universities admit students by entrance exam nowadays? Anyway, I'm not the kind of person who would turn in a blank exam paper."

"It's a pity Zhang Tiesheng's* way of getting into college doesn't work."

"We're still young. We should learn something useful, don't you think?" He finished his dumplings and hurried off, leaving the puzzle unsolved.

He was punctual, and came at the same time as before. This time he ordered beancurd jelly, the grey bean curd jelly with green chive flowers and mud-like sesame jam with red pepper spread on top of it. Why is it that people in China and abroad know the name of the first emperor of the Qin Dynasty but not the name of the scientific genius who invented beancurd jelly?

"You lied to me."

"No, I didn't."

"You told me you didn't have a job."

"It's true. I came back from the north only three months ago. The reason I gave for leaving was 'personal business'. But I start a job next month."

---

*Zhang Tiesheng was a student who turned in a blank paper in a university extrance exam and was later admitted to college. He was held up by the "gang of four" as a hero who rebelled against the "old educational system".

"In a scientific research institute?"

"No, in a neighbourhood service centre. I'll be apprenticed to learn how to repair umbrellas."

"That's terrible!"

"No, it's not. If you've got a broken umbrella, bring it to me."

"What about your optimization methods, palaeontology and foreign languages?"

"I'll go on studying."

"Are you going to repair umbrellas by the optimization method, or make an umbrella out of dinosaur bones?"

"Well, optimization could also be applied to umbrella repairing. The thing is, however.... I'd like another bowl of beancurd jelly, not too much pepper, please ... you can see the perspiration on my forehead ... thank you. You know, you take a job to make a living and also to do your duty. But a person should be more than just his trade. A job isn't everything, nor does it last for ever. Human beings should be the masters of the world and their work, and above all, masters of knowledge. Suppose both of us are umbrella repairers, and we each earn eighteen yuan a month. But then if you know about dinosaurs whereas I don't, you're better off and richer than I am. Am I right?"

"I don't know what you're talking about."

"Yes you do. In fact, you already did. Otherwise, why would you be talking to me? Look, that customer from Shandong over there is getting angry because he got some grit in his boiled peanuts and he's hurt his teeth. Goodbye!"

"Bye! See you tomorrow."

On uttering the word "tomorrow", Susu flushed. Tomorrow was, like the streamers tied to that "botty curtain", simple and unadorned, easy and unrestrained. It was like bamboos, clouds, dreams, ballet, a note from a G string, like autumn leaves and spring flowers. But it was a "botty curtain" only a poor, bare-bottomed child could afford to fly.

He didn't come the following day. Nor did he come the day after that. And looking for that foal, Susu lost her own way and moaned like a sad whinnying mare. It was as if her residence registration, grain certificates and ration cards had been revoked in one fell swoop.

"It's you! You're ... back again!"

"My grandmother died."

Leaning against the wall, Susu felt as if she had fallen into an ice pit. It was some time before she realized that this bespectacled young fool's grandmother was not her own grandmother. Yet she still felt saddened and cold all over.

"One's life is short, and time is the most precious thing."

"But my most precious time is spent carrying plates." She smiled heavily and seemed to hear the distant sound of a galloping colt.

"You've carried plates for a lot of people. We should thank you. But it's more than that."

"What else? They don't really even need me to carry dishes. It wasn't easy for my dad and mum to get this job for me. They had to go to a lot of trouble."

"It's the same everywhere," he said with an understanding smile. "I suggest you learn some Arabic since this is a Muslim canteen."

"What's so special about a Muslim canteen? Anyhow, the Egyptian ambassador won't be coming here for fried dough chips."

"But you might be the ambassador to Egypt. Have you ever thought of that?"

"You're joking," she said. The colt raced into the Muslim canteen and trod on her feet. "That's just dreaming."

"Dreaming, joking, what's wrong with that? Otherwise life would be too dull, wouldn't it? Besides, you should be confident that you could develop the talents, the qualifications and abilities to be an ambassador to Egypt, or, better still, overtake him. You may not serve as an ambassador, but you should be able to surpass him. The key to achievement is study."

"You sound like a rather ambitious careerist."

"No. Like Adam."

"What is Adam?"

"It's the first Arabic word I am going to teach you. Adam means person. It's a beautiful word. Adam in the Garden of Eden. It is a transliteration. And Eve is pronounced *Hawa*, meaning sky. Human beings need the sky and the sky in turn needs human beings."

"So that's why from childhood onwards we fly kites?"

"See, you're an exceptional student."

Lesson one: Human beings. Adam needs Eve and Eve needs Adam. Human beings need the sky and the sky needs human beings. We need kites, balloons, airplanes, rockets and spaceships. That was how she started to learn Arabic. It made people roundabout a little uneasy. "You should keep your mind on carrying dishes. Be careful not to make a bad impression. Do you have any friends or relatives abroad? If the purification-of-class-ranks movement starts again, strange people, strange things and strange phenomena will be examined. You'll be placed under investigation as a special case." "I haven't dropped a single plate. I don't wish to be promoted to director. I know Muhammad, Sadat and Arafat. You are entirely welcome to be chief of my special-case examination group."

Besides, she was in love with Jiayuan. The news soon reached her father's ears. It was as though cameras and bugging devices, all shadowing the young girl, were omnipresent. "What's his name, his original name, any other names he's ever used? His family background, his own background? What was their economic situation before and after land reform. His personal history since he was three months old? His political record? Are there any members of his family or immediate relatives who were sentenced to death or imprisonment, put under surveillance, or were landlords, rich peasants, counter-revolutionaries, bad elements, Rightists? When were they labelled as Rightists? And when were the labels removed? How did he act in past political movements? His and his family members' incomes and expenditures, bank deposits and balances...?"

To all of these questions, Susu had no answers. Her mother was so frightened she cried. "You're only twenty-four years and seven months old. You're not supposed to think about marriage for another five months yet. There are bad people around everywhere, you know." Dad was resolved to see the young man's neighbourhood committee, his work unit, local police station, personnel department and file department, anywhere he might be known. To get things moving, he planned to give a hot-pot dinner for the relevant people and accordingly started to make preparations. His favourite Yixing teapot was flung to the ground and smashed into pieces.

"The way you are doing things, you might find counter-revolutionaries but you would never find a friend!" Susu shouted and then burst into tears.

The director, members of the management, group leader and instructor all raised questions like her father's and gave advice like her mother's. A proletarian love should grow out of a shared belief, a shared point of view and a shared ideology, and a mutual and deep understanding should be cultivated seriously, cautiously and sincerely over a long period. One must always be on the alert for enemy activities. The choice of one's love should follow the five conditions for a young revolutionary. She couldn't throw the restaurants' teapot on the floor since she had been trained since childhood to protect public property.

Chairman Mao passed away. Susu shook and cried bitterly. She had wanted to cry long ago, to cry for Chairman Mao, to cry for herself and for others.

"China is finished!" said her father, but instead it was the end of the "gang of four". Susu was close to Chairman Mao a second time when she paid respects to his remains. "I once came to present flowers to you," she said quietly and calmly.

She knew that everything was changing. She could openly and casually learn Arabic although the fact remained that admission to the Party and promotion came easier for those who spent the whole night playing poker than for those who studied foreign languages. She could walk hand-in-hand with Jiayuan, although some people went crazy at the sight of young men and women together. But they still couldn't find a place to talk. The chairs in the park were always occupied. After trying hard they eventually did find one but it turned out that there was a pool of vomit in front of it. They moved on to a large, ramshackle park where loudspeakers hung from the telegraph poles beside every bench. The loudspeakers were blaring out "Information for Visitors", "... fifty fen to fifteen yuan fine", "... will be sent to the relevant law-enforcing authority", "conscientiously observe the regulations and obey the administrative personnel", etc. The regulations were so complicated a person wouldn't even know how to stroll in the park without first taking a week's training course. How could they possibly sit there and talk about their love? They left.

But where to? By the side of the moat was a place without loudspeakers, but it was somewhat out-of-the-way. Once, it was said, a courting young couple had been whispering there. All of a sudden, they heard "Don't move!" and a masked man appeared, dagger in hand. Next to him stood an accomplice. Their watches were stolen and the money taken from their pockets. Lovers are always powerless in the face of violence. The case was cracked by the police and the perpetrators arrested. Why do some people dislike the police department? No one could do without them.

What about going to a restaurant? Well, first you have to position yourself behind someone's chair and watch him eat, mouthful by mouthful, then light a cigarette and stretch himself. Not long after you take this hard-to-come-by seat and pick up your chopsticks, your newly-arrived successor places his foot on the rung of your chair. As he moves his leg, the diced meat and slices of tripe you're eating begin to dance in your throat. Should you want to go to a bar or a coffee shop, you won't be able to find one because those are decadent places. Taking a walk will keep you in trim and is a fashion in America. But in winter it's too cold. Of course they did go out together in that cold weather, twenty degrees below zero, wearing padded coats, fur hats, woolen scarves and face masks. Hygienic and infection-free. But what often happens to courting couples is that naughty children playing in the lanes burst out laughing, or curse and throw stones at them. It makes you wonder how these brats ever came into this world.

Jiayuan was easy-going about things. He didn't mind where they went. Whether it was leaning against a railing, or sitting beneath a parasol tree or on the river-bank, he just wanted to stop and sit awhile, speak in Arabic and English and snuggle up to Susu. But Susu was always dissatisfied, difficult to please. No, she didn't want to accept that kind of substitute, in the same way that the customer from Shandong couldn't tolerate the grit in his peanuts. For three years now they had spent their weekends looking for somewhere to sit down. They kept on looking and whole evenings disappeared. Oh, my boundless sky and vast land, on which tiny piece of you may young people court, embrace and kiss? All we need is a small, small place. You can hold great heroes, earth-shaking rebels, vicious destroyers and dissolute scoundrels. You can hold battlefields, demolition sites, city squares, meeting halls, execution grounds ... why can't you find a place for Susu, 1.6 metres tall and 48 kilos in weight, and for Jiayuan, just under 1.7 metres and 54 kilos, who are head over heels in love?

Susu rubbed her burning eyes. Had she touched some pepper? Had she rubbed her eyes because they were burning or were her eyes burning because she'd rubbed them? "Can we find a place to stay this evening?" she wondered. Though the weather was getting colder, it wasn't yet necessary to wear a face mask. Jiayuan said that he would go to see the Housing Administration Department. They would get married as soon as they found a place. They wouldn't have to walk in the lanes any longer.

"Hey, Comrade Elder Sister, can you tell me where Dashi Street is?" asked a man with an accent, a big bundle on his back and dust all over his new clothes. He was actually much older than Susu.

"Dashi Street? This is Dashi Street," answered Susu, pointing to the intersection where the traffic lights were changing, and the cars, buses and bicycles were surging ahead, stopping and then rushing forward again like the tide.

"Is this really Dashi Street?" His back bent, the middle-aged man looked up and rolled his eyes, expressing doubt.

"It *is* Dashi Street," Susu repeated emphatically. She wished she could show this honest, skeptical person the department store and the big roast duck restaurant by holding them all in the palm of her hand. The man hesitantly took a few steps. He went to cross the street, but not at the pedestrian crossing. A white-uniformed traffic policemen shouted at him through a loudspeaker. Alarmed and confused by the tongue-lashing, the man halted in the middle of the road, surrounded by a whirlpool of automobiles. "Comrade Elder Brother," the man asked, tilting back his head, "where is Dashi Street?"

"Susu!" Jiayuan arrived, breathless, his hair dishevelled, his forehead dripping with sweat.

"Did you just burrow up out of the ground? I've been waiting ages for you. You don't show up and then all of a sudden you appear out of nowhere."

"I know how to make myself invisible. In fact, I've been following you."

"If only we both knew that trick...."

"What do you mean?"

"Then nobody could see us if we danced in the park."

"Why are you talking so loudly? People are looking at you."

"Some people think dancing is vulgar because they're so ugly themselves."

"You're sounding more and more sarcastic. You weren't like this before."

"It must be the autumn wind sharpening up my tongue. We can't even find a place to shelter from it."

Jiayuan's eyes were dim and Susu lowered her head. Multitudes of lights, windows and houses were reflected in the lens of his glasses.

"No flat?"

"No. The Housing Administration Department refused to let us have one. They told me there are people who've been married for several years and have kids that still don't have a place."

"Well, where did they get married then? In a park? In the kitchen where the dough chips are made? In the traffic policemen's kiosk? That would be a good place with glass on all sides. Or maybe in a cage at the zoo? But that would send up the price of tickets."

"Don't get so touchy. What you...." He pushed back the glasses which were unlikely to slip off. "What you said is no doubt correct. But you can't expect houses to drop out of the sky. There are so many people who need houses. And some of them really are in a more difficult position than we are."

Susu was reduced to silence. Lowering her head, she began to kick a non-existent pebble.

"Well, have you had supper? I haven't." Jiayuan changed the subject.

"What did you say? Oh, I only remember serving meals, never whether I've eaten myself."

"I take it you haven't then. Let's go to that won ton canteen. You stand in the queue and I'll try to get a seat. Or I'll get a seat while you line up."

"You're repeating yourself. You sound like somebody making a speech at a meeting."

The won ton canteen was crowded. You would have thought the won ton was free, or better yet that you'd be paid to eat it instead of paying twenty fen per bowl. "Let's forget about the won ton and buy some sesame cakes instead. Oh, there's a queue for that too. Then let's go and get some buns from the store across the street." But just as they got there and reached out for the buns, the salesclerk was selling the last two to a little old man wearing a Qing-dynasty robe lined with badger fur. "Well, let's forget about the buns. But what can we do?"

"It would have been great if we just hadn't been born in the first place," Susu said coldly. "If Ma Yinchu's* new population theory hadn't been mistakenly criticized we would never have come into this world."

"Why are you in such a bad temper? Anyway, we actually came into the world before his population theory existed. Since the fruit buns are sold out, let's buy a couple of bags of biscuits. We have biscuits. We wait on customers and repair umbrellas. We study, we do good things and help people. And there can never be too many good people — on the contrary, there aren't enough."

"What's the reward for being a do-gooder? To have to hand over seven yuan and two jin's worth of grain coupons to somebody who's having you

---

*Ma Yinchu, ex-president of Beijing University, was criticized during the "cultural revolution" for his theories of family planning and population control, and was rehabilitated after the fall of the "gang of four".

on?"

"In any case, I still should've helped the old woman, even if they had extorted seven hundred yuan.... I suppose you would've done the same thing, wouldn't you? Susu!" Jiayuan suddenly shouted. Thunder and lightning. The electricity wires and lights were swaying.

"Try one of my biscuits," said Jiayuan.

"They're the same as mine."

"No, mine are particularly good."

"Why?"

"Why not? Even two drops of water aren't exactly the same."

"Try mine then."

"Alright, I'll try yours."

"You try mine after I've tried yours."

They exchanged biscuits and then shared them one by one. When they had eaten them all Susu laughed. Hungry people are worse-tempered than the well-fed.

There was a drastic change in the weather. Electricity wires were whining. Billboards were roaring. The street lights became hazy. A rustling cold wind dispersed the pedestrians. In a matter of seconds, the street was broad and empty. Traffic policemen retreated into the kiosks Susu had reckoned were an idea bridal chamber.

"We must find some shelter!" Icy sleet, falling at an angle, offered a stern caress. They held hands, unable to hear each other speak. Against nature and against life they were undefended. But the big hand and the smaller hand were both warm. Their own inextinguishable fire was all the property and power they had.

"Let's find somewhere to shelter," they mumbled, chewing dust and rain. They started to run. Whether Jiayuan was pulling Susu, Susu was pulling Jiayuan, or the wind was pushing the two of them was hard to tell. In any case, a burst of energy pulled and shoved them forward. They made their way to a recently-finished fourteen-storey block. They had longed for a place in this newly-born row of high-rises. But they were strangers. And aversion to strangers was one of the characteristics of the old woman who'd been run down and the old man in the badger fur robe. What a look the old boy had given the two of them when they went to buy buns! As though he thought that any minute they would take out daggers.

There had been widespread criticism of this row of high-rises. A family living on a top floor had been unable to carry a wardrobe up to their flat. They then tried to hoist it up through the window. What a marvellous spectacle. The rope broke and the wardrobe fell and was smashed to pieces. A new *Arabian Nights* story. But Susu and Jiayuan thought otherwise. They always felt a little shy approaching the buildings, their longing being a kind of unrequited love.

The snow and rain gave them the courage to dash in. They climbed up storey after storey. The staircase was filthy. There were no lights. There were sockets but no bulbs. Fortunately the street lights were on all night and that was enough. After making numerous turns they eventually reached the corridor on the top floor. It seemed uninhabited. There was a smell of cement and fresh paint and it was warm. No wind, rain or snow. It was devoid of loudspeakers broad-casting instructions, people in masks, pedestrians and impatient customers jiggling your chair to make you leave. Here there were no parents who looked down on umbrella repairers and waitresses. No mischievous children who would, seeing a courting couple, use foul language, abuse and throw stones at them. From here, the lights of the twenty-five storey Dongfeng Hotel were visible. The melodious chiming of the railroad station clock was audible and the electric clock on the customs building could be seen. Looking down, they saw green, orange and silver lights. Electric sparks flashed from the trolley wires. Headlights and red signal lights blinked on and off. They heaved a deep sigh of relief, as though they had reached paradise.

"Are you tired?"

"No, not at all."

"We've climbed fourteen stories."

"I could climb another fourteen."

"So could I."

"That man was a real idiot."

"Who?"

"That country bumpkin we met a while ago. He was at the bottom of Dashi Street but he was still wandering all over the place looking for it. I told him but he wouldn't believe me."

They began to speak in Arabic. Stammering, like their heartbeats, enthusiastic, unconventional. Jiayuan was going to take an entrance exam for graduate school. "We may not succeed," he urged the less-than-confident Susu, "but we should try our best." Jiayuan took her hand in his. It was tender and firm. Susu moved closer and nestled against his ordinary, strong shoulder. Her hair was like warm black rain. The lights — glimmering, flickering and twisting — formed the lines of a poem. An old German ballad goes: "There is a flower called 'forget-me-not', its blossoms are blue." A Northern Shanxi ballad goes: "Words of love I have for you. Fearing the laughter of others, I hesitate to let you know." Blue flowers floated in the air. Waves washed over them. Why fear being laughed at? Youth is more fiery even than fire itself. It is a pigeon's whistle, fresh flowers, Susu and Jiayuan's tear-filled eyes.

Clatter ... clack....

"Who's there?" barked a loud voice. Jiayuan and Susu suddenly became aware of several people at either end of the corridor. Many of them were carrying things: rolling pins, spatulas, shovels. Man is a tool using animal. You might have thought this was an uprising of primitive citizens.

A harsh and hostile interrogation began: "Who are you? What are you up to? Who are you looking for? Did you say you weren't looking for anyone? That you came here to take shelter from the wind and rain? Damn you! Sneaking around and hugging like that. I bet you were up to no good. Young people nowadays are just impossible. China will be destroyed by the likes of you. Where do you work? Your names? Your original names, any other names you've ever used? Have you got your resident's cards, employee's I.D. cards or letters of introduction? Why don't you stay home? Why don't you stay with your parents, your leaders or the broad masses? No, you can't leave. Did you think nobody would see you? Whose doors have you pried open? A public place? This public place is ours, not yours. Shame on you! Hooligans! Disgraceful! What? An insult? What do you mean insult? Don't you know we were given half-shaved heads? We were beaten. We were made to do the 'jet-plane'.* Get out of here or we'll show you what we can do. Get the ropes ready...."

Susu and Jiayuan both kept calm. A moment earlier they had been happy. The two of them knew, though not well, several languages. But neither of them could understand this strange language spoken by their dear compatriots. If dinosaurs could talk, they would be more intelligible than this. Confused, they looked at each other and smiled.

"We're going to do something about this," a "dinosaur" plucked up enough courage to say. No sooner had he finished than he went and hid behind the others.

"We're really going to do something about this," others echoed and then shrank back. Jiayuan and Susu were still encircled and blocked, unable to get away.

Suddenly a brave man with a drainpipe in his hand shouted, "Aren't you Susu?"

Susu nodded. With a doubt.

The misunderstanding was cleared up. "Sorry. We apologize. We were afraid of the thief. People say there've been thefts in this building. We have to take precautions. There are some bad types about. We thought you were.... How stupid. Sorry."

Susu vaguely recognized the long-haired young man as a classmate from elementary school. He was white-skinned, plump, like a bun made from fine white flour, a food which should be popularized.

"Now that you're at my door...." her schoolmate invited them in. "All right," Susu and Jiayuan winked at each other. They followed her schoolmate to the dazzlingly bright lift. Now they had a legitimate status as the guests of a resident. The door closed and the lift began to drone. Thanks to this kind-hearted schoolmate their security and dignity were assured.

---

*Punishments inflicted on "bad" elements during the "cultural revolution". In the "jet-plane" the victim was forced to bend down with arms forced upwards for long periods of time.

The Arabic numerals on the lift wall changed quickly, from 14 to 4, and now the ear shaped number 3 lit up. It stopped and the door opened. Leaving the lift, they turned one corner after another until they reached his flat. The serrated key, the real trouble-shooter, opened the door confidently with a click. A flicked switch and the lounge and kitchen lights were on. The white walls looked as though they were wearing too much powder. The bedroom door creaked open. A bluish light from the street lamps filled the room. Before Susu could ask her schoolmate not to switch on the light it was on. "Sit down." A twin bed, wardrobe, a red leatherette sofa, a chest of drawers, a tin of malt-and-milk extract, an unopened "ten-delicacy" tonic wine. Her schoolmate continued to introduce his new home: space, amenities, design. Water, heating, gas. Lighting, ventilation, sound-proofing. Fire-proofing, earthquake-proofing.

"You live here all by yourself?"

"Yes," rubbing his hands, the schoolmate was becoming prouder by the minute. "My dad got this place for me. My parents are really anxious for me to get married. I plan to take care of that next May Day. You must come. Good, that's settled. I've got someone to give a hand. He's my friend's uncle and he used to work as a cook at the French embassy. It's going to be both Chinese and foreign food. His best dish is sugar-coated yams. You can wind the sugar threads round and round and they won't break. Don't give me any presents, by the way. Don't buy me furniture or a desk lamp or bedding. I've got everything I need."

"What's your fiancee's name? Where does she work?"

"Oh, that hasn't been decided yet."

"Is she waiting to be assigned a job?"

"No, I mean I haven't made up my mind yet who I'm going to marry. But I'll get somebody before next May Day. No problem."

Susu picked up a balloon from a table and rubbed it vigorously against the leatherette sofa. She tossed it upwards and it clung firmly to the ceiling. Looking up, she delighted in a game she had loved since childhood.

"Oh, good heavens! Why doesn't it come down?" asked the schoolmate, his mouth agape in astonishment. "It's still up there!"

"It's a kind of magic," Susu replied, looking sideways at Jiayuan and pulling a face. They left. Flabbergasted, their hospitable host had yet to regain his composure as he saw them off at the lift. His mind was still on the balloon on the ceiling.

Susu and Jiayuan left their lovely high-rise. It was still snowing and a wind was still blowing. As it fell on their hands and on their faces and trickled down their necks, the damp snow seemed to express a kind of affection for them.

"It's all my fault," said Jiayuan. "I've got no way of getting that sort of place. I'm sorry I've put you in such a difficult position." Laughing,

Susu covered his mouth with her hand. In her happiness, her smiling face would have put a blossoming pomegranate to shame.

Jiayuan understood. He began to laugh too. They both understood their own fortune. They knew that life and the world belonged to them. The laughter of the young couple seemed to halt the wind, snow and rain, and the glow of the night sky over the city was the sun.

Susu ran ahead and Jiayuan chased after her. Beneath the street lamp, the sheets of rain seemed even heavier and more dense.

"This is Dashi Street. It's right here!" shouted Susu at the top of her voice, pointing to the hotel building.

"Of course. I never doubted it."

"We've had a wonderfully happy evening. Now we should shake hands and say goodbye."

"Well, goodbye. We won't meet tomorrow. We must work hard. We both want to pass that entrance exam."

"Well, it's just possible that we will."

"Pleasant dreams!"

"Dreams about what?"

"Dreams about ... a kite!"

What? A kite? How did he know about that? "You know about the kite too, do you? Do you know about the streamers hanging from that kite?"

"Why, of course. How could I not?"

Susu ran back to embrace him and kissed him right there in the street. Then they each headed home, turning frequently, as the distance between them grew, to wave to one another.

Translated by Lu Binghong

Chen Huansheng's Adventure in Town

●

──── GAO XIAOSHENG ────

Born and raised in Jiangsu, Gao Xiaosheng began to publish stories in the 1950s, but it was the series of stories such as "Li Shunda Builds a House", "The Poverty-Stricken Household" and "Chen Huansheng's Adventure in Town" that he wrote after 1979 to reflect the life and psychology of Chinese farmers in the period of economic reforms that brought him fame. Two of his short stories won national awards in 1979 and 1980.

1

ONE day, Chen Huansheng went to town.

The cold spell had passed, and the weather was turning warm and breezy. With a full stomach, a suit of new clothes and a clean holdall, Chen walked briskly, as if the bulging holdall weighed nothing at all. The thirty li to town was no effort for his sturdy, long legs. He had often gone there on foot carrying a heavy load. Now, as he was carrying practically nothing, there was even less reason for him to take a bus. Besides, there was no point in getting there too early, so he slowed down to a leisurely pace, enjoying the scenery.

He was going to sell fried twists. The rice had been harvested, the wheat planted. Having paid agricultural tax in kind and sold his surplus grain, he had taken home his grain and fuel rations for the year. Since there was no farm work for the time being, he could earn some extra money in town. The free market had been reopened. As long as he did not try to speculate, he was permitted to sell his produce.

He had made the twists with his own flour and oil. They were fresh, crisp and delicious, better than those in the state-owned stores. His holdall was cram-full of them, five or ten to a plastic bag, looking tempting. If he sold them all, he would earn three yuan.

He wanted to buy a new hat with the money, a good new hat. He had not worn one for forty-five years, ever since he was three. Before Liberation, he couldn't afford one. After Liberation, he was in his prime and didn't need one. During the "cultural revolution", although he was getting on and felt the cold, he again lived from hand to mouth. Clothing was a luxury item on his budget. After the autumn harvest of 1978, his income had increased, but he was too happy to mind the cold. This year, however, he seemed to have become more delicate, hunching his shoulders in the cold weather, sneezing and catching a cold. He decided he must have a hat. That was not too difficult — just a trip to town and earn some money.

Free of worries, Chen was a different man. Having lived in poverty most of his life he was confident things would continue to improve. Content and happy, his face was fuller and brighter. When he awoke at night, he was too excited to go back to sleep at the thought of his full barn and wardrobe, even to the extent of waking up his wife for a chat.

Conversation had never been his strong point. Besides his wife, he hardly talked to anyone. He wasn't anti-social; he just had nothing to say. How he envied those who could make witty small talk, marvelling at their experiences and adventures. How they could tell shocking stories in a spell-binding way. He was a hopeless case, never discovering anything interesting to talk about. Back from town, all he could relate was, "There were many (or few) people in town today." Or, "There were pigs for sale, and the vegetables were cheap and didn't sell well." His life had been nothing out of the ordinary either. All he could recall was, "My mother often spanked me when I was a boy. My father seldom did." Or, "I had four years of schooling. But I've forgotten all I learned." And, "During the drought in '39, we caught fish in the dried-up river. In '49, the Communists defeated the Kuomintang." And, "After our marriage, my wife gave birth to a son and a daughter." It wouldn't have mattered if he had kept his mouth closed. He couldn't read novels or remember the operas he had seen and the stories he had heard. Nobody cared for his boring descriptions of farm work either. As for selling fried twists, that was nothing extraordinary. People had been doing that for some time. The recipe, packing, price which included the profit, where and when to make a good sale — all these were taken from others. To brag about this would be ridiculous. He would become a laughing-stock. "Fancy that, not a penny to his name, yet selling fried twists now!" Better to keep his big mouth shut.

He developed an inferiority complex. When people gathered in the evenings chatting, he never ventured a word. No one even threw him so much as a glance. He hadn't known there was such a thing as "cultural life". But when his life improved, he thirsted for it. He liked going to films and operas; life was dull without them. When asked, "Whom do you admire?" he piped up, "Lu Longfei." "What's so special about him? He's only a story-teller." "That's just it. I like his way of talking." His reply caused much amusement.

He felt ashamed. He should never have opened his mouth. How he wished he could have some adventures to tell people.

2

When he felt embarrassed and awkward, this wish would sometimes pop into his mind; nothing more than that. On his way to town, however, his sole concern was his new hat.

Walking slowly, he still arrived before six p.m. He bought himself a cup of tea and ate the pancake he had brought for supper before heading for the station, window-shopping all the way. He went into three department stores to investigate the price of hats till he finally found one he liked. Then he remembered he had no money but his savings. He had planned to buy it with his earnings that night, not realizing that the stores closed early. So he would have to buy it the next morning. But how could he stay overnight, having no friends or relatives in town? He would have to brave the cold a few days more.

Disappointment made his head feel colder. He arrived at the station after eight, still too early, but it gave him time to find a good place to sit. The people waiting for the trains had already eaten. They wouldn't buy his twists. Some children pestered their parents for one. He would be busy only when the trains arrived. One was due in at 9:40 p.m., another at 10:30 p.m. By then most shops were closed, and the hungry passengers would crowd around him. Another train was scheduled to arrive at 11:20 p.m., but that was too late. He wouldn't wait for it even if he still had some twists left. He would go home and sleep.

It happened just as he had expected. When the 10:30 p.m. train arrived, the passengers rushed over, helping themselves to his twists, making it difficult for him to serve them all at the same time. When he counted the money afterwards, he was thirty cents short. He counted it again. Still thirty cents short. Someone must have taken his twists without paying. He sighed at his misfortune. He had been on the alert against people like that. But there had been such a crowd. He would have to swallow the loss. Still he had made more than his three yuan.

He sighed again, preparing to go home. When he rose, his legs buckled under him and he felt weak. He was frightened. Was he ill? He had been too busy to feel anything and had thought his hoarseness was due to so much haggling. But he felt really awful, his mouth parched and feverish. He touched his forehead. Any draught made him feel terribly cold. He craved a cup of hot tea, but the stalls were shut. Then he remembered that the station supplied hot water. He shambled over. There were no cups. Most passengers brought their own and the station did not take the trouble to supply any. Having no alternative, Chen cupped his hands and drank. The water didn't burn his hands, which were also hot. He felt better after a drink. Going home would be difficult. It suddenly seemed a long way away. He could hardly stand and had to sit down. It was all because he had not bought the hat. Now he had caught a chill. Everything had gone wrong! What was he to do? If he should really fall ill here, without friends or relatives, and could not see a doctor in time, he might not survive. A decent honest fellow like him had no reason to die. Why the haste? He had a few more years' hard work ahead. Cheered up again, he opened his mouth to laugh, but no sound came. Only the corners of his mouth moved, his right hand tapping his thigh appreciatively, as if he were beating time to beautiful music. He let out a long sigh and lay down on a bench.

3

It was broad daylight when he woke up. He was listless and coughing, his mind hazy. He didn't want to open his eyes. When he turned over, intending to go back to sleep, he felt the bed give, while his heart jumped. He put his hand beneath him. It felt very soft. He took a careful look and found himself sleeping on a comfortable big bed. He lay in disbelief, his eyes shut, trying to figure out how he had got there. He thought hard. He vaguely recalled seeing Secretary Wu of the county Party committee and his jeep. Then all the details fell into place.

It had been Chen's lucky year, always someone around to help him out. While he was lying unconscious in the station waiting-room, a jeep had driven up with Secretary Wu in it. He was catching the 12:15 a.m. train to go to a meeting in the provincial capital. Arriving half an hour early, he had strolled around in the waiting-room, his driver remaining until he entered the train in case Wu needed him. As few people were around at midnight, Wu soon caught sight of Chen asleep and laughed. The previous autumn Wu had spent two months with Chen's brigade. "What was this simple hard-working peasant doing here?" Wu wondered. "He might miss his train." He noticed the empty holdall below Chen when he reached out to wake him. Goodness! Had he been robbed? But however hard he shook Chen, he could not rouse him. Chen was feverish to the touch. Wu quickly helped him to sit up.

All Chen knew was that when he opened his eyes and saw Secretary Wu, he clutched at him. "Are you ill?" Wu had inquired. Chen had nodded. When Wu asked him why he was there he put his hand on the holdall. "Where are your things?" Chen had smiled, but he was not sure if he had explained. Anyway, Wu seemed to understand him and together with the driver, helped him into his jeep and took him to a clinic. A man in a white coat, who must have been the doctor, examined him and told

Secretary Wu that he had flu. The doctor gave him some medicine and pills, without asking for payment. Putting him into the jeep, he told Secretary Wu, "Sorry, we've no spare beds. You'd better take him to a hotel. He'll be alright after a good night's sleep." As the jeep moved away, Chen remembered Secretary Wu saying to the driver, "Only thirteen minutes before my train leaves. Take me to the station first. Then you find him a hotel. Get him a single room. Say he's my friend...."

Tears welled up in Chen's closed eyes, and slowly rolled down his cheeks. What a good person Secretary Wu was, treating him like a friend, helping him when he was in trouble. He had probably saved his life.

In fact, they were only acquaintances, hardly friends. Their only previous contact was the day Wu had dropped in at Chen's home to have a meal, intending to find out how much Chen's life had improved. He had brought the children some expensive sweets, costing a lot more than the simple meal. Though he was not really a friend, Secretary Wu was close to the ordinary people.

These thoughts made Chen feel happier. He wiped away his tears with the quilt and opened his eyes to look carefully at the room he was in. To his astonishment, everything in the room was new and shining! The ceiling was a dazzing white, the lower half of the walls were varnished, the upper half white-washed, while the dark red floor gleamed. There were two big leather armchairs, a dark red chest of drawers and a cream-coloured desk. The sheets had a beautiful flower print and the quilt was new, with a silk top cover and snow-white back. Instinctively, Chen drew himself up for fear that his feet might soil it. He got up stealthily, as if he were a thief, and dressed quietly. Carrying his shoes in his hands, he walked barefoot. Unable to resist the two armchairs, he went over to touch and feel them, afraid to sit down in case his weight damaged the springs. Then he opened the door and silently let himself out.

The corridor chilled his feet. When he saw other people wearing their shoes, he put his own on. Secretary Wu had sent him to a high-class hotel. Too good for him! He had heard that hotels were expensive. A room like this must cost a lot. Perhaps the price of a hat. What a waste!

Very worried, he decided to ask for his bill and check out right away.

"Please, may I have my bill, comrade?" he said to the girl reading a newspaper behind the counter.

"Room number?" she asked, her eyes glued to the print.

"I don't know. The last room in the east wing."

The girl tossed away the paper and smiled sweetly at him. "So you came in Secretary Wu's jeep! Are you feeling better now?"

"I'm all right. I want to go home."

"No need to hurry. Are you Secretary Wu's old friend? Where do you work?" The girl was quite chatty, as she handed him his bill, smiling even more. Chen found her very beautiful.

Chen looked down at the bill. His hand shook as if it were red-hot. He couldn't believe his eyes. "How much?" he couldn't help asking, as the blood rose to his head.

"Five yuan."

"For one night?" He sweated.

"Right."

His heart thumped vigorously. "Goodness me," he thought. "It costs not one hat, but two!"

"You're not well!" cried the astonished girl. "You're still sweating."

"But I only came at midnight." Chen should never have protested so naively.

The girl, realizing at once that he was a nobody, snapped with a poker face, "I don't care when you came. You have to pay a day's charge till noon." She had not ridiculed him for his relationship to Secretary Wu.

Her icy face told Chen that his foolish remark had displeased her. That shut him up altogether. His trembling hands pulled the notes out of his pocket, counting them three times before he handed them over. The banknotes were already wet with sweat.

The girl, who returned to her paper, frowned at the small change, but her manners made her accept them politely.

Chen was indignant. That large sum of money did not earn even a smile from the girl. He was on the point of walking out, when he remembered his holdall and returned to his room.

He hesitated at the door, looking at the glistening floor, wondering if he should take his shoes off. Then he thought, "Damn it! I paid five yuan." He strode right in and plunked himself down on the armchair. "What if the springs should break? I've spent five yuan!"

Feeling hungry, he took out his last pancake and began eating. Then he rose and poured himself a cup of hot water from the thermos flask. When he turned back, he found that the chair was alright. He brought himself to his full height and then flopped down, repeating this three times. The armchair remained the same. An excellent chair! He lay back in it, eating his pancake. He felt much better, his head had cleared and he had sweated away his fever. He believed he had got rid of his bad luck, or he could look upon the expense as part of the cost of his cure.

Once he had washed down the pancake, he regretted the money again. The hat he had fallen in love with cost 2.5 yuan. Why should the room be as expensive as two hats? Even a rich man would become poor in no time staying here. He was just a commune member earning 70 cents a day. Seven working days couldn't cover the costs. What a joke! He had only been there seven hours, a day's earning for each hour. How could such a pauper lie on such an expensive bed? Since the girl had said the room was his until noon, he would have his money's worth, not leaving a minute before then.

He proceeded with his plan. As he had sweated and eaten, he wanted to wash. Finding no towel, he used the pillowcase to give his face a good rub and then got into bed without undressing. He had no scruples now, having paid his five yuan. He wouldn't care if he turned the room into a pigsty. Nothing was worth so much money!

Unable to fall asleep, his thoughts turned to Secretary Wu. In a hurry to catch his train, he had not bothered to find out if the room was too expensive for Chen. Chen blamed himself for not buying the hat. Besides spending all he had earned, he now had to eat into his savings. What about the hat? He must buy it still, so as not to fall ill again.

At the thought of the twists, he began to feel hungry. The pancake had not filled his stomach and he had sold all his twists. Lying there would only increase his appetite. But where could he get lunch? He had no grain coupons on him. If he got too hungry to walk, he might have to stay another night. At the thought of that, he leapt up, kicking away the quilt. He grabbed his holdall and left immediately. However nice the room was, it was no place for him. He would forfeit his three remaining hours.

He made straight for the department store, where he bought the hat, put it on his head and left.

Enjoying the scenery, he covered the 30 li home easily. As he was nearing his village he began to worry. How was he to explain everything to his wife, who might raise hell at his extravagance? Suppose he told her that he had lost the money gambling? But he never did that. Spent it eating? He was no glutton. Stolen? He would get a piece of her mind for being careless. Charity? No. He needed that himself. Gave it to a girl? That might make his wife jealous.... What should he say?

He couldn't find a good excuse. Then he slapped his thigh in glee, when it dawned on him that his adventures were worth a lot more than five yuan. Now he had something to boast about. Who in his whole brigade, cadres and peasants alike, had ever sat in Secretary Wu's jeep? Who had ever stayed in such an expensive room? He would tell his story. Now who would dare to sneer that he had nothing to say? Who would look down on him any more? ... As his spirits rose, he seemed to grow in stature too. He was no longer afraid of his wife. He would just mention the name of Secretary Wu. Well, every dog has his day. He had purchased spiritual satisfaction for five yuan. It was dirt-cheap! He strode on happily and was home in no time.

Sure enough, his prestige in the brigade rose considerably. The villagers listened to his adventures. Even brigade cadres became more friendly. On the streets, people often pointed him out, saying, "He rode in Secretary Wu's jeep," or, "He stayed in a room costing five yuan a day." Once, the purchasing agent of the commune farm machinery plant patted him on the shoulder saying, "I've never had your luck! When I go to town on business I often stay in that hotel, but I'm never given such a nice room."

Since then, Chen has become very satisfied and works more energetically.

Translated by Yu Fanqin

Pages from a Factory Secretary's Diary

●

—— JIANG ZILONG ——

Jiang Zilong, born in 1941 in Hebei, started work in the Tianjin Heavy Machinery Plant after graduating from middle school in 1958. Conscripted into the navy in 1960, he spent five years there, working as a surveyor. After demobilization he went back to the machinery plant. "Manager Qiao Assumes Office", "Pages from a Factory Secretary's Diary" and "New-Year Greetings" were all national prize-winning stories. The hero of "Manager Qiao Assumes Office" is well-known throughout China. Jiang Zilong's novels include The Snake Raiser.

March 4, 1979

I went to the factory an hour earlier than usual today because I wanted to say goodbye to Manager Wang, who was leaving for good. I reckoned that a man like him wouldn't kick up a fuss about it but would go quietly before the workers arrived.

Wang himself had asked for the transfer, but in fact, I'm pretty sure he felt unable to continue working in this factory. He was simply squeezed out by Assistant Manager Luo Ming. It was an open secret, yet people kept mum, especially in front of Wang. No one would rub it in. It was really awful.

As a factory secretary for four years, I've seen off two managers. Now Wang is the third.

When something is wrong with the management in a factory, a transfer is the most convenient remedy. That's probably true everywhere. Each time I say goodbye to a manager, I examine myself. It takes me a week to get over it.

I decided to use my power for the first time to order our only jeep to take Wang to his new place.

But a janitor told me that he had left half an hour before!

"All on his own?" I asked.

"Party Secretary Liu carried his luggage for him."

"But where's our jeep?"

"Luo had it out on business last night."

I was very upset. I'd hoped to get to the factory to give Wang a hand. But obviously the man behind all this dirty business had pipped me at the post.

I had a sudden feeling of resentment against Liu, the number one in our factory. What a weakling! Shandong, his home province, has been famous for its heroes since ancient days. Where were his guts? Numbers one and two squeezing into a bus with all that luggage!

As I was musing, the jeep sped in in a cloud of dust. Luo got out, beaming.

"Hello, Wei!" he said in a mocking tone. "Why so early? Seeing Wang off? Has he left?"

"Yes."

I'm laconic, especially when I'm in a bad mood. The least said, the soonest mended! A secretary must watch his tongue. A blunder can bring a lot of trouble.

Luo fumbled in his pocket and fished out a few firecrackers. Passing them to me, he said, "Have some fun!"

Refusing to take them, I replied, "I don't dare light them."

He snorted, "You're no man!"

"You often carry them in your pockets?"

"Left-overs from the Spring Festival. I'll set them all off and clear the air!"

Crack! He lit one and guffawed.

A cold shiver went down my spine. Wang was lucky to have left already. How would he have felt about this?

Manager — a post which is so enticing to certain people! In an attempt to remove the word "assistant" in his title, Luo had pushed out three men. But twice new managers had been appointed. Will another come or will Luo be promoted? If the latter, I'll have to consider leaving too, quitting the manager's office and going back to the production department to work on statistics again.

March 11

"Wei, have you heard that Luo's been promoted to manager?" Quite a number of workers tried to sound me out.

"No, I haven't." My answer was the same.

Then someone would probe, "Oh, come off it! Surely you've heard it."

Poor fellows! Having no say whatever in the factory, yet wanting to know everything. Pointless curiosity! No matter who's the manager, you'll have to work all the same. It's none of your business!

"Manager Luo, you're wanted on the phone!" People have begun to address him like this these days. Even some workshop reports start with "Manager Luo". "Assistant" has been omitted. Those cunning cadres, who have already trimmed their sails to suit the wind, are more pitiful than the workers.

"Wei, don't you smell a rat? Luo works hard these days. He's got a finger in every pie. He's all over the place. Always with a smile on his face. Even his voice is louder."

"No, I don't." You're here to work, I thought, not to watch others' expressions. Perhaps it's my professional weakness, my nerves have gone dull or numb. I've got used to all kinds of speeches and facial expressions. I take nothing to heart.

Since I know there are some who watch my expressions and weigh my words carefully, when I have to address Luo, I always take the trouble to say his full title — "Assistant Manager Luo".

When certain documents require a manager's perusal, I give them to Liu, the Party branch secretary, according to the rules. I then pass them on to whomever he tells me. I don't intend to flatter Luo. He's probably sensed it. However, since I haven't been officially informed about his promotion, he can't do anything about it.

I don't care whether or not he's going to be the manager. That's none of my business. If the higher-ups ask my opinion, I'll object. He's been in this factory for ages, knows everything about it and he has quite a following, yet he'll never be a good manager. What he cares about is power, not responsibility. He lacks the necessary qualities and abilities of a good manager.

March 12

It's strange. Luo's daughter, Luo Jingyu, came to my office and chatted for some time.

She's been job-hunting since she came back from the countryside two years ago. The trouble is, she's too choosy. She won't work in a collective-owned factory, nor in a job she doesn't like and she refuses to go somewhere a bit far from home. As she rarely comes to our factory, I couldn't work out at first what she was up to, yacking away in the office. Then she mentioned the question of her job at last and said, "I want to work here."

"You must be kidding!" I said doubtfully. "Though we're state-owned, we're small, only two hundred people. Nothing to write home about. Besides, there's no job you'd fancy here."

"It's difficult to get a good job, and I've been waiting for two years." She told the truth. "I'm already twenty-six. I can't afford to wait any more. A chemical factory has its advantages. The production costs are low, but the profit's great. So your bonuses are high."

"That's quite true. Have a word with your father then."

"He would find it embarrassing to help me. Wei, will you do me a favour?"

Here was an opportunity for a man who wanted to butter up his superior and climb up the social ladder. If it was inconvenient for a manager to do something, then it was up to his secretary to help him out. He should run errands and do the job in all kinds of names if necessary to achieve his superior's aims.

When I had failed to resist the Party branch committee's decision to appoint me as the factory secretary, I made a rule for myself that there would be nothing personal between my superiors and me. No matter who he was, our relationship was strictly business! Public affairs should be conducted in an orthodox way. Personal considerations shouldn't intrude.

"Wait till I ask the Party branch committee," I replied.

She was totally unprepared for such an answer. She thought that, as she was the daughter of the manager and I was her father's secretary, I should naturally serve her too. She was very cross and, after a snigger which was just like her father's, left with a slam of the door.

Marcg 15

"Our new manager will come soon," Secretary Liu told me jovially in a low voice.

This down-to-earth man was as innocent as a lamb. He had received three managers in the same jovial mood and sulkily seen them off, carrying their bags. Today he was again in high spirits.

I was neither very happy nor disappointed. I was simply bored.

March 18

The telephone in the office kept ringing. I heard it from quite far away. People mock those who enter the factory gate just as the bell is ringing. But I enter the office five days out of six just as the phone is ringing.

Calls at this time are usually for managers. It is the right time to catch them. Half an hour later and they're nowhere to be found. Even I have no idea of their whereabouts, let alone what they are busy with.

Brr....

As a secretary, I was used to it. No matter how urgent it sounds, I am never in a hurry. I opened the door, hung up my bag, had a bite of my bun and finally picked up the receiver.

"Hello! Is that Secretary Wei? Would you do me a favour, Wei? My father died yesterday and he's to be cremated today. Could you have a word with the manager and say that I want to borrow a car? Do help me out, please!"

Startled, I inquired, "Who is it?"

"This is Pang. Pang Wancheng. Sorry to trouble you."

"Why didn't you let me know earlier?" I complained.

"How could I know he would die so soon?"

I was hard put to it. "You know that we've only one jeep and one lorry. But they went to fetch raw materials from the countryside yesterday. They won't be back for a day or two. What can I do?"

Pang was a very simple, honest crane-operator and he would never ask the factory for help if he wasn't desperate. Despite what I told him, he stubbornly continued pleading, "Wei, I'm in no position to ask Manager Luo for such a favour. But you've been a secretary for years. You know much better than me how to solve the problem. I've no one to turn to. The time for the cremation has been fixed. All our relatives will come soon. What shall I do if I can't get a car?"

In the eyes of the workers, I seem to be a man of power too. They don't realize I'm just the manager's errand-boy and mouthpiece. However, I couldn't explain that to him at that moment. It seemed that I was the only "important person" he knew, his last hope.

While I was still talking, a stout, short fellow suddenly appeared behind me and said smilingly, "Let me speak to him."

Astonished, I asked, "What — what are you doing here?"

This bloke had a charming round face with a pair of big sparkling eyes.

He looked like a salesman from a factory who had come on business. Pointing, I said, "The production department's the third room on the left."

He shook his head and introduced himself, "My name's Jin Fengchi. I'm sent by the Bureau of Chemical Industry to work here."

The new manager! My heart missed a beat.

I cursed myself. A secretary shouldn't be so snobbish. Why did I judge a man by his appearance?

I handed him the phone. When he spoke, his voice became serious and concerned, "Don't worry, Comrade Pang. Tell me, when do you need a car?"

He took a biro from his breast pocket and I gave him a piece of paper. While repeating Pang's words, he scribbled on the paper. "Ten o'clock, fine. Your address? No. 8, Fifth Lane, Jinzhou Street. Good. What's your name again? Pang Wancheng. OK, Wancheng, wait at home and I'll send you a van. Don't be so polite. Anything else I can do for you? My name isn't important. Anyway you can stop worrying now. But don't be too upset. Better take care of yourself. Have a few days off and rest."

He rang off. Taking the receiver in his left hand, he dialled a number. "Is that the Chemical Machinery Repair Plant? Who's speaking? Du! Guess who's speaking to you? Ha! Ha!... Yes, I'm in my new job. No choice. Very sad to leave you and our factory too. Look, I've a slight problem here. Can I borrow your van? Excellent! Ten O'clock. Tell Young Sun to go to No. 8, Fifth Lane, Jinzhou Street and look for a man named Pang

Wancheng. Sorry to trouble you. Phone me whenever you want me."

Having put down the receiver, he turned to ask me, "How many telephones do we have?"

"Ours is a small factory, so there are only three. There's one here, one in the production department and another in the reception office."

Pulling over a stool and sitting down, he produced a cigarette case and handed me a cigarette. Having lit his, he said slowly, "Surely you must be Secretary Wei, a very capable man I hear."

"My name's Wei Jixiang. I'm a square peg in a round hole, not really qualified."

I wanted to impress on him that I had no interest in my present job.

"I'm new here," he said politely. "I need your help."

I quickly waved my hands to show I could do very little.

His face fell. "I'm not being polite," he said seriously. "Cadres learn from the people and a manager from his secretary. It's the secretary who drafts the manager's speech for mass meetings. All a manager does is to read it aloud from the platform. A manager's competence largely depends on his secretary's level. If the secretary's lousy, the manager probably won't be any good either. You read all the documents first and then pass them on to the managers concerned. Besides, you have to attend to the managers' odd jobs. Managers may be the leaders of the factory, but you're their boss."

I was fidgeting, feeling, in turn, comfortable and uneasy. My face was burning. I couldn't figure out whether he was flattering me or being sarcastic. I am considered a man with some education in the factory. But today I was all at sea, unable to tell whether or not he was serious.

It is too early to jump to conclusions, but one thing is certain, he's no fool!

At noon, Pang came straight from the crematorium and asked me to take him to the new manager.

Secretary Liu was showing Jin round the workshops as Pang, a black band round his arm, and I searched everywhere for him. Not knowing what had happened, many people followed us.

On seeing Jin, Pang went over and kowtowed in the traditional way. I was shocked!

Jin was surprised too. He hurriedly helped him up and said, "Comrade Pang, what on earth are you doing?"

Pang was very grateful to him. Too emotional, he stuttered when he spoke, "A th-th-thousand thanks, M-M-Manager Jin. If you hadn't sent the van, goodness knows how long my father's body would have remained at home. He'll be grateful to you too in the nether-world. Thank you very much."

Jin wanted to pat him on the shoulder to comfort him but he was too short. So he gripped Pang's arm instead and said earnestly, "Don't talk like that, Pang. Nowadays those who have influential connections use them. Those who have power use it. But what about the workers who have neither? We can't blame the workers for their resentment, nor can we complain that they are less enthusiastic than before 1958. We can't say that they're selfish and only thinking of themselves. If nobody seems to care about them, they have to look after themselves." I was flabbergasted. He was really bold to talk like that! Though new, he seemed very frank with the workers. He talked in a way as if he were defending them.

What he said touched their hearts. The admiration in their eyes and their whispered comments showed that his words were more effective than an "inaugural address" at a mass meeting.

Liu was delighted to see the workers responding positively to the new manager and said earnestly to Jin, "The workers of this factory are a fine lot, aren't they? They like you."

Jin turned to Pang and continued, "Wancheng, your father's dead now, but don't let it get you down too much. Take a few days off. Your must look after yourself too."

He had said that over the phone and now he was repeating himself in public.

Deeply moved, Pang didn't know what to say. Flushing, he replied, "No. I won't have a rest. I'll come back to work today."

Having said that, he began to put on his overalls. He had only taken half of his three days' leave for the funeral.

Liu led the manager to another workshop. As I turned to go to my office, I spotted Luo standing at the back of the crowd. Gazing after the two receding figures of Liu and Jin, he puffed vigorously on his cigarette. The pale pock-marks on his face became more distinct, an indicator of his feelings. When he was in high spirits, they disappeared. When he was furious, his red face seemed to make the marks whiter.

He went to Pang and said smilingly, "Pang Wancheng, I never thought that a big man like you could be so yellow-bellied! So a van can make you grovel on your knees!"

Unprepared for this, Pang stammered, "Manager Luo, you're...."

Luo is a ruthless man, liable to get nasty any minute. Very often, he would suddenly scold for no obvious reason. I pretended not to have seen them and went to the office.

But he caught me up and walked abreast with me.

"Wei," he spoke up, "our new chief certainly knows how to win friends and influence people!"

I said nothing. I've always avoided rivalry between managers. I'm impartial to all.

But no doubt our little factory will soon have troubles again.

March 23

"The first thing Manager Jin did was to borrow a van from outside for the most honest worker of our factory."

The news soon got round. After much exaggeration, it assumed an air of romance.

How easily people are satisfied and moved!

April 2

Manager Jin and I got into the jeep and went to the company to report on our work. However, neither of us spoke for some time.

But suddenly he asked me a very peculiar question, "'I may be a dragon here, but I'll be no match for you, a snake in its old haunts.' Do you know which opera that line is from?"

"Shajiabang," I said, throwing him a glance.

Another silence. But I understood perfectly what he meant.

It was not until we got out and entered the office block of the company, he ventured again, "We must speak first. At the beginning, people tend to be formal and the big shots would like to listen to others first. So it's an opportunity for a small factory like ours. Besides, at the start of the meeting, leading comrades are attentive and listen carefully. But later their concentration wanes. They'll begin smoking, drinking tea or going to the lavatory. No one will really be listening."

He was sharp. But I was still worried. What had he got to say? He'd been in the factory less than a month!

The company had notified us that there would be a managers' meeting. Liu, thinking Jin was far too new, suggested that Luo attend the meeting. I knew Luo liked to appear on such occasions. But Jin smiled and said, "Better I go." It was very subtle. Was he against letting Luo attend the meeting as a manager or was he eager to seek the limelight himself?

Sure enough, as the meeting was declared open, he spoke first. He was eloquent and his example of Pang only taking half of his three days' leave was vivid and moving. While he commended the worker, he impressed the listeners with his art of leadership.

We were praised at the meeting, unusual for a tiny factory like ours.

I felt more and more that Jin was not as simple as he seemed.

When the second man began his report, Jin whispered to me, "Jot down the good points, Wei, particularly others' experiences and the company directors' instructions. I'm going out for a moment."

He was away for several hours, only reappearing shortly before the meeting ended. Very strange!

April 25

It gets more and more peculiar. The marks on Luo's face are less visible. Has the power struggle come to an end? Luo is not a man to easily knuckle under. Has he thrown in the sponge? Not likely!

When I entered the office at noon after lunch, I saw Jin talking over the phone, Luo beside him, wearing an obsequious look, which was very rare.

"... Her name's Luo Jingyu, a relative of mine. You must help her however difficult. I'll expect your answer within a week. OK. So it's settled?"

The penny dropped. I have no admiration for Jin's way of doing things, but I have to admit that he certainly has a good head on his shoulders. Luo is a difficult man to co-operate with, but he knows thoroughly our production and has quite a following. If he is under Jin's thumb, Jin can consider himself really settled in the factory.

But I had never expected that Jin would do such a thing. He certainly knows how to win over a philistine. No wonder people remark behind his back that he is as slick as a snake.

May 10

Jin and I went to a meeting at the bureau. Not long after it had started, he again whispered to me, "Keep notes, Wei. I'll be out for a moment."

Whenever we had meetings either in the company or the bureau, he always played the same trick. What on earth did he go out for? What could keep him that busy?

After a short while I left the meeting too. It was quite warm and many offices had their doors open. As I went up to the second floor, I happened to see Jin wandering from room to room. He seemed to have dropped in to have a chat or a laugh with practically everybody from the department heads to staff members. He had brought with him plenty of good cigarettes and offered them generously to everyone who smoked. But it was not just one-sided, he was given cigarettes too. He was very familiar with the people working there. Drinking and smoking, he was utterly at ease. Sometimes he had business to do, sometimes he came just to chat. A couple of hours were easily killed this way.

Our factory is a tiny unit in the Bureau of Chemical Industry. That a manager of such a factory is on good terms with many people including some cadres higher than himself in the bureau is really something remarkable!

On the way back to our factory after the meeting, I told him, "I hear you've got a lot of friends in the bureau."

"Didn't you realize that this afternoon?" He grinned at me.

I couldn't cover up my embarrassment.

"Wei," he said buoyantly, "we've been together for some time now, and I've come to know that you're a very good comrade. Your handwriting's absolutely beautiful and you write quickly. Day after day, you run your legs off, working harder than any manager. However, I must say, you're a bit of a stick-in-the-mud. Tell you what — in capitalist countries, money counts, but in our country, it's your connections. That's something I've learned through experience. This certainly won't change in the next three to five years. Ours is a small factory and we've no big cadres. That means we've neither power nor position. If you don't have good connections and don't butter people up, you can do nothing."

An amazing theory! I could not decide if he was admirable or despicable.

May 12

Luo was all smiles when he spoke to me in a cheerful voice, "Wei, I've got a job for you. Will you bring Manager Jin to my home for dinner tonight? He probably won't come alone, so I'm roping you in too. Do everything you can to persuade him."

"Toadying to the boss!" I thought. "So humble, just because he's found your daughter a job."

But what else could I expect of someone who had been a pump-keeper, then joined the Party and become an assistant manager by chance? I'd never have dinner in his home! In the past, I always made some excuse. "Just my luck!" I said. "My son's got pneumonia! I'll have to take him to hospital after work today."

His face darkened at once. "I suppose I'm not important enough! Well, don't trouble then. Just send Jin to my home, OK?"

What could I do? I was a factory secretary after all. Gazing after his back, I cursed, "I'll be damned if I'll let my son be a secretary!"

I went to Jin when it was time to knock off. He accepted the invitation bluntly and urged me to accept. I told the same lie again. Narrowing his eyes, he grinned and said, "Don't make it up, Wei. You're no good at lying. Your face gives you away!"

"But it's true, every word!" I defended myself hastily.

"Oh, come off it!" he guffawed. "You don't even bother to change your lies! Always the same story. Your little fib is known all over the factory. People say, 'When Wei doesn't want to go somewhere, he excuses himself by making his wife or children ill.' You're an educated man. Can't you invent some other story?"

I shook my head, smiling wrily.

Patting me on the shoulder, he continued, "You poor innocent! The assistant manager is throwing a dinner for us. That's our good luck, you know. I won't take a sip of any liquor under two yuan a bottle! Come with me. You don't have to say a word, just eat your fill! Isn't it great?"

I didn't go anyway. But I learned that Luo's daughter had started work in a state-owned radio factory today. So that was why Luo threw the dinner. Jin is really quite a character to have tamed a fellow like Luo.

When the Party spirit, discipline and laws don't work for someone, personal feelings and favouritism may have their place.

But I'm unimpressed by Jin's way of doing things. In fact, his simplicity and kindness, which made such an impression on me the first day he arrived, have changed. (*I have omitted my diary entries from June to September.*)

October 9

The complications among the leading comrades reflect those in society and people's thinking.

Now Luo and Jin have ganged up, while there's a growing tension between Jin and Liu. This morning, there was the inevitable show-down over bonuses at the Party branch committee meeting.

A government document circulated in September said that a factory was entitled to bonuses proportionate to its profits. The raw material our factory needs is others' waste material. The capital is small, but the profit remarkable. As a rule, the smaller the number of workers in a factory, the easier the bonus is given. It was calculated at the end of September that each worker could get a fifty-yuan bonus and an office worker more than forty. That meant most of the workers would get double their rate of pay.

Being an honest and straightforward man, Liu was astonished to hear this. Forty yuan a month extra was, of course, something he needed, for his living standard was the lowest among the top leaders of the factory. But he was against it. Shaking his head, he protested, "That won't do! Such a big bonus? Out of the question!"

"What's there to be afraid of?" many workers countered, disappointment showing on their faces. Everybody welcomed having some extra cash. But the members of the Party branch committee sat on the fence, staring at the manager and the Party secretary, waiting for a decision. They wanted the money but were hesitant about bearing the responsibility.

"Speak your mind, Luo," Jin urged the assistant manager.

Luo was very blunt, "Give the bonus to the workers. Act according to the document."

Liu retorted, "The document applies to enterprises in general. But ours is an exception. We can't take advantage of this. We must thoroughly understand the spirit of the document. Besides, the leaders might not approve of it if they knew."

"What would you do with the money?" Luo asked. "Hand it over to the state for nothing?"

"Put it in the bank for the time being. It'll come in handy for the community welfare fund."

Silently Jin smoked. No one knew what he was thinking. He is expert in handling people, always weighing the pros and cons carefully. He would never risk his position for a few dozen yuan for the workers. What if he should offend the company or the bureau? Surely he knew which side to back. He would never lose a lot to save a little. Besides, the Party secretary had already made his attitude clear. He wouldn't oppose Liu.

I thought too that Jin would surely be against the large bonus.

As I'd expected, Jin said, "Liu's right. The sum's a bit on the large side...."

"You —" Luo uttered, his face suddenly red.

Jin wagged his finger at him, as if there had been an agreement between them. I realized all of a sudden that Jin was making use of Luo, a headstrong fellow, to sound out Liu first.

Jin continued, "We're the leaders of the Oriental Chemical Factory. We needn't worry about the state. Our chief concern is the welfare of the workers of this factory. If we offend them, we'll certainly get into trouble. We've read the document to the workers. If we don't issue the bonus according to the document, we'll be breaking our promise and damaging the image of the state. It'll put us in a bad light for sure. Even worse, the workers will be disheartened, and production will drop. So I vote for giving the bonus, every cent of it. If the company inquires into it, we can say we were carrying out the instructions in the document. If other factories raise questions and poke their noses into our affairs, we'll tell them we acted according to the principle of 'more pay for more work'. Our factory's doing well. We've made a good profit for the state. Of course we're entitled to a big bonus. Now what do you think?"

As most of the members agreed with what he'd said, it was decided thus. Liu felt it wrong to give such a big bonus, but he had no convincing argument. Though it was a majority vote, he was still uneasy. He asked Jin to stay behind after the meeting.

Work had already ended, but I didn't go home since I still had some urgent business to attend to. The window above the door leading to Liu's office was open. While writing, I could hear clearly the conversation in Liu's room. I am worried about him. He is too old-fashioned, too inflexible. In the past, he'd been fretting a great deal about the friction between the manager and the assistant manager. Wang had suited him very well, a decent and upright man, honest and frank to both his inferiors and superiors. But he was narrow-minded, and often sulked. He couldn't brazen it out and finally left after less than a year in the job. Jin is shrewd and able and hits it off well with everybody. Even Luo has succumbed and co-operates with him. Liu should be having an easy life. Yet he goes looking for trouble. In the past, he and Wang had failed to contain Luo. How can he now deal with Jin and Luo single-handed?

Liu's voice in the next room became louder and louder. "... To be a leader, one must play fair. It's wrong to pander to one faction or try to please everybody. What's worse is to curry favour by giving away the state's money. Jin, some people have complained to me about you. You ought to watch your step."

It was terrible. How could a Party secretary speak to a manager like that? To ease the tension, I hurriedly sent them the material I'd just written.

Jin was really smart. He listened with patience, no sign of anger on his face. Seeing me, he smiled and remarked, "You've come at the right time, Wei. Let's talk it over together. This Party secretary of ours is really impossible! No wonder the leading body of this factory was so ineffective and always at odds with each other. Instead of helping his subordinates out of difficulties, he needs them to help him out. Now tell me, Liu, how am I not playing fair? You accuse me of currying favour by giving away the state's money, but didn't I do it according to the spirit of the document?"

Liu sighed, waving his hand and replied, "As for money, the more the better. I know the workers won't be very happy if we lessen the bonus. But as leaders, we must think about their long-term interests. We must guide them, educate them. Doesn't the document also say that part of the bonus can be used for the community welfare fund?"

"If you hold back the fifty yuan, you'll enrage the workers. What exactly do you want that money for?"

"For some future use. For instance, we must ensure that we can give a bonus every month, no matter how small. Even if we fail in fulfilling the production quota, we can still give a bonus, just in case. Besides, if we've put aside enough money, we can build a few more houses for the workers."

"Forget it, Liu! Haven't you had enough?" Jin then turned to me, "As a secretary, Wei, you must have learned this lesson. Act promptly while you've power in your hands. The document says you can give the bonus, so give it! If you hesitate now, you can do nothing about the money later if the directive is changed. As for the housing problem, I tell you frankly, it won't be easy to build a dozen houses for a small factory like ours. The construction departments will want a couple of them when the houses are put up. Then there are those in charge of electricity, water, coal and even food stores.... How many rooms will be left for us? You'll spend the money, sweat over it, and then what will you get in return? Troubles, abuse! What benefit will the workers of this factory really get? Better put a lump sum in their hands!"

Though Liu didn't quite agree, he said nothing more, however.

Jin offered us cigarettes, but Liu refused. Instead, he took out his own. Jin wasn't offended, lighting his cigarette calmly. Drawing on it deeply, he continued, "Liu, the way you handle things was OK before 1958, but it won't work now. Take the document. Abide by it, but don't be too strict. There's a lot to learn. For example, how many times have you got yourself in a fix? Those who had been sent to the countryside during the "cultural revolution" were allowed to come back to town and were allocated jobs.

But you didn't act quickly enough, and it was soon stopped. You lost the opportunity and everyone was mad at you. Then all those whose wages had been frozen were to be refunded. Those who got in first were lucky. Those who were slow got nothing. There are lots of examples. If you're inflexible, you'll lose every chance."

Jin hoped sincerely that Liu would change a bit. But I think, Liu was disgusted by his theory.

October 10

The bonus was issued, and everybody talked about it. What upset me was that they seemed to know all the gory details about the disagreement the previous day, even better than my minutes! Liu became the target of all their gripes, while Jin was worshipped as a hero.

It is unfair to put Liu in such a bad light.

Jin decided to hold a mass meeting to mobilize the workers at this favourable time. At the meeting, he made a short yet moving speech. There was no draft, but he knew what he was talking about.

"All the bonus is given to you, every bit of it. Some people were shocked at such a big sum. Frankly, if we work harder, our profit will rise even more, and next month you'll probably get an even bigger bonus. So long as I'm in charge of the money, I assure you that all that you're entitled to will be given to you without delay, without a cent deducted!"

November 2

It was just my day! From early dawn till mid-afternoon, I only caught a couple of small carp. On my way home, I ran into Jin. He's got a crateful, so I asked where he had been fishing. Instead of replying, he smiled. I reckoned that he must have known the keeper and had fished in his pond. Despite my refusal, he gave me half his fish. When I passed his home, he invited me in. It was difficult to refuse. Besides, I wanted to have a look at his home. A capable man like him, I guessed, must have a nice flat with fashionable furniture. But to my surprise, it was so simple that I could hardly believe it was his.

He asked his daughter, who was doing her homework, to cook, while he offered me a drink. Glowering at him, the girl took up her satchel and went into her granny's room.

So he had to turn to his mother. Reluctantly, the old woman went to the kitchen grumbling. I soon learned why from her complaints.

Jin earned seventy yuan a month, but he only contributed a little for the house-keeping. He smoked good cigarettes and drank good alcohol. Every evening after work, he boozed. When he got home, he made do with a snack. So his wife had to keep his mother and the two children on her salary.

He was no boss at home, not like in the factory.

I never realized Jin was such a bloke.

December 31

The bell had long since rung but the cadres still stayed in the factory at the request of Jin, who had phoned from the bank. The bonus for each worker at the end of the year was a hundred yuan. However, the bank refused to pay the money. Jin had gone to the bank taking the document with him. Trying to persuade them to agree, he had stayed there for a whole day, not even returning for lunch, but no one knew why he asked the cadres to wait for him.

He returned at last. Elated, he told the cadres, "Make it snappy, everybody! We must divide the money and give it to the workers today."

Overjoyed, everyone was raring to go. Under the direction of the head of the financial department, they put into each red envelope a hundred yuan.

Liu called Jin to my office and said emotionally, "Jin, we can't do this. It's all wrong to give bonuses at random! It's not stated in the document that the workers should be given a big sum at the end of the year, is it?"

"But it doesn't say we shouldn't either, does it?" Jin was edgy after a hard day.

"Jin, it's a mistake. We're not going to close down after the New Year, are we?"

"Oh you! You're impossible!" he snapped, barely concealing his irritation. "How many times have I told you that we must give all the bonus to the workers? And we must do it today. Or why did I waste my time at the bank? The higher-ups keep changing their minds. Who can predict the new rule next year? If a new document comes freezing bonuses, then we'll be in trouble! The workers will be furious with us."

"Don't worry! I'll answer for it!"

"But it's been decided at the Party branch committee meeting. You can't change it now." Jin pushed open the door and left. This was the first time I had seen him in a rage.

January 3, 1980

As soon as I began work today I received several documents, one of which stated that all the 1979 bonuses were frozen.

I showed it to Jin. He chuckled and said, "I knew it would happen."

When it was read among the workers, they felt all the more grateful to the manager. Even the cadres couldn't help talking about it. It was really lucky! One day's delay and the bonuses would have been lost. Our manager was a man of vision and action!

This afternoon, we elected a delegate to the People's Congress. The candidate was chosen by the workers themselves this time. It was really democratic. The whole factory was divided into five groups: four workshops and one group of cadres. Jin won the election by an overwhelming majority in the three workshops. He almost got full votes in the cadres' group except three. It had been expected. But one person from the fourth workshop wrote on his voting slip, "Jin Fengchi is an old fox!"

The workers, who were chosen to count the ballot, told someone about this, and it was a blow to Jin's pride.

After work, Jin came to me, a bottle of alcohol in his hand. "Don't go, Wei," he said. "Have pity on a homeless man! Have a drink with me."

He produced some peanuts from his pocket.

"Why don't you go home?" I asked.

"My wife and I had a quarrel last night. I can't go home today, or we'll fight again." He poured himself a drink and gulped it down.

"Jin, you ought to look after your family," I chaffed. "From next month, I'll take most of your salary to them."

He smiled. "Chin-chin! Even an upright official finds it hard to settle a family quarrel. We've been at odds for twenty years, and she can never get the better of me. You want to try? Cheers!"

He drank like a fish. There was nothing to eat except the peanuts, which he nibbled. Before long, his eyes became bloodshot.

He stared at me and remarked all of a sudden, "It's very difficult to please people nowadays. They're a mixture of any and every sort. No matter how hard you try, somebody's always grousing."

I knew what he meant. But it was hard for me to say anything. He had another sip and continued, "I've offended the Party secretary in the interest of the workers. If I'd pleased the Party secretary, I'd have offended the workers. Do you know who cast the three votes against me?"

I was startled. How could he know who voted against him? He must have suspected Liu. But Liu was open and obviously wouldn't vote for him.

"I don't know," was all I could say.

"Luo's one of them. No question!"

I was so shocked, I could hardly believe it. "But he admires you a lot, doesn't he?"

He grinned. "I did him a favour. Anyway, his little tricks can never fool me. He's a ruthless character and very ambitious. But he was right not to vote for me."

"What about the third one?"

Pointing at himself, he said, "That was mine."

He was either drunk or making fun of me.

"It's true," he said, tossing down his drink. Now the liquor had really gone to his head. "I know you must think that I'm as slick as a snake. But I wasn't born like that. The longer you muddle along in this society, the smarter you become. After a few slips and falls even you'd wise up. The more complex the society, the sharper the people. Liu's a good man, but he didn't get as many votes as I. How can good men like him cope in future? If I'd listened to Liu and run the factory in a rigid way, production would have dropped. I'd have offended the workers and there'd be no profit. The state and our leaders wouldn't have been happy about it. Don't think I'm glad because I've got most votes. On the contrary, I feel very bad. I knew Liu wouldn't vote for me, but I voted for him...."

"You're a bit tipsy, Jin," I said, helping him to a bed which was for those on night duty. "Have a rest. I'll go home and fetch you some food."

I deeply regretted that I'd voted in his favour. Though he got most votes, he is not of the calibre of a people's delegate, even in these times.

I'm certain that he'll lose the next election.

Translated by Wang Mingjie

Lulu

—— ZONG PU ——

Since her graduation from Foreign Literature Department of Qinghua University, Zong Pu has worked as an editor and a researcher of foreign literature. Her works possess all the qualities of a woman writer: exquisite, lyric and profound. In 1957 she published "Red Beans" a story which brought her first fame but then criticism too during political campaigns. "Melody in Dreams" won a national award for short stories in 1978. Her recent works include the novelette "Three Generations' Stone" and many short stories and essays.

SAT on the ground, Lulu howled piteously. The rays of the crescent moon filtered through the leaves and the courtyard was splashed with the mottled shadows of the trees and the dull glow of moonlight. Lulu's sad howls went through the walls of the courtyard and started off other howls in the little mountain valley village. Howls in the night always have something sad about them, but Lulu's cries were so bitter and so desperate that they slashed through the warm and still springtime night like a knife.

He barked for all he was worth, long drawn out barks that sounded like sobs, horrible to hear. Could the master that had left him hear him? Where was he? Lulu felt like he was in the wilderness again, a wilderness where there was nothing and where to prove his existence he had to howl out....

Three old rooms extended along the north end of the yard. In the room on the eastern side there was still the glow of lamplight; the room on the western side was already pitch dark, but it was in this room that the faint noise of footsteps and voices were heard all of a sudden followed by the door being opened. Two children in off-white coloured pyjamas came out on tiptoe. A girl of about ten years held a bowl of rice; her little six year old brother hid behind her as soon as he saw Lulu and gripped her pyjama top tightly.

"Lulu, eat this. There's meat in it." The young girl put the bowl of rice down in front of him. Another bowl of rice was already there, untouched.

Lulu looked at them with sad eyes and seemed to calm down. He had very short legs, a pointed fox-like muzzle, and pure white fur. There was a black collar round his neck and this was attached to a tree by a rope.

Lulu's master had been an old Jew. The old man had lived quite close to the village and had died two days earlier. His death, like his birth, had meant nothing to the village. The funeral was soon got out of the way; all that was left was this short-legged white dog, whining constantly, determined not to leave his master's house. Pople had beaten him, but he just kept circling the house. The owner of the house had had an excellent idea: "Give him to Mr Fan. That sort of dog's only fit for that lot downstream." "That lot downstream" was what the villagers called people from other provinces. So Lulu had been taken to the Fans against his will and had been tied to a big tree in their courtyard. He had been there for three days already.

The two children had always been Lulu's friends. They used to go round to the old Jew's to play; they were probably the only guests the old man ever had. Th old man used to make lovely fully-furnished little paper houses. The children would roll a little glass marble that they had brought from home through the house. The old man would make Lulu shake hands with them; Lulu would stretch out his paw and shake hands with them one at a time, time and time again. Lulu would often jump onto the arm of the armchair, press his white muzzle against the white head of the old man and look at the two children. Those days his eyes were docile and warm and even seemed to laugh.

Now the old man was gone and there was just Lulu. A miserable, howling Lulu.

"Lulu, stay with us. Do you understand Chinese?" the girl asked softly. "Do you want to shake hands?" She had repeated the question many, many times those last three days, but Lulu no longer stretched out his paw, he just started howling again.

But this time Lulu didn't howl, he just panted heavily as though he had been running a long distance. The little girl stretched her hand to stroke his head. Her little brother tried to stop her as Lulu was famous for biting people; his speciality was biting them in the heels, making no noise. "It's okay," she said. "You won't bite me, will you Lulu?" As she spoke, she rested her hand on Lulu's head. Lulu trembled at the contact and his hair bristled slightly. The old man was always stroking him, from his head down to his tail. The old man's hand had been heavy whereas this hand was light, but its softness soon put him at ease. Panting, he stretched his paw to the girl.

"Good Lulu!" The girl shook hands with him happily. "Mum, Lulu wants to come and live with us!"

Mum came out into the courtyard and after the little girl introduced her, she shook hands with Lulu too, as did little brother of course. Mum reproached her daughter gently: "Why did you give all the meat to Lulu? What are we going to eat tomorrow?"

The girl hung her head down and said nothing, but her little brother came to the rescue: "Let's just eat nothing tomorrow."

"But what about your father?" sighed mum. "He's so tired." Then she turned to Lulu: "Just don't bark tonight, okay?"

They all went to bed. Only dad was still up, writing by the dim glow of the paraffin lamp. Lulu felt a lump in his throat several times, but looking through the window and seeing the figure hunched over the table, he gulped back his sobs and there was just a sort of gurgling noise in his throat.

Lulu began eating again and although he did whine every now and then, he took a definite turn for the better. The girl and her mother let him off his rope, constantly reminding little brother not to leave the courtyard door open. The courtyard was part of a large, sprawling old temple. The temple had many rooms and many of the townspeople had taken refuge from the bombing there; so the previously deserted temple was now full of the signs of human inhabitation.

When the young girl took Lulu to meet her father, her father demanded that Lulu sit down and wave his paws in front of him in greeting. "Go on, Lulu!" shouted little brother. Lulu hadn't recovered enough to be in the mood for playing games, but he did it anyway. "He understands Chinese!" the two children cried delightedly. Lulu put down his front paws and then shook hands with Mr Fan too. Mr Fan cast aside his habitual indifference for a moment and looked at Lulu carefully. "What does the name Lulu mean? Is it Hebrew or something? He looks like a fox. We ought to call him silver fox." Although he was well respected in the school he taught at, at home no one took any notice of what dad said, and so Lulu remained Lulu.

Lulu was soon on good terms with the family's cat, Feifei. At the start, Feifei was terrified of Lulu. She would arch her back and retreat spitting, to show him that she wasn't to be provoked. For his part, Lulu displayed not the slightest hostility, knowing that he was supposed to protect everything belonging to the family. He stuck his paw out to the cat and the children fell about laughing. Eventually Feifei understood that this was a friend and cat and dog sniffed each other as a sign that they would live peacefully together.

Ten days later, everyone thought that it would be safe to let Lulu out. As he never stayed out very long, everyone soon set their minds at rest about him. However, one day Lulu hesitated a little by the door and then went back to the old Jew's house. When he found the door locked, he sat on the doorstep and howled. It was always the same sadness, the same deep sorrow. He remembered his misfortunes, and his heart broke. Lulu tried hard to remember what direction that old man had gone. Suddenly he was surrounded by people: "What are you howling at, dog?" They threw stones at him and he ran off, but instead of going home, he headed downhill towards the town.

Lulu ran along with his tongue hanging out, his short legs preventing him from going very fast. He ran as fast as he could as there was a mystery he wanted to clear up.

The country road had no traffic and few pedestrians; by each side of the road there were all sorts of wild shrubs forming two natural hedgerows. The white dog looked like a fluttering white feather moving in the hedgerow. Now and then other dogs would run up — those big, clumsy looking dogs that the villagers called "four-eyed dogs" because of the white hairs that circled their eyes — and they wanted to sniff Lulu or scrap with him. But Lulu just dodged them and ran on desperately towards the answer of the mystery.

He ran most of the day and arrived in the town at dusk. He stopped in front of an old foreign style building. He lay down in front of the closed door and let out a sigh from time to time. This was where he and the old man had lived together once: maybe his master was there now. Couldn't he hear Lulu crying? People opened the windows and came outside to take a look, but none of them had white hair. Someone said, "That's the old Jew's dog." "Why's he come back here?" No one asked what had become of the old man.

For two days and two nights Lulu crouched by the door. Then people got fed up and decided to do something about it. On the morning of the third day, several people approached Lulu armed with ropes and sticks. Someone threw him a bone and called his name. Despite being hungry, thirsty and completely exhausted, Lulu didn't budge an inch. Then he remembered the off-white pyjamas and those gentle little hands offering him the rice. He looked back at the door one last time, hoping that the old man would walk out of it at this precise moment. But he didn't. Lulu jumped up, slipped between the mens' legs and ran out of the town.

The solution of his mystery was that he'd never see the old man again. He didn't know that the place where the old man had gone was a place that everyone, including Lulu, goes to sooner or later.

Mum and the little girl both blamed little brother, saying it was he who had let Lulu out. The little boy wanted to show he was tough and so he went to play by the tree alone. He said nothing but he felt pretty bad inside. Stupid Lulu! How could he leave the people who loved him? Mum came to collect Lulu's food dish and drinking bowl, ready to throw them in the bin. It was dusk on the third day and he wouldn't be coming back.

The little girl put the dish back in its original place. It had only been three days, he'd be back.

All of a sudden there was the noise of something scratching at the courtyard door. The little girl pressed her ear against the door and listened carefully, then she suddenly rushed to open the door. "Lulu!" Sure enough it was Lulu. He sat in the threshold, panting and staring at the three of them. The little girl leaned over and hugged him and he licked the little girl's hand. "Lulu!" Her brother rushed over to welcome him. Lulu licked his hand too, and then ran around him twice, taking care not to knock him over. Next Lulu greeted mum, clasping his paws in front of him, but avoiding licking her as he knew she didn't like it. Then he went indoors to find Mr Fan. He slipped under the desk and rubbed against Mr Fan's legs. That evening everyone was happy. Even Feifei welcomed Lulu, timidly sniffing noses with him.

From then on, Lulu was part of the family. He guarded the house faithfully, obeyed orders strictly, and apart from the fact that he often went out at night, his behaviour was irreproachable. He was more than a dog; he even helped Feifei catch mice. When a mouse dived down the sewer and Feifei was rushing frantically back and forth to prevent it escaping, Lulu would go and guard one end of the sewer with Feifei at the other end, and then he would stick his muzzle through the gap in the flagstones covering the sewer and growl softly. The mouse would naturally go charging out the other end, only to end up under Feifei's claws. Dad remarked that this proved that Lulu was a hunting dog, or at least the descendent of a hunting dog.

When the little girl and her brother went into town to buy beancurd, Lulu would always accompany them. Lulu would have loved to carry the basket for them, but his legs were too short and so he just had to run along carrying nothing whatsoever. He would often run ahead of them, disappear, and then burst out from a hedge a moment later. Somehow he always managed to stop himself in time and never knock the children over. Sometimes the old beancurd seller would give Lulu a bone and Lulu would thank him by clasping his paws in front of him. This always made the old man hoot with laughter. Sometimes the little girl and her brother would play with the village children. On these occasions Lulu would sit patiently to one side as though he were interested in their games too.

A clear little stream flowed by the village, with wild flowers growing on its banks and flanked by shady willows. The three of them often came here, running around in the shade of the willows or sitting down and telling each other stories. Mr Tang, a friend of dad's who lived in the neighbouring province, visited the Fan's once and seeing the three of them like this, he sighed that if he was a painter he would do a canvas of the two coarse-clothed children and the white dog sitting under the willows by the river. Such a picture would help him to forget the scars of war, he said.

According to Mr Tang, Lulu was from a noble race of dogs. However, that was of no concern to the Fan family. Lulu, if anything, cared even less.

In fact, Lulu usually didn't take much notice when stories were being told. He would often plunge into the little stream for a swim. He was a born swimmer, his pointed muzzle always keeping above the rippling green water. Mum didn't approve of them going down to the river, and every time Lulu came back soaked she would reproach him: "Where have you been taking them? What would happen if they fell in?" Lulu's ears would prick up as he listened to her. It was like he was the big brother who had been left in charge.

Although mum reproached them, since they promised they wouldn't go in the water, the children were still allowed to go down to the stream pretty often. There was nothing wrong about that. However, one time Lulu really did make a really bad mistake. Mr Fan used to go and teach in town, and as a rule, usually stayed in town three days out of the week. Mum had to go and look after a neighbour's child who was ill. Mum had attended nursing school for two years and in the mountain village she found herself duty-bound to act as a nurse. As she left she said to Lulu, "If you weren't here, I couldn't leave the children at home ... but since you are, I can go without worrying. I'm going to leave them with you, okay?" Lulu listened attentively and wagged his tail. "No going out at night. You sleep indoors, okay?" Lulu felt the strength of mum's hand stroking his back. He wouldn't let her down.

Lulu often went out hunting at night. On the thickly wooded mountain there were plenty of hares and squirrels. He would hunt all night and would always return full of energy, his coat glistening with an aura of wildness and life. The prey helped to supplement the mildewed rice of the Fans. The rice was Mr Fan's wage but its mildewy taste overpowered any nice flavour that it might have had. Actually, Lulu was interested in neither the rice nor the many little worms that were in it. Those few days Lulu didn't leave the children for an instant, even staying in at night. If they hadn't gone to the market on the fourth day, then Lulu's canine weakness wouldn't have been revealed.

The road that passed below the mountain village was the place where all the neighbouring villages held an always bustling market twice a week. Chicken, fish, meat, eggs, basins and jars, birds and cats were all up for sale. The little girl had come to buy pine needles, which are excellent for kindling fires. She bought a bundle and pulled little brother away by the hand, preferring not to look at all the lovely things that they knew perfectly well they couldn't afford. Little brother agreed with her and strode off on his little legs with added vigour. When they had gone a little distance they discovered that Lulu was missing. "Lulu," the little girl called softly. Then they heard laughs and shouts coming from the area where the meat sellers were: "Do some tricks for us, whitey. Do a somersault!" The two children rushed forward and saw Lulu sitting up and begging, desperate for the meat.

"Lulu!" The little girl shouted angrily. Lulu jumped up and ran over to her side, his head turned back and staring at the dangling piece of beef. There was also pork, mutton, donkey and horse meat on display, but it was the beef that fascinated Lulu and that he longed to eat. Fresh, bloody meat like he'd eaten every day before. The smell of the raw meat brought back the chase, the kill, the victory, the freedom; it brought back the boundless forests and the wild mountains and made him feel confused and disorientated.

The meat seller recognized the girl and her brother and laughed. "That's the Fan's dog," he said and then sliced off a bit of meat and put it in the little girl's basket. The villagers all sympathized with destitute teachers: they were very learned, but they had no idea how to raise dogs.

The girl wouldn't take the meat at any price. Dragging little brother with her, she walked away. At this moment Lulu pounced in from the side, grabbed the meat, and took to his heels.

"Lulu!" Carrying the basket full of pine needles, the little girl tore after him out of breath, with little brother following behind. The men all laughed. It was an unmalicious, happy laugh, but it grated upon the little girl's ears.

When they got home, Lulu had put the meat down in front of him and was sitting there staring at it. Lulu went to welcome the girl and tried to ingratiate himself, obviously looking for permission to eat the meat, but the little girl just threw the basket down, held her head in her hands, and burst into tears.

Her little brother gave her his handkerchief anxiously and stamping his foot with rage, he had a go at Lulu: "If you like meat so much, why don't you leave? Go into the mountains and find somebody else to live with!" Lulu circled anxiously round the girl, prodding her gently with his paw and nudging her with his head. He didn't look at the meat again.

The little girl buried the meat under the tree in the courtyard. Later her mother paid for the meat but she didn't reproach Lulu. Since the incident was over and done with, there was no point in recriminations. Lulu gradually got used to eating less meat, only going out hunting every now and then. He seemed to prefer the warmth of his loved ones to the thrills of the wild. Dad said that dogs too could learn to eat simply.

Lulu made one other serious mistake, this time an irreparable one. He and his friend Feifei the cat often used to play together. He would push Feifei with his muzzle, she would jump up and pounce on him, and then they would have a sort of play fight. When the days got colder, Feifei used to leave her basket to go to sleep by Lulu. That year Feifei gave birth to a litter of kittens and began to get more aggressive towards Lulu. The hapless Lulu stuck his muzzle in her basket to sniff the kittens and Feifei took a swipe at his nose, making him bleed. Lulu was angry, but he still wanted to play with her, so he picked her up gently in his mouth and took her outside. Suddenly Feifei gave a horrible screech, lay shaking on the ground for a few moments, and then stopped breathing. Lulu stood there petrified, then he walked over to her and prodded her with his muzzle. He rolled her over a few times but she didn't fight back like she had before. She just didn't move.

When mum came out to have a look she found Lulu sitting next to Feifei, whining. Seeing her, he stared dumbly and then went down on his stomach and crawled towards her, looking up at her furtively. She was livid: "You stupid dog! See what you've done! What about those little kittens? Are you going to feed them?" She pushed the basket of kittens under his nose. Lulu scuttled backwards terrified, still not daring to stand up. The little girl and her brother both tried to intercede on Lulu's behalf, but mum was determined to give him a thrashing. Lulu moved backwards into the inner room. Thinking he was going to run off, the three of them followed him in and saw him at dad's feet. He sat up and clasped his front paws together, his face a picture of misery, begging dad to speak up for him. Dad stroked Lulu's head, and seeing mum's murderous expression, said, "Only give him a couple of clouts, okay?" Now mum calmed down for the first time and said that she wouldn't hit him excessively, but that he had to be beaten as he was a dog and wouldn't remember the lesson otherwise. She dealt Lulu three heavy blows and, although he whimpered piteously, he lay there submissively with no thought of running off, in spite of the fact that the doors to both the room and the courtyard were wide open. Dad left his desk and came over to Lulu: "Most people can stand light punishments, but run off if the punishment is heavy. You stood a heavy punishment. Well done."

After his beating, Lulu sneaked off to his basket. The little girl and her brother were forbidden by their mother to go to him, because she said he needed time to repent first. The little girl was sad for Feifei and her kittens, but sad for Lulu too, knowing that he hadn't killed Feifei on purpose. There was no food for Lulu that evening so she secretly took him some water and leftovers. Lulu licked her hand and whined.

If you weighed up Lulu's mistakes and his good points, his good points were by far the more numerous. One afternoon mum was called out to look after an expectant mother. She had originally arranged to deliver some medicine to a far off village that day, and now this task passed to her daughter. The little girl wrapped the medicines up happily. Her little brother and Lulu wanted to accompany her, but it was too far for them; anyway, the little boy wasn't feeling too good, so it was decided that Lulu would stay at home with him. Mother and daughter left the house together and then went their separate ways. Lulu and little brother came as far as the monastery door to see them off and watched the pale yellow of the girl's home-spun clothes disappearing into the green thicket.

When mum got to her patient's house, she found the woman already in labour. She attended to her until the baby was born and didn't leave until she was satisfied everything was as it should be. When she got home that evening it was past ten already and all she could see in the house was the baleful glow of an oil lamp. Lulu was whining and padding about restlessly and the moment little brother saw mum, he rushed over and burst into tears: "Sister's not back yet!"

Father was away, so mother calmed herself down, went to the house of a colleague nearby, woke the professor up, then woke the owner of the house up, and then woke up all the people that these two thought would be needed. Lanterns and torches were prepared hastily. Lulu stood whining at mother's side and trod on her feet to get her attention. Little brother suddenly understood: "Let Lulu find her!" Mother hesitated a moment and then said, "Go on, Lulu. Find her!" Lulu shot off like an arrow and disappeared quickly into the night.

Lulu ran with all his might. The light aroma that was a mixture of the little girl's own scent and the herbs she was carrying guided Lulu as he ran. He was dead to the existence of anything else: the night, the trees and the gurgle of running water on either side of the road were all unreal; only the barely discernable scent of the girl was real. One moment he lost the scent. He avoided the bridge, went down to the stream, swam across it, clambered onto another little road and there was the scent again. Lulu felt no smugness at his cleverness, he just carried on running hard. He ran all the way to a village in a neighbouring valley.

The village was pitch dark and everyone was asleep. He ran up to a house and scratched anxiously at the door. The scent stopped here, so it was obvious that the girl had gone in. He scratched at the door a few times, then followed the courtyard wall round to the back door. Suddenly he picked up the scent again, this time minus the herbs. The little girl had walked out of the back door, crossed the village and then taken the little winding path to the mountains. Lulu ran on for another quarter of an hour, not daring to rest, running his heart out with his tongue hanging out. The trees became more numerous and the grass deeper. The thick nocturnal smell of the plants confused Lulu and he strained to catch that familiar scent again, seeking it in the thick grass. The little animals in the wild grass fled in all directions in their fright, but Lulu was too absorbed to notice them. At that moment, even if the most delicious prey had appeared he wouldn't have given it a second glance.

At last, under a tree and by a rock Lulu saw the pale yellow home-spun cloth again. The little girl was leaning against the rock, fast asleep. Lulu leapt forward joyfully. He frisked about a moment then sat down and stared at the little girl. After a while he circled her twice before finally pawing at her gently.

She woke and looked around her, astonished: the crescent moon lit up the dark trees, the rank grass, the mountain and the rocks. Suddenly she cried out: "Lulu, we've got to get home. Mum'll be worried sick." She wanted to hold Lulu by the collar but she was too tall so she took off her blouse and tied one end to his collar. Lulu led the way obediently, constantly turning his head back to look at her, making happy little whining noises.

"Lulu, I just wanted to try and have a really long dream like Rip van Winkle," the little girl confided. "I hadn't dreamt it was so late, but at least it wasn't twenty years."

As they came to the dyke they first saw a twinkling light far off in a thicket and then in no time at all, the rise and fall of human voices: it was the search party. The men saw snow-white Lulu first. Many voices started calling him and asking him questions, as though he could answer. His answer was to lead the little girl to them. The little girl threw herself into her mother's arms and Lulu looked up apprehensively from where he lay, scared that the little girl was going to be punished like everyone who worried or angered mother, but mother just squeezed her and asked her tenderly: "Weren't you scared of not seeing me when you woke up?" "Just before I went to sleep I got scared that I really would sleep twenty years. But I couldn't help it, I just fell asleep anyway." Everyone laughed and then talked about the terrible danger she'd been in with all the wolves that there were in the mountains. No one took any notice of Lulu.

When dad came back from the town, he found Lulu and shook his paw gratefully. Lulu had already more or less forgotten his exploit, but the fact that the last few days he'd been getting beef in his food made him very happy.

Time passed by and the girl and her brother started going to the nearby school which had moved to the village from the city: the girl at the secondary school, her brother still at primary school. Everyday Lulu would stand at the monastery door, watch them go, and then go to the bottom of the hill and wait for them to come back. Lulu still played in the grass and accompanied them when they went to buy beancurd. Then the young girl started falling ill frequently. Every time she had to stay in bed Lulu became very nervous as though he could smell some sort of danger. The old beancurd seller said that she must have offended the mountain gods and that the family should lay an offering at the place where Lulu had found her. Mum and dad thanked him but mumbled something about "malnutrition" and "tuberculosis". Lulu didn't understand. If he had done he would have gone to visit the mountain spirit himself, in place of his little friend.

Fortunately, most of the time the girl was like everybody else, and so Lulu's worrying never lasted long. The days flowed by gently and happily like the bubbling little stream by the village. If Lulu had died at this point in time he would have been the happiest dog in the world. However, Lulu was very healthy, his white coat glistened and he was in superb physical condition. Nobody knew how old Lulu was, but it was obvious that he would live a long time yet.

The little stream gurgled gently, unaware of the torrents and waves of the large rivers. Finally the news of Japan's surrender reached the village and the whole village seethed with an excitement greater than that of any market day. It was an end to all the suffering. To the other three's surprise, dad squeezed mum tight, and said with tears in his eyes, "You've had it too hard, too hard." Mum sobbed, dad embraced daughter and son, and the four of them hugged each other. Lulu rushed to and fro, shoving his head between them. In this dear little family that had suffered so much, there had to be Lulu.

"Let's go to Beiping!" said little brother with a pleased look on his face. His graceful elder sister crouched and hugged Lulu. At that point no one had thought that Lulu wouldn't be able to go with them.

The family were completely destitute, and the house contained nothing but two precious children and the manuscripts that dad had written over the years by the light of the paraffin lamp, so moving house posed no difficulties in itself, only the problem of what to do about Lulu. If they left him here, he would go mad. In the end they decided to take him as far as T city and leave him there with the dog-loving Mr Tang.

After several days of bustling preparation, the family boarded the bus. During that time Lulu had been a bag of nerves, and at night he had been having nightmares constantly. He dreamt he saw dad, mum, the girl and little brother all leaving with just him left behind, running alone in a wilderness. He couldn't smell any familiar scent, which made him frightened and upset. During his dreams he whined out loud, and then mum would walk over to him and wake him up. Mum asked dad: "Do you think dogs can dream?" "I think ... well, Lulu can at least."

To his surprise, Lulu boarded the bus too. He was besides himself with happiness and completely reassured. He made a special effort to please mum and rubbed himself against her, but she just yelled: "Go away! It's already bad enough on this bus without you doing that!" Lulu hastily squeezed between the girl and little brother. The three friends were jolted around by the bus, and they watched the green hills slowly getting left behind. At each corner the road would disappear and then reappear suddenly, stretching away into the distance.

The day after they set off, the girl got ill again. Dad remarked that it was a shame she couldn't enjoy the scenery. She lay down when she was on the bus and stayed laid down when they got to the hotel. Lulu was more worried now than he had ever been when she had been ill before. He refused to leave her side even for an instant, and the panic-stricken and miserable look in his eye gave mum a terrible feeling of foreboding and unhappiness: "She's not that bad, Lulu, don't worry." Mum chased him out of the room, so he took up post at the door. Little brother felt sorry for him and gave him a detailed explanation of what was happening: how they could cure sister's illness at Beiping, but that owing to the traffic they couldn't take Lulu along; about what a good man Uncle Tang was and how he would certainly be nice to Lulu. Lulu didn't understand, but he listened quietly, licking little brother's hand from time to time.

Near T city there was a huge waterfall whose noise could be heard ten li away. When the bus arrived there, everyone got out and climbed up to the pavilion for admiring the waterfall. The little girl was running a temperature but insisted on getting out of the bus. With dad on her left, mum on her right, Lulu in front and little brother bringing up the rear, they went up to the pavilion. The raging water fell down over a hundred metres of precipice and formed a lttle lake in the emerald hills; a mist of water vapour reached the pavilion. The girl felt as though the thick, white, semi-translucent curtain of water and the raging thunder were far, far away from her. She wanted desperately to get a closer look but they seemed to retreat before her until she could see nothing and fainted on her father's shoulder.

That was the last time Lulu saw his friend. Within a few days he was looking sallow, his white coat having lost all its lustre. His food at the Tangs always had beef in it, but he would just sniff at it and walk off, no matter how much little brother tried to encourage him. Little brother was now taller than his sister and Lulu could no longer knock him over. Lulu stood outside the big house, whining: he hated the smell and he wanted to leave. If he had known that at that moment the litle girl was looking out of the first floor window and watching him for the very last time, he would gladly have stood there a lifetime, never leaving it.

The day the Fans left, Unle Tang locked Lulu in the garden. The Fans went to the hospital to pick up the girl and then went straight to the airport. Knowing that they would never see Lulu again, brother and sister cried bitterly together. They didn't hear the heart-rending, distorted howls, didn't see Lulu fighting to break free of the rope, the fur on his neck all rubbed off. They flew away, leaving their childhood friend behind them.

Lulu searched desperately for his masters, searching so long that Uncle Tang thought he had gone mad. Uncle Tang kept trying to shake Lulu's paw and saying in a friendly voice: "You'll stay here, won't you, Lulu? It's all settled, eh?"

Eventually Lulu began to gradually calm down. Then one day he disappeared. Six months later, after everyone had assumed that he was dead, he suddenly reappeared at the Tangs. He was much thinner, and what coat he had left was now completely grey; there were bare patches where his pink skin showed through and his collar had disappeared, being replaced by an identification disk from another province. He had obviously gone back, searching for the answer to the mystery. If Lulu had been able to write, he would probably have written about how he had braved dew and frost, how he had crossed mountains and forded rivers; how he had been beaten and tied up but had managed to escape and continue his odyssey each time; how he had seen the monastery on the mountain once again but had not been able to find his masters. Or maybe he just would have written nothing, blind to the miseries of the outside world, obsessed only with solving the riddle in his heart. He went, and then he undertook every hardship to return, so as not to upset the arrangements his masters had made. Of course no man or dog could ever really understand what really went on in his heart.

The Tangs had known about Lulu's activities, but what they didn't know was that he delighted in going to watch the waterfall. He would often go and sit in front of the fall, watching the cascading water and howling sorrowfully.

June, 1980

Translated by Christopher Smith

The Story of a Living Buddha

●

—— MALQINHU ——

Malqinhu, a Mongolian, was born in 1930 in Tumud Banner, Liaoning Province. In 1945 he joined the army as a cavalry reporter, and went on to become a writer in a cultural troupe. While working on the Horqin Grasslands in 1951 he published his first story "People on the Horqin Grasslands". Since then, he has published many works, most notably the novel The Boundless Grassland, *and three short story collections. He has also written several film scripts. "The Story of a Living Buddha" won a national literary award.*

MY home was a village named Bayan Hot, the seat of our Banner Prince. In this village I passed my "golden childhood", now shrouded in a somewhat dim and mysterious light which evokes a deep nostalgia in me.

Our neighbour was a lama named Tegus. According to tradition, lamas should not marry. However, Tegus was not only married, but even had a family. I still have not managed to understand how this could have come about.

Lama Tegus had three sons. The eldest was called Hasenjiab, the second Garhe and the third Malaha. Malaha was the same age as I. When we were only beginning to learn to speak, the two of us with our bare bottoms played together on the sand dumps in front of our houses. By the time we were old enough to wear open-seat pants, we had already become fast friends.

Little Malaha was a very handsome boy. He had fine eyebrows and clear eyes, red lips, white teeth, a round face, a high nose and a full head of jet-black curly hair. Only his ears were too long, and rather unattractive. But our elders said that this was a "feature of Buddha", and that persons who had such long dangling ears were destined to have good fortune. I am not too sure exactly what is meant by good fortune. But anyhow Malaha was then much wiser, abler and bolder than I. I admired him very much.

My family was extremely poor. His was a little better off. In the spring of the year when I was about six years old, our village was afflicted with famine. With the exception of the Banner Prince and a few households of Bayan,* the families in our village had nothing to eat. One evening little Malaha came to me and said, "Get your basket, let's go and climb the elm trees and collect elm-pods!"

"Where shall we go on a dark night like this?"

"That large pasture in front of the Banner Prince's mansion, where we can climb up those big elms."

I was frightened on hearing this, and said quickly, "They are holy trees. Haven't you seen people go there every year to kowtow to them? Who'd dare climb up them? The Prince would cut off our legs if he knew."

Malaha waved his hand and said, "*Ha*i! Holy trees, what's that? Who's ever seen a holy spirit? Have you seen one?"

I shook my small bald head.

"Let's go then before the moon comes up. Hurry up and climb the trees and get the pods!"

Elm-pods were good to eat, mixed with flour chaff and steamed. Especially in famine years, they were a rare relish for the poor. Knowing that we had nothing to cook tomorrow, I summoned up my courage, took my basket and followed him to the large pasture in front of the Banner Prince's mansion.

Little Malaha was a real devil. He saw not far from us an old spotted cow grazing with her neck stretched out. Telling me to do as he did, he lay down on the grass and crept slowly like a frog towards the cow. At first, I didn't know what was in his mind. Then I saw him drive the cow before him with a branch, to shield us so that we could proceed behind her towards a holy tree. I then realized that this would prevent the sentries on the fort of the Banner Prince's mansion from discovering us. The old spotted cow was quite obedient. Covering us with her huge body, she led us to a large holy tree and then swaying her long tail moved aside to graze.

The dark night made the large holy tree appear intensely black, swaying to and fro in a way that struck terror into me. While I was standing there dumbly, little Malaha had already nimbly climbed up the tree. Following him, I also climbed up. It was truly a holy tree, still flourishing in such a dry season. Soon we had gathered two large basketfuls of elm-pods. A red, big moon had risen in the eastern sky, seeming so tender, mysterious and affectionate. Malaha and I were both fascinated by the bewitching and majestic sight of the moon rising. We carefully hung our baskets full of elm-pods on a branch, and waved our hands happily at the smiling moon from our stations high up the holy tree....

The moon rose higher, casting its silvery light all over the pasture. I

---

*The Mongolian word for "rich man".

suddenly thought about our return home and asked Malaha anxiously, "The moon's so bright, how can we escape from the pasture?"

"We must ask the old cow to help us again," he said.

When we had got away from the pasture, we put the two baskets of elm-pods on the ground and rolled about in high glee. After the tension of the escape followed by our joyous play, we were quite tired. We lay down with outstretched limbs on the dew-soaked meadow and gazed silently at the deep blue night sky. Our limited powers of imagination now had free play. What is the sky made of? Why is it such a deep blue? Is there another world behind the deep blue sky, and are there virtuous and cultivated persons residing there, as the old Buddhists said? There certainly wouldn't be a fierce Banner Prince, nor wretched poor people, and what's more, there wouldn't be any need to live on elm-pods....

The following day, both our households had a sweet-smelling meal of steamed elm-pods mixed with flour chaff.

That year we had a dry spring and a water-logged summer. Rain fell continuously from early summer, and the stream in our neighbourhood rose high enough for people to catch small fish in it. One day, little Malaha came running to find me, his brow beaded with sweat.

"Let's go and catch fish in the stream," he said. "It's nice and cool."

I was feeling unbearably bored at home, so I went with him without a murmur.

The flooding had ended. The water in the stream was so clear that one could see down to the bottom. At first sight, the multi-coloured pebbles in the stream appeared like so many leaping small fish. We stripped off our clothes and plunged in. A pleasant feeling of coolness spread rapidly all over my body, and even penetrated into my heart. We stood stark naked in the stream, splashing water on each other and frolicking about, forgetting our original object of catching fish.

The next day, around noon, what was to me an almost unthinkable piece of news circulated through the village. Little Malaha, who just yesterday was my bare-bottomed fishing companion, had been chosen by the Gegen Monastery as a living Buddha! To say that he was chosen as a Living Buddha is not quite correct. According to Buddhist teaching, a Living Buddha is a reincarnation of another in a previous life. This is to say, the Living Buddha in his previous life writes down in liquid gold on red satin where and in which family he will be born again, puts it in a sealed engraved silver pot and keeps it in a certain secret place. After the death of the Living Buddha, a conference of senior lamas, presided over by his erstwhile "sutra teacher", is held, the silver pot is unsealed in public and the testament is read out to the meeting. Then, in accordance with the directions given in the occult and riddle-like posthumous script, a search for the reincarnated Living Buddha is made.

It was reported that the previous Living Buddha of the Gegen Monastery had written in his posthumous document that the characteristics of the family he was to be born into were as follows: First, the first syllables of the names of the three sons were in the order of the Mongolian alphabet — A, Na, Ba, Ha, Ga, Ma...; thus if the first syllable of the name of his eldest brother was "Ha", that of the second brother would be "Ga" and that of himself "Ma". Secondly, eight hundred and ten steps to the southeast of their house was a large tree which could not be encircled by five persons with their hands joined together. And thirdly, eight hundred and ten steps to the northwest of their house and three feet underground was a lump of granite as big as an ox head. It was not enough to find a family with three sons whose names began with the syllables Ha, Ga and Ma, but the family's home must conform to the two other circumstances described. Only then could the lamas declare that the new Living Buddha's family had been found.

The envoys sent out by the Gegen Monastery took several years to make secret investigations and inquiries according to the directions given, and finally concluded that my little companion Malaha was the new Living Buddha they were looking for. Thus little Malaha who was catching fish in the river with me yesterday changed overnight from a boy into a deity the eighth Living Buddha of the Gegen Monastery.

This was a momentous event. All the Buddhists in the village seemed to share some of the glory. Every one of them was smiling and the whole village was bubbling over like a cauldron of boiling water. At noon, the leading Senior Lama of the Gegen monastery announced that, beginning from two o'clock in the afternoon, Living Buddha Malaha would receive the worship of the villagers.

My mother was a devout Buddhist. She told me to wash my hands and face and get ready to go at the appointed time to pay homage to Living Buddha Malaha. Hearing this, I couldn't help laughing aloud. Seeing me act in such a sacrilegious manner, she gave my ear a sharp tug and sternly bade me, "Don't laugh!" I dared not laugh again.

Soon it was two o'clock, and Mother took me to kowtow to Malaha. My childish curiosity made me want to find out what my little companion who had become a Living Buddha now looked like.

I followed my mother to the gate of Malaha's home. A large number of men, women and children had already gathered there. As Malaha was now a Living Buddha, the distinction of generations in the outside world did not apply to him any more. Those he called uncles and aunts or even granddads and grandmas yesterday had also to come and pay homage to him and receive his benediction today. When after some time it was our turn to go inside and kowtow to the Living Buddha, my heart began to beat fast, for I was somehow afraid. I was pushed indoors.

I saw Malaha sitting upright in the centre of the *kang*, with a borrowed redwood *kang* table in front of him, upon which was placed a volume of Buddhist sutras and a silver pot containing "holy water" with a peacock feather stuck in it. This peacock feather was used to spray "holy water" on worshippers. When I entered, little Malaha at once smiled at me. I don't know whether I myself smiled or not. On either side of Malaha sat his mother and his "sutra teacher". The old sutra teacher's eyelids and lips were loose and pendulous, and there were two deep furrows on each side of his mouth. His face was gloomy and he looked quite frightening. I dared not keep looking at him. My mother had already knelt down on the ground, putting her palms together devoutly and kowtowing three times. I hastened to imitate her and kowtow to Malaha. When I had kowtowed a first time and lifted my head to look at him, our eyes met. He smiled his usual innocent smile, waved his hand and made a face at me. I dared not smile, but he was so pleased with himself that he laughed outright. The sutra teacher was evidently much offended at such behaviour, and made two loud sniffs in warning. Malaha's mother became alarmed and hastened to caution him in a kind but stern tone, "Living Buddha, sit quietly and don't be naughty!"

When my mother and I had finished our worship, Malaha took up the sutra volume, of which he didn't know a word, and with it touched our foreheads lightly. He then sprayed some drops of "holy water" on our heads with the peacock plume. The ritual was concluded. When Mother was taking me out of the house, I boldly looked back once again at little Malaha to take leave of him. My little companion raised his eyebrows and knowingly winked at me as if to say: You just wait; we'll go and climb the tree again to gather elm-pods, and to catch fish in the stream.

I could not help thinking: Malaha had not been changed into a Buddha, he was still my little companion.

At four o'clock the next morning, Living Buddha Malaha was to set out on his trip to take his place in the monastery. All our villagers went very early to the sides of the earthen road which was sprinkled with water, to wait there and see him off. I woke up at dawn that day, and the thought that I would soon have to part with my little companion made me extremely sad. I wanted to cry when standing among the crowd outside the village. But the atmosphere was so solemn and quiet that I did not dare. I just stared at the entrance of the village where Malaha was to appear.

Soon there came the boisterous sounds of a lama band, which consisted of gold and silver bugles, ram-horn trumpets, a big bass trumpet more than ten feet long and borne by two small lamas, eight drums and ten pairs of cymbals. There was nothing musical about the fearful, ear-splitting din produced. In this great hubbub, a large golden yellow object moved towards us, coming nearer and nearer. The people kneeling waiting on the sides of the road began to kowtow incessantly as the golden yellow object approached. The Living Buddha Malaha's train was now before us. Hoping for a final look at my little companion, I knelt there dumbly, forgetting to pay my respects. "Kowtow, kowtow!" Mother urged. In confusion I bent over once, and then lifted my head again to look at Malaha. Ha! I saw a train of nine big tall horses each covered with a large yellow satin cloth, reaching almost to the ground. Apart from the lamas who were acting as grooms, the priests and members of Malaha's family followed behind the nine horses. Malaha, dressed in a yellow robe, looking lonely and pathetic, rode on the fifth horse. Although there were four lamas looking after him on both sides, he was still very much afraid of being thrown, and was gingerly holding fast the reins. When he came before me, he looked over our bent heads. He seemed to have seen me, and again, not to have seen me. His thick eyebrows were closely knitted and his face was full of the pain and sorrow of parting from his native place, his relatives and companions. It seemed to me that there were tears in the corners of his eyes.

The golden yellow object gradually moved away and was lost in the yellow dust. The villagers got up one after another, their foreheads all stained with earth. Those who had kowtowed more had more earth on their foreheads. These people were so deeply immersed in religious devotion that they forgot to wipe their foreheads with their cuffs.

When I followed the crowd back to the village, I felt as if robbed of something, or as if two young oxen were fighting inside my heart. It was unbearable! I did not eat or drink that whole day. I went alone to sit silently with fixed eyes in the shade of the trees on the large pasture ground. When it had grown very late Mother found me and took me home.

Three years elapsed, and I entered a western-style school.

On day when I returned home from school, I found my mother's poverty-wrinkled face bright with happiness. "Living Buddha Malaha will come home tomorrow to receive the worship of his fellow villagers," she told me. In my mind filled with the letters of the Mongolian alphabet there appeared once more the image of my beloved little companion Malaha.

Living Buddha Malaha was to receive the worship of his fellow villagers on the top of the high white marble steps before the main hall of an ancient lamasery in the eastern part of the village. It was said that to kowtow to a Living Buddha could dispel misfortune and turn disaster into good luck. Consequently, some old people, hoping to atone for the "sins" they had committed in their present lifetime and to enjoy "peace and happiness" in their next life, would prostrate themselves and kowtow at every step right from their doorway until they came before the feet of the Living Buddha. In order to do so, some even got up at midnight. Having been a pupil in a western- style school for several years, I was already quite indifferent to religion. I was not interested in looking at the magnificent structure of the monastery, or in the solemnity of the ceremony but concentrated on elbowing my way through the crowd to a place near the

Living Buddha to take a careful look at my childhood companion, to find out what, after all, he was now like. Amidst the dense smoke of incense-sticks I was carried by the stream of people to the front of little Malaha, no, Living Buddha Malaha. He was sitting on a thick yellow satin cushion at the top of the steps, while I was kneeling beneath at the bottom of the steps on a hard flagstone. I raised my head, opened my eyes wide and stared. I quickly discovered that my little companion Malaha had completely changed. His cheeks were emaciated, his eyesockets deeply sunken and his face was ashy white, devoid of expression. His eyes especially appeared weary and lack-lustre. He seemed to have recognized me, and rolled his eyes once. But without waiting for my reaction, he immediately resumed his "Buddha appearance"; his eyes were again motionless. Alas! Only three years and my little companion had changed from an innocent lively child into such a cold and apathetic "god". I felt cut to the heart.

In the summer when Malaha had been a Living Buddha for a full five years, a grand gathering was held by the Gegen Monastery, during which Living Buddha Malaha would expound Buddhist sutras. I went with our neighbours to witness this magnificent occasion. On the last day, the Leading Senior Lama of the Gegen Monastery declared: Living Buddha Malaha would receive the worship of the laity that evening.

In the evening, the monastery was filled with a large crowd of worshippers. I stood at the end of a long stream of hurrying people, and looked from a distance of about a hundred metres at the Living Buddha's throne. I saw several ever-burning lamps in the lofty main hall. Although every bronze oil cup of each lamp could contain fifty catties of butter, the light was still not strong enough for me to see his face clearly. All I could see was a figure draped in a yellow cloak, with a yellow satin hood on his head, his palms together, sitting there motionless like an earthen idol in a large monastery.

I made a detour from the back of the main hall to the front of the Living Buddha. All the devout Buddhists there were in a frenzy, unable to restrain their emotion. Some were praying loudly, others begging tearfully for his blessing. They were bowing low, ready to kneel down at any moment. The Living Buddha Malaha, however, with his eyes closed, took no notice of his devout, fanatical worshippers; he did not even deign to move an eyelash. To attract his attention I deliberately straightened up and walked right up to him, hoping that he would turn his eyes to look at me again. But my hopes were disappointed. Suddenly I was emboldened, I don't know how, to call softly several times to the living idol draped with yellow satin, "Malaha, it's me! Hello, it's me, Malaha!" Although my cry was not loud, I was sure he could hear me. But he made not the slightest response. My heart sank like a stone: Was it possible that he had really become a Buddha? In these overpowering and mysterious religious surroundings, I went down involuntarily on my knees before him and kowtowed several times in succession. When I got up again and dragged myself out of the monastery, I was heart-broken, crying loudly at the thought of having lost my dear childhood companion for ever.

Several more decades passed. And now our people were masters of the new society.

Nurtured on the people's milk, I had grown from a poor, illiterate boy into a writer. I frequently recollected my own "golden childhood", the months and years of struggles, and my many childhood companions and comrades-in-arms of my youth, who had become models for the characters that appeared in my writings, but for some reason I had failed to include little Malaha. Perhaps it was because he was no longer a man in my memory, but had become a Buddha. In my literary works, which depicted real life, what I required were men of flesh and blood, men of feeling, not earthen idols who could not even turn their eyes or react when their own names were called.

Rat-tat-tat!

I was sitting in my study and writing one quiet winter night when I heard someone knocking at the door. My eighty-six-year-old but still healthy mother answered "Coming, coming," and went to open the door. Then I suddenly heard my younger daughter crying, "Papa, come here quick, grandma has fainted!" I dropped my pen and hurried out. My old mother had not fainted, she was kowtowing repeatedly. Because my daughter had never seen this done before, she thought that her grandmother had fainted. Meanwhile, the guest had taken a stride forward and was carefully helping my mother up, saying, "Aunty, you shouldn't do that now, I am a man, an ordinary man, not a Buddha!"

I turned to look at the visitor. He was neatly dressed. His temples were grey, the corners of his mouth drooped, and the hair on his balding head was brushed tidily backwards. He turned directly towards me after helping my mother up. Then, from his smiling eyes I recognized him: it was Malaha my little childhood friend!

"Where have you been all these years?" I asked him after inviting him to my study and exchanging some words of greeting.

"I was travelling around practising medicine, staying wherever I could; but you mustn't think I was an itinerant quack peddling dogskin plasters." He drank a mouthful of the tea I offered him and spoke calmly, with a note of self-mockery. "As soon as our area was liberated, I turned over the affairs of the monastery to the Leading Senior Lama and began to study Mongolian and Tibetan medicine in the temple where I lived. The traditional medical knowledge of the Mongolian and Tibetan people is extremely rich." So saying he took out an elaborately bound book from his bag. "Here's the result of my forty years research, recently published," he told me.

I took the book from his hand and saw embossed on its cover the title,

Mongolian and Tibetan Pharmacopoeia, in big golden characters in the Mongolian, Tibetan and Han languages. Underneath was printed the name of the author: "Malaha".

"In the nineteenth century these parts produced the well-known writer and historian Yinzhannaxi, and now in the twentieth century we have our celebrated doctor Malaha. This is something our people can be proud of!" I said elatedly.

Malaha's face was now quite mobile and it was clear that he felt deeply honoured. His intelligent eyes glowed.

"I've just attended a national conference on medical science in Shanghai, and came especially to see you on my way back."

Malaha stayed with us for three days. On the eve of his departure I prepared some dishes and wine to bid him farewell. He was not a good drinker, but that evening he finished three cups in a row. The wine warmed our faces. The affection we had felt for each other as children came back to us again. We were both very happy. Thanks probably to the wine I had drunk, I blurted out a question which I had not yet had the courage to ask:

"Are you now Doctor Malaha, or Living Buddha Malaha? A doctor is a man. But if you are still a Living Buddha, then you are not a man but a deity."

Malaha sat in a reclining chair, a cup of tea in his hand. He smiled sadly, and said in a voice neither hurried nor slow:

"Ah! Of course, there are no deities in this world. But then, out of foolishness and to find something in which they can place their hopes, men create gods for themselves. A man worshipped as a god by his fellow creatures has at first only a vague sense of being one. As time goes by he becomes convinced that he is one, and therefore acts like a god. Men then worship him more devoutly and believe in him more fanatically. They don't know that they have been made fools of. Creating a god is also making a fool of the man thus converted. And the man converted into a god then assumes the manner of a god to make fools of the people who have deified him. We have passed many thousands of years in this comedy of mutual trickery. These years have been a time of absurdity. But history ultimately will be written by the people themselves and these years of absurdity have already passed."

Beijing, June 10, 1980

Translated by Wen Xue

The Log Cabin Overgrown with Creepers

●

—— GU HUA ——

Born and raised in a remote mountain village in the southern part of Hunan, Gu Hua is a writer influenced by local customs and folk art forms. Upon graduation from middle school he began his studies at an agricultural school. Later still, he became an agricutural worker at a local agricultural science institute and stayed there for fourteen years. He began to write in the 1960s and has since published a great number of works. "The Log Cabin Overgrown with Creepers" was voted one of the best short stories of 1981, while his outstanding novel A Small Town Called Hibiscus *won a Mao Dun Literary Award in 1982.*

FOR many years the story of a Yao girl has been told in the forests of the Wujie Hills, a young woman called Pan Qingqing, or Azure, who was a tree warden deep in those ancient and mysterious forests. She was born, grew up and married in the hills, and in all her life she only once went to the forestry station, which was itself remote enough. The young men there had only heard of this marvellous woman but had never set eyes on her. Her family had lived in Green Hollow for generations in a log cabin overgrown with creepers, a cabin built of fir trunks so strong that no axe would make an impression on them or wild boar shake them. The parts of the trunks that were sunk into the ground had long since turned black and grown layer upon layer of wavy mushrooms in lace-like patterns. Behind the cabin a mountain stream ran clear throughout the year.

The cabin's links with the outside world were a narrow track and a telephone line that had been put up before the "cultural revolution" to carry fire reports but had been cut by a heavy fall of snow one winter. Since the beginning of the "cultural revolution" there had been a never-ending succession of bosses at the forestry station, and they had all been too busy cooking their political pies to send anyone to reconnect the line, so that this symbol of modern civilization no longer reached this ancient forest. But for the occasional sound of a hen, a dog or a baby from the cabin and the column of light blue smoke rising from its stove the thousands of acres of woodland around Green Hollow would have been peacefully sleeping day and night. Not all the songs of the birds in the hills and all the blossoms opening and falling on them would even have woken it.

Azure had lost both her parents early. Her husband was a Han Chinese called Wang Mutong, a tall, powerfully built man strong enough to kill a tiger. Husband and wife were both forest wardens. Mutong liked a couple of cups of Azure's corn wine before his meals, and except that he got drunk occasionally and beat her black and blue he was not a bad husband. He cared for his wife, never sending her up the hills to fetch firewood, of which he always kept plenty ready cut in stacks. He did not make her cut and clear firebreaks through the trees, and for over ten years there had never been a forest fire in Green Hollow. Nor did he expect her to till the soil and plant the crops. He saw to it that their big plot of land by the stream always had more onions, pumpkins and other fresh vegetables than the four of them could eat. All that Azure had to do was to feed the pigs, suckle the babies, wash, make and mend the clothes, and look after the house. At twenty-six or twenty-seven she was still as lively and fresh as an unmarried girl. Mutong could not read a word but he was bursting with self-confidence and he knew everything. He felt that he was the real master of Green Hollow: the woman was his, the children were his, and the cabin and the hills were his, though of course he did come under the forestry station. As the leadership had sent him to look after this part of the forest, that made him like a minor vassal in charge of his own fief. Before she'd had the babies Azure had often asked to visit the forestry station that was some 45 kilometres away but he had never let her go, sometimes hitting her savagely or even forcing her to kneel for long periods as a punishment. He was afraid that if his beautiful wife had her eyes opened by that lively, bustling place she would start getting fancy ideas. She might have been led astray by those smooth and pushy young men at the station. He only stopped worrying after she had given him the babies, first the boy and then the girl, which left her firmly tied to his belt and truly his woman. It was now the turn of the younger generation to be hit and forced to kneel. He ran the whole household by strict rules. The places of husband and wife, as of father and children, were all clearly set out in Green Hollow. Difference of status counted for a lot in this miniature society.

Mutong and Azure lived in virtual isolation from the world. It would be an exaggeration to say that she followed him in everything, but they were both used to each other and they got along without trouble. Mutong would go to the forestry station once a month to collect their wages and bring back the rice, oil and salt for the family. Every time he came back he would tell her what had been happening at the station and the news he had heard there. Azure would listen with her dark and gleaming eyes opened wide and her mind filled with amazement. It was as if her husband were describing some foreign country on the other side of the world. In the last few years her husband had been telling her a lot about young students rebelling and making trouble. Teachers who wore glasses were being dragged around the hills with placards on them like performing monkeys. The forestry expert who had studied for half a lifetime was supposed to have drowned himself in a little pond so shallow that he had not even got his back wet. "We're better off as we are in Green Hollow. The gleaming black earth here is ever so fertile. You just have to stick a piece of firewood into the ground for it to grow and come into leaf. We're not educated. We bother nobody and nobody bothers us."

Some of what her husband said Azure understood and some she didn't. She was thoroughly confused, and was worried for those learned scholars who lived beyond their hills. Book-learning was a disaster, and she found herself thinking that she and her husband were lucky to have avoided it. She had heard him saying "We're better off as we are in Green Hollow" so often that she came to believe it herself. She did not ask much of her husband, but simply wished that he would not hit her too hard when he lost his temper and started laying about him. Every evening at nightfall they shut the door of their cabin and went to bed. Half a pint of paraffin that he brought back from the station was enough to keep that lamp burning six months. Only when the moon and the stars happened to shine in through the wooden-framed windows set high in the walls could they spy on how the couple spent their nights.

"Azure, I want you to give me more babies."

"We've got Little Tong and Little Qing. You told me the forestry station won't let people have big families any more. Don't women have to be sterilized?"

"Never mind that. Five more wouldn't be too many."

"Don't you care about how I'll have to suffer?"

"Suffer? Women don't mind a bit of suffering at child-birth."

"I'm scared of the people at the station telling us off."

"To hell with that. The worst they can do is refuse to give us extra grain rations. We've got soil and water here in Green Hollow. Just look at my hands: they're as big as rice-measures. Do you think I couldn't raise a few more kids? I'll clear a cotton field next winter, and you can fetch the spinning wheel and handloom your mum left you and clean them up."

"Get on with you. You think I'm a pheasant that you can keep in these hills."

"You're mine."

Azure said no more as her husband held her tucked under his armpit that smelled so sharply of sweat. She was very docile. She belonged to him. If he wanted to beat or swear at her that was only as it should be. She was in the bloom of youth, and could bear children as painlessly as a tree bearing fruit. When she fed the babies the milk flowed endlessly like sap from her white breasts. Her husband was young and strong. He could kill a tiger or catch a wild boar. When he embraced her, his arms were like a ring of iron; they did what husbands and wives probably do in other places, and he had so much strength it was as if he did not know what to do with it.

In the summer of 1975 the One-hander came to Green Hollow. Let there be no confusion: he was not a man in authority but a city youngster who had come to settle on the forestry station in 1964. His real name was Li Xingfu and they said he had been born in the year of Liberation, 1949. He was tall, slender and rather elegant, and quick at selecting seeds and looking after saplings. He knew how to get on with any of the forestry workers or officials he met. But he had been carried away by his enthusiasm for travelling around the country exchanging revolutionary experience as a Red Guard in 1966, and had left a perfectly good hand lying by the railway track when hitching a ride on a train. From then on one of his sleeves had hung empty. After a few years hanging around in the city he had come back to the forestry station and this was when the workers there had nicknamed him the One-hander. From then on the station's leadership had been down on him. They had telephoned each of the felling districts and forest management teams but they had all refused to take him. Apart from the fact that the One-hander could no longer do heavy manual work he had been one of the "young revolutionary warriors". If he started exchanging revolutionary experience in some mountain hollow he would be as useless as a piece of wet beancurd dropped in a pile of ash that you couldn't either blow or wipe clean. One day, while Wang Mutong, the warden of Green Hollow, came to the station to fetch the grain for his family the station's political director bumped into him. Smiting himself on the back of the neck the political director thought: Yes! Why not send Li Xingfu off to Green Hollow to be a forest warden with Wang Mutong and his wife? The work was not too light or too heavy but just right, and on top of that there was nobody else for dozens of miles around apart from the very reliable and straightforward Wang Mutong and his wife. There was no one Li Xingfu could exchange revolutionary experiences with but monkeys and pheasants. Wang Mutong's first reaction to being given someone to work under his leadership was delight, which turned to disgust when he realized that this subordinate Li Xingfu was the One-hander. "Wang, my friend, you've been wanting to join the Party for years, haven't you? This is a test that our organization is setting you," said the political director, slapping him on the shoulder. "You'll have no problem keeping him in order — he's only got one hand. I'll have a word with him myself in a moment and make him agree to three conditions: in Green Hollow he'll have to obey your instructions in everything, he'll have to report everything to you, and he'll have to get your permission if he wants to leave the hollow. Show a bit of spirit. Try to reform this educated youngster who's gone wrong." Only then had Wang nodded his assent and decided to take the test that the organization was setting him by shouldering the burden of "education and reform".

Thus the One-hander had come to Green Hollow and become an important new member of the little society headed by Wang Mutong. Some twenty or thirty paces from their own ancient log cabin Wang Mutong and his wife built him a little, low cabin with walls of upright logs and a roof of fir bark on the bank of the jade-clear mountain stream. The new cabin and the old, the little one and the big one, became neighbours. At first Wang Mutong had felt no hostility towards the One-hander and liked being called Elder Brother Wang by him.

The One-hander was captivated from the very first by the beauty and peace of Green Hollow. Every day Wang Mutong would send him to sit in the watchtower on the ridge, so that each morning he would climb the narrow path that snaked through the mists of the great forest. It was like walking in a very hazy dream. The milky-white mist that covered the mountain and filled the valley was so thick it seemed to be a liquid on which you could float. When the sun showed through and the mists began to disperse at nine or ten in the morning he felt he was in another, enchanted world as he sat in the watchtower on the ridge with the brilliant greens of the foliage above him and below his feet clumps of tall Guangdong pines and Chinese hemlock trees rising through the rolling mist. But the One-hander knew the woods and the valley were no fairyland. He was aware that Wang Mutong and his wife were both young, and that she was tender and beautiful, with big, dark eyes that could talk and sing, although she tactfully kept a proper distance between them. But young people cannot bear loneliness. Was he destined to exchange experiences and make friends only with the golden monkeys, the thrushes and the grouse in this green valley?

Wang Mutong's boy Little Tong was seven and his daughter, Little Qing, five. At first the children had been rather afraid of "one-arm", but the situation had changed after the One-hander caught Little Tong some birds, brought Little Qing back some blossoms from the mountains to wear in her hair, and let her look at herself in a little mirror. The children started to call him "Uncle Li" or "Elder brother". A few days later Little Tong insisted on going to sleep in the One-hander's cabin and refused to go back when his mother called for him. Mountain children are lovable in their own special way. When a snake slithered into the little cabin, making the One-hander shake with terror, Little Tong told him that snakes never bit people unless they were trodden on. Little Tong went on to tell him with graphic imitations about the three kinds of snake in Green Hollow. "Green bamboo snakes are very lazy. They usually lie coiled up in the bamboo without moving." He put his head back, closed his eyes, and pursed his lips as he went on, "They spit their poison out like this" — he blew through his lips — "to lure birds, and as soon as the bird comes close they pounce and get a good bite on it. Then they coil round the bamboo again and take their time eating it up. The shouting snake is different. Its skin's the same colour as mud. It looks terrific going through the grass. It rears up about waist high, pushing the grass aside, like this." He made his eyes bulge, opened his mouth wide, and kept stretching his head forward. "It goes 'Hoo, hoo', and it's really scary. There's another sort that's thick as a chopper handle and as long as a carrying-pole. Dad calls it a forty-eighter, and when it goes along it shakes its head all over the place. You'd think it was crazy." The One-hander, afraid that Little Tong was going to do another imitation, put his hand on the boy's head and asked, "How do you know all that?" "I've seen green bamboo snakes myself and Dad told me about the shouting snakes and the forty-eighters. Dad catches snakes and sells them outside the mountains." The One-hander looked at the boy, of an age to be going to school, imitating the snakes, thought of that long, cold thing slithering out of the cabin, and felt miserably sad.

Adults observe children and children observe adults. The One-hander brushed his teeth and rinsed his mouth out every morning. Little Qing always poked half of her face out of the door of their cabin to gaze wide-eyed at this amazing sight. One morning she came timidly over and asked, "Uncle, does your mouth smell bad?" The One-hander, whose mouth was full of toothpaste, did not understand what she meant.

"If your mouth doesn't smell bad why do you rub it with that brush every day?"

The One-hander had to laugh. When he had finished washing his face he said to Little Qing, "Ask your mum to buy you and Little Tong a toothbrush one day and brush your teeth every morning. Then they'll be lovely and white."

Little Qing was not convinced. "Mum never uses a brush, and her teeth are lovely and white."

"Does your mum's mouth ever have a nasty smell?" the One-hander asked, trying to press home his argument.

"She loves kissing me, and her mouth smells ever so nice. If you don't believe me kiss her yourself and see."

"Stop talking such nonsense, you little devil. Come back at once," Little Qing's mother called from inside their cabin.

The One-hander's face felt hot and his heart pounded as if he had just done something wicked. He shot back into his own little cabin.

It was a trivial incident, but Wang Mutong had heard. He dragged

Little Qing to the doorway of their cabin and made her kneel there as a punishment. It was obvious that he wanted the One-hander to see. Although nothing suspicious had happened he now had eyes in the back of his head and was on his guard.

The life of the two households in Green Hollow flowed as calmly as the jade-green mountain brook behind the cabins. Although the deep places only came up to your calves and the shallow parts just covered your heel it could reflect the dancing trees, the clear blue sky and the leisurely floating clouds. It now reflected something new, a tall fir pole that the One-hander had put up outside his wooden cabin: a radio aerial.

This was to stir up trouble. The little black box in the One-hander's cabin could talk and sing. It broke the immemorial silence of the night among the ancient mountain forests. At first only the children took their courage in their hands to go to listen to it in the little cabin after nightfall, but after a while Azure herself began to drop in for a while on the pretext of fetching them home to bed. Of course, the next thing every evening was for Wang Mutong to appear to take his wife and children back to bed. Once his tone of voice was a little rough and "It's too early," Azure answered back with something like petulance. "If we go to bed the moment it gets dark I hate having to wait so long for daybreak." When Wang Mutong heard his wife say that she hated the long wait in bed till dawn a dark cloud fell over his heart. The tall and strongly built forester never went to listen to the devilish voices singing in the black box. He was going to preserve his inviolable dignity as a man and watch closely to stop things from developing any further.

Soon afterwards the One-hander organized Azure and the children to tidy up the piece of ground between the two cabins and make neat stacks of firewood and other things by the doors. The muddy and uneven ground that used to be filthy with dogshit and pig's urine was now level and clean. The One-hander said that he wanted to plant flowers there and teach Azure and the children to read and do the radio exercises. The thought made Azure's face all smiles. The children followed the One-hander round all day, and it was always "Uncle says this" or "Uncle says that's wrong". Anyone would think he was closer to them than their own father. This upset Wang Mutong, who did not like what he saw. Although the One-hander had only one arm he was gradually changing life in Green Hollow, like a worm silently turning the earth over. "Bloody show-off. He wants to impress us all in Green Hollow with his education. Anyone would think he's better than me."

He was not surprised when the One-hander made four suggestions about the work. The first was that the forestry station should be asked to repair the telephone line that had been out of action for years and to install a loudspeaker for cable radio between the two cabins. The second was that they should put up painted wooden notices on all the mountain paths into Green Hollow with the Forestry Code on them. The third was that he and Wang Mutong should have a system for patrolling the mountains and fire-watching with two eight-hour shifts a day; when on duty they should not make traps with bent saplings, dig up edible roots, or do any other work on their own account. The fourth was that there should be a politics and literacy class that the children could join in. When Azure heard this suggestion she smiled and gave her husband a wordless look with her big, bright eyes that obviously said, "Look how educated he is. He has such clever ideas — they sound wonderful."

Wang Mutong saw all this at once. It was very painful. His face went hard, he tightened his lips, and his eyes spat fury. "You smell good, don't you, just like a brand-new latrine," they seemed to say. "You can keep your fancy nonsense." He glared savagely at his wife then said to the One-hander very bluntly, "City boy! They always used to say that a stranger should follow the local customs, and the guest do what suits the host. You may not be a guest, but you're certainly not the host. There hasn't been a forest fire here in fifteen or twenty years. All the leaders we've had in the forests of the Wujie Hills have always said my work's good. I've been a model worker every year. I don't need any wires or boards or shifts or classes. You'd better sharpen your billhook and get yourself fit. The forestry station made me the boss here. The three conditions the political director told you about weren't just hot air."

Wang Mutong was an intimidating sight as he stood there, his arms akimbo and his eyes flaming with anger. The One-hander gazed wide-eyed with horror, his mouth hanging open and his face pale from shock. Azure could not bear to see it, but she dared not provoke her husband's savage and violent fury by showing her own anger or speaking out of turn, so she could only try to ease the tension by saying to the One-hander, "Li, he's not very educated. He talks a bit rough...." But when she saw that her husband was on the point of exploding she shut up. "Rough I may be," Wang Mutong said with a mocking laugh, "I suppose you're very smooth. The roughs control the smoothies these days. The roughs are in charge, Li Xingfu. Don't you forget that the leadership sent you here to be educated and remoulded." With that he turned his massive body away and stormed off, putting his feet down so hard that they left deep footprints.

The One-hander's four suggestions had run up against the rock of Wang Mutong and disappeared without trace. He felt deflated. Yes, he had been sent to Green Hollow to be educated and reformed, but he could not help feeling afraid of Wang Mutong. He knew that there was very little he could do to improve his present state, but he was full of energy and could not let himself stay idle, because idleness made him depressed, lonely, fed up with life, and thinking he would do better to jump off a precipice and be done with it. He had two books that he had kept from before the "cultural revolution": *Trees* and *A Forest Fire Prevention Manual*. He took *Trees* with him on his daily patrols of the mountains and taught himself to recognize the hundreds of different kinds of broadleafed evergreens that grew there with the help of the illustrations in the book. To prevent his time here from being completely wasted he decided to do a survey of the forestry resources of Green Hollow that would be of use when felling began in the future. Thinking that Azure would understand him he told her of his plan, and she was as warm and friendly with him as if he'd been her own brother. "Silly thing. Go ahead and do it, but don't talk abut it to anyone else." "Won't Wang mind?" "You won't be doing anything wrong. You...." When she said "You...." she drew the word out. Her dark eyes shone so bright he could see himself reflected in them; they shone straight into his heart. He was afraid to look into them, though he did not know why. Azure's "You...." echoed over and over again in his heart.

It was autumn. The One-hander collected the seeds of some rare and valuable trees, including a rare fir, golden-leaf magnolias and south China camphor trees that he intended to raise in a little nursery. He planned to carry them into the forestry station later as seedlings for the technicians to raise. Some land had to be burnt and cleared for his nursery, and as he knew that Wang Mutong would not be at all interested he had to ask Azure to help him.

That day Wang Mutong was in the mountains setting traps. The One-hander and Azure had chosen the slope where wild aubergines grew next to the vegetable patch, a piece of land that Wang Mutong was intending to clear for cotton. They set it alight and soon thick smoke was billowing out above the roaring wind and flames. The two of them were relaxed and happy, laughing and shouting like brother and sister. They never expected Wang Mutong to come rushing down the mountainside in a high temper. He glared coldly at them, took the billhook from his belt and cut down a little pine tree that he wielded with both hands to put the fire out. The One-hander tried to explain, but Wang Mutong gave him a terrible glare and roared, "Cut out this newfangled nonsense! I've got other plans for this land. Li Xingfu, write a self-criticism tonight for burning land without my permission." "Who am I to hand it to?" "Who to? Do you think that just because I don't read I can't be your leader? I'm telling you, you'd better behave yourself when you're under me." Hearing these awful things said Azure gave her husband a tearful look. "Go back and feed the pigs — the swill must be cooked by now," he said harshly as if he were some malevolent deity.

The One-hander stole a lingering look filled with pity at Azure and watched her turn and go back without saying a word, wiping her tears away with the back of her hand.

Everyone needs to feel self-confidence and self-respect. Fail to mend a little crack and a yawning gap will open up: even the earth itself will split open. Wang Mutong felt that the One-hander had flung down a challenge. His own wife was getting out of hand: she wasn't as docile and tender as she used to be.

One day Wang Mutong had to go to the forestry station to fetch the family's grain. Normally he would spend the night there, but this time for some peculiar reason he had felt very uneasy as soon as he set out that morning. There was a worry nagging at him that he could not get out of his mind. He was a powerfully built man and his blood was up, so he did the journey of some ninety kilometres there and back the same day, with a load of sixty kilogrammes of rice on the return leg. When he got back that night he stank of sweat. The door of his cabin was half open and the lamp was still on. His wife must still be up. That was odd. He went inside to find nobody there. Then he heard laughter and singing coming from the One-hander's hut. He felt the stove: It was cold. He was now ablaze with an anger that nothing was going to calm down. He rushed out and stood outside the One-hander's window. He could see it all clearly: his own wife sitting with her chin in her hands, Little Tong leaning against her knees, and both of them listening with rapt attention to a woman singing devilish songs in that accursed box. And the One-hander had Little Qing on his knee with his face touching hers. He could hear that the song coming from the black box was a Yao love song.

"It's lovely. My mum loved singing it when she was alive...." Wang Mutong could see his wife's eyes shining devilishly as she gazed at the One-hander so sweetly. "You Yaos have always been wonderful singers and dancers...." The One-hander was looking at her in that shameless way too. Wang Mutong could bear to see no more. He had to control the flames of his anger to stop himself from shouting obscenities when he said, "Little Tong, Little Qing, like going to the music hall, do you? Is this your way of shortening the wait till daybreak?" Only then did Azure realize that her husband was back. Pulling Little Tong with one hand and Little Qing with the other she rushed to the door. "Just look at you, you're so worn out you're soaked in sweat," she said. "Why didn't you spend the night at the station?" He ignored her, and by keeping his teeth clenched he prevented himself from saying something that he did not want to say: "If I'd stayed the night at the station I dare say you'd have spent it at his place."

Back in their own cabin Azure quickly lit the stove and heated his water while cooking him a meal. She did not warm him up any wine because she was afraid he might beat her up if he got drunk. That night Wang Mutong showed exceptional restraint. His silence was terrifying, freezing the atmosphere in the hut. He gave himself a rub down and washed his feet with the warm water then went to bed and to sleep without a word, paying no attention to the food his wife had set on the table. She seemed to understand what was upsetting him: several times she tried to make up with him by pushing hard at his naked back with both her hands, but he lay there as heavy and immobile as a gunpowder barrel. It was terrifying.

Wang Mutong was not only physically strong: he could work things out and think for himself. He felt that his position in Green Hollow was under threat, and the spark of mutiny was spreading from Azure to Little Tong and Little Qing. Was he going to sit there calmly watching the One-hander gradually luring away his wife and his children? Was an upright, tough and hardworking model forest warden going to be beaten by a weedy little one-armed city boy sent to the countryside? He decided to start by consolidating his position in his own cabin. The next morning his face was set and his eyes glaring as he announced in a voice like thunder, "Little Tong, Little Qing, kneel to your father! Kneel! Now, listen. From today onwards if either of you or your mum sets one foot inside the little cabin I'll gouge your eyes out and break your legs." Azure's face went pale as she heard this ban being proclaimed. Little Tong's and Little Qing's teeth were chattering as they knelt behind her. They were trembling like a pair of saplings in a cold wind.

Before the One-hander set out to work Wang Mutong went to his cabin to ask for the self-criticism he had demanded several days before. When the One-hander said he had not yet written it he said, "Do you think that what I say is just hot air that counts for nothing? I tell you frankly, Li Xingfu, that the leadership at the station put you completely in my power. From now onwards you won't be allowed to talk or act out of turn. All you'll be allowed to do is behave yourself. I'm giving you another day's grace. I want your written self-criticism first thing tomorrow morning."

Wang Mutong glared at him with his leopard eyes and shook two fists that were like sledge-hammers as he went on to lay down three new rules. "Listen! As from today you will report to me every evening here in your cabin on what you've done each day. If you're busy you can ask me for leave, and when you're not busy don't come into my cabin whenever you feel like it. And, thirdly, if you try to lead anyone in my family astray with that devilish box of yours you'll catch it from my fists. With just one finger I could pull out your fir pole with that wire on it and throw them over the hill."

He worked along two lines: internal pacification and resistance to outsiders. He also took some practical steps to enforce his prohibitions. Previously they had always gone past the One-hander's cabin whenever they left their own hut to take the dirt track that led east to the forestry station or to cross the stream westwards to sit in the fire watchtower on the mountain or to patrol. Wang Mutong now wielded his pick and shovel to cut a new path for his family. Of course, this meant making a detour of a good hundred paces when going to the mountain or the station.

This was the situation that the One-hander had no choice but to accept. Wang Mutong's status and position in Green Hollow was as strong and stable as that of a ruler of an ancient forest kingdom and it brooked no questioning. He had never gone to the One-hander's cabin very often before, but now that his wife and children dared not come any more he would go and sit there every evening to hear the One-hander's report on what he had done that day. He evidently enjoyed this taste of being a powerful leader and kept the One-hander as docile and well controlled as a so-called class enemy.

Thus it was that the One-hander withdrew into his little cabin like a snail pulling back into its shell. Even the songs from the little black box were quieter now. In the face of harsh reality, which had once again given him a black eye, the One-hander had to admit that he was beaten. Life in Green Hollow went back to its usual sleepy pace.

The weather was very odd that winter: it thundered constantly but there was no snow. Older people took it as an omen of a winter and spring drought. Every morning Green Hollow's vast ancient forest was hung with hoar frost shaped like dog's teeth, and the evergreens seemed to be wearing suits of jade sewn together with silver thread. It was a gleaming white world that did not disappear before noon. The two cabins at the bottom of the valley were crowned every morning with white jade, and the gurgling flow of the mountain stream behind them was now silenced by the hard shell that lay on it.

On these freezing frosty days Azure had no work to do outside apart from feeding the pigs twice and cooking a couple of meals, so she would turn out her basket of rags to sew soles for the children's shoes. When her husband took Little Tong and Little Qing out to play in the hills Azure would sit by the stove with a piece of cloth in her hands. Sometimes she would sit there lost in thought for half a morning. Every day Wang Mutong would bring back hares and badgers that he had caught on the mountains and take off their skins to be nailed up on the wall. The fat meat being stewed in the earthenware pot could be smelt for miles around. The strange thing was that the smell of the meat now made Azure feel sick, just as if she were expecting again. A great stone was crushing her heart, and underneath it there was still something alive. Her husband had been beating her a lot recently and she was covered in bruises. She could scarcely breathe in peace from morning till night as she watched his expression and his eyes. When he started hitting her she could only hope that his fists would land on her back or her legs or other places that did not matter. She wept till her tears ran dry and then till they flowed again; her fate was so bitter, and her husband so cruel. She felt that it was only the One-hander who respected her and treated her as a human being. That tyrant of a husband treated her like a criminal. She felt as sorry for the lad as she did for herself. But she was angry with him too. Of all the places he could have gone to why did it have to be Green Hollow? He'd ruined their lives.

The worst thing of all now for Azure was smelling her husband's acrid sweat in bed at night. Many nights of silent weeping gradually developed a spirit of resistance in her. Every evening when she went to bed she would obstinately turn her face to the wall. She might have been nailed there: she would not turn over however much he tugged and pushed. "I'll kill you," he muttered through teeth clenched in fury. "Go ahead!" "Whore! You just want your fancy man." "Are you going to beat me again? He'll hear, and the story will get out." "Bitch!" "Help! Mum! Hit me again I'll scream." Azure now had the courage to stand up to her husband. She did not know why, but he was afraid of the One-hander hearing their secrets, and she was worried too about him knowing how she was mistreated and beaten every night.

Life can be very abnormal, and so too can emotions. Azure felt herself changing, though she did not know whether it was for the better or the worse. This freezing cold winter she wanted to dress herself up a little, which she had not before. She now liked wearing the silver gray woolen headscarf that she normally kept at the bottom of her trunk and her rose-red corduroy outer jacket. She kept herself as clean and tidy all day as if she were just about to go visiting, and even filled the copper basin her mother had left her with clear water from the stream to look at her own reflection. Some years ago she had asked her husband to buy her a looking-glass to hang on the wall from the forestry station, but every time he came back he said that he had forgotten. Now she realized that he had been doing it deliberately. He had been afraid that she'd see how pretty she was: a face like the moon, bright eyes, a mouth like a petal of red magnolia wet with dew, and two dimples. She looked lovely when she smiled and lovely when she didn't. Anyone would fancy her. The One-hander? No! How shameful. Her heart started to beat wildly. Her mind was in a whirl. She covered her burning cheeks with her hands and would not look up. It was as if she had done something wicked. Recently she hadn't been able to stop herself stealing looks at the One-hander's little hut. The strange thing was that the more her husband refused to let her go there the more attractive it seemed to her. The One-hander's radio, soap, face-cream, and all those other amazing things from the four corners of the globe were as alluring as a new world. Li Xingfu's name Xingfu meant "happiness", but was that skinny, pale-faced lad happy? Every day he had to chop the firewood, wash his clothes and cook his meals, all single-handed, and he did not so much as glance at her. When he saw Wang Mutong the poor thing looked as if he'd seen a tiger. She felt sympathy, tenderness for him often with the bewitching shyness of a Yao girl.

Once the One-hander came back from the forestry station with some sweets wrapped in silver and gold paper that he slipped unobtrusively into the children's hands. Little Qing was clever enough to unwrap one of them and pop it into her mother's mouth. Azure at once hugged her daughter tight and kissed her over and over again' on the lips. "Little Qing," she asked as if in dream, "does your mum's mouth have a nasty taste?" "No, no." "Does it taste sweet?" "Yes, very sweet." Heavens! What a thing to be saying to her own daughter! She blushed deeply, and as the sweet in her mouth slowly dissolved the delicious juice seemed to flow straight down into her heart. She covered her daughter's soft pink cheeks with her own sweet kisses. Her strict husband saw none of this, and it was none of his business. If he had seen her he might have killed her there and then.

One day when Wang Mutong had gone into the mountains to set tree traps Azure went to the stream to fetch a bucket of water. She saw the One-hander rinsing his clothes in the water so icy it cut to the marrow of the bone. His only hand was red with cold. Putting the bucket down she went over to him, took the clothes, and started rinsing them out for him. He stood up at once and took a couple of paces back. "You shouldn't, Azure," he said. "If Wang sees you he'll...."

She carried on rinsing without looking up. "Why shouldn't I? I'm not doing anything wrong."

"I know.... But he'll hit you again."

She stopped for a moment, not moving.

"Look. Your arm's all purple."

"Shut up, you fool. One of the pigs charged me in the sty."

It took all her self-control to hold back the tears that welled up. She longed to run somewhere where she could howl aloud. She rubbed and shook out his clothes several more times, then picked them out of the water, wrung them till they were a huge twisted knot, and dropped them without a word in his galvanized pail. She did not look back at him as she picked up her bucket and went, forgetting all about the water she had come to fetch. Once back in her cabin she leant against the door, weak in the limbs and completely drained of strength. Her heart was pounding so hard it seemed to be about to leap out of her chest. She did not cry. Indeed, she wanted to laugh. This was the first time in her life she had done something for another man behind her husband's back. This terrifying first time comes sooner or later in everyone's life. After the pounding of her heart had subsided Azure felt happy for a very long time. Her husband noticed nothing when he came back from the hills that night. She had won a victory.

The winter drought and the freeze went on till the end of the year. The branches of many of the broad-leaved evergreens around Green Hollow were stripped bare, and they stretched their withered bony arms out to heaven like so many starving and thirsty old men. The hillsides were thickly covered in fallen leaves of every shape and colour that rustled as they blew around in the frosty wind, making the mountains resplendent with their rich colours of gold and jade.

The long drought made it impossible for the One-hander to go on lying low in his little cabin. He was up before dawn every morning to patrol the mountains with his billhook at his belt and his fire prevention manual under his arm. Several times he plucked up his courage to suggest to Wang Mutong that they ought to clear all the firebreaks and sweep the dead leaves from the paths. Because of his hostility to the One-hander Wang Mutong paid no attention to him and ignored nearly all of his suggestions. Wang Mutong was in charge of Green Hollow, and other people had better keep their mouths shut and stop being so bloody keen. But this time the One-hander had some kind of premonition and he did not give in. He decided to take some precautions himself. He persuaded Azure to clear all the undergrowth, firewood, dead leaves and fallen branches away from the two log cabins. He also used every spare moment he had to read aloud from his fire prevention manual to the children, which really amounted to reading it to their parents too. One morning Wang Mutong heard a conversation between the One-hander and Little Tong.

"Uncle Li, what does 'running into the wind' mean?"

"If there's a forest fire you can get away by running towards where it's coming from."

"Uncle, what do we do if our cabin catches fire?"

"Go and crouch down in the stream. Stay on this side where there aren't any big trees."

"Rubbish!" Wang Mutong was going to hear no more. "You're trying to bring us bad luck, talking like that." Having scared the boy off with his angry words he turned to the One-hander and demanded, "Li Xingfu, are you planning on starting a forest fire in Green Hollow?"

The question left the One-hander dumbfounded.

"Why else do you spend all day thinking about how to escape from one?"

"Brother Wang, fires and floods are cruel things."

"In that case do you think that there's bound to be a bush fire in Green Hollow this winter?" Wang Mutong contemptuously snatched the fire prevention manual from Li Xingfu's hand, flicked through it a couple of times without being able to read a word and threw it back to him. "I suppose this teaches you how to tell fortunes. You know what's going to happen, do you?"

"Brother Wang, the drought's gone on for so long and the hills are covered with fallen leaves. Every night the radio says...." The One-hander always looked sordid, guilty, pale and weak in Wang Mutong's presence. The word "radio" made Wang Mutong laugh derisively. "Has that black box of yours been singing any of those disgusting love songs recently?"

The One-hander did not know whether he wanted to laugh or to cry. Keeping a straight face, he replied, "Wang, I've got a suggestion to make. Shouldn't we put in a request to the forestry station asking them to get the telephone line repaired? Otherwise if there were an emergency here by any remote chance we'd have no way of contacting the outside world."

"If you want to make your request, go to the station and make it. I'll give you two days' leave. Why don't you see if they'll send a firefighting team to Green Hollow while you're about it?" Wang Mutong gave the One-hander a mocking glance, yawned unconcernedly, and added, "I can tell you without boasting that in the twenty or thirty years I've lived here I've never seen a forest fire."

After the evening meal Wang Mutong went to the One-hander's little cabin as usual. What the One-hander found different this evening was that instead of his usual hectoring manner as if he were dealing with a public enemy Wang Mutong spoke very pleasantly. "Young Li, you're planning to go to the station, aren't you? I wonder if you could do me a favour." He produced a sheet of paper that he had brought with him and asked the One-hander to write out his application to join the Party. This was surprising enough, but the next thing was that Wang Mutong put his finger in his mouth and bit it open with a loud crunch. He waved the bleeding finger in front of the One-hander's face as if it were a tiny flag. "Soak your brush in this and write it quick for me. 'Dear forestry station leadership, I'm writing this letter in blood to apply for Party membership. I'm not educated, I'm a rough person, but I have a red heart and I do what the Party tells me....'" The horrified One-hander quickly found a battered old writing brush, soaked it in the fresh blood from Wang Mutong's finger, and wrote the application in blood as quickly as he could. The very sight of the blood made him tremble. He was covered in cold sweat.

When the blood letter was written Wang Mutong folded it up carefully and put it into an inner pocket next to his skin. When it came down to it he could not trust the One-hander and allow a political unreliable to hand his sacred application in to the station.

The next morning Wang Mutong was out burning the undergrowth by his vegetable garden, which he was planning to extend. He had not ever bandaged up the wound on his finger. He was a good worker and already had about a quarter of a hectare of land cleared for vegetables. The station required him and his wife to raise three pigs a year. These had to be smoked and handed over as cured meat at the end of the year; the rest they could slaughter and eat themselves. He cared nothing about ideology and isms, but he trusted the Party just as he trusted himself. He liked the party and the Party liked him, and he reckoned that the Party ought to consist of people like himself. He collected huge piles of fallen branches and leaves, rotten stalks and dead plants from the hillside that he carried to his plot to burn. he collected ashes for fertilizer like this every year, and winter drought or no winter drought this year was going to be no different. The One-hander was very worried about him doing it in so dry a winter, but he did not dare say anything to Wang Mutong's face. He slept badly at night, troubled by nightmares of monstrous and terrible fires as beautiful as sunsets, fires flowing like great rivers. One or two nights he got up quietly, went to cut himself a fir sapling from the hillside, and stood on guard by the bonfire that Wang Mutong had burned the previous day. He stayed there for most of the night, the icy wind cutting into his hand, feet and face as painfully as a knife. Why was he watching over the bonfire? He hadn't written a letter in his own blood, and even if he had nobody would have believed him. The flames were shooting up from the fire and the sparks were flying. It only needed a few of them to set the dry twigs and grass on the hillside alight for a forest fire to spread with the speed of the wind. He wondered whether he should go to the station and put in two requests, one for them to get the telephone line repaired straight away, and the other for someone to be sent to inspect the fire precautions in Green Hollow and persuade Wang Mutong to see sense. He secretly told Azure of what he wanted to do. The last few days her eyes had been swollen like peach stones and she wept as she nodded in reply. Her expression showed that there was much that she wanted to say to him, for whom she felt pity, love, resentment and anger.

That afternoon the One-hander was crouched over his stove cooking some rice to eat on his journey when Azure suddenly rushed into his cabin, openly defying the strict ban her husband had imposed on her. The One-hander stood up in confusion, not knowing what to do. She looked as if she had just come back from working on the vegetable patch. She was wearing only a thin shirt on her top half. It was rather tight and the top button had come open, showing the most alluring glimpses of her full breasts.

"Azure, you...." The One-hander had not even the courage to finish asking his question. He was so flustered that he did not even look up.

"Idiot. Sometimes you're ever so clever, but sometimes you're such a fool. I'm not an evil spirit come to bewitch you." The sight of the One-hander's embarrassment and confusion made her feel more tender towards him than ever. It was a maternal tenderness.

"Azure ... you...."

"I've come to ask if you'll do something for me when you go to the station."

Only then did the One-hander calm himself enough to look her in the face.

"Here's a hundred yuan. I want you to buy us a radio like yours, and a round mirror, and some soap, and some of that cream with a nice smell you put on your face on frosty days, and a brush each for me and Little Tong and Little Qing to brush our teeth with every morning, and we want to put up a pine pole with a wire on it...."

He stared at her with wide-eyed and utter astonishment. This woman from the forests was a goddess of beauty. Her breasts were full, her limbs were exquisitely proportioned and she was brimming with health. She was also tender and gentle, and her body was full of youth and life.

"What are you staring at me like that for? I'm a victim too, just like you." She turned aside with a touch of winning anger as her cheeks flushed and tears began to roll down them.

"All right, all right. Azure, you are good. I, I...." The One-hander was as if spellbound by something about Azure that glistened and shone. A moment later he came to and blushed. "Azure, if you spend all that money at once, won't you be afraid of what Wang...?"

Azure had been gazing at him with happiness and pleasure until "...won't you be afraid of what Wang...?" ruined everything. It was a handful of salt thrown into a heart full of sugar.

"Afraid? I've been afraid of him for ten years and more.... He's been catching animals every winter and selling their skins every spring. Besides, we both earn wages and don't spend much of them. There are piles of ten yuan notes at the bottom of our trunk.... He's too mean to spend them.... I'm not afraid.... Living with him here.... The worst he can do is kill me."

As she spoke the tears welled up in her eyes, as they did in his too. "Azure, I'll take the money and buy the things for you. Don't cry, don't cry. You're a victim too. I'm very sorry for you. I hate myself, hate myself.... Stop crying, Azure. There, there. If Wang sees you when he comes down the mountain he'll beat you again and swear at me...."

"You're no man," said Azure. "You're even less than one of the creepers on our cabin." She shot him a glare filled with all the anger in her heart, turned and went out of his cabin.

"Azure! Azure!" The One-hander followed her to the door and made an involuntary gesture, stretching out both his hands as if to embrace something beautiful. But all there was instead of his left arm was an empty sleeve.

The One-hander went to the forestry station. Big new slogans were being painted all over the place, such as "Down with the Rightist Reversal of Verdicts", "Criticize the Bourgeoisie Within the Party".* Cadres and workers were arguing vociferously and going in and out of the spacious office of the station's political department. The One-hander felt that the right person to report to was the director of the political department, as he had sent him to Green Hollow in the first place. He had waited outside the office nearly all morning and only managed to squeeze in just before the lunch break.

"Oh, it's you, Li Xingfu," said the political director. "Why are you

---

*These were slogans raised in the political movement started by the "gang of four" to attack Comrade Deng Xiaoping in 1975.

back here?" He was standing in front of his desk and just about to go out; Li Xingfu's arrival made him stay. He patted his aching head, then put his hands on his hips and fidgeted with the lower half of his body. But his manner was reasonably friendly.

The One-hander grabbed the chance to tell the director as briefly as he could about the need to restore the telephone line to Green Hollow.

"Restore a line that's been out of action for ten years or more?" The political director put on an expression of amazement. "Is that Wang Mutong's idea? Oh, it's yours. You'd better understand, Li Xingfu, that Wang Mutong's our man in Green Hollow. He may not have much education but he's politically reliable. He's been a model forester for a dozen years or more.... A telephone would need investment capital and material. It couldn't be repaired just by shouting an order. Besides, a big movement's just beginning. The whole county from top to bottom is going to be attacking the rightist tendency to overturn verdicts. That will be the main thing and much more important than everything else. Do you understand?"

The One-hander then made his request for the station to send people to inspect the forest protection and fire prevention in Green Hollow and reported how Wang Mutong was making bonfires in the dry season. He was terrified that the political director would be too impatient to knock off work to hear him through to the end.

"Oh dear, and it looked as though you'd been making a lot of progress recently, Li Xingfu." The political director put on another show of great astonishment, then looked very solemn as he continued, "Let me tell you once again. The station leadership has complete confidence in Wang Mutong. You should follow his leadership in Green Hollow and let him educate and reform you. Don't try to run your own show. And they say.... Well, his wife's young and very good-looking. Don't start getting any funny ideas. What would you do if someone cut off the arm you've got left? Eh? You're an educated youngster. You've got a future...."

Thus it was that so far from being able to report the state of affairs to the station the One-hander was given a very cold dressing-down. It was perfectly obvious that the leadership did not trust him at all. He felt that there was no point in going on living like this as if he were a mangy, scabies-ridden dog who got kicked and driven away wherever he went. He spent a couple of days hanging around the co-op and the tree nursery on the little street at the forestry station. He wished his parents had never sent him to school and longed to be an illiterate, stupid boor like Wang Mutong. The way the world was now ignorance was something to be proud of. It had been decided that the more you knew, the more reactionary you were, and that only the likes of Wang Mutong could make revolution. Finally he started to miss Green Hollow, Azure, Little Tong and Little Qing. At least there were three people in that remote and isolated corner who didn't look down on him and regard him as evil. The thought made the One-hander feel a little easier in his mind. He went to the station's grain store to buy two months' supplies of oil, salt and rice and then to the co-op to buy a transistor radio, soap, face-cream, toothpaste, toothbrushes, and a mirror the size of a small basin for Azure. Finally he went to the food store for steamed buns equivalent to a kilogram of flour. Early the next morning he set out back to Green Hollow with his purchases suspended from a carrying pole.

He carried on till the sun was starting to set, by when he had reached Black Cwm. There was only one more ridge to cross before Green Hollow, and he would be back before dark in the little log cabin where he was to settle down and find his destiny. He had already noticed the black smoke rising above Green Hollow. Was Wang Mutong still making bonfires for ash? But why was there so much smoke? It didn't look like the smoke from bonfires.

Although he was exhausted he did not stop to rest but hurried up towards the pass. He could smell the fire on the other side of the mountain and hear the crackling of the flames. Had a forest fire really started in Green Hollow? Where else could the smell and the noise be coming from? As dusk gradually fell the sky reddened on the other side of the ridge. Was it the glow of sunset or the glare of a blazing forest?

He rushed up the path, his body soaked in sweat, and beads of it the size of fingertips on his forehead. Some kind of supernatural power seemed to be driving him towards the pass. All of a sudden the valley was filled with a sheet of red, flowing fire that shimmered beneath his eyes. Green Hollow! He almost passed out. Green Hollow was a sea of flame. The mountain wind whipped up tongues of fire, line after line of them, thousands of giant red centipedes writhing all over the hillsides around the hollow. Thick smoke poured up from the galloping flames in the valley. Ancient trees that had stood for a thousand years were now pillars of fire lighting up the heavens. Rocks were exploding in the heat like landmines. Rolling fireballs, red arrows and dancing crimson snakes merged into a burning torrent, the strange and terrifying beauty of a forest fire.

"Azure! Little Tong! Little Qing!"

Leaving his carrying pole at the top of the pass the One-hander ran shouting down towards the blazing valley. In this crisis he could not abandon Azure, Little Tong and Little Qing. They were the only three people who meant anything to him in this valley. He ran flat out and only luck saved him from tripping over. He did not know how far he had run through clouds of choking smoke when he saw a woman crawling towards him, her hair matted, her face covered in soot, and her clothes in tatters.

"Azure, dear Azure! What's happened? What's happened to you all?"

The One-hander shouted aloud for joy when he realized that this was Azure. But when she saw him she could only stretch her arms towards him imploringly and collapse on the ground. He rushed over to her and half squatted as he put his arm round her. "Dear, dear Azure. It's me, Li Xingfu, Li Xingfu. Dear Azure...."

The One-hander's throat went dry and his voice hoarse as he called to her and wept for ten full minutes until she came round. She opened her eyes and could only murmur, "It's you, it's you, I've found you...." before lying back in his arms, sobbing.

"Don't cry, dear, don't cry. Tell me how the fire started. Where are Little Tong, Little Qing and Wang?" The One-hander shook Azure's shoulder as he asked.

"Let's go. Help me up." As she spoke she struggled to her feet and staggered up the mountainside. The One-hander helped her as he listened to her story. "That evil man ... the cruel bastard.... At about noon on the day you went to the station he found out that there was a hundred yuan missing from the wooden box. He kept saying I'd stolen it to give my fancy man. He wouldn't believe a word I said. He just beat me up, and went on till every inch of me was bruised and aching.... May Hell take him. Then he locked me into your little cabin and left me there for three days and nights. He didn't even give me a drop of water. It was only very late last night that I finally scratched and pulled a plank loose and crawled to the stream for a drink. Then I saw that the mountain was on fire. It started from his bonfires. Let it burn. Let it kill all the animals in the mountains."

"What about Little Tong and Little Qing?"

"The hellhound! Once the fire started he put the box with the money in it on his back and took Little Qing and Little Tong down the stream ... the way you taught them." Her body went weak and she leaned against the One-hander's shoulder. She was not weeping any more. There was even a kind of exultation in the way she ran her fingers through her own hair than stretched her hand out to run them through the hair plastered to the One-hander's forehead by his sweat.

The catastrophe numbed him with horror. They climbed till they reached the top of the pass and found the carrying pole he had left there. Only then did he remember his steamed buns and his bottle of cold water. He got them out at once for her to eat. She was so hungry that she downed a steamed bun in three of four mouthfuls. After she had eaten four he would not give her any more, he only let her drink. She went on leaning against his chest, resting with her eyes shut.

He hugged her tight as he gazed in fascinated horror at the galloping flames twisting wildly in the wind. Suddenly he remembered that behind the mountain opposite was Love Hollow, where there was a stand full of rare firs and golden-leaf magnolias that the specialists in the station said were precious survivals from he last minor glaciation, living fossils on the verge of global extinction. At the thought of this he said to her, "Azure dearest, let's make our way round to the back of the mountain opposite while the fire's still only halfway up the mountainsides. We can go by the firebreak that runs along the top of the ridge. If we can save the trees in Love Hollow we'll at least have something to say for ourselves should we ever go back to the station."

As he spoke the One-hander looked back at the narrow track that led to the forestry station. His expression showed that it was a last farewell.

"Whatever you like. Wherever you go I'll go with you." Food and the short rest had restored the life force in the Yao woman. She was strong.

The forest fire in Green Hollow was spotted by a military radar post over fifty kilometres away, and the forestry station of the Wujie Hills was immediately informed by telephone. Only then did the station's bosses begin to panic and mobilize large forces to go into the mountains to fight the fire. But by then a third of the thousands of hectares of primeval mixed broadleaf forest had been destroyed. All that was left in the valley were bare, charred trunks and branches looking like devil prisoners just released from hell.

A week later Wang Mutong turned up with the two children at the forestry station, his wooden box on his back. Nobody knew where he had gone to escape the disaster. Azure and Li Xingfu had disappeared. Wang Mutong swore with tears streaming down his face that the fire had been started by Azure and her lover, the One-hander. It had been nothing to do with his own bonfires. The station had made him a model forester for a dozen or more years now. To show where his heart lay he respectfully presented his application to join the party written in his blood to the station Party committee. Naturally the station leadership believed his tearful story and sent militia to search for the culprits. But after combing the blackened mountains for several days all the militia found were the charred bones of wild animals. Nobody knew whether the One-hander and Azure were dead or alive.

As it happened the forestry station, like every other corner of China, was then preoccupied with a great class struggle that was supposedly going to settle the destiny of the country and the Party. Rather than disturb or deflect the main direction of the movement to "counterattack against the rightist tendency to reverse correct political verdicts" they explained it by their usual class struggle theory and reported to their superiors that "the forest fire started by class enemies has been put out in good time by the revolutionary cadres and masses". There the matter ended.

Wang Mutong refused on his life to go back to Green Hollow. Fortunately the station was then also responsible for a stretch of ancient forest at Heaven's Gate Cave, next to the borders of Guangdong and Guangxi, where the old forest warden had died. So the leadership sent Wang Mutong with his two children to succeed the old warden in that rough, hard, self-sufficient way of life. It was said that Wang Mutong married a widow from Guangxi the same year. As before, he set out each day at dawn and went to bed at nightfall, and he was as full of energy and strength as ever. It happened that the widow had a son and a daughter too. It would only be natural if when they all grew up they married Wang Mutong's children and lived in the ancient log cabin at Heaven's Gate Cave for generations.

But after the fall of the "gang of four" there was a great deal of talk in the forestry station. Some people said that if the One-hander and Azure were still alive somewhere far away they would be living quite differently. Even more reckoned that with so many wrong and unjust verdicts being put right across the country Azure and Li Xingfu might turn up any day at the station demanding that justice be done to them too. Why not? In the last couple of years the mighty trees in Green Hollow that had survived the fire gaunt and blackened had been putting forth fresh green branches and new leaves.

April 1980

Translated by W. J. E. Jenner

Daft Second Uncle

●

—— SU SHUYANG ——

Upon graduation from the Chinese People's University in 1960, Su Shuyang taught in a college. He began to write in his spare time in 1956 but it was not until 1977, when he wrote the plays Loyal Hearts *and* The Neighbourhood *that he became famous. He started writing novels and short stories in 1979 and has since published* Native Land, "The Street Under the Sunset" *and many other works. All his works describe the lives of the ordinary people in Beijing and have a strong local style.*

NEW life will always replace the old regime, that's certain. But bidding farewell to the past is not necessarily a laughing matter; it may be nostalgic, painful or elegiac.

For instance, I long to move into a high-rise building, no matter how high, so eager am I to leave the big compound which I have to share with other families; but Second Uncle is dead against moving into a "pigeon-cote" — he detests all the new tower-blocks. Tastes differ.

In the old days Second Uncle was a paper-hanger. I say "in the old days" because that trade of his is a thing of the past in present-day Beijing.

Before Liberation he made paper figures and horses. When a well-to-do family had a funeral, if the householder could afford it he would make a whole streetful of emblems. Young boys and girls, that goes without saying, as well as carriages, horses, sedan-chairs, chests, crates and clothes, in fact everything needful. There were little blue-faced demons and pink-cheeked fairies too stuck up on sorghum stalks. As a senseless child the sight of those paper effigies made me wonder how the dead could ride in paper carriages and use paper ingots to buy paper cakes to eat while speeding to the gate of Hell. The King of Hell and his demon soldiers guarding the gate would graciously let pass those who paid them paper money — didn't they know that it couldn't be used like the official banknotes? Apparently when someone died his brain stopped working and he imagined that things made of paper were real. That made me think the living contemptible, using fakes to trick ghosts while snivelling and moaning for them. What sort of behaviour was that? So I disliked Second Uncle, whose livelihood was cheating ghosts at the expense of the living, yet who was forever boasting about his skill. If one day ghosts were to take medicine which cleared their minds (they were said to have to eat befuddling medicine), they would surely pay him back. I called him Daft Second Uncle, he called me Daft Little Three, but which of us is really daft has never been clarified.

After Liberation, when Second Uncle's skill in making paper figures was uncalled-for, he became a paper-hanger.

"Daft Little Three, see what a good job I've done, better than a plastered ceiling." He went on boasting endlessly of his skill. As most houses in Beijing had papered ceilings, he had plenty of chances to show off and was kept very busy each spring and autumn. I saw him at work, and he knew the tricks of his trade, no doubt about it. He could dispense with a ladder, simply using a T-shaped support of sorghum stalks for the big sheet of white paper he had pasted over; then standing on the floor he raised this up and with a swish of a long-handled broom stuck it evenly over the boards above. In this way he papered a ceiling in next to no time. He told his client the sheets of paper he needed. If a sheet or two was left over he cut it into strips to paste over cracks. Not even a scrap the size of a finger was wasted. By the time the ceiling was dry you could hardly make out where the sheets of paper had been stuck together. It did indeed look better than a plastered ceiling.

"This is an art, Number Three! If I didn't know a trick or two how could I boast?" Second Uncle added, "Like that writing of yours, this takes practice." At this point I would make haste to buy him some liquor. Unable to resist liquor, he would drink himself tipsy and then sleep. Once asleep, of course, he stopped blethering, and I could get on with my writing. Otherwise, once he started holding forth I had to listen respectfully for hours, not allowed to show the least sign of impatience. If I did, he would wag his finger at me and sneer, "So you can scribble a few characters, eh? Look down on your uncle, do you? I used to dandle you, but never mind that — what writer wasn't once dandled — quite apart from that, I'm a worker. Doesn't literature have to serve the workers, peasants and soldiers? You ought to serve me."

"That's fine, Second Uncle, I'm going to right away. I'll send out to buy liquor and half a catty of pig's head."

When he nagged me I had to treat him to liquor and pork. Why not take preventive measures and lay in liquor to forestall his lecture? So whenever he bragged I treated him to drinks.

But his homilies often showed nostalgia for the life in old Beijing, and this sometimes upset me.

"Nowadays everything is collectivized. That's no good." Once when he had indigestion he drank tea instead of liquor, which made him more garrulous, and he came out with this remark, which threw me off balance. I protested, "Second Uncle, tea's not intoxicating, don't talk as if you were tipsy."

"What's wrong?" He glared at me with his beady eyes. "You've got a nerve! I'm not against collectivization. I'm just saying it was too hard and fast, not flexible enough. For instance, wasn't beancurd good to eat with sesame oil, chives and chili sauce? But now it's disappeared. If they happen to sell beancurd in that small eating-house up the lane it's not what it used to be, tastes more like cotton-wool. He curled his lip. "Aren't stiff-dough buns tasty? On a winter night with the wind howling through the telegraph wires, when you heard a clapper sounding some way off you knew stiff-dough buns were coming. The pedlar would shout stiff-dough — buns! Didn't that sound good? You don't hear it nowadays."

That carried me back to my childhood, as if those mournful cries borne on the cold wind were still ringing in my ears. They had something poetic about them. Yes, life in Beijing then had the beauty of a prose poem.

"Everything has disappeared!" complained Second Uncle, and went on to cite other examples.... I must admit that his talk made me nostalgic for life in old Beijing, though I have no idea whether or not it's right to feel this way.

"Don't harp on about such things," I urged him. "Life's getting better every day. Why keep dwelling on the past? Of course there were some tasty things and colourful sights, but it is all linked with the past. When the new replaces the old, some good things are bound to be swept away, but better things will take their place. Don't you agree?"

"Not I," he said. "I think everything tasty and colourful should be kept. Chocolate's new-fangled, but it's too expensive and sticks in your gullet. Give me caramels any day."

"If a girl in a blouse with permed hair and high-heeled shoes walked down the street holding a sorghum stalk, rolling a caramel to eat, would that look good to you?" I asked.

"What's wrong with our national style?" he retorted.

We couldn't see eye to eye. He grew more and more crusty because every day more one-storied buildings were being replaced by tower-blocks, while those lucky enough to survive had mostly given up papered ceilings for plastered ones. He retired and was "out of work", unable to paper plastered ceilings however much superior his papering was. But he kept his own papered ceiling and rejected five offers from the Housing Bureau to plaster it for him. He also ordered me not to follow the fashion of outlawing that sacred paper ceiling, to retain a last entrenchment for his past glory. Unable to withstand him, I had to let my room remain antiquated. At night rats paraded overhead, their feet drumming on the taut paper, and sharpening their teeth on the sorghum stalks while savouring the taste of dried paste and white paper. Dust kept falling from the roof, some motes drifting down through the little holes made by the rats to land softly on my head. My wife told me with a smile, "In the future you should wear a straw hat while you're writing. You'll look fine, like Don Quixote's man Sancho." I hated that paper ceiling. Apart from the diversions already described, in the rainy season that clean expanse of white became a map of the world. But Second Uncle loved it, and wished it would rain every day so that he could keep himself busy repapering the ceiling once a week. The fact is, mine has been papered eight times this year. Eight times in less than four months. You figure it out. To say nothing of the expense, how could I write in peace?

One Sunday this month Second Uncle came rushing in. "Number Three, do me a favour. Go and ask the Housing Bureau not to pull down my house."

"What's up?"

"Our house is to be torn down and all the families in our lane are to be moved out, so a high-rise can be built!"

"Splendid, I envy you the chance to live in a high-rise building."

"A high-rise? Damned if I will! Do go and tell them."

"I don't have the face. Besides, if the other houses are pulled down how can they leave yours? Do you expect the tower-block to leave a space for your two rooms or the road to bypass them? No way."

The old fellow said nothing but sat gulping down his spittle.

"What's good about living in that shack of yours?" I asked.

"In the first place," he retorted, "can you grow flowers in a high-rise? Nothing planted on concrete will grow, and you can't hear crickets chirping."

"You could keep a couple in a jar," I chuckled.

"Pah." He scorned the suggestion. "That would be bogus. And how about chatting round the stove on winter evenings. Those flats have central heating, can people sit chatting round a radiator? You can't roast jujubes on a radiator, can't brew yourself jujube tea. Who thought up this idea of spoiling Beijing by building tower-blocks all over it? That's how foreigners live. There's nothing Chinese about it."

"Don't go making it sound like a question of principle," I put in. "I'm off to buy liquor. I just saw some pigs' ears on sale, real whoppers."

"If you cut off Pigsy's ears now I wouldn't eat them. Huh, you want to put me to sleep, can't stand me, eh? Nothing doing. I'm not drinking today."

The old fellow was really worried. But he knew, no matter how he worried, he had no way of stopping tower-blocks from encroaching steadily on old Beijing. His line of retreat was rapidly being cut.

"I'll move!" he decided. "Swop houses, even if it means exchanging two rooms for one. I'm not going to live in a tower-block."

I asked, "Is my cousin willing? Besides, exchanging houses isn't easy."

"If she's not willing we'll split up. I'll post up notices everywhere to swop with someone at once."

My cousin is a doctor, still unmarried, and normally the most dutiful of daughters. If not for her devoted care he might long ago have gone to be sued by those ghosts who had ridden in his paper carriages. His willingness to leave her now so as to live in a one-storied building where he could listen to crickets showed the extent of his determination.

The next day I saw on a telegraph pole near by his SOS for a house in exchange for his. But written appeals, however desperate, are powerless to stop progress. The lane where he lived and his home along with it were doomed to be razed to the ground.

The roar of a dozen bulldozers was like the thunder of drums declaring war on the old. Those iron path-finders lined up outside the lane waiting for the command to raze and pulverize those relics of the past.

Daft Second Uncle plumped himself down by his gate, from which the door-frame had been dismantled. Gripping the brick wall he declared, "I'm not leaving. This is my home. I'll die here. That's fine with me."

He was surrounded by neighbours taking leave of their old homes, by demolition workers, by grown-ups and children come to watch this drama. Their expressions conveyed bewilderment or derision. They failed to understand how anyone in his right mind could let a tumbledown shack hold him back from entering upon a new life. With all their eyes on me, I had to brace myself to reason with him. But before I could even open my mouth he snubbed me.

"It's no use your talking. If you had any conscience or feeling for Beijing, you'd go and take it up with the city council. Doing away with our lane and our one-storied houses with papered ceilings built round courtyards is like doing away with our temples and the Summer Palace — it's no longer Beijing. Well? Go and tell them that's what your Second Uncle says."

Though I had no way to dissuade him, my cousin had. She said soothingly, "Don't shout, dad, or you'll have another heart attack. Yes, your heart's palpitating." Rubbing his chest she turned to me. "Here, Third Brother, hold him up, I must give him an injection."

"I won't have it!" Second Uncle shouted.

"Even if you don't, that won't stop the bulldozers," she said. "And if your health breaks down how can you paper Third Brother's ceiling for him."

Well, doctors must be the smartest people on earth. Her words carried such weight that at once Second Uncle piped down. He looked at me, at a loss, then meekly held out one arm. His daughter deftly gave him an injection. Very soon he calmed down, and his eyes glazed over. Then she told me to hurry up and call a cab. I asked her, "Was that shot for heart disease?"

"Of course not," she answered. "It was a tranquilizer."

So it was a sedative! The old fellow would enter his new life in a dream and would open his eyes high in a tower-block to greet the red morning sun. How ingenious of her.

The cab came, and Second Uncle, half asleep, was bundled into this modern transport. Just before getting in he gripped my hand and mumbled:

"Mind now, mind you keep that papered ceiling of yours."

Swift as the wind, the taxi carried off this staunch defender of old Beijing while roaring bulldozers charged at the one-storied houses which were obstructing progress, to open up a new road. One by one the houses, their roofs ripped off, crashed down sending up clouds of dust in the sunshine. Those who had lived in this lane stood in silence nearby to watch this spectacle. Some were shedding tears. Were they mourning their old homes, recalling the years spent here, or savouring past griefs and joys? At all events a new life not yet experienced was waiting for them.

I stood there in a daze, wondering when the same fate would befall my home. How would I react to it? Would I still laugh at Daft Second Uncle?

Yes, the old must always pass away, its pleasant and beautiful features too, because after all it belongs to the past. But was there no sense in Daft Second Uncle's assertion "All that's good should be kept"? Especially in the case of old Beijing and its way of life. I was really confused about this.

I rushed off to find Second Uncle, afraid that when he woke to discover himself in a tower-block he might take it too hard or, not being used to stairs, might trip up and fall down....

Translated by Gladys Yang

A Tale of Big Nur

●

—— WANG ZENGQI ——

Wang Zengqi, a student of the celebrated minority writer Shen Congwen, graduated from the Chinese Literature Department of the Southwest China United University. He began to write short stories in 1940 and has published many collections of short stories including An Unexpected Encounter, Night in the Sheepfold *and* Story After Supper. *He is also a scenarist and an essayist.*

1

IT is a queer name for a place, Big Nur. Mongolian they say, perhaps from the Yuan Dynasty (1271-1368). However, there is no way now to ascertain what people called it before that time.

A *nur* is a large expanse of water, not as big as a lake but much bigger than a pond. When the water level is high in spring and summer, Big Nur looks vast. As the source of two rivers, it has a narrow sandbank in the centre covered with cogon grass and reeds. In spring when the water is warm, the purplish-red reed shoots and the greyish-green southernwood on the sandbank turn emerald. In summer, the snow-white ears of the cogon grass and the reeds sway in the breeze. When they turn yellow in autumn, they are cut for thatching the roofs of houses. The sandbank is the first to turn white when it snows in winter and the last to thaw. The snow remains there glittering, while the ice melts in the river and the land grows green.

In the old days on the northwestern side of the sandbank were several heated buildings. Through the clumps of green willows on a whitewashed wall could be distinguished four conspicuous characters in black paint: "Chick and Duckling Breeders". There was a small clearing in front where some people sat on tree stumps chatting in the shade. Now and then someone came out carrying two bamboo baskets full of cheeping yellow fluffy chicks and ducklings. East of the sandbank was a size shop. People starched their clothes and the underneaths of their quilts, for they liked to hear them rustle. Outside the shop dazzling white lumps of size were being sunned. Close to the shop were several stores selling fresh river produce such as water chestnuts, arrowheads, water caltrops and lotus roots. A fish market was collecting and distributing fish and crabs, and there was also a grass purchasing station. Beyond these were fields, cattle sheds and waterwheels. Big pats of cow dung were neatly pasted on cottage walls to dry. It was a truly rural scene. To the north were the villages in Beixiang, to the east the neighbouring prefecture of Xinghua.

On the southern shore of Big Nur stood a green wooden house, formerly the office of a boat company with a waiting-room at one side. At the waterside was a quay. A small steamer had plied between this spot and Xinghua, leaving on odd-numbered days and returning on even-numbered ones. Brightly painted and hung with colourful bunting, the boat had been a thrilling sight with its chugging engine and black smoke pouring from its funnel. While porters loaded and unloaded goods, passengers embarking or disembarking mingled with the pedlars selling beef, sorghum liquor, fried peanuts, melon seeds and candy covered with sesame seeds. After some heavy losses, the shareholders sold the boat and closed down the company, but the wooden building remained intact and empty. Only some mischievous boys living in the vicinity played in the waiting-room, fighting with rods and sticks or peeing from the quay. Standing seven or eight in a row, they pissed into the water to see who could aim the farthest.

Big Nur was also the name of the land around the water where the town and the countryside met. There was a long alley south of the boat company leading to a street outside the north gate of the town. There the hubbub of the town was faintly audible. Without a single shop, the place had its own colours, noises and odours. Even the residents were different. Their lives, customs and morals were quite unlike those of the town dwellers, who wore long gowns and studied Confucian philosophy.

2

To the east and west of the boat company were two small settlements, each dissimilar. The one to the west was characterized by some scattered low houses with tiled roofs. Most of the inhabitants were from places along the Lixia River. They were pedlars selling radishes, water chestnuts, Chinese hawthorns and lotus roots boiled with glutinous rice to fill in the holes. One man who sold spectacles was from Baoying, while another from Hangzhou sold bamboo chopsticks. Like migrating birds, they would rent a room from an acquaintance and stay for a period of time, some longer, some shorter, leaving after they had sold their goods. They began work at sunrise and rested at sunset. After breakfast they went out carrying their wares, hawking and crying out for customers in various accents and tones. At dusk, they returned like birds to their nests. Before long smoke from damp fuel, a sweet yet pungent odour, wafted out through the low eaves. Because these men were from different places and made little money, they were polite and amiable. Their settlement was always peaceful, as bickering or scuffles were rare.

Among the residents were also about twenty tinsmiths from Xinghua. Tin articles were in demand, and every household had tin incense burners, candlesticks, spittoons, canisters, kettles, teapots and wine pots. Even chamber pots were made of tin. When marrying off a daughter, the parents would give her tin utensils for her dowry; at least two big tin containers which could hold four to five kilos of rice to put on top of a chest. When a woman gave birth to a baby, her parents traditionally sent, apart from two hens and one hundred eggs, two pots of glutinous rice porridge in the tin containers from her mother's chest. So even twenty tinsmiths did good business.

The tinsmiths were not highly skilled, and their tools were simple: a shoulder pole with a bellows and some tin plates on one end, a charcoal stove, and two bricks, two foot square with several layers of paper pasted on one side or the other. A tinsmith usually set his load on the porch of a customer's house or on the open ground by the roadside. There he worked the bellows, put the old tin to melt in the pot, and poured the liquid in between the two bricks to press it into a plate which he then cut with a pair of metal shears and beat with a wooden mallet on his anvil. In about the time it takes to eat a meal, the article began to take shape. To give it a finish, he scraped it, polished it with sandpaper and finally rubbed it till it shone with a kind of gloss.

These tinsmiths were very loyal and helpful to each other, looking after their sick companions and never competing for customers. If they went into partnership, they shared the profits. Their leader was an old man whom they all obeyed. An upright fellow, he was very strict with his juniors and apprentices, not letting them gamble, drink or flirt with women. He advised them to be honest, not cheat and avoid trouble. Except for business, they could not loiter on the streets.

The old tinsmith was good at Chinese boxing and taught the others. When they were not at work, he would take them out to practise in pairs, claiming this was a good way of passing time as well as useful for self-defence. For amusement, they also sang local operas. Whenever it rained and they could not go out, they sang. Girls and married women nearby crowded round to watch and listen.

One of the apprentices was the old tinsmith's nephew, whose pet name was Eleventh Boy, as he was the eleventh child in his family. Very intelligent and handsome, he was a worry to his uncle. Tall, broad-shouldered, with a slender waist, he was well proportioned. Beneath his bushy brows shone a pair of large eyes. He wore a straw hat, neat, well-fitting clothes and black shoes. In hot weather, he unbuttoned his shirt, revealing his chest and spotless white cummerbund, five inches wide, wound tightly round his waist. He walked with a spring in his step. The old tinsmith was well aware that when the girls and women gathered to hear them sing, they really came to admire his nephew.

He constantly warned Eleventh Boy to steer clear of the local girls and women, especially those living at the east end. "They're different from us," the old man told him.

3

To the east of the boat company were houses with adobe walls and thatched roofs. The residents there had been porters for generations. Men and women, old and young, lived by their shoulders.

They mostly carried rice from the boats which landed at Big Nur. The rice was taken away by these porters to rice shops or the granaries of rich families, or to other big boats, moored at Loquat Sluice outside the south gate of the town, to be transported along the canal to other places. Sometimes they had to carry their loads to wharfs as far away as Cheluo or Mapeng Bay, one to three miles away. Without stopping for a rest, they walked with quick, even steps, chanting all the way. In a line of ten or twenty, each carried a load weighing two hundred catties. They shifted their loads from shoulder to shoulder in unison when the man at the front put his hand on his shoulder pole. For each load they were given a bamboo tag with one end painted red, the other white. At dusk they were paid according to the number of tags they had accumulated.

Apart from rice they also carried bricks, tiles, lime, bamboo poles, tung oil.... All year round they worked and never went hungry.

When their children reached their teens, they began work carrying half a load in two willow baskets. After one or two years, they were strong enough to bear the whole load and earned as much as the adults.

The porters led a very simple life, daily exerting all their strength, and eating three meals cooked on a small stove. No money was spent on fuel. Villagers carrying reeds to sell at the market always dropped some on the road. Children, too young to be porters, collected these with a bamboo rake and were nicknamed "Raking Devils". Sometimes, to save trouble, they simply snatched a bundle of reeds from a villager and took to their heels. By the time he had laid down his load and shouted curses, they were nowhere to be seen. Because there were no chimneys, smoke poured out from the windows or doors, drifting to the surface of the water and lingering there. These households never stored grain. They bought enough food only for each day. At meal times the men squatted outside their homes, holding big bowls of brown rice with vegetables, small fish, preserved beancurd or pickled hot peppers. They wolfed down their food with such relish that nothing in the world seemed more appetizing.

They celebrated New Year's Day and other festivals by changing into clean clothes, feasting and gambling. Each gambler took a stack of ten or twenty coins, then threw in turn another coin at the pile, keeping the coins that fell down. Another game was rolling the coins. Piles of coins were placed on the ground and a brick was propped up at one end to form a slope. The gambler rolled a coin down the brick. If it stopped at a spot five inches from a pile, he could take the money; if seven inches, he had to forfeit the same amount as the stack. The porters enjoyed themselves, while onlookers cheered loudly, adding to the fun.

The girls and women were as strong as the men. They concentrated on carrying fresh water products, perhaps because the men disdained carrying dripping loads. They had slender figures and put pomade on their thick black hair. The buns at the back of their heads were large and tied with red wool visible from far away. At one side of their buns they liked to wear a decoration — a tender willow twig twisted like a ball at the tip at the *Qingming* Festival, some mugwort leaves at the Dragon Boat Festival, a gardenia or an oleander in season, or a big red velvet flower when they could not get a fresh one. Because they carried their loads with a shoulder pole all year round, nearly all the shoulders of their blouses were patched. An old blouse, with new and different coloured patches, was the distinctive dress of the women at Big Nur. Twenty women with loads of purple red water chestnuts, green water caltrops and snow-white lotus roots walking in single file, like willows swaying in the wind, were a wonderful sight!

They earned the same amount of money as the men and adopted their fast way of walking like a gust of wind, or sitting with legs wide apart. They also wore straw sandals and dyed their toenails red with garden balsam. They did not avoid raw or cold food. They talked and cursed like men. They even chanted the same rude songs....

Unmarried women were more reticent, but once married they behaved as boorishly as they liked. There was an old bachelor called Huang Hailong, who had been a porter when young. Later he hurt his leg and was assigned to the wharf to look after the rice boats and collect the bamboo tags. Old as he was, he loved to fondle this woman's breast or pinch that one's bottom. According to his age, the women ought to have addressed him politely as grand-uncle, but all of them called him "Old Bawdy Beard". One day as he was up to his old tricks again, several women made a plan. Following a signal, they took immediate action. In the twinkling of an eye, the old man's trousers were thrown up to a tree-top. When the old fellow heard the bamboo clappers for selling noodles with dumplings, he regained his high spirits.

"Who dares take a bath in the nur?" he challenged. "I bet each one of you two bowls of noodles with dumplings you won't!"

"Really?"

"Sure!"

"OK!"

The women stripped and splashed in the water. A moment later, climbing ashore they cried, "Boil the noodles!"

People here seldom married in a regular way, so sedan carriers and trumpeters were of no use. Women came to men of their own accord. Girls generally chose their spouses themselves. They were rather casual in their sexual relations. There was nothing strange about a girl giving birth to an illegitimate child at her mother's home. A married woman could have a lover. The only criterion for a woman to take delight in a man was her consent. Most girls or women asked their lovers for money to buy flowers, but some gave money to their lovers instead.

The townsfolk looked down on their morals and manners, but were theirs any better? It was difficult to say.

4

To the east of Big Nur, there was a household of only two members — a father and his daughter. Huang Haijiao, the father, was Huang Hailong's cousin. He had been a fine porter, capable of going up steep gangplanks with his load. The grain bins of the big grain shops here were thirty to forty feet high with the planks sloping very steeply. One had to ascend them at one go. Whenever an older man or a woman hesitated at the foot, Huang would take their two hundred catty load and shoot to the top like an arrow. Raising his hands, he would pour the two baskets of rice into the bin and then stride down with only a few steps to the ground. Honest and faithful, he had not married until he was twenty-five. That year, when he carried grain to Cheluo, he met a girl asking the way. With a long fringe and a bun on the back of her head, she wore a little rouge on her face. Flurried and anxious she could not give the exact name of any place. Huang saw at a glance that she was a maidservant running away from some rich and influential family. He talked with her for a while, and finally she agreed to live with him. She called herself Lianzi, a common name for maidservants in the region.

A year later she gave birth to a girl. It was July when rosy clouds filled the sky, so they named her July Cloud.

Lianzi was deft and hard-working, but she liked to wear tight silk trousers, eat melon seeds and nibble between meals. She sang ballads such as "The cold moon rises and sheds light on my chamber. Giving a yawn, I stretch myself and feel sleepy. *Aiyo, aiyo,* I'm feeling sleepy...." All this was quite different from the local customs.

When July Cloud was three years old, Lianzi eloped with an actor who played young gentlemen's parts in a theatrical troupe passing through the village. That day Huang had gone to Mapeng Bay. Lianzi washed and starched all her husband's clothes, gathered together her daughter's, cooked a pot of rice and purchased half a catty of wine. Entrusting the little girl to her neighbour, she said she had something to do. She locked the door and was never seen again.

Huang did not feel too sad, for things like that were not unusual. A caged bird sometimes flew away. But he adored the little creature she had left behind. Unwilling to see the child suffer at the hands of a cruel stepmother, he determined not to marry again. Shouldering the responsibilities of both father and mother, he brought her up by himself. He taught her how to make fishing nets and weave reed mats by the age of fourteen, because he was loath to see her be a porter.

At fifteen she was as beautiful as a flower, her figure and face like her mother's. With a dimple in one cheek, her face had an oval shape with long dark eyebrows. The corners of her eyes slightly tilted upwards and their long lashes made them look narrow. But when she suddenly looked round, they opened wide in a somewhat surprised and absorbed expression, as if someone was calling her from a distance. When she made a net or wove a mat by the waterside, some youths walked past her, pretending to be on business. If she went to the market to buy meat, vegetables, oil, wine, cloth or cosmetics, she got more and better quality than others for the same price. The women caught on to this and asked her to purchase things for them. Whenever she went to the market, she had to carry several bamboo baskets, returning home with aching arms. If there was a theatrical performance in the Taishan Temple, people had to carry a bench or a stool to sit on, but not July Cloud. She went there empty-handed and was always offered a good seat. Few people applauded the wonderful performance, because most feasted their eyes on her.

Soon she reached sixteen, the age she should consider marriage. But who would win such a beauty? First Boy at the breeders? Second Boy at the size shop? Third Boy at the fresh water food shop? Both Huang and his daughter knew they all desired her, otherwise what was the point of hanging around July Cloud all the time? But the girl did not take them seriously.

At the age of seventeen, fate stepped in. Her father fell from a plank and injured his spine. At first he thought it was not serious. But the large quantities of medicinal wine and plasters did not produce the desired result. Eventually his legs were paralysed. Sometimes he got up from his bed and, taking hold of a high stool, shuffled a few steps forward. Most of the time, he lay propped up against a pile of quilts in bed. He could no longer earn money to buy his daughter new clothes or velvet flowers. Instead he had to depend on her to support him. Though still less than fifty, he could only do some old women's work, such as preparing bundles of string for his daughter to make nets. The girl did not neglect her poor invalid father. If anybody was willing to marry her, he must also be willing to live with her and provide for the sick man. Who was prepared to do that? The only property they had was their thatched three-roomed house. The girl and her father each occupied a side room. The one in the middle was a small hall. First Boy, Second Boy and Third Boy came from time to time, glancing at the slender figure behind the fishing net or sitting on the snow-white mat. In their eyes admiration still shone, but their enthusiasm was dampened.

In spite of the old tinsmith's warning, Eleventh Boy still went to the east side of the nur frequently. Middle-aged women, young married women and girls liked to entice him there to mend old kettles. On the way from Big Nur to the town, there was a shady spot under the willows in front of July Cloud's house, a nice place to seek customers. One wove mats, while the other melted tin. Eleventh Boy and July Cloud were an ideal pair to keep each other company. Sometimes July Cloud stopped to help the young tinsmith work his bellows. When she went indoors to check on her father, she would ask Eleventh Boy if he wanted to have a smoke or a drink of water. He would cover the stove and take her place weaving. Once when her finger was cut by the sharp bamboo, he sucked the wound for her. Through their exchanges she knew that he had no sisters and that his mother had remained a widow for years, doing needlework for others, straining her eyes. Eleventh Boy feared she would become blind some day....

People expected the two to fall in love, but how could they marry? One family needed a son-in-law, while the other a daughter-in-law. As for the two, they loved to sit side by side talking. They were old enough to love, but nothing was settled; they were like clouds floating back and forth in the sky, unable to form rain.

One moonlit night July Cloud went to wash some clothes on a boat. A naughty boy crept stealthily up and tickled her from behind. Caught off her guard, she fell into the water. She could swim a little, but since she was scared and the current was swift, she struggled, then shouted for help. After swallowing a lot of water, she was washed away by the current. It happened that Eleventh Boy was practising Chinese boxing on the level ground outside the breeders. He saw someone being carried along, her hair floating on the surface of the water. Quickly throwing off his shoes, he jumped into the nur and rescued her.

July Cloud was still unconscious. He had no choice but to lift her in his arms like a child and carry her home. Dripping wet, she was soft and warm. His heart throbbed as he sensed her nestling closer to him.

In her room she came to. As a matter of fact she had been conscious long before. He lay her on the bed. As she changed her wet clothes the moonlight shone on her beautiful body. He snatched up a bundle of grass and boiled her half a pot of sugary ginger soup. After she had eaten it, he left.

She got up, bolted the door and lay down again. She seemed to sense how she had looked, lying in bed. The moon was exceptionally fine.

"You're an idiot!" she thought to herself. Then she repeated it aloud. Before long she was sound asleep.

That same night a man prized open her door.

5

West of a street near an alley opposite the boat company there was a Taoist temple named Lianyang Temple, in which was stationed a local armed force under the jurisdiction of the prefectural government in name, but paid by the local trade association. Bandits were rampant in the region. They kidnapped people by hiding their boats amid the reeds in the nur, from which they could easily escape when chased. The merchants felt they needed the protection of a special armed force. Well-equipped, the troop had a boat with armour on three sides and bullet-proof iron plates chest high. Before setting out on a mission, the soldiers could be seen shouldering two machine-guns and carrying more than half a crate of bullets aboard the boat.

A week or a fortnight later they would return triumphantly with few casualties. Once ashore, in a column four abreast, they marched through the long alley led by a dozen trumpeters, heading for the big street leading to the prefectural government. When they reached the main street, the trumpeters began to blow. Behind them were the soldiers with loaded rifles. Their captives were sandwiched in the middle, sometimes three, five, or only one, with their hands bound behind their backs. What was amazing was that the captives also marched boldly and spiritedly in step with the music. They even followed the officer of the day, shouting loudly, "One, two, three, four!" All the shops and stores were informed beforehand to withdraw their birdcages of mynas or grey thrushes, because it might make the bandits unhappy to see them. As the captives would be thrown into prison after they arrived at the prefectural government, if they saw the caged birds, they would feel depressed. The glittering brass trumpets and bayonets and the militant column, with some legendary bandit heroes, made a fascinating spectacle for the residents living along this street. It was as wonderful as watching lion dances, dragon lanterns, stilt performances, children in fancy dress on high frames or a big funeral procession with all the required Taoists and monks.

Suppressing bandits in the countryside was the soldiers' sole duty. They seldom drilled, except for taking the two machine-guns to the waterside and firing several rounds of ammunition. What made others aware of their existence were the twelve trumpeters practising at the edge of the nur from eight to nine in the morning and four to five in the afternoon, first blowing one long note, then some sections separately and finally playing marches together. After that they were free to do whatever they liked. Some slipped away to the doors of certain households and with a cough, stepped inside, closing the doors behind them.

Most of the trumpeters liked to dress well. They had plenty of free time and earned their money. Their pay did not amount to much, but each time they returned from the countryside they got a reward. Sometimes they held secret talks with the bandits and did a deal with them. That was why they could spend lavishly. Because they protected the local gentry and merchants, they had strong backers, so even when they caused trouble, nobody made a fuss.

Their leader, Liu, was familiar with the women of several households. He was the man who had prized open July Cloud's door!

He left ten dollars when he took himself off.

It was not the first time something like that had happened. July Cloud's father learned about it that very night. Holding the money in his hand, he heaved a long sigh. When their neighbours heard, they did not say much. "That dirty beast!" the girls and women cursed.

July Cloud did not shed tears or try to drown herself in the nur. That kind of thing happened to a girl sooner or later, she thought philosophically. But why him? It should not have been him! What was to be done? Get a kitchen knife and kill him? Burn down Lianyang Temple? No! She had to consider her invalid father. Upset, she sat on the bed utterly confused. Then it dawned on her that it was time to get up and prepare breakfast. She had to make nets, weave mats and go to the market. She thought of her childhood when she had watched a bride wearing a pair of pink silk embroidered shoes. She missed her mother, who was now somewhere far away. She did not remember what her mother looked like, but recalled that she dipped a dropstick in some rouge to make a red dot between her eyebrows. She picked up the mirror and stared at her reflection. It seemed that she saw herself for the first time. She reflected how Eleventh Boy had sucked her wound. She felt unworthy of him. Overcome with regret, she sighed, "Why didn't I give myself to him?"

This idea grew in her mind after each visit of the trumpet squad leader.

Then the troop went off on a mission again.

One day she went to see Eleventh Boy and said, "Come to the east bank this evening. I've something to tell you."

When Eleventh Boy arrived at the appointed spot, she stepped aboard a sampan for tending the ducks. It was too small for more than one person. Local people also used it to cut reeds or grass or gather wild duck eggs on the sandbank. She punted the sampan towards the sandbank, shouting over her shoulder. "Follow me!"

In no time Eleventh Boy swam to where she was waiting.

There they stayed in the grass until the moon was high in the sky.

6

The older apprentices knew about the affair but kept it secret from the old tinsmith. They left the door unlatched for Eleventh Boy and oiled its hinges to muffle the squeaks. Eleventh Boy often did not come back before dawn. One day he pushed the door open as usual and was about to slip into bed, when the old tinsmith boomed, "Are you courting death?"

Affairs of that kind could not be concealed. The news finally reached the ears of the trumpet squad leader. In fact, nobody had to tell him. He knew it himself, for July Cloud was cold and detested the sight of him. They were not married, so it was nothing to him if they broke up. But it was a loss of face to let a young tinsmith steal her away from him. That was unprecedented! He could not swallow such an insult, nor could his colleagues, who liked to bully others. If they ignored this, what would happen next?

One day before dawn, Liu with several men kicked open July Cloud's door, dragged the young tinsmith out from under her quilt and bound him up. They also tied up the girl and her father in case they summoned people to the rescue.

They dragged Eleventh Boy to the graveyard at the back of Taishan Temple and beat him up, wanting him to pack up and go back to his home in Xinghua.

The young tinsmith remained silent.

They ordered him not to enter Huang's house or lay a finger on July Cloud again.

He still refused to say a word.

They tried to make him beg for mercy and apologize.

He gritted his teeth.

His toughness enraged them all the more. "See how stubborn he is!" one of them said. "Beat him to death!" Seven or eight sticks rained down on him again.

He was beaten almost to a pulp.

Hearing that Eleventh Boy had been kidnapped by the trumpeters, the other tinsmiths searched high and low for him until they finally came to the back of the temple.

Feeling there was still some life in him, his uncle hurriedly sent a man to fetch an old chamber pot. He knew that only the scales inside the pot could save the life of a dying man in such a condition.

Eleventh Boy clenched his teeth so tightly that the liquid could not be poured down his throat.

July Cloud took over and whispered in his ear, "Eleventh Boy, drink it!"

Seeming to hear a faint voice, he opened his eyes. The girl poured it down.

There was no knowing why, but she herself also tasted it.

Then the tinsmiths took off a door, laid Eleventh Boy on it and carried him away.

They reached the east end of the nur and were about to move westward, when July Cloud stopped them and said, "Carry him to my home."

The old tinsmith nodded.

July Cloud took all her fishing nets and reed mats to sell in the market and bought medicine for Eleventh Boy's injuries.

Women killed their laying hens for him.

The tinsmiths pooled money to buy ginseng.

Porters, tinsmiths, women and girls came constantly to see him, expressing an affection and kindness they seldom showed in their hard, dull lives. They believed that what Eleventh Boy and July Cloud had done was correct and were proud that Big Nur had bred such a young fine pair. They felt as pleased as if they were celebrating the New Year.

Liu dared not show his face. His gang also barricaded themselves in their quarters with double sentries posted at the gate. Those "heroes" turned out to be cowards!

The tinsmiths held a meeting and submitted to the prefectural government a petition demanding that the trumpet squad leader be handed over to them.

The local government gave no reply.

Then tinsmiths took to the streets and demonstrated. It was a rare sight for there were no banners or slogans, just twenty men with their loads, parading slowly through the town. Silent and grave, they were dignified and determined.

The demonstration lasted for three days.

On the third day they sat in front of the screen wall facing the gate of the prefectural government. On each head was a wooden tray with incense burning in a burner. That was an ancient custom. When people had suffered grievous wrongs, and the officials concerned refused them redress, they could burn down the court with incense and go unpunished.

The tinsmiths never wavered. If they took action, the result would be serious. The prefectural magistrate invited the local gentry and merchants to talk the matter over and reached a consensus that the case could not be ignored any longer. So the head of the trade association invited an assistant as the representative of the prefectural magistrate, the adjutant of the troop, Eleventh Boy's uncle and two of the older tinsmiths, Huang Hailong of the porters, the spectacle seller from Baoying and the chopsticks pedlar from Hangzhou to meet in a big teahouse to settle the matter.

Agreement was reached. All medical expenses were to be borne by the troop (actually the trade association gave the money), and Trumpet Squad

Leader Liu was to leave the area and sign his consent to this. The old tinsmith accepted the terms but insisted that Liu add one more point. If he set foot in their prefecture again, the old tinsmith would settle accounts with him.

Two days later Liu left, quietly escorted by two of his men holding a gun. He had been transferred to Sanduo Prefecture to work as a customs officer.

When Eleventh Boy was able to take some food and speak, July Cloud asked him, "They said they'd stop beating you if only you promised not to come to my home again. Why didn't you agree?"

"You would have liked me to?"

"No."

"I knew you wouldn't."

"Was it worth it?"

"Yes, it was!"

"Oh, how wonderful you are! I love you! You must get well quickly."

"Kiss me and I'll recover soon."

"Yes, I will!"

There were three mouths to feed now and only one wage-earner. They had no savings, and nothing to sell or pawn. Making fishing nets or weaving mats did not bring in money right away. Eleventh Boy's injuries would not heal quickly. July Cloud took the two baskets her father had used, knocked away the dust and went to earn money immediately. The local girls and women admired her. At first they were worried, but later they relaxed when they saw her carrying her loads with quick, steady steps. From then on, July Cloud worked as a woman porter, wearing a big red flower on one side of her hair. Her eyes were as bright as ever, but their expression was more profound. She had become a capable young wife.

Would Eleventh Boy recover?

Certainly!

1981

Translated by Kuang Wendong

The Destination

—— WANG ANYI ——

Wang Anyi, a young woman writer, was sent to do farm work in the countryside after graduating from junior middle school in 1969. In 1972 she joined a Jiangsu drama troupe and in 1978 moved to Shanghai to work as an editor at Childhood *magazine. She published her first story in 1976. Her publications include the novels* The Old Course of the Yellow River *and* The Lapse of Thirty Years *and several collections of short stories. "The Destination", "Lapse of Time" and "Little Bao Village" were all national prize-winners.*

1

OVER the loudspeaker came the announcement, "The train is arriving at Shanghai terminal...."

Dozing passengers opened their eyes. "We're arriving in Shanghai."

"We're nearing the terminal."

The impatient ones removed their shoes and climbed onto their seats to reach for their luggage.

A group of middle-aged men from Xinjiang began making plans. "We'll take a bath as soon as we check into a hotel. Then we'll call the heavy-machinery plant and go out to a Western-style restaurant."

"Right. We'll have Western food." Their spirits rose. They had gone to work in Xinjiang after their university years in Beijing, Fuzhou and Jiangsu. Though they retained their accents, their appearance and temperament were "Xinjiangized", weather-beaten and blunt. When Chen Xin asked casually about Xinjiang after he got on the train at Nanjing, they gave him a detailed and enthusiastic account of the region: the humour and wit of Xinjiang's different ethnic minorities, the beautiful songs they sang, the graceful dances and lively girls. They also described their own life there, how they fished and hunted. Expressive and eloquent, they painted an appealing picture.

"How long will you be in Shanghai?" asked one of the group, a man from Beijing, patting Chen Xin on the shoulder.

With a smile, he turned around from gazing out the window. "I've come back for good."

"Got a transfer?"

"Right."

"Bringing your wife and children?"

"I haven't any," he blushed. "I couldn't have come back if I'd been married."

"My, you must be determined." Chen Xin's shoulder received a heartier slap. "You Shanghainese can't survive away from Shanghai."

"It's my home," Chen Xin justified himself.

"But there's a big wide world outside."

Chen Xin smiled.

"One should be able to find interesting things anywhere. You skate in Harbin, swim in Guangzhou, eat big chunks of mutton with your hands in Xinjiang and western food in Shanghai.... Wherever fate lands you, you look for something interesting and enjoy it as best you can. Maybe that's what makes life interesting."

Chen Xin only smiled. Absent-mindedly, he kept his eyes on the fields flitting past his window, fields carefully divided into small plots and planted like squares of embroidery — there were patches of yellow, dark and light green and, beside the river, purple triangles. To eyes used to the vast fertile soil of the north, the highly and carefully partitioned land struck him as narrow and jammed. But he had to admit that everything was as fresh and clean as if washed by water. This was the south, the outskirts of Shanghai. Oh, Shanghai!

The train hurtled past the fields and low walls and entered the suburbs. Chen Xin saw factories, buildings, streets, buses and pedestrians.... Shanghai became closer and tangible. His eyes moistened and his heart thumped. Ten years ago, when classes were suspended during the "cultural revolution", he and other school-leavers left for the countryside. At that time, as Shanghai faded into the distance, he had not expected to return. No. He probably had thought about it. In the countryside, he ploughed, planted, harvested wheat, dredged rivers and tried to get a job or admittance to a university. He finally enrolled in a teachers' college. After graduation he was assigned to teach in a middle school in a small town. Able to earn his own living at last, his struggles should have ended; he could start a new life. But he felt he had not arrived at his destination. Not yet. He was still unsettled and expectant, waiting for something. He only realized what he had been waiting for, what his destination really was, when large numbers of school-leavers returned to Shanghai after the fall of the "gang of four".

In the past decade, he had been to Shanghai on holiday and on business. But with every visit he only felt the distance between him and Shanghai grow. He had become a stranger, an outsider, whom the Shanghainese looked down upon. And he found their superiority and conceit intolerable. The pity and sympathy of his friends and acquaintances were as unbearable. For, at the back of that lay pride. Still he was forced to admire Shanghai's progress and superiority. The department stores were full of all kinds of goods and people dressed in the latest fashions. Clean, elegant restaurants. New films at the cinemas. Shanghai represented what was new in China. But above all there was his home, his mother, his brothers and his dead father's ashes.... He smiled, his eyes brimming with tears. He would make any sacrifice to return. He had acted as soon as he learned that his mother was retiring and that one of her children could take her job. He had gone here and there to get his papers stamped, a troublesome and complicated business. He had fought a tense and energetic battle, but he had won.

The train pulled into the station. As Chen Xin opened the window, a cool breeze, a Shanghai breeze, rushed in. He saw his younger brother, now grown tall and handsome. Seeing him, the youth ran beside the train calling happily, "Second Brother!" Chen Xin's heart shrank with regret. He calmed down remembering how ten years earlier, his elder brother had run beside the train too at his departure.

The train came to a halt. His younger brother caught up, panting. Chen Xin was too busy talking to him and handing him his luggage to notice that the cheerful group of middle-aged men were bidding him farewell.

"Elder Brother, his wife and Nannan are here too. They're outside. We only got one platform ticket with your telegram, saying you were coming. Have you got a lot of luggage?"

"I can manage. How's Mum?"

"She's OK. She's getting dinner ready. She got up at three this morning to buy food for you."

A lump rose in his throat; he lowered his head in silence. His brother fell silent too.

They moved quietly out of the long station. At the exit his elder brother, his wife, and his son, Nannan took his suitcases from him. They struggled under the weight for a few steps and then gave them back to him. Everybody laughed. His elder brother clasped him round his shoulders while his younger brother took his arm. Sister-in-law followed carrying Nannan.

"Have you got all the necessary papers?" his elder brother inquired. "Tomorrow I'll ask for leave and take you to the labour bureau."

"I can take him. I haven't got anything to do," offered his younger brother.

Chen Xin's heart trembled again. He turned to him with a smile. "OK. No. 3 can take me."

It took three buses to reach home. His mother greeted him, lowering her head to wipe away tears. The three sons were at a loss for words, not knowing how and also too shy to express their feelings. All they could say was, "What's there to cry about?" It was his sister-in-law who knew how to stop her. She said, "This calls for a celebration, Mum. You should be rejoicing."

The tension lifted. "Let's eat," they said to one another. The table was moved from his mother's six-square-metre room to the big room his elder brother and wife occupied. Chen Xin looked around. The room where he and his two brothers had once lived had a different appearance. The light green wall paper was decorated with an oil painting and a wall light. Smart new furniture had been made to fit the room. The colour was special too.

"What do you call this colour?" asked Chen Xin.

"Reddish brown. It's the fashion," answered his younger brother with the air of an expert.

Nannan moved a stool over to a chest of drawers, climbed on it, and turned on a cassette recorder. The strong rhythm of the music raised everybody's spirits.

"You live well!" The excitement in Chen Xin's voice was obvious.

His elder brother smiled apologetically. After a long pause he said, "I'm glad you're finally back."

His sister-in-law carried in some food, "Now that you're back, you should find a sweetheart and get married."

"I'm old and ugly. Who'd want me?"

That made everyone laugh.

More than ten different dishes were placed on the table: Diced pork and peanuts, braised spareribs, crucian carp soup.... Everybody piled food onto Chen Xin's plate. Even Nannan copied them. They went on serving him even when his plate was like a hill, as if to compensate for the ten hard years he had spent away from home. His elder brother almost emptied the stir-fried eel, Chen Xin's favourite dish, onto his plate. Though younger by three years, Chen Xin had always been his brother Chen Fang's protector. Chen Fang, tall and slender, had been nicknamed String Bean. His school marks were high. Outside of school he was poor at sports and had slow reflexes. His legs always got caught in the rope when it was his turn to jump. When playing cops and robbers, the side he was on was sure to lose. Chen Xin always fought for him when no one wanted him. "If you don't want my brother, I won't play either. And if I don't play I'll make sure there'll be no game." And he meant what he said, so the boys compromised, fearing the terrible havoc he'd wreak on the one hand and hating to lose a popular, funny playmate on the other. Later, when Chen Fang had to wear spectacles, he looked so scholarly that his nickname became Bookworm. For some reason Chen Xin considered this even more insulting than the previous one. He brought an end to it by bashing anyone who dared to utter it. When classes were suspended during the "cultural revolution", he had finished junior middle and his brother senior middle school. The government's policy was clear; only one son could work in Shanghai, the other must go to the countryside. His heartbroken mother had mumbled tearfully, "The palm and the back of my hand.... They are both my flesh and blood." Feeling sorry for her, Chen Xin volunteered, "I'll go to the countryside. Brother's a softy; he'll get bullied. Let him stay in Shanghai. I'll go...." When he set out, Chen Fang had seen him off at the station, standing woodenly behind a group of friends, not daring to meet his eyes. As the train pulled out, Chen Fang moved forward to grasp Chen Xin's hand and ran beside the train even after the speeding locomotive pulled them apart.

Chen Xin had finally returned. Overcome by all sorts of emotions, no one was particularly good at expressing them, so they transformed them into action. After supper his elder brother served tea while his wife made up a bed in the hut they had constructed in the courtyard. His younger brother stood in a queue for Chen Xin to go to the public bath house. When Chen Xin had eaten his fill and bathed, he lay on the double bed he was to share with his younger brother, feeling as relaxed as if he were drunk. The clean, warm bedding had a pleasant smell. The lamp on the desk beside the bed gave the simple hut a soft glow. Someone had placed a stack of magazines beside his pillow; the family knew and had remembered that he always read himself to sleep. Oh, home. This was home! He had returned home after ten years. Feeling a peace that he had never felt before, he closed his eyes and dozed off without reading. At dusk he woke up. Someone had come in and turned off the light. He opened his eyes in the darkened room and peacefully drifted back to slumber.

2

Early in the morning Chen Xin and his younger brother went to the labour bureau to start the formalities. The triangular lot beside the bus stop was filled with tailors' stalls and sewing machines. A young man with a measuring tape hanging round his neck accosted them. "Do you want something made?" They shook their heads and walked away. Curious, Chen Xin turned to look back at the young man who was dressed up like a model, soliciting customers.

His brother tugged at him. "The bus's coming. They're all school-leavers waiting for jobs. Shanghai's full of them." Chen Xin was astonished. His brother, shoving his way onto a bus, stopped at the door and called out to him, "Come on, Second Brother."

"Let's wait for the next one." The bus was filled to bursting and the crowd at the bus stop made Chen Xin hesitate.

"More people will come. Get on quick." His brother's voice seemed to come from afar.

Chen Xin was strong. He could push. He shoved and squeezed until he caught the door handle and placed his feet on the steps. Then he mustered his strength and, amid cries and curses, pushed deeper into the bus to stand beside a window where he could hang on to the back of the seat. But he was crammed and uncomfortable, bumping against people's heads or backs, having a hard time fitting in. All round him the passengers grumbled.

"Look at the way you're standing!"

"Just like a door plank."

"Outsiders are always so awkward on buses."

"Who're you calling an outsider?" An indignant No. 3 squeezed his way over, ready to pick a quarrel. Chen Xin tugged him. "Don't mind them. It's so crowded. Don't fight."

Softly, No. 3 gave him a tap. "Turn this way. Right. Hold the seat with your left hand. That's better. See?"

It was true. Chen Xin heaved a long sigh. He finally fitted in with his chest pressed against a back and his back against someone else's chest. At least his feet touched the floor. He turned his head to look and noticed a silent understanding among the passengers. Facing in the same direction, they all stood in a straight line, one behind the other. This way, the bus could fill to capacity. He thought of the remote town he had lived in where passengers squeezed in any old way, no scientific method at all. The bus held fewer people while the crowding and discomfort were the same. Shanghainese could adapt themselves to smaller spaces better.

The female conductor's voice came through a loudspeaker in Beijing and Shanghai dialects, "The next stop is Xizang Zhong Road. Those who're getting off please get ready." With royal airs, this woman looked proud and disdainful, like a strict disciplinarian. But these announcements helped passengers. He recalled again the buses and the woman conductors in that little town: battered, dusty buses shooting off before their doors were closed; unenthusiastic conductors never announcing stops but closing doors on passengers and catching their clothes in them. They had no rules at all. Things were in shipshape order in Shanghai. In that sort of environment, you had to do things properly.

When they got off the bus, No. 3 took Chen Xin down a street to one of the city's free markets. There were vegetables, fish, poultry, woollen sweaters, sandals, purses and hair clips, and stalls with fried food and meat dumplings. Below a placard announcing folk toys were paper lanterns and clay dolls. Seeing a market like that, Chen Xin had to laugh. What a strong contrast with Shanghai's wealthy, modern Nanjing Road.

"There are a lot of markets like this in Shanghai," explained No. 3.

"The government encourages school-leavers to be self-employed."

The mention of the unemployed youth made Chen Xin frown. After pausing, he asked, "What was the matter with you, No. 3? Why did you fail the university entrance exam again?"

No. 3 lowered his head. "I don't know. I guess I'm stupid."

"Will you take it again next year?"

After a long silence, No. 3 said haltingly, "I might fail a third time."

That made Chen Xin angry. You've no confidence in yourself.

No. 3 smiled honestly. "I'm not cut out to study. I forget what I learn."

"Your elder brother and I didn't have the chance to continue our studies. You're the only one in the family who can attend a university. But you've no ambition."

No. 3 fell silent.

"What are your plans then?"

No. 3 gave a laugh but said nothing. Just then someone called out behind them, "Chen Xin!"

They turned to face a woman leading a handsome little boy. She was in her thirties, with long permed hair and fashionable clothes. Chen Xin couldn't place her.

"Have I grown so old that you don't recognize me?"

"Why, it's you, Yuan Xiaoxin! You don't look older, just prettier," Chen Xin laughed.

Yuan laughed with him. "Come on. We were in the same group in the countryside for two years, and yet you couldn't place me. What a poor memory!"

"No. It was just that I didn't expect to see you. Weren't you among the first batch to get a job? Are you still at Huaibei Colliery?"

"No. I came back to Shanghai last year."

"How come?"

"It's a long story. How about you?"

"I returned yesterday."

"Oh." She didn't show surprise. "Zhang Xinhu and Fang Fang are back too."

"Good," Chen Xin's voice showed excitement. "So half the group have returned. We must get together sometime. Our hard times are finally over."

She gave a faint smile, revealing fine wrinkles at the corners of her eyes.

"Uncle," chirped the little boy. "You've got white hair like my grandpa."

Chen Xin laughed, bending down to take the boy's hand. "This is your son?" he addressed Yuan.

"He's my sister's son," she explained blushing. "I'm not married. If I were I couldn't have come back."

"Oh." Chen Xin was surprised. Having graduated the same year as Chen Fang, Yuan must be thirty-three or thirty-four. "But why didn't you marry after your return?"

"Well, how shall I put it? One has to wait for an opportunity."

Chen Xin said nothing.

Caressing the little boy's fluffy hair she said softly, "Sometimes I felt that the sacrifices I made to return to Shanghai weren't worth it."

Chen Xin tried to console her, "Don't say that. It's good to be back."

"We'll be late for the film, aunty," cried the boy.

"Right, we ought to be going." She looked up and smiled at Chen Xin. "Sorry if I dampened your spirits. But you're different. You're a man, and you're young. You'll find happiness."

Chen Xin's heart grew heavy as he watched her disappearing into the crowd.

No. 3 commented, "She's a dead crab."

"What do you mean?"

"She's over thirty and hasn't got a boyfriend. She's like a dead crab. No hope."

"It isn't that she can't find one. She said she was waiting for someone to come along. Don't you see?"

Whether he understood or not, he answered disapprovingly, "Whatever you say, she's got a big problem. Men in their thirties are married, or else handicapped or ineligible. Eligible ones are hard to please and like young beautiful girls. There are handfuls of twenty-year-old girls up for grabs." Chen Xin meant to say that some people were waiting for love. But then he had second thoughts. That was beyond No. 3. Youngsters like him were so different from his generation. Throwing a sidelong glance at his brother, he said instead, "You really know a lot."

No. 3 looked very proud. The sarcasm was lost on him. Feeling apologetic, Chen Xin added in a kinder tone, "What do you do every day?"

"Nothing much except watch TV, listen to the radio and sleep."

"What are your plans?"

He said nothing. When they were walking up the steps of the labour bureau, No. 3 confided, "I'd like to get a job."

Chen Xin halted. No. 3 turned to urge him, "Come on." His eyes were frank and sincere. Still Chen Xin avoided them.

3

He started work at his mother's factory, which was a long way away. It took him an hour and twenty minutes and three buses to get there. Assigned to work at a lathe, he had to learn from scratch; mockingly, he called himself a thirty-year-old apprentice. What he found hard was not the lathe but the adjustment to the new life and the fast pace. He had to run from the first bus to catch the second and then the third.... He mustn't miss any of the connections, which meant no smoking or daydreaming. He also found it hard to adjust to three rotating shifts. After a week on night shift it took more than two weeks to catch up on his sleep. As a result he was always tired. Within two months his face grew thinner. People said he looked better that way for the weight he had gained before he came home was not healthy. It was the result of the flour and stodge he had eaten in the North, whereas in Shanghai people ate rice.

Still he was glad he had returned to Shanghai even though his contentment was marred by a feeling of emptiness. Something was missing. The longing of the past ten years, an ache that had affected his sleep and appetite, had come to an end. But it had given him a goal to fight for. Now he was at a loss and felt empty. Maybe he was too happy being back? He must start a new life even though he had not given much serious thought to what it should be like. Things were only just beginning.

Ending the early shift, he dragged his legs, numb after eight hours' standing, to the bathroom, had a bath, changed and left the factory. At the bus stop passengers spilled from the pavement onto the middle of the street. At least three buses were late. He waited for ten minutes but there was no sign of a bus. The passengers complained, assuming there must have been an accident. Losing patience, Chen Xin started to walk the few stops to catch the second bus. Li, a worker a year younger than he, had once shown him a shortcut. Relying on his memory, he went along a lane to a narrow cobbled street where people on both sides were washing honey buckets, cooking, knitting, reading, doing homework, playing chess or ping-pong, or sleeping on door planks, making the little street even narrower. The houses lining it resembled pigeon cotes or the squares of a harmonica. Through the small, low windows he saw only beds, large and small, bunk and camp beds. So, recreation, work, other activities, all had to take place out of doors. What would they do when all those at work came home, or on rainy and snowy days? Suppose a grown-up son found a wife? If behind the colourful shop window, dazzling billboards, glamorous clothes and the latest film posters, there existed streets that narrow, rooms that crowded, lives that miserable, Shanghai was not as wonderful as one imagined.

It took him half an hour to reach the second bus stop. He shoved in and fitted his six-foot-high body into the smallest space as he had now learned to do, so that he wouldn't be taken for an outsider. It was already six when he got home, hungry and tired, expecting to find steaming hot food waiting for him, but supper was not ready. His mother had been shopping on Huaihai Avenue and had got home late, as it was impossible to rush through the teeming crowds on the streets, in stores, on buses. His sister-in-law had started to cook when she returned home from work. His mother helped to wash and chop the vegetables. "No. 3 does nothing but sleep and listen to his transistor radio," his mother said, showing her annoyance. "You could have sliced the meat for me, you layabout."

Frustrated, Chen Xin went over to his dark hut. A transistor radio was buzzing jarringly, half-talking and half-singing between two stations. He jumped in fright when, groping over toward his bed, he almost fell over a leg. His brother sat up, "You're back, second brother?"

Chen Xin turned on the desk lamp, "You're too lazy, No. 3. Why don't you give Mother a hand when you've nothing to do?" he stormed.

"I bought the rice and mopped the floor this afternoon," No. 3 said, defending himself.

"So what? When I was your age I was ploughing and harvesting in the countryside."

No. 3 fell silent.

"You're twenty this year. You should use your brains and do something useful. Get up. How can you while away your time doing nothing? Pull yourself together and act like a man."

No. 3 walked out silently. Chen Fang, just back from work, joined in. "You're an adult, No. 3. You should behave like one. We all need some rest when we come home from work. You should've helped."

Chen Xin added from the hut, "If you were studying for the university entrance exam, we wouldn't blame you, but would let you have as much time as you needed...."

No. 3 remained silent. His mother interrupted to make peace. "It's all my fault. I didn't tell him what to do before I left. Supper'll soon be ready. Eat some biscuits first. Go and buy some vinegar for me, No. 3." When No. 3 had left, she told her two elder sons, "I'd rather he stayed at home and didn't roam around and get into trouble. Of all the unemployed youngsters, he's one of the nicest."

Supper was at last ready at half-past seven. They ate in his mother's small room. No one felt like talking after the episode with No. 3, and with no chatting, no one enjoyed the meal. In an attempt to liven up the atmosphere, his sister-in-law broke the silence by saying, "My bureau has set up a club to help young bachelors who want to get married. Shall I get a form for you to fill in, Chen Xin?"

Chen Xin forced a smile. "Certainly not. I don't want to get married."

"Nonsense," his mother piped up. "Everyone gets married. With your looks, I'm sure you'll find a wife."

"Tall men like you are very popular nowadays with young girls," said a smiling No. 3, who had forgotten all about the reproaches he had received. He was still young.

"Getting married's no joke," his sister-in-law added. "You need to have at least a thousand yuan."

"We'll help even if we go bankrupt. Right, Chen Fang?" his mother asked.

"Hmm," his elder brother mumbled stupidly.

"But even if you've money, but no room, it's still hopeless," his sister-in-law went on.

"If we can't find a room I'll move out and sleep in the lane if he's getting married. Right, Chen Fang?" his mother asked again.

"Sure," his elder brother agreed.

"You mean what you say, Mum?" asked his sister-in-law, smiling. His mother laughed. "Haven't I always meant what I said?"

"What sort of a joke is that?" Chen Xin put down his bowl. Although the three of them smiled, he sensed they were serious and full of hints. It was highly unpleasant.

He watched TV in his brother's room. Before long he felt drowsy and could hardly keep his eyes open. He had to get up very early to go to work. He rose and retired to his hut where No. 3 was already in bed listening to the transistor radio, laughing at a comedy show, looking happy and comfortable.

"Bed so early?" Chen Xin asked.

"The TV programme was awful," No. 3 answered, but only when the programme ended in applause. He reluctantly turned off the radio.

As usual, Chen Xin read for a few minutes and then switched out the light. In the darkness he heard his brother say, "I wish Dad was still alive. Then you could take his place while I took Mum's. Dad had a better job. He worked in an office."

Chen Xin's nose tingled. He wanted to hold his brother in his arms but he only turned and said hoarsely, "You should have tried to go to university."

After a while No. 3 began to snore. But Chen Xin's urge to sleep had vanished.

No. 3 could have had his mother's job but for him....

He had called long distance saying, "No. 3 is living in Shanghai. He'll have a way out somehow. This is my only chance...." His mother was silent at the other end. He had repeated, "I left home at eighteen, Mum, and I've been alone for ten years. Eighteen, and I've been all alone for ten years. Ten whole years, Mum." Still silence. He knew that his mother must be weeping and repeating to herself, "The palm and the back of my hand.... Oh, the palm and the back of my hand...." In the end, No. 3 gave him the chance, which was only natural. Ten years ago, he had done the same for his elder brother. Like him, his younger brother had not complained or grumbled but was nice to him. Turning in his sleep, No. 3 stretched one leg across him again. He did not push it away.

His brother was too lazy. Wouldn't everything be fine and everyone happy if he could enter university? But not everyone could do that or go to a technical college. No. 3, ashamed at not having passed the exam, was amiable to everyone and never defended himself when he was criticized.

Chen Xin sighed. Life in Shanghai was not easy.

4

One evening, Aunt Shen, who worked in his mother's factory, was to bring a girl round to meet Chen Xin. As this had been arranged by his mother, he couldn't give a flat refusal although he found the situation awkward and silly. "You must start building a new life," said his elder brother. The statement had stunned him. When his new life became so concrete, he was not prepared for it and found it hard to accept. But, on second thoughts, he couldn't imagine a more significant and important new life. Maybe it just meant marrying and having a child? Shaking his head, he smiled wryly, while an emptiness filled him. The ten years of longing for Shanghai, though gnawing, had been mixed with sweetness. It was like a dream, a yearning suffused with imagination. Anticipation was perhaps the best state. He remembered that when he was a child Saturday had always been better than Sunday.

But everyone in the family was full of enthusiasm. Preparations started after lunch. His sister-in-law swept and dusted her room, while his elder brother bought cakes and fruit. They planned to put Nannan to bed early in case he made a *faux pas*. It had happened once before when his grandmother was matchmaking and the young couple met at their place. Having always been present when grown-ups talked and not really understanding what it all was about, he suddenly pointed at the young man and girl and asked his mother, "Are they getting married, Mum?" It had been very embarrassing.

No. 3 was the busiest of all. He suggested that his mother cook lentil soup and offered Chen Xin his best clothes to wear. Chen Xin was annoyed by his excitement, which was just because he had nothing better to do.

His enthusiasm dampened, No. 3 still helped to cook a large pot of lentil soup and made Chen Xin put on his bell-bottomed trousers.

The girl arrived at seven-thirty; hiding shyly behind Aunt Shen and moving quickly over to an armchair in a corner, where she picked up a book to read. With her head lowered in the darkness, no one could see her features clearly.

"Chen Xin is a promising young man. The workers in the factory are very pleased with him. The ten years he spent in the small town in the countryside gave him a lot of experience. He's not irresponsible like new school-leavers," began Aunt Shen.

"Yes. It was hard for him, having to stay far away so long," said his mother, her eyes glancing over to the girl in the corner.

"How do you like working at a lathe, Chen Xin?" Aunt Shen turned to him. "Standing on your feet for eight hours is quite tiring."

"It's OK. I don't mind it. I did all kinds of work in the countryside," replied Chen Xin, his attention fixed on the corner. He could see nothing except her profile, short hair and wide shoulders.

"Where's your son, Chen Fang? He must be a lively boy."

"He's sleeping. He's a nice boy," Chen Fang answered absent-mindedly.

"He isn't so nice," countered his wife. "He's a little scamp. I don't want him."

"Don't talk like that. No one can take him away from you. Naughty boys are clever boys."

"That's true...." Chen Xin's sister-in-law moved over to the corner. "Come and have some lentil soup."

Someone quicker had got to the corner first and switched on the standard lamp, saying, "You need some light to read." It was No. 3 who had slipped in unnoticed. Chen Xin was ready to throw him out, but he was grateful for his clever intervention.

The girl was bathed in light. All stopped talking and turned to her. Then all turned back to look at each other with disappointed expressions. After a while, his sister-in-law collected herself and said, "Don't read now. Come and have some lentil soup."

Very embarrassed, the girl finished her bowl of soup, wiped her mouth with a handkerchief and announced that she was leaving. No one made any attempt to stop her. After some polite remarks — "Please come again", "Take care of yourself" — they all rose to see her to the door, while Aunt Shen saw her out of the lane alone. This was the custom and all scrupulously obeyed it. Chen Xin, recently back, didn't know the rules. But No. 3 stood beside him, showing him what to do.

His mother asked, "How did you like her, Chen Xin?"

He laughed in reply.

"She's no good. Her cheekbones are too high. It's a sign that her husband'll die early," said No. 3.

"Don't be silly. No one's asking you."

"She's a bit short on looks," commented his elder brother.

"She's not pretty. I wonder what sort of person she is," said his mother.

The comments stopped when Aunt Shen returned. She addressed Chen Xin with a smile, "She seemed to like you. It all depends on what you think now."

Chen Xin remained silent, smiling.

Realizing something was wrong, she added, "She's a nice girl, honest and simple. She's twenty-eight. Her parents are well-to-do. They don't mind whether the young man is well off or not, provided that he's nice. If he has no room, he can live with them. They have a spare room.... You'd better talk it over and give me a reply as soon as possible.... You must trust me, Chen Xin. I won't let you down. I've known you since you were a kid."

The whole family saw her to the entrance of the lane.

When they returned, his elder brother asked, "What's you impression of her?"

Chen Xin gave a frank reply. "Not good."

"Looks aren't important. You can date her for a while," suggested his sister-in-law.

"Looks are very important. Otherwise, my elder brother wouldn't have married you," Chen Xin teased her, causing general laughter.

His sister-in-law punched him on the shoulder, half laughing and half angry.

"I too think you could date her, Chen Xin. You mustn't go by looks alone," said his elder brother.

"Looks are very important when two people are introduced to each other. What would I fall in love with if not with her looks?" Chen Xin had his reasons.

"She doesn't have to be a beauty, but at least presentable." No. 3 had to voice his opinion.

"I think she's OK, Mum," his sister-in-law said, turning to his mother. "Besides, she has a room. That's very important in Shanghai."

Chen Xin retorted, "I'm marrying a girl. Not a room."

"But it's an important factor. She's not ugly except that her face is a bit wide. Her eyes and eyebrows are all right."

"Forget the eyes and brows. For one thing, she doesn't attract me at all."

No. 3 laughed. This was something new to him.

"It's all for your own good. You can't live on attraction," said his sister-in-law.

"I agree," his elder brother added.

His mother broke in, "Let him decide for himself."

"Yes, yes," his elder brother seconded.

"We'll, let's leave it at that," cried Chen Xin. It was all so pointless. "Don't bother about it any more, Mum. I'll find my own wife. If I can't find a good wife, I'll remain a bachelor all my life." He retired to his hut.

In his dreams, a pair of eyes smiled at him, a pair of jade black eyes, in the shape of a new moon, eyes that smiled sweetly and gently. He woke up. From his window, only one-foot square, he saw a new moon.

Ah, eyes like a new moon. Where was she? Who was she? In the school where he had taught, every morning on his way to breakfast in the canteen he saw a girl on an old-fashioned bicycle taking a shortcut from the back gate to the front. Elegant and petite, she always turned to look at him with those eyes.... He was confident that if he had asked where are you going? she would have replied. He had never asked, and he would never know where she came from and where she was bound. Many people took a shortcut though his school. The front gate led to a hospital, cultural centre, cultural troupe and a machinery plant. At the back gate were a department store, playground, and cotton mill. She had passed by him hundreds, thousands of times and he had let her go even though he liked her and the sight of her made him happy. But his mind was set on Shanghai, his sole destination. He had finally returned to Shanghai, while she had become something in his past, something that would never return, leaving only a beautiful memory. He had few regrets as Shanghai carried more weight than a girl. Still he was a little sorry.

He remembered his school with its big garden, bigger than any school in Shanghai. The campus had a boulevard and a grove. In summer he iced melons in the well in front of his room. Several students used to bring food to him. But he had left these loyal students without saying goodbye, afraid of complicating matters. He missed that school. That part of his life had touched his heart.

5

One morning, his elder brother surprised them by telling his mother that his family wanted a separate residence card. He stammered, "Then ... we can have ... two rations of eggs ... two rations of everything."

He avoided his mother's eyes when she looked up silently. Chen Xin wondered why he stuttered, as if it was something very embarrassing. After all it was a bright idea to get extra rations, which were given according to residence cards. He laughed. "What brainstorm. How did you ever think of it?"

But his joke had made his brother flee in shame. His mother fixed her eyes on him, saying nothing.

Chen Xin left for work. Following behind him, No. 3 whispered as if it were a secret, "You know why elder brother wanted to have another residence card?"

"He wanted more eggs...."

"Of course not," No. 3 cut him short. "He's after the room."

"The room?" Chen Xin halted puzzled.

"Right," No. 3 affirmed. "The twenty-two-metre room belongs to him once he has his own residence card. It must be our sister-in-law's idea."

"Let him have it," Chen Xin moved on. "You don't put your brains to good use, yet you're very quick in such matters."

That day, Chen Xin was preoccupied, his brother's suggestion recurring in his mind. He had a feeling it implied something more. Then his younger brother's words rang in his ears: "He's after the room." He also recalled how his sister-in-law had harped about his marrying a girl with a room. Did it really mean that? Instinctively he waved his hand to deny it. "It can't be," he said almost aloud, scaring himself. Then he had to laugh.

When he returned home after work, he heard his mother saying to his elder brother, "You can't separate from us. Chen Xin has a right to that room too. He has been away working in the countryside for ten years. If he marries, you must divide it. Isn't that right?"

His mother asked again when he didn't answer, "Isn't that right?" Only then did he echo, "Right." Bringing in a dish, his wife banged it loudly on the table. By coincidence?

A heavy cloud hung over the dinner table. His elder brother and wife sulked while his mother apologetically piled food in their bowls. No. 3 kept throwing meaningful glances at Chen Xin. "See?" he seemed to say. Disgusted, Chen Xin turned away, looking at no one. Luckily Nannan brightened the atmosphere by standing up and sitting down on the chair asking for this and that. He had thrown away his spoon and was grabbing with his fingers. His grandmother caught his hand and spanked him lightly on the palm. No. 3 made a face and cried "Hurrah!" while Nannan declared proudly, "It didn't hurt at all."

Everybody laughed. But Nannan's mother dragged him down from his chair and scolded, "You rude boy. You don't appreciate favours. You should thank your lucky stars that you're not kicked out." The laughter froze as everyone wondered whether to continue laughing or look solemn. "Oh, boy!" No. 3 said softly to ease the embarrassment.

Chen Xin's mother's face fell. "What do you mean?"

"Nothing," his sister-in-law countered.

"I know what you were driving at." His mother brought it into the open. "It's the room."

"No. I don't care about the room. But when my son grows up, I won't let him marry a girl if he doesn't have a room."

"Don't rub it in. I may be poor but I love all my sons and treat them all equally. The palm and the back of my hand, they're all my flesh. Chen Xin had to leave home because of Chen Fang. You shouldn't be so ungrateful." The old lady wept.

"Ungrateful? When other girls marry, they all get a suite of furniture including chairs and a standard lamp. When I married Chen Fang what did he have? Have I ever complained? And we never failed to send Chen Xin parcels and money every festival. What complaints can you have about such a daughter-in-law?" She wept too.

Chen Fang was stunned, not knowing whom to console.

No. 3 fled. He was useless, disappearing whenever a real crisis occurred.

"Don't cry." Chen Xin stood up. He was disturbed and agitated. "I don't want the room, Mother. I'm not marrying. I'm quite happy just being back in Shanghai."

His mother was even sadder. Stealing a glance at him, his sister-in-law wept more softly.

At night, when everybody had retired to bed, his elder brother entered the hut smoking a cigarette. "Don't mind your sister-in-law," he said.

"She's not mean, though she likes to grumble. I had no savings when we married. We had nothing except a bed and she's never complained. These last years, by scrimping and scraping, we bought some furniture and decorated the room. She was content with the improvement and wants to keep it. She's not bad and knows we should divide the room into two for you but just finds it hard to accept. I'll talk her round gradually."

"Forget it, Brother," Chen Xin stopped him. "I meant what I said. I swear I don't want the room. Please reassure her. Just don't separate from us. The old lady likes to have her whole family together."

His brother broke down, putting his arms around Chen Xin's shoulders. Though Chen Xin wanted to take him into his arms, he pushed him away and pulled the quilt over his head. Ten years had toughened him.

It was not easy to live in Shanghai.

6

Chen Xin, used to a carefree life, was very disturbed. The following morning, his day off, he got up at daybreak and went out, telling no one. He wanted to take a walk. Accustomed to the vast spaces in the north he found Shanghai oppressive. High-rise buildings blocked out the breeze and the crowds made the air stale. Where could he go? He would go to the Bund.

He got off the bus and moved ahead. He could see the ships anchored in the Huangpu River on the other side of the road. On the bank there were green trees and red flowers; and old people doing *taijiquan* exercises, children playing and young people strolling and taking photos. He felt lighter. He crossed over to the river, the symbol of Shanghai. It was not blue, as he recalled, but muddy and stinking. Everything should be viewed from a distance, perhaps. A closer look only brought disappointment.

He came to the Bund Park, bought a ticket and went in. A fountain cascaded down a rock into a pool, rippling the water. He recalled that long, long ago, the water didn't fall directly into the pool but onto a statue of an umbrella under which a smiling mother and two children sheltered. He had liked the sculpture so much when he first saw it as a child that he had stared at it refusing to be led away. It was like a symbol of his life. His father had died early and his mother had brought up her three sons, overcoming many difficulties. By sticking together, they had given one another warmth in hard times. When a tornado hit Shanghai, the four of them had huddled together on the bed. The lightning, thunder, and howling wind had frightened and excited them. His younger brother had made exaggerated shrieks, his mother playfully blamed the sky, while Chen Xin, acting as a protector, sat beside the light switch, which his elder brother, having just learned something about electricity, was scared of. The storm was frightening and exhilarating. And there was a warmth. It was this that had attracted and drawn him home.

Water, falling on the pond, caused monotonous, empty ripples. A drop fell on his hand. He suddenly realized that it was from his eyes. What was the matter with him? When he had left home and his mother had sobbed her heart out, he hadn't shed a tear. Today ... he experienced a tremendous disappointment, as if a most precious thing had suddenly been shattered. He turned and left the park.

The stores were opening, salespeople were removing the shutters outside the shop windows, which displayed a dazzling array of goods. The pedestrians on the street, so well dressed they looked like models, made his head spin. Unconsciously he stopped outside a shop window: Plump dolls with enormous heads were shooting down a slide, two others were swinging in each other's arms. In the background several Young Pioneers were flying model planes, which circled in a blue sky.

He couldn't move. It all reminded him of his childhood, his youth and the golden memory he had when he left Shanghai. He had mistaken this memory for Shanghai, to which he had struggled to return. Back home, he found he could never recapture the past.

The pedestrians increased, edging from the pavements onto the street. They seemed to be walking in file, and it was hard to move quickly. Life in such a compressed world was difficult. He remembered the struggles on buses. In restaurants, he had to stand beside tables for seats, and then others waited for him to leave while he ate. In the parks three couples sat on one bench and in the Yuyuan Park lined up to have a picture taken on a rock mountain. Humans created not only wonders, but also problems. Why must he squeeze in? Why?

People rubbed shoulders, toes touched heels. Though they lived so closely, they were all strangers. Not knowing or understanding one another, they were proud and snobbish. He remembered a song his brother had recorded a few days ago: "People on earth are thronged like stars in the sky. Stars in the sky are as distant as people on earth."

That town was different. It was calm, maybe a little too deserted. One could run and stroll at ease on the streets and breathe freely. And in a small town, the same people meeting constantly knew one another by sight, nodding to and greeting all acquaintances, creating a warm, friendly feeling. So a big city had its drawbacks, a small town its advantages.

He moved with the stream of people, not caring where he was heading. He was dazed. The bittersweet yearning in the past decade disappeared, and with it the fullness he had felt in the past ten years. He had arrived at his destination. What was his next step? One must have a destination. Should he follow the new trend and equip himself with Western-style clothing, leather shoes, bell-bottomed trousers and a cassette recorder ... then find a sweetheart and get married?... Yes. He could start doing that though it required effort and hard work. But would he find happiness if fashionable clothes concealed a heavy and miserable heart? If he married for the sake of getting married and the wife he chose was not understanding, wouldn't he be adding a burden to his life? Again he missed the new-moon eyes and the chances he had lost. A man's destination must be happiness, not misery. He suddenly felt that the destination he sought ought to be something bigger. Yes, bigger.

His spirits lifting, the dark clouds parted slightly to let through a dim light. Dim and hazy, it was still a light.

"Chen Xin."

He halted. Someone had called him.

"Chen Xin." He heard it again. He turned and saw a bus ploughing slowly through the crowds on the street. His elder brother was leaning half way out of the window, reaching out to him. Behind him was his sister-in-law. They seemed agitated.

Shocked, he chased the bus. His elder brother grabbed his hands and gazed at him speechless and wooden, as he had done ten years ago when he ran after the train. Chen Xin was touched. His sister-in-law grabbed him too. "Chen Xin, you mustn't do anything drastic." She broke down.

"What nonsense!" Chen Xin laughed, tears rolling down his face.

"Come home," said his brother.

"Yes. I'll come home." Home was, after all, home. Quarrels were caused by poverty. I made you suffer, my loved ones. He was suddenly ashamed of having used the ten years as a trump card. His mother, two brothers and sister-in-law had also endured those difficult years. And besides, life meant joy, fun, pleasure. For instance, the boulevard, tree groves, the well, innocent pupils, and eyes like a new moon.... He had overlooked them all. But ahead of him there would be another ten, twenty and thirty years, a long, long time. He must give his future some serious thought.

Another train was leaving the station. Where was it bound? He knew that his destination would be farther, greater, and he would have to wander more than a decade, maybe two or three decades, a lifetime. He might never settle down. But he believed that once he arrived at his true destination, he would have no doubts, troubles, or sense of rootlessness.

Translated by Yu Fanqin

Eight Hundred Metres Below

●

—— SUN SHAOSHAN ——

Born and brought up in Shandong, Sun Shaoshan started doing farm work at home upon graduation from junior middle school. In 1968 he went to reclaim wasteland in Heilongjiang and later became a miner. He began to publish short stories in 1981. "Eight Hundred Metres Below" won a national short story award in 1982.

Trapped in an Impasse

THE earthquake stranded four men in a shaft eight hundred metres below ground where they were squashed into a corner by a huge rock fall. Eight hours later they had hewn out a path with their picks only to find all exits to the surface blocked. They were practically buried alive. As they had come to this particular shaft to do a quick job, nobody knew they were there. What could anyone do even if they knew their exact location? It would take six months to reach them with the normal methods.

They could only wait for death to come. Their lives would ebb away slowly through cold and hunger. Death would only take them when it got tired of toying with them. Despair gnawed at their hearts. Someone began to groan.

Zhang Kun, the foreman, was a small man of fifty-five. His eyes were bleary from having worked forty years underground but they had a fierce expression. Now their steely coldness was menacing. He fixed them on everyone in turn before saying, "Keep cool. We aren't dead yet."

That gave them a shred of hope. According to Zhang, if he remembered clearly, behind the wall of coal was a deserted seam from which all the coal had been mined dozens of years back. If they could make their way there, they could escape though an air shaft, that is, if it hadn't collapsed. Anyway, it was a forlorn hope.

Leng Xijun, a miner in his thirties and the strongest among them, threw all his weight behind his pick, sending sparks and bits of coal flying, permeating the area with the smell of sulphur. He wielded his pick tackling the wall of coal, despair and fear transformed into hatred. To live he must break through it, but it was harder than rock. With only his pick, it was an impossible task even in normal circumstances.

Wang Jiang, the youngest, was barely twenty. He was a despondent middle-school graduate, who had failed to pass the university entrance exam four months previously.

The middle-aged man with a long neck like a grasshopper was nicknamed "Chatterbox" because he talked non-stop and was a poor worker. He was amazed at Leng, who hadn't eaten all day, hacking away for all he was worth.

Leng admired only Zhang, a man who courageously faced any hardship, but he was getting old. The task of finding a way out naturally fell on his shoulders.

An Unexpected Sound

Suddenly, Leng was asked to stop. Startled he halted. His three friends put their ears to the opposite wall listening hard.

"Thud, thud, thud!..."

Such a rhythmic sound could only be made by man. Surprised, he walked over and knocked the wall with his pick. He got a response. The sound of knocking can carry through a twenty-metre thick wall of coal. Judging by the loudness of this sound, the wall was only two to three metres thick. The sound of a voice, however, can only carry through a thickness of half a millimetre, so they could not find out who was on the other side.

Chatterbox straightened up and announced, "I know who it is."

"Who?"

"Li Gui."

Doubtless it was that rascal, no, thief! No one else could be in the area. They were a team of five men. At the first tremor, Li Gui had run off with all their bread, and was cut off from them when the roof collapsed. He must have thought the earthquake was a cave-in, in which case he would wait until rescued, eating everybody else's bread. He had never dreamed of being stuck in such an impasse and now had to beg help from those he had robbed.

Everybody fell silent. The man had stolen their means of survival eight hours ago. Did they want to save him? The ticking of their watches could be heard in the silence.

Zhang commanded, "Break through it!" He pointed at the wall separating them from Li.

There was no response from the tall miner.

"Did you hear me?" the old man demanded. He was an absolute authority in this world of darkness. Even the mine director obeyed him when Zhang led a rescue operation after an accident, his short arms waving vigorously as he snapped out orders left and right like a general commanding an army.

The tall miner replied bluntly, "Nothing doing!"

"Why?"

"You know why."

"My orders don't count any more?"

"Of course they do. You were appointed foreman by the mine Party committee and the bureau Party committee agreed. But, as things go now, we're all facing death and death is the great leveller. It's hard to say who should give orders."

"But remember, we miners should always die together. We can't leave a man to die!"

"I don't want to die with him."

Nowadays the younger generation had minds of their own and could best their elders in arguments. Exasperated, Zhang shouted to the rest of his team members, "What are you doing then? Take his pick."

He forgot he had only two men under his command now, and neither was Leng's match.

"I dare you!" Leng looked murderous, raising his pick above him. Embarrassed when no one made a move, he confessed, "I'm not being mean. But we're like clay buddhas crossing a river. We've no guarantee we'll survive, so who wants to be lumbered with that bastard? Let's put it to a vote. If the majority are prepared to die for him, I'll do the same."

No one was over-anxious to save Li Gui.

What kind of a man was he? Let's examine his relationship with others.

Wang Jiang and Li Gui

As luck would have it, the first day the unfortunate middle-school graduate Wang Jiang began working in the shaft his path crossed Li Gui's. Wang's tub was derailed and, try as he might, he couldn't get it back on the track. Li, the only one behind him, looked on with folded arms and a smile. When Wang finally gave up, he walked over and said, "Don't you want your coal any more?"

"No," replied Wang, utterly helpless.

"Sorry about that, little brother. I'll take it."

Strong as an ox, Li heaved and righted the tub and slowly hitched it to his own, leaving the gaping Wang rooted to the spot. They were on piece work. Wang had pulled the tub and filled it with coal and now would not get a cent for his back-breaking work since Li had just appropriated it. Furious, he felt he couldn't bear to be a miner. Later Li often taunted him, "Might means right down here, little one."

Once, when Li was pushing his tub too quickly down a slope Wang warned him, "Take care, somebody's walking ahead."

This only prompted Li to give the tub a sudden shove so that it rumbled down even faster. If the man hadn't nimbly leaped out of the way the tub with its load of half a ton of coal would have sent him flying. Wang was almost scared out of his wits while Li remarked flippantly, "It went so fast, I couldn't brake it!"

Wang indignantly exposed him, but he retorted, "If I hadn't let go of the tub, who would make way for me?"

Then he tried to appease Wang by giving him a friendly tip. "Nowadays everyone looks after number one."

Yes, he was only thinking of saving his own skin when he grabbed all their bread. Had the world really come to that? The apprentice miner wondered.

Chatterbox and Li Gui

Chatterbox was filled with a sense of satisfaction knowing that Li was trapped. Heaven is just, he thought. The rascal has got what he deserved.

His long thin neck had suffered a lot at Li's big hands. Whenever a quarrel arose, Li would pin him down, clutching his neck with his pincer-like hands, almost breaking it and demanding, "Tell me, Chatterbox, do you dare to argue with me?"

"No, I don't."

"Who's in the wrong?"

"I am."

Chatterbox only dared to curse under his breath behind his back. "Son of a bitch! Some day you'll die a violent death if Heaven is just."

Li was cunning as a fox. The accidents he had been in maimed his work-mates but never him. He always came out in one piece. "This time the old fox is caught," thought Chatterbox. "Thank heavens!"

Everyone is pleased when a bad person is punished. But if one is given a rod and told, "Teach him a lesson!" it isn't so easy. Now Leng's suggestion of voting was like putting a rod in everyone's hands. Chatterbox, who since childhood had been used to receiving blows instead of giving them, did not know what to do.

Leng Xijun and Li Gui

Leng had first seen Li in a bathhouse soon after he joined this team. A large, dark, naked man was groping about in the public baths. "There are more wolves than meat," he cursed. "I just dropped a big cake of soap. Which bastard picked it up?" His knotted muscles intimidated even Leng, who was six feet tall and a basketball player. When Leng happened to step on the cake of soap, he hesitated and then refrained from saying anything or picking it up for him. But that episode made him wary of Li.

Strong as Li was, no one wanted to be his partner. His temper drove everyone away, so he had to work alone. If somebody brushed against him or inadvertently stepped on his foot, he would pay him back right away. When the other man explained he had done it accidentally, Li would retort with a glare, "Me too!"

At the break one day, a piece of coal falling from the roof had hit his head. He jumped up and his eyes narrowed, scrutinizing everyone. But he kept calm. The following day, Leng found him sitting all by himself in the same spot throwing coal at the roof, trying to figure out who had taken him unawares the day before. Leng shuddered.

No one dared to stop Li when he pushed his rumbling tub like a tank. Even the tall basketball player was all nerves, wondering if he happened to get in Li's way, should he step aside for him like the others? He was afraid to cross his path, yet at the same time he longed to pit his will against Li's. He felt that sooner or later, they would clash. But it had never happened. Li had cunningly sensed the tension between them and greeted Leng cordially every morning.

Leng had told people more than once, "Three years with Li in one team is enough to turn anyone into a beast." He had snatched up a pick to attack Li when he was dirty enough to steal all the bread. But a stronger tremor had separated them. Now he was asked to save Li with the same pick. Hell, no!

Zhang Kun and Li Gui

At the end of 1980 there was a lot of talk when the bonuses were being handed out. The workers each got three hundred yuan, while members of the revolutionary committee got nine hundred. The workers complained that the cadres had grabbed too much money, while the cadres retorted that the workers were greedy, not satisfied with getting three hundred yuan for nothing. Li was the only one who considered the division reasonable. He said, "Listen, when good cadres grab money, I support them. They're at least practical. Everyone likes money. Beware of those who don't reach out for those crisp notes. They're ambitious like Lin Biao and the 'gang of four'. They want more money. They're really bad, devouring people without even spitting out their bones.... This is what the world has come to."

Old Zhang, who happened to hear this, was infuriated. He wasn't a money-grubber. A Party member for thirty years, he was the only one of the thirteen leading cadres to give up his bonus, feeling his good salary was ample reward. He didn't want a lot of money and he was not ambitious. He was due to retire after three months.

He had cried, "You're talking rubbish, Li Gui! So anyone who refuses to take the bonus is a follower of the 'gang of four'?"

Not knowing his foreman had not accepted the money, Li added ingratiatingly, "It's the truth. Honestly, when I see money, I want to pocket every cent. Nowadays, what leader isn't after money?" Zhang knew he and Li would never see eye to eye, so there was no use arguing with him. So Zhang mocked, "You seem to know the situation quite well, young man. How much of the world have you seen anyway? Is it a long time since you were wet behind the ears?"

"I haven't seen much. Still it's thousands of li around."

"You find things the same everywhere?"

"More or less. My hometown was poor and there were no bonuses. My county built a few new socialist villages, which were known all over the country. The newspapers carried articles about them; the radio made broadcasts. People even came from Xinjiang to learn from them. Travelling by car they saw blocks of nice brick houses along the straight streets. Anyone would think that the villagers were living in paradise. No one knew their actual state of poverty. I bought my wife a pair of woollen trousers when we got married. As I forgot to buy her a belt, she had to use a piece of cloth instead. Can you believe that? Two years after all the publicity, our county Party secretary was promoted to the provincial level, while the villagers had to leave home to make a living."

"Before I left, my weeping mother sewed five yuan in the lining of my padded jacket. I travelled three thousand li without touching it. When I was caught bumming a ride on a train, I was made to get off at a small station. I was so scared of that god-forsaken spot that I pleaded on my knees for mercy. One man pushed me off the train with a swift kick to my behind. It was night and the station was on a mountain far from anywhere. I hated the world and made up my mind right there to get rich...."

Because of this, Zhang was not as surprised or indignant as the others at his action. It was natural for a man who had only seen the seamy side of life.

Li feared neither the Party secretary, nor the mine director but only Old Zhang, knowing that he stood to lose if he offended him. Although a foreman was not a high official, he had certain powers such as giving extra work for more money, allocating easy work or turning a blind eye when Li slacked. Strong as he was, Li always flattered this little man whom he could knock out with one blow.

Zhang, who had worked in the mines since he was fifteen, knew of Li's weakness for money. He never ticked Li off when he played a trick, but let his pocket suffer making sure Li realized it was a punishment. Since it conformed to the rules and regulations Li couldn't complain. As soon as he repented, Zhang would find ways for him to make up his loss. Li feared and hated the old man, while at the same time admiring him too. Zhang liked Li for his spirit, never sparing himself where money was concerned. He called the young men in his team lazy, claiming that miners in their forties would sweat for ten cents while they wouldn't lift a little finger for one yuan. When they called Li a money-grubber, Zhang scolded them, "What do you know? If nobody wanted money there would be no mines in the world."

"You mean socialism depends on people like him?"

"It can't depend on you, coddled as you are. You don't work a hundred days a year, and drown yourselves in booze all day long, drinking as if you were going to kick the bucket sooner than we. And you have the nerve to mock him!"

The old man could do nothing with those who didn't care if they were demoted or fined. No one could be fired after all. In comparison, Li had his merits. Although Leng hated Li, Zhang admired his work. Even a black sheep was better than no sheep at all. Leng's disobedience annoyed Zhang, who was used to giving orders. Now at this crucial moment, his words fell on deaf ears. What the hell was this voting business? He was furious.

Voting

Leng solicited opinions. "What's your idea, Xiao Wang? You speak first."

The young apprentice was in very low spirits. "I don't mind what you do. You're older than me. You decide."

"What about you, Chatterbox?"

Leng fixed his gaze on his peer, who hurriedly replied, "All right. I'll say something. Li is selfish, cruel and mean. He makes me puke. He's such a rat that today he stole from all of us. Let him stew in his own juice!"

He stole a glance at his foreman and then hedged, "But, to leave him is too ... too.... Well, even if we did, we're not to blame. It's his own fault. Whatever we do, we're in the right...."

"You haven't said a thing, damn you!" Leng was furious. Chatterbox, who had been bullied about by Li was now vacillating. Banking on a quick vote Leng became impatient. Neither Zhang nor he had won any support yet.

Zhang was moved. He realized no one wanted to risk their lives for Li or voice their opposition right away. As foreman he was responsible for everybody's safety. So he tried to persuade them, using a coaxing tone he had never used before in all his years underground.

"I know Li can be a swine, but he's not an enemy. We don't know whether we'll come out alive, but if we do we'll regret not having tried to save him when we see his wife and children. You're young. He'll be on your consciences all your lives. Life won't be worth living. That's why people die together in the mines. No one ever hesitates to save another."

Chatterbox chipped in, "Right. That's exactly what I said...."

Leng cut him short with a glare. "What did you say?"

"I mean it, although I did not say it; we ought to think of his wife and children."

Leng threw the pick down. "You do what you want. I won't lift a finger. Wait till he joins you. He may turn cannibalistic and eat you up too when he gets hungry!"

Their Nerves

The digging began. While one worked, the others turned off their lamps and sat in the dark. Once the batteries were used up, they would be doomed.

A soft moan pierced their hearts. They knew who it was. The more the man tried to control his sobs, the harder it affected them. He was only twenty, so young. Zhang felt so harassed, his breathing became difficult. If they missed their chance of survival because of Li, he would be killing the youth. But what could Zhang do? How could he console him? Certainly not by saying, "Don't worry, we'll come out alive." How could he guarantee that? "It's glorious to die for the revolution." That didn't hit the right note either. There were so many middle-school graduates, why had he been chosen to work here? If that was such an honour then the sons and daughters of the officials, who were given other surface jobs, were not doing glorious work. Zhang knew Wang had been assigned to his team because his father had offended some leaders. Why should he pay for his father's mistakes? Zhang couldn't think how to comfort him.

Chatterbox tried to crack a joke. He couldn't ask the boy, "Do you miss your wife?" so he joked at his own expense. "My wife will miss me tonight. She'll have to sleep alone."

"Don't worry," Leng sneered, "someone will look after her. If you do go home, don't forget to cough at the window."

His spirits rising, Chatterbox offered, "Let me tell you a funny story."

In the darkest place in the world, the foulest language was habitual. A newcomer, who found it shocking at first, would gradually get used to it and appreciate the raciness.

Chatterbox began, "In my son's language class, the teacher wrote the word 'blanket' on the blackboard and asked my boy to read it. My darling son only stared at it. So his teacher prompted him. 'What's on top of the mattress in your home?' Blinking stupidly he answered, 'My mum.' His fellow pupils laughed. Then the teacher prompted again, 'What's on top of your mum?' 'My dad.'"

The trapped men laughed uproariously until they grew hysterical.

"Shut up! Stop that cackling!"

The old man shouted to no avail. He turned on his lamp. The madly laughing faces horrified him.

To bring his men out safely, he must make sure they remained in a normal state of mind and kept their will to live. Excessive excitement could cause a nervous collapse and total apathy. Most of the time, people broke down not from a lack of energy but a lack of morale. He must stop them.

One by one he slapped them. Shocked, they grew quiet.

Their eyes, wild with laughter, scared themselves. Leng jumped up to curse Chatterbox.

"You skunk! You stole the story. I've heard it many times. You pretended it was your son's."

He was covering up his agitation and his gratitude to the old man. Leng grasped the pick and attacked the rock with a will.

Meeting Li

Another eight hours passed. The sun would be shining on the mine. Though darkness reigned eight hundred metres below the surface, everybody felt fresher out of habit. Li on the other side had a very good tool and the sounds he made showed that they were getting nearer.

When Leng's turn came again, he struck through with a hard blow. Air gushed in as Li made a small hole with his pick.

If it had been any man but Li, Leng would have made a big opening for him right away. As it was, his energy flagged. "Crawl through yourself!" he called into the hole, threw the pick down and sprawled on the ground. The three other men moved over. No one stirred on the other side. Wasn't it Li after all? Why didn't the man speak? Then a loaf of bread appeared in the hole. A brown, round loaf. Their eyes and mouths watered as the maddeningly sweet smell assaulted their senses. Four pairs of eyes followed the bread as it rolled over. All of them leaned forward, but none picked it up. Then a huge hand pushed another loaf through. It was Li. Thank god the heel hadn't already eaten up all the bread! He had saved some for them. Happiness filled their hearts, not because of the food, but because Li had proved himself human. They hadn't wasted their efforts. One by one the loaves kept rolling through until they counted ten. The entire lot. Li's portion was still untouched. What willpower he had shown! Anxiously they all reached out together to pull the big burly man through. The small opening tore his clothes at the shoulders. His high cheekbones were streaked with sweat and coal dust. He got to his feet and looked alertly at his mates. There was no hatred, only concern, warmth and pleasure. Tears welled up in his sunken eyes. He squatted down, his hands covering his face, and broke into violent sobs. The tears poured down between his fingers.

No one uttered a word. In the silence that followed, it was as if a strong ray of sunlight had pierced the cold dark pit. Warmth drove away hatred and estrangement. They felt a closer tie than they had ever felt above ground. They would give their lives to achieve such a closeness. They were united into an organic whole, which would never be destroyed whatever happened.

Silently, the old foreman passed out the bread.

The Outlet

People crossing oceans, deserts and forests are prone to lose their bearings. In a mine one doesn't use the points of the compass either. Relying on his memory, or the instincts of the old, Zhang led his men on. Exerting the little strength they had left, they groped their way forward, sometimes having to crawl on all fours, helping and encouraging each other. Each was not fighting for himself alone, but for the group. Individually, they would have given up long ago. After five days, they finally found the air shaft.

Chatterbox, the last to reach the opening, looked up at the patch of sky. "My darling wife," he cried with mixed feelings, "you're not fated to be a widow!"

Like a broken stalk, his head hung on his narrow neck. He crouched down and wept. Tears rolled down the faces of these men who had cheated death.

Eight hundred metres above were the blue sky and clouds. The sun shone brightly on the earth where the green mountains rolled and the leaves rustled in the trees. How beautiful life was!

The Last Mission

After resting for a while Leng, exhausted, began dozing off. They were safe now, he thought. They could sleep a little before starting the difficult ascent. Sleep was what they needed and wanted most. He closed his eyes. Zhang shouted hoarsely, "Get up, damn you! All of you get up!" He called them all sorts of names, but nobody heeded him. Leng closed his eyes, ignoring him totally.

"Get moving! Heaven gave you a big body, so put it to good use. When I was a young man...."

Why is he picking on me? Leng thought. What's got into him? Has he gone crazy? This was Zhang's favourite beginning when he wanted to give the young people a piece of his mind. "When I was a young man...." Leng's retort, "You were damn all. After so many years you're just a little foreman," would drive the old man crazy.

Leng wouldn't take that now. As he jumped up angrily he saw stars and his head throbbed with an excruciating pain. Startled, he realized that the foreman was trying to save them. Past experience told him that if they lay down for half an hour, they would never get up again. Zhang didn't want to scare them by telling them directly.

After an earthquake, all the gas from the broken coal seams seeped out of the mine through the air shafts poisoning anyone in the area. They daren't linger.

Leng gave Zhang a hand in pulling everyone to his feet. He grabbed Wang's hand, urging him, "Buck up and get a move on. You can rest when you're out."

The boy flopped down like a noodle when Leng let go and pleaded, "I'm so sleepy. Let me rest, you go ahead. I can find my way now."

The foreman bellowed, "Shit! You're useless! No wonder you had to come here. Did you sleep during your exams?"

The young man leapt up like a scalded cat. He had never expected Zhang, whom he respected, to taunt him like that. Quivering with fury, he dashed towards the air shaft. Groaning, Chatterbox went after him.

"You go and get someone to come and help me out," Zhang told Leng.

"No."

"Why not?" the old man demanded impatiently.

"You know why." Leng was worried. "Before someone could rescue you, you'd be...."

"You...."

The truth was like a blow. The old man dropped his head. Presently he straightened up.

"Get going and stop talking. As long as I...."

His efforts to rise were unsuccessful. He stumbled, bumping his head. Leng was appalled. He thought that Zhang had only lost confidence, but he was, in fact, totally drained of all strength. For forty years he had worked in the mines and now he had used up all his energy for others. He had none left to save himself. In desperation, Leng wanted to throw his arms around the old man and cry. Zhang stopped him with a severe glance, standing firmly with his head leaning against the rock. "Quit it! Get going!"

Leng looked around at a loss. Only then did he notice Li was still there.

Li tore up his trousers and made a rope. "I'll carry you," he told the old man. "We'll stick together."

Leng tied Zhang on Li's back.

They began the climb. Ordinarily the two men could have easily carried Zhang any distance. Now it was different. Li moved his legs with difficulty, slipping down when he had made a little advance.

Leng crouched down and cried, "Stand on my shoulder! I'll push you up." Li hadn't the heart to put all his weight on Leng's shoulder. Leng cursed in fury. "Lost your guts? Stand on my shoulder! That's it." Leng straightened up, pushing Li and the old man up bit by bit.

The two enemies had united together to save Zhang's life. It could not be done alone. Each step took them that much closer to life and that much farther away from death.

"People die together in the mines. No one ever hesitates to save another." They pushed and climbed, advancing along the air shaft towards a new life.

1982

Translated by Yu Fanqin

The Seven-Tined Stag

●

—— WURE'ERTU ——

Wure'ertu is an Ewenki, an ethnic minority in Northeast China. After graduating from junior middle school in 1968, he went to live in a remote mountain village, where he became a hunter, then a worker, a policeman, and finally a local cadre. He published his first short story "The Little Guard of the Big Mountains" in 1976. Very prolific in recent years, he has published three collections of short stories and won three national short story awards.

THIS is a story from my boyhood.

With one hand covering a swollen cheek, I scrambled up from the elk-skin mattress, gazing at him, tears trickling from my eyes.

"What have you got to blubber about, you brat? Just staying in the tent all day long waiting to be fed like a cat!"

As he growled these words, he raised his bear-like paw again.

"I'll go, I'll go tomorrow," I cried, clenching my teeth.

"What for?"

"To hunt. Give me the gun my father left me."

He stared bleary-eyed at me for a moment, as if regarding a stranger.

I stopped crying. I never wanted to cry again. Squaring my shoulders, I stood facing him, feeling I'd suddenly matured. No longer a thirteen-year-old, I never wanted again to cower before him.

My father had died some years earlier. To stay alive, my mother had married this man, but after a few years, she died of illness, leaving me an orphan to eke out an existence with him. How I longed to grow up quickly into a tall, strong man whom nobody would dare bully! Each time he got drunk he treated me like this, beating me till I was black and blue. I'd had enough of it.

Sensing my resistance, his anger mounted, but he hesitated to bring down the threatening fist suspended over my head, and merely stared at me silently. Suddenly he turned round to wrench a gun from a tent pole and thrust it at me.

"Take it, brat, and go into the mountains tomorrow and hunt squirrels and deer or whatever you come across. I'd like to see you do it!"

The gun was almost as big as I and nearly knocked me over. But I grasped the barrel and said defiantly, "I'm not afraid and I can hunt as many animals as you!"

"Shut your big mouth! Hunting isn't as easy as drinking wine," he declared, grabbing the wine bottle and gulping it down with a gurgling noise.

That night, lying under a torn bear-skin quilt and hugging the gun, I fell asleep despite my hot painful cheek. At midnight I woke with the cold. Curling up like a hedgehog, I clasped the gun still tighter. The tent vibrated with his loud drunken snores. I really hated him and had never honoured him by calling him father. To my mind he was just Teji — the name he was known by. Because of my painful right cheek I could not go to sleep again, so I thought of my mother and fancied I saw her mournful eyes resting on me and, with a warm hand caressing my cheeks, she seemed to be speaking to me. Tears filled my eyes and I hurriedly hid my face. After a while I was tired and fell asleep again. In my dreams I came to a lake — the one I'd visited often in the spring — where I saw a flock of snow-white swans, big and small, sporting on the lake, clinging to each other. They were free. If only I could be a swan!

The next morning found me up earlier than usual. I lit a fire and as it blazed it drove away the cold. I put some elk meat into a pot and buried two wheat buns in the hot charcoal embers. Soon the meat was done and the buns baked. Sitting cross-legged beside the fire like an adult, for the first time I ate till I nearly burst.

I knew that hunting in winter was no joke. So I carefully examined the soft elk-skin boots left me by my mother. Though not new they were still solid. I stripped them off, took out the damp grass lining, separated into two parts the feathers and soft grass I'd stolen from a squirrel's nest, wrapped them around my feet and put the boots on again. My elk-skin trousers and deer-skin jacket were full of holes, but I liked to wear them all the same, because they had been sewn by my mother and gave me some comfort. The cartridge belt and hunting knife had been left by my father. Now with these plus my courage, I would become a real hunter recognized by everyone.

Stepping out of the tent, the snow crunched under my feet, making me wonder whether it was laughing at me or just groaning in the icy cold. The bitter north wind went through my fur jacket, cutting my chest and back like a knife. But with my back straight, I strode on in high spirits towards the slumbering, dim, snow-covered forests.

I'd been out hunting several times, so the forests were not strange to me. Walking in them, I felt an incredible personal happiness, which made me momentarily forget that I was an orphan. This indescribable feeling would help to dispel hunger and fatigue, especially when I was on my way home after a day's climbing and hunting with sable and squirrel on my back. I became aware of my own strength.

But what would I encounter today? The forest looked lovely, with the blue sky hanging above, white snow on the slopes and no mist or wind in the woods. Silence reigned and the pines and birch trees seemed to be dreaming sweet dreams, perhaps waiting for me to awake them.

Carefully I climbed up a mountain where a huge peak loomed large. A lush growth of brown pines and white birch trees grew on the back face, and the front was covered with smooth snow. One side presented a sunken slope facing the sun, forming a haven from wind and cold. On its shoulder was a majestic overhanging cliff looking like a man holding up his head in pride. There must be some animals there. I walked softly with the faint crunching sound of snow under my feet. I was not disappointed, and soon discerned the vague form of an animal moving in the woods. My heart began beating fast, my body trembled and all the strength drained from my legs. This was the first time I'd encountered a wild animal alone.

Pressing forward a few steps, I was able to locate it. I leaned against a tree trunk, lifted my rifle and gritted my teeth. The gun went off with a crack. The animal staggered a bit but quickly began to run unsteadily towards the edge of the forest. Now I could see clearly it was a wild stag, sturdy and stately-looking with his pale seven-tined antlers shining from much rubbing. He gave a shiver at the sight of me and turned to cry, whereupon five other terrified deer — the doe and fawns — appeared and raced along with him in a flurry. The stag remained behind them. From time to time he turned his head to give me hostile and suspicious glances. I knew he was protecting the herd. Quickly they crossed the hill and vanished into another dense forest.

Dazed for a moment, I pulled myself together and felt a sense of elation. Picking up my rifle, I set off in pursuit. I knew I'd hit the stag.

The snow was dotted with drops of red blood like flowers.

By that time, however, the sun was already behind the mountain top and the sky became gloomy, the forests dark. It was too late to follow the stag today. Anxious and annoyed, I had to drag myself home.

That evening, seated by the fire, I felt in my heart a flame dancing too.

"I hit a stag today," I told Teji, who, when sober, was not so sinister-looking, but always surly.

"Did you?" He didn't bother to raise his head.

"It's a big stag with seven-tined antlers. I hit him with my first shot."

"Really?" This time, he squinted at me.

"He bled so much. I would have chased him but it was getting dark...."

"Hum, you fool! So, you wounded him and made him shed a little blood, and you call that hunting a stag! A real hunter, to start with, should skin the stag, cut out the kidneys and bring them back for everyone to have a taste.... The stag is a real man, not like you blubbering for the slightest reason. He would rather die than give in. Do you understand?

It was as if some snow had been thrust down my collar. I was both annoyed and piqued. "I'll bring you the stag's kidneys tomorrow then."

"Fine. Tomorrow morning I'll go to meet the furrier. In the evening I'll be waiting for you with an open mouth — to eat venison."

The day had just broken when I reached the slope where I'd hit the stag the previous day. Following the hoofprints in the snow, I felt sure I could catch up with him, because he was wounded and could not possibly get too far away. Maybe he was lying in the nearby woods. I crossed the mountain and the valley when my eye caught another trail of spoors, strange, fresh and petal-like, which appeared to be following those of the stag's too. It was some time before I recognized it as the hateful tracks of a wolf. What did it mean to do? Was it after my stag too? But when I reached the mountain top and looked down I was surprised to see I'd circled back to the slope from where I'd set off. There was the cliff high before me and the vertical precipice like a dagger thrusting sheer into the valley, at the bottom of which lay a peaceful big river.

Suddenly a clatter sounded in the birch forest to the left at the foot of the mountain. Running into view came six deer including my wounded stag at the rear, and a wolf chasing them three hundred metres behind. By the time the herd had reached the poplar forest the stag's steps grew increasingly slow and unsteady. Worried, I saw the wolf was shortening the distance between them. Just then, with a backward glance, the stag left the herd abruptly and started hobbling up the slope, while the wolf chased close behind.

Having reached the top, the stag cut straight towards the cliff, below which he slowed down his pace and started ascending step by step. His wounded leg hurting him, he looked in agony.

"Be quick! The wolf's coming up!" My whole attention was so absorbed by the peril of the wounded stag that I completely forgot my own situation and the hunt.

The wolf suddenly rushed forward and snapped at the stag's hind leg. But almost at the same time the stag kicked it and sent it rolling down with a harsh shriek. I saw a bloody mass torn from the stag's leg.

To beat the wolf the brave stag would rather lose a piece of his own flesh. What a pity his kick had missed the wolf's forehead.

The wolf rolled on the ground, its tongue licking its wound. After a while it crawled up and rushed towards the cliff again, its claws gripping the rocks to support the climb. As it was drawing near the stag turned round to block the path, resting his dauntless gaze on his opponent. When the wolf charged forward again, the stag lifted his hoof to strike a hard blow, which sent the wolf rolling down the slope howling once more. This time its neck was injured. Crazed with pain, it writhed on the ground, twisting its mouth in an attempt to reach the wound.

At last the wolf struggled to stand up, humping its back, baring its fangs, its eyes bloodshot, its hair standing on end. Stepping backwards, it then made its third attack. Meanwhile the stag calmly lowered his head, propping his thick pointed tines against a rock by his hooves in readiness.

The wolf took several running steps, which provided it with the momentum needed to leap up and swoop down on the stag. My heart missed a beat. But just in time, the stag threw up his antlers, which caught the wolf, then hurled it over his head like a stone. The next moment the wolf fell down the cliff and vanished.

Well done, my seven-tined stag! Just like an experienced hunter, I thought. The stag held up his head in triumph, his large antlers spread beautifully and his sturdy body silhouetted against the sky. He was a magnificent sight. Watching him I could not help feeling an urge to cry out, "My stag, you're the victor! You've proved you're not afraid of the wolf."

Standing on the cliff, the stag gave a short cry — he was calling his herd.

The echoes filled the valley.

Descending, the stag passed in front of me leisurely. I sheltered, in the direction of the wind, so he couldn't scent me. Fascinated, I watched his sturdy antlers, his shining eyes showing both love and hatred, courage and intelligence, his slim upright neck suggesting unyieldingness, his curved body with its yellowish coat and his straight legs concentrating all his strength. He was so very beautiful that I recalled Teji's words, "The stag is a real man.... He would rather die than give in."

Exhausted but still maintaining his dignity, he went past me. I could not resist giving a long sigh, which caused him to halt on the alert. I felt something jog my memory and recalled I was the hunter here. Automatically my eyes shifted to the wounds on his legs. The bullet had left a wound but missed the bone, but the wolf's bite was a dreadful sight, pouring blood. There was no doubt that I could kill him easily. Unconsciously my hand moved to my rifle and rested there, as I watched him limp away till he faded in the distance....

"Farewell," I said to myself, "my seven-tined friend!" As I looked at the distant ranges, I experienced a lonely feeling for the first time.

It was dark when I finally arrived home after countless tumbles. Never had I felt so exhausted before. Ducking into the dark tent, I lit a fire with a trembling hand, then slumped down as if nothing could make me rise again. Soon I was racked with hunger pangs, so reaching a hand into a birch hamper, I grabbed a piece of meat and stuffed it into my mouth. Suddenly the tent flap was flung open and Teji appeared.

"Well, the stag hunter's back at last?"

His harsh voice sounded intimidating. I tried to sit up, but failed after much effort. My waist and legs felt like stiff wooden clubs which were not in my control.

"What have you brought me?" he asked in a low yet threatening voice, thrusting his face close to mine.

I smelled the strong odour of wine.

"Didn't get him, eh? Like a bird with two empty claws."

All I could do was nod my head at him.

"He walked past you, step by step. If you had wanted you could have ridden him."

I was astonished. How had he seen all this?

"You fool! I went out to see off the furrier and found the stag's tracks and yours which I traced downhill. To me prints can speak for themselves. I need none of your explanations."

I had no mind to explain. The furrier had indeed come, which could be proved by the absence of over a dozen bundles of squirrel, sable and lynx pelts. Even my elk-skin mattress was missing. In place of them was a small pile of things including a few bottles of wine, a packet of salt and two cakes of tea. That was all the skins were worth.

"What are you looking for? Your mattress? Didn't you promise to get me a stag? Now out with it, why didn't you shoot?"

Not willing to utter a word, I bit my lips, aware that I would not be able to make myself understood. But I'd no regrets.

"You were scared of him? Afraid of his large antlers?"

"I didn't want to kill him."

" 'I didn't want to kill him.' How nice it sounds! Aren't you an Ewenki? You idiot!" He took up a stick and beat me hard.

Calmly I suffered the pain with dry eyes. In my mind was the image of the unyielding stag.

That night, sleeping on a straw mattress, I dreamed of the stag and the sporting swans on the lake.

Spring set in at last, the season for collecting antlers. However, this year Teji was not in luck. He hadn't got a single one, and he had placed his last hope on waiting at the salty ground in the marsh.

He took me to the hunting ground, and after supper, when the campfire was out, we followed the path to the marsh, our guns over our shoulders and an animal-skin mattress in our hands. It was a patch of salty ground in a grassy swamp, so messy from the hoofs of the deer, it was like a muddy cattle pen. There was a sparse growth of green grass on the darkish alkaline soil.

We selected a spot, separated the grass, spread the mattress and sat down to hide ourselves waiting for the wild deer to come to lick the salty soil. An experienced hunter, Teji told me that the evening breeze was blowing from the valley, the same direction the deer would leave the dense forests, so even those with the keenest noses would not be able to scent us.

Gradually the forest grew quiet, the dew could be heard dripping on the ground. Clumps of bushes nearby became less distinct and blurred. The whining mosquitoes commenced their assaults, getting on my nerves. They were in my ears and hair and stung my face and neck. There were so many of them that with a sweep of your arm you could catch a handful.

Teji was seated beside me, watching the marshy ground like an eagle. But I soon became sleepy and dozed off with my hands supporting my head. When it was almost dawn, he woke me up.

"Damn it!" he cursed. "No luck. During the night, some deer did come but they wouldn't approach the ground and just wandered about. I could hear them but couldn't see them."

His face, full of mosquito bites, indicated he had kept watch the whole night.

"Before the sun rises, the deer will come again. Just wake me up then and do it gently. Or you shoot, picking out those with large antlers." Saying this, he lay down to sleep, clutching his gun.

Little by little the forest grew light and the outlines of trees could be seen clearly, but silence still reigned as the birds had not yet woken up.

After a while I heard some noises like hooves. I ducked my head down in the grass and peeped out from between the blades. A dark form with an erect neck stepped out of the bushes. It paused, then headed gently for the patch of ground. My hand moved to the gun and clutched it so that it would not make any noise. Only twenty or so paces in front of me, the form turned out to be a stout stag with reddish hair and shining dark four-tined antlers. While his ears twitched, he lifted one of his front legs carefully, put it down tentatively, then picked up the other. Wasn't he my stag? I was startled by the recognition, but his particular limping tread told me I was right. Also I knew that his four tines would grow into seven in autumn. When he came nearer I could even see the old scars on his leg. Oh, my friend, my hero, did you come here intentionally to meet me? I could feel my heart beating fast and my hands trembling: I'd sworn that I would never shoot him, nor allow anyone else to injure him.

While I stared fascinated, he calmed down and bent to lick the alkaline soil, chewing leisurely. His antlers, his neck, his body, even his wounded leg were so beautiful that I recalled the magnificent sight on the cliff, an indelible memory.

Just then Teji turned over, talking in his sleep. I gave a start: what if he woke now and found my stag? Scenes flashed before my eyes: the stag, shot in the chest, falls to the ground, blood streaming from his wound.... No, it was too dangerous! He must escape! Thinking of this, I stood up abruptly amidst the grass.

The stag was shocked. Leaping, he fled, but in the swamp, however, he stopped to glance at me, gave a cry and ran on towards the bushes.

Teji woke up with a start. Jumping up he grasped the gun, looking round. But it was too late. He only caught a glimpse of a form flashing past. His face suddenly changed. It became ugly and menacing as he stared at me, his facial muscles twitching. "You ... you brat! Why didn't you shoot?"

I didn't reply.

"You let it go deliberately, you brat! What will you eat and wear without antlers?"

He raised his gun and beat me with it.

I lost consciousness and fell to the ground.

That was how my brief second meeting with my seven-tined stag ended. The third one took place in the autumn of the same year.

That morning, Teji and I left the camp together and headed for our respective hunting grounds.

As soon as I set foot in the pine forest, my eyes caught some animal spoors. A closer look told me that those were made by wolves and were fresh. Since my acquaintance with the stag, I hated wolves more and whenever an opportunity presented itself, I never failed to shoot them.

Following the tracks took me into dense undergrowth where I discovered even more prints. What was strange was that there was a stag's spoor mixed up with them. This showed that a fight had occurred here. A certain ominous presentiment made me hurry.

Soon I came to a birch forest, charming in the autumn, with its white tree trunks, golden leaves and bars of red rays shooting through the tree tops like transparent silk ribbons. Just then some horrible sounds came from the forest. Quickly removing my gun from my shoulder, I groped my way forward. An amazing spectacle greeted my eyes after I had parted some branches: four wolves were attacking a stag by rushing, swooping, tearing and snapping. The latter was none other than my friend — the seven-tined stag who was engaged in a life-and-death struggle around a birch tree. His antlers were lifted high and every muscle taut to display strength, which demonstrated his indignation and unyielding spirit. When two wolves dived at him, he reared up, his hooves beating them alternately in mid-air. One of the wolves was hit and dropped to the ground, the other shrank back fearfully, while the two behind sprang up and snapped at his rump from both sides. Mad with fury, he jumped to run around the birch trees with the wolves hanging upon him like a honeycomb dangling on a branch.

There was no time to delay. I raised my gun and when it fired, one of the hanging wolves dropped dead, the other three gave up and fled.

Now that the stag was out of danger, I propped my gun against a tree and walked up to him. This time he did not run away from me, but stood there panting, looking at me, his eyes full of pride and courage. Like an old friend I approached him, only to be shocked: his body was covered with wounds, running with streams of blood and perspiration. My heart was broken. It was unthinkable what agony he was suffering. Besides, I felt ashamed that I could do nothing to help him.

After a short rest the stag recovered his energy. He tried to run away only to be tugged to a halt. Something had caught his antlers so that he threw them back and his body reared up. In desperation, he started tumbling around a birch tree, as his hooves thudded and churned up dirt and grass. His antlers had become entangled in an iron wire screwed on the tree.

My heart contracted with pain: he could die this way. Without a second thought I unsheathed my hunting knife and moved over. When he paused to gather breath, I rushed up to cut the wire. Before it was done, however, I felt a hard bump, and the next moment I was sent flying and lost consciousness.

After some time, how long I don't know, I got to my feet, though I felt searing pains in my chest. Trembling and soaked with perspiration, I knew the blow had been severe, but I felt no resentment towards the stag.

With much effort, I dragged myself to where the gun stood. Leaning against a tree, I raised the gun to aim at the thin wire.

The first shot missed, so did the second. Although my hands were shaking and I felt dizzy from the pain in my chest, I fired one shot after another till the wire snapped.

Like an untamed horse breaking free, the stag darted forward. As if riding the wind, he was out of sight in a moment.

Heaving a sigh of relief, I suddenly felt weak and collapsed on the ground.

There I lay quietly. The sky looked unusually blue and clear, which made me relax, so I closed my eyes. Then the stag appeared in my mind in his final lightning dash out of the forest. What force he had displayed! His irresistible desire for freedom again touched me and brought happy tears to my closed eyes.

It was time to go home. I gave up the attempt to skin the dead wolf because I felt too weak. Leaning on my gun, I struggled to stand up but had to bend my head because of dizziness.

Two huge feet unexpectedly appeared under my gaze. Slowly I raised my head — there was Teji.

We looked at each other.

There were a few leaves on his shoulders. He must have waited a long time without letting me know, and taken in all that had passed between the stag and me.

He looked at me as if he understood me for the first time, and had found something he had failed to find before. Then his stare moved to my chest. I glanced too. My jacket was ripped to pieces in front, revealing, some bleeding flesh. The sight at once made me feel sick and dizzy, but with the gun's support I stood firm, clenching my teeth and holding my head up to face him. My defiant look was saying, "Now I've let him go again, and I did it deliberately because I regard him as my friend."

Instead of looking angry, however, he gazed at me strangely. Then reaching out the hand he used to beat me with, he gently stroked my hair. After that he turned round, squatted down in front of me, put his arms behind and carried me on his broad back.

A shaft of sunlight penetrating through a dark cloud shone down upon us, while I pressed my face against Teji's shoulder.

From afar came the cries of deer.

Translated by Yang Nan

Black Walls

●

—— LIU XINWU ——

Born in Sichuan, Liu Xinwu began to teach Chinese in a Beijing middle school after graduating from a teacher training school in 1961. Between 1976 and 1980 he worked as an editor at a publishing house in Beijing. In 1977 his short story "The Class Teacher" brought him recognition, and won first prize in the 1978 nationwide short story competition. His representative works are The Drum Tower, *a novel, and* The Grade Separation Bridge, *a collection of novelettes.*

SUMMERTIME. Sunday.
A courtyard in an alley. Three fruit trees, five or six households.
Early morning. 7:30 a.m.
The room at the eastern end of the courtyard is the Zhou's. Actually there is just one certain Mr Zhou, about thirty years old, who lives there on his own. One might assume that he has never been married, though he uses a basin with a large, red double happiness design. One might also assume that he has been married and divorced but then why does he lower his head, study the ground and walk off in the other direction when he sees an unmarried woman in the courtyard? He only recently moved in and his work unit has a long and complicated name so his neighbours have not been able to work out exactly what he does for a living. By reckoning on their fingers they can work out that at his age, having been sent to the countryside for eight years, he can only have been working for about seven years at the most. Consequently, the amount of money in his monthly wage packet is not interesting enough to keep them guessing for long. Since he moved in he has never caused any trouble. He never drops in on anyone; nor does he receive any guests. When he meets neighbours in the courtyard they may first ask him: "How are you?" He will reply neither shyly nor arrogantly: "I'm very well, thank you"; or he may first ask the neighbour: "Finished for the day?", and the neighbour will reply: "Lord no! I'm just

sitting in the cool breeze awhile" But he will not stop and chat. Sometimes when he goes to the communal tap in the courtyard to fetch water, wash his clothes, or wash some rice and he bumps into a neighbour, of course they have to say something to each other. He only speaks when forced to reply to a question. If he answers, he will not follow it with another question. The other families who have lived in the courtyard a long time cannot say that they like him, nor that they dislike him.

He was busy very early one morning. First he moved everything out of his room, then he mixed some sort of liquid in a large wash basin. He must have borrowed a foot operated spray gun yesterday. Clearly, he was going to paint his room.

This began as nothing out of the ordinary. When the neighbours bumped into him at the communal tap, they asked him: "Are you painting your room today?" "Yes, yes I am ." Then they asked him politely, "Do you need some help?" He thanked them: "I've got a spray gun so it should be an easy job! Thank you anyway." After collecting the water he calmly walked away. A calling cicada was hiding in the umbrella-like crown of a scholar tree whose trunk was only as wide as the mouth of a bowl. The noise was getting louder, but they had all grown accustomed to it and so did not find it annoying anymore.

7:46 a.m.

"Chi — chi — chi...."

It was a new sound but it was clear what it was. Zhou had started spraying his room.

7:55 a.m.

Several of the young people from the courtyard had the day off and went out one by one. Naturally they were all dressed up in the latest fashions, each one different from the next. One girl, a meat cutter during the week, was wearing imitation jewel earrings and cream coloured high-heels. As she left the courtyard, she opened a blue-flowered, nylon, automatic umbrella. There was also a young man who worked in the foundry's workshop. On his upper half, he was wearing an Indiana State University T-shirt, printed in English. On his legs, he wore grey corduroy hunting trousers originally made for export. He put on a pair of large-framed, purple sunglasses as he walked out, pushing a small-wheeled bicycle. A second girl hurried out of the courtyard. She studied business management at the local branch of the university. She was wearing a pale green dress, loose at the waist, which she had made herself, and was carrying a round, rattan hand-bag. The events which followed may have occured because they all went out, but it is hard to say if things would have been different if they had not done so, as there was still one young person who remained behind the entire time. This young man sold glassware in the local market and was enjoying a day off. After breakfast, he lay on his bed, reading *The Lamp Without Light*. When his mother called him to join in the following events, he smiled, lay back down and continued to read his book.

8:15 a.m.

The atmosphere in the courtyard was heating up. It is not quite correct to say "in the courtyard"; it would be better to say "in the room". It was not in every room, but it was in the north room in the middle of the courtyard. That was where the Zhao family lived. Mr Zhao was fifty-six years old. He had retired early so his second daughter could take over his job. Soon after his retirement, he went to another work unit to "fill in" for a time. Recently, that unit began making cutbacks, leaving Mr Zhao out of work. Currently, he was trying to arrange another job in a different work unit.

Several of the neighbours gathered at his house. They told Mr Zhao the news: Mr Zhou was not spraying his walls white but black! He was actually spraying his walls black! They did not know what kind of paint he was using but it was black as ink! Pitch black!

Mr Zhao was both astounded and strangely pleased at the same time. Ten years before, he had been the deputy-in-charge of the Workers' Propaganda Team in a song and dance troupe. At that time when some "activists" came to inform him about some "new trends", his manner and tone were just as they were now. Mrs Zhao felt much as her husband did. Eight years before she had been the head of a "socialist neighbourhood committee". Once when some people told her about the remains of a reactionary slogan written at the base of the wall behind the date tree, the atmosphere was much as it was now. Who could guess that something would happen to bring the dead issues of a decade or so ago back to life again?

"That's just not right," Mr Zhao proclaimed.

"How dreadful," said Mrs Zhao indignantly.

8:25 a.m.

"Ch — chi — chi...."

Mr. Zhou was still spraying his room.

Newsflash: He had sprayed the ceiling black, too!

Mr Zhao asked them all to sit down, giving the room the feeling of a meeting hall. Meetings can take on all forms: at some, everyone is bored; at others, only you are interested; at still others, it is you who is bored. Mr Zhao enjoyed the present meeting. He put forward the motion: "In this sort of situation we should inform the police as soon as possible."

If this were eight or ten years ago, this would not have been a mere proposal but a conclusive decision; not just a man giving his own opinion, but a leader's directive.

But, this was the present, not the past. Tall, thin Mr Qian went so far as to immediately oppose him, saying, "As I see it, we shouldn't go to the authorities.... that is, we have no basis. What can we tell the police?"

Mr and Mrs Zhou both stared hard at him. They were both thinking: Damn tailor! Years ago when he was an entrepreneur he never dared to open his mouth, much less oppose our suggestions, but now he does some private business at home, buys a colour television and his whole tone of voice changes.

Mr Qian sat up straight and began fervently expressing his opinion: "Brother Zhou may be suffering from a recurring illness. There are such diseases; I've read about them in the paper. Sufferers have been known to behave strangely under stressful conditions.... Young Zhou was airing his quilt outside his front door last Sunday. Perhaps no one noticed but the quilt cover was made of bright red silk while the underside was duller red. Really, very odd! So I say we should not go to the police but fetch a doctor instead. There is a retired doctor of traditional medicine just down the alley. Although I have heard that traditional medicines don't work on these kinds of illnesses, it would not hurt to consult him."

Not many people responded to Mr Qian's words because as he talked they could not help gazing out of the window, through the shade of the scholar tree, to where they could see "Brother Zhou". Perfectly calm and collected, he continued to spray his walls. Faintly, they could hear him humming a song. Was this the manner of a sick person?

Mr Sun, who was sitting by the door, passed his little finger through his thinning hair and suggested: "Shouldn't we just go and ask him why he is spraying his walls black? If he can't give a good reason, we can just forbid him — no, advise him not to — yes, advise him not to do it anymore."

Another neighbour, Mrs Li, who was sitting in the middle of the crowd, took the opportunity to say, "Why don't you go and ask him for us."

Everyone agreed to this suggestion.

8:36 a.m.

When Mr Sun made his suggestion he thought it would naturally be Mr and Mrs Zhao who would confront Mr Zhou. He never imagined it would be he who would be sent to ask. He regretted sitting by the door. For the past thirty years, he had worked in a primary school in charge of general affairs. He had not taught a class in his life. Consequently, he had picked up many of the mannerisms of a teacher but, now faced with a situation where he had to straighten his back and go to investigate a "strange phenomenon", he felt as though he had been forced to the front of a podium to deliver a speech. His hands and knees shook uncontrollably and he was completely tongue tied.

8:37 a.m.

"Chi — chi — chi...." The spraying continued.

"Bzzzzzzz...." Inside the room, they continued talking in hushed voices.

Mr Sun flicked the long nail of the little finger on his left hand and stared at the tips of his shoes. He was not willing to go to question "Brother Zhou". How could he ever face them again if he received a brash refusal? How could he explain such a failure? What if the idiot said something incriminating? Should he report it directly and be responsible for the unknown consequences, or should he keep the information to himself and risk being accused of protecting Mr Zhou? And what if some evidence came to light in the future....

He gave it tremendous thought. Beads of sweat broke out on his forehead as he said, "Maybe ... maybe Mr Zhao could go and ask instead?"

As no one else wanted the job, everyone agreed and said in chorus, "Yes! Let Mr Zhao go!"

Mr Zhao did not make any immediate move, but waited for them to stop urging and start pleading with him. Only then did he abruptly stand up and declare, "I'll go and ask!" He turned and left the room.

Everyone gazed out the window and watched the receding figure of Mr Zhao walking straight towards Mr Zhou's front door. They all listened attentively, hoping to catch a part of the conversation. All they could hear was the incessant call of the cicadas, high in the scholar tree.

8:41 a.m.

Ashen-faced, Mr Zhao returned to the room and reported, "That rascal says he will come and explain to me when he has finished. I knew he would pull some trick. He doesn't respect us, his neighbours."

Mrs Zhao pointed out of the window and said, "That's the man come to read the water meter, isn't it? He'll go and look in Mr Zhou's room! He'll probably spread all kinds of rumours about black paint and our courtyard, and give us all a bad name!"

Mrs Li, whose job was fluffing cotton into quilts, had a very placid nature and so put forward an explanation to make them all feel better, "Perhaps the black paint is just the undercoat. When it's dry he'll spray a top coat of white paint."

8:43 a.m.

"Chi — chi — chi...." The noise from the spray gun continued. Looking towards the room all they could see was blackness. No one really believed Mrs Li's explanation. The more Mrs Li looked, the more she could not help despairing.

What could one say? Black walls! In this very courtyard! Mr Zhou is not afraid of doing evil things himself, but he should not get others involved.

8:45 a.m.

Everyone in the room agreed about one thing: he should not spray his walls black! How could anyone spray his walls and ceiling black? Most people would not dare even think of such a thing. He did not just think about it, he actually did it! Extraordinary! Weird! Half-mad! Reactionary!...

Mr Zhao still thought the police should be informed. Just as he was about to go and do so, he had second thoughts: The police station is not the same as it was eight or ten years ago (at that time there was not a police station but a "group to smash the leaders of the judicial and public security institutions". It was in the same courtyard as the present-day police station). Today the police are not as extreme nor do they think themselves as important as in the past. They always talk about "going by the book" but once you start doing things "by the book" then problems like the black wall dilemma will drag on and possibly never be resolved. Mr Zhao hestitated. He felt strongly about it and really did want to report it. It was a responsibility he could not shirk, a duty he had to take quick action to deal with. Could he be doing it for his own good? But what possible benefit could come of reporting it?

Mrs Zhao realized what her husband must be feeling and felt very bitter. How different it was eight or ten years ago! Her husband was actually suffering now because he lacked any real skills, and could only work as an assistant or warehouse watchman. Was it because he had not tried to learn a trade? Certainly not. For the past thirty odd years he had been transferred to work in various campaigns. The campaigns had come and gone, so now he had no way of earning a living. Formerly all his pride had come from his political sensitivity. Now he had a chance to display this talent, but his eyes, wrinkled face and the corners of his mouth showed hesitancy. Why was it? What was all this exertion for today? Could it be just for the good of his own family?

More and more, Mr Zhao believed that "Brother Zhou" was suffering from a recurring illness. He admitted that what he had just been thinking was wrong. Traditional doctors were unable to treat this sort of illness. Could he not just let the doctor take his pulse? Not really. He would still have to get a Western doctor. But doctors didn't make house calls nowadays. It would be extremely difficult. Who could persuade him to go to the out-patient's department?

Mrs Li wanted to go home and get her lump of a son to stop reading his novels and think of what to do. Perhaps he could bring Mr Zhou to his senses, and even help spray the walls white again. White is so nice! Why should anyone want anything different?

Mr Sun wanted to go home but was too embarrassed to make the move. In this sort of situation a person ought to make clear his position on the matter, so in the future he could not be accused of "sitting on the fence". Of course a person should not leave it so that in any future situation he could not be accused of having played a part in a "misjudged case". Ideally one would avoid any sort of criticism in the past, present or future. He had already shown enough "intention" to go to Mr Zhou's, so he should now make an early retreat. But it would be hard to slip out without being noticed....

8:48 a.m.

Mr Zhao had a grandson affectionately known as "Little Button" who was not much more than ten years old. At the start of all this he had been painting in the back room. At length, he came and leaned on the doorway between the two rooms, curiously listening to the adults' discussion. He thought the room crowded, muggy, hot and disordered. Why did adults have to torment themselves like this?

Once again they began to discuss the matter and once again the atmosphere heated up. Little Button stood before his grandfather, turned his head and asked: "Grandpa, what are you all doing?"

Mr Zhao said to him firmly, "Off with you! Go and play! There's nothing for you here!"

Little Button was not convinced and thought to himself: Are you angry with Uncle Zhou for spraying his walls? Uncle Zhou is a very nice man. He's such fun. Once he called me to his room. He took some pieces of card from a drawer. The pieces were of every colour under the sun and were as big as the Evening News. He kept changing them and pressed them up to my eyes so that all I could see was that colour. Then he asked: "Do you like it or not? Does it feel hot or cold? Dry or wet? Pleasant or nasty to smell? Does it make you want to go to sleep or go out and play? What does it make you think of? Or does it make you think nothing at all? Does it make you feel frightened or calm? Does it make you thirsty or not? Do you want to go on looking at it or not?" He jotted down every reply that I made. See how much fun he is! If you don't believe me, go over to his place and see for yourselves!

Little Button thought this far, then raised his head and said loudly, "Grandpa, you still haven't finished your discussion. You must be awfully tired. Can I say something now?"

There was nothing for it but for everyone to stop talking. They all looked at him.

Mr Zhao waved his hands as if he had been wronged and said, "Right, right! Go ahead!"

Little Button asked: "When Uncle Zhou has finished his room, will he go from door to door spraying everyone else's rooms as well?"

8:49 a.m.

Everyone went blank.

8:50 a.m.

Mr Zhao blurted out: "I'm sure he'd dare!" Mrs Zhao echoed, "He'll try!". Mrs Li and Mr Sun said at once, "He wouldn't, he'd never...." Mr Qian thought carefully before saying, "He doesn't look like a trouble maker. His illness only seems to recur in his own home...."

8:51.30 a.m.

Little Button turned round, blinked his round, black eyes, blacker even than the walls, shining black. He smiled innocently and said in a shrill voice: "So that's settled! Uncle Zhou is spraying the walls of his own room, and it has nothing to do with us, so what are you all going on about?"

8:52 a.m.

Everyone went silent.

The "chi — chi — chi...." of the wall spraying drifted over, mingling with the sound of the cicadas, becoming even more pronounced.

Summer 1982

Translated by Alice Childs

The Tall Woman and Her Short Husband

•

—— FENG JICAI ——

One of China's best-known writers, Feng Jicai was born and brought up in Tianjin. He started out as an athlete but after an injury was transferred to work in the Chinese Traditional Painting Press in Tianjin where he began to paint and write. In 1974 he started teaching Chinese traditional painting at the Tianjin Workers' College of Decorative Art and continued to write in his spare time. In 1978 he became a professional writer. Since 1976 he has published the novels The Boxers, Magic Light *and* The Miraculous Pigtail *and six collections of novelettes and short stories.*

1

SAY you have a small tree in your yard and are used to its smooth trunk. If one day it turns twisted and gnarled it strikes you as awkward. As time goes by, however, you grow to like it, as if that was how this tree should always have been. Were it suddenly to straighten out again you would feel indescribably put out. A trunk as dull and boring as a stick! In fact it would simply have reverted to its original form, so why should you worry?

Is this force of habit? Well, don't underestimate "habit". It runs through everything done under the sun. It is not a law to be strictly observed, yet flouting it is simply asking for trouble. Don't complain though if it proves so binding that sometimes, unconsciously, you conform to it. For instance, do you presume to throw your weight about before your superiors? Do you air your views recklessly in front of your seniors? When a group photograph is taken, can you shove celebrities aside to stand swaggering and chortling in the middle? You can't, of course you can't. Or again, would you choose a wife ten years older than you, heftier than you or a head taller than you? Don't be in a rush to answer. Here's an instance of such a couple.

2

She was seventeen centimetres taller than he.

One point seven five metres in height, she towered above most of her sex like a crane over chickens. Her husband, a bare 1.58 metres, had been nicknamed Shorty at college. He came up to her earlobes but actually looked two heads shorter.

And take their appearances. She seemed dried up and scrawny with a face like an unvarnished ping-pong bat. Her features would pass, but they were small and insignificant as if carved in shallow relief. She was flat-chested, had a ramrod back and buttocks as scraggy as a scrubbing-board. Her husband on the other hand seemed a rubber rolypoly: well-fleshed, solid and radiant. Everything about him — his calves, insteps, lips, nose and fingers — were like pudgy little meatballs. He had soft skin and a fine complexion shining with excess fat and ruddy because of all the red blood in his veins. His eyes were like two high-voltage little light bulbs, while his wife's were like glazed marbles. The two of them just did not match, and formed a marked contrast. But they were inseparable.

One day some of their neighbours were having a family reunion. After drinking his fill the grandfather put a tall, thin empty wine bottle on the table next to a squat tin of pork.

"Who do these remind you of?" he asked. Before anyone could guess he gave the answer, "That tall woman downstairs and that short husband of hers."

Everyone burst out laughing and went on laughing through the meal.

What had brought such a pair together?

This was a mystery to the dozens of households living in Unity Mansions. Ever since this couple moved in, the old residents had eyed them curiously. Some registered a question mark in their minds, while others put their curiosity into words. Tongues started wagging, especially in wet weather when the two of them went out and it was always Mrs Tall who held the umbrella. If anything dropped to the ground, though, it was simpler for Mr Short to pick it up. Some old ladies at a loose end would gesticulate, finding this comic, and splutter with laughter. This set a bad example for the children who would burst out laughing at sight of the pair and hoot, "Long carrying-pole; big, low stool!" The husband and wife pretended not to hear and kept their tempers, paying no attention. Maybe for this reason their relations with their neighbours remained rather cool. The few less officious ones simply nodded a greeting when they met. This made it hard for those really intrigued by them to find out more about them. For instance, how did they hit it off? Why had they married? Which gave way to the other? They could only speculate.

This was an old-fashioned block of flats with large sunny rooms and wide, dark corridors. It stood in a big courtyard with a small gatehouse. The man who lived there was a tailor, a decent fellow. His wife, who brimmed over with energy, liked to call on her neighbours and gossip. Most of all she liked to ferret out their secrets. She knew exactly how husbands and wives got on, why sisters-in-law quarrelled, who was lazy, who hard-working, and how much everyone earned. If she was unclear about anything she would leave no stone unturned to get at the truth. The thirst for knowledge makes even the ignorant wise. In this respect she was outstanding. She analyzed conversations, watched expressions, and could even tell what people were secretly thinking. Simply by using her nose, she knew which household was eating meat or fish, and from that could deduce their income. For some reason or other, ever since the sixties each housing estate had chosen someone like this as a "neighbourhood activist", giving legal status to these nosey-parkers so that their officiousness could have full play. It seems the Creator will never waste any talent.

Though the tailor's wife was indefatigable she failed to discover how this incongruous couple who passed daily before her eyes had come to marry. She found this most frustrating; it posed a formidable challenge. On the base of her experience, however, and by racking her brains she finally came up with a plausible explanation: either husband or wife must have some physiological deficiency. Otherwise no one would marry someone a whole head taller or shorter. Her grounds for this reasoning were that after three years of marriage they still had no children. The residents of Unity Mansions were all convinced by this brilliant hypothesis.

But facts are merciless. The tailor's wife was debunked and lost face when Mrs Tall appeared in the family way. Her womb could be seen swelling from day to day, for being relatively far from the ground it was all too evident. Regardless of their amazement, misgivings or embarrassment, she gave birth to a fine baby. When the sun was hot or it rained and the couple went out, Mrs Tall would carry the baby while Mr Short held the umbrella. He plodded along comically on his plump legs, the umbrella held high, keeping just behind his wife. And the neighbours remained as intrigued as at the start by this ill-assorted, inseparable couple. They went on making plausible conjectures, but could find no confirmation for any of them.

The tailor's wife said, "They must have something to hide, those two. Why else should they keep to themselves? Well, it's bound to come to light some day, just wait and see."

One evening, sure enough, she heard the sound of breaking glass in their flat. On the pretext of collecting money for sweeping the yard she rushed to knock on their door, sure that their long hidden feud had come to a head and avid to watch the confrontation between them. The door opened. Mrs Tall asked her in with a smile. Mr Short was smiling too at a smashed plate on the floor — that was all the tailor's wife saw. She hastily collected the money and left to puzzle over what had happened. A plate had been smashed, yet instead of quarrelling they had treated it as a joke. How very strange!

Later the tailor's wife became the residents' representative for Unity Mansions. When she helped the police check up on living permits, she at last found the answer to this puzzle. A reliable and irrefutable answer. The tall woman and her short husband both worked in the Research Institute of the Ministry of Chemical Industry. He was chief engineer, with a salary of over 180 yuan! She was an ordinary laboratory technician earning less than sixty yuan, and her father was a hard-working low-paid postman. So that explained why she had married a man so much shorter. For status, money and an easy life. Right! The tailor's wife lost no time in passing on this priceless information to all the bored old ladies in Unity Mansions. Judging others by themselves, they believed her. At last this riddle was solved. They saw the light. Rich Mr Short was congenitally deficient while poor Mrs Tall was a money-grabber on the make. When they discussed the good luck of this tall woman who looked like a horse, they often voiced resentment — especially the tailor's wife.

3

Sometimes good luck turns into bad.

In 1966, disaster struck China. Great changes came into the lives of all the residents in Unity Mansions, which was like a microcosm of the whole country. Mr Short as chief engineer was the first to suffer. His flat was raided, his furniture moved out, he was struggled against and confined in his institute. And worse was to come. He was accused of smuggling out the results of his research to write up at home in the evenings, with a view to fleeing the country to join a wealthy relative abroad. This preposterous charge of passing on scientific secrets to foreign capitalists was widely believed. In that period of lunacy people took leave of their senses and cruelly made up groundless accusations in order to find some Hitler in their midst. The institute kept a stranglehold on its chief engineer. He was threatened, beaten up, put under all kinds of pressure; his wife was ordered to hand over that manuscript which no one had ever seen. But all was to no effect. Someone proposed holding a struggle meeting against them both in the courtyard of Unity Mansions. As everyone dreads losing face in front of relatives and friends, this would put more pressure on them. Since all else had failed, it was at least worth trying. Never before had Unity Mansions been the scene of such excitement.

In the afternoon the institute sent people to fix up ropes between two trees in the yard, on which to hang a poster with the name of Mr Short on it — crossed out. Inside and outside the yard they pasted up threatening slogans, and on the wall put eighteen more posters listing the engineer's "crimes". As the meeting was to be held after supper, an electrician was sent to fix up four big 500-watt bulbs. By now the tailor's wife, promoted to be the chairman of the neighbourhood's Public Security Committee, was a powerful person, full of self-importance, and much fatter than before. She had been busy all day bossing the other women about, helping to put up slogans and make tea for the revolutionaries from the institute. The wiring for the lights had been fixed up from her gatehouse as if she were celebrating a wedding!

After supper the tailor's wife assembled all the residents in the yard, lit up as brilliantly as a sportsground at night. Their shadows, magnified ten-fold, were thrown on the wall of the building. These shadows stayed stock-still, not even the children daring to play about. The tailor's wife led a group also wearing red armbands, in those days most awe-inspiring, to guard the gate and keep outsiders out. Presently a crowd from the institute, wearing armbands and shouting slogans, marched in the tall woman and her short husband. He had a placard hung round his neck, she had none. The two of them were marched in front of the platform, and stood there side by side with lowered heads.

The tailor's wife darted forward. "This wretch is too short for the revolutionary masses at the back to see," she cried. "I'll soon fix that." She dashed into the gatehouse, her fat shoulders heaving, to fetch a soapbox which she turned upside down. Mr Short standing on this was the same height as his wife. But at this point little attention was paid to the relative heights of this couple facing disaster.

The meeting followed the customary procedure. After slogans had been shouted, passionate accusations were made, punctuated by more slogans. The pressure built up. First Mrs Tall was ordered to come clean, to produce that "manuscript". Questions and denunciations were fired at her, hysterical screams, angry shouts and threatening growls. But she simply shook her head gravely and sincerely. What use was sincerity? To believe in her would have made the whole business a farce.

No matter what bullies sprang forward to shake their fists at her, or what tricky questions were asked to try to trap her, she simply shook her head. The members of the institute were at a loss, afraid that if this went on the struggle meeting would fizzle out and end up a fiasco.

The tailor's wife had listened with mounting exasperation. Being illiterate she took no interest in the "manuscript" they wanted, and felt these research workers were too soft-spoken. All of a sudden she ran to the platform. Raising her right arm with its red armband she pointed accusingly at Mrs Tall.

"Say!" she screeched. "Why did you marry him?"

The members of the institute were staggered by this unexpected question. What connection had it with their investigation?

Mrs Tall was staggered too. This wasn't the sort of question asked these days. She looked up with surprise on her thin face which showed the ravages of the last few months.

"So you don't dare answer, eh?" The tailor's wife raised her voice. "I'll answer for you! You married this scoundrel, didn't you, for his money? If he hadn't had money who'd want such a short fellow!" She sounded rather smug, as if she alone had seen through Mrs Tall.

Mrs Tall neither nodded nor shook her head. She had seen through the tailor's wife too. Her eyes glinted with derision and contempt.

"All right, you won't admit it. This wretch is done for now, he's a broken reed. Oh, I know what you're thinking." The tailor's wife slapped her chest and brandished one hand gloatingly. Some other women chimed in.

The members of the institute were flummoxed. A question like this was best ignored. But though these women had strayed far from the subject, they had also livened up the meeting. So the institute members let them take the field. The women yelled:

"How much has he paid you? What has he bought you? Own up!"

"Two hundred a month isn't enough for you, is it? You have to go abroad!"

"Is Deng Tuo* behind you?"

"That day you made a long-distance call to Beijing, were you ringing up the Three Family Village?**"

The success of a meeting depends on the enthusiasm worked up. The institute members who had convened this meeting saw that the time was ripe now to shout a few more slogans and conclude it. They then searched Mrs Tall's flat, prizing up floorboards and stripping off wallpaper. When they discovered nothing, they marched her husband away, leaving her behind.

Mrs Tall stayed in all the next day but went out alone after dark, unaware that though the light in the gatehouse was out the tailor's wife was watching her from the window. She trailed her out of the gate and past two crossroads till Mrs Tall stopped to knock softly on a gate. The tailor's wife ducked behind a telegraph pole and waited, holding her breath, as if to pounce on a rabbit when it popped out of its burrow.

The gate creaked open. An old woman led out a child.

"All over, is it?" she asked.

---

*Deng Tuo (1912-1966), historian, poet and essayist, was the Party secretary of Beijing in charge of cultural and educational work, who was considered a counter-revolutionary after the start of the "cultural revolution" in 1966.

**In 1961 Deng Tuo, Wu Han (a historian) and Liao Mosha (a writer) started a magazine column "Notes from the Three Family Village" and published many essays which were well received. During the "cultural revolution" the three writers were falsely charged as "The Three Family Village".

Mrs Tall's answer was inaudible.

"He's had his supper and a sleep," the old woman said. "Take him home quickly now."

The tailor's wife realized that this was the woman who minded their little boy. Her excitement died down as Mrs Tall turned back to lead her son home. All was silence apart from the sound of their footsteps. The tailor's wife stood motionless behind the telegraph pole till they had gone, then scurried home herself.

The next morning when Mrs Tall led her son out, her eyes were red. No one would speak to her, but they all saw her red, swollen eyes. Those who had denounced her the previous day had a strange feeling of guilt. They turned away so as not to meet her eyes.

4

After the struggle meeting Mr Short was not allowed home again. The tailor's wife, who was in the know, said he had been imprisoned as an active counter-revolutionary. That made Mrs Tall the lowest of the low, naturally unfit to live in a roomy flat. She was forced to change places with the tailor's wife and moved into the little gatehouse. This didn't worry her, as it meant she could avoid the other residents who snubbed her. But they could look through her window and see her all alone there. Where she had sent her son, they didn't know, for he only came home for a few days at a time. Ostracized by all, she looked older than a woman in her thirties.

"Mark my words," the tailor's wife said, "she can only keep this up for at most a year. Then if Shorty doesn't get out she'll have to remarry. If I were her I'd get a divorce and remarry. Even if he's let out his name will be mud, and he won't have any money."

A year went by. Mr Short still didn't come back and Mrs Tall kept to herself. In silence she went to work, came back, lit her stove and went out with a big shabby shopping basket. Day after day she did this, the whole year round.... But one day in autumn Mr Short reappeared — thinly clad, his head shaved, and his whole appearance changed. He seemed to have shrunk and his skin no longer gleamed with health. He went straight to his old flat. Its new master, the honest tailor, directed him to the gatehouse. Mrs Tall was squatting in the doorway chopping firewood. At the sound of his voice she sprang up to stare at him. After two years' separation both were appalled by the change in the other. One was wrinkled, the other haggard; one looked taller than before, the other shorter. After gazing at each other they hastily turned away, and Mrs Tall ran inside. When finally she came out again he had picked up the axe and squatted down to chop firewood, until two big boxes of wood had been chopped into kindling, as if he feared some new disaster might befall them at any moment. After that they were inseparable again, going to work together and coming back together just as before. The neighbours, finding them unchanged, gradually lost interest in them and ignored them.

One morning Mrs Tall had an accident. Her husband rushed frantically out and came back with an ambulance to fetch her. For days the gatehouse was empty and dark at night. After three weeks Mr Short returned with a stranger. They were carrying her on a stretcher. She was confined to her room. He went to work as usual, hurrying back at dusk to light the stove and go out with the shopping basket. This was the same basket she had used every day. In his hand it looked even bigger and nearly reached the ground.

When the weather turned warmer Mrs Tall came out. After so long in bed her face was deathly white, and she swayed from side to side. She held a cane in her right hand and kept her left elbow bent in front of her. Her half-paralysed left leg made walking difficult. She had obviously had a stroke. Every morning and every evening Mr Short helped her twice round the yard, painfully and slowly. By hunching up his shoulders he was able to grip her crooked arm in both hands. It was hard for him, but he smiled to encourage her. As she couldn't raise her left foot, he tied a rope round it and pulled this up when she wanted to take a step forward. This was a pathetic yet impressive sight, and the neighbours were touched by it. Now when they met the couple they nodded cordially to them.

5

Mrs Tall's luck had run out: she was not to linger long by the side of the short husband who loved her so dearly. Death and life were equally cruel to her. Life had struck her down and now death carried her off. Mr Short was left all alone.

But after her death fortune smiled on him again. He was rehabilitated, his confiscated possessions were returned, and he received all his back pay. Only his flat, occupied by the tailor's wife, was not given back to him. The neighbours watched to see what he would do. It was said that some of his colleagues had proposed finding him another wife, but he had declined their offers.

"I know the kind of woman he wants," said the tailor's wife. "Just leave it to me!"

Having passed her zenith she had become more subdued. Stripped of her power she had to wear a smile. With a photograph of a pretty girl in her pocket she went to the gatehouse to find Mr Short. The girl in the picture was her niece.

She sat in the gatehouse sizing up its furnishing as she proposed this match to rich Mr Short. Smiling all over her face she held forth with gusto until suddenly she realized that he had said not a word, his face was black, and behind him hung a picture of him and Mrs Tall on their wedding day. Then she beat a retreat without venturing to produce the photograph of her niece.

Since then several years have passed. Mr Short is still a widower, but on Sundays he fetches his son home to keep him company. At the sight of his squat, lonely figure, his neighbours recall all that he has been through and have come to understand why he goes on living alone. When it rains and he takes an umbrella to go to work, out of force of habit perhaps he still holds it high. Then they have the strange sensation that there is a big empty space under that umbrella, a vacuum that nothing on earth can fill.

January 16, 1982

Translated by Gladys Yang

Ah, Fragrant Snow

●

—— TIE NING ——

Tie Ning, a young woman writer, was already displaying a rare literary talent during her middle school days. Upon graduation from senior middle school in 1975 she moved to the countryside to experience rural life rather than go to university. She published "Ah, Fragrant Snow" in 1982, which won her fame. This story and "Buttonless Red Shirt" won national awards. Her publications include the collections of short stories Path in the Night, Buttonless Red Shirt *and* Ah, Fragrant Snow.

IF trains had not been invented, if nobody had laid railway tracks into remote mountains, small villages like Terrace Gully would never have been found. The village and its villagers, in fifteen houses, hid in the deep wrinkles of an old mountain, silently accepting the willful mountain's tender caress and brutal temper.

But now, two slim, glittering railway tracks stretched over the mountain. They bravely spiralled halfway up, then quietly felt their way further, wound and curved before finally arriving at the foot of Terrace Gully. Then they made their way into the gloomy tunnel, dashed ahead to another mountain, and hurried away into the mysterious distance.

The villagers jostled to watch the green dragon whistling past. It carried an unfamiliar, fresh wind from some strange place beyond the mountains, and hastened away from poor Terrace Gully. It went at such a pace that the sound of the wheels rolling on the tracks was like an eager voice: can't stop, can't stop! It had no reason to stop at Terrace Gully. Did anyone in the village need to go on a long journey? Did someone from beyond the mountains want to visit relatives or friends at Terrace Gully? Were there oil deposits or gold mines? Terrace Gully had no power at all to invite the train's attention.

Nevertheless, a new stop was added to the railway timetable, "Terrace Gully". Perhaps some passengers had made a suggestion, and one of them who had some influence was related to the village. Perhaps the train attendant, a jolly young fellow, had noticed the pretty girls of Terrace Gully. Every time the train passed, they would come in groups, stick out their chins, and stare at the train with greedy eyes. Some pointed at the train, and occasionally you could hear coy screams when they poked each other. Perhaps none of these was the real reason. Perhaps Terrace Gully was just too small — so small it made your heart ache, so small that even the gigantic dragon couldn't bear to stride proudly ahead without stopping. Whatever the reason, Terrace Gully was on the railway's timetable now. Every evening at seven o'clock, the train from Beijing to Shanxi would stop here for one minute.

One minute, so fleeting, yet it threw Terrace Gully's peaceful evenings into disorder. It had been the custom in the village to go to bed right after dinner, as though everyone heard the old mountain's mute order at the same time. The small stretch of stone houses would suddenly become completely noiseless — so quiet that it seemed the village was silently confiding its piety to the old mountains. But now, the girls of Terrace Gully served dinner in a flurry, absent-mindedly grabbed a quick bite, put down their bowls, and went straight to their dressers. They washed off the dust and stains of the day, revealing their rough and ruddy complexions, combed their hair, and then vied with one other in wearing their best outfits. Some girls put on new shoes which they were supposed to wear only for Spring Festival; others even secretly put a little rouge on their cheeks. Then they ran to the railway, where the train passed. Fragrant Snow was always first; her next-door neighbour, Frail Phoenix, followed right behind.

At seven o'clock, the train slowed down as it approached Terrace Gully, gave a loud crash and a shake, then stopped. The girls rushed toward it, their hearts thumping violently. As if watching a movie, they looked into the cars through the windows. Fragrant Snow hid behind her friends and covered her ears. She was the first to come out of her house to watch the train, but retreated when it arrived. She was frightened by its gigantic head. The monster spurted out magnificent white smoke, as though it could suck Terrace Gully into its stomach in one breath.

"Fragrant Snow, come here!" Frail Phoenix dragged Fragrant Snow to her side. "Look at those golden rings in that lady's hair. What do you call them? It's the lady in the back seat with that big round face. Look at her watch, it's smaller than my nail!"

Fragrant Snow nodded. At last she saw the golden rings in the woman's hair and the tiny watch on her wrist. But soon she found something else. "A leather schoolbag!" She pointed to a brown leather satchel on the luggage rack.

Fragrant Snow's discoveries usually did not excite the other girls, but they still rushed up around her.

"You stepped on my toes!" Frail Phoenix cried out and complained to another girl who was pushing to the front.

"What a loud voice! You want to show off so that white-faced man will talk to you, don't you?"

"I'll tear your mouth off if you repeat that!" Frail Phoenix cried, but couldn't help looking over to the gate of the third car.

The fair-skinned young attendant stepped down from the train. He was tall and had jet-black hair, and spoke with a beautiful Beijing accent. Perhaps this was why the girls called him "The Beijingese" behind his back. "The Beijingese" crossed his arms on his chest, kept a distance neither too close to nor too far from the girls: "Say, young ladies, don't hold onto the windows, it's dangerous!"

"Oh, so we're young; are you so old?" the bold Frail Phoenix retorted.

The girls broke into laughter. Somebody gave Frail Phoenix a shove, and it made her almost bump into him. Instead of being embarrassed, this boosted her courage.

"Hey, don't you feel dizzy staying in that train all day long?" she asked.

"What do you do with that thing hanging on the ceiling? It looks like a broadsword," another girl asked. She was referring to the electric fan in the railway car.

"Where do you heat the water?"

"What if you run into some place and they haven't got any roads?"

"How many meals do you city people eat every day?" Fragrant Snow asked in a small voice, hiding behind other girls.

"Bah, I'm at the end of my rope," grumbled "The Beijingese".

They wouldn't let him go till the train was about to start. He glanced at his watch as he ran toward the train, and shouted back: "Next time! Next time I'll answer all your questions." He had long, nimble legs and stepped on the train agilely. Then, the green door shut with a bang. The train dashed into the darkness, leaving the girls beside the ice-cold tracks. For a long time they could still feel the slight quiver in the tracks.

Everything became quiet again. On the way back home, the girls quarreled about trifles.

"She's got to bind the nine golden rings together first, then stick them in her hair."

"No. She didn't do it that way."

"Sure she did."

"Frail Phoenix, why don't you speak up? Still thinking about that Beijingese?"

"Get lost. You talk because it's you who's thinking about him."

Fragrant Snow didn't say a word. She just flushed with embarrassment for her friend. She was only seventeen and had not yet learned how to rescue someone from this sort of talk.

The same girl kept teasing Frail Phoenix, "I know, you like him but haven't got the nerve to admit it. He's got such nice skin!"

"Nice skin? That's from staying in that big green house all year long. Let him try Terrace Gully for a few days," someone in the shadows said.

"There you go. Those city folks all hide in rooms from the sun. They should see our Fragrant Snow. Our Fragrant Snow was born with this pretty skin. If she only did her hair into a bunch of curls like those girls on the train."

Frail Phoenix had no response except to let go of Fragrant Snow's hand. Frail Phoenix couldn't help feeling defensive about the fellow, as if the girls had belittled someone related to her. She firmly believed that his fair skin was not from hiding in rooms. It was natural.

Fragrant Snow put her hand back into Frail Phoenix's. It seemed to her that she had somehow wronged her friend, and she was asking forgiveness.

"Frail Phoenix, have you lost your tongue?" the same girl attacked again.

"Who's lost whose tongue! You girls look at nothing but whether a fellow's got nice or ugly skin. You like him, why don't you go with him?"

"We aren't the right match."

"Don't you think he's got his own girl?"

No matter how heated these quarrels were, the girls would always part amicably because an exciting idea would arise in everyone's mind: tomorrow, the train would pass again and they would have another wonderful minute. Compared to this, a little quarrel was nothing.

Ah, that colorful minute was filled with the joy, anger, grief and happiness of the girls from Terrace Gully.

As the days went by, the girls added a new dimension to this precious minute. They began to carry rectangular wicker baskets full of walnuts, eggs and dates, and stood under the train's windows to quickly strike up bargains with the passengers. They tiptoed and stretched their arms all the way up to raise basketsful of eggs and dates to the windows, taking in exchange things that were rare in Terrace Gully: fine dried noodles, matches, or the girls's favourites: bobby pins, gauze kerchieves, sometimes even richly coloured nylon socks. Of course it was risky to take the latter items back home, for they might get scolded for making decisions based purely on their own fancy.

The girls seemed to have a tacit agreement to assign Frail Phoenix to "The Beijingese". Nobody else but Frail Phoenix, basket in hand, would ever go to him. It was amusing to see how she made a deal with him. She always dawdled on purpose, putting a full basket into his hands just when the train was about to start. The train began to move before he had time to pay for her eggs. He put the basket in the train, and made gestures to explain something to her, while she stood by the train feeling happy; she was glad that he took her eggs without paying. Of course the fellow would bring money to her the next time, and would bring a bundle of noodles, gauze kerchieves, or something else. If the noodles weighed ten *jin*, Frail Phoenix would insist on taking out one *jin* to give back to him. She felt this was only fair. She wanted their contact to be a little different from a regular business sale. Sometimes she would remember the girls' remark: "Don't you think he's got his own girl?" As a matter of fact, whether or not he had his own girl was not Frail Phoenix's concern, because she never thought of going away with him. But she wanted to be nice to him. Did she have to be his girl to treat him nicely?

Fragrant Snow was taciturn and timid, but her sales were the most successful of all the girls. Passengers loved to buy from her because she looked at them so trustingly with her pure, innocent eyes. She had not learned how to haggle over the price; she simply said: "You offer as you think fit." They looked at her face that was as pure as a new-born baby, her lips as soft as red satin, and a beautiful feeling would come over them. They couldn't bear to trick this little girl.

Sometimes she would seize an opportunity to ask passengers about things from the outside. She asked if the universities in Beijing would want students from Terrace Gully, and what "musical poetry" was (she happened to see this term in a book a classmate brought to school). One time she asked a middle-aged woman with glasses about a pencil-case that could close automatically, and how much it would cost. But the train started moving before the woman could answer. She ran quite a while after the train. The autumn wind and the whistling wheels rang in her ears; then she stopped and realized how ridiculous she was being.

The train was soon out of sight. The girls surrounded Fragrant Snow. When they found out the reason for this train chasing, everybody laughed.

"Silly girl!"

"It's not worth it."

They tapped her mockingly on the shoulder like the venerable elders would do.

"It was my fault. I should have asked her earlier." Fragrant Snow would never think that this was not worthwhile; she only blamed herself for acting too slowly.

"Bah, you might as well ask about something better," said Frail Phoenix carrying the basket for Fragrant Snow.

"No wonder she asked that; our Fragrant Snow is a student," said someone else.

Perhaps this explained everything. Fragrant Snow was the only one in Terrace Gully who had passed the entrance examination for middle school.

Terrace Gully had no school. Fragrant Snow had to walk five miles every day to the commune school. Although she had a quiet disposition, with the Terrace Gully girls she always had things to talk about. However, at the commune middle school she did not have many friends. There were a lot of girls, but the way they acted, the expression in their eyes and their soft laughter made it seem that they wanted Fragrant Snow to realize she was from a small village, a poor place. They asked her over and over: "How many meals do you eat every day at home?" She was ignorant of their intention, so she always answered innocently: "Two meals." Then she would ask, "What about in your village?"

"Three meals," they would always answer proudly. Afterwards, they felt pity and anger that Fragrant Snow was so slow.

"Why don't you bring your pencil box to school?" they asked again.

"There it is." Fragrant Snow pointed to the corner of her desk.

Actually, everybody knew that the little wooden box was Fragrant Snow's pencil box, but they all looked shocked. The girl sitting next to Fragrant Snow started fiddling with her big plastic pencil box, closing it up with a click. This was an "automatic" pencil box, and only long afterward did Fragrant Snow learn the secret of how it shut automatically. It was because there was a small magnet hidden inside. The little wooden box was a special present made by Fragrant Snow's father, who was a carpenter, to celebrate her success in the entrance examination. It was unmatched in Terrace Gully, but here in the school, it looked awkward and outmoded. The little box shrank back timidly in the corner of the desk.

Fragrant Snow's mind was no longer at peace. The meaning of her classmates' repeated questions suddenly dawned on her. She realized how poor Terrace Gully was. Her eyes were fixed on her classmate's pencil box now. She guessed that it must be from a big city, and the price must be quite outrageous. Would thirty eggs buy it? Or forty? Fifty? Her heart sank.

What am I thinking about? Did Mother collect eggs so I could go off on wild flights of fancy? Why is that inviting click always ringing in my ears?

Late autumn came to the mountains. The wind grew colder and the days short, but Fragrant Snow and the other girls never missed the seven o'clock train. Now they could wear their colourful cotton-padded jackets. Frail Phoenix wore two pink barrettes, and some girls tied their plaits with braided elastics. They had traded eggs and walnuts for these things from the train. They carefully dressed up from head to toe, imitating the city girls in the train. Then they lined up by the railway tracks, as if they were waiting to be reviewed.

The train stopped and heaved a deep sigh, as if it were complaining about the cold weather in Terrace Gully. Today the train showed an unusual indifference towards Terrace Gully; all of the windows were tightly closed, and passengers were sipping tea and reading newspapers in the dim light. Nobody glanced out of the windows. Even those familiar passengers seemed to have forgotten the Terrace Gully girls.

As usual, Frail Phoenix ran to the third car to look for her "Beijingese". Fragrant Snow tightened her red scarf, switched her basket from her right hand to her left, and walked by the train. She tiptoed so that passengers might see her face. Nobody noticed her, but on a table, something among the food caught her eyes. She put down her basket, held onto the window sill with a violently pounding heart, and assured herself that it was a pencil box with a magnet. It was so close she could have touched it if the window had been open.

A middle-aged woman attendant dragged Fragrant Snow away, but Fragrant Snow kept watching the pencil box from a distance. When she had assured herself that it belonged to the girl by the window who looked like a student, she ran over and knocked on the window. The girl turned about and faced her. Seeing the basket on Fragrant Snow's arm, she waved her hand apologetically and showed no intention of opening the window. Fragrant Snow ran toward the door and when she reached it, grabbed the hand rail. If she had still been a little hesitant when she was running toward the door, the warm air from the car would have strengthened her resolve. She leaped onto the footboard. She intended to run into the carriage as fast as she could and in the shortest time trade the eggs for the pencil box. She had so many eggs. She had forty today.

At last Fragrant Snow stood in the train. She held her basket tightly, and stepped cautiously into the car. Just then, the train gave a lurch, and the door closed. The train began to move. She threw herself at the door only to see Frail Phoenix's face flashing past the window. It did not seem like a dream; everything was real. She had left her friends, and was standing in this familiar yet strange train.

The train gained speed, carrying Fragrant Snow with it, leaving Terrace Gully behind. The next stop was West Pass, ten miles away from Terrace Gully.

Ten miles in a train or a car is nothing. Passengers chatted for a while and then came the West Pass stop. Many got on, but only one got off. Someone in the train seemed to try to bar her way, but she jumped down resolutely, just as she had confidently leaped onto the train a little while ago.

She had no basket in her arms, for she had quietly put it under the girl's seat. On the train, she had told the girl that she wanted to trade the eggs for the pencil box. The girl had insisted that she would give the pencil box to Fragrant Snow. She had also said that she didn't want the eggs because she lived in a dormitory and ate in a dining hall. She had pointed to the "Mining College" school badge on her coat to convince Fragrant Snow. Fragrant Snow had taken the pencil box but had left her eggs on the train after all. No matter how poor Terrace Gully was, Fragrant Snow never took anything without paying for it.

Earlier, when the passengers had learned that Fragrant Snow was getting off at West Pass, what could they say to her? They had tried to persuade her to stay overnight at West Pass, and the warm-hearted "Beijingese" had even told her that his wife had a relative living at this train station. Fragrant Snow did not want to find his wife's relative. His suggestion made her a little sad, for Frail Phoenix, for Terrace Gully. Thinking of this sorrow, how could she stay on the train? Hurry away, hurry home, and hurry to school tomorrow. Then she could open her schoolbag proudly and put the pencil box on the desk. So she told those on the train who were still trying to talk her out of returning home: "Don't worry, I'm used to walking." Perhaps they believed her. They had no idea what mountain girls were like. They believed that mountain people were not afraid of walking at night.

Now Fragrant Snow stood alone in West Pass gazing after the departing train. Finally, it was completely out of sight and a wild emptiness surrounded her. A chilly gust of wind blew on her and drained the warmth from her body. Her shawl had slipped down to her shoulders. She wrapped it closer about her head, then sat on the railway tracks curled up with cold. Fragrant Snow had experienced all kinds of fear. When she was a young girl she used to fear hair: if a hair stuck to her shoulder and she couldn't remove it, she would cry in terror. When she grew older she was afraid to go to the front yard alone at night; she feared caterpillars and being tickled. Now she feared this strange West Pass, feared the gloomy mountains, and the dead silence all around. When the wind blew in the nearby grove, she was afraid of the rustling sound. In ten miles, there were so many groves and thickets she would have to walk through.

A full moon was rising. It bathed the silent valley and the pale-gray trails; it bathed the withered autumn leaves and the rough tree trunks. It lit up the overgrown brambles and queer-looking stones as well as the troops of trees rolling over the mountain sides. It lit the glittering small box in Fragrant Snow's hand.

Only then did she remember it and hold it up to take a closer look. She had not even looked at it on the train. Now, under bright moonlight, she found it to be light green with a pair of white lotuses. She opened it cautiously, then closed it the way her classmate had done. It closed tightly with a click. She opened it again, and felt that she should put something into it right away. She fished a little cold cream case out of her pocket and put it in. Then she closed it once more. Only now did she feel that this pencil box really belonged to her. She thought of tomorrow. How she hoped that they would question her over and over tomorrow at school.

She stood up. All of a sudden her heart was full and the wind felt much milder. The moon was bright and clean, and the mountains, shrouded in the moonlight, reminded her of a mother's breast. The leaves of walnut trees had been blown by the autumn wind, and curled up into golden bells. For the first time, she heard clearly their nocturnal singing in the wind. Her fear was gone and she walked forward on the ties with vigorous strides. So this is how the mountains are. This is how the moon is. And the walnut trees. Fragrant Snow seemed to recognize for the first time the mountains and the valleys in which she had been reared. Was this how Terrace Gully had been? Not knowing why, she walked faster. She was eager to see it and she was curious about it as if she had never seen it before. Surely, some day the girls of Terrace Gully would no longer beg from anyone. All the handsome fellows in the train would come to the village to court, and the train would stop longer: maybe three or four minutes, maybe eight or ten minutes. It would open all its windows and doors, and anyone could get on or off easily.

But it was still tonight, and the situation was still in progress: the train had carried Fragrant Snow away from Terrace Gully. Forty eggs were gone. What would mother say? Father worked day and night, stripped to the waist, his back the colour of red copper, making chests, cupboards, and trunks. This was how he earned enough money to pay Fragrant Snow's tuition. This thought made Fragrant Snow stop. The moonlight seemed too dim, the ties became vague. What was she going to say to her mother and father? She looked around at the mountains; the mountains were silent. She looked around at the nearby poplar groves; the poplar groves rustled but refused to give an answer. Where was this sound of running water coming from? She saw a shallow brook some metres away. She went over and squatted by the brook. She remembered a story from when she was a little girl. One day when she and Frail Phoenix were washing clothes by a river, an old man selling sesame candy came over. Frail Phoenix advised her to trade an old shirt for some candies. Frail Phoenix had also suggested that she tell her mother that the shirt had been accidentally washed away by the running water. Fragrant Snow wanted the sesame candies very much, but she hadn't traded after all. She still remembered how the old man had waited patiently for her to make a decision. Why was she thinking of this tiny incident now? Perhaps she should fool Mother this time? The pencil box is far more important than sesame candy. She would tell her mother that it was a magical case and whoever used it would have luck in everything he did: go to college, take trains and travel everywhere, have whatever he wanted, and not be scorned. Mother would believe all this because Fragrant Snow had never lied.

The singing of the brook shifted into an elated tone. It ran forward happily, dashed on the stones, and occasionally splashed up in small sprays. Fragrant Snow wanted to resume her trip now. She washed her face with the river water and smoothed her tangled hair with wet hands. The water was chilly but she felt refreshed. She left the brook and went back to the long railway track.

What was that ahead? It was the tunnel. It stared blankly like an eye of the mountain. Fragrant Snow stopped but did not step back. She remembered the pencil box in her hand and imagined her classmates' amazed, envious gazes. Their eyes seemed to glimmer in the tunnel. She bent over to pull up a weathered weed, then stuck it in her braid. Her mother had told her that this way one could ward off evil spirits. Then she ran toward the tunnel.

Fragrant Snow began to feel hot from walking. She untied her shawl and let it hang around her neck. How many miles had she walked? She did not know. She only heard small, unknown insects chirping in bushes, and she felt loose soft weeds caressing her trouser legs. Her plaits had been blown loose by the wind, so she stopped to braid them neatly. Where was Terrace Gully? She looked ahead and saw many dark spots wriggling on the tracks. They became clearer as they moved closer. They were people. It was a crowd walking toward her. The first was Frail Phoenix. Behind her were the girls of Terrace Gully. When they saw Fragrant Snow, they stopped.

Fragrant Snow guessed that they were waiting. She wanted to run to them but her legs became heavy. She stood on the ties and looked back to the straight tracks. The tracks were suffused with a dull glow under the moonlight, recording Fragrant Snow's journey. She suddenly felt her heart tighten, she began to cry. They were tears of joy, and of satisfaction. In front of that stern, good-natured mountain, a pride she had never felt arose in her heart. She wiped off the tears, took the weed out of her plait, then holding up the pencil box, ran toward the crowd ahead.

On the opposite side, the motionless troop began to flow as well. At the same time the girls' joyful cheers burst in the silent valley. They cried Fragrant Snow's name, their voices so warm and spontaneous. They were laughing that kind of bold, hearty laugh that had no restraints. Finally the ancient mountains were moved and trembled. They echoed in a sonorous, low, and deep voice, cheering together with the girls.

Ah, Fragrant Snow! Fragrant Snow!

Translated by Zha Jianying

A Land of Wonder and Mystery

●

——— LIANG XIAOSHENG ———

Liang Xiaosheng went to do farm work in Heilongjiang after graduating from junior middle school in 1968. Later he worked as a farmer, a tractor driver and a primary school teacher. In 1974 he entered the Chinese Department of Fudan University in Shanghai, and after graduation became an editor at the Beijing Film Studio. He began to publish stories in 1979, and won recognition with the tale "A Land of Wonder and Mystery". Since then, he has won three national literary awards. His recent works include the novel Snow City.

1

IT was a deathly silent and boundless swamp, covered the whole year round with dried branches, rotten leaves, and poisonous algae. The surface, dark brown and stagnant, had a deceptively peaceful appearance. Below it was an oozing abyss which contained the decomposing skeletons of bears, hunters' guns and tractors belonging to reclamation teams. It sent out a morbid odour for a hundred li and was known as Spirits' Swamp.

When I first arrived in that Great Northern Wilderness, I heard many legends about this Spirits' Swamp: deep in the starless, moonless night one could see across the slumbering wasteland the eerie greenish glow of the will-o'-the-wisps; one could hear bears roar as they were swallowed by the swamp, gunshots fired by hunters for help and the desperate cries of those caught in the mire ... sometimes one could hear a strange bird's song which sounded just like a sad woman wailing, "What a pity, what a pity...." But no one had ever seen what kind of bird it was. The local Oroqen people called it the bird which "summons back the spirits". They thought that it was really an incarnation of the God of the Earth and that deep in the night it came to comfort and call back the spirits of people and animals who had died in Spirits' Swamp. And the will-o'-the-wisps were its lanterns.

Spirits' Swamp, like the ferocious nine-headed dragon of Greek myth, forcibly occupied the land behind it, a fertile land of more than ten thousand hectares, and no one dared cross the swamp to reclaim it. The Oroqen people used to call this land the "Devil's Reach". During winter they occasionally crossed it, but they never killed any animals for fear of inescapable punishment by the "Devil".

It was my third winter in the Great Northern Wilderness. A detachment of a dozen or so educated youths had been sent by our reclamation company to Devil's Reach.

As a result of being wrongly situated from the outset, our company was located in a natural depression with fairly limited arable land. If harvest happened to coincide with a rainy season, the combine harvesters got bogged down in the wheat fields like paralysed toads. So we had always had bad harvests and that particular year could not even produce enough for the following year's seeds. We couldn't afford to live off the land, much less send grain to the state. That was why the reclamation regiment decided to disband our company and re-allocate the more than two hundred young people to other companies.

What more profound humiliation could there be than this decision? Many of us burst into tears as we listened to the old company leader's announcement. Li Xiaoyan, the company's deputy instructor, was the first to stand up and indignantly refute the decision.

"The company should not be broken up! We can reclaim Devil's Reach. We ought to have thought of it earlier. We must rebuild our company there. Let Devil's Reach be covered with our reclaimers' footprints for the first time. We'll guarantee the regiment that we'll get a crop the same year we reclaim the land. The following year we'll have our new company base. Take our word for it!"

Though usually we listened indifferently to her ambitious words, this time her rousing speech actually did encourage us and many of us felt the same way.

Finally the regiment cancelled their decision and accepted our guarantee.

Several days later, we set off for the vast snow-covered wilderness with two first-rate 54 h.p. tractors decorated with red ribbons and flowers, a newly-made wooden sled trailing behind each. The whole company had lined up to see us off. Hope, confidence, trust and a silent concern was in their eyes, and each of us felt a strong sense of responsibility. Everyone cried.

The first sled held our food and luggage and we squeezed ourselves into the tent set up on the second.

We sat silently shoulder to shoulder. Beside me my younger sister cuddled a wicker cage which contained a small squirrel. She looked pale, her expression dull, her eyes sad and, like a deaf-mute, said nothing the whole journey. I had no other brothers or sisters. Although I had loved her very much since childhood, I felt a mixture of pity and hatred towards her then because she had recently acquired a bad reputation and I was thoroughly ashamed of her.

Li Xiaoyan, the deputy instructor, sat opposite with the blacksmith, Wang Zhigang, a sturdy man with a tanned, rough complexion, who gave the impression of being powerful, strong and determined. It seemed natural for us to compare him with Othello, and we had nicknamed him "Moor". He liked to be alone, and had a just and ethical character. He didn't seek the limelight, and had a strong influence over the younger people. I rather envied him for that. It was the deputy instructor who had nominated him specifically to join our detachment. Now I stared with jealousy as Li rested her head on Moor's broad shoulder to take a nap.

I asked myself why I was attracted to her. Was it her beauty? Certainly she was beautiful, a girl from Shanghai, with a lovely face, white, delicate skin, large, shining eyes, and thin, curved eyebrows. Her face always had an expression of wonder. Her slender figure seemed to confirm what we'd heard, that she had been a good ballet student in Shanghai and that many dance troupes had wanted to recruit her but that she'd refused them all. She had come to the Great Northern Wilderness of her own free will. From the first moment I saw her, I couldn't help being aware of her. But I wasn't usually someone who was easily seduced or overwhelmed by pretty girls. On the contrary, whenever I meet a girl, the more beautiful she is, the more aloof I am. It's one of my maxims — never be a slave of love through indiscretion. Was it her seriousness, her solemnity that enticed me? Not really. I rather preferred girls with enthusiastic, frank and open-minded characters. Sometimes I thought Li's solemn bearing was hypocritical and it disgusted me. It was true she'd sworn not to pay a home visit to Shanghai for three years in order to reinforce her determination to settle in that border area. She also made the suggestion that other girls in the company ought not to wear make-up or colourful clothes. But some of them passed it around that Li still worried about her white, delicate skin and that in summer she stealthily went to the river bank to get a suntan. Unfortunately the sunshine only turned her white skin pink, not the brown she wanted. She also tried to be more masculine, wearing what the boys wore, doing the same manual labour they did. She wanted to change her figure, to adopt the so-called "beauty of the labourer", but she remained slim and graceful. Strong and healthy, she was like a small white birch, erect and tall during those three years in the Great Northern Wilderness. She had not been home once during that time. In the first year she had become the head of the platoon, in the second, a Party member, and in the third, the deputy instructor of the company, a model for the whole regiment, showing others how to strike roots in the frontier reclamation areas.

One summer evening in that third year, right after she was appointed deputy instructor of the company, I suddenly heard someone singing when I was sketching on the river bank.

Under the bright sky of early spring,
My eighteen-year-old lover sits on the river bank.

It was a "decadent" song strictly prohibited at the time. Who was singing it? If our deputy instructor heard about it, an "ideological struggle" would inevitably ensue. Whoever it was sang well. Her voice was very sweet. Burning with curiosity, I picked up my home-made drawing board and went quietly along the bank to find out who the singer was. Suddenly I came upon someone sitting on a large, smooth grey stone beneath a reclining willow tree on the opposite bank of the river. It was none other than our deputy instructor! She was washing her clothes, dangling her bare feet in the water, her trouser legs rolled up above the ankles and her white calves uncovered.

Under the bright sky of early spring,
My eighteen-year-old lover waits for his sweetheart, Yinglian....

After scrubbing, kneading and wringing out the clothes, she stood up on the large grey stone and tiptoed cautiously across a group of cobblestones to hang them over some branches. Afraid the cobblestones might hurt her feet, she moved gingerly, with quick light steps, just like the dance of the cygnets in *Swan Lake.* Having spread the clothes across the shrubs, she returned to the river bank with the same steps. She collected a few wild flowers, taking in their scent and placing some in her hair, two on the right and three on the left. Then, squatting in front of the river, she stared for a long time at her own reflection in the water. She was admiring her own beauty! After a while she rose slowly. Then suddenly she jumped up onto the grey stone's smooth surface and, her arms outstretched, made an elegant semi-circle and performed a Mexican folk dance with quick steps.

The drawing board slid from my hands and dropped into the water, causing a slight noise. Alarmed, she stopped dancing and saw me watching her from the opposite side of the river. She appeared stunned, like a bewildered fawn or a startled crane about to take flight.

The river between us, we stared at one another in astonishment.

The first to recover my composure, I jumped into the river to retrieve my drawing board. Feigning a casual manner, I waded through the shallow water to the opposite bank. By then, the wild flowers in her hair had disappeared and the trouser legs had been rolled down.

"You ... what are you doing here on the river bank?" she asked, intending to gain the upper hand, and with it the psychological initiative. She tried her best to conceal her embarrassment, assuming a relaxed manner as much as she could. She became again a solemn, reserved young woman in the presence of a young man, a deputy instructor with the requisite dignity. But she hadn't had enough time to button up her jacket, faded from many washings, and underneath she wore a pink shirt, short and tight, with a V-neck through which I caught a glimpse of a white neck and bosom, round white shoulders and even the cleavage of her heaving breasts. Immediately I averted my eyes and felt my heart racing with excitement. I flushed, feeling an inexplicable kind of shame, guilty about debasing her and myself as well, though I could swear to Heaven that I didn't, even for a moment, desire her. I didn't even feel the instinctive response which ordinarily occurs when a young man meets an attractive girl, the passion which originated with Adam and Eve.

She was so very sensitive. As my eyes took her in, she immediately covered her jacket flap and turned round. When she turned back again I saw the old familiar deputy instructor, jacket buttoned right up, and feet burrowed deep into the sand to hide the fact that she had no shoes on.

I felt humiliated by her behaviour and tried to find words to break the awkward silence, but ended by blurting out something very foolish, "You're ... so beautiful!"

"What!" Her face blushed like a crimson cloud. My sudden appearance had caused her problems, placing her in an impossibly awkward position.

"What I ... I meant is that you danced beautifully. If I'm not mistaken, it was a Mexican folk dance, wasn't it?"

"Mexican dance? Don't make fun of me. I was just doing the radio limbering-up exercises for middle school students."

"Does that mean you're going to deny you were singing as well?"

"Singing a song? Why should I deny it? I did sing a song." In addition to her feigned puzzlement, she now added one more thing, an artificial directness. She began singing:

Near the Qinghe River, on Tigerhead Hill,
Is situated Dazhai Production Brigade....

After singing two lines she said to me, "That's the song you heard me singing."

The blush had receded and she had completely recovered her normal complexion.

I felt that she had made a fool of me and treated me as though I was blind and deaf. I couldn't stand any more such insults. Suppressing my anger with great effort I said coldly, "No, that wasn't the song I heard. You sang: 'My eighteen-year-old lover waits for his sweetheart, Yinglian'!"

"Eighteen-year-old lover? His sweetheart Yinglian? I've never even heard of such a song. Don't talk nonsense!" She raised her slender eyebrows with a surprised and astonished expression, as if I had called her a thief.

So many hypocritical changes of expression had taken place on that lovely face.

I had nothing more to say, and just looked at her in astonishment. To me she looked like the Sphinx, with her lion's body and human face, only the Sphinx was more honest. As I remember, even the Sphinx said the same thing to everyone: If you fail to solve my riddle, then I will devour you. But the Sphinx was less shameless than this deputy instructor, since ultimately she had jumped down from the rocks and died when Oedipus correctly answered the riddle. The deputy instructor wanted me, a normal person of sound mind, to believe myself to be an idiot, a daydreamer who talked in his sleep.

"You hypocrite!" Indignantly I turned around and abruptly strode off.

"Wait!"

I halted without turning around, but I could sense her anxiety.

"You ... are you going to report me to the company leader?..." she murmured, with an imploring tone.

Still with my back to her, I softened and shook my head. After walking a distance I could not help looking back. She remained standing beside the river like a statue, motionless....

I never told anyone else about the incident.

I couldn't be that mean.

But from then on, whenever she made speeches she would become uneasy when our eyes met. I regretted that and felt sorry for her.

Not long after that I got a telegram saying that my mother was seriously ill, but I was unable to get permission from the company leader to return home. The reason was clear, since I was the combine harvester driver and it was then harvest season. Actually, I knew that the company leader didn't believe the telegram was genuine. That was another reason he didn't approve my request. He had been deceived several times by phoney telegrams which parents or their children sent in order to arrange a reunion. Some of them even invented the death of a parent. As a consequence, the company leader had become an empiricist. It was no use pleading with him to let me go, nor would any kind of explanation help. But I couldn't remain indifferent to the telegram. My father had died early and my mother, a worker in a small factory, had brought up my younger sister and me through all kinds of difficulties and hardships. It had not been easy for her, and only I understood how she had put her heart and soul into looking after us. Now my younger sister and I had come to this Great Northern Wilderness and left her at home alone. She was a woman of strong character and would never use deceitful measures even though she was yearning to see us.

I decided I had to return immediately to see her.

That day I stealthily left the company....

My mother! This woman who had tasted her fill of the bitterness of life! She was so unyielding, so concerned for her children. She knew she was dying but she only cabled us that she was "very sick" instead of "mortally ill". She didn't want to alarm us with such frightening words.

During my mother's last five days I lived with her and gave her as much care and love as I could to thank her for bringing us into this world and helping us to grow up. I did this not only for myself but also for my younger sister who was unable to return.

Five days, only five days! No matter how I expressed my love or took care of my mother during those five days, it was only a symbolic compensation. How can a mother's love and concern for her children ever be compensated?

My mother's last words were, "Look after your sister. You're all the family she has."

Numbed by grief, I went back to the company.

The day I returned, on the instruction of the company leader, the Youth League branch held a meeting to discuss what disciplinary action should be taken over my desertion. Before the meeting, someone had disclosed that I was certain to be expelled from the League. The meeting itself was purely a formality and I would be used as an example to warn the others.

I myself was totally indifferent to whatever punishment I had to have.

The meeting was conducted by the deputy instructor. I thought she would certainly use the opportunity to take her revenge and I was determined to keep my mouth shut and listen to her long criticism of me.

At first she asked me to say something about my mistake.

I looked down and muttered, "My mother ... died ... three days ago...." Finishing this sentence, I put my head in my hands and felt everyone's eyes focussed on me.

For an instant, it seemed that everyone at the meeting was holding their breath. Suffocated by the sudden silence, even the air seemed unnaturally still. Following this pause, the deputy instructor said in a low but clear voice, "The meeting is over...."

She was the first to leave.

As I passed by the company office, I heard the deputy instructor and the company leader arguing fiercely. I was surprised, since the deputy instructor was used to carrying out the company leader's instructions. Wondering what they were wrangling over, I stopped to listen.

"I am the head of this company. Don't I have the right to punish a subordinate?" It was the angry voice of the company leader with his heavy Sichuan accent.

"I am the Youth League branch secretary. Punishing League members is the duty of the League branch." The deputy instructor's voice was raised too.

"All you're doing is making excuses for a deserter!"

"A deserter? Did he desert the battlefield? Did he cross to the other side of the Heilong River? Do you know that his mother died? Three days after her death he came back...."

"Oh, his mother died, did she!?"

"Company leader, I am an educated youth too, with an elderly father and mother. They're longing to see me. I'd go back home this very minute if I hadn't taken an oath. But I can't. I don't agree that he should be expelled from the League. Company leader, please, put yourself in his position and think it over!"

I heard her start to cry. As I stood outside the company office, tears welled up in my eyes too.

I felt thoroughly grateful to her. Not because she had defended me, but because she had said, "I am an educated youth too...."

All of my misconceptions and prejudices about her were erased by this sentence and I felt I would go through hell for her.

Hearing this I knew she was a good person with a noble character and a sympathetic heart. Nevertheless, two days later this same person told me something which hit me like a bolt of lightning.

That day, while helping me to turf out the weeds in a long stretch of ground, she asked, "After work would you mind coming with me?" It was the second time in three years that she had talked to me. The first had been the encounter by the river not long ago. This time her sullen and serious expression seemed an omen of some misfortune.

As we shouldered our hoes and lined up to return, she said to me in front of everyone else, "Please wait. Let's go together." The others looked at both of us with curious expressions.

After they had moved off a distance, she looked me in the eye, and said, "Without consulting you, I've arranged to have your younger sister transferred to our company."

"Why? What's happened? Tell me!"

"When you were home...."

"Tell me!"

"She had an abortion...."

Shocked, I felt my body swaying and nearly fell.

She steadied me with her hands.

I roughly pushed her aside, shouting, "You're lying!"

She staggered backward. Eyes wide with fear, she uttered two words, "It's true!"

I felt suddenly as if I was glued to the ground. I wanted to shout out but it was as if there was something stuffed down my throat and I couldn't. The only sound coming from my voice was a hoarse moan. My vision blurred and she became indistinct.

Like someone crazed, I raced towards the tent.

I wept through the whole of that night, biting the quilt corner to avoid disturbing my soundly sleeping roommates. I remembered my mother's last wish, but before I could carry it out, my younger sister had acted scandalously. Now she was to be transferred to my company so she could be under my wing. Never! With the right of an elder brother, I would punish her severely, on behalf of my dead mother.

The next day I was called to the office by the deputy instructor and there met my younger sister. On seeing her, I sprang at her like a leopard, took her hair and forcefully hit her head against the earthen wall.

"Stop!" I heard the deputy instructor shout. She dashed forward trying hard to loosen my frenzied grip.

"Get away!" I roared at her.

I tortured my younger sister as though I was torturing myself. My hysteria seemed to relieve the pain.

Suddenly, I received a sharp slap on the face.

I released my grip.

The second slap was much harder.

The two slaps had sobered me and unconsciously I stepped back, rubbing my burning cheek.

My younger sister didn't utter a single word, or moan, shout or plead. Her dishevelled hair covered a pallid face bathed in tears, and her large eyes were full of humiliation.

Her face drained of colour, the deputy instructor held my younger sister tightly and stared at me, determined to fight if necessary.

"You bloody animal!"

That was the first time I ever heard her use foul language.

From that day on I was in love with her.

Now she was sitting opposite me. As the covered, tractor-drawn sled slogged on through the whirling snow, we were chilled by the northwesterly wind. It carried snowflakes into the tent through an open flap which no one wanted to draw. We looked at the white world outside, the white land, the white mountains, the white river, the white forests. The blizzard violently pursued us, like millions of maddened, galloping wild oxen.

After silently looking round at everyone, the deputy instructor then said, almost to herself, "Should we have someone tell a story? Or perhaps sing a song together?"

There was no response to her suggestion. Everyone was exhausted.

Her eyes fell on me.

I cleared my throat and began to sing *The Reclaimers' Song*:

Every reclaimer has a sun in his heart,
One hand holds a gun, the other a pickaxe.

No one joined in and so naturally I halted after the first two lines of the song.

Just then, Moor started to whistle. He wasn't a good singer, but he could whistle quite tunefully. What surprised me though was that he was whistling the famous Russian folk song, *Troika*. He wasn't at all afraid of the deputy instructor's interference. His whistling had an enchanting quality, like a clarinet or a trumpet. His lyrical, rhythmic melody produced in us a sense of sadness, of deep melancholy.

Someone started humming quietly, then another and a third, gradually converging into a chorus.

My younger sister looked up, stared uneasily and then, lowering her head again, heaved a long sigh. I felt sorry for her.

I gazed across at the deputy instructor's face, guessing that she would immediately put a stop to this sentimental song. But she remained indifferent. Her head was still resting on Moor's shoulder. Her eyes closed, she pretended to be falling asleep, but I noticed her hand covertly beating time.

I felt that my pride had been hurt and bit my lower lip. The song continued:

The Volga is covered with ice and snow,
The Troika is driving over the icy river.
Someone is singing a melancholy song,
The singer is....

Night fell unobtrusively and the merciless blizzard stopped its howling. Maybe it surrendered itself or maybe, with our tractors driving at full throttle, we left it behind in that silent wilderness.

Now we were enclosed by the chilly darkness, a huge natural tent flap.

2

Travelling like the migrant Oroqen people, we drove swiftly across the vast snowy plateau for two days and two nights. When we looked at the map, we were convinced that we had arrived at the snow-and-ice covered Spirits' Swamp. A solemn wilderness dawn was just breaking.

Spirits' Swamp! It was not as dreadful as the legends described. Perhaps it was in hibernation and its true ferocious appearance was hidden deep beneath the snow. It seemed as if the largest lake in the world lay frozen in front of us. Devil's Reach — it looked so flat we could hardly believe that it extended only as far as the remote horizon.

"Hey! Devil King, where are you? Show yourself!" shouted one of our companions.

But the "Devil" did not appear.

Suddenly, Moor pointed to something in the distance, "Look!" A round wooden stake with a notch cut into it stood at an angle.

Curious, we walked over to have a look. The deputy instructor brushed the snow from the stake and we saw a wooden tablet with something carved on its rough surface. Most of the words had been eroded by wind and rain, but some poor handwriting was still faintly visible: "... died here...."

Each of us shuddered.

"There's another one over there!" My younger sister had discovered a similar evil omen. She was the first to walk back to the tractor.

The deputy instructor said softly, "Let's go back. Don't disturb their rest."

If someone asks me what the hardest and bitterest work of all in the Great Northern Wilderness is, I'll answer "reclamation".

And if someone asks me what work in the Great Northern Wilderness I feel most proud of, my answer will also be "reclamation".

Because we were eager to discover the best sources of water and timber, nearly every part of Devil's Reach was covered with our footprints. We finally discovered a stream — not marked on the map — which was the only clean water source. We named it the "Wanderer" since it had been wandering across the flat wasteland for countless years before we discovered it and set up a tent next to it.

When the snow melted, our gleaming ploughs sank into the bosom of Devil's Reach. Who but a reclaimer could experience the joy of ploughing the first plot of virgin land by tractor? There were many wolves on this flat land. In threes and fours they swaggered along behind the tractors, preying on field rats startled by the ploughing, and at night they would howl around our tent. The hardship of this work had transformed all the young men in the detachment into saints. All of us, including my younger sister and the deputy instructor, lived in the same large tent. Their small "world" was separated from ours by a hanging blanket, behind which existed a sacred, forbidden place.

One night, I suddenly woke and could not hear the usual night shift tractor roaring outside the tent. I immediately sprang to my feet and, without thinking, barged into the "forbidden place" to shake the deputy instructor awake.

"What do you want?"

"Moor is out ploughing, but the tractor has stopped!"

With the tractor silent for such a long time, there must be something wrong with Moor. Everyone in the tent got up. Just as we were all about to run out, Moor suddenly appeared at the entrance, his hands gripping the two front paws of an old wolf which was clinging to his back. The animal was still half alive, its mouth wide open, its two back paws clinging to either side of his waist.

"It's still alive! Quick! Hit it!" shouted Moor.

We immediately took up sticks and clubs and beat the large grey animal to death.

Moor flung himself on a pallet, gasping for breath. After a long pause he told us, "The steel cable on the big plough broke and I was changing it when that damned thing came at me and got me round the shoulders with its claws...." His face and hands were cut and bloodstained, his clothes in tatters. Frowning, he took off his padded jacket. His sweatshirt and skin had also been clawed.

The deputy instructor ordered my younger sister, "Quick, get the first-aid kit!"

Just then we suddenly realized that the deputy instructor, feet bare, was wearing only her underclothes. She had just become aware of it herself and felt uneasy at our stares. But she remained calm, and said coolly, "What are you looking at? Haven't you got anything better to do? Go to bed again, all of you!" Submissively, one after another, people went to bed and buried themselves in their quilts once again. But I remained, holding the lantern above Moor's head.

It was the first time the deputy instructor had ever given me such a tender look. Without saying a word, she took the first-aid kit from my sister and carefully bandaged Moor's wounds....

My younger sister was the "minister of domestic affairs" of the detachment and did all our washing and cooking. The frozen vegetables brought from the company had all been eaten and no edible wild herbs could be found in such a cold winter, so she did her best to make different kinds of food for us with the remaining two bags of flour.

If I had joined this reclamation work because of the deputy instructor, then my younger sister had come to Devil's Reach because of me. I was her only family member. If I went to the ends of the earth she would go with me. Although I had treated her cruelly, she still wanted my protection and shelter. On the surface, I still appeared indifferent towards her, but in truth I had already wholeheartedly forgiven her.

Only those who are guilty of monstrous crimes do not forgive others. After all, she was my younger sister, my only sister.

I was duty-bound to take care of her. Both before and after the scandal occurred, had I carried out my responsibilities as an elder brother? No, I hadn't. The first day we arrived in the Great Northern Wilderness, she had become fascinated by deer, and had asked if we could work at the deer farm together. I had refused. I thought her fragility and wilfulness would cause me endless trouble and worry. Instead I had looked after my own affairs and shirked my duties as an elder brother. After her mistake, which had left her open to public censure, my first thought was that she had tarnished my reputation. I had detested her without feeling the slightest ounce of pity or sympathy for her....

Now, in countless sleepless nights on Devil's Reach, I gradually realized my true nature. I had to confess to myself what a selfish brother, what a mean coward I was.

One day, when just the two of us were alone in the tent, I called over to her with a soft voice, "Sister!"

She was kneading flour on the chopping board. Hearing me calling, she raised her head and looked at me with a frightened expression, tears welling up in her eyes.

"Younger sister, are you still angry with me?" I moved to her side.

Tears, large tears, trickled down her pallid face on to the dough she was kneading.

"Younger sister...." My voice was hoarse.

Turning around and throwing herself into my arms, she hugged me with flour-covered hands and sobbed.

After a long while she stopped. The first thing she asked me was, "Is mum better?"

It was as though I had been stabbed in the heart.

Oh, mother! If only you had heard what your daughter was saying, you would cry too.

May you not hear, and have no more worries about your children. But I wish that somehow you could know what your daughter had said, because she was the one who loved you most.

I hadn't the courage to tell my sister that our mother was dead. I worried about her delicate feelings and the fragile heart which wouldn't be able to bear such a shock.

I answered in a gentle voice, "She's not sick. She's been missing us terribly. When I told her that we were both alright, she felt better."

A wan smile appeared at the corners of her mouth, a pained and anguished smile. It was the first time she had smiled for several days.

"Tell me who the young man is. I want to teach him a lesson."

My sister firmly shook her head.

"Do you ... love ... him?"

Silent, she nodded.

"He.... How about him? Does he love you?"

Another silent nod.

I stared at her. The angelic expression on her face was obviously a reflection of her true feelings. I felt lost.

Suddenly she asked, "Elder brother, do you love her?"

"Who?..."

"The deputy instructor!"

"Where have you heard such nonsense?"

"I discovered it for myself. She likes you a lot too."

"Really!?" I grabbed her tightly by the arm.

"Yes!"

"But she likes Moor!"

"She trusts him and so do I. He's worthy of our trust. Any girl would trust someone like him. But you're the one she's fond of. She told me that you have an artistic nature. She also knows that you're in love with her...."

Suddenly she stopped talking.

Almost at the same time, both of us saw the deputy instructor standing by the entrance to the tent. She had obviously overheard our conversation.

"*Aiya*! I must go and collect the clothes I left drying by the river." Finding an excuse, I fled from the tent, racing wildly across the flat land. Devil's Reach seemed to be the most beautiful place in the whole world.

That day after eating our evening meal, we all gathered together in the tent to tell stories, something we did quite often to amuse ourselves. We told all sorts of stories: fairy stories, ghost stories, horror stories, humorous stories.... Each of us, including the deputy instructor, freed of the company's fetters, seemed to have come into his own at Devil's Reach.

The deputy instructor told us a tale from the *Odyssey*, of how the great Odysseus, returning to his homeland of Ithaca after attacking Troy, was detained by a headwind in an isolated island with his companions. She told us how the residents of the island presented them with a magic plant, common on the island, which was so delicious that upon eating it a person would forget all of his troubles. Odysseus and his companions forgot their homeland, their parents, their brothers, sisters, wives and friends when they ate this plant and so they stayed on the island for the rest of their days....

To my surprise, the deputy instructor told this story in such a natural, unexaggerated manner that we were all moved by the depth of feeling she expressed.

She finished her story and left us all deep in thought. Only my younger sister heaved a long sigh, and said to herself, "I'd like to get a lot of those magic plants."

The deputy instructor sat next to Moor, her head resting against his shoulder as usual. The flames from the big stove cast a red glow across her face. As the light flickered over her pretty features, an expression of longing and sadness appeared before my eyes.

I inevitably felt a deep sympathy for her. Had she not been restrained by the oath she had made three years earlier, she could have visited her family. Three years! She must have missed her parents and friends more than any of us.

I opened my board and said, "Don't move, Moor, I want to draw both of you." Actually I really only wanted to draw the deputy instructor, so beautiful was she, but I dared not openly say so. However, Moor thought that I was publicly mocking him, something he could not endure. It was obvious that he had misunderstood.

When the deputy instructor subconsciously moved her head away from his shoulder, he clutched her hand and stared at me coldly, "Don't move! Let him draw. Don't disappoint him!" There was a hint of challenge in his intonation. The deputy instructor obediently leaned her head against his shoulder again and looked at me with a faint smile.

Without saying anything more I began to sketch. I was determined that the drawing would be meticulous, would really convey her beauty. So I looked up at her and drew several strokes, took another look, and drew several more. Never had I worked so carefully on a sketch. Finally I finished it and intentionally broke my pencil lead on the very last stroke.

"I'm sorry, I haven't done it very well." I handed it over to the deputy instructor.

Everyone gathered around admiring the sketch.

"Not bad! It looks just like her!"

"Ah! That's really quite a talent you've got. Why have you kept it a secret from us? Will you draw me one day?"

"*Aiya*, you've only drawn me!" The deputy instructor threw a glance at Moor.

"I'm sorry. My pencil broke." I flushed slightly.

The deputy instructor took the sketch and looked at it carefully for a while and then said, "May I have it?"

"Certainly. You can keep it if you like."

"I'll look after it." She looked down. As she did, Moor stood up and slipped out of the tent. From that day on he was much more reticent.

Everything in life can be eventually forgotten except love.

I would persist in my pursuit of her, never give up my love for her, never love another, never....

The first spring rain came.

The soil of the reclamation fields, dark and rich, was like a baby greedily sucking Mother Nature's milk. People often compare spring to a gorgeously dressed young maiden, but it was travelling over Devil's Reach more like a solemn woman, walking slowly and with measured paces. Carrying her uniquely soft dye with her, she turned the world green.

One day the deputy instructor fainted by the banks of the Wanderer. She was ill and did not come to for two days. While in a coma, she kept mumbling, "Wheat seeds, wheat seeds." None of the medicines in our first-aid kit could reduce her temperature. On the third day she came to, called my sister to her bedside and asked, "How much food is left now?"

"Only a little," answered my sister.

The deputy instructor looked about with an expression of deep concern, and said with a smile, "My dear friends, on behalf of the company I want to thank all of you. I am going to suggest that the Party branch record your merits. Now, except for one or two of us, everyone should return to the company and give them a hand moving here. This must be finished before the ice on Spirits' Swamp melts!" She gently took my sister's hand, "You have to stay with me, otherwise I'll feel lonely."

"I want to."

"I'll stay too," I said.

Moor looked over at the deputy instructor. "I'd like to stay as well, if you agree."

She nodded her approval.

Now only the four of us remained on Devil's Reach.

One day, a second ... four days passed. The company still had not arrived. A company of more than two hundred people on the move would inevitably mean many difficulties. But, within those four days, Spirits' Swamp had completely melted. Our trusted friend the Wanderer River had betrayed us and collaborated against us with the Spirits' Swamp. When my sister and I went out on the fourth day, we were stunned by the change in the environment: in one night, the clear, meandering Wanderer had become a rushing current, turbid and muddy, like a wild galloping horse with hairpin turns and whirlpools, lumps of snow and ice, withered branches and broken trees. The river had overflowed and poured water across the swamp. Spirits' Swamp was now a vast expanse of water.

My sister was worried. "If the company doesn't arrive today, we won't have anything to eat."

Moor and I shot her a glance but said nothing. What we were most worried about was how the company would cross the swamp.

Without saying anything more, my sister went back into the tent, and Moor and I followed. She sat on a pallet beside the deputy instructor, who was still in a coma, and tears filled her eyes. Catching sight of us, she quickly wiped them away, picked up a sickle and a small basket and said, "I'm going out to dig some wild herbs."

It was almost noon when suddenly we heard my sister calling out from a distance, "Brother, brother, quick, come here!"

Moor and I immediately jumped to our feet and ran out of the tent where we saw my sister, like a small terrier, chasing after a weak roe deer. Tossing her sickle, she hit its rear leg and it fell. She sprang at it, but failed to hold it. Struggling free, the deer ran towards the swamp. My younger sister was on its heels. At the edge of the swamp it stopped for a moment, as if looking back at her, then jumped and fled, limping.

"Stop!"

"Sister!"

Moor and I shouted at her.

My younger sister was at the very edge of the swamp, pacing up and down. She finally came to a halt and looked at the deer with its mired feet. After a slight hesitation, she made a first cautious step into the Spirits' Swamp.

"Come back! It's dangerous...." shouted Moor as we ran towards her.

She turned round to look at us and then waved her hand as if to say, "Leave me alone...."

When Moor and I reached the edge of the swamp, she had already caught the deer. Struggling with the small animal, she suddenly sank deep into the mire. Before we could even think what to do, all we could see was her small hand repeatedly grasping the air. In an instant, both my sister and the deer had completely disappeared from sight.

"Keep away...." Her last words in this world still echo in my ears.

"Sister...." I shouted and raced recklessly towards the swamp.

With his strong arms Moor grabbed me from behind. I struggled against him and then lost consciousness.

When I recovered I found myself lying in the tent, the image of my younger sister's tiny hand appearing repeatedly before my eyes. My mother's last wish rang again in my ears and tears welled up. I struggled to get up and saw Moor standing still outside the tent. His tall figure was silhouetted clearly against the pale moon. The eerie song of a bird rang out over the swamp and sent cold shivers down my spine. Perhaps the bird was calling back my younger sister's soul. I wasn't superstitious, but the thought suddenly flashed across my mind. I stared at Moor and blazed with hatred towards him. Had he not restrained me, I believed I would certainly have been able to save my younger sister. I was consumed with guilt over her death.

I stood up and staggered out of the tent. When Moor heard my footsteps, he turned slowly round, his eyes wide open, and stared at me in astonishment. Maybe he knew I was enraged, for he instinctively stepped back.

I abruptly raised my fist.

"You...." Stunned, he stepped back again.

"I hate you!" I growled, clenching my teeth.

He fixed his eyes on me and said in a low, deep voice, "If it's because of your sister, then I have the right to defend myself. Do you think I have the heart of a devil? Don't you think I'm upset about your sister's death? If I could change places with her, I'd willingly be caught in that swamp myself. If it's because of her...." he threw a glance at the tent, "then go ahead and hit me! So long as I'm still alive, and she's not your wife, I have the right to love her."

His words made me shiver. As though paying condolences to my younger sister, I lowered my head. A silence reigned over the night. The flat wilderness was quiet and sullen, and even the song of the eerie bird who called back lost souls had died away.

Moor slowly turned and walked away into the darkness. Soon his figure was lost in the hollow black night.

"What are you two quarrelling about?"

I looked over my shoulder to see the deputy instructor standing by the tent. In the past four days she had become so weak that, had she let go of her grip on the tent flap, she would most certainly have collapsed.

After a long silence two words fell from my lips, "The wolf...."

"Wolf?..." Scrutinizing my expression, she asked, "You're hiding something from me. Where's Moor? Where is your sister? Where have they gone? Tell me! What's happened?"

"My sister ... died in the swamp...." I couldn't hold back my sorrow any longer and covered my face with my hands, sobbing aloud.

On hearing this, she uttered only a short "Oh!" and fainted, as if she'd suddenly received a heavy blow.

Moor had not returned even though it was now deep into the night. Where could he have gone? Would he come back and share the same tent with me again? Had he met with some mishap? If he had any kind of accident I would be responsible....

I was plunged into confusion, and waited anxiously for his safe return, feeling the dark night move on its long course. I took care of the still-unconscious deputy instructor. It was the first time in the unlimited vastness of that flat wilderness that I experienced such dreadful loneliness. The whole night long I could not fall asleep.

At dawn I heard the hurried clatter of hoofs in the distance and ran out of the tent to find Moor dismounting from a horse.

"Where did you get the horse?" I said in a friendly manner, trying to put aside all of the unpleasantness between us.

"Several days ago, I found a branch with a trail marker cut into it and knew there must be some Oroqen hunters nearby. I found them yesterday and borrowed it from them. How is the deputy instructor?"

"Still unconscious."

"The Oroqen hunters told me that maybe she has haemorrhagic fever."

"Haemorrhagic fever?!" I froze. I had once heard of someone dying of that like a leaf ripped down by the autumn wind.

"Take this horse and escort the deputy instructor back to the company right now," ordered Moor. "You must go back the way we came and you will probably meet up with our company and be able to save her."

"No, I'll stay here and you take her."

"I'm too heavy. If I try and take her, the horse will certainly collapse halfway there. It's already exhausted. The two of you go together. If you head westward fifty li you can cut around Spirits' Swamp, and go due west beside it!"

To continue arguing with him would have been useless.

Moor tied the unconscious deputy instructor to my back and then helped me mount.

"Take the gun!"

"You keep it."

"No, you should take it. You need to be prepared for any incident." He fastened the gun to the saddle, reined the horse around and then gave the animal a strong punch on its rump.

The horse neighed and raced westward at full gallop.

Although the westward route was thirty li less than the eastward one, we had to cross a vast grassland. We were fortunate in having a well-bred Oroqen hunter horse, a short and compact animal, not handsome but able to bear hardships and stand up to gruelling work. It really is the hunters' friend, the camel of the wilderness.

Having passed the Spirits' Swamp I continued urging the horse on. It seemed to understand what I wanted, and galloped on without slackening. After travelling nearly thirty li I felt my cotton-padded trousers drenched by the animal's sweat. Suddenly it snorted several times and began to stagger. It tried to continue with all its strength, but its forelegs buckled. As soon as I dismounted, it instantly inclined to one side, stretched out its neck, and collapsed.

The horse's belly rose and fell, warm air spurting from its nostrils, its mouth dribbling white foam. Before lying down, the intelligent animal had paused to prevent its full weight crushing down on its rider's leg and had looked at me almost apologetically with its clear eyes.

"Put me down! Put me down! Where are we? What are we doing here? Where are you taking me?"

The deputy instructor had come to, and struggled against the rope tying her to me.

I untied the rope and gently put her down on the ground, her head and shoulders leaning against my chest.

"I'm taking you to meet the company. You're seriously ill."

She murmured, "Am I going to die? Is that it?"

I felt upset hearing my beloved say such words and replied in a loud voice, "No, of course not!"

She forced a smile, "I'm not afraid of death. Really. Don't you remember the lines in our oath to settle in the wilderness: 'It's not necessary to be buried in our home village, everywhere in the wilderness is our home.' The only thing I regret is that in a few months I would have been able to visit my parents. I really miss them. They're longing for my visit, nearly going crazy over it. I've written them a letter promising to go after the autumn harvest here, but now...."

I sobbed, my tears falling on her face.

"Don't cry." She gently took my hand. "If I do die, please bury me beside Spirits' Swamp and let me keep your younger sister company. She was a good girl. My only request is that on my grave tablet, I would like the word 'reclaimer' carved together with my name...." Large tears gradually filled the corners of her eyes.

I held her tightly and sobbed loudly and bitterly.

"Look, what's that? It's like that magic fruit in the legend. Would you break off a branch for me, please?" Her large, beautiful eyes were fixed on something nearby.

Following her line of vision, I saw a cluster of purplish-red azaleas in bud. I helped her to lean against the saddle and went over to break off the branch. She was dead when I returned.

She and the Oroqen horse had stopped breathing at the same time.

Beneath me I felt the ground spinning; above, the blue sky turned black.

Wiping my eyes and pinning the azaleas to her chest, I knelt down and kissed her pale lips for a long time. I think that had she been alive, she would not have blamed me.

Carrying her body on my back, I walked on.

I saw the company caravan appear on the distant horizon.

The whole company expressed sorrow at the death of the deputy instructor. Everyone cried.

......

When the company caravan, the carts, sleds, tractors and trucks drew near the swamp, it was already dusk. Someone found a cotton-padded hat stuck on a wooden pole temporarily used as a grave marker. I went ahead and removed the hat. It was Moor's dog-skin hat. A slip of paper inside read: "I've discovered a way through Spirits' Swamp and have marked it with twigs. A li east of here...."

That night the whole company passed safely across the swamp leaving behind only the carts which might get stuck. But nowhere could we find Moor.

The next morning, beside the Wanderer we discovered bloody strips of Moor's clothing, a big axe and three dead wolves.... There had been a fierce fight between him and the wolves. We imagined how he had fallen after having fought with all his might against them.

During those sorrowful days we began to seed Devil's Reach.

In accordance with her last wishes, we buried the deputy instructor by Spirits' Swamp. From Camel Mountain, a hundred miles away, we transported a huge grey stone which the old mason in our company chiselled into a grave tablet and on which he carved the words: "In memory of reclaimers Li Xiaoyan, Wang Zhigang, Liang Shanshan, our beloved comrades...."

On Camel Mountain we felled more than a thousand pine trees to make a road across Spirits' Swamp along the markers placed by Moor, and named it "Reclaimers' Road". The following year several other companies came to settle on Devil's Reach.

At last we conquered Spirits' Swamp.

One silent dusk when I visited the reclaimers' graves I saw a stranger standing there and found a bunch of azaleas on the tablet. Azaleas had been my sister's favourite flower.

In an instant, I understood that the stranger was the young man who had been in love with her.

From the expression on his face, I could see that he would never leave

Devil's Reach.

We exchanged a glance and he turned and walked slowly away.

I didn't stop him to ask his name, nor even think to ask where he came from....

He was one of our generation — that was all I needed to know.

We had experienced the blizzards of the Great Northern Wilderness, the hardships and the joy of reclaiming this land of wonder and mystery. From then on, no matter what the difficulties were, whether we stayed or whether we left, nothing could produce fear in us or make us surrender.... The Great Northern Wilderness!

1982

Translated by Shen Zhen

Han the Forger

●

—— DENG YOUMEI ——

Deng Youmei became a messenger in the Chinese Communist Party's Eighth Route Army at the age of eleven. Being too small, however, he was sent back to Tianjin, where he led an itinerant life until he was forced to go to Japan as a labourer. In 1945 he returned to China and joined the New Fourth Army as a journalist. In the 1950s he was wrongly criticized for writing "On the Precipice" and sent to do manual work for over a decade. Following his rehabilitation in 1978, he started writing again and his short stories "Our Army Commander", "Three Woman Soldiers in Pursuit of Their Troops" and "Han the Forger" won national awards. His recent works "Snuff-Bottles" and "Na Wu" are all set in Beijing and have a strong local style.

HE hadn't walked down this road for more than thirty years. Now it was asphalted and lined with buildings and a school. In his youth Gan Ziqian used to come along here to Taoran Pavilion Park to sketch. Now, standing beside the historic lake, he felt lost. "Where on earth can Han be?" A man who would be useful for the country's modernization, Han had been ousted from the antiques trade decades ago. Like a sputtering candle, Gan knew his days were numbered. If he didn't find Han he wouldn't find peace even after death.

The misunderstanding between Gan and Han had started with a prank. Gan could paint well in the traditional style, and sometimes copied old works. Seeing a masterly copy of an early painting one day tempted him to do likewise. On an impulse he made a painting called *The Cold Food Festival* and attributed it to the celebrated 12th-century artist Zhang Zeduan, using a well-preserved sheet of Song paper and ink. Originally he did it just for fun, never expecting his copy would attract a newspaper correspondent, Na Wu, who came from an impoverished Manchu noble family. Na Wu took it away and asked a famous craftsman to mount it, colour it with tea and then fake the seal of the Qing emperor Qianlong. When this was done he brought it back to Gan saying, "Look, it exceeds even Master Zhang's skill. And it's certainly as accomplished as Han's."

As a dealer, connoisseur of paintings and well-known copyist, Han had been appointed assistant manager of the Gongmao Pawnshop.

"You flatter me. I don't think my skill is nearly as great as Han's," he protested.

"Flatter you? Never!" retorted Na Wu. "If you don't believe me, let's put it to the test."

"How?"

"I'll take it to Gongmao Pawnshop. If Han tells me it's a fake, then I'll say we were only joking. But if I can fool him, then it proves that you do have a remarkable skill. What's more we can share the money between us. Then you can treat me to a roast duck." With this, he carried the painting away wrapped in a blue cloth.

At first Na Wu had only wanted to pawn the painting in order to make the bet with Gan and it was only when he actually had it in his hands that he changed his mind. To fool people he needed to be dressed in his finest clothes, since the pawnshop looked first at the customer and then at the goods. So on the appointed day, he wore his silk gown, a fashionable waist coat, black satin slippers and white silk socks. Between his fingers he balanced an exquisite cigarette-holder with a fine cigarette, lit but unsmoked. Placing the painting on the counter, he asked a price of a thousand yuan and then turned away to look at the wall. From his appearance, Han assumed that he must be a ne'er-do-well from an impoverished Manchu family and that he had stolen the heirloom to pawn. Men of his ilk never sold things and usually never redeemed what they pawned.

Fooled perhaps by Na Wu's appearance, frightened by the high asking price or owing to sheer negligence, Han, after haggling for a long time, chanted in his Shanxi accent, "An antique painting. We can loan you six hundred yuan...." In those days, a bag of flour was only two yuan and forty fen so six hundred yuan was an enormous sum. When Na Wu returned and told him the story, Gan laughed heartily. But on second thoughts, he was scared stiff. If the story got about, it would discredit him with his friends, and offend them as well. Although the relationship between them was not particularly close, they were still friends. And both were fond of Beijing opera, especially of performances by Sheng Shiyuan. Whenever an opera was staged starring Sheng, they would both go to see him. As a result of their frequent attendance and vocal support, Sheng was convinced that if they were not at the theatre cheering, his performance would be below par.

Seeing Gan's misgivings, Na Wu coaxed, "Don't get so worried about it. Everybody already knows Han makes a living from forged paintings. It's time he got his comeuppance. If you're worried about your reputation, we won't do it again. Nobody will find out if neither of us let on. What we did this time wasn't to make money but to put your technique to the test. Now that he's offered us money though, we mustn't be so foolish as to turn it down. Are you really going to pay it back with interest and redeem the painting?"

"I can't afford to."

"You couldn't even if you had the money since the pawn ticket belongs to me now."

Gan had no choice but to give him three hundred yuan. Finishing his duck, Na Wu declared, "Now I'm going to take the ticket to the Japanese pawnshop. I should be able to bluff him out of two or three hundred yuan. So let me pay the bill."

"You're a little too clever at times," remarked Gan.

"Well, don't you agree that to cheat a Japanese is patriotic?"

And soon Gan heard others gossiping, saying that Han was used to cheating people with his fakes, but that he had never expected to be swindled himself. Shortly thereafter Gan received an invitation from Han to celebrate his birthday on August 16.

When the day arrived, Han rented the Listening to Lotus Hall overlooking a lake in a garden behind Beihai Park and set ten tables under a corrugated iron shade to treat his friends. Gan expected to find a dispirited Han but instead he looked more cheerful than ever. After three cups of wine, he stood up and bowed to the guests with his hands folded, saying, "It's not only because it's my birthday that I invited you here today. I also want to tell you that I've made a blunder."

"I'm sure you've already heard — I've been taken in by a fake. When I was poor, I lived on fake paintings. Now I've been caught myself. It is a sort of retribution, and I've no one to blame but myself. But I think all of us are basically honest men, so to save you from suffering a similar loss, I've brought it here for you to have a look at. Bear this lesson in mind and don't make mistakes yourselves." Then he ordered the painting to be brought out.

With this, his two apprentices approached, one holding the painting, the other carrying a pole with a double-pronged tip which he used to hang the painting on to a bronze hook. All the guests gathered round to examine the work. "Looks genuine all right. How amazing!"

"Don't you be taken in by it. Try to spot its weakness and then we will learn something from it." Turning to look at Gan, Han smiled, adding, "Ziqian has a good eye. You try first."

Gan's face had already turned crimson, but since he had been drinking, no one became suspicious. Moving forward, he first looked at the lower left-hand corner of the painting and spotted his thumb-print, positive proof that the work was his, but he was unable to detect any discrepancies. Had he known of any, of course, he would have corrected them in advance. Secretly he admitted that his brushwork was not up to that of the original painting. He commented, "The brush strokes are weak, and the style a little vulgar. Mr Han's really been deceived by the fact that the artist has used 12th-century paper and ink."

Han laughed saying, "I was duped this time not because the faker was so skilful but because I was too conceited and negligent. So today I'd like to advise you all, don't follow in my footsteps and always keep your eyes open. The painting looks genuine but if you're observant enough, its weakness can be easily detected. For instance, the subject is *The Cold Food Festival* and that takes place in spring. The painter Zhang Zeduan lived in Kaifeng where at that time of year people would have been wearing spring clothes. But look, the boy in the painting is still wearing a cotton-padded hat with flaps. Do you think Zhang would have made such a mistake? For another thing, the young woman by the grave is weeping over her dead husband. The word 'husband' has a closed syllable at the end, but her mouth is open saying 'ah'. Judging from this, I would venture to suggest that this painting is not by Zhang Zeduan."

It was an explanation that won everyone's admiration, even Gan's.

At this, Han threw a cup of wine over the fake, struck a match and set fire to it. Then he laughed again, saying, "Getting rid of it saves anyone else from being swindled. Now let's have another drink before the opera begins."

With the destruction of the painting, Gan felt greatly relieved and calmly sat enjoying the entertainment. As a gesture of friendship, Sheng Shiyuan appeared and performed especially well. Han, on his part, cheered loudly and Gan couldn't refrain from following suit. When the performance was over, Han went backstage to express his appreciation. Sheng asked, "The man who often accompanies you to the theatre hasn't come to see me for a long time. Who is he? Won't you introduce us next time he comes?" Since he'd been cheated, Han had felt so miserable that he hadn't been to the theatre for several days and consequently wasn't aware that Gan had also been staying home. Sheng's words startled him. He knew that the forger must be someone from the same trade and had therefore invited a number of them in order to watch what would happen during dinner. However, he had never been even remotely suspicious of Gan. Immediately he looked around to find him but was told by his apprentice that Mr Gan had just been called away unexpectedly.

Later, called to the side door of the garden by Na Wu, Gan was annoyed. "What the devil did you come here for?" he growled.

"I apologize but I must tell you. I went to pledge the pawn ticket with the Japanese but he asked me to let him inspect the painting first. Dare we run the risk? If it passes, then there's no problem. If the Japanese spots anything wrong with it though, he won't be as easy to deal with as Han — we'll be sent to prison."

"You're too greedy!" Gan scolded. "In any case, the painting has already been destroyed by Han."

At first Na Wu was stunned by the news. Then all of a sudden he slapped his thigh and exclaimed, "Wonderful! It's time Han got what was coming to him."

"What are you going to do? We've already made him lose six hundred yuan. Don't be so cruel! He and I are friends and see one another frequently."

"Friends? No. Business is business. It's foolish to let a good opportunity slip through your fingers. Come, stay awhile. I'll treat you to some crabs."

After Na Wu's departure, Gan was uneasy. Han was a better man than Na Wu and even if he himself had nothing further to do with this, he didn't have the heart to let Na Wu extort any more money from him. So he made up his mind to visit the pawnshop and inform him of Na Wu's intention in order to avoid any further trouble.

When he arrived at Gongmao Pawnshop, Han came out to meet him and graciously ushered him into a private room behind the accountant's office. Shortly an apprentice appeared bringing Gan a cup of tea. Han puffed at his hookah for a while before breaking the silence, "I haven't seen you lately. Where've you been?"

Before Gan could reply, the accountant, looking upset, scurried in and stuttered, "Something's wrong, sir!"

"What's wrong?" Han asked nonchalantly.

"There's a man here to redeem his pledge."

"Redeem his pledge? What's wrong with that? It's natural that people come here to redeem their pledges."

"But, he wants to redeem the...." The accountant glanced at Gan, then approached Han and whispered.

"Speak up!" ordered Han. "Mr Gan is not a stranger."

The accountant couldn't help blurting out, "... that painting!"

"Which one?"

"*The Cold Food Festival* that you burnt yesterday."

Gan, shocked, felt a shiver run down his spine, for he had never expected that Na Wu would carry his trick so far.

But Han said calmly, "Tell him the painting he pawned is a fake and that he should be content with the sum he got from me. If not, I'll take him to court."

"I'm sorry, sir. But you can't speak to a customer that way. He came here to redeem his pledge and even if the pledge was a bit of toilet paper, we are still supposed to return it to him. If we can't, then we should pay him twice the loan. Even if we do, I'm not sure he'll take it. How can I tell him we'll go to court?"

The accountant's argument reduced Han to silence. Just then they heard a commotion outside. Na Wu shouted, "What! You want to keep my heirloom, do you? If you're not going to return it to me, you'd better pay me a proper price for it!"

"Outrageous! I'd better go and see what's happening," said Han. "Excuse me, Ziqian."

Angry and embarrassed, Gan ignored protocol and followed Han out of the room.

The shop's counter was over a foot higher than the customer. Behind the counter stood Han, surrounded by his accountant and assistants, all looking down at Na Wu, who challenged, "If you have the painting here, then return it to me. If not, we'll have to settle the matter another way."

Gan peered out from behind Han and saw a swarthy, heavy-set fellow standing behind Na Wu. He was dressed in grey clothes, his sleeve cuffs covering his hands. Beneath his unbuttoned jacket Han could see a white calico vest edged with black trimming, and recognized him immediately as a police detective. It certainly looked as though Na Wu was determined to continue hounding Han. Winking at him, Gan began tentatively, "Oh, it's you, Mr Na. Well, we're all friends here. Why do you want...."

"Mr Gan, what we're talking about it no laughing matter. Please don't get mixed up in this. I pawned a scroll painting inherited from my forefathers. Today I've come here to redeem it. First they tell me it's a fake. Then they promise I can get it back another day. Does it surprise you that my patience has run out?"

As Gan was about to try and coax him out of continuing, Han edged forward saying to Na Wu, "So you've run out of patience, have you? Well, I'm much more impatient than you are. I reckoned you'd be here as soon as the shop opened. Why did it take you so long? You want to redeem the painting, do you? Then first please show me the money!"

"So you're afraid I haven't brought it." With this, Na Wu threw a white packet on to the counter containing the principal and interest, amounting together to over eight hundred yuan. Having counted the sum and placed the interest to one side, Han handed six hundred yuan to the accountant, then removed a package from under the counter and handed it downwards.

"Here. Now take it away."

Hearing this, Gan and the assembled assistants were taken aback. Na Wu stood stunned before nervously reaching out for the package, his hands trembling so much that he could not even hold it. The detective reached out and steadied him, saying, "You'd better have a look. Is it the one you pawned?"

No sooner had he untied the bundle than the sweat stood out on his brow, and his lips trembled. Pretending to talk to himself, he said so that Gan could hear, "Wasn't this burnt yesterday?"

"If I hadn't burnt it yesterday, would you have come here today?"

replied Han sarcastically.

"So there are two such paintings in existence!" uttered Na Wu.

"If you like, I'll produce another one for you tonight," added Han.

Incredulously Gan asked, "What on earth is it, Mr Na? Won't you let me have a look?"

Holding the painting, Gan blushed scarlet with shame. First of all, he examined the lower left-hand corner, and looked hard at the thumb-print, which though very pale could barely be distinguished from that in the destroyed painting and had they been placed together in front of him, he would have been unable even to identify his own work. It was said that some craftsmen were so skilful they could peel off the top layer of a painting to make two. "Can Han do that?" he wondered.

"It looks like there's nothing for me to do here." The detective was growing impatient. "Settle with me and I'll be off."

Paying him, Na Wu turned towards Han with a contrite smile and folded his hands in a gesture of respect, "I've learned a lesson from you and paid two hundred yuan for the privilege."

"Take the interest back!" Han handed it over to him and laughed. "It was you who brought the painting here and I imagine your slippers must be worn out, so you'd better use the money to buy a new pair. By the way, please tell the man who made the fake...." With this he turned to the dumbfounded and embarrassed Gan before going on, "Does he think he's clever enough to fool me? Not until he can fool the painter himself with his fakes, will he be properly qualified. So I suggest he study for another couple of years."

Ashamed, Gan slunk out of Gongmao Pawnshop, head bowed, and from then on never appeared when Han was around. Although Han was a man of good reputation, his master dared not run the risk of losing any more money and in the first month of the following year he was dismissed. Later he was reduced to working as a junk dealer for two years, but since business was bad, he finally supported himself by collecting and selling scrap. Gan, despite suffering a temporary loss of credibility, got a good job restoring damaged paintings.

As a result of his background, clear record, progressive ideology and loyalty to the Party, Gan was elected to the leadership of the antiques trade after Liberation and became vice-chairman of the trade association during the socialist transformation of capitalist enterprise.

To reinforce the leadership after the changeover, someone suggested that they should appoint Han to a job. The authorities did not know much about his past and asked Gan for his opinion. Gan was evasive, saying he didn't know much about him and asked them to wait until he found out a little more. Returning home, he turned the affair over in his mind. Though he hadn't intended to cheat Han, he certainly wouldn't be able to explain it easily. "If Han isn't hired, then no one will rake up the past," he thought. "If he is, however, he may raise it against me. What's more, I'm applying for Party membership. Why should I bother to recommend him?" But Gan also couldn't lie to the authorities. When asked for his opinion, he said, "Han lived on fakes and used to be an assistant manager in a pawnshop. He was quite well-off before Liberation. On his birthday the famous Beijing opera actor Sheng Shiyuan even performed at his home...."

"It's said that he's an able man. What do you think about our employing him?"

"The decision rests with you," Gan replied evasively. "My political experience is low, and I'm not sure."

In the end Han was rejected.

According to the conventions of the antiques trade, people who had been vetted could do anything except assess or deal in antiques. From that day on Han sank into obscurity.

Many years passed. Gan didn't feel guilty and, as time went on, forgot about Han.

During the "cultural revolution", Gan was deeply wronged. After the fall of the "gang of four", he was rehabilitated and had his savings, which had been confiscated, returned. What pleased him most was that he was able to go and work at an antiques studio, where he could put his knowledge to full use. But time takes its toll. When he was elected a people's representative, he was given a medical certificate stating that if he didn't rest, his chances of recovery were nil. At length he recalled Han.

In the antique world some old craftsmen had died, and others had fallen ill. During recent years few talented successors had turned up, and a shortage of able people became a big problem. The international antique market was brisk. Han was good at both assessing and copying ancient paintings and should have had a position which would have given full play to his unique skill. Instead, the man had been barred for many years.

Gan was so filled with remorse that he confessed everything to the Party committee. The secretary praised him and asked him to try and locate Han.

But Beijing was so big, where was Han? First Gan was told that he was a boilerman for a teahouse at Tianqiao, but when he got there he found the place had closed down. Then he was told that Han and another old bachelor had rented a house to breed goldfish near the Goldfish Pond. When he went to look for him, the house had been razed. Half a month passed but Han was nowhere to be found. All Gan knew was that he was still alive, and sometimes went to Taoran Pavilion Park to practise shadow-boxing at dawn.

He was determined to find him. Despite the doctor's warnings, he went with his cane first thing in the morning to the park. As the sun had not yet risen, only a few dim figures could be discerned running along the edge of the lake. Others were singing, walking or fishing. But whom should he approach?

Just then an old man with a beard and a cane, wearing traditional-style clothes, came towards him. He was so absorbed in humming a Beijing opera aria that he didn't notice the people around him. Out of habit, Gan spontaneously cheered, "Wonderful!"

The old man stopped to look up towards the shaded trees by the lake. "Why, that cheering sounds familiar to me, but I haven't heard it for more than thirty years."

"I haven't heard such a sweet voice for over thirty years either," Gan chimed in. "Aren't you Mr Sheng?"

"Oh my goodness!" The old man stepped forward, and grasped Gan by the hand. "It's you, the man who used to come with Han to see my performances."

"Yes. My name is Gan Ziqian."

"I've heard of you. Once after a performance, I wanted to meet you, but you had already left. Thirty years have passed since that day. How are you getting along? Where do you work now?"

Told that Gan was an adviser at an antiques studio, Sheng said, "I'm with a Beijing opera company now. I lost my voice in 1945 when the Japanese surrendered and was jobless. But after Liberation, the government showed a lot of concern for us and gave us the opportunity to use our talents, so I became a teacher at a Beijing opera school, but that was interrupted by the 'cultural revolution'...."

"Mr Sheng," Gan cut him short, "you mentioned Mr Han to me just now. Do you know where he is?"

"Why yes. He lives with me."

"Eh?" surprised, Gan stared at him for a long time before he asked cautiously, "Really?"

"Of course. Anybody who comes here to practise shadow-boxing knows he's lodging with me. During the 'cultural revolution' the teahouse where he worked closed down. Since he couldn't earn a living, I told him not to worry and to stay with me for the time being. My wife died and my son was transferred to another province, so I was alone. I told him he could come and keep house and that as long as I had an income, he wouldn't go hungry. So he's been living in my place for the past ten years."

"If he's there now," Gan said impatiently, "may I go with you to see him?"

"No."

"Why?"

"Because he's gone into hospital with a stroke."

Gan heaved a sigh.

"Don't worry," Sheng added. "He's out of danger, but the doctor won't let him have any visitors yet."

Relieved, Gan asked again, "What caused it?"

"Overwork. Last year the doctor insisted that he take it easy, but he was busier than ever with his work. He said that his ancestors were connoisseurs of paintings, and had the knack of being able to tell genuine works from fakes. While he was able, he wanted to write it down so that the knowledge would not be lost."

Gan sighed. "If only he could have done it earlier!"

"Years ago he used to complain to me that the higher-ups in the antique world were a bunch of laymen who'd insulted him and that he would rather die with his skills than teach others. However, in the last couple of years, since I've been cleared of the false accusations made against me in the 'cultural revolution' and we've had a bit more money, he's changed his mind. Now he says he won't withhold his knowledge any longer and has decided to write it all down. I was delighted and provided him with paper, ink, fine tea and tobacco, but I forgot to remind him to take care of his health."

Hearing this Gan was moved. "You really have been a loyal friend!"

"Oh, I owe a great deal to the way things have improved since those chaotic years, otherwise I couldn't have afforded to help him."

With a heavy heart Gan walked silently beside Sheng for a while before asking, "Is he able to talk?"

"Yes, but his tongue gets a little stiff sometimes."

"So he can still be cured." Gan was cheered, thinking he should suggest sending someone to Sheng's house to have Han's speech recorded. When the next National People's Congress opened, someone should propose helping old scholars and craftsmen to pass on their knowledge.

Saying goodbye to Gan, Sheng promised, "As soon as I have the doctor's permission, I'll take you to see him."

On his way home, Gan felt much more at ease; at long last he had found an opportunity to make amends for his error. Now he could die with a clear conscience.

1981

Translated by Song Shouquan

My Faraway Qingpingwan

●

—— SHI TIESHENG ——

Shi Tiesheng, a young writer, was born and brought up in Beijing. After graduating from middle school in 1969, he was sent to do manual labour in the countryside. In 1972, ill health forced him to return to Beijing. He published his first story "The Professor of Law and His Wife" in 1979. He wrote many short stories subsequently, including the 1983 and 1984 national prize winners "My Faraway Qingpingwan" and "My Grandma's Star".

GENERALLY speaking, northern cattle can be divided into two types: Mongolian and Huabei. Of the Huabei type, those from Qinchuan and Nanyang are the best, for they are tall and strong. A Huabei-Mongolian cross is an even more attractive animal, with its crooked horns pointing forward, fighting ability and fine hide, and is easy to rear. I know a little about Huabei cattle. Let's say, if somebody wanted to buy one right now, I could guarantee to buy him the best. Everybody knows you should look at an animal's build, teeth and temperament. By doing that, you can perhaps get one that isn't too bad, but you won't necessarily get a genuinely good one. The key thing is to check its temperament by taking a whip and cracking it in the air, at which a good animal will glower and thrash about. This kind of animal will work hard and trot spiritedly. A lazy animal, when it hears the whip crack, will slump, close its eyes and put up with it. Don't choose this kind of animal.

When I was sent to the countryside, I looked after cattle for two years in a small mountain village in northern Shaanxi called Qingpingwan. Although our village was on the Loess Plateau, one found only yellow loess and nothing like a plateau there. Land frequently caved in because of floods which washed soil down ditches, dams and rivulets into the Yellow River. From Luochuan northward, the yellow mountain ranges and ridges went as far as the eye could see. There were few trees, so few that the villagers remembered clearly the exact number and type on each mountain.

When I herded cattle on the mountains, I often thought how wonderful it would be if that yellow earth could be changed into piles of millet and wheat, and the wild grasses and thistle in the ditches and gullies into cypress groves. The old fellow who herded the cattle with me always smoked a long-stemmed pipe. He would laugh and say, "Then we could have steamed buns the year long and my wife and I might get a wooden coffin."

This old man's name was Bai. He had a few teeth left and a straggly beard and he liked to sing, although he had a voice like a broken gong. At dusk, when we herded the cattle back to the village and the last ray of the setting sun fell on the river bank, the old man would hoist the bundle of wood tied to the end of his pick and walk along singing: "Red flowers blossom along the river bank, the poor long for a good life..." drawling out the words. Although it wasn't a particularly robust voice, it was melodious with a slight *vibrato*. Sometimes, by chance, we'd see a couple of small heads appear, perhaps foxes or wild goats, prick their ears up to listen for a bit and then run away. Anyway, you couldn't have lived by hunting there, animals were so scarce. The most outstanding feature of the place was its poverty, with its barren mountains and empty rivers, so the "good life" was something the poor only dreamt of. When it was nearly dark, the children who'd gone out looking for edible wild herbs would come back, the older ones leading the little ones, the little ones pulling even smaller ones, each with a basket on their arm full of amaranth, or garlic and mushrooms. They would all follow behind the cattle, shouting and laughing, vying with each other to scoop up the cattle droppings to take home.

The poorer a place is, the harder the work is. Sowing in spring, harvesting wheat in summer, planting corn, sorghum and millet in the autumn, and in winter, building dams and terraced fields. Work went on non-stop. Take spring sowing for example. Manure had to be carried up the mountain with poles and baskets, each load weighing about sixty or seventy *jin*. Every morning you had to make four or five trips, which earned you only two workpoints. That was equivalent to six fen. With that you could buy two popsicles in Beijing. In that place of course, there weren't any popsicles. People who worked in the mountains would drink whatever water they could get. Before sunrise, people tilling the fields would pick up their wooden ploughs and drive their cattle up the mountains. By the time the sun appeared, they would already have ploughed several mu. A blazing sun imprinted the elongated shadows of cattle and men on to the mountain slopes, of people spreading fertilizer in the wake of the ploughs, of others behind them sowing, and to the rear others breaking up clods of earth, all in a line moving slowly, rhythmically forward to the cattle driver's long cry. Sometimes the cries were exhausted and sad, sometimes cheerful and humorous. It was a scene which made me forget the time I lived in and silently reflect on mankind's long and remote history. It seemed to me that this was exactly how we had walked through the centuries.

At the Qingming Festival I got ill and had terrible pains in my back and legs. At first, I thought it was only sciatica or a strain and never imagined it would become as serious as it has. It's very windy at Qingming in north Shaanxi and even the sky was yellow with dust. The sun became hazy and the winds beat against the paper panes of the cave house windows. One day I was lying alone on the earthen *kang*....

That day the team leader brought me a bowl full of steamed buns.

It's a north Shaanxi custom that at Qingming every household, even poor ones, must eat several of these steamed buns. They are dyed red and green and the villagers call them *zi chui*. Everyone in Qingpingwan enjoyed eating them, especially the children, who'd been clamouring for them for days.

That day the team leader placed a bowl of *zi chui* on the *kang*, and invited me to eat. He sat down on the edge of the *kang*, puffing on his long-stemmed pipe. *Zi chui* are made with fresh white flour on the outside and black flour inside, sometimes mixed with bran. Without saying anything, the team leader watched me. As he was leaving, he blew into the bowl of his pipe, and said, "It's not easy for a young boy like you to be so far away from home."

The next time the team held a meeting, the team leader suggested I look after the cattle. All the commune members agreed. "Young man, don't hurt yourself. Take good care of our cattle." Everyone spoke to me that way. In that place everything was done by hand, carrying manure and water, chopping wood, making beancurd at Qingming, noodles at the Dragon Boat Festival, pressing sesame oil, digging out cave houses. Your body was your capital; cattle were the only thing that could replace manual labour. I was very moved that the peasants had given me such important work. I didn't say anything. The peasants liked deeds rather than words.

I looked after ten head of cattle and Old Bai the other ten. We were in the same corral, which had been set up in the highest place in the village. It was on flat land, with two rows of cowsheds and three stone caves piled high with fodder. The shallow Qingping River gurgled through all day long and just before it reached the village it made a turn and formed itself into a pool. On one side of that river bend was a cliff, on the other an expanse of beach. In summer the village children would romp about naked, somersaulting and jumping into the pool. Sometimes, with whoops and squeals of delight, they caught a crab. Old Bai would sit on top of the cave by the corral watching them, smoking one pipe after another. "The little ones don't have a worry in the world," he would say. Then he would begin singing in his husky voice: "My hometown, that well-known place,

Thirty-li Village, Suide County...." Old Bai was originally from Suide. He'd come to Qingpingwan to work when he was young and had been living there ever since. Suide was even poorer and you could only get work as a seasonal labourer, or a stone mason, or a storyteller.

Some of the Suide people also worked as musicians. Around the Spring Festival, sitting by the corral, you could often hear the pleasing sound of the *suona*. Some of the players were from Mizhi, some from Jiaxian, but most were from Suide. They wandered about the village and would casually blow their *suonas* in front of somebody's cave house. If they chanced upon a family about to have a wedding, they could play for a day and eat their fill. If they were unlucky, they could only ask for a few scraps or some money. Everyone gave something, some more, some less. Old Bai in particular gave a lot. "Everybody has hard times," he would say. He'd once been a musician too and though he'd had enough to eat, he'd often been short of clothes. If no one asked him to play, he would have to spend the night in a cold cave. Now, putting out hay for the cattle, he would sing: "What a hard, hard life for the labouring man, January through October, suffering like horses and cows, eating like pigs and dogs." Old Bai was full of songs.

Ever since my childhood I'd liked Shaanxi folksongs. Shortly after I arrived in Qingpingwan, I asked the villagers to sing. Everybody said that Old Bai liked to sing, and that he sang well. Some commented, "Old Bai's had a miserable life and only those who've suffered sing the best mountain songs." Actually most of the north Shaanxi songs have a melancholy flavour. But, whenever they are sung, they liven things up. Sometimes when Old Bai was driving the cattle out of the village, he would sing in falsetto *Run Away to Xikou*: "Darling you're going off to Xikou, I can't keep you any more. Holding my darling by the hand, I see him off at the door. Don't keep to the path, take the road instead. You will meet other travellers and not be lonely...." The women working at the threshing-ground would call out to me laughing, "Get Old Bai to sing *The Bachelor Weeps for a Wife*. He sings that really well." Old Bai pretended not to hear, and sang *A Young Girl's Marriage*: "At the first watch, my darling slipped into my room; when mother asked me what the noise was, I told her it was the north wind rattling my door...." The verses that followed were a little suggestive. When Old Bai and I drove the cattle off, we could still hear them complaining and scolding us. Old Bai winked at me and drove the animals with a willow branch, singing as he went.

Usually we got up into the mountains by noon. The sun would scorch the yellow earth a flaming red colour. Nameless tiny insects buzzed around us. Even the mountains seemed exhausted as they listlessly leaned against one another. For a radius of a dozen li, there were only Old Bai and myself; only the sound of our voices urging on the cattle. Old Bai knew how to find spring water there; he made a small hollow with his hoe and after a bit water began to appear. Beads of water like tiny pearls oozed into it; not a lot, but it was cold and sweet. Old Bai drank some water and then wiped his mouth, singing, "You've taken an interest in me, I've taken an interest in you too." I didn't know what was on his mind....

Taking care of cattle in summer is not an easy job. All the fresh grass grows at the edges of fields, near the crops. The two of us had to run about, shouting and swearing at the cattle to shoo them away. Old Bai cursed them as if he were cursing people. If we were off guard for a minute, the crafty ones would steal the seedlings. The worst was a black bull looked after by Old Bai. He was an old hand and could easily distinguish seedlings from weeds. He pretended to eat the grass growing at the edge of the field. Then he would slowly move near the seedlings, head lowered, watching me out of the corner of his eye. When I was watching him, he appeared to be indifferent, and wouldn't touch the nearby seedlings, but as soon as I turned around, he would immediately snatch a stalk of millet or corn and run away. After a while, I caught on to him and pretended not to look while he was edging near the seedlings. When his tongue reached into the forbidden territory, I shouted at him. The old boy would stagger backwards with a frightened, ashamed look. It was a little bit sad to see.

The cattle in north Shaanxi had a hard life too. Sometimes they were even too tired to eat grass. They would puff and blow until their bodies shook and I was really worried that sooner or later they might all collapse. Seeing them vying with one another to lick the saline drops which oozed from the ground, I was angry at the unfairness of nature. Several times I thought of buying salt for them, but I was greedy and had spent the money my family had sent me on buying eggs.

Every night, Old Bai and I had to work until eleven or twelve feeding the cattle. We had to feed them at regular intervals, not too much at any one time. Liuxiao'er, his seven-year-old granddaughter, followed Old Bai like a shadow. She always had a couple of potatoes or corn kernels in her small handkerchief. Old Bai liked to make a fire with the hay left by the cattle and Liuxiao'er would put the corn kernels or potatoes in the hot ashes. If it was a corn cob, she would poke it with a branch until the kernels made a crackling sound. That was the favourite snack of the mountain children.

Liuxiao'er always asked me about Beijing. "Do you really watch movies in caves?" "It's not a cave, it's a cinema." "Last time you said it was a cave." "Oh, that was television. A square box. It's just like watching movies." She thought for a while, her head tilted to one side, then asked another question. "Whenever you want to eat meat you can, right?" "Yes." "You're lying!" "It's true!" "What, getting meat three meals a day?" "You can if you want to." She asked the same questions time and time again and even though she knew what kind of answers I would give, she still continued, "You say that people in Beijing don't like eating white meat?" She was surprised to hear that Beijing people didn't like fatty pork. Lifting her tiny face upward she would stare at the stars; to her, the mysteries of Beijing were as great as those of the Milky Way.

"The children here in the mountains don't understand much," the old man said. He'd seen a lot himself, having joined the Party in 1937, fighting southwards to Guangzhou with the troops. He often talked about Guangzhou: its neon lights, the Cantonese fancy for snakes, the skyscrapers and elevators.... Liuxiao'er would listen, unable to fall asleep. "City people don't know much about things in the country. Can they handle dogs?" Liuxiao'er giggled. She was referring to the time we first arrived in Qingpingwan, when we'd been chased all over by the village dogs. "The students from the city couldn't tell bullocks from cows," Liuxiao'er said as she went over to stroke the feeding cattle. She counted, "Red Bull, Little Bull, Dappled Cow.... Grandpa, maybe Old Black Bull is sick. He refuses to eat." "He's old and tired," Old Bai answered. Nights in the mountains were so quiet you could only hear the the cattle grazing, crickets chirping and sometimes the distant howling of wolves. Old Bai had a poor *erhu* which he played and, of course, would sing.

Liuxiao'er asked most frequently about Tian An Men. "Did you go very often to Tian An Men?" "Yes." "Did you see Chairman Mao a lot?" "No, I've never even seen him once." "What! He lives there. How could you not see him if you went there?" She thought Chairman Mao was always standing in Tian An Men, the way he did in the pictures. Once she whispered to me, "Will you take me to see Tian An Men this winter when you get home?" "I'm afraid your grandpa won't allow you to go." "You can persuade him. He trusts you. I've got enough saved up." "How did you do that?" "Selling eggs. My grandpa doesn't want the money. He gave it to me to buy a jacket." "How much have you got?" "Five yuan." "That's not enough." "Hey, I'm just teasing you. See, I've got eight and a half." She fished out a small cloth bag and opened it to show me the money. Except for two one-yuan notes it was all small change, ten or twenty cent notes. Most of them were what I had paid Old Bai for his eggs. That was the only way to improve my diet. But how could I explain that to Liuxiao'er? I really would have liked to take her to Beijing in the winter. But that winter, I became seriously ill.

Actually, raising cattle is not that difficult. As Old Bai says, all it needs is hard work and careful attention. Raising cattle doesn't need physical strength, but it is arduous, getting up several times each night to feed them. You can't get a whole night's sleep all year round. In winter, getting up from your warm quilt in the middle of the night is not an easy thing to get used to. It was especially hard mixing the fodder at dawn. While the cattle lowered their heads to eat I would usually doze off several times as I sat on the grey stone slabs beside the trough. Old Bai would chatter incessantly in my ears about the price of black-market rice shooting up again; about the supply of striped corduroy and marketing cooperative; about how worn and threadbare Liuxiao'er's padded jacket was.... I just answered with grunts, since I was dreaming of the Beijing Duck at the Quanjude Restaurant. Once I suddenly fell into the icy hole of Shichahai pool — that woke me up with a start. Old Bai was still chattering. "You'd better go back to sleep in the cave. I'll mix the fodder for you next time," he said. A light flashed across the sky, a shooting star. The moon had hidden itself in the valley, leaving only stars and mountains facing each other, perhaps forgetting each other. "This kind of work isn't for young people. This is the time when they should be having a sound sleep." He sighed and complained, while I dozed off into my dreams once again.

When it was raining or snowing, the two of us would take refuge in the cattle shed. The floor was covered in dung and urine and there was nowhere for me to doze off. My legs and back ached constantly. "Damned weather," Old Bai cursed and then said to me, "Beijing's pretty good, why on earth did you come to this mountain area?" "Why didn't you stay in Guangzhou?" I asked casually. He stroked his brown moustache, and then made to fill his pipe. He stared at me for a long time, "Yes, you've got me. I don't know why I was so obsessed at the time." Then he stopped, as though searching his memory for the reason. "Ah, you can't make felt from feathers, and mountain people can't became officials," he said. "If I hadn't come home then, I might be living in one of those high buildings with a bodyguard. You see, we mountain people were foolish, and only thought of returning home as soon as the war was over. There's nothing better than life in a cave house. Damn it! If I'd stayed, would my Liuxiao'er have to worry about not getting her corduroy jacket?"

Every time I got money from home, Old Bai would ask me to buy cigarettes for him. "Okay," I said. "How about a pack of Peony?" "Oh, a pack of Yellow Leaf will do." "But I have a suggestion," I whispered. "Send some cigarettes to the back gully!" "You're a naughty pup!" he scolded. I was referring to the widow living in the back gully. She was a dozen years younger than Old Bai and all the villagers knew that she treated him well. Old Bai smoked his cigarette and stared off into the distance. I sang: "You've taken an interest in me, I've taken an interest in you..." while passing him a few cigarettes and motioning to the back gully. He didn't speak, and seemed to be lost in thought, smiling. At last he put the cigarettes into his small tobacco pouch, "Wait until Liuxiao'er gets married to someone in Beijing." Then he laughed, knowing what he'd said was nonsense.

When we drove the cattle over the mountain, and saw the cave house in the far distance, I asked Old Bai, "What's she like?" "You mean Liang Liang's mother? She's nice," he answered. "Then why don't you live with her?" "I, I'm too old, too old..." he said evasively. "Don't talk rubbish," I said, "then why do you go there so often in the evenings?" Actually I was teasing him. "Ah, don't tease me." He pretended to look serious. I tried to bluff him, "I saw everything. Why don't you admit it?" He was silent and looked a little uneasy. I hadn't actually seen anything.

Old Bai gazed down at the cave house at the foot of the mountain. Liang Liang's mother was chopping a tree-stump with difficulty and a little boy was helping her; it was Liang Liang. "I think you'd better marry her. It's not easy for her to live alone with the boy. What's more, you'd have someone to mend your clothes." "Ah, how can I leave Liuxiao'er and who'll look after her?" "You can all live together." "Her Liang Liang is too spoiled. If we live together, Liuxiao'er'll come off worse. Anyhow stepmothers are usually not so kind." "What do you mean stepmother? Liuxiao'er ought to call her grandma." "What's the difference?" There were only the two of us, so we could talk to each other without any inhibitions. The old man stared at the smoke which rose from Liang Liang's home and wafted around the gully. A school bell rang. The sun had set behind the mountains. In the twilight the villagers were returning from the fields. Shepherds were driving their bleating flocks back to the village. Old Bai still sat there silently smoking his pipe. Obviously he wanted to marry the woman, but he was worrying about Liuxiao'er. Liuxiao'er's father had died a tragic death. No one dared ask Old Bai about his son's death. It was said that whenever Old Bai thought of it, he would cry and thump his forehead. Someone said that Old Bai had not sent gifts to the doctor when his son was sick and thus delayed medical treatment; actually a dozen or so *jin* of rice or flour would have been enough. What miserable times!

In autumn, grazing cattle in the mountain is a joy. All the crops have been harvested and the fields are bare. The wild grass in the gullies and ditches is so thick that a cowherd can sleep at the entrance to a gully as soon as he shoos his cattle into it. Sometimes I would drive the cattle up the mountain and sit at the bottom of the path reading. In autumn the mountains change their drab colours. There are red leaves on the bushes halfway up, yellow leaves on the birch-leaf pears, and wild jujube trees full of tiny fruits like coral beads ... rows of light blue wild blossoms stretch across the slopes. Small grey voles poke their heads up from behind yellow clods of earth, wild ducks emerge from caves and fly up into the blue sky, clucking pheasants sometimes appear at the tops of cliffs, or sometimes disappear into the thick grass.... I thought it odd that even though they were so poor, no one hunted these little creatures. Perhaps it was because they had no guns, or maybe because the birds were too small, but there had to be another reason. In spring, when the swallows came, every family would open their windows, inviting them to make their nests;

many families had swallows' nests and no one harmed them. If anybody suggested that swallows could be eaten, the villagers would glare and say, "Swallows!" as though something sacred had been blasphemed.

After harvesting the wheat, the cattle got their rest and we drove them to graze in the mountains all day long. Old Bai didn't rest. When we found a good grazing spot, he would disappear after telling me what to do. Sometimes I would suddenly see him halfway up a cliff chopping down a shrub. It was difficult to get anything to eat as well as to get fuel, so we often had to climb high up to get a little wood. Old Bai told me that it had been different in the old days, when there were fewer people and more good trees. The forests had been so dense people didn't go into them much. The old people now still cherished the memory of how the Red Army had overthrown the landlords and given the peasants their own plots to till.

In the mountains, even though I was sometimes by myself, I never felt lonely because I had the cattle with me. I would watch them all day long and got to know their every movement. Ordinarily the cows didn't bellow except when they were nursing their calves. When the sun set, a nursing cow would be eager to return to the village and if you didn't let her go, she would moo incessantly and circle round anxiously, unwilling to eat. I remember once falling asleep in a gully and when I woke up, the sun was already approaching the mountain top. As we herded the cattle together to go back, Old Bai and I suddenly discovered we were missing one. At first we were worried that the animal might have fallen down one of the hidden crevices created by the rains. Old Bai became very concerned, but then realized what had happened, "It doesn't matter. She missed her calf and has gone back by herself." I found out that the missing cow was nursing. When we were still a distance from the village, we could hear mooing. One of ours responded as it seemed that the mothers and offspring had a lot to chat about after a day's separation. The cows looked so gentle, kind and serene while their calves were suckling. I liked the cows and the calves, but my favourite was the red bull with the sturdy build who was capable of pulling a heavy plough all by himself. He had fine horns, big and long, which pointed forward, and he could defeat the strongest bulls in the neighbouring village. I always used to give him a little more to reward him. However he still wasn't the head of the cattle. I disliked the old black bull most. He was not only crafty and a bully, but he also lacked strength. When he was pulling the plough with another bull, he would run out of breath. He occupied the leading position and he looked courageous enough to repel an invasion from other villages' "chiefs", but he would run away faster than usual after a couple of rounds. The old cow was different. Although she was older than the black bull she was considerably more amiable. Whenever the small calves poked their heads towards him she would patiently lick their coats.... It was a great joy being with the cattle. There wasn't another person within a radius of a dozen li, just the mountains. Occasionally, a lone shepherd would pass over one of the ridges and give me a shout. The black goats ran along the precipitous cliffs as though they were on flat ground. From afar, it was just like looking at a chess board suspended in the sky, with the white sheep like white chessmen at the bottom of the board. There was spring water in the gullies. When you were thirsty you could drink and if you were hot you could bathe in it. It was a carefree sort of life although we were often hungry.

Old Bai had a younger brother who'd been a herdsman, but I had now taken his job. People said that he was a bit shady and that he had stolen fodder and speculated on the side. He'd once been put into the county jail. I didn't think he was so bad. He had made some steamed buns to sell at a higher price to the water conservancy station a dozen li away and made a small profit in order to buy sorghum seed and corn. It was said that his steamed buns were mixed with low quality flour. They also said he caught crows and sold them as chicks. Old Bai looked down on his brother. He respected the honest poor.

Singing a song Old Bai came back with two *dan* of firewood and asked me, "Are you hungry?" "I've already finished your share," I said. "Oh, you can have that with pleasure!" He seemed very happy. As he hummed, he took me to a large birch-leaf pear tree on the other side of the mountain. "Let's have a delicious meal!" He climbed the tree. He was fifty-six years old then, although he looked older than that, but he climbed trees better than I did. Perching in the tree, he broke off a fruit-laden branch and threw it down to me. The fruit was about the size of a small fingernail, bronze-coloured and dotted with yellow specks. They were sour and set your teeth on edge. Old Bai sat in the tree eating them and singing *Xintianyou*, an old north Shaanxi revolutionary song: "Rivers flow through the opposite gully, guerrillas stream down the mountainside...." He was probably thinking of those days. He once told me that he had carried the coffin of Liu Zhidan, the north Shaanxi revolutionary base leader, and had also kept vigil beside the coffin. Some people thought Old Bai boasted. Sometimes he did. He started singing *Xintianyou* again: "The morning glories blossom while the sheep mate, I haven't seen you since last February." "You just saw her last night," I shouted. "My lad, hadn't you better find a sweetheart right away? Otherwise you'll be losing time," he counter-attacked. "The 'back gully' lady's got you." "You mean Liang Liang's mother? She's nice." "I suppose those two bundles of firewood you cut are for her." "Whoever wants them can take them." That was true enough. Although he was poor, Old Bai wasn't stingy.

Once I got up at midnight and groped my way into the cave in the dim moonlight. It was piled high with hay. As soon as I touched a bundle, two people suddenly jumped up and frightened me out of my wits. I cried out, terrifying them. An older man immediately said, "Don't be afraid, we're not villains." Old Bai came in with a lantern thinking there was a wolf. Actually the two people were storytellers from Suide. When night came, they'd gone into the cave to sleep. Old Bai invited them to his home and gave them some food. In north Shaanxi there was a saying: When people from the same town meet, they talk to each other with tears. Old Bai and the two blind men chatted the whole night, sighing and complaining all the time.

The following evening, Old Bai arranged for the whole village to donate something for a performance by the two men. There were people everywhere, on top of the caves, on the courtyard walls, on the millstone too. Everyone was spellbound, although nobody knew quite what they were talking about. Storytelling in north Shaanxi is actually a kind of singing accompanied by a three-stringed instrument. The melodies, full of melancholy tunes, were like the gurgling water of the Qingpingwan River just outside the village. The moonlight was shimmering on the river. The sorghum and millet, rustling in the night breeze, was accompanied by an occasional donkey's bray. Holding Liuxiao'er in his arms, Old Bai sat among the crowd singing along in a low voice. Liang Liang's mother, neatly dressed, sat on top of a cave house with her son. Liuxiao'er fell asleep in her grandfather's arms, though she'd planned to pop some corn at the enclosure after the performance, and her tiny hand was still clutching her small handerchief. It was rare for the village to have such excitement.

I was more interested in watching the bulls fight. That was really exciting and gave you a true sense of strength and challenge. I studied the fighting quite carefully. All twenty cattle, primarily the bulls, had their own rank. But on what basis? At first I was puzzled. The red bull I looked after revered Bai's old black bull. The red one was young and strong, with muscles on his shoulders like little hills and a springy gait, but the latter was already senile and lean, not much more than a large, bony skeleton. All the same, the old black bull was the chief. He always stayed near any of the cows in heat and wouldn't let other bulls come close. I tried several times to get the red bull to challenge the old black one, but all the latter would have to do was wave his horns and the red bull would flee. I was annoyed at the despotic arrogance of the old black bull and the red one's timidness. Later on I realized that the ranking order of the bulls was based on the results of their yearly fighting. The bull who won the annual battle would be honoured as the chief and endowed with privileges throughout the year. Even if he became ill or enfeebled during the time, he would still be revered by the others. That was the influence of tradition at work. But each year when spring came, the bulls having rested over winter, would start fighting again. Naturally the strongest bull (sometimes two) would be elected to compete with the old chief for the championship. That spring my red bull was a candidate and began butting heads with the old black bull. I took the opportunity to try and set up a decisive fight and drove them to an open space near the river (otherwise it would have been dangerous). I did it behind Old Bai's back to avoid a scolding. At the beginning, the red bull was still a bit timid, and the old black bull still had his prestige. Perhaps it was the lure of the cows in heat. Whether it was out of contempt or passion, the red bull finally cried out a challenge to the old bull. The two assumed a fighting stance and confronted one another, their hooves digging into the ground, glowering fiercely. Suddenly they started. The first time was for testing strength and courage. Strong protruding horns are very effective, since they can easily pierce the opponent's weaknesses. Both of the bulls had good horns. The most important thing was wisdom. The former champion, however, depended too much on his strength and power, and the contender, more careful and nimble, occupied a favourable position on higher ground and forced the older bull on to the defence. Taking advantage of the opportunity, the red bull lowered his head and rushed at the opponent's neck. The old black bull had no alternative but to turn and flee. The red bull caught up with him and gored him on the rump, a sure mark of his defeat. That ended the first round. Ordinarily such a fight would have five or nine rounds, and whoever won three out of five or five out of nine would become the new chief. The old champion would have to voluntarily resign to review his heroic past.

Old Bai later looked unhappy about the fighting. I smiled and offered him a cigarette. He smoked and looked at the old black bull's wounded rump, saying, "He's old, but once he saved someone's life...."

It was said that one New Year's Eve everybody was celebrating, eating fried buns and drinking rice wine, when suddenly Old Bai heard an ox crying and a wolf howling. He went to the cattle pen and to his surprise saw that the old black bull had gored a wolf and impaled it against a wall. Though the bull's head had been scratched by the wolf and blood oozed from the wound, he still stood firm. Old Bai killed the wolf and later sold the pelt and bought cigarettes for the whole village.

"No, we shouldn't treat him like that," Old Bai went on, "one year most of the oxen in the village met their end, some died, some were slaughtered. Only the old black bull and the old cow were left and if we hadn't had them the village would have been in a bad way." Old Bai stroked the old black bull's horns with respect, "When this bull dies we must bury him and no one must eat him."

But the old black bull was finally taken to the river bank and killed. He broke his legs that winter stumbling into a hidden crack on the slopes. It's true that oxen cry tears while being killed. Only Old Bai and I refused to eat his flesh. That day the village air was thick with the smell of beef. Old Bai and I sat by his empty trough chain-smoking.

There's one other thing I remember: one night I got up several times to feed the cattle and found the old black bull still standing, puffing and blowing. At first I thought he was ill. When I stepped up to him and reached out to touch his ears, I saw that beneath his belly was a calf lying fast asleep. If the old black bull had lain down, he would have definitely injured the calf. So I drove the calf away and the old black bull immediately settled down. He stared at me and I at him. He was grateful to me, but he would never realize who ought to have been grateful to him.

That winter I suddenly felt the strength go out of my legs and not long after I returned to Beijing, both legs gave way.

While I was in the hospital, one of my classmates, who'd also gone to north Shaanxi, came to see me on his home visit. He brought me the things the villagers had sent: millet, green peas, red dates and sesame.... I recognized the small handkerchief which had held the corn kernels.

He fished a ten-*jin* rice coupon out of his pocket and told me that Old Bai had sent it. The crumpled, greasy coupon was stuck on a piece of white paper.

"I told him that this coupon is only good in Shaanxi. He wouldn't believe me. He said, 'What's so superior about Beijing? I got this in exchange for ten *jin* of good millet. I don't believe it can't be used in Beijing.' So I had to take it and bring it to you. Old Bai said it would be useful when you want a doctor."

I remembered how Old Bai's son's treatment had been delayed. Old Bai thought that Beijing was like Shaanxi.

Ten years have passed. The year before last, Liuxiao'er came to Beijing twice. She really had saved enough money to pay the cost. She told me that in the last couple of years life in the country had improved a lot. The villagers had enough to eat and they also had more meat. She also told me that lean meat really was tastier than fatty meat.

"Is the Qingpingwan River still flowing?" I don't know why I asked such a stupid question.

"Of course," she giggled.

"What about my red bull, is he still alive?"

"Yes, but he's getting on."

I couldn't imagine what the red bull, who'd been so full of energy, looked like in his old age. Perhaps he was like the old black bull, despotic but also generous....

Liuxiao'er bought her grandfather an *erhu*. She wanted to buy a sewing machine for herself but she could not find a suitable one.

"Does your grandpa still like to sing?"

"He sings all day long."

"Does he still sing *Run Away to Xikou*?"

"Yes."

"And the *Hired-hand's Song*?"

"He sings them all."

"Not only when he's sad?"

"Who ever said that?"

As to the origin of those songs, that's better left to musicologists to study. I will always remember the sight of the cattle licking the saline earth and think of Old Bai's songs: red flowers blossom along the river bank, the poor long for the good life.... Now the "good life" is not just a vague hope. What Old Bai sings about now isn't the faint red light of the setting sun, but a scarlet wild flower called morningstar lily, which blossoms every year.

My Old Bai, my cattle, my faraway Qingpingwan....

Translated by Shen Zhen

An Encounter in Green Vine Lane

●

—— LIU SHAOTANG ——

One of China's best known contemporary authors, Liu Shaotang is famous for his ability to capture the flavour of rural life in north China. A native of Tongxian in the suburbs of Beijing, he began publishing essays and short stories at the age of thirteen, his first collection appearing in 1953. In 1954 he entered Beijing University where he studied Chinese literature. He has published many collections of short stories and novels including Catkin Willow Flats, Songs from Hawthorn Village, Mid-Autumn Festival, The Earth's Fire, Spring Grass *and* Flames of War.

1

FOR twenty-five years I've lived in Green Vine Lane.

My home is situated in a small separate courtyard, with five date trees inside and four scholar trees outside, all of which have been there since the Qing Dynasty. The five rooms under these date trees have changed their occupants six times, though they were built less than half a century ago.

At first this small courtyard was used as a back yard. As far as I know, the original owner of this mansion was a dandy, a descendant of the Qing royal family. With a legacy of a dozen or so residences inherited from his ancestors, he led a life of debauchery in this big mansion together with his wife and two concubines. In order to entertain his guests, he later added a back yard with three additional rooms on the south side and two on the east according to the location of the date trees, and used it as a place to play mahjong, smoke opium, sing Beijing opera, hold feasts and so on. After Liberation, in spite of his advanced age and ailing like a candle guttering in the wind, he failed to overcome his addiction to opium and was arrested for buying the drug on the black market. As his health had been completely ruined by alcoholism and his licentiousness, he died soon after he was sent to jail. A fight immediately began involving his wife, two concubines and twelve sons and daughters. The feud was so fierce that even his burial was postponed for nearly a month. Finally, acting as a mediator, the local court made a decision that each member of the family should share equally the money accumulated from auctioning his more than ten residences. As a result, in order for the house to fetch a higher price, a wall was quickly erected between the back yard and the main front buildings so that the five additional rooms formed a separate courtyard. When I bought this small courtyard, it had already become dilapidated.

Usually, a person would hold a house-warming party when he moved into a new home, but in my case it was different. Soon after we moved in something unfortunate happened. Everyone in my family, young or old, fearful and nervous night and day, kept to the house most of the time. Then I was sent to Tongxian to do physical labour in the countryside. For twenty out of the twenty-five years, I lived alone in a thatched cottage in a small village along the banks of the North Canal. Every month, whenever I took a few days leave of absence to go home, I always returned when it was dark and stayed indoors. I never went out of the small courtyard. In recent years, though I have lived in the city since my rehabilitation, I've still no time to go out in the streets. Instead, I keep myself busy reading, writing or entertaining guests. Unlike those years in the village along the banks of the North Canal, where I was on intimate terms with every villager and could recognize which hen of which household had just laid an egg upon hearing it cackle, I know no one here in Green Vine Lane, not even my nearest neighbours living in the next courtyard separated by only a wall.

One morning in June, while leaving to attend a literary forum, I spotted an old man sitting under the dense shade of the scholar trees. No sooner had he heard the creak of my gate than he turned his face in my direction and watched me cross the threshold. He stood up immediately, bowed and greeted me with a broad smile. "Are you going downtown, sir?"

He was in his seventies, thin, with grey hair, long eyebrows like those of the God of Longevity, smiling eyes and a few wrinkles, all of which suggested that he was a genial sort. Dressed in a small jacket with buttons down the front and a pair of black silk trousers with legs as wide as lanterns, he held a folding fan more than a foot in length. Though physically small, he had quite a large mouth and a loud, husky voice.

Unable to recollect if I had seen him somewhere before, I thought he was just a talkative old man. Out of politeness, I replied, "Are you enjoying the breeze here?" With that, I nodded courteously and left in a hurry to go to my meeting.

Little did I think that when I came back at noon, he would still be sitting under the dense shade of those scholar trees. Having spotted me from afar, he rose to his feet and greeted me again, "You've come back!" Though somewhat hoarse, his voice had a pleasant ring.

"And you're still here enjoying the breeze!" I answered with a smile. Since I didn't want to appear rude, I stopped to exchange a few words with him. "May I know your name, sir?" I asked, handing him a cigarette.

"Thanks, but I'm not a smoker or drinker." While speaking, he stood there gracefully. "Don't be so formal. My name's Wang Jiekui."

I noticed the calluses on both his hands and felt closer to him. Then I asked, "Are you from the countryside?"

At this, he grew more relaxed and replied smiling, "Mr Liu, I was born at Green Poplar Village and so have the honour to be one of your neighbours, separated only by the canal."

"Have you known about me for a long time?" Upon hearing him speak my surname, I felt even closer to him.

"I've watched you on TV several times." He narrowed his eyes and smiled broadly. "Besides, I enjoyed listening to your novelette *Catkin Willow Flats* on the radio."

"I hope you won't spare your criticisms," I said quickly.

"I really don't deserve this." He grew serious. "May I ask you: Did you ever hear or see the woman ballad singer Yun Zheyue you mentioned in your story?"

"Yes, I saw her in my childhood." The old man's inquiry reminded me instantly of that brave, pretty woman, who had led a wanton life as a travelling entertainer. "Later, I heard that the Japanese and the puppet government's secret police had posted a reward for her arrest on charges of advocating resistance against the Japanese. She died in prison at Tongzhou. I haven't the heart to go on writing about her."

"It was very kind of you to make her a character in your work. She was my junior fellow apprentice. Now her name will live in history." Tears welled up in his eyes. "If she were alive today, she'd be sixty-nine. As far as I remember, she was born in the year of the tiger."

"Are you a ballad singer too?"

"I've been a story-teller for thirty years."

"Where did you perform?"

"At Jade Spring Teahouse in Nanxiaojie Street, inside the Chaoyang Gate."

"In 1948, while studying in Beijing, I used to go to Jade Spring Teahouse almost every Sunday."

"I related the complete novel *Cases of Prefect Bao*."*

"But I remember that was Liu Jingting Junior's performance."

"Liu Jingting Junior was my stage name." The old man chuckled.

---

*Prefect Bao was a just official in the Song Dynasty.

"Are you ... are you that young scholar 'Ten *jin* of Beancurd'?"

This rarely-heard nickname brought back long forgotten memories. Events from thirty-four years ago flashed into my mind.

2

At that time, I was twelve years old.

Soon after I passed the entrance examination that year and obtained an official tuition grant, I left my home and came to Beijing to attend middle school. However, my scholarship always came late, never once on time, leaving me no choice but to find a way to fend for myself. Having handed in a five-dollar note borrowed from a classmate, the son of a rich family, as my cash deposit, I began work as a newspaper boy after school. In those days, more than twenty newspapers, large and small, circulated in Beijing, varied in form and bad in content. As a matter of fact, the success of a newspaper at that time relied solely on its distribution, which was controlled by a handful of men. Each manipulated a number of distributors who were in charge of selling a certain number of newspapers, while every distributor in turn controlled a group of newspaper boys running all over the city. The biggest group had scores of boys, whereas the smallest had only ten or so.

In order to collect the newspapers in time, I had to get up at three o'clock every morning, and then run from my school to Dengshikou, where I would stand in a line in front of the Jianguo Dongtang Theatre. Only after the newspaper boys had waited there for a long time was a creaking sound heard in the distance, and then a tricycle and trailer appeared loaded with ten or more bundles of newspapers and pedalled by our boss, the distributor. As the heavily loaded tricycle zigzagged under the dim street lights, it still took some minutes to reach the top of the queue. Then our boss would distribute the newly printed newspapers to us one by one. Those who stood in front could pick any best-seller, but their quantity could not surpass their cash deposit.

At the very beginning, as I had handed in five dollars, I was allowed only one hundred and fifty newspapers. Before long, I increased my deposit to fifteen dollars after making a small profit, so the distributor permitted me to get more than three hundred and fifty copies. Once the newspapers were in my hands, I clutched them under my arm and ran as fast as I could, shouting all the way at the top of my voice: "Hey, today's newspaper! *The World Daily! The North China Daily! The Beiping Daily! The Xinsheng Daily! The Xinmin Daily!*... Read all about the huge robbery at Dong'an Market in broad daylight, about the case of a strange corpse discovered in a trunk at Qianmen Railway Station!" I used to finish this in one breath like a prolonged tune.

At that time each newspaper boy had his own route. I went from

Ganmian Lane to Chaoyang Gate, running along the big streets and small lanes within that district. As a rule, customers liked to read newspapers as early as possible, while we newspaper boys did our utmost to sell them quickly since the price varied with each hour. For instance, a newspaper worth four cents could sell for twenty cents a copy at four o'clock in the morning, fifteen cents by five o'clock and ten cents by six o'clock. By seven o'clock we neither made a profit nor loss, but after half past seven, the remainders were worth nothing, fit only to light a stove. Every Sunday, in addition to the newspapers, I could sell fifty magazines. My income thus doubled.

I was born and raised in the countryside. At five or six years old, I began to chase wild rabbits, and at twelve, I could run as swiftly as the wind. Because I ran fast, I could sell all my newspapers before half past five. Every morning, in Nanxiaojie Street on my way back to school, I would usually go into a small restaurant where I would order either a bowl of noodles with beef ribs or seasoned millet porridge with two deep-fried fritters. Then, with my stomach fairly full and sweat streaming down my face, I would go to school to attend the morning self-study class.

This small restaurant was run by an ugly, fierce-looking woman in her forties who wore gaudy clothes and heavy make-up. Her lover was none other than my boss, the newspaper distributor Zhang Deshou. By then, Zhang was around twenty-two years old. He suffered from acne and had two gold teeth. While speaking or walking, he tried to imitate the coy, coquettish style of the well-known actor Xiao Cuihua.

The majority of customers in this small restaurant were poor — those who pedalled tricycles, water carters, vegetable sellers who carried a pair of baskets on a shoulder pole, peddlers who sold peanuts, watermelon seeds and cigarettes in small baskets, fortune-tellers, and chemists with trade banners selling rat poison. There were also occasional peasants and poor students. Whenever the woman couldn't manage the business by herself, Zhang would give her a hand, playing the role of waiter, either carrying plates or adding up the bills.

In my school, the food was revolting and the menu monotonous: steamed maize bread with vegetable soup. Sometimes meat would not be served for months at a time. Consequently, I was unable to bear it and decided to give myself a feast in the restaurant.

Although I had my breakfast there every morning, I hardly ever ordered a meal inside, and what's more, I usually ate standing at the entrance and then left in a hurry as soon as I'd put down my chopsticks.

One rainy day, when I stepped into the restaurant, I found no customers there except the woman and her lover Zhang. Sitting facing each other, they were having their meal: fried pork and pancakes and an egg soup.

"Hurry up, the food's getting cold!" Zhang urged his lover after he had eaten and drunk his fill, while picking his teeth with a match sliver. "Manager Liu has ordered a plate of *shijin* beancurd, I've got to take it to him quickly."

Just at that moment, I entered the restaurant.

"Oh, Little Scholar, what do you want to eat?" the woman asked while chewing the pancake.

"*Shijin* of beancurd!" With Zhang's voice ringing in my ears, I posed as an expert and ordered the same.

"Ten *jin* of beancurd! How the hell can you eat that much?"* Alarmed by my order, the woman widened her cherry-like eyes, straightened her neck and stopped swallowing the food in her mouth.

"If that fellow Liu can eat such a large amount of beancurd, so can I!"

Upon hearing this, the woman laughed so much that she spat her food all over Zhang's face. Splitting her sides, she exclaimed, "Good heavens, what a joke! Ten *jin* ... of beancurd, like a mountain. It'll surely ruin your ... small, white belly."

After hurriedly cleaning his face, Zhang was so angry that he turned to me, his teeth showing, snorting in contempt and smiling coldly. "What a shame! Fancy a little scholar like you, mixing up your words whenever you open your mouth. Remember, it's *shijin* beancurd, not *shi jin* of beancurd...!"

"Little Scholar. Ten *Jin* of Beancurd! Little Scholar. Ten *Jin* of Beancurd!" Clapping her hands and stamping her feet, the woman proprietor rocked with laughter.

Blushing, I fled. From then on, I was nicknamed "Ten *Jin* of Beancurd". Only after I finally left that place, did I succeed in ridding myself of it.

Opposite the small restaurant was the Jade Spring Teahouse, which consisted of a couple of rooms without partitions and holding twenty-eight square tables. The teahouse could seat more than one hundred customers at a time. Born into an old official family, the owner of this teahouse knew the rudiments of writing and took an interest in reading newspapers. Since I used to give him a free copy of a paper every morning on my way back to school, he allowed me to sell magazines in his teahouse. At the entrance hung a blackboard posted with playbills, announcing the two performances played every day. The one during the day featured the *Cases of Prefect Bao* performed by the celebrated Liu Jingting Junior, while at the night show *Strange Tales of Liaozhai* were recounted by the master story-teller Zhao Yingpo. The popular name of *Strange Tales of Liaozhai* was *The Stories of Ghosts and Fox-fairies*. Zhao was good at telling ghost stories

---

*The words *shijin* (mixed flavoured) and *shi jin* (ten *jin*) sound almost the same in Chinese, so the author mistook the name of this popular dish, ordering the quantity ten *jin* of beancurd.

and his narration was horrible and bloodcurdling. Some, while listening to his performance at night, would more often than not be so frightened that they would rather pee in their trousers than pluck up their courage to go outside. Nor did they dare go home without someone to accompany them. In a small alley, they would panic at the mere rustle of leaves in the wind. However, whenever Zhao performed in this teahouse, the audience, under the spell of his mastery, would never miss a chance to listen, even at the risk of peeing in their pants once again.

I had been addicted to listening to stories since I was six. Nearly every Sunday, immediately after I had sold my newspapers and magazines, I would spend my spare time in the Jade Spring Teahouse.

As a rule, before the performance began, on a small stage in the teahouse's hall was a desk on which lay wooden clappers and a folding fan. When the old wall clock began to strike eight o'clock, a waiter went to the small stage and hung in front of the desk a red curtain embroidered with the performer's name in big characters. As soon as he withdrew, there came a loud cough behind the curtain at the entrance to the stage, and the noise in the hall instantly died down. As Liu Jingting Junior raised the curtain, making his appearance on stage, the audiences applauded. Then, with a broad smile, he walked up to the front part of the stage, and made a deep bow to the audience, polite and relaxed. After that, he raised his head, straightened his back and quietly took his seat at the desk. Picking up the wooden clappers in two fingers and holding the folding fan in his right hand, he composed himself and cast a sweeping glance around the entire hall. Shortly afterwards, with a sudden strike of the wooden clappers on the desk, he commenced his performance in a tone neither fast nor slow, neither high nor low.

"Last time, the narration was suspended when I came to...." On account of his clear pronunciation and elegant tune, every word was filled with emotion, touching the hearts of the audience.

Craning my neck to look at the stage, I saw an emaciated man of about thirty-seven years old with short hair and dressed in a rather worn cloth gown. To tell the truth, there was really nothing extraordinary about him. He looked like an ordinary person.

In front of me, Zhang suddenly whispered in a low voice, "Amazing! This yellow-skinned skeleton has such a golden voice!" I saw that, sitting cross-legged, Zhang had fixed his shifty eyes on something behind the story-teller. Following his gaze, I spotted a young woman aged about twenty on a bench near a teapoy in front of the entrance to the stage.

Her skin was fair, her eyebrows drawn elegantly and her small mouth painted scarlet. She combed her hair back in the banana-like style quite fashionable at that time. Her lotus-pattern short jacket was unbuttoned as she nursed a baby girl, changing her breasts, as big as gourds, from right to left. She did it casually as if no one else was present.

"Who is that woman?" I asked Zhang in a low voice.

"Master Liu's wife," Zhang whispered in my ears, slobbering. "She's called Sweet Sister, the daughter of the teahouse owner. She's made Liu Jingting Junior earn a lot of money for her father."

Usually, whenever the first performance came to a close, Liu would leave the stage to take a rest, and then, rising to her feet, Sweet Sister would go to collect money from the audience with her baby in one hand and a small bamboo basket in the other.

"Is there anyone here who feels like being the first to give money?" In contrast to Master Liu's voice, this young woman sounded affected and sweet in spite of her big build.

Whenever I listened to Liu's story-telling, I noticed that it was always Zhang who first offered money generously. Smiling and grimacing, Zhang chucked a big banknote into the basket and said to her, "Take it and buy some tonic for your man!"

Sweet Sister spat at him on the spot, yet Zhang, shaking his head, seemed quite pleased, as if she had spat perfume.

Once the small basket was filled with coins and notes, she would go back to her seat and count it. Then Liu would resume his performance.

Sometimes, when the collection was taking place, some mean fellows would slip away and a few others would try to follow their example, throwing the entire hall into confusion.

"Now, now! Those who have money should help us, whereas those who have forgotten to bring any should assist us by standing still." In an attempt to maintain order, Sweet Sister went on explaining at the top of her voice, "So, gentlemen, you needn't be nervous even if you really haven't any money. Just sit still!" At this point her voice suddenly became sharp and hoarse. "Of course, that gentleman who left a moment ago had his reasons. Though as frightened as a stray cur, he is, in fact, a dutiful son. He hurried off to buy medicine for his sick mother. However, I think he ought to leave here openly. There was no need for him to slink out as he did. Otherwise, when he dashed out of the entrance, he might have collided with a tramcar."

The Jade Spring Teahouse was located at the entrance to Nanxiaojie Street and a tramcar was approaching with its noisy bell along the route inside Chaoyang Gate.

With a kind of irresistible magic force, Sweet Sister's words nailed the audience to their seats, though some of them had planned to steal away.

"Look at that woman. What a sharp tongue she has! She has cursed those stingy fellows in an ingenious way!" Zhang thought highly of her eloquence, and smiled broadly.

On one occasion, when the collection happened to be lower than usual, Sweet Sister insisted on keeping the audience waiting till they offered a bit more. Though Liu tried to go on stage several times, he was driven back by his wife's glowering looks.

Feeling sorry for him and impatient to listen to the rest of the story, I fished out the money earned from my magazines that day and handed it to Sweet Sister.

"Thank you very much!" she said as she beamed at me. "Just look, though he normally stands to listen, this little scholar is so generous that he would even cut off his own flesh if necessary. I dare say he'll become a Number One Scholar or obtain a doctor's degree!"

Upon hearing this compliment, I was so embarrassed that sweat beaded my face.

I was about to leave after the performance when Liu called out suddenly, "Little Scholar, wait a minute, please!"

"What's the matter, Master Liu?" I asked him, halting.

He took out a banknote from Sweet Sister's small bamboo basket and walked up to me, saying, "Take your money back! Keep it and buy some books for yourself." Though Sweet Sister rolled her eyes, he pretended to have seen nothing.

Greatly embarrassed, I hurried away.

"Ten *Jin* of Beancurd! How can you be so ungrateful to Master Liu!" Zhang grabbed the money from the story-teller. Catching up with me, he grasped one of my hands, urging, "Quick, let's go and have a plate of *shijin* beancurd!"

Zhang pulled me along till we reached the small restaurant, and the money thus landed in his lover's wallet.

On the following Sunday, I went to the teahouse again. At the sight of my entrance, Sweet Sister nodded, giving me special treatment: she not only invited me to sit next to her, but also poured me a bowl of strong tea. When the first performance came to an end, she put her daughter in my arms, saying, "Little Scholar, please hold Rong'er for a while!" Then, taking up her small bamboo basket, she began collecting money from the audience.

Rong'er, whose pet name was Niuniu, had a small pigtail standing upright in the centre of her head and a pair of lovely round, dark eyes, looking like two fresh grapes. Oddly, the baby didn't react to me as a stranger. But she eventually wet my pants, and they were soaked as if they had just been washed.

On that day, I played the role of Sweet Sister's baby-sitter, so that she had time to give her father a hand pouring tea, boiling water or soliciting customers.

It was getting darker and darker. As Rong'er was as heavy as a small stone roller, I grew exhausted and dizzy. Then Liu's loud voice suddenly boomed into my ears, "Immediately after his master, Prefect Bao, had ordered tea, Bao Xing went out of the chamber with a teapot in his hand. Walking through the winding corridor, he came to the kitchen. But as soon as he pulled aside the door curtain, he exclaimed, '*Aiya!*' If you want to know what happened next, please come again tomorrow, and I'll explain it in detail." With a flourish of his wooden clappers, Liu ended his performance.

This episode made me nervous. Bao Xing had gasped when he raised the door curtain. What had he seen? Was there an assassin bursting through the window with a sharp sword? Or did someone throw a man's head into the kitchen, the blood still dripping?

"Master Liu, what did Bao Xing see?" I inquired impatiently when the story-teller left his seat and came down from the small stage.

However, instead of answering my question right away, Master Liu took the towel handed him by Sweet Sister and cleaned his face calmly. Beaming, he replied in a low and soft voice, "Don't worry, Little Scholar, it's nothing serious!"

As I insisted on being told, Sweet Sister, a bit annoyed, snapped at me, "He's just stopping the story at a climax to keep the audience in suspense. Don't spoil our business!"

I had no choice but to go back to school distracted.

That night, I tossed and turned: The first half I suffered from insomnia, while in the latter half I had a nightmare. I had not even calmed down when I came back to school soon after selling my newspapers, so I asked leave on the pretext of having a stomach ache. No sooner had the bell begun to ring than I sneaked out of the school gate.

As I reached the entrance to the teahouse, I heard Liu just begin to return to his story. "Last time, I'd stopped at the point where, ordered by his master Prefect Bao to make some tea, Bao Xing went to the kitchen with a teapot in his hand, but, no sooner had he raised the door curtain than he exclaimed in alarm, '*Aiya!*' Well...." Blinking his eyes, Liu paused for a while as I entered.

All at once, my heart sprang into my mouth.

What did he mean? What had happened? Staring at Liu, I thought over and over again that it must be an assassin, or a man's head dripping with blood.

To my surprise Liu answered the riddle, "The water on the stove hadn't boiled yet!"

At this, the whole hall rocked with laughter. Some, overwhelmed with admiration at his superb skill, thumped the tables and shouted "Bravo", whereas I felt as if I had been made fun of. Greatly disappointed, I left the teahouse, returning to school with tears streaming down my face. What lousy luck! When I reached school, the supervisor was standing in front of the gate looking stern. He questioned me, and I confessed my misconduct. I had made a fool of myself. It was noted down that I had cut two classes and I was publicly warned at morning assembly. From then on, I avoided the teahouse, and I never met with Master Liu, Sweet Sister and their daughter Niuniu again.

After thirty-four years, I felt that past life belonged to another world.

3

I stood under the shade of the scholar trees together with Master Liu, who was now seventy years old.

"What have you been doing all these years?" I asked him impatiently.

"It's hard to explain in a few words!" He sighed and his shining eyes suddenly grew dim. "When you have some time, I'll tell you in detail the story of my family's separations and reunions over the years."

"Please visit me at home after four o'clock!" As I crossed the stone step in front of my door, I halted, adding, "I've finished another novelette entitled *The Lotus in the Breeze*, in which both Yi Taixi and Huo Shaoyun are mentioned."

"Oh, them. I'm quite familiar with them!" A trace of a smile appeared on the old man's sad face. "Yi Taixi was my senior fellow apprentice, while Huo Shaoyun, who took Yun Zheyue as his teacher, calls me uncle."

"Be sure to come this afternoon!" After urging him once more, I entered my courtyard.

When I awoke from my noontime nap, there was no one else at home, for all the others had gone either to work or school. The branches and leaves of the five date trees in my courtyard were so thick that they looked like an umbrella. I placed two rattan chairs and a round table in their shade and prepared a pot of green tea before I watered the flowers as I waited for Liu's arrival.

At four o'clock sharp I heard footsteps outside my door. I hurried to welcome him, but instead of Liu my visitor was a woman of thirty-five or so.

Tall and slender, with a pale complexion, sad eyes and two pigtails, though her hair had been permed, she wore a white blouse embroidered with light golden flowers and a black skirt. She seemed to be in mourning, but for whom?

Before I had time to open my mouth, she smiled shyly, asking, "Are you Comrade Liu?"

Nodding my head, I asked in reply, "May I know your name?"

"I'm Xu Rong." She was on the verge of tears. The daughter of Liu Jingting Junior.

"So you're Niuniu!" I exclaimed.

"Yes, I am." She lowered her head bashfully. "My father told me that when I was a baby you used to listen to his story-telling and hold me in your arms."

"Come in and sit down, please!" Recalling the old days, I was deeply moved. "Why hasn't your father come with you?"

"Oh, he's gone to hospital to see my mother." Standing motionless, Xu Rong lowered her eyes. "He said he would come to visit you tomorrow."

"What's wrong with your mother?"

"Cancer of the esophagus. She may not live till tomorrow."

I was startled to hear this. I sighed and asked her sadly, "Did your mother suffer a lot in the countryside these past years?"

"She divorced my father twenty-five years ago, but she's been living all the time in the city...." While speaking, Xu Rong looked miserable, tears streaming down her face.

"Why did they divorce?"

"My mother got involved with a scoundrel, and then it was too late."

Then Xu Rong made to leave. As I did not want to press her to stay, I had no alternative but to see her off. While walking with her, I asked her, "Where are you working?"

"At a street-run toy factory."

"What does your husband do?"

"He died long ago."

Upon hearing this, I felt sad again. Who would have thought that little Niuniu, whom I used to hold in my arms thirty-four years ago, would have met with such a tragic fate!

When we reached the door of a neighbouring courtyard, Xu Rong took out her handkerchief to wipe away the tears from her eyes. It had not occurred to me that my little Niuniu's home was so close to mine.

That evening, concerned about Liu, Niuniu and her mother Sweet Sister, who was probably also fifty-eight years old now, I crossed the threshold of a neighbouring courtyard for the first time in my twenty-five years in this small lane.

The appearance of this courtyard had changed completely. There were small, low houses that looked like dovecotes, and it was difficult to find a way through them. The whole place was full of children weeping, adults shouting, the clatter of dishes and bowls, the raucous mixed music of Beijing opera, a TV play, assorted songs and a chorus from TV sets, radios and tape recorders. What a row! When I inquired where Xu Rong lived, someone indicated with his lips that she lived in a side room at the back of the courtyard.

The side room was, in fact, a very small, narrow and shabby one hidden in an innermost corner. Yet despite the small size, Xu Rong had set up in front of her home a wire fence and a wooden gate. The fence was sparsely covered with ivy which brought a bit of vitality to the place.

"Is Comrade Xu Rong at home?" I inquired, standing at the gate.

"Who's there?" The light in the house was suddenly switched off.

"It's me, Old Liu."

"Oh, wait a minute!"

"Has your father come back from the hospital?"

"No. He didn't want to leave my mother."

"Then I'll come again tomorrow!" As it was suffocating in this crowded compound, I hurried back to the street, breathing the fresh air.

Once out of the north entrance to Green Vine Lane, I turned into Fuyou Street. Instead of returning home right away, I continued to stroll along the pavement under the dim streetlights slanting down through branches and leaves of the trees by the roadside.

Before I could walk far, Xu Rong chased after and finally caught up with me.

"I'm going to the hospital." While buttoning up her blouse, she ran with quick, short steps. "Would you like me to give a message to my father?"

I stopped and said, "What worries me most is your mother's condition."

"I'm afraid she won't last the night!" Xu Rong was choking with sobs. "When my father arrived at her bedside, she was already unable to speak, let alone raise her hands. She just weeps."

Then we began to walk together.

"Why did they get divorced?" I asked.

Xu Rong sighed. "Soon after Liberation, my maternal grandfather died, so the Jade Spring Teahouse became my mother's property. Originally my father had made up his mind to join a folk art troupe, but my mother disagreed with him, insisting that the teahouse would profit by his remaining there. Being progressive in his views, my father decided to tell a story reflecting contemporary life. But, the novel from which he adapted this story was written by a writer who later was labelled a Rightist. So my father got involved in this problem, and was punished along with the writer. Fearing that the teahouse would be confiscated and that we would lose our livelihood, my mother readily placed her confidence in a scoundrel and divorced my father. As I was only eleven the court decided I should live with her."

"How did your father end up at Green Poplar Village?"

"He sought refuge with his apprentice He Chuansheng, and ever since then he has lived there, more than twenty-five years in all."

"Why didn't I ever hear about this?"

"In 1951, when my father went on tour to several places, he accepted He Chuansheng as an apprentice, but my mother abused him, so the boy left before his apprenticeship was finished."

"Are there any others at his home? As an outsider, how could your father stay there all the time?"

"Chuansheng was an orphan. Only his grandparents lived with him. When my father went there, Chuansheng got a father and his grandparents another son. All four got on very well together."

"This He Chuansheng seems a loyal friend." I praised him, but after thinking for a while, I realized there was something strange about it. "With only four of them that means He Chuansheng never got married?"

"He was married, but out of consideration for my father he divorced his wife." At this point, Xu Rong began to sob once again. "She was so selfish and used to snub my father, banging bowls down loudly or hinting bad things about him. Unable to endure it any longer, Chuansheng decided to divorce her."

"I'm going back home the day after tomorrow, so I'll go and visit your friend Chuansheng."

"But he's in Beijing at present."

"Where's he staying? I'll go and see him right away."

"Since he accompanied my father here, he's been staying at a small hotel in Xiheyan Street outside the Qianmen Gate." Xu Rong paused and then went on, "He's worried about my father so he's keeping him company at the hospital. I'll tell him to call on you as soon as possible."

"Your father's a fine man!" I sighed. "He's not bitter and still tries his best to be with your mother on her deathbed. You should show more respect for him than even He Chuansheng has."

"Oh, no, it was my mother who wanted to see my father." Xu Rong wept some more. "Realizing she was dying she longed to see my father once again. As soon as they received my telegram, my father and Chuansheng rushed here, arriving the day before yesterday."

"But why did they meet only today?"

"Because my stepfather forbade them to meet before."

"How narrow-minded of him!"

"He's a beast!" Xu Rong snapped. "The dirty swine made a false charge against my father twenty-five years ago, and then he mistreated me eleven years later."

My heart pounded. "What happened?"

"Several years ago while working as a buyer for a street-run factory, apart from having some political problems before Liberation, he was also guilty of corruption. So in an attempt to join a so-called revolutionary organization during the 'cultural revolution', he forced me to marry its leader, a man twenty years older than I."

"When did your husband die?"

"Soon after he was promoted to leader of the public security section of the industrial administrative office of our district. The people's government discovered that he had murdered three people in the past, so they went to arrest him. Frantic with worry, he died from a cerebral hemorrhage within a few hours."

"Then how was your parents' reunion arranged today?"

"Chuansheng gave my stepfather one thousand yuan, so we bought the right to their meeting!" Filled with anger and hatred, Xu Rong trembled. "You know that scoundrel pretended that because of my mother's hospitalization he had spent one thousand yuan in medical bills, so if my father wanted to meet her, he had to pay. Chuansheng was furious but went home, got all his savings, which he'd accumulated bit by bit to build a house of his own, and gave them all to that rat."

"But you should stand up to him!"

"He's a creep and his superiors think highly of him."

"Anyway, you can take him to court. I'll find a lawyer for you."

By then we'd reached the north entrance of Fuyou Street where a trolleybus was about to stop. Xu Rong ran to board the one going to the hospital. Gazing after her, I felt very upset. Liu, He Chuansheng and Niuniu had been bullied by that bastard, yet, I, an outsider, would never stomach such treatment. I am a born meddler. Sure enough, once a lawsuit was filed, we could settle matters in court.

4

The next afternoon I was sleeping on my bed. All of a sudden, I was awakened by someone pounding at my door. Putting on a jacket, I rushed to open it.

Xu Rong was there, wearing a black armband.

"Is your mother...?" Though it was to be expected, I was upset when I saw her in mourning.

"Please help us sort things out now!" she asked in tears. "That beast insists on keeping my mother's ashes."

Hurriedly buttoning up my shirt, I went to the neighbouring courtyard again.

At this, the inhabitants of those honeycomb-like houses poked their heads out of their windows and stared at the small side room. Close behind me, Xu Rong dared not raise her head, and she seemed to tremble.

"My master wants to have the ashes of my mistress!" An angry voice exclaimed from the window of the side room. "Are you going to give them to him? Yes or no?"

"Help!" someone shouted in a voice just like the squeal of a pig about to be slaughtered.

Xu Rong gave me a push and we rushed to the gate together and saw a middle-aged man brandishing a kitchen knife in one hand and grasping the front of a wretched old man's jacket with the other.

"Let him go, Chuansheng!" Xu Rong shouted. "Here's Comrade Liu. He'll settle the problem fairly. Let him judge the case for us!"

The middle-aged man put the kitchen knife down on a chopping block.

"I don't care who's here. If a person has an offensive weapon, it's proof enough that he wishes to resort to violence. Let's go to the police station!" Picking up an oil-stained handbag, the old man rose to his feet, ready to go.

"Don't move!" He Chuansheng barred his way.

"Sit down! None of you is allowed to raise a hand to fight!" I shouted from the fence. "There's a saying, 'With justice on your side, you can go anywhere; without it, you can't take a single step.' Now, who wants to speak first?"

"How ashamed I feel!" Standing woodenly, Liu wept. "While on her sickbed, Rong'er's mother often said that, after her death, her ashes should be given to me. But ... but Zhang Deshou wants more money for them."

"Zhang Deshou? Zhang Deshou?" Pulling aside the ivy, I put my head through and looked around.

"That's me!" the old man answered, nodding his head.

In spite of his changed appearance due to age, I recognized at first glance from the speaker's crafty eyes and gestures that this was none other than my old newspaper distributor. I smiled coldly and asked, "Zhang Deshou, do you recognize me?"

"What's your name then?"

"Ten *Jin* of Beancurd!"

"This man's an out-and-out scoundrel!" Filled with indignation, He Chuansheng declared. "He forced my master to pay him one thousand yuan for medical expenses, and now he wants five hundred yuan for the ashes. Is there any humanity in him?"

"Anyway, Sweet Sister was my wife, alive or dead!" Trembling on his sorghum-like thin legs, Zhang stamped his feet. "If I give him her ashes, that means I'm a cuckold. No. I won't do it for nothing!"

"But, Zhang Deshou, you're going too far!" With that, I turned round to ask Xu Rong, "Did your mother leave a will?"

"A few days before she died, I borrowed a tape-recorder and recorded all she said."

"Good! Play it right now."

Xu Rong went into the inner room and returned with a tape-recorder. As soon as she put the cassette in the machine, the conversation that had taken place several days ago between Sweet Sister and her daughter was heard.

"Niuniu...." The sick mother gasped for breath at almost every other word. "I'm dying.... Probably, I can't live much longer.... You see ... I've so much ... to say to you!"

"Mum, don't worry, you take it easy and stay here, and you'll get better soon," Xu Rong cried in a low voice.

"Everybody must die. Now, my time has come...." The old woman struggled for words. "All my life, I've only done one thing that weighs on my conscience. I treated your father unfairly.... Do you still remember him?"

"How can I forget my own father?"

"Try to find him for me! I want to see him. How I wish that he could beat or curse me! This is the only way I can die in peace."

"But no one knows where he is."

"I think ... perhaps, he might have gone to He Chuansheng's home. But I'm not sure if he's still alive."

"Why do you think he went to live with him?"

"Because Chuansheng always respected his elders and superiors. How sorry I am now that I.... You see, I thought he was stupid, so I used to beat him...."

"Where does he live?"

"At Green Poplar Village along the canal."

"I'll write to him immediately."

"Hurry!... I miss your father so much. I long to see him.... Give him my ashes...."

"I'll send him a telegram right now."

As Sweet Sister gasped, the tape made a noise.

"What a damned bitch! Uttering a pack of lies even as she lay dying!" Zhang butted in, taking advantage of the pause.

"Shut up!" yelled Chuansheng.

"Rong'er, after I pass away...." The old woman resumed her speech with difficulty, "You must go back to your father! Zhang Deshou ... is a beast, simply a beast!" The speaker stopped to catch her breath. "When he fell out with that woman who owned the small restaurant immediately after Liberation, he came to kowtow to us, begging us to hire him as a waiter in our teahouse. Your father felt sorry for him and agreed. Who would have thought that ... in 1957 he lied to hurt your father, and later on, with sweet words tricked me? He did us all great harm and broke up our family."

"Damned bitch! Damned bitch!" Zhang grabbed the machine, exclaiming, "I'll smash this along with the ashes of that damned bitch!"

"Give them to me!" Xu Rong shouted grieved. "Give me my mother's ashes!"

When He Chuansheng turned round to pick up the kitchen knife again, I stopped him with one hand and pointed at Zhang with the other. "How dare you behave like a brute? Once Xu Rong files her lawsuit, I'll be her witness in court!"

Zhang smiled wryly, saying, "Rong'er, if you want the ashes, how can I refuse you? But, you must give the tape to me."

"All right! All right!" Xu Rong promised him, confused.

"No, don't!" I told her. "This is proof of his crimes."

"Give it to him and get him out of my sight!" Waving his hand, Liu spoke in a weak voice. "If he remains here longer, I'll die of disgust."

So, an exchange was made of the tape for the ashes.

"Comrade Liu, thank you for helping us!" Zhang bowed and smiled in a sinister way. "We've been friends for decades. If you have time, will you do me the honour of visiting my humble home for a chat? I'll entertain you with a dish of *shijin* beancurd, with a true Beijing flavour like in the old days."

With that he left.

"Comrade Liu, thank you for coming to our rescue and settling the problem!" His eyes brimming with tears, He Chuansheng clasped my hands.

Silence reigned in the narrow, small courtyard. Only then did I take a long look at He Chuansheng. He was five or six years younger than I. Though he was a peasant, his appearance and manners were more elegant than mine, perhaps because he had once been apprenticed to a story-teller. He acted just like a country school teacher both in speech and manner.

Ashamed at his gratitude, I hastened to say, "Don't mention it. I only put in a word or two for you. I'm a writer, with no power, so what great role could I play?"

"In fact, even if you hadn't appeared, I wouldn't have dared kill him." He smiled. "I just wanted to frighten the bastard, but if he was obstinate, I'd have given him the five hundred yuan in my pocket."

"It seems that your family is the most prosperous one in Green Poplar Village, otherwise how can you afford to throw your money away like that?"

"That's not true. But in the past two years, we villagers have all become richer. My family's just average."

"You've proved a loyal friend," I praised him, patting him on the shoulder. "I'll urge the county broadcasting station to interview you."

"Oh no, don't do that, please!" He blushed at once. "In fact, if you'd like to visit us and see how Mr Liu has been a good son to my grandparents, you'll realize I've still a long way to go."

"Learn all the fine skills of your master."

"You know, I was only his apprentice for less than two years. I can't learn all his skills completely." Shaking his head, He Chuansheng took out the five hundred yuan from his pocket. "I've wanted for a long time to buy a tape-recorder and some cassettes to record all my master's skill so they won't be lost for ever."

"That's a good idea!" I exclaimed in delight. "I'll ask the county cultural bureau to get some cadres to help you write them down."

"There's no need for that." He spoke as if he had already a plan. "I can do it by myself."

"But your education...." I wondered whether he clung to the traditional idea that a performer in the old society preferred to keep his own rough manuscript to himself rather than hand it over to others.

"But Chuansheng has some education!" Sitting all the while with his eyes closed, Liu suddenly opened them. "Soon after being driven away by

Rong'er's mother, he returned home and went to primary school and then junior middle school. But because I went to live at his home, he gave up his original plan to take the entrance examination for senior middle school. So, he lost the chance to go to university...."

"My master encouraged me not to abandon my studies." He Chuansheng blushed and added, "Old Liu, forgive me if I've offended you, but I've adapted your novelettes for story-telling."

"Wonderful. How kind of you!" I was overjoyed at this news. "When do you plan to return home?"

"Well...." He Chuansheng exchanged a glance with Liu and went on, "We thought we'd leave tomorrow."

"Then, let's go together!" I issued an order. "Niuniu, you'd better ask for leave to spend some days in Green Poplar Village. It will broaden your horizons."

At half past eight the next morning, a Beijing jeep came to drive me to the countryside and I took Old Liu, He Chuansheng and Xu Rong with me as well. Leaving the south entrance to Fuyou Street, we passed Chang'an Street, Tiananmen, Wangfujing, the railway station and Jianguo Gate. As soon as we were beyond the city wall, the jeep sped along the highway from Beijing to Tianjin, taking only two hours to reach our destination.

Sitting in the jeep, I had time to think. Before getting out I had already made my decision.

Being meddlesome by nature, I liked very much the idea of playing the role of matchmaker!

1983

Translated by Hu Zhihui

The Last Angler

●

—— LI HANGYU ——

Born in Hangzhou in 1957, Li Hangyu worked first as a farmer and then as a motor mechanic after graduating from junior middle school. In 1977 he was admitted to the Chinese Department of Hangzhou University, and on graduation he became an editor at a county broadcasting station. He began to publish short stories in 1979. His collections of short stories "The Last Angler", "The Old Customs of Brick Stove Beach" and "At the Corner of Human Society" all have a strong local flavour.

AT sundown, Fukui remembered that he should check his fish hooks. He crawled out of his boat shelter, stood on the slope of the dyke and, full of anticipation, inhaled the salty breeze like a homeless dog sniffing food. His nose seemed to be able to tell if there were big fish on his hooks.

Over the ditch below the dyke he had built a boat shelter, which looked from afar like a local tomb, for the deceased were not buried underground but had waist-high little brick tombs with tiled roofs and little windows — it made the living green with envy. Fukui's boat shelter was thatched. Poor as he was, he would never have such a nice abode at his death. He would go to the other world on a straw mat.

Of course he did not expect to die for a long time yet, as he was as strong and healthy as an old turtle. Though fifty, he was as much a rake as in his youth and could still take some loose woman as his lover. Muscles bulged on his broad tanned back, like an unevenly planed door plank, with a deep red scar below his right shoulder like the handle. The scar had been made by the sharp point of a pole in a fight over a net.

With a jar of earthworms in his hand, Fukui strode over the sandy bank to reach the river. He was stripped to the waist and wore a pair of big loose shorts of home-spun cloth in a tiny floral pattern, so big and breezy that he felt as cool as if he were naked while he walked. He liked to sleep in the buff too — very comfortable and pleasant. This pair of shorts had been given to him by No. 7, who would have married him had he not been so poor that he had to ask her for them. He was her first lover in her widowhood.

The ebbing tide had beached his boat. His big bare feet, tramping over the soft sand, still hot from the day's sun, did not feel the heat for their soles were as thick as if shoemakers had reinforced them with extra leather. He picked up a rope tied to a hole in a plank of the boat and hauled it into the water.

The boat's flat bottom was not much bigger than Fukui's big body. Lying on his back he used to think that it would make a suitable coffin. All it needed was a lid.

He gave it a shove, lay down in the stern and, lifting his hairy thick legs, began rowing with his feet. All anglers on the Gejiang River did that, to free their hands to cast a net or pull in the hooks. Big as bear's paws, Fukui's feet were as nimble as a cat's. His toes, huge like mushrooms, clamped around the oars, his legs bending and stretching, the oars rising and falling....

The setting sun seemed to have cast a handful of gold coins on the water. The river was gilded.

The boat reached the middle of the river. Not far away was a big red-and-white striped bamboo float. There were eight altogether spaced out every thirty metres or so. They were attached to the rolling hooks Fukui had placed there more than two hours ago. He rowed harder and brought his boat over to the first one.

The hooks were set with the current and Fukui began collecting from the first one. On one end of a nylon rope, as thick as a single wire, was a big stone. The rope, with the help of the floats, rose slantingly to the surface. Every three to five feet was a smaller float from which hung a hook ranging from two or three metres to a dozen metres in depth, for the different shoals of fish. The rolling hooks were bigger than those used on fishing rods and thus caught bigger fish. Once a fish bit, it would pull the float down so the angler knew which one to haul up and which to leave. If an extra big carp struggled vigorously, the rest of the hooks would converge. The more it struggled, the more hooks it would draw. These hooks were really formidable.

Regrettably, these hooks could exercise their prowess less and less as pollution was increasing and the anglers fished ruthlessly, not waiting for the fry to grow and the fish to spawn. By now fish had become so scarce in the river that their number was probably smaller than that sold at the West Stream free market. Big ones were a rarity.

Fukui sailed along the floats, a few of which were bobbing up and down, half-submerged in the water. To his annoyance, he got a few butterfish weighing less than half a catty each. He could have got more with a net. It didn't pay to set the rolling hooks for such small fry.

Nowadays even the fish were smart. Small butterfish would dive down and bite his hooks. It was something he couldn't fathom. He replaced the fish with earthworms.

On the west bank a woman walked down the quay onto a sampan, heading in his direction. Her body swayed as she rowed. Even from a distance Fukui could tell it was No. 7 and he knew that she had come from Guanfa's place.

The west bank, the southern outskirts of Binzhou, the provincial capital, was a large residential area and an ideal place for a sanitorium with its beautiful scenery. Some years ago, there were around a hundred anglers on this stretch of the river among whom seventy lived in Xiaochai. Throughout the year, they moored there, fishing early morning and evening, and selling their catch to the people of West Stream Village nearby, while during the day, they mended nets and sorted out their rolling hooks. What a happy life that had been! The river teemed with fish, Fukui's pot was filled with wine and on the bunk in the boat was a little woman with big breasts and a large bottom. Her cursing had sounded like music to his ears. That was the life. Most important, Fukui was a respected, handsome man. With the prestige he enjoyed, he was complacent too. He was the only one on the west bank who was never addressed by the slightly derogatory term "angler". He had even made friends with a VIP from the sanitorium whom Guanfa brought to him, who chose several big fish he had just caught. That gave him a chance to chat and drink with the man.

Guanfa, a cook in the sanitorium, came from Xiaochai Village. He was a useful person to the anglers of Xiaochai who looked upon him as a powerful person and gave him a few fish now and then. His neighbours envied his constant supply of free fish. Then people began to ask him to buy fish for them and he readily complied, having a sense of responsibility and being willing to help whenever he could. His importance was not felt at first as the river was teeming with fish and he was always able to satisfy the needs of all the residents, except once or twice during bad weather. Then, as the fish decreased year by year, the stalls in the market sold their supplies in less time than it took to smoke a cigarette. Guanfa began to be busy. He banned the stalls and made all the anglers give him their fish, so he decided the prices and the buyers as if he were the state price control organization. In the course of time people gave this "helpful" person a bad name — the fish despot.

Fukui and Guanfa were cousins and had been good friends. In recent years, business between Guanfa and him had slackened because he, the last and only angler in Xiaochai Village, had no luck fishing. Guanfa was no longer a fish despot. No. 7's crawling from his bed to Guanfa's had embarrassed both of them. Guanfa was apologetic while Fukui felt he had been humiliated. Thus they drifted apart.

As the boat came closer he could make out the blue dots on her brand-new white blouse.

Some time ago he had heard that No. 7 often stayed the night at Guanfa's. He remained dubious. No. 7 was forty years old. Ten years ago, when her husband was drowned, she had meant to remarry, but had not found a suitable mate. Slanderous remarks about her were not reliable since she had a bad reputation and the villagers liked to gossip about her. But today, he had seen with his own eyes her coming from the west bank in an attractive blouse as if she were still a young girl.... So the rumours were probably eighty per cent true. There's no smoke without fire.

He suddenly felt a weight under the line in his hand. Before he could pull up the fish, No. 7, drawing abreast, jeered, "Oh, Fukui." She pointed at the heap of little butterfish in his boat. "What a size! it must be your lucky day," she said giggling.

Fukui reddened, regretting that he hadn't thought of covering them with his straw hat. Catching such tiddlers was mortifying, like a useless dog stealing chicks to fill his stomach. And he particularly hated to lose face before her. He lowered his head and gathered the line hesitantly, hoping that fate would be merciful.

"Oh, it's a shad," No. 7 cried, her eyes bulging with excitement. "Goodness me, the Dragon King must have done this. Your luck's certainly changed. No one has seen a shad in this river for years. I almost forgot what it looks like. My, it weighs at least three catties.... Didn't I say you'd be lucky today?"

"I'm not an idiot." Fukui was pleased too. "You were being sarcastic."

"Certainly not. I meant to drive away your ill fortune."

"What a liar!"

"Of course. My appearing here brought you luck. Even before I finished what I was saying, this big fellow popped up. Don't be ungrateful, Fukui. You owe me something."

Fukui replaced his hooks, brought around his boat and headed for home with No. 7 rowing beside him. He had not checked the rest of the hooks though some of them seemed to have fish at the end. He believed like other anglers that after an exceptionally good catch he must stop to avoid changing his luck. He should save that for the next time.

"The shad's worth more than ten yuan, Fukui."

"I'm not selling it."

"You're not?"

"I'm going to eat it myself." He meant it. He hadn't had a shad for at least five years. When he pulled it out of the water he couldn't believe his eyes. Gechuan River was famous for its shad. Tender and delicious, they sold for at least three yuan a catty in the free market. He would be rolling in money if he could catch one every day. Just one. Regrettably it was a rarity now, almost extinct. He wondered how this one had sneaked in. He would enjoy it all by himself.... Maybe he should invite No. 7?... Look, how her mouth was watering. Just like a cat....

Fukui stared at No. 7's swaying bottom. She was rowing standing up, her sampan abreast of his boat. As before, he was lying in the stern rowing with his feet, his head turned towards her bottom. She had lived with him for eight years, at first in secret of course. She wouldn't let him stay overnight for her son watched her carefully. When his father died, Baozi was a big boy. She was only sixteen years old when she had become a mother, still a slip of a girl. She didn't want to act wantonly under her son's nose. After he married and had a home of his own and because her reputation was already bad, she openly kept Fukui as her lover, sleeping together every night and going places as man and wife, though they did not refer to each other as this in public. The villagers accepted them and waited for their wedding. Although it would be a second marriage for both, there would still be wine and food.

"Why are you staring at me? Haven't I got pants on?"

Fukui turned away. He couldn't understand what magic No. 7 possessed, giving him funny ideas at his age. If they had not been on the water, he would have thrown her on the ground and threatened her with his fist. "Marry me, No. 7, stop fooling around with Guanfa. I'm getting on. It's too lonely fishing on the river. Keep me company."

Instead, he said, "How is Guanfa these days?"

"How did you know I'd been to Guanfa's?"

He hummed and hawed. He was jealous. That looked bad in a man of his age. What was the matter, he scolded himself. Had he never touched a woman before?

"He's recovering." No. 7 told him. "But he's unhappy. He can't be a fish despot any more since most of the anglers in our village have turned to farming. He's like a baby without milk. Formerly, in the eyes of the villagers, Guanfa was as important as the head of the sanitorium. Now, he's as worthless as dog's dung. He's retired because of his health. Alone at home with nothing to do, he drinks all day. His face is sunken.... He needs a woman to look after him." She stopped rowing, straightened up and said hesitantly, "Fukui, there's something I want to talk to you about...."

"What?" His legs stopped. The boat was left to take its own course.

"After my son got married, I felt lonely.... Guanfa wants me to be with him."

He almost cried out, "Aren't I lonely? I need a woman too...." But he realized at once he couldn't compete with Guanfa who, being a government employee, had a pension while he didn't even have a presentable home.

"I've no secrets from you. You've been kind to me for many years."

"It's none of my business." Fukui became angry. "You can marry whoever you like."

"Don't lose your temper." No. 7 was annoyed too. She let go of her oar and stood arms akimbo, ready for a fight. "I've treated you well. I was thirty when my husband died and I waited for you for ten years. I've not expected much, only that you could save some money, build a house and lead a man's life. But you wouldn't listen to me. You're stubborn, sticking to this river as if it were your father's grave. Those fry you catch can't even feed a cat. And see how poor you are, can't even buy yourself a pair of shorts. You're not ashamed to wear the ones your lover gave you. By not listening to me, you've become even poorer. Yet you still dare to be rude to me? I can't be your lover for life.... Why don't you build a house, send a match-maker and marry me."

"You think I'm too poor." He felt wronged.

"So what? You deserve it. Poverty's nothing honourable like in the past. Why can't you get rich, Fukui, when others can? Try and get rich." She put down her arms and took up the oar again. "To tell you the truth, I hate poverty. I've suffered all my life. Now I want to live a little. I don't want to sleep in your shed and have nothing to eat."

Fukui did not reply. Despondently he rowed his boat. As the sky darkened, a grey mist rose from the river to wash out the colour from the sky and land.

"When are you going there?" he inquired.

"Soon. But before I go I want to do you a favour." She threw him a loving glance, hating to part from him. "You've helped me bring up my son, Fukui. I owe you something."

"Forget it." He felt better now. She hadn't forgotten their past love.

"When I marry, the commune monosodium glutamate factory will need a new monitor. I've talked to the group leader who has agreed to give you my place. It will be yours if you'll just mention this to Dagui. The work's easy and you'll have a stable income. It's more reliable than fishing on this empty river. Listen to me, Fukui. One needs something more solid when one gets old."

Dagui was a member of the commune managing committee and the son of one of Fukui's cousins. But Fukui had never asked favours from him.

They came to the bank. It was three more li along East Stream to Xiaochai Village. Fukui moored his boat in his shelter. No. 7 was rowing home in her sampan. After he had secured it, he put the shad and the butterfish into a creel and climbed up the dyke to walk home. He soon caught up with No. 7.

"Come and eat the shad with me, No. 7."

"OK. See you later." She laughed.

Fukui quickened his steps. He must make haste and prepare the fish. The best way to cook it was to steam it with a few spring onions. Passing by a vegetable garden he grabbed some and broke them into inch-long bits as he hurried on.

Xiaochai Village sprawled out on the north bank of East Stream. Across the arched bridge was Dachai Village, which was growing into a town as the commune offices were located there. Along both banks fishing boats were moored higgledy-piggledy like corpses strewn on the ground. Most of the boats were never used, some were rotting or in pieces, others were overgrown with moss and barnacles as if they had been there for hundreds of years.

Fukui's hand stank of fish. When he reached home, the spring onions smelled as if they had already been cooked with the fish.

His home was a bamboo and straw shed, while others lived in tiled-roof houses or thatched huts. His was worse than a hut or even the pigsties of the rich. As Fukui shoved open the door with his shoulder, the door frame came crashing down almost braining him. Closing the door was no easy matter either. He tossed the creel to the ground, held the half-rotten frame in place with one foot and pushed the door to. He couldn't leave it open as the mosquitoes would devour him at night since he had no net.

It was getting late. He should quickly gut and wash the fish. Sitting on a big tree stump beside his water vat, he scaled it. He had two rooms, a bedroom and a kitchen where he cooked and ate. He had no other needs besides food and sleep. The kitchen was cluttered with all sorts of junk. Torn fishing nets adorned the walls, spotted fungi grew under the west wall. A fat black cat sat on his stove, staring calmly at the big fish in his hands. The cat lived well, having lots of fish to eat and no work to do, since Fukui was so poor that even mice disdained to call.

A spider zoomed down from the roof and landed on the tip of his nose. Feeling it tickle, he brushed his nose with his hand and the spider shot up again.

Suddenly he heard the chugging of a mini-tractor approaching and stopping at his door.

It was Dagui, who blared like a trumpet the minute he made his entrance. "Good for you, uncle. No. 7 told me you caught a shad. It's been years since I tasted one. They don't live in the fishpond I've contracted from the brigade. But thanks to you, I'll have a taste of it today."

Reluctantly, Fukui asked him into the bedroom, while cursing No. 7 in his heart for her loose tongue.

"Is the fish ready?" Dagui sat down on the bed, sniffing loudly in the direction of the kitchen.

"No hurry.... I'm cooking the rice first," mumbled Fukui. He returned to the kitchen and stared woodenly at the shad on the big plate. He wasn't a mean person. He would have welcomed anyone but Dagui to share his luck. His reluctance was caused by something that had happened in the past. He could never forget how this man who called him uncle had once swindled him.

One unlucky spring day two years before, his set of rolling hooks became entangled with a blasted steam boat which went off with them, leaving not a single one behind. He had cursed and shouted himself hoarse. Later, when he calmed down, he began to wonder where he could get another set. He went to many stores in vain. One shop assistant in Dachai Village told him that such old-fashioned hooks were no longer available. As anglers on the river had taken to farming, no one would specially produce such hooks for him. "Forget it, uncle," the man tried to persuade him. "Scientific and modern methods are being used in fishing now. Those rolling hooks are too primitive. Besides, the pollution in recent years has killed all the fish. Look at Dagui, he's contracted to tend a fishpond and is taking good care of it. It's teeming with fish. He can catch them with his bare hands. Last year, he earned 8,000 yuan and bought a tractor. How about you, uncle?" Fukui snorted with disapproval. He couldn't understand such terms as "scientific", "pollution" and "primitive". Let the oxen puzzle over those. They had big heads. To him, the fish in the river were like fruit on the trees, which were plentiful some years and scarce others. Would he have a large catch the following year? Formerly, on lucky days, he caught a hundred catties a time, and the biggest fish fetched more than twenty yuan. Those good days might come again if he could bide his time for a few years. So he sought out Dagui, knowing that he had a set of superior hooks, well-wrought, eighty per cent new, the work of old Hu from Shibalipu. "Old Hu is dead and his three sons have gone to the city and become workers. It's the end of their family profession," said Dagui, throwing him a glance, waiting for him to see the significance of Old Hu's death. "To tell you the truth, uncle, this is possibly the last set of hooks he ever made. I want it as a souvenir. You know, this will be very valuable in future. A museum might want it for their collection.... Some time ago Wuxi wanted to trade it for six big carp, but I refused."

Fukui understood the last sentence all right. After that talk, he had to give Dagui ten carp in two months before he was able to get the hooks. As an angler might not experience any important event his whole life, it was much more humiliating for him to be swindled. When you were cheated you could pretend you hadn't realized it. But swindling was done openly so it was much more mortifying.

Fukui wasn't so generous that he was willing to share his fish and wine with that cocksure son-of-a-bitch. To kiss the ass of somebody who had slapped you in the face was too much.

But no fisherman would kick out a guest. Fukui lifted the lid of his pot and stared uncertainly at the shad sprinkled with spring onions.

The black cat jumped onto the stove, moving timidly over to it.

"You want a bite too?" He grabbed the cat, meaning to throw it out of the window. But then he had second thoughts and tossed the fish at it instead.

This animal could help him to get the better of Dagui. Wonderful! He would prefer not to eat it himself.

As he watched the cat tearing at the fish, he felt he was tearing Dagui apart with his own teeth. He trembled with exhilaration.

When he returned to the bedroom, Dagui inquired, "Is the fish steamed, uncle?"

"Damn it, the cat got it."

"What?" Dagui jumped up like a fire-cracker and dashed into the kitchen, almost stepping on the cat eating.

"The blasted beast!" The cat shot off. The fish was in shreds. "You're too careless, second uncle. What a pity.... That damn cat.... If I were you, I'd have killed it."

Anyway, the fish was no longer edible. After chatting a little, Dagui left depressed.

Fukui hummed happily as he watched Dagui's tractor bounce up the bridge. But he lowed out of tune like an ox.

He prepared the butterfish. He could only give No. 7 that when she came. They were delicious, although too bony. He put the fish into the pot and lit the fire.

He fed the fire slowly, thinking hard as he waited for No. 7.

It was after nine and there was still no sign of her. She said she would come. Had she changed her mind?

He couldn't wait. He had to check his hooks. He wolfed down some cold rice and left with a lantern.

The villagers were sitting in the cool air talking and laughing. The mournful aria of a *yueju* opera over the loudspeaker was often drowned by dogs' barking. As the salty river breeze blew over Fukui's body under his torn shirt, he felt as relaxed as if a woman's soft hand was caressing him.

She was waiting ahead for him. To reach the river he had to pass by her home. In spite of the darkness she knew it was he from his build, strong as a bull's.

"You two spent a long time over your wine? Were you drinking it as if it were medicine?" she demanded.

"The hell I was!"

"You didn't drink?"

"Who with?"

"Dagui, of course. Didn't he call?"

"He did.... But he got nothing to eat."

No. 7 stared suspiciously at Fukui's excited, boyish face as he gave a vivid account of how he had played the trick on Dagui.

"You're a fool."

She was on the point of letting out a stream of invective when her heart melted into pity for him. She had arranged for Dagui to go and "enjoy" his fish to give Fukui an opportunity to mention his wish to fill the vacancy to be left by her in the factory. Dagui couldn't refuse after drinking his wine and eating his fish. Once Fukui had a stable income she could marry with an easy mind. After all, one night's love lasts a hundred days, as the saying goes. They had been lovers for eight years. Slightly hopeful, she inquired, "Did you mention the replacement to Dagui?"

"Shit. I couldn't bear to work in a factory." Fukui didn't appreciate it at all. "Going to work on the dot in a small factory can't compare with fishing. It's suffocating."

He had spoken the truth. He had been fishing since he was fourteen in the open air and would hate changing his life at his age. He was as used to it as if he had been born an angler, knowing how to arrange a net's hooks even in his mother's womb.

No. 7 realized it was impossible to change him. She could only stare helplessly at Fukui as he walked towards the river to try his luck.

In the summer night the river was like a woman decked out in her jewelry. Fukui saw, on the other side, street lamps dancing like a fire dragon along the new Jiangbin Boulevard. Lately, at seven every night, in the twinkling of an eye, this fire dragon lit up as if by a magic wand. The majestic sight often made Fukui marvel at how the fools in the city could work controlled by the clock.

He approached the river, lit his lantern and brought his boat out of its shelter. The chirping of insects faded away as small fish churned beside the boat, chasing his light. They escorted him to the middle of the river like shrimp soldiers and crab generals crowding around their dragon king. If he cast his net every night, he wouldn't be so poor. The greedy city folks ate small fry too. He could have earned some money even if he fished just once. But he preferred not to do that. He had a beautiful plan. Since he was the last angler, all the fish belonged to him. He would wait until they grew bigger. Then he would have his former luck. He would live as before.... Life was beautiful in the past. He had drunk wine with a VIP.

But in the past, there was no fire dragon on the other side of the river. Every night he counted the lamps, and he had never got it right. They fascinated him. In spite of the explosives shaking heaven and earth and frightening away all the fish when the road was under construction, he was still bewitched by their grandeur.

In the middle of the river he rowed along his rolling hooks and back. There was nothing. All the floats lay lazily on the river.

Fukui settled down, with his head resting on the seat in the stern, his bare feet stuck in a space at the prow. It would be nice to die peacefully like this when his time came, to die on this river which enchanted him like a seductive woman. It would be a pity to die on land, because he wouldn't have a tomb with an airy window. He would be buried underground. The people who buried him would pound the earth on his grave with spades so he couldn't breathe. To die on the river was like sleeping in the arms of a wanton woman. He would have no complaints.

The small fry following his boat increased in number.

Fukui picked up his jar and emptied the earthworms into the river....

In days gone by, it was shameful for an angler to feed the fish. But now, many of the old taboos no longer held fast.

Translated by Yu Fanqin

Nobby's Run of Luck

●

—— ZHANG JIE ——

Zhang Jie is an outstanding woman writer. Brought up in a village in Liaoning Province, she had a passion for literature while still a child. In the late 1950s she entered the Chinese People's University to study economics. Upon graduation she worked in an industrial bureau, and then in a film studio. She began publishing short stories in 1978 and since then has written many stories, essays and novellas. Her novel, Leaden Wings, *won a Mao Dun Literary Prize. Most of her works have been translated into foreign languages.*

NOBBY was an intelligent dog. Whereas other circus dogs could only add and subtract, he had also learned division and multiplication. He had achieved this, frankly speaking, because Feiffer was such a good trainer, as he never failed to point out.

Feiffer was said to have a grandiose plan to teach Nobby algebra, geometry and trigonometry too.:..

The townsfolk of A — set little store by the circus as a form of entertainment. When this circus was first set up, certain local authorities objected based on the fact that their citizens had such refined tastes, such a scientific tradition, from drinking the special water from the river which flowed through the town. For a long time the interested parties had made qualitative analyses of its chemical composition to prove the positive effect of this water on those who drank it. The fact that they finally condescended to appreciate the circus was due entirely to Nobby's mathematical brilliance.

This made Nobby apprehensive. He trained more conscientiously than ever. Whether at the height of summer or in the depth of winter, he tried his best. He even resolved to remain a bachelor to devote his entire energy to the circus.

His skill increased day by day. Each time he responded to a curtain call the audience applauded loudly, excitedly shouting his name. That made him more apprehensive and, his tail between his legs, he sidled away or backed out.

In addition to the regular circus rations, Feiffer supplemented his diet to make up for all the energy he expended on training and performing. Nobby did not keep these extras to himself but shared them with his colleagues, no matter how limp, dizzy or shaky he felt from a lack of calories.

A little monkey in the troupe whispered in his ear, "Don't be a fool, mate, you've sweated blood for this food. What capital do we have apart from our health? Why don't you think of the future?"

Nobby gaped and lolled his long tongue out, sitting blankly there for some time, bewildered by the monkey's warning. What bearing had this on his future?

From this brief introduction it should be clear that Nobby was a dog with a good mass line. Though he had won a name for himself, he was so modest and prudent that he did not arouse the jealousy of his colleagues. Though comfortably off, he did not swagger like the newly rich. Though Feiffer's favourite, his master's belief in him did not make him arrogant or domineering. Acting with propriety he led a peaceful life, steering clear of disaster. All who saw him agreed that he was a good dog.

Time flashed by, swift as an arrow. Thanks to Feiffer's careful training, Nobby mastered the four main branches of mathematics.

Feiffer took no risks and did nothing unless sure of success; consequently, for the time being, he did not let Nobby display his new accomplishments. Nonetheless, the word was spread by a black dog in the circus, a newsmonger.

A dog able to do arithmetic, algebra, geometry and trigonometry — this was sensational news! The world's major newspapers carried all kinds of pictures of Nobby, with accounts of his diet, sleeping habits and performances.

Nobby!
Nobby!
"Nobby and the Prospects for the Exchange of Mammals' Viscera";
"The Value to Medical Science of Nobby's Brain";
"Nobby and the Rise and Decline of Cynicism";
"Atkins' Law and Nobby."

It was said that Mr Atkins won several valuable prizes on the strength of this dissertation.

Someone looked up "I.Q.Charts" compiled by Binet and Simon and on the basis of it deduced that Nobby had stayed down in the fourth form owing to acquired bad habits, not because of any innate stupidity. Feiffer had to fill in all sorts of forms for him: Did he wet his bed? Did he write with his left hand or his right? At what age did he start smoking?...

Those forms which Nobby found most tiresome were finally rejected as unsuitable for A —'s specific conditions, because they continued to use the old French methods.

The interested parties working outside town by the river sent in a pile of statistics five metres thick, to prove that Nobby's intelligence was related to the river water. But this was also rejected because it blurred the distinction between higher and lower animals.

Nobby was taken to a laboratory and put in a transparent glass box where all day long instruments of every kind monitored his brain, heart, liver, pancreas, lungs, gall, stomach — unfortunately he had no womb, hence was better at logical thought than thinking in images — as well as his nervous, digestive, respiratory and circulatory systems, his bowel and bladder movements.

All that he ate and drank was prepared according to a scientific ratio of vitamins A, B, C, D, E.... Moreover, he ate fixed amounts at regular hours.

Every day crowds came to watch him regardless of whether he was asleep or whatever he was doing, which greatly embarrassed Nobby.

Once Feiffer brought all the other dogs in his troupe to see him, so exciting Nobby that he longed to bound over and playfully bite them or sniff at them. For fear of breaking the lab's rules, though, he simply gave a low growl and rhythmically wagged his tail a few times in welcome. Feiffer and the other dogs stood nervously by the door, not daring to come in. Awe-stricken, they stared at the various tubes, electrodes and wires attached to his head, chest, four paws and hind legs. Their eyes showed deep sympathy and concern, as if he had been carved into eight parts or transformed into an immortal and was no longer a dog.

A savant finally declared that if Nobby had really mastered all the main mathematical operations he should give a demonstration to prove that he was no charlatan.

Feiffer took him back to the circus. In his excitement Nobby jumped up and down, dashed three times round the little yard and piddled in each corner, turned his musty litter upside down, then rolled in the mud till he reeked. After that he went to the kitchen to gnaw on two bones, thumping his tail against Feiffer's lean legs....

The performance took place in the grandest theatre in town, because many celebrities wanted to attend it.

Feiffer had made Nobby a crimson velvet waistcoat and a white satin bow tie. Nobby saw from the mirror that he cut a handsome, imposing figure. He was going to prove to all that he was no charlatan.

The theatre was agog.

"They say Nobby eats thirty walnuts a day."

Walnuts? What were they? Nobby had never seen any, let alone eaten thirty a day.

"Why so many?"

"Good for the brain. Otherwise how could he do those calculations?"

"No wonder."

No wonder what? As if his intelligence was not the result of Feiffer's painstaking teaching and his own hard work, but was due to something called walnuts. Who knew, though, maybe when shut up in the lab he had been fed these things called walnuts.

Nobby felt he had been cheated.

"Know what?" said a lady. "I was the first to discover this dog prodigy." For Feiffer's sake Nobby was tempted to bite her.

The second bell sounded. Nobby made his entrance. At once every voice in the big theatre was hushed.

Nobby squatted solemnly in the middle of the stage, his confident eyes sweeping over the audience.

Feiffer started explaining this act. Told the audience what it meant when Nobby stretched his left or right foreleg; stretched his left or right hindleg; moved his left or right ear, or both simultaneously; closed his left or right eye, or both eyes together. If he stretched his left foreleg that signified a chicken's leg, and the number was indicated by the number of times he barked; if he stretched his right foreleg that signified a rabbit's leg ... and so on and so forth.

Nobby saw a high-class lady in black evening dress in the middle of the sixth row put her handkerchief to her mouth to stifle a yawn. That yawn was so contagious that others in the audience followed suit, while a sound like the buzzing of swarms of bees broke out.

Nobby's nose twitched as if he scented danger.

Feiffer hastily concluded his introduction. Then Nobby gave an impeccable demonstration of calculation. But the audience was very lukewarm. Having forgotten Feiffer's explanations, they simply did not understand the performance.

Everyone left before the final curtain. Nobby heard the high-class lady say, "Ridiculous. If a dog could do mathematics, what would men be needed for?"

Feiffer stood motionless for a long time on the empty stage, hunching his shoulders as if he had received a hard blow on the head.

After that he stopped teaching Nobby to calculate. He either muttered incoherently or sighed or threw things about. Sometimes he hugged Nobby, patting his neck, and said: "They're wrong, Nobby, you're a good dog, honestly. Remember I shall always love you."

Nobby thought: Why say that? Of course I'm a good dog, Feiffer.

People started investigating Nobby's history.

"Who's your father, Nobby?"
He had no idea.
"Who's your mother?"
Again Nobby had no idea.
They measured his ears, legs and tail, cut off a tuft of his hair, and X-rayed him....

Before long the experts produced monographs about Nobby's ancestry. Judging by the length of his ears and the way they stood up or drooped, he must be Mongolian; judging by his skeletal structure he must be Turkish; judging by the length of his legs he must be English. They all held different views.

Again it was Mr Atkins who received the highest fee for his brilliant composition, for his theory was one no professor or scholar could refute. "From his name we can deduce that he is a nobody."

A nobody!

A nobody!

"I realized long ago that this dog was a rascal, when he stole a leg of mutton from my house."

"He's actually a bad, stupid dog. Those calculations were done by a dog robot."

When spring came Mr B returned after a long absence to the circus, bringing a small dog the colour of camel's hair. Nobby dashed forward to welcome his old friend back.

Before Nobby became famous and was just beginning to display his talent, to win recognition for him Mr B had visited all the best families in town, gaining admission to each imposing mansion and making a name for himself as a man who stood up for justice.

But now that he had no eyes for Nobby, he went straight up to Feiffer. This puzzled Nobby. Had he changed so much that even such an old friend could not recognize him?

Mr B picked up his small camel-coloured dog. "See this dog?" he said to Feiffer. "It has a nose like a chestnut, and a long thin neck. And take a look at its ears — they rotate like wind vanes. I bet you he will soon make a great name; you can't go wrong backing him. How about it, Feiffer? I'll sell him to you cheap, eh?"

Feiffer said nothing, stroking Nobby at his feet. Mr B urged, "Want him or not? Speak up."

Feiffer spoke then, saying, "Dear Nobby."

Nobby, still wondering if he had really changed, gazed in bewilderment at Feiffer's face, not knowing what he had said.

With the tip of one shoe Mr B kicked Nobby in the stomach and said to Feiffer: "What an ungrateful dog. You trained him to become a star, but he's forgotten your kindness and doesn't recognize you as a friend. See, he's ignoring you."

"No, you're wrong there. Nobby's ill, and has something on his mind. Can't you see that he's upset? He's been in the dumps all day long,... we should make allowances for him."

Nobby looked at Feiffer with tears in his eyes. Though he still didn't understand what he had said, he was sure it was something kind and affectionate.

Nobby suffered from insomnia. Even when he managed to sleep he often had nightmares.

He kept dreaming that the high-class lady in evening dress had tucked her long skirt into her pants and brought people to chase him into the pond. Though he choked and tried to climb out, they wouldn't let him. They just kept cursing and stoning him.

He dreamed that he had gone mad, and was wandering like a wild dog in the wasteland.

He dreamed that Feiffer did not want him. When he said, "I'm Nobby, Nobby...." Feiffer glanced at him like Mr B as if he did not know him, and said, "Scram, you disgusting dog!"

Nobby often woke in the middle of the night in tears. He heard passers-by in the street say: "Listen, a dog is crying."

"Can dogs cry?"

"Sure. It may be having a nightmare."

"Can dogs dream?"

"Sure they can."

Nobby lost weight. He could neither eat nor drink, and his coat lost its gloss. What had become of his appetite? He'd once eaten five catties of beef in a single meal.

He had stopped frisking about, had lost his former energy and couldn't do a single sum.

He gave up training, and Feiffer didn't want him to train. He spent the whole day lying in a corner, his jaw resting on his front paws, brooding as he stared at the distant meadows and hills.

The black dog who liked to gossip kept squatting apologetically at one side, watching over him from a distance. He gathered the courage to say, "Forgive me, Nobby. I never knew it would come to this. I didn't mean to harm you."

"Forget it. Really, mate. It wasn't your fault."

One evening Nobby thought he heard his name called in the distance.

Was it the wind? Evening mist? The setting sun? Running water? Autumn insects?

He pricked up his ears to listen. He twitched his nose to sniff.

The wind carried the faint scent of flowers, the delicate fragrance of bitter herbs and the fermenting odour of over-ripe fruit. As Nobby sniffed and listened, it seemed to him that his long lost soul had come back.

He walked out of his corner, yawned, shook himself, then ran off down a sandy path.

Nobody ran after him or threw stones at him as he loped along. In the stillness he heard the pads of his feet, springy and rhythmical. His heart at peace, his mind a blank, all he knew was that he must go far, far away.

How long did he run? Nobby had no idea. Suddenly he started — he was at the sea.

Stunned, Nobby squatted down on the seashore. He had never seen such a majestic sight before. The waves roared, leaping skyward as they surged in from far away as if to pound him to pieces; but he was not afraid.

He was not afraid, knowing that here was nothing to fear.

He ran towards the sea, his paws wet and cold. He ran on till he was soaked up to his middle, chilled to his heart. He ran on till the waves gently lifted him up and he entered infinitude.

"Nobby — Nobby."

He looked back and saw Feiffer standing on the beach, his lean arms thrashing about like willow boughs soon to be snapped by a typhoon. His long sparse hair stood up like straw in the wind.

"Nobby —"

Nobby couldn't see him clearly, but was sure that tears were streaming down his cheeks. He could still go back, he wasn't yet exhausted; there was still time. But no. Don't take it so hard, Feiffer, you can find yourself another good dog, only don't teach it mathematics, mate.

"Nobby — I love you!" Feiffer shouted hoarsely.

"I love you too." Those were Nobby's last words.

He let himself go, and the waves carried him farther out to the deep ocean.

I shall never go back, he thought.

Translated by Gladys Yang

The Tavern

●

—— ZHENG WANLONG ——

Zheng Wanlong began work in an agricultural chemical factory in Beijing after graduating from the Beijing Chemical School in 1963. In 1974 he moved to work as an editor in the Beijing Publishing House. He started writing in 1963. His publications include the novel Gurgling Water Bay *and a collection of short stories.*

THE old miser was heating wine with damp charcoal again. The room was filling up with acrid smoke that slithered across the tables like flocks of dirty grey sheep. The smoke made Chen Sanjiao's nostrils twitch and put him off his wine.
    Chen Sanjiao picked up the smell of smoke before his sledge pulled into the paddock in front of the tavern. He was a trapper, and sensitive to smells. Even as a young man, he could tell how long ago an animal went by simply by sniffing its droppings.
    People and horses milled about the paddock. The men from Oroqen were bartering pelts and odds and ends for salt, gunpowder and flour with a man called One-Eye from the Heyuansheng Firm. They knew they would get the short end of the stick dealing with One-Eye but they weren't willing to go another hundred and fifty odd li to the nearest trading post. A blizzard was brewing to the west that would certainly close the mountain pass. Before that happened they had to make camp.
    Inside the paddock, a thin dusting of snow on the ground had been churned into a sea of mud. A thin layer of slick, black ice had crusted over the top. One-Eye balanced a black-wood abacus in one hand and dabbed at the gummy empty socket of his missing eye with his other sleeve. He had lost the eye fighting a hunter over a woman. The hunter's knife took out the eye. Had it not been for that fateful fight, One-Eye would have gone to the Urgunar River, and with his cunning, would have made it rich within a few years. As it was, One-Eye was not doing badly. Although he

couldn't read or work the abacus well, he had the gift of the gab. Chen Sanjiao could tell how the bartering was going. The men of Oroqen were being swindled. One-Eye was after the leopard pelts and he would get them at his price too. Chen Sanjiao watched. He was too weary and did not have the energy to interfere. He had to conserve what strength he had.

People were afraid of Chen Sanjiao. As soon as his sledge pulled into the paddock, people scattered like frightened deer at the sound of a hunter's rifle, their eyes practically popping out of their heads. These people were startled to see him alive, for it was rumoured that he was dead.

They watched him heave a short snouted bear off the sledge. It was a big beast of about three or four hundred kilos. The knife had gone in at the throat, and had torn a gash right down its middle, spilling its guts everywhere.

"Hey, Master Jiao, are you here to trade?" One-Eye smiled unctuously.

Chen Sanjiao turned his back on him, squatted down to unharness his horse.

"In three days the mountain pass will close. I'll make you a fair deal on the bear."

"Of course you will, you bastard," Chen Sanjiao tethered his horse to a hitching post, and walked over to the bear. "Get some men to carry this inside for me."

His eyes swept over the people in the paddock contemptuously, as if they were a collection of idiots. He had no use for any of them, although they too lived off the wilderness. Chen Sanjiao was not particularly conscious of it, but he had a reputation. His eye was as sharp as a knife. There was neither man, woman nor beast that did not fear him. He was a man of courage, and it was said that he once killed a wolf with three kicks. He broke his big toe that time, and earned himself the nickname of Sanjiao, meaning "three kicks". Behind his back people called him "Chen the Yellow Beard". No one dared call him that to his face. No one really knew him: how old he was; whether he'd been married or ever loved a woman; whether he was a Han or a Daur. He never smiled. No one remembered ever seeing him smile. Even when he was drinking he was morose. It was as if there had never been a happy moment in his life.

Chen Sanjiao sat at a table next to the window. He had thrown it open to let in the wind to blow out some of the smoke.

Old Corncob, the tavern-keeper, was chopping turnips on the counter. Chen Sanjiao always had a big plate of shredded turnips tossed with sugar.

"You haven't been here for a long time," Old Corncob was saying almost casually, his little gimlet eyes watching Chen Sanjiao's every move.

"I almost didn't make it back," Chen Sanjiao replied, absently playing with a sliver of beef on his plate.

"You mean the business at Xinzi Creek?"

"I've been on that trail for a month."

"They say it started snowing up there a month ago."

"I got on the boat at the mouth of the Humar River the day the snow began. The wind came up after we left Raozhu. The waves on the Heilongjiang River were as tall as the mast. The boat was driven ashore, and smashed to smithereens. You couldn't find a whole plank afterwards."

"What happened to the people?"

"I'm all that's left. The boatman and his whole family drowned. His youngest kid was only a week old. They died quickly. The bodies were never found. He still owes me twelve gold pieces. I won't forget that."

"Well, I guess that'll be a debt for the underworld."

"Actually I wasn't planning to collect it. I just wanted him to remember that. I helped him buy his boat. He was new in these parts, and he seemed a decent sort."

The shredded turnips arrived. Chen Sanjiao started in on them crunching them between his teeth as loudly as a cow chewing its cud, his Adam's apple bobbing with every swallow. Then he started cursing, complaining that the wine was watered down and the turnips weren't sweet enough and had no bite.

Old Corncob stood there meekly taking this abuse. He gritted his teeth and hatred flashed from the depths of his little gimlet eyes. He hated the man with the yellow beard, for since the day the tavern opened Chen Sanjiao had been eating and drinking there, and had never paid a cent.

Chen Sanjiao did not look up at the tavern keeper standing beside him. He knew what was going through Old Corncob's head. To him Old Corncob was a wounded wolf. Actually it was Chen Sanjiao who gave him the name of Old Corncob. Their paths crossed for the first time when the man with the shifty eyes first came to the border area, before he got established. They met on the road. Chen Sanjiao stopped his horse across the road. In his hand was a curved hunting knife with a blade about a foot long, which he played with deliberately, turning it this way and that, gazing at the man before him as if he were an animal ready for the kill.

"You're here because you've made a fortune."

The man flashed him a look of surprise. Sanjiao could see he was struggling to remain calm.

"It's none of your business!"

"Oh, no," Sanjiao said almost conversationally. "You haven't been around long enough to know, but everybody around here knows this knife of mine minds everybody's business."

The man stared at the stranger with the yellow beard, and the knife he kept twirling restlessly between his fingers. "I'm a businessman," he said. "I came here to do business."

"You don't fool me. I've been around animals all my life, and these nostrils tell me you have the blood of at least two men on your hands. I can smell it...."

The little gimlet eyes looked positively frightened now.

"You'd better watch your tongue! That's a serious accusation!"

Before he finished, his rabbit skin hat had been knocked to the ground, and the tip of Sanjiao's knife was pricking his throat.

"You old corncob," Sanjiao hissed under his breath. "You'd better play it square with me. Get me riled and I'll slit you open, and fix it so your head and your body will part company."

Chen Sanjiao never mentioned that incident again, but the memory of it weighed on Old Corncob like a ton of bricks.

Old Corncob had been running a tab. It was about time he collected, he thought. Friendship is friendship, and business is business. Old Yellow Beard was hardly a friend. He was more like a rash. Every time Old Corncob thought of the man the rash itched. In the last few months when he had seen neither hide nor hair of him, Old Corncob had gone about asking for him. "Old Chen Sanjiao owes a huge debt and hasn't paid. What kind of man is that, tell me!" Now the urge to ask for his money stuck in his throat. Somehow he just couldn't get it out. Chen Sanjiao slammed the empty copper wine jug down in front of his face.

"Give me another half jug."

"You want more?"

"What's the matter? Scared I won't pay?"

"Of course not. I wouldn't dream of bothering you with a paltry thing like that!"

"I won't cheat you blind. I pay my debts."

Old Corncob filled the jug and brought it back to the table, pulled up a stool and sat down across from Chen Sanjiao. As he sat down he noticed Chen Sanjiao had a towel wadded under his shirt that was black with congealed blood. Through the open shirt he could see a great gash in Chen Sanjiao's neck. The blood had clotted over the wound, but with every breath blood and water oozed from it. Old Corncob was startled. It looked bad. Whoever did it had done a good job. That's justice, he thought, triumphantly.

Chen Sanjiao's face was like a sheet of old parchment. Not even sorghum wine could take away the look of impending doom. No wonder he pulled his hat down so low, Old Corncob mused. He didn't want people to see that look on his face, or notice the wound. He wanted people to see him as he used to be: fearless and arrogant.

He hasn't much time left, thought Old Corncob. Perhaps it's time to bury the hatchet, and forget the debt. He felt he ought to say something but couldn't think what. Should he try to be comforting, or should he chew him out?

"What the devil are you staring at?"

"Nothing! I didn't see anything."

Although Chen Sanjiao hadn't looked up from his wine cup, Old Corncob could feel a sudden chill creep into his bones. He sensed that Chen Sanjiao was capable of anything to keep his condition a secret.

"A lot of people are going to get their wish. But I won't let them gloat."

"You're not badly hurt, are you?"

"There's still breath in the old carcass." Chen Sanjiao unsheathed his hunting knife and laid it on the table between them. "Fetch your accounts."

"No, Master Jiao, I have no intention of collecting from you!"

"I want you to record what's owing to me."

Old Corncob produced a book of accounts and writing implements. Chen Sanjiao shut his eyes, one hand crept under his shirt where his wound smarted. He spoke slowly, "Zhang with the scarred eye owes me twenty gold pieces. That idiot Zhang Zhao owes me a measure of wheat, and four gold pieces. Lu Laoliu owes me for a pair of bear paws, that's ten gold pieces. And Liu with the beard owes me six horses...."

Old Corncob wrote it all down.

"Is that all?"

Chen Sanjiao drained the rest of the wine in one draft. "That's all," he said.

"You want to pay your tab with that money?"

"I want them to remember they owe me, and to mend their ways. Wang Fengxiong is dead. He brought three men against me. I was alone. They had done some pretty bad things to widow Zhang. Anyway we met at the mouth of the Naren River. He ran up against my knife. That's justice."

"Yes, justice has been done!"

"Wang Fengxiong left the bear. He was a crack shot, but he wronged too many people, and finally he had a reckoning with me." He laughed mirthlessly through his nose. Perhaps the laughter aggravated the wound, and he paled. "Take the bear to the trading post, and barter it for flour." He took out a purse made of dog skin and threw it on the table. "Take the flour and the purse to widow Zhang."

Old Corncob picked up the purse and gave it a toss, and said knowingly, "They say when you were young, you and widow Zhang...."

Before he could finish, Chen Sanjiao leaped to his feet, one hand closed on Old Corncob's collar and twisted. Old Corncob's greenish eyes bulged from their sockets. Chen Sanjiao brandished a fist under Old Corncob's nose. "If you've got an itch in your bones, I can still oblige."

He let go, and Old Corncob slumped to the ground.

The room was deathly silent. The few men who had been drinking there had quietly slipped away. Even the paddock was deserted.

Chen Sanjiao sat down again and emptied the wine jug into his cup.

"I've paid my way through life," he said. "Total up what I owe, and you'll be paid."

"You have no children, so who's going to pay for you?"

"I have forty-two scars on my body. Now there's one more. That's gold."

"Yes, I understand. But I'm not asking to be paid."

"I'm going to settle with you anyway."

"No, no. Please! There's no hurry!"

Old Corncob could feel a chill rising through the soles of his feet. His whole body trembled.

Chen Sanjiao slipped a gold ring off his finger and handed it to Old Corncob. It was a curious ring shaped like a dog. Chen Sanjiao had it specially made for him in Harbin. It was said that the dog had followed him everywhere for years. Someone stole it, ate it and sent the pelt back to Chen Sanjiao. In his grief, Chen Sanjiao had stabbed himself in the throat. Fortunately he was discovered in time. Otherwise he would have left many a keg of wine untapped.

"Take the ring to Miller's Ridge and ask for Liu Santai. He will pay every cent I owe."

Old Corncob palmed the ring. Something suddenly occurred to him then.

"You mean you're leaving and never coming back?"

"I'm never coming back."

"Never?"

"Never."

"Where are you going?"

"Past Moling Ridge to Xiaosu Creek. There's a gold mine there. That's where I came from and that's where I'm going."

"But that's madness. With this weather coming up, in three days the snow will seal off the mountain passes. You'll freeze out there...."

"Me? Freeze?" Chen Sanjiao snorted. He lifted the wine jug to his lips and sucked out the last dregs, strapped on his hunting knife, slipped into his leopard skin coat, pulled on his fox skin hat and lumbered out the door like a great bear.

Old Corncob hurried out after him. Chen Sanjiao was already hitching up his sledge.

"You can't go like this," Old Corncob pleaded. "Rest here a few days until you're better then leave."

"And let everybody know I'm licking my wounds under your roof?"

He finished hitching the horse, climbing into the sled and was gone.

Night fell in the northwest. The clouds rolled down on the mountains like a lid, and the forests stood, black and menacing, waiting to close in on the sledge.

It was the last time Old Corncob ever saw Chen Sanjiao. Ever since that day a year ago, something seemed missing from Old Corncob's life. He felt empty. He was listless. Although winter was the time when the tavern could really turn a profit, and he could dilute the wine as much as he liked, making money didn't seem that important any more. There was no news of Chen Sanjiao. Old Corncob was like a rabbit in a burrow, cooped up day after day in the tavern, drinking himself into a stupor.

He could not understand why Chen Sanjiao chose to "go" that way. Some said he was a hard man, some called him a hero; others said he was mad. Whatever he was, after he'd gone he became legend. The young people took to wearing leopard skin coats, and caps stitched together with three strips of fox fur. Even One-Eye came round with ten kilos of the best tobacco from Guandong, and left it for Chen Sanjiao, saying that he had also come from the gold mine at Xiaosu Creek.

Finally the spring thaw came. The earth began to show a hint of green, but for whom?

People from the village going up to Xiaosu Creek asked for Chen Sanjiao but no one had heard of him. It seemed he had never been there, or if he had been, he had quietly slipped away again, like the melting snow.

Old Corncob went up too, carrying with him the parcel of tobacco, a keg of wine and some meat. But it was all in vain. On the way back he decided to stop at Moling Ridge and look up Liu Santai.

Moling Ridge was such a small settlement that all one had to do was stand in the middle of the road and shout for Liu Santai, and he would appear. Old Corncob was amazed that the person who answered to the name was a lad of about fourteen, in a shabby padded jacket, his cheeks and chest ruddy from the cold.

The boy piqued Old Corncob's curiosity.

"Are you Liu Santai?"

"There is no other around here," the boy answered evenly. "Who wants to know?"

"Do you know Chen Sanjiao?"

"I do."

"He told me to give you this ring."

"Is he dead?"

"I don't know. All I know is he went to Xiaosu Creek just before the blizzard closed the mountain pass."

"Then he won't be back."

"How do you know?"

"When I was ten years old he told me when he goes to Xiaosu Creek, he won't be back. He didn't want people to see him die. Did he say anything before he left?"

"Only that you'd pay me for the wine he drank."

"Alright. I will."

"You're only a kid. What are you going to use for money?"

"What's your hurry? I'll grow up and pay you back every cent he owes. You're Old Corncob, aren't you?" the boy flung the nickname at him like a challenge. He slapped the ring into Old Corncob's hand. "You hold onto this as a pledge. Just keep alive and wait for me. One day I'll come and pay you, and you'd better be able to give that ring back to me, or I'll have your hide."

Before Old Corncob could gather his wits, the boy was gone.

Old Corncob watched Liu Santai walk away. Suddenly there was a flash of recognition. The leather belt the boy was wearing belonged to Chen Sanjiao. The pieces of the puzzle began to fit together. He yelled after the retreating figure of the boy, "The debt is cancelled! You don't have to pay!"

The boy walked on without a backward glance. Whether he heard or not, he gave no sign. Old Corncob stood there in the middle of the road, gazing at the ring in his hand. The design of the dog winked in the sunlight.

Translated by David Kwan

A Soul in Bondage

●

—— TASHI DAWA ——

Tashi Dawa, a Tibetan, was born in 1959 at Batang, Sichuan. He worked in theatre before becoming a full-time writer. He began publishing short stories in the late 1970s and endeavours to portray young Tibetans in the context of modern Tibet. In recent years he has espoused magical realism. "A Soul in Bondage" won a national award in 1985.

THERE is a Peruvian folk-song called *El Condor Pasa* that I have not heard for a long time. But its simple, yet solemn melody lingers in the mind. Whenever I hear it, it conjures up a vision of high plateaus and deep valleys; of bits of farm land carved out of hillsides; of straggly crops; mill houses beside streams, and low stone cottages; of mountain folk struggling under heavy loads, the sound of cow bells, and the lonely dust-devils whirling in the wind, under a dazzling sun.

My visions are not of Peru and the foothills of the high Andes. They are visions of the Pabunaigang Mountains in the south of Tibet. I am not sure whether I have actually been there, or merely dreamt of those mountains. I cannot be sure, for I have been to too many places to keep reality and fantasy separate. I realize now that the Pabunaigang Mountains in my mind were only the reflection of a 19th century landscape by Constable until I finally went there.

Although it was still a quiet mountain area, the lives of the people had quietly slipped into the modern era. There was a small airport, from which a helicopter made the trip into the city five times a week.

Nearby was a electric generator powered by solar energy. In a small restaurant next to the gas station at Zhelu Village, I sat with a man with a beard. He was a talker who went on and on. He was actually quite well known, the chairman of the Himalayan Transportation Company; the only outfit in Tibet that owned container trucks built in West Germany. I went to a carpet factory where designers worked out their ideas on computers.

A satellite disc picked up five channels and broadcast thirty-eight hours of programs a day.

In spite of the material progress that has been made, some of the old traditions live on among the people of Pabunaigang Mountains. For instance, the village chief who has a doctorate in agriculture still makes the curious "lo-lo" sound with his tongue when he speaks to me as an expression of respect. And when people ask a favour they still say, "gu-ji, gu-ji" in a plaintive voice. Old men remove their hats and press them to their breasts as a sign of respect. Although weights and measures have been standarised ages ago, people here still measure lengths by holding out one arm and indicating the length they mean by chopping at it with the palm of the other hand, from the wrist upwards, all the way to the shoulder.

Sangjiedapu, the living Buddha, was dying. He was the twenty-third incarnation of the Buddha at Zatuo Monastery. He was ninety-eight years old, and after him there would be no successor. Sangjiedapu and I had been friends. I had come to write an article about him. When a religion as mysterious and as steeped in legend such as Lamaism fails to produce a successor to its many petty leaders, it declines. Those were my sentiments. Sangjiedapu thought otherwise. He shook his head at me, and his eyes took on a faraway look. "Sangbala," he said slowly, "the battle of Sangbala has been joined."

According to legend there is a paradise on earth to the north — the kingdom of Sangbala. It is said that the secret sect of the Yoga began there. The first king, Suochadenapu was a disciple of Buddha, and later, went about preaching his message. Scriptures prophesy that one day, the kingdom of Sangbala will be invaded by a great host. "You will ride on, never turning back. Twelve divisions will follow you. You will aim your spear at the heart of Halutaimeng, chief of demons and arch-enemy of Sangbala. And the demons will be routed." This was the anthem of the last king of Sangbala. Sangjiedapu had touched on the battle of Sangbala once before. He said the battle of Sangbala would go on hundreds of years, but the demons would be vanquished in the end. Then the tomb of Zunggeba would open, and once more the message of the Buddha would be preached. This would continue a thousand years, and then great winds and fire would sweep the earth. Finally, a deluge would bring about the end of the world, but a handful of souls would be spared. The world would begin again, with religion revived. Sangjiedapu lay in his cot, his eyes fixed on someone that only he could see, and it was this unseen presence that he addressed when he spoke: "When you've crossed the Kalong Glacier you will be standing in the palm of the Lord of the Lotus. Ask nothing. Seek nothing. In prayer you will find inspiration, and inspiration will bring visions. You will see out of the criss-crossing lines of that palm, one line leads to earthly paradise."

I seemed to visualise in that instant how it might have been when the

Lord of the Lotus ascended into heaven. I seemed to see a chariot driven by two angels whisking him away into the southern sky.

"Two young people from Kangba are searching for the way to Sangbala," said the living Buddha.

"You mean to tell me, in the year 1988, a man and a woman...." I asked wearily.

He nodded.

"And the man was wounded?" I asked.

"Then you know the story," replied the living Buddha.

Sangjiedapu, the living Buddha began to recall the story of the young man and woman who had come to Pabunaigang Mountains, and the things they encountered on the way. As the story unfolded, I realised that I was listening to a tale I had written some time ago, and locked away in a trunk, without showing it to anyone. Yet he seemed to be reciting the story, word for word. The place was a village named A on the road to Pabunaigang. The time was 1984. There were only two characters: a young man and a young woman. The reason I never showed the manuscript to anyone was because I did not know how to end the story. Listening to the living Buddha tell it made everything clear. The only difference was that at the end of my story the young man meets an old man in a tavern, and it is the old man who tells him where he must go. I did not describe the way ahead. I could not, because I did not know it at the time. Yet the living Buddha claimed that it was he who showed the two young people the road they must travel. There was yet another coincidence: both the old man in the story and the living Buddha spoke of the lines in the palm of the Lord of the Lotus' hand.

Others drifted into the room, and gathered round the cot. The living Buddha's eyes glazed, and gradually he slipped away.

The funeral preparations began. There were those who wanted to bury him in a stupa so that there would be a lasting monument. But Sangjiedapu was cremated. I left there shortly afterwards, musing on the source of inspiration in creative writing.

When I reached home, I opened a trunk labelled "Precious Rubbish". In it were all the manuscripts that had been rejected, and some that I did not wish published, all in neat brown paper envelopes. I found an envelope marked "840720" which contained an untitled short story. This is the story:

Jade first saw the man as she drove her sheep down the mountain. From where she stood he was no larger than a black speck moving slowly across the pebbly bottom of the dry riverbed. She could tell it was a man and that he would be coming towards her hut. She cracked her whip, and drove the sheep quickly down the incline.

It would be dark before the man got here, thought Jade. A few low huts built of stones from the riverbed stood on a small knoll. Behind were pens for the sheep. It was a desolate place. Two families lived here: Jade and her father, and a mute woman of about fifty who lived next door.

Jade's father was a story-teller and a singer. People came from all around to hire him. He had even been invited to perform in the cities. At times he would be gone a few days, but he was also known to stay away for months on end. When they came for him, they would usually bring an extra horse. And he would ride off with them, his six-stringed zither strapped to his back. The horses picked their way down the mountain gingerly, their copper saddle bells jingling and echoing through the wilderness. Jade would watch him go from the top of the knoll until the horses rounded a bend and were out of sight, stroking the big black dog that stood close to her.

It seemed that all her life was marked by the mingled sound of hoof beats and saddle bells. When she sat high on the mountain tending her flock, in her lonely daydreaming, she seemed to hear music rising out of the valleys, a wordless song of the spheres full of the irrepressible life of the wilderness, loneliness and yearning.

The mute woman who wove all day, clambered on to the knoll every morning at dawn, threw a handful of barley in the air, and cried out soundlessly to the Goddess of Mercy. Then, taking up her greasy prayer wheel, she faced the east and prayed. Now and then, Jade's father would steal into the woman's house in the dead of night, and tiptoe back to his own bed at the break of day wrapped in his long, shabby robe. Jade milked the goats, wolfed down a bowl of gruel, put up a bundle of food, picked up her soot-blackened pot, and drove the flock up the mountain. That was life.

Jade prepared some food and made the tea. Then she sprawled on the bed to wait. When the dog started barking, she rushed outside. It was already dark. At first she could see nothing. Then suddenly he stepped out of the darkness.

"It's alright; the dog won't hurt you," said Jade.

He was a tall, handsome young man. A red tassel pinned to one side of his wide-brimmed hat trailed passed one temple.

Jade led the young man into her hut, and put food before him. Her father was away, and the mute woman's loom was the only sound that broke the silence. The young man was weary. After he had eaten and thanked the girl, he threw himself on the father's bed, and was fast asleep.

Jade stood on the threshold for a moment. The sky was filled with stars, and the silence of the night enveloped her. The moonlight threw the peaks and the valleys into sharp relief. The big, black dog moved about in a restless circle, straining on its tether. Jade crouched beside it, and drew it close. She thought of herself, of this lonely place where she had changed from a child into a young woman. She thought of her father too, and of all the grim and silent men who came for him. And she thought of the young stranger sleeping in the hut, who came from a distant place, and would be gone again in the morning. She wept. She knelt on the ground and hid her face, and prayed for her father's forgiveness. She wiped her face on the dog's neck, and went back into the hut. For a moment she stood uncertainly in the dark, trembling in every limb. Then silently she slipped under the sheep pelt beside the young man.

When the morning star rose in the east, Jade rolled up her thin blanket, and in the flickering light of the oil lamp, stuffed strips of dried beef, a bag of barley, some salt and a piece of yak butter into a sack. Then she hung the little blackened cooking pot on her back. She had all the things that a young girl ought to have when she leaves home.

"I'm ready," she said.

The young man took another pinch of snuff, dusted the last particles from his hands and got to his feet. He rubbed the top of her head, put an arm about her shoulders and guided her out of the hut and turned westward where it was still dark. Jade carried everything on her back. She never even thought to ask where the young man would take her. Her only thought was that she was finally leaving this lonely, lifeless place. The young man carried a string of camphor wood prayer beads. It was all he owned. He walked erect, his head held high, filled with an unshakeable faith in the long journey ahead.

"Why do you wear a leather thong round your waist? You look like a dog on a leash," he said.

"It's for counting the days," Jade replied. "See. There are five knots. That means we've been away from home five days."

"What's five days? I've never had a home."

She followed Tabei. They spent the nights on threshing floors, or in sheep pens. Sometimes they slept among the ruins of abandoned temples, or in caves. When they were lucky, they slept in a farmer's hut or in a shepherd's tent.

Whenever they came to a temple, they would kneel before each altar and touch their foreheads to the ground. Whenever they encountered a Manni cone they would find a few white pebbles to put on the top. There were many pilgrims along the way, slithering along on the ground. The heavy canvas aprons they wore were worn through at the chest and the knees, and patched over and over. Their faces were covered with grime, and on their foreheads were great black bruises from repeated knockings on the ground. The pieces of wood with nails hammered through them, which pilgrims used to pull themselves forward, left two deep furrows in the ground as they passed. Tabei and Jade walked and soon left the pilgrims behind.

The mountains of the Tibetan Plateau stretched into infinity. There were few people. They travelled for days at a stretch without seeing another soul or a village. They were battered by the cold blasts that blew out of the valleys, and the blazing sun scorched the earth. If one stood still and gazed up at the sky long enough, one would feel the earth shift under foot, as though one were in danger of being tossed into space. The mountains were wrapped in eternal silence. Tabei walked quickly, his lithe body held stiffly erect. Jade, carrying a heavy load on her back, gradually fell back. Tabei climbed on to a high rock and sat down to wait. They seldom spoke. When the silence became too much to bear, Jade would sing. It was a crude, tuneless sound that she made, more like an animal bellowing in distress than singing. Tabei would give her an impatient look, and she would fall silent again. Jade followed Tabei doggedly, speaking only when they stopped to rest.

"Is the wound still bleeding?"

"It's alright. It doesn't hurt anymore."

"Let me look at it."

"Catch me some spiders. I'll mash them and rub it on the wound. It will heal quicker."

"There aren't any spiders here."

"If you look in the cracks between the rocks you'll find some."

Jade dug up a few rocks that were half buried in earth. She searched diligently, and in a little while caught five or six spiders. Tabei mashed them between the palms of his hands and rubbed the sticky substance on the wound on his calf.

"That dog was vicious. I kept running and the pot on my back was banging the back of my head so hard that I felt my eyes were popping out."

"I should have killed the dog!"

"The woman gave us one of these," Jade made a lewd sign with her hands.

Tabei scooped up some earth and sprinkled it on the wound, letting it dry in the sun.

"Where did she keep her money?"

"In the cupboard behind the counter. She had a wad like this," he held up two fingers to show her the size of the wad. "But I only took about ten notes."

"What are you going to buy?"

"There's a monastery at the foot of the mountain. I'm taking it to the Buddha, and keeping a bit for myself."

"Do you feel better now?"

"I feel fine, but I'm so thirsty I could die."

"I'll fetch some kindling."

Tabei stretched out on the rock and pulled his wide-brimmed hat over his eyes, chewing on a stalk of grass. Jade knelt in front of the fireplace built of stones, blowing on the smouldering kindling. The wood caught, sending out a spray of sparks. Jade scrambled to her feet, rubbing the smoke out of her eyes. A lock of hair on her forehead was singed.

Two shadowy figures appeared on a distant peak. They were probably shepherds tending their flocks, sitting there like a pair of vultures. Jade raised her right hand and waved. The distant figures waved back. They were so far away that a shouted greeting would not be heard.

"I thought we were the only people here," said Jade to Tabei.

"I'm waiting for the tea," Tabei replied shortly.

Jade suddenly remembered something. She took a booklet out of her robes and gave it to Tabei. She had lifted it out of the back pocket of a youth she met in a village the night before, who had made advances. Tabei flipped through the booklet. He did not understand the drawings, nor could he read the text. On the cover was a picture of a tractor.

"It's useless," he pronounced and flung it back at Jade. Jade was crestfallen. It seemed she could do nothing right. Thereafter she used the pages to light fires for tea.

At dusk they saw a village at the foot of the mountain half hidden by trees. Jade's mood lightened. She sang, and taking up her staff did a wild dance, poking Tabei in the armpits and below the waist, trying to make him laugh. But Tabei seized the end of the staff and flung it aside with such force that it sent Jade sprawling in the dust.

They went on in silence. Once they reached the village, Tabei went off alone to drink in the tavern. They had agreed to meet later at the new school building where they would spend the night. The school was not yet completed and there were still no windows or doors, only openings. A film was being shown in the village square, and someone was hanging a screen on wooden poles. Jade went into a clump of trees to gather firewood. Suddenly she was surrounded by a swarm of children who threw stones at her. She tried to take no notice, though she was hit on the shoulder. It was not until a young man wearing a yellow cap came along that they ran off hooting and yelling.

"They threw eight stones at you and one hit you," smiled Yellow Cap. He had a pocket calculator in his hand which he showed to Jade. The numeral eight flashed on the screen.

"Where are you from?"

Jade looked at him dumbly.

"How long have you been travelling?"

"I don't remember," replied Jade, then she showed him her leather thong. "Help me count."

"Does each knot represent a day?" He knelt beside her and counted ninety-two. "That's very interesting...."

"Really?"

"Didn't you count them yourself?"

Jade shook her head.

"Ninety-two days. Let's say you travelled twenty kilometres a day," he tapped the keys of his calculator. "That makes one thousand eight hundred and forty kilometres."

Jade did not understand numbers.

"I'm an accountant," the young man volunteered. "This thing helps solve all my problems."

"What is it?" asked Jade.

"It's a calculator. It knows everything. For instance it can tell me how old you are." He pressed some buttons, and showed the flashing figure to Jade.

"What does it mean?"

"It says you're nineteen."

"Am I really nineteen?"

"You tell me."

"But I don't know."

"Tibetans didn't used to keep track of their ages. But this knows, and it says you're nineteen."

"I don't think it's right."

"Let me look again. Maybe I misread it. I'm not quite used to the numbers yet."

"Does it know my name?"

"Of course."

"What is it then?"

He pressed some keys and filled the screen with figures.

"See? What did I tell you; it knows."

"What is it?"

"Don't you know yourself? You're really ignorant."

"How do you read it?"

"You read it like this," he held up the calculator for Jade.

"Do all those little flashing things say 'Jade'?"

"Of course it says 'Jade'."

Jade giggled delightedly.

"That's nothing. Foreigners have been using these for ages. I've been thinking about a problem. We work from day to night. According to economic theory the value of labour should equal the value of goods produced." He rambled on, throwing in bits of labour relations, the ratio between the value of labour and value of manufactured goods. He even mixed in something about the year, the month, the day, addition, subtraction, multiplication and division. It was a hodge-podge that made no sense. Finally a figure flashed on the calculator screen.

"Look at that! We end up with a debit. That means at the end of the year we have to go cap in hand to the state for supplies of grain.... That's against all the laws of economics! Well, what are you staring at?"

"I was thinking if you haven't any food, you could eat with us. I was just gathering firewood to cook the evening meal."

"Damn it, you must have come out of the dark ages. Or maybe you're from another planet!"

"I come from a faraway place...." she reached for her thong. "How many days did you say?"

"Eighty-five, I think."

"That's not right. You said ninety-two, you liar." Jade laughed.

"I think I'm drunk," he muttered shutting his eyes.

"Will you eat with us? I still have a bit of dried beef."

"Girl, why don't you come with me? I'll take you to a place where there are happy young people. There is music and beer and disco. Drop that bundle of twigs and come with me."

Tabei pushed his way out of the crowd watching the film. He had been drinking but he was not drunk. It was the coloured images, now large, now small, flitting across the screen that made his head ache. He stumbled into the unfinished building. Jade's little black pot was perched on a pile of stones, and her things were stowed in a corner. Tabei felt the hearth stones. They were cold. He gulped a mouthful of cold water and leaned against the wall, deep in thought. The villages ahead would lose their original tranquillity more and more; they would become noisy and clamorous. There would be the roar of machines, laughter, music, voices raised in joy and anger. He wanted none of those things. He wanted to be rid of the confused sounds of humanity. He was seeking something quite different.

Jade finally stumbled into their camp. She leaned heavily against the wall, and even at that distance she reeked of liquor. But Tabei could tell she had been drinking something better than he had.

"They are so happy," she gurgled between laughter and tears. "They are as happy as the gods.... Let's not leave the day after tomorrow.... Let's stay a day longer...."

"No," he said. Tabei never stayed more than one night in a place.

"I'm weary. I'm so very tired." Jade shook her head.

"You don't know what it is to be weary. You have the legs of a cow. You're never tired."

"You don't understand," she protested. "It's not the body that I'm talking about."

"You're drunk. Go to sleep." He dragged her down, and pressed her onto the ground. Afterwards he made another knot on her leather thong.

Jade was weary. Every time she lay down to rest, she felt she could not get up again. She did not want to go on.

"Get up. Don't lie there like a lazy bitch," Tabei ordered.

"I don't want to go on," Jade lay in a patch of sunlight, gazing up at him through half-opened lids.

"What did you say?"

"You go on alone. I don't want to follow you day after day. You don't know where you're going. You'll wander for ever."

"Women don't understand anything." He knew where he was going.

"Maybe I don't understand," she shut her eyes again.

"Get up!" He kicked her in the rump, and raised his hand to strike her. "Get up or I'll beat you!"

"You're a devil!" cried Jade, scrambling to her feet. Tabei turned and walked away, leaving Jade to scramble after him as best she could.

One night, Jade ran away. She strapped the little pot on her back and stole away into the night. She picked her way down the mountain by the light of the moon and stars. The next day, as she rested beside a deep chasm, she saw a figure approaching from a distance. It was as it had been the first time she saw Tabei. He had caught up with her and she turned on him with the ferocity of a cornered beast. She seized the pot and smashed at him with all her might. But the blow went wide. He knocked the pot from her grasp and sent it bouncing into the chasm. They heard it rattling down to the bottom. She climbed down the chasm after it. It was hours before she pulled herself up again. The little pot was full of dents.

"Look what you've done to my pot," wailed Jade.

Tabei took the pot from her, and they examined it together.

"There's only one small crack," he remarked. "I'll fix it."

Tabei turned away, and Jade followed reluctantly.

Suddenly she threw back her head and sang, and her strange, wild song echoed from peak to peak and down into the valleys.

The truth was Tabei was weary of Jade. He believed that in a past life he had accumulated enough merit to have escaped the underworld and been reborn. But on his way to nirvana woman and gold were the stumbling blocks that he must rid himself of.

Soon after they came to a village called A. By that time the leather thong around Jade's waist was a mass of tight little knots. The villagers came out to greet them with drums and gongs. The militia formed a guard of honour, holding up semi-automatic rifles with red rags stuffed in the muzzles for safety's sake. Four villagers dressed as cows danced in the road. The village chief and some young girls came forth to greet them carrying hadas whose spouts had been smeared with yak butter. There had been a drought in the village. A soothsayer had prophesied that a couple would come from the east that day, and they would bring rain. At dusk when Tabei and Jade appeared, the villagers believed them to be the two people they were expecting. So they came out to meet the strangers in their festive garb. Tabei and Jade were hustled onto a tractor and driven into the village. The houses in the village were decorated in coloured prayer flags. Many of the onlookers thought they recognised the traits of the Goddess of Mercy in the way Jade spoke and carried herself. To them she was the manifestation of the Goddess. For the first time Tabei was totally ignored. However, Tabei knew Jade was not a manifestation of a divine being. He had watched her in her sleep, and come to loathe her ugliness, for her face grew slack and saliva dribbled from her half-opened mouth.

Tabei went to a tavern bent on getting drunk and picking a fight. If he annoyed someone enough to pull a knife, so much the better.

There was only an old man drinking in the tavern. Tabei sat down insolently across from him. A village wench with a coloured kerchief tied around her head put a glass before him and poured the wine.

Tabei quaffed the wine, slammed the glass down and cried out, "This wine is like horse's piss."

No one took any notice.

"Do you think it's horse's piss?" Tabei asked the old man.

"I drank horse's piss once when I was young. Right out of the thing dangling between a stallion's legs."

Tabei chuckled.

"I was trying to get my herd back from the bandit Amelia. I followed her all the way from Geze to the Takalamagan desert."

"Who was this Amelia?"

"That was a decade ago. Amelia was a bandit queen, a cossack who came from Xinjiang. She was a terror in Ali and the north of Tibet. She would sweep down on a herd under the cover of night, and in the morning all that was left were a jumble of hoof prints. Even the government troops couldn't stop her."

"Then what happened?"

"Well, I took my gun, got on my horse and chased her into the desert. And a few mouthfuls of horse's piss saved my life."

"What happened then?"

"The bandit queen wanted to keep me as her...."

"Husband?"

"As her goat herder. And I was the owner of a herd of ten thousand! But she was beautiful, as dazzling as the sun, and no one dared look at her. In the end I escaped. To tell you the truth, aside from heaven and hell I've been everywhere."

"But you haven't been where I'm going," said Tabei.

"Where is that?" asked the old man.

"I'm not sure." For the first time Tabei was uncertain of the way ahead. The old man seemed to understand.

The old man pointed to the mountain behind him and said, "Nobody's been there. This village used to be a post station once. There was nowhere you couldn't reach from here, but nobody has been in those mountains. Back in 1964," he went on dreamily, "the communes were just beginning. Everybody was talking about communism, but nobody knew what it was. They said it was some kind of paradise, but nobody knew where it was.

The Tibetans didn't know where it was. Neither did the Alis, nor those from Qinghai. But no one had been across the Kalong Glacier so it had to be there. A few people sold all they had and went off to find communism. They never came back. No one cared to follow them, no matter how hard things got."

Tabei gripped the rim of his glass between his teeth and gazed at the old man thoughtfully.

"But I know a secret that lies at the foot of the Kalong Glacier," added the old man.

"Tell me."

"Are you prepared to go there?"

"Maybe."

"When you reach the top of the mountain, you will hear a weeping sound. It sobs like an abandoned child. But it's only the wind blowing through a crevice. It will take you seven days to reach the top. It will be sunrise. Rest. Don't be in a hurry to descend. The light reflected off the snow will blind you. Wait till dark, then begin your descent."

"That's no secret," said Tabei.

"That's not the secret. Two days after you have crossed to the other side of the mountain, you will come to a plain criss-crossed by a thousand creeks and gullies that seem to run in all directions. It's like a maze. That's not a secret either, but don't interrupt. Do you know where those creeks and gullies come from? They are the lines on the right palm of the Lord of the Lotus. Aeons ago, the Lord of the Lotus battled a demon called Shibameriru. They fought for one hundred and eight days, and though the Lord of the Lotus used all his magical powers he could not vanquish the demon. Finally, the demon turned himself into a flea, that he might evade the Lord. But the Lord stretched out his hand and smashed the flea straight into hell. The force of that blow left the print of his right palm on the earth. It is said that humans who enter that maze will be lost for ever. However, there is one route out. But there are no markings on it whatever."

Tabei stared at the old man solemnly.

"That is only a legend, I don't really know whether it's true," muttered the old man.

Tabei made up his mind to go there. The old man came to him then and proposed that he leave Jade behind for his son. The son had recently bought a tractor. These days every family wanted one. In the mornings, the rumbling of the tractors drowned out the crowing of the roosters. And while they drank the cool, clear water of the mountain streams, they smelt the faintly pungent odour of gasoline. The old man operated a mill powered by electricity, and his wife farmed ten mu of land. Not long ago he had attended a meeting of farmers who had prospered, and received an award. His picture was in the newspapers. No generation in their family had been as prosperous or as busy as they. Now they needed a sensible woman to take charge of the household, and a wife for his son. While they were still talking the son came in. He flashed a wad of notes in front of the stranger. He wore a wrist-watch, and a walkman was strapped to his waist. Earphones were stuck to his ears. He danced to music that no one else could hear. He was the epitome of the young man of the city. Tabei was not impressed. What interested him was the tractor parked outside. The engine had not been switched off, and the tractor emitted a put-put sound. Tabei ran his fingers over the steering-wheel enviously.

"I'll leave Jade for you," said Tabei. From the way he smiled, Tabei knew the young man had probably already had Jade.

"Can I drive this contraption?" asked Tabei.

"Of course. You can learn to drive it in half an hour," the young man said expansively. He quickly showed Tabei how to control the machine; how to regulate the gas, shift the gears, and how to start and stop.

Tabei drove the tractor along the dirt path in the gathering dusk. Jade watched from the side of the road, her eyes brimming with joy, for she was going to stay. Just then a heavier tractor towing a load came careening down the path. The driver saw Tabei in front of him but it was too late to stop. Tabei panicked, not knowing what to do. The young man shouted for him to drive the tractor into the ditch by the side of path. At the last moment, Tabei leaped from the driver's seat. The tractor slid into the ditch, but the oncoming tractor caught Tabei and knocked him to the ground. Everyone rushed to him. Tabei picked himself up. He had been struck in the side, but to everyone's relief, aside from a good dusting, he was none the worse for wear.

Tabei was leaving. He took Jade in his arms and touched his forehead against hers, and went off towards the Kalong Glacier. That evening it rained, and the whole village celebrated. On the way Tabei began to spit blood.

The manuscript ended there.

I decided to return to Papunaigang, and cross the Kalong Glacier to the place they called the palm print of the Lord of the Lotus. Perhaps I would encounter my protagonist again.

The distance from A Village to the Kalong Glacier was farther than I imagined. The mule I hired went lame. It lay on the ground, white froth dribbling from its mouth, its eyes rolled back in the throes of death. I unstrapped the saddlebags, and shouldered them myself, and leaving a handful of meal beside the mule's muzzle, went on my way. At the top of the mountain the wind roared. Yet the air was calm but bitterly cold. The snow lay in unbroken undulations for as far as the eye could see.

I began the descent. I had goggles so I did not have to wait till dark. Slowly I zig-zagged my way down. The saddle bags grew heavier and heavier, as they slipped down to the small of my back. I stopped to adjust them. As I leaned forward, the weight shifted, I lost my balance and pitched forward. I felt myself helplessly sliding down the mountainside. I drew myself into a tight ball, and tumbled head over heels down the mountain. When I came to I was lying at the foot of the mountain. A deep furrow marked my passage had through the snow ending where snow and mist melted into one another. I had looked at the time when I was on the mountain top and distinctly remembered it was 9:46, yet now my watch registered 8:03. Beyond the snow line, the earth was covered with moss, and further down there was grass, which gave way to low brush and then short, stubby trees, and finally forest. Beyond the forest, the vegetation grew sparse again. Great boulders jutted out of the dry earth. I noticed all this while I had been checking the time, comparing what I thought it should be to what my watch registered. I concluded that somehow after I crossed the Kalong Glacier time began to move backwards. The calendar and the hands on my watch spun in reverse, five times faster than normal.

The landscape took on a dreamlike quality. There was row upon row of Bodhi trees with elliptical leaves and yellowish-white bark, and roots that were so neat they might have been deliberately carved. To one side there stood the ruins of an ancient monastery. Suddenly a huge elephant came lumbering towards me across the clearing. The landscape took on the nightmarish quality of Salvador Dali's *Temptation of St. Anthony*. I hastened to put some distance between myself and the beast, and did not stop till I reached the banks of the hot springs. I was exhausted but I dared not sleep for fear that I might never wake again. Beyond the hot springs the plain was littered with gold saddles, bows and arrows, rusted spears, armour, scripture cases and tattered banners. It appeared to be an ancient battlefield out of some forgotten epic. If I was not so tired I would have ventured forth for a closer look. As it was I gazed at this curious spectacle from a distance. Long exposure to the steam had melted the metal, so that the various objects melded into indistinct masses. I was beginning to wonder if I was seeing things. Long isolation plays strange tricks on the mind. But my reasoning and memory were unaffected. The sun still rose from the east and set in the west. Though night still followed day, the backward spinning of the dials on my watch was disconcerting. It disturbed my metabolism, and shifted my centre of gravity.

At dawn I woke under a huge red boulder. I found myself at a point where a thousand creeks and gullies fanned out in every direction. I had reached the palm of the Lord of the Lotus. I clambered up the side of a gully and looked over the rim. The empty plain swept onto the horizon. Some of the gullies that criss-crossed it were bottomless. The plain must have endured a long drought, for the earth was cracked and scorched to a cinder; not a blade of grass grew. It reminded me of the final scene of a film I once saw. The earth was emptied of life by a nuclear holocaust. Only a man and a woman survived. They struggled painfully towards each other, and embraced at the fade out. They were the new Adam and Eve.

But my protagonist did not appear.

"Tabei ... Tabei ... Where are you?" I shouted. The sound travelled far but there was no echo. I felt he could not have found his way out of the maze.

A while later a figure appeared in the distance, moving slowly towards me. I ran to meet it, shouting Tabei's name at the top of my lungs. When I got closer, I found it was Jade.

"Tabei is dying," she sobbed.

"Where is he?"

Wordlessly she led me into a nearby ravine. Tabei lay at the bottom of the ravine. He was pale and wan, and his breathing came in short painful gasps. Moss covered the sides of the ravine, and water dripping from the cracks in the rock had collected into a small pool. Jade soaked her belt in it and squeezed the water into Tabei's half-open mouth.

"Master, I have been waiting. I comprehend and the gods will inspire me," Tabei said, lifting his eyes to me beseechingly.

"He has a serious wound in the side," Jade whispered to me. "He has to keep drinking water."

"Why didn't you stay in the village?" I asked.

"Why would I stay there?" she retorted. "I never considered staying. Besides, he would never let me go. He took my heart and tied it to his belt. I can't live without him."

"That's not so," I objected.

"He wants to know what that is?" Jade pointed in the direction from which I came. I looked back. Before me was a deep gully, as straight as an arrow. At the end of it was a huge red boulder. That was where I spent the night. On the rock was carved the symbol of a bow. It was the pictorial representation of a sound Tibetans made when they had recited the six syllables of their chant a hundred times. I concluded the strange marking must either mean that this was a place which gods and demons frequented, or it marked the resting place of a dead hero. I had seen such a rock on the banks of the Quimixingu River commemorating the Tibetan hero Benlatin II who fought the British invaders in 1904. But I felt no need to explain all this to Tabei. It was too late to explain the truths I discovered. I had given life and purpose to all my "children", who like Jade and Tabei were consigned to a serial numbered brown paper envelope. But I had made a grave error in their creation. I should have made them human beings of the new era. The act of creation is objective. How would I answer to letting characters like them wander the world in our time?

I crouched beside Tabei, pressed my lips close to his ear and tried to tell him in words that he could grasp that the place he sought all his life did not exist any more than Thomas More's *Utopia*.

But it was too late. In the last moments of life, nothing would shake his faith. He turned his body and pressed his head against the earth.

"Tabei," I said, "you will get better. I have some medicine in my saddle bags over there."

"Hush," Tabei pressed his ear hard against the moist damp earth. "Listen! Listen!"

I listened but all I could discern was the wild beating of my heart.

"Help me up there! I must get up there!" Tabei pushed himself up to a sitting position, shouting and gesticulating.

I helped him to his feet. Jade climbed to the top of the ravine and I, holding Tabei round the waist with one arm and dragging myself forward with my free hand, gradually inched our way upward. It was a painfully slow climb. I gashed the palm of my hand on a sharp rock. At first it was numb, then a sharp pain shot down the length of my arm, and the blood trickled down the sleeve of my jacket. I hung on doggedly. Finally we were almost level with the edge of the ravine. Jade reached down and seized Tabei by the armpits, and I pushed from below and in this way half dragged and half lifted him over the edge. The sun was peeping over the horizon. Tabei dragged the air into his lungs in greedy gulps, looking round all the while as though he were searching for something.

"What are they saying, Master? I can't understand. Tell me please, I beg of you!" Tabei prostrated himself before me. Then Jade and I heard it too. It was a sound that came from the sky.

"It's temple bells," cried Jade.

"It's church bells," I corrected her.

"It's an avalanche!" said Jade.

"It's a thousand people singing," I corrected her again. Jade looked at me quizzically.

"The gods are speaking," said Tabei simply.

This time I did not attempt to correct him. How could I explain that the man's voice was speaking in English; that this was a live broadcast from the 23rd Olympics in Los Angeles that was beamed to every corner of the globe by a space satellite? Finally, the sense of time came back to me. The dials on my watch stopped all at once. It read: July 1984, 7:30 a.m. Beijing time.

"It's not the gods speaking, it's man's challenge to the world, my son," I said to him.

I didn't know whether he heard me, or if he understood. He curled up as if he were very cold, his eyes shut tightly as if asleep. I knelt beside him, and gently arranged his body in the shape of a bow. The blood of my injured hand stained his tattered clothes. I felt a pang. I had killed him, as surely as I had killed so many other protagonists. It's time I stopped.

"I'm all alone now," Jade said pathetically.

"Never mind. You've endured enough. I'll remould you."

I looked up at her, and she gazed back at me, full of innocence and trust.

The leather thong around her waist dangled before my eyes. I took hold of it and counted the knots that marked the days of her long trek. There were one hundred and eight, the same number as Tabei's string of prayer beads.

The sun had risen. I took Tabei's place and Jade followed behind. We were going back, but time was moving forward.

Translated by David Kwan

Return

●

—— HAN SHAOGONG ——

Han Shaogong was born in 1953 in Hunan. In 1978 he entered the Chinese Department of the Hunan Teacher Training University and in 1982 became an editor of a magazine. In 1985 he became a professional writer with the Hunan branch of the Chinese Writers' Association. He has published several collections of short stories and won national awards in 1980 and 1981.

MANY people have said that sometimes, the first time that they go to a place, they feel that they already know it well without knowing why. That is the sort of experience that I am having now.

I am walking. The mud track has been badly washed away in some parts. It has left behind a ridge of earth and nests of pebbles, like flesh scooped out, exposing muscle and bone and wizened internal organs. Several sticks of rotting bamboo and a cow rope in the ditch herald the imminent appearance of a village. A host of black shadows dance on the pools of water at the side of the road. Not looking closely, I think they are the shadows of rocks. Taking a closer look, I see they are calves' heads staring furtively at me. They are all wrinkled and moustached, hoary at birth, hereditarily old. On the other side of the banana grove ahead there is a square blockhouse with cold gun embrasures and walls blackened as if by smoke and flame or the congealing of many nights. I have heard that there were many bandits in this region in the past. If they had been left uncaptured for ten years there would be no people left on the land. It is hardly surprising that the villages have blockhouses or that the mountain peoples' homes cluster together one against another, sturdy and cowering, with windows set high like eyelets that bandits cannot climb through easily.

This all looks so familiar and yet so strange, as it often happens a word becomes both more and less recognizable the more one looks at it. Damn it, have I or have I not been here before? Let me guess. That flagstone road up ahead runs around the banana grove, and then turns to the left beside the oil press. From there perhaps one can see an old tree behind the blockhouse. It is either a ginkgo or a camphor which has been struck dead by lightning.

Sure enough my guesses are soon proved right. Even that hollow tree, with two young boys amusing themselves by burning grass in front of it, seems to have been in my imaginings.

I guess again with trepidation. Perhaps there is a low cowshed behind the old tree, in front of which there are several piles of cow dung. Under the eaves there is a rusty plough or harrow. As I walk over, sure enough they become closer and more distinct. It seems as if I have even seen the uneven pestle and mortar made of rough stone, the silt in the bottom of the mortar and those two fallen leaves before.

Of course the stone mortar of my imagination does not have silt in it, but now I think carefully, it has just rained, and wouldn't the water from the roof of the building flow into here? There are cold shivers running up and down my spine once again.

I definitely have not been here before. There is simply no way. I have never had meningitis; I have never been mentally disturbed. My brain is still in working order. Perhaps I have seen it before in a film? Heard friends talk about it? Or in a dream.... I am madly trying to think.

Even more strange is that the mountain people seem to recognize me. Just now when I was looking for stones as I crossed the stream with my trousers rolled up, a young man, shouldering two trees bound together in the shape of the letter "A", came down. When he saw me slipping and sliding he took a dried branch from a shed at the side of the road and threw it to me. Inexplicably he showed his yellow teeth and laughed.

"You've come?"
"Ah, yes, I've come."
"Must be ten years."
"Ten years...."
"Go up to my house and rest a while. Sangui is ploughing in the field out front."

Where is his house? Who is Sangui? I'm confused.

I follow the path up a small slope, and a tiled courtyard rises in front of me. I can see the outlines of several people threshing something on the flat land. I can even hear the clacking of the wooden flails, sometimes loud, sometimes soft. They are all barefoot and all have short hair. Their faces have a brown glaze of sweat, the edge of which is breaking up unevenly. In the dazzling sunlight, there is a small section of reflected light on their cheekbones. Their jackets all hang too short, revealing a soft belly and navel. Their trousers hang loosely from their hips. Not until I see one of them go towards a cradle and undo the clothes around her breast, and see that they are all wearing earrings, do I realize that they are women. One of them opens her eyes wide at me.

"Isn't this Ma...."

"Glasses Ma," another reminds her. Finding this name amusing, they all laugh.

"My name isn't Ma, it's Huang...."

"Changed your name?"

"No, I haven't changed it."

"So you still like to tease? Where have you come from?"

"From the county, of course."

"A really uncommon visitor."

"What about Young Liang?"

"What Young Liang?"

"Wasn't your wife called Liang?"

"Mine is called Yang."

"Could I have remembered wrongly? No way, no way. At the time she even told me it was the same as my family name. My mother-in-law is from Sanjiangkou, Liangjiashe, you know."

Know what? Anyway what has her name got to do with me? It is as if I really wanted to see her but came here instead. I do not even know myself how I got here.

The woman lays down her flail and leads me into the house. The doorstep is extremely high and wide. So countless have been the people, both young and old, who have crossed the threshold or sat on the step that little by little the middle has been worn into a dip. The yellow grain of the wood is as if tainted by a moon spreading its rays on the doorstep before congealing into a fossil. Small children have to crawl over the threshold. Adults have to pick their legs up high before, with difficulty, they can swing their bodies through the door. It is pitch black inside. Nothing can be seen clearly. There is just one high eye of a window that lets in a few rays of light, cutting open the damp blackness. There is also the odour of pig swill and chicken droppings. It takes a long time for one's eyes to become adjusted and see that the walls and beams are covered with soot. There is also an equally black hanging basket. I'm sitting on a block of wood. Strangely enough they do not have chairs here, just wooden blocks and benches. The women, young and old, all crowd twittering in the doorway. The one breast-feeding her child is not in the least bashful, but pulls out the other large breast and puts it in the baby's mouth. Looking towards me she smiles while the removed breast drips milk. They are all saying very strange things.... "Young Qin...." "It is not Young Qin." "Is that right?" "It is Young Ling." "How come? Isn't she still teaching?" "Couldn't she come back for a break?" "Did you all return to Changsha?" "Was it in the city or countryside?" "Have you had any children?" "One or two?" "Has Young Luo had any children yet?" "One or two?" "And Chen Zhihua?" "One or two?" "What about Bearhead? Has he found himself a wife?" "Children too? One or two?..."

I quickly realize that they have all mistaken me for a "Glasses Ma" who knows a Young Ling, a Bearhead and others. Maybe he looks a lot like me. He also hides behind his glasses looking at people.

Who is he? Must I think about him? From the laughing faces of the women, it looks as if board and lodging will not be a problem today. Thank God. It is not a bad thing to be taken for Mr Ma. I'll reply to their questions of "one or two", surprise them a bit and gain their sympathies. It shouldn't take much.

The elder woman from Liangjiashe brings in a tea tray with four large bowls of fried flour gruel. I find out later that this is in hope of a peaceful year, the four bowls symbolizing the four seasons. The sides of the bowl are black, and I do not dare touch my lips to them, but the gruel is good. It tastes of fried sesame and polished glutinous rice. She picks up two dirty articles of children's clothing from the floor, puts them in a wooden washing bowl and carries it into the bedroom, so that one sentence is split in two: "We had no news of you for so long. According to Master Shuigen..." (she does not come out of the room for a long time) "... when you went back you were sentenced to a long term in prison."

I am so astonished that I nearly scald my hand on the gruel. "No. What term in prison?"

"Old Shuigen doesn't know anything, blast him! Caused my father-in-law to worry no end. He burned many incense sticks on your behalf." She covers her mouth and laughs. "Ah, I'm going to die laughing."

All the women laugh. One with a mouthful of yellow teeth adds: "He even went to Daigongling to beg for Buddha's help."

How dreadful: seeking the Buddha's help. Maybe this Mr Ma really got into some big trouble that landed him in prison, and here am I in his place eating gruel and laughing like an idiot.

The woman has brought in a second cup of gruel. As before one hand gripping the wrist of the hand carrying the bowl. This must be polite custom in these parts. I have not finished the first bowl yet, but it has dried, and the sesame and the glutinous rice have not slipped down the sides of the bowl. I do not know how I am going to drink it with any refinement. "He was always concerned about you. He said you were very kind and had a good conscience. He wore your coat for many winters. He's dead now, and I have turned the coat into padded trousers that my youngest can still wear...."

I want to talk about the weather.

The room has suddenly darkened. I turn my head to look. A black shadow seems to be blocking the whole door. I can tell it is a man, naked to the waist. His bulging muscles are not rounded but have corners and edges like rocky crags. What is he carrying in his hand? From the silhouette, it looks like a cow's head. The black shadow has enveloped me without allowing me to see his face clearly. He throws the thing he has been carrying on to the ground with a thud. Two large hands grip mine and lock together.

"It's Comrade Ma. Ha ha ha...."

I am not a caterpillar, so what am I afraid of?

As he turns towards the stove his side is plated with light. Only now can I see clearly that it is a smiling face with a large, black, cavernous mouth and both arms are tatooed.

"Comrade Ma, when did you arrive?"

I want to say I really am not called Ma but Huang, Huang Zhixian, and I have not come in search of a place I know well out of deep feelings for it.

"Do you still know (remember? recognize?) me? The year when you left I was still in the mountains building roads. My name is Aiba."

"Aiba, yes," I reply humbly. "You were team leader at the time."

"No, I wasn't, I recorded work points. Do you still know my wife?"

"Yes, I know her. She makes an excellent gruel."

"I went with you to catch meat. Do you remember? (Catch meat: does that mean hunting?) I wanted to make an offering to the mountain gods, but you said it was superstitious. Afterwards you blundered into a patch of poisonous grass and got a rash all over. That time you came across a muntjac deer, it went right past your hip but you didn't prang it...."

"Er, no, I didn't. Just missed. My eyes aren't very good, you know."

The black cavern of a mouth bursts out laughing. The women slowly get up, swaying their large hips, and go out of the door. The man who calls himself Aiba takes out a bottle gourd and politely pours me a drink in my large bowl.

The drink is very cloudy. It is sweet, peppery and bitter, apparently an infusion of herbal medicine and tiger bone. He will not smoke my cigarettes but uses newspaper to roll himself a homemade one. He draws on it once, and the paper flares up. He's not the slightest bit worried, does not even look at it. Not until I have been anxious for a good while does he calmly put out the fire in just one breath. The tobacco is still in good shape.

"There is plenty of food and drink for you nowadays. At Spring Festival every household killed a cow." He wipes his mouth. "In the year when we had to learn from Dazhai* no one had any income. But you know that already."

"Right."

I want to talk about the good times.

"Have you seen Delong? He's now the county head. Yesterday he went to Zhuomei Bridge to plant trees. He may be back now, or maybe not.

---

*A production brigade in Xiyang County, Shanxi Province which was the so-called pacesetter for Chinese agriculture.

Maybe he is." He is talking of people and affairs which totally confuse me: so-and-so has built a new house, five metres high; so-and-so has built a new house six metres high; so-and-so is about to build a new house five metres high; the way so-and-so is digging foundations, maybe it will be five metres, or maybe six. I listen nervously, trying to catch the train of thought behind the words. I find the speech of these parts a little odd: "see" has become "regard", and they say "clear" for "peaceful". Another word is "gather". Does it mean rise? Or does it mean stand?

I feel a little tipsy and confusedly express my happiness at either five or six metres.

"You haven't changed a bit, coming into the mountains like this to have a look." Once again he draws the cigarette paper into a small bright fire, making me secretively anxious for a few seconds again. "I've kept the book you gave out when you were our teacher." He shuffles up the stairs. It is quite a while before he re-emerges with threads of spiders' web in his hair, patting a few pages of a small, mimeographed book. It is probably a character learning textbook. The cover has already been ripped off, and it smells of mold and tung oil. Crudely printed inside there is an old night-school song, miscellaneous characters used by the peasants, the 1911 Revolution, Marx's discussion on peasant movements and a certain map. Each character is very big, with blobs of printing ink. There is nothing strange about these characters: I could indeed have written them.

"You suffered too. You were so hungry that all that was left of your face were your eyes, but still you came and taught classes."

"It was nothing, nothing."

"In the snowy twelfth moon. It was so cold."

"So cold that my nose nearly froze off."

"But still we had to work the fields, lighting pine torches to see by."

"Ah, yes. Pine torches."

He has suddenly grown mysterious. The patch of light on his cheekbone and his spots close in on me. "I want to ask you something. Did you kill Shorty Yang?"

What Shorty Yang? My skull suddenly contracts, the inside of my mouth stiffens, and I repeatedly shake my head. I'm really not Mr Ma and have never seen Mr Shorty Yang. Why lay the whole criminal case on my shoulders?

"Everyone says you killed him. That man was a two-headed snake. He deserved to be killed!" He's growing angry. When he sees I won't confirm it, he starts to doubt a little and look disappointed.

"Is there any more to drink?" I change the subject.

"Yes, yes as much as you can take."

"There are mosquitos."

"They're hard on strangers. Shall I light some straw?"

The straw is lit. Another group of people have come to see me. They turn in through the door and as usual ask after my health and about each member of my family. The men take my cigarettes and smoke them with loud puffs, sitting against the door or the walls narrowing their eyes into smiles, not saying much. I listen to their occasional remarks. Some say I have put on weight. Some say I have lost it. Some say I have aged. Some say I still have a young face, of course because of the greasy food of the city. As soon as they have smoked their cigarettes, they laugh again and say they must go to chop trees or shift cow dung. Several little children run up and spend some time looking closely at my glasses. Then in nervous high spirits, with a real feeling of terror, they shout, "There's a ghost inside! A ghost!" and run off in all directions. A girl is standing by the door, a piece of straw in her mouth, idiotically looking at me with glittering tears filling her eyes. I do not understand why. It makes me feel very uncomfortable. I had best politely keep my eyes continuously on Aiba.

I have come across this sort of thing more than once. Just now I went to look at their variety of opium. On the way I met a middle-aged woman. As soon as she saw me she was obviously terrified. Her face was like an oil lamp that had suddenly dimmed. She quickly picked up her heels, lowered her head, chose a road and left. I did not know what this meant.

Aiba says I should go and see Third Grandpa — who in fact is not here any more. I'm told he died from a snake bite not long ago. This is just a name that lingers in conversation. His solitary little house still stands near the brick kiln. It is already half falling down. Just one look and it would collapse. Beneath the two tung trees there is lush green grass that has grown waist high. It has grown all around the house, sinisterly covering the steps up to the front door with shaking tongues of grass about to swallow up the little house, as if trying to gobble up the last remaining bones of a family. The padlocked wooden door is already full of black holes bored by worms. I wonder if the house was in such a bad state when the owner was here. Is it possible that man is the house's soul, and once the soul has left the outer body rots at this speed? In the grass there is an overturned rusty barn lantern, on top of which are white bird droppings. There is also a broken earthernware jar. At a touch hundreds of mosquitos come buzzing out. Aiba says it was always used to pickle vegetables and I often came to Third Grandpa's house to eat pickled cucumber. (Really?) Painted on the flaking wall are several fading characters. Only the edges of the brush strokes have not totally faded: "Take a broad look at the world...." Aiba says it was I who wrote these characters. (Really?) Aiba pulls up a bunch of weeds and peeps at a bird's nest in the trees. I turn to the window and glance in. I can see half a basket of lime in the corner. There is also a large, round disk. Taking a closer look I realize it is an iron barbell, rusted and out of shape. I am surprised. How does this piece of sports equipment come to be in the mountains? How did it get here?

I had better not ask. Was it I that gave it to Third Grandpa, gave it to him to be made into a hoe or a rake, but he did not do it after all? Is that right?

Someone up the slope is calling cows: "Ooma — Ooma." And in the wood opposite the faint ring of cow bells can be heard. The way they call cows here sounds oddly like calling mamma miserably. Perhaps it was these calls that turned the brick walls of the blockhouse black.

An old granny carrying a bundle of firewood on her back comes down from the mountain. Her waist is almost bent double. Step by step, her chin sticking out like a rake, she comes, raking as she steps. She looks up at me with deep eyes. It is as if she is not looking at me but looking right through my brain to the tung trees beyond. Her blurry pupils bore through her eyelids with absolutely no expression in them, just a wrinkly face which makes me feel very nervous. When she sees Third Grandpa's old house she turns again to look at the old tree at the end of the village. She mindlessly murmurs, "The tree is dead too", then slowly rakes her way in to the distance. The withered strands of silver on her head are pressed down by the wind, pressed down.

Now I am convinced I really have not been here before. I am quite mystified by her words, as by a deep pool I cannot get to the bottom of.

Dinner is a very solemn occasion. Big chunks of underdone beef and pork smelling raw and greasy are laid imposingly on the table. The meat, in palm-sized pieces, is piled up in a bowl. Grass is used to hold the meat overflowing from the bowl so that more can be piled on top. People have been eating in this same way for thousands of years. One person has not come. The host puts some rough straw paper in the empty place. As each person takes a piece, a piece is put on the paper just as if he were eating. During the meal I ask about their sweet-smelling rice. They then determine to give me some as a gift, refusing to mention a price. As for opium, no matter whether this year's crop is good or not, the national pharmaceutical industry has a monopoly on it. I do not dare say anything more.

"Shorty Yang deserved to die." Aiba slurps a mouthful of hot soup and pats the spoon back in its sticky place on the table. Fixing his eyes on the bowl of meat, he knocks his chopsticks: "With his turned-up bottom and his rounded palms, he botched any job he did. Him build a house? Very crafty!"

"That's right, is there anyone who didn't suffer under his iron rules? There are still two scars on my wrists. That son-of-a-bitch!"

"How did he die in fact? Did he really bump in to the old devil and fall over the cliff?"

"No matter how fierce he is, a man can't escape his fate. If it is man's lot to have one litre, he will want ten. Hongsheng from Xiajiawan is just like that."

"That man is diabolic. He even eats rats."

"That's dreadful. I never heard that before."

"Bearhead also suffered from his fists. It was obviously several bags of dye — I saw them myself — but it wouldn't dye cloth, it was only good for painting the Buddha in the temple."

"It was also partly because of Bearhead's low social status."

I pluck up all my courage and interpose a sentence.

"Were the authorities sent to investigate the affair of Shorty Yang?"

Aiba, chewing on a piece of fat, mumbles: "Investigate? Investigate my bollocks! The day they came to find me I went to look for the old chicken. Oh, Comrade Ma, why haven't you touched your drink? Come on, eat up, eat."

He forces another piece of meat on me. My throat tightens. The best thing is to pretend to go and get some more rice, and while in a dark corner, I give the meat to a dog sqeezing past my leg.

After supper they insist on me taking a bath. I suspect it is one of the customs of this area. I have to pretend to understand it all. They don't have a wash bowl, only a large tub, which can hold several large pans of hot water. It is put in the corner of the kitchen. Women come and go in front of the tub. The woman from Liangjiashe occasionally adds water with a gourd ladle, making me very embarrassed. I squat lower and lower into the tub. Only when she takes the bucket to feed the pigs do I let out a sigh of relief. I have been in for so long that I am hot all over, and sweat is pouring off me. The water was heated with wormwood, so the red spots all over my body where I have been bitten by mosquitos do not itch any more. The lard lamp above my head, shining through the steam, creates a bluey mist and tinges my flesh blue. Before putting my shoes on I look at my blue body. I suddenly feel very strange, as if it is someone else's, which is odd. There are no clothes or accessories here, no strangers, so there is no one to hide anything from or to pretend to. There is only bare, exposed me. The real me. I have hands and feet, so I can do things. I have a gallbladder and a stomach, so I have to eat. I have genitals to reproduce. The world has temporarily been shut outside the door. In the world one is busy with work and so has no free time to think about these things. Our ancestors came into existence only by the coincidence of a sperm joining with an ovum. Not until this ancestor coincidentally met with another was there another fertilized ovum and a latter-day me in existence. I am one of many coincidentally fertilized blue eggs. What am I in this world for? What can I do? I stupidly think too much.

I am wiping an inch-long scar on my calf. It comes from being struck by a football boot on the playing field, and yet it could almost be ... a bite from a certain short man. Was it on that rainy, foggy morning? On that narrow mountain path? He came up carrying an umbrella, so terrified that he was trembling under my stare. Then he knelt down and said he would never do it again, never again, and said that Second Sister-in-law's death had nothing to do with him, nor was it he who made off with Third Grandpa's cow. At the last he put up some resistance, his eyes bulging as if they were about to fall out as he bit my leg. His hands began to grasp the cow rope around his neck, and then abruptly stretched out like two crabs crawling, convulsing on and digging into the ground. At some point they slowly came to rest and were calm....

I do not dare go on thinking, I do not dare even look at my own hands — do they not smell of blood and still hold traces of cow rope?

I must try hard to convince myself that I have never been here before and do not know any Shorty something. I have not seen this bluey fog even in dreams before, never.

The central room is very noisy. An old man has come in, trampling out the pine torches and saying that he once had me buy some cloth dye for him and still owes me two yuan. He has come to repay the money and to invite me to eat at his house tomorrow and stay the night. This is what has got Aiba angry. Aiba says he is going to fetch the tailor tomorrow. He has already bought the meat. Tomorrow, no doubt about it, I have to go to his house....

Whilst they are still arguing I sneak out of the door. I stumble off, hoping to go and see "my" house that I used to live in — Aiba says it is the cow shed behind the old tree. Not until the year before last was it turned into a cow shed.

I pass beneath the tung trees again and through the grass that is about to swallow up old Grandpa — the shadow of the sloping thatched house. It is quietly looking at me, using the call of a crow to cry hello, using the whispering of the leaves on the trees to talk with me. It even feels as if there is the odd drop of alcohol in the air.

My child, you have come back? Get yourself a chair and come and sit down. I told you to go far away and never come back again.

But I missed your pickled cucumbers. I learned how to make them myself, but they are never as good as yours.

What is so good about those dreadful things? I saw you were hungry. It was dreadful. You'd ploughed all the way to the edge of the field, and you were so hungry that you pulled the broad beans from the stalks and ate them. Then only thing for it was to give you pickled cucumbers.

You were always concerned for us, I know.

Everyone leaves home at some point. It was only right.

Once when we were carrying branches, we only brought nine loads, but you put it down as ten, so that we could have more work points.

I don't remember.

You always wanted us to shave our heads, saying that hair and beard suck blood and left to grow long are bad for the health.

Is that right? I don't remember.

I ought to have come to see you before. I never thought things would have changed so drastically. You left in such a hurry."

"I ought to be gone. If I'd lived much longer I would have turned into a spirit. I did like a drink, and now I've had my fill I can sleep soundly."

"Won't you have a cigarette, Grandpa?"

"Help yourself if you want some tea, Young Ma."

I have left the smell of alcohol, holding high the pine torch that is about to die out, and I think about the farming activities of tomorrow. I can often hear frogs at my feet, jumping into the pond. I am going to my home, but now I don't have a torch, and my house is a cow shed. Obviously it will be unfamiliar, cold and detached. I cannot see anything clearly. I can only hear the sound of the cows chewing the cud and smell the odour of warm cow dung from the straw in the shed. The cows think it is their owner who has come; their heads jammed together crane out against the door of the pen.

As I go, footsteps echo from the earth walls of the shed, as if there is someone else walking by the wall or even in the earthern wall. This person knows my secret.

The mountain cliff opposite is black and gloomy. It is even higher and closer at night than during the day, making one catch one's breath. Looking up through the thin space to the starry sky, the earth seems close, the sky far. One feels held down by some force, about to be pressed down and down into a deep crack in the earth.

The huge moon comes out, surprising the dogs in the village, which start to bark. I tread on the moonlight sieved through the shadow of the trees. I tread on the dots of moon, which are like algae or floating duckweed, and walk towards the stream. There may be someone sitting by the river, perhaps a girl with a straw in her mouth.

There was no one by the stream, but when I turn back I at last see someone's shadow under the old tree. The night is so clear that there ought to be a silhouette.

"Is that Young Ma?"

"Yes, it's me." Surprisingly my reply was not in the least rushed.

"You've come from the stream?"

"Who ... who are you?"

"Fourth Sister."

"Fourth Sister. You've grown so tall. If I bumped into you in the street I really would not recognize you."

"Now you've been out in the world you think everything has changed here."

"How is your family?"

Suddenly she turns gloomy, looking at the house over by the press, and her voice changes a little. "My sister hates you...."

"Does she?" I am so nervous that I dart a look at the path out to the light and the level ground, wanting to run. "I ... you never can tell. I told her...."

"Why did you put corn in her basket like that? A girl's basket, and you just put things in it? She gave you a lock of her hair, you know."

"I ... I didn't understand. I didn't understand people's ways here."

It seems that my reply passes. I can still muddle through.

"Everyone says that. Are you deaf? I saw it all. You taught her acupuncture."

"She liked to study, wanted to be a doctor. In fact, I didn't understand it myself and was just sticking needles in anywhere."

"You city people don't know what friendship is."

"Don't be so...."

"It's true! It's true!"

"I know. Your sister is a good girl, I know. She sings beautifully and is excellent at sewing. Once she took me to catch eels. She just put her hand in, and there was an eel. I was ill. She cried so hard.... I know all that. But there is a lot that you do not understand. I'm going to be rushing back and forth all my life, I ... have my own career."

At last I've said the word career, though it was not easy.

She covers her mouth and sobs. "That man Hu, he's vicious."

I seem to know what she means by this, and continuing to probe, I reply, " So I've heard. I want to find him to settle the score."

"What's the point? What's the point?" She stamps her foot and cries even more broken-heartedly.

"If only you had said something earlier, it wouldn't have turned out like this. My sister is a bird now. She comes here every day and calls you. Calls you. Can you hear her?"

In the moonlight I see her gaunt back rising and falling. Above is her smooth neck and white scalp clearly visible through the parting in her hair. I want to wipe her tears away and grasp her shoulders, kiss her head like kissing a younger sister and let her salty tears stick to my lips, and then to swallow them.

But I don't dare. This is a strange story. I don't dare lick open the wound.

There really is a bird calling in the tree, "You can't do that, brother. You can't do that, brother," — a solitary sound like a sharp arrow shooting high in the air and quickly dropping into the mountains, dropping into the green trees, dropping into that black cloud and silent flash of lightning over there. I smoke a cigarette and look towards the storm as if talking to silent history.

You can't do that brother.

I leave. Before going I leave a letter for Fourth Sister, asking the woman from Liangjiashe to pass it on to her. In it I say that her sister wanted to be a doctor but never made it. I hope that the younger sister can achieve the elder's ambition. One must forge one's own road. Is she willing to sit the exam for the hygiene school? I will send her lots of material to help her study. I promise. I also say I'll never forget her older sister. Aiba caught the parrot in the tree. I am going to take it back with me and let it sing in my window every day and be my friend for ever.

It feels like I have absconded. I did not say goodbye to the people from the village, nor did I ask for their sweet-smelling rice. What do I want with rice or opium? That is not what I came for. The whole village, the whole baffling me is suffocating. I have to escape. I turn round to look and see that old tree killed by lightning at the end of the village. It is stretching out its withered branches like convulsing fingers. The owner of the hand was struck down in battle and turned into a mountain but still holds up a hand, struggling to grasp something.

I enter the inn in the county town centre and sleep to the sound of the parrot at the head of the bed. I have been dreaming of walking on and on along the winding mountain road, its mud washed away by mountain water, so it looks unfleshed, retaining only tendon and bone and withered organs to support the mountain people's straw shoes. The end of this road can never be reached. I look at my watch. I have already walked for one hour, one day, one week ... but it is still the same road under my feet. No matter where I go after this, I will always have the same dream.

I wake up in the night to drink three cups of water, pee twice and then make a long distance phone call to a friend. I intend to ask him whether he has beaten Scabby Cao at cards, but when I start to speak I ask about the exams for self-study courses.

My friend calls me Huang Zhixian.

"What?"

"What do you mean what?"

"What did you call me?"

"Aren't you Huang Zhixian?"

"Are you calling me Huang Zhixian?"

"Why shouldn't I call you Huang Zhixian?"

I am stunned. My brain is empty. That is right. In this inn where mosquitos swoop about in the dimly lit passageways, I have a temporary bed. Beneath the mouthpiece of the telephone is a grunting, fat head. But — is there anyone in the world called Huang Zhixian? Is that Huang Zhixian me?

I am tired. I can never leave this immense being which is me. Mother!

Translated by Alice Childs

The Mountain Cabin

●

—— **CAN XUE** ——

Can Xue, a young woman writer, was born in 1953 in Hunan. She discontinued her studies after she finished primary school and became a worker in a street factory. Later, together with her husband, she set up a tailor's shop. She began to write in 1985 and has since published the novel Performance of Breakthrough *and the short story collection* Dialogue in Paradise.

ON the barren mountain behind my house there was a wooden cabin.

Every day I sat at home tidying my drawer. When I stopped, I sat in my armchair with my hands flat on my knees and listened to the howling. The north wind blew the fir-bark roof of the little cottage with violent rage. And the howl of wolves echoed in the mountain valley.

"Hmph, your drawer can never be cleaned well enough." My mother sported a false smile.

"Is everyone deaf around here?" I continued speaking with constraint. "There are so many thieves wandering around outside our house at night that when I turn on the light I see countless holes poked through the window by human fingers. In the next room you and father are snoring so heavily that all the bottles and jars tremble in the kitchen cabinet. I kick the mattress and turn my swollen head, listening to the captive man in the little cabin beating violently on the wooden door. The beating lasts until daybreak."

"Every time you come to my room looking for something, I quiver with fear." Mother studied me cautiously, retreated to the door, and I saw one of her cheeks ridiculously twitching with fright.

One day I decided to climb the mountain to see what was really happening. I set off as soon as the wind dropped. I climbed for a long time, and the sunshine penetrated my eyes so fiercely that I felt very dizzy. White flames gleamed on every rock. I was coughing as I wandered on the mountain. Beads of salty sweat from my brow dripped into my eyes, and

I could neither see nor hear anything. I returned home and stood outside the door for a little while. I could see in the mirror the man's shoes were covered with mud, and there were two purple clouds masking his eye sockets.

"This is an illness." I could hear my family secretively laughing in the pitch dark.

By the time my eyes had adjusted to the darkness in the room, they'd already hidden themselves laughing and hiding. I found that they had messed up my drawer while I was absent. A few dead moths and dragonflies had been thrown on the ground, and they knew those were my favourite things.

"They helped you re-organize the drawer while you were away," my younger sister said, glaring steadily at me, her left eye turning green.

"I heard the wolves howl." I intended to frighten her. "Packs of wolves run around the house and squeeze their heads through the cracks in the door. This happens immediately after dark. You're so frightened in your dreams that cold sweat breaks out in the arches of your feet. Everyone in this house sweats from the arches of their feet. Look how wet the quilts are and you will know."

I felt annoyed because some things in my drawer were missing. Mother pretended to know nothing about it and lowered her eyes. But then I felt her eyes staring ferociously at the back of my head. Every time she stared at the back of my head, that part of my scalp went numb and swelled. I knew they'd already buried my *go* set by the side of the well behind our house. They had done that countless times, but each time I dug it up at midnight. They always turned on the light while I was digging and poked their heads out the window. They remained calm in the face of my resistance.

When we were eating I told them, "There's a little cabin on the mountain."

They all lowered their heads, wolfing down the soup noisily. Probably nobody heard my words.

"Hundreds of rats scurry about in the wind." I raised my voice and put down my chopsticks. "The sand and rocks on the mountainside rumbled down towards the wall behind our house, and you were all so scared that you sweated in your arches. Do you remember? Just look at your quilts, and you will know. When the weather cleared, you had to air your quilts in the sunshine. And the lines were always filled with your quilts."

With that wolf-like eye of his, Father gave me a quick glance. Suddenly I realized that Father became one of the wolves every night, chasing around the house with chilling howls.

"White gleams everywhere." I grasped my mother's shoulder with one hand and shook her. "Everything pierces my eyes, making them tear so that I can't make anything out. But whenever I return home and sit in my armchair with my hands flat on my knees, I can see clearly the fir-bark roof of the little cabin. The figure is not far away. You must have seen it, too. In fact all of our family has seen it. There really is a person squatting inside whose sockets are covered with two purple clouds, caused by sleeplessness."

"Every time you dug up and scraped at the stone beside the well, your mother and I would be suspended in mid-air, shivering and kicking in bare feet, unable to reach the ground." Father evaded my eyes and turned his face towards the window. The panes were daubed with fly droppings. "I dropped a pair of scissors down the well. I made a secret decision in my dream to get them out of the water. Yet when I woke up I always found I was mistaken. I have never dropped any scissors into the well, and your mother is quite sure of that. But I couldn't give up the idea altogether, so I thought of it sometimes later. I would suddenly feel sorry when I lay down, for not retrieving the scissors as they rusted on the well bottom. It has vexed me for decades, and wrinkles have been etched into my face like knife cuts.

"Eventually I came to the well and tried to lower the water bucket. The rope was heavy and slippery, and it tore through my loose grip, the bucket splintering against the bottom of the well. I rushed home, looked into the mirror and found my left temple completely white."

"The north wind is really fierce." I winced, my face purple and blue. "Ice fragments have frosted my stomach. When I sit in the armchair I can hear their restless tinkling."

I always wanted to clean my drawer well, but Mother secretly set herself against me. She would pace in the next room, tapping loudly on the ground and dismantling my thoughts. I wanted to dismiss the sound of her steps, so I laid out playing cards, murmuring, "One, two, three, four, five...," and the steps suddenly stopped. Mother stretched her little, dark green face around the side of the door, droning, "I had an erotic dream, and my back is still in a cold sweat."

"And the arches of your feet," I added. "Everybody's arches sweat. Yesterday you aired your quilt again. It's quite normal."

My little sister ran to tell me privately that Mother intended to break my arms because the sound of my drawer being opened was driving her mad. Every time she heard the sound, she dipped her head in cold water tormentedly until she got a serious cold.

"These things are not at all accidental." My little sister set her eternal stare on me until red, measle-like spots stung my neck. "Take father for example. I have heard him talking about that pair of scissors for twenty years, perhaps. Everything has been going on for so long."

I oiled the sides of my drawer, opening and closing it lightly, soundlessly. I experimented with it for many days, and the steps in the next room were also soundless. She was deceived by me. So you see, deception can hide many things, if you are just a little careful. I was so excited that I worked energetically throughout the night. But while my drawer became cleaner, the bulb suddenly burned out, and Mother tittered in the neighbouring room.

"My eyes were stung by the light in your room, and I heard a popping come from within my veins like beating drums. Look here," she pointed to her temples, where a plump earthworm pulsated. "I'd rather have scurvy, so that every day it was my own body knocking, rumbling. You've never tasted this. Because of this disease Father once contemplated suicide." She stretched a plump hand toward my shoulder and let it rest lightly. The hand was frozen and dripped with water.

Someone was conspiring by the well. I heard him drop the bucket into the well repeatedly. The suspended bucket struck against the side. At daybreak he threw the bucket into the well with a loud crash and ran away. I opened the door of the next room and found Father in a deep sleep, grappling with the side of the bed. The blue veins stood out on his hand, and he moaned miserably. Mother held the broom and thrashed about wildly with her hair in disarray.

She told me that at the very moment of daybreak a great swarm of long-horned beetles had flown in through the window, striking the wall and falling in great heaps to the floor. She had got up to sweep, and when she was putting on her slippers, her toe had been bitten by a beetle hiding inside. Her leg had swollen into a great lead pillar.

"He," Mother pointed at Father, who still slept soundly, "he was dreaming of being bitten himself."

"In the little cabin on the mountain there is another person moaning. The leaves of the wild vines tossed in the black wind."

"Did you hear?" Mother put her ear to the ground conscientiously in the dim light. "These things threw themselves on the ground and passed out. They rushed into the room at the very moment of daybreak."

That day I did climb the mountain again. I remember it clearly. First I sat in a rattan chair, resting my hands on my knees, and then I opened the door and walked into the white light. I ascended the mountain, and my eyes were brim-full of the flames of the white rocks. There were no wild vines and no little cabin.

Translated by Mei Zhong

Touch Paper

●

—— JIA PINGWA ——

Born and raised in a mountain village in Shaanxi, Jia Pingwa entered the Northwest University to study Chinese in 1975. Upon graduation he worked as an editor first for the Shaanxi People's Publishing House and then for Chang'an magazine. He is now a full-time writer. He has published more than twenty works including novels, short stories, poems and essays. All his works are set in the southern part of Shaanxi where great changes have been taking place during the period of economic reforms. "Two Sisters" and "The Lunar December and January" were both national prize-winners.

1

SLENDER green bamboo clung steadfastly to the gaps in the cliff face. A youth threw bundles of bamboo down onto the rocks below, then tossed his cutting knife down too. It fell silently, and shone with a cold brightness, like a lost cresent moon.

It was dusk over the Han River, and after a hard day's work one could finally rest. The young man took three pieces of syrup cake out from under a rock and sat gazing dreamily over the river where it flowed past the cliff. Syrup cake is wrapped in the leaves of the Mongolian oak then steamed, so it looks like a glutinous rice cake, and when you open it the veins of the oak leaves are clearly printed on the cake. Just as he was about to eat them, a crow began circling overhead. Although it had not discovered the cakes when they were hidden under the stone, now it came down and snapped up all the crumbs that fell to the ground as the young man ate, and even snatched a piece from the youth's hand before swiftly flying away. At that moment a shuttle boat sped by, so fast that it would soon disappear behind the cliff where it jutted out into the river. At the bow of the boat stood the boatman holding a punt pole. He sang in a wolf-like voice:

*When you take my hand,
I want to kiss your lips.
Take my hand.
Kiss your lips
Deep in the mountains the two of us stroll....*

This boat carried men along the river to the dense forests in the mountains in the north where they cut lacquer. It set out from Twin River Pass, and moored for the night at Huluzhen.

At Huluzhen was Sun Erniang's teahouse. It was said that men from the river would arrive there worn out from their work, flop into the bamboo chairs, sip tea, have a smoke, and listen to Sun Erniang play her *pipa** and softly sing mountain songs. After you had heard a number of her songs you began daydreaming about being out on the river in your boat wearing a raincoat made of woven rushes, singing those scandalous ditties and letting your imagination run riot.

Dad had taken this boat up to the forests in the mountains to cut lacquer, mused the young man. He had gone miles to cut and cut for a bit of lacquer, his clothes ripped to shreds as he cut incisions into the rough lacquer trees and inserted shells into the incisions. The fate of the lacquer tree was a bitter one indeed. Every spring and summer they would be lacerated by knives. When the bark of the thicker parts had been cut until it could be cut no more, then it was the turn of the thinner parts, until all the good bark had been cut and the sap dried up. Then the tree died. Dad died too. Dad had been poisoned by lacquer. He was not at all scared of it. However, when lacquer got spattered on your clothes you could not wash it off, and nor could you wash it off your face and hands, so your face and hands festered. They festered until, like the tree, you had no good skin left, then you died.

Below the cliff somebody yelled in a piercing voice, then shouted abuse, "Dog Ah Ji, what on earth are you doing up there?" Ah Ji was the youth's nickname. His real surname was Liu and his given name Ji. Dog referred to the dog that belonged to Pockmarks Wang who ran the touch paper mill at Seven Mile Flat. Dog often followed Pockmarks Wang's daughter Chouchou around, so when the other youths wanted to make fun of Ah Ji they said he had never seen a girl in his life and was therefore even more unfortunate than Dog.

Ah Ji wandered down to the base of the cliff, watching as he went the evening sun light up the Han River. The cliff face glowed with the dim red of the fading sunlight, while he himself still cast a clear shadow in the bamboo grove and his skin and hair was tinged with the green of the foliage around him. Down on the river bank, the others had already made

---

*A four stringed instrument held vertically and plucked.

wooden rafts and piled the bundles of cut bamboo onto them, so they helped Ah Ji make his raft. They blew up two tyre tubes and tied them to the bottom of the wooden platform, then piled the bamboo onto it.

"Ah Ji, have you seen Wang Qi?"

"No"

"He was sitting on the shuttle boat. He cut thirty pounds of lacquer — made even more money!"

"And he's swollen all over. I'm not going to cut lacquer!"

"Do you think you can get anywhere near a woman with your bamboo cutting? If you don't produce a son for your Dad, what sort of son are you?"

"Let's go back. It's getting late."

Ah Ji jumped onto the raft and pushed off with his puntpole. His raft shot out into the middle of the river and he followed the current downstream. The others soon caught up and formed a straight line behind. By the time they reached Seven Mile Flat it was already dark. The window of the touch paper mill, which was at the entrance of the village, was a blood red colour, and the water wheel made a deep splashing noise as it slowly turned and plunged heavily into the water. Ah Ji shivered involuntarily. Every time he heard the sound of that water wheel he became agitated. He dawdled around behind the others.

"Ah Ji, are you handing in your bamboo?"

"You go first, I'll be there in a minute."

The others hauled the wet bamboo to the open ground in front of the workshop, and looked towards the door of the bamboo crushing room. An oil lamp hung from the main beam of the room and cast an even, reddish light, like the sun. The water wheel stood vertically and turned, driving a large square wooden crusher, while Chouchou sat beside it pulling out the crushed bamboo. When the crusher rose, you could see the outline of Chouchou's body and her pale face. When it dropped, her body and pale face disappeared from view. Ah Ji really worried that one day Chouchou would forget what she was doing, or doze off, and the wooden crusher would make mincemeat out of her. Of course Ah Ji's concern was unwarranted, for Chouchou had been pulling bamboo out from the crusher for two years and had not lost a hair.

Just then Dog came rushing out from the workshop, barked loudly, and launched an attack on Ah Ji. The sight of Dog who could not speak the language of humans attacking Dog who could amused the other bamboo cutters no end.

"Chouchou, your dog is going to bite Ah Ji to death. Aren't you going to do anything about it?"

The water wheel inside the crushing room was very noisy, so Chouchou did not hear them. Instead Pockmarks Wang came out from the paper pressing room and yelled viciously, "What are you saying? If you don't get over here and weigh the bamboo, I won't take any in today!"

Ah Ji cursed Pockmarks to himself. "Ten Pockmarks and nine demons; if just one doesn't die it's a calamity!"

2

The greatest worry in Pockmarks' life was those youths who cut the bamboo, but he couldn't get too offended because the touch paper mill was privately run and the raw material for touch paper was the green bamboo which the bamboo cutters sold to him. He could not stand the sight of them, but at the same time he could not do without them. As he was not able to get along with them, life became so very tiring.

Actually Pockmarks was not a bad man. During communization he had held a post as chairman of the Poor Peasants' Association. Because of his honest nature, he never held a high post, and lived a life of strict frugality. While other people took every chance to grab whatever they could for themselves, he remained in his three roomed stone house, with a stone table, stone mortar and pestle, and a gnarled pomegranate tree outside the door. People often said, "If one has a big family, they never have money; if they have money, they never have a big family." What he lacked was money. He had nothing except his wife, who was ill and died three years later. When his wife died his daughter was only two, yet he never remarried nor got involved with other women, putting all his effort into bringing up Chouchou instead. Chouchou was his meticulously created work of art. He would carry her on his back to meetings, where he told her not to cry or make a fuss ... and cry and make a fuss she did not. When a family in the village was dividing up their household to go and live in separate homes, he would go and oversee. Chouchou would be told not to eat other people's things, and she would not do it even if it meant starving to death. By the time Chouchou was sixteen she was a grown-up.

Then the communes were done away with and replaced by the township government, and the land was divided up and allocated to families to work themselves. Once father and daughter were up on the hillside digging together in their field, to the side of which grew a peach tree that had blossomed magnificently. Chouchou broke off one of the flowers and put it in her hair. Her father said, "Take that out of there now! It makes you look as ugly as a goblin!" Another time, some youths in the village had gone down the Han River to Huluzhen, Baihe County and on to Xiangyang, and come back with trousers that were tight at the waist and wide at the bottom, which made one seem instantly taller. Chouchou sewed the waist of her trousers a little tighter too, but when her father saw it he grew angry, saying, "You've turned into a demon," and demanded she loosen them back to their original style. Old Man Pockmarks enthusiastically welcomed the contract system of farming, but complained day after day about the decline in people's morals, saying people were no longer as pure and honest as they once were. At home he said to Chouchou, "See, people are really selfish. During communization they all loafed about and didn't work hard, but when each person got their own land to work, they started working like crazy! Crazy they might have been, but at least they were still honest peasants. Now they've all started going out and getting involved in trade, and there's never been a crook who wasn't a trader! In the old days if a family was building a house, there wasn't a family in the village that did not go and help. If there was a toilet to be dug, six or seven people would turn out to give a hand. Now they only care about money. If there's no percentage in it, nobody will do any work — they've all become snobbish and self-seeking. This policy has got to go!"

However, the countryside no longer had a poor peasants' organization, so Pockmarks' words were in vain. The policy did not change. The only change was that Pockmarks' prestige had declined, his relations with others had turned for the worse, and that he was in bad financial straits. As you need money to do anything, he had no choice but to set up the touch paper mill: he converted his three roomed home into a mill. Pockmarks could make paper pulp, and Chouchou's uncle — an old man who could eat but not speak — was called in to scoop out the paper. Chouchou's job was to dig three big pits in the open ground in front of the workshop, then put in a layer of bamboo, spread a layer of lime over it, cover the lime with a layer of straw, pour water over it, then bury the whole lot. Two or three months later, when the bamboo had rotted, she would dig it up and dry it in the sun, then sit by that thick square crusher day after day crushing the bamboo into fine fibres.

When the water wheel was turning, it seemed nothing else existed outside the bamboo crushing room. Splash, splash. Thump, thump. At first Chouchou's insides had turned at every thump, but by now she did not even hear the noise. All she heard was a heart beating in her chest and a pulse beating in her wrist.

She often thought: How strange things are in this world. Touch paper is fire, green bamboo is water, so water can become fire. Was she, the papermaker, operating this process of fusion and change between fire and water? Chouchou had not had much schooling, and there were many things she never thought of, or if she did she could never explain them.

She had to grease the axle of the water wheel, so she went outside the bamboo crushing room and breathed in the fresh air, looked at the solitary tree on the hill opposite and at the single cloud that floated above it. As she was watching the mist and waves on the river, she saw the bamboo cutters' rafts drifting down towards her.

The bamboo cutters were sitting on the rafts, their heads shining and ears sticking out. When they got near the mill and saw Chouchou, they all shouted, "Chouchou, come and weigh the bundles of bamboo for us!"

At first Chouchou laughed, but the sun got in her eyes and made her blink. "Chouchou, do you like mushrooms? These mushrooms aren't those dog piss ones. They're fleshy and really moist!"

Chouchou ran over. She had a good body, but her clothes didn't fit, so she hitched them up as she ran. When the bamboo cutters said that Chouchou had worn her clothes out, she blushed.

Pockmarks saw all this, so naturally he told Chouchou to go off and crush bamboo, and was as impatient as ever while doing the weighing, separating the bamboo into groups of shoot bamboo, stalk bamboo and trunk bamboo, dividing them into grades according to size. He haggled with the youths over the price and grew extremely angry.

"Aren't you being too hard on us?" said one of the youths.

"Who's being hard on you? I've learnt to treat people as they deserve to be treated."

"You're not as good as Chouchou."

"Get off with you!"

When Chouchou saw that her father and the youths were arguing she came over and said, "Dad!" Pockmarks' face went all shades of red, and he yelled at her, "Go back and crush your bamboo!" The youths quickly took their money and left, while Chouchou went not to the crushing room, but instead to the channel where she sat and sobbed, taking no notice when her father called her.

When Pockmarks saw Chouchou was crying, he calmed down, and taking his tobacco, he went over and crouched down beside her, and lit up a pipe. After exhaling a few times, he said, "Chouchou, are you still angry with your dad? I'm not blaming you, I'm just worried that the modern-day society will spoil you. We're decent folk. We're working this mill, but we're not doing anything disreputable; we live cleanly, so when the government changes its policy, nobody will be able to say anything against us."

As Chouchou listened to her father, her thoughts somehow turned to her mother. Her memories of her mother were very vague, and ten years of memories of her father rushed up in their place. Much of what her father said was correct, and who else in this world loved her so much? But what had she done wrong? Where had she lacked circumspection? Chouchou's mind was in a turmoil. She sat completley still, watching the water in the channel babble and flow past her. After a while the water wheel started making its noises and the wooden crusher began its thumping. Chouchou could not stand it. She went into the factory and stood behind her father who was pulling crushed bamboo out of the crusher. Her father stood up and she stepped down into his place and began putting bamboo under the crusher. She heard her father say, "So my Chouchou does have some sense after all!"

From then on Dog lay across the entrance to the bamboo crushing room. He was snow-white except for two black eyes. For some reason, every time Chouchou saw the dog she thought of those young men who cut bamboo, but every time they came to hand in bamboo, Dog stood barking loudly by the door of the mill.

One day, as Ah Ji was bravely making his way towards the crushing room, Dog went for him. Ah Ji had guts and bared his teeth even more fiercely than Dog. Chouchou stood up and said, "Ah Ji, that dog will really bite you! What do you want?"

Ah Ji said, "Chouchou, can't you get out and come for a walk?"

"I want to crush bamboo," she answered.

Ah Ji said, "Your dad never gives up. He really makes life tough for you!"

Although Chouchou did not return Ah Ji's abuse of her father, she was not happy. As Dog bit hold of Ah Ji's heel, Ah Ji called Chouchou's name and threw her a yellow mountain apricot. Dog managed to pull one of Ah Ji's shoes off. Chouchou caught the apricot and threw the shoe back, and then her father came in. Chouchou stuffed the apricot in her mouth and went back to crushing bamboo. The apricot was really ripe, so ripe in fact that it dissolved into delicious sweet and sour juices as soon as she tried to chew it.

Ah Ji walked down to the bank of the Han River, cursing Pockmarks for being such an old fogey, and vowing to marry Chouchou whenever he got enough money. The other youths laughed at Ah Ji's wishful talk, but after teasing him a while they sighed, got on their rafts and made their way back to their respective villages. On the river they passed a shuttle boat headed for Huluzhen, upon which the boatman was singing boastfully:

> That's her opening her 'brella over there,
> Taking a cold kettle to boil herself some tea.
> Cold kettle boiling tea, tea doesn't boil,
> Made me laugh all the way to the mountains.
> Upon the ivory bed, on the lovers' pillows,
> Under the bedclothes I go looking for that flower,
> All of her white flesh soft like tender tea.

3

Ah Ji's house was also built of stone, which did not leak when it rained but was filled with spots of light when the sun came out. Ah Ji lay on the *kang* and stared at a shaft of sunlight that shone down through the roof and at the myriad things that flew about in it, and thought about how to make some money. If he could make money, everything would be alright. He could fill his pockets with cash, go to the touch paper mill and say, "Pockmarks, I'll buy all your touch paper!" Pockmarks would be thrilled for sure, and would not treat him with his usual bad temper. Then he would raise the matter of marrying Chouchou, and next thing you knew he'd be calling Pockmarks "Father-in-law"! But how to make money? Cutting bamboo he got a cent per pound, and if he worked hard he made three dollars, which was just enough to feed himself on. There was no way he was going to cut lacquer, so if he wanted to earn money he would just have to keep cutting bamboo, but there was not much money in that. Ah Ji said to himself, "Pockmarks, Pockmarks, you stubborn old fogey. You've been inflexible all your life and you want Chouchou to be the same. You'll see! I'll marry Chouchou and take her to see the world. When you kick the bucket we'll take no notice and there will be nobody to act the dutiful son at your funeral. And although you make touch paper now, when you meet your end nobody will come and burn paper at your grave!"

Ah Ji had thought it all out, but as soon as he arrived at the touch paper mill he grew scared of Pockmarks and of the dog. So he went back to the cliff to cut bamboo, which he did until he was worn out and fed up, and then he made himself a *xiao**. The people who lived by the Han River knew nothing of musical notation, but the art of playing the *xiao* had been passed down from generation to generation. He played a song of mourning, with such long doleful tones that the others in the bamboo grove felt a chill run down their spines. His mates said, "Ah Ji, Ah Ji, stop playing like that!" But Ah Ji kept playing, and the others could only sigh, "Chouchou's really stolen his heart!" When they called Ah Ji "Dog" before, it was just a joke, but now that he had really fallen in love with her, his mates tried hard to help him find a way to get her.

"Ah Ji, do you really want to marry Chouchou, or are you just doing it out of spite?"

"For real, and for spite!"

"O.K. then, you little love bird, here's what you do. Go to Chouchou and put a bun in her oven. Pockmarks will hate you for it of course, but he'll want to save face, so he'll just have to take it on the chin and let you have your way. There you are. Are you game?"

Ah Ji shook his head.

The other bamboo cutters really did want to help, so when they went to hand in the bamboo some of them crowded around Pockmarks and led him into the paper pulp room, and the others took a bone and led Dog away from the mill. Meanwhile Ah Ji slipped into the bamboo crushing room from behind the water wheel to see Chouchou.

Chouchou panicked. "You're crazy! As soon as the dog barks, Dad will be in here screaming at me."

Ah Ji said, "Are you that scared of your old man? Your dad's seventy, and you're only eighteen!"

---

*The *xiao* is a kind of bamboo flute, played vertically.

Chouchou said, "My dad doesn't trust you lot, you're not straight."

"Your father's talking rubbish. I'm as straight as a die!"

The two of them stood beside the crusher. When it rose it came up to their shoulders. When it dropped the ground upon which they were standing shook with the thump. There was no bamboo under the crusher, so it fell with a hollow sound, and Ah Ji had trouble hearing what Chouchou was saying. For a while Ah Ji said nothing, then he took the *xiao* out from his belt and gave it to Chouchou. She laughed and said, "I can't play it."

Ah Ji replied, "I'll teach you. It's really easy to learn!" Whereupon he put it to his lips and began to play. The tune he played sounded like water, only softer, and was in time with the splash, splash of the water wheel and the thump, thump of the crusher. Ah Ji looked up at the rainhat shaped spider web in the rafters, at the green moss growing on the axle of the water wheel, then looked at Chouchou's pale face and at where her breasts pushed out against the loose coarse fabric shirt she was wearing. Chouchou became engrossed in Ah Ji's playing. Her eyes would grow bright, then go dim. His head lowered and she wondered at Ah Ji's mouth, cleverer than that of a nightingale.

But then Pockmarks appeared at the door and howled, "Damn you, bastard!" A bamboo rod came down on Ah Ji's legs with a whack, and the *xiao* fell under the crusher and in a moment was pounded to smithereens. As Ah Ji ran out of the bamboo crushing room, he heard Pockmarks beating Chouchou and yelled, "If you're going to hit someone, hit me! Hitting Chouchou's too easy!" Hearing the commotion, Dog rushed back and bit Ah Ji on the leg. Ah Ji fled.

Pockmarks stood on the open ground in front of the mill and pointing at the distant Ah Ji, yelled, "Ah Ji, you scoundrel, if this mill ever buys bamboo from you again, it'll be over my dead body!"

So with this Ah Ji's avenue for earning money was shut off. He lay at home for three days completely dispirited and with nothing to do. Without Ah Ji the other bamboo cutters felt listless, so they took some wine and went across to Ah Ji's house to comfort him with a drink. Wine is supposed to relieve one of one's cares, but on this occasion it only made things worse, and Ah Ji got drunk for the first time. In his drunken state he repeated Chouchou's name over and over again. When he sobered up he was so ashamed that two days later he caught the shuttle boat to Huluzhen.

When Ah Ji arrived at Huluzhen, there were people coming and going everywhere, but Ah Ji did not know any of them, nor did he have a place to stay. All the boats going up and down the Han River stopped here, and while in port the boatmen would go to Sun Erniang's teahouse, so Ah Ji went there too. The teahouse had three rooms, but the dividing walls had been removed leaving four posts. To the left and right was a row of cane deck chairs, where people sipped tea and listened to Sun Erniang play the *pipa* and sing. Nobody really knew for sure if Sun Erniang was her real name or just what everybody called her. In any case, she wasn't old, somewhere between thirty and forty. She had a pale face, shining hair, and two large breasts that bobbed around under her clothes. She had a good voice.

> *The man takes the boat down the Han River,*
> *The girl burns incense there in her room.*
> *The incense she places in the incense burner.*
> *One look, two looks, seventy-two looks.*
> *The lands about Nanjing, the walls of Beijing;*
> *Old Goddess of Mercy, please protect my man — may he come home soon.*

So as my heart does not break in two.

Ah Ji listened and thought of Chouchou back there in the touch paper mill, and tears came to his eyes. He went into a daydream and finally fell asleep in the deck chair, only to wake to the voice of Sun Erniang yelling, "Young man, is this your *kang*?" When he opened his eyes he found he was the only one left in the teahouse, so he got out as fast as he could and began wandering about the streets looking for somewhere to stay.

4

Huluzhen had been in existence for about three hundred years, and was one of the most thriving and lively towns along the Han River. Just to the north mountains rose and fell like a sleeping dragon, ignoring the narrow town that stood like a reed on the hill below. The Xun River flowed down from the Qinling Mountains, winding and carving its way around three sides of the town before entering the Han River. Between the rivers stood a jumble of buildings large and small. When Ah Ji was a child he had once come to the town with his father, but now his memories of it were very vague. This time the thing that struck him most strongly was the streets. It was said there were five streets, but in fact there was really only one. It began by the steps that led up from the crossing, went through bustling River Street, wound its way around to the right bank at the back of the town, zig-zagged up the slope and over to the left bank, then twisted its way all the way up the hill to the top. On the top was a tall building, the seat of the local people's government. Four little, stone-stepped lanes leading straight uphill branched off this winding street. There was one of them that Ah Ji did not know the name of, so he called it "Real Man's Lane." In this area of criss-crossing, winding streets, all the houses were built in strange designs, no two houses were the same, and small houses wedged amongst large ones. Before Liberation, Huluzhen had been a large port. There had been many warehouses, shops, inns and stalls, and wealthy people had the means to construct large and richly ornamented homes. Because they were built according to the lie of the land, these homes spread in all directions, twisting with the land on which they stood. Now these old homes had been divided up and given to the people, and had fallen into disrepair. However, at the same time new concrete buildings of all different shapes and sizes had been constructed wherever a place for them could be found. There was not a single bicycle in the whole town, but everybody carried a torch in their pockets. Ah Ji had nothing to do, so he wandered through every nook and cranny in the town. He saw some people wearing clothing made of straw and felt hats, and others with sunglasses and long hair — new and old jumbled together, handsome and ugly side by side. Ah Ji could not help heaving a sigh, regretting that he had not come here more often, and feeling sorry for Chouchou who had never been here in her life. "If Chouchou could come here once, then she'd stop listening to her father!" Thinking of this, his stomach began to rumble, and as he looked around at the shops selling little cakes and things, his mouth began to salivate profusely. People are always thinking of ways to make a living, and Ah Ji had a quick mind, so he soon thought up a plan. He went down to the crossing and asked the people who had come up from the towns for sightseeing if they wanted to stay in the state-run guest house upon the hill. As the streets in the town were winding and steep, he would be their porter and carry their bags up the hill. City people had money but no strength, so Ah Ji had a steady income. On a few occasions, delicate girls would get off the boat, take one look at the hill and not know how they were ever going to get up it. Ah Ji would then sit the girls on his shoulders and carry them up Real Man's Lane. From his shoulders the girls would see the town — the labyrinthine old buildings and the taller new structures — besides themselves with delight. There was one small courtyard house with a well in the centre and surrounded by square buildings with traditional sloping roofs in particular that often caught their attention. Seeing all these wonderful sights, the girls would start singing with joy. Although Ah Ji was used to climbing mountains and carrying bamboo, he found carrying live people extremely tiring, as eighty pounds soon felt like a hundred and twenty. What comforted him and more or less made him forget his weariness were the girls' songs and the fragrance that seemed to emanate from their bodies.

Now Ah Ji had money. After he had eaten his fill he went and sat by the gate of the temple of the River God. By the gate was a strangely shaped rock many feet high, and on it grew lichen and a gnarled old tree with red autumn leaves. At the foot of the rock was a spring with ice-cold water, into which had been tossed many silver coins. The boatmen threw these in and wished for good luck, then went into the temple and burnt a whole bunch of touch paper to the River God. As soon as he saw the touch paper catch alight and the black smoke fly up into the air like a vulture, Ah Ji thought of Chouchou and became melancholy. He gazed at the Han River winding its way through the mountains, mists and sandbars towards him, with its rugged banks and swirling eddies.

With that, Ah Ji made his way down to Sun Erniang's teahouse on River Street. There he mixed with the boatmen. If they said the tea was good, he said the tea was good, if they cheered Sun Erniang's singing, so did he. These visits to the teahouse became a habit, and Sun Erniang came to know Ah Ji, asking his age, where he came from and whether he was married or not. Asking this last question, Erniang laughed, and pinching Ah Ji on the cheek, exclaimed, "So you're a bachelor, eh!" Ah Ji did not really understand exactly what she meant, and played dumb anyway to give the others a bit of fun. Although he laughed foolishly, he had sharp eyes and nimble hands, and began helping Erniang stoke the boiler and fill the boatmen's teapots. Erniang liked him and let him sleep by the boiler at night, but warned, "If you're a thief, I'll skin you alive. No matter where you hide, the boatmen can find you anywhere along the length and breadth of the Han River, and they'll bring you back to me! At night, sleep quietly, and if you hear any movements upstairs, don't call out!"

Now Ah Ji had his own nest, he slept like a log. However several nights later he could not get to sleep, and in the middle of the night he heard footsteps upstairs, then a chair moved, and he heard talking and laughing. Ah Ji thought: Erniang lives upstairs, so could she be talking to her husband? But he had never seen her husband, nor any children! Puzzled, he waited until a time when there was nobody in the teahouse and asked, "Erniang, does uncle do business in another town?"

"He's dead."

"Dead? So you haven't got any children?"

"I've got you for a son!"

Ah Ji choked on his words, and could not say anything. Then Erniang asked, "Ah Ji, what did you hear last night?"

"I heard you talking to someone."

"Stuff your ears with donkey hair!"

Ah Ji thought: "Erniang is a widow. Could it be that she has a lover come in the night?" He didn't dare ask. He observed every boatman who came into the teahouse, but none of them seemed likely to be her lover. All of them seemed close to her. When they came in they would give her edible dried fungus, or walnuts, or headscarves, and make cheeky comments that exceeded the limits of propriety, or were just outright crude. She greeted them in a hundred different ways, the worst of which was to scowl and abuse the boatmen as if she were scolding her son. Ah Ji did not think Erniang was a bad person, but rather looked upon her as an elder sister, or mother, or Goddess of Mercy, and at night when he was in bed he would also think of that pair of large breasts moving about under her clothes.

One day, Ah Ji was doing his porter job on "Real Man's Lane". On the way up his legs felt weak, and on the way back they ached. He finally arrived back at the teahouse, and while he was taking off his hat and socks and brushing them, Erniang said to him, "Are you going to be a porter all your life?"

"I don't know how to do anything else," Ah Ji replied.

Erniang said, "If you had some capital I could introduce you to a boatman and you could go into trade. But you haven't got any capital, so no boatman will take you. Why don't you go up into the mountain and cut lacquer?"

"I'll do anyting else, but there's no way I'm going to cut lacquer," Ah Ji answered.

"Then go back to the fields, and get a wife to accompany you."

"I want to marry Chouchou," Ah Ji blurted out.

Erniang asked, "Who's Chouchou, with such an ugly sounding name?"

As he could not fool Erniang, he told her the whole story of his relationship with Chouchou. Erniang listened in silence, then sighed, "Poor Chouchou. If you are a real man, you should go and marry her!" Ah Ji pondered ruefully the fact that he had no special skills nor any money, and could not think what to do. Erniang said, "I heard there's a hunchback at the temple of the River God who can tell fortunes by analysing characters. Go and have your fortune told and find out what's best for you to do. You can't believe all these superstitions, but you shouldn't just disbelieve them all either."

Ah Ji went to the temple and found the hunchback by an ancient stele to the right of the large rock and spring. He could tell fortunes and cure illnesses by massage. An old man who had angina was carried to the hunchback, who immediately set to kneading the old man's abdomen, but still the old man could not stand up straight. The hunchback said, "That's O.K., that's O.K.", whereupon he put his finger on an acupuncture point on the old man's abdomen. When he started rubbing it, the old man died. But the hunchback continued to massage the man's abdomen until the clot dissolved, then he gave the same acupuncture point another knead and the old man revived, his illness cured. People watching exclaimed, "What a miraculous doctor!" Somebody said, "Not only can he bring the dead back to life, he can also tell fortunes by analysing characters!"

Ah Ji immediately went forward and asked to have his fortune told. The hunchback asked him which character he wanted analysed. Ah Ji said, "My name is Ji, so analyse 'ji'!" The hunchback muttered to himself for a moment, then putting his hands together said, "You have a good future. At present you have financial problems, but all the signs are propitious and good things will come to you!" Ah Ji only half believed him, so quickly asked where he should go and what he should do. The hunchback replied, "The character 'ji' has a leftward sloping stroke at the top, which is a black dragon raising its head. In the middle is wood and at the bottom is the character 'zi'. 'Zi' belongs to the water element, and if water is below wood, then the wood grows profusely on account of the water. This is a really good character. You should do things in the north, east or west, but avoid the south, as south belongs to the fire element and burns wood." Ah Ji did not understand *yin* and *yang* and the five elements, but he understood that if he met water he would thrive, and if he met fire he would suffer. He found himself thinking about cutting bamboo. Then he thought, "Pockmarks loathes me, and if he won't take my bamboo, what can I do?" He became despondent. Raising his head again, he saw groups of boatmen going into the temple, and all of them bought touch paper from the stall at the gate. He got a sudden inspiration and rushed back to the teahouse to tell Erniang, "I've found something I can do!" She asked him what it was. He explained that he would go back to Seven Mile Flat and buy Pockmarks' touch paper, then come back and sell it outside the temple. The profits would be huge. Erniang was happy for Ah Ji and encouraged him to go and do it.

From that time on Ah Ji spent much of his time travelling between Seven Mile Flat and Huluzhen. When Pockmarks saw Ah Ji had come to buy his touch paper, he did not mention their previous quarrel. At first Ah Ji only bought a few bundles of paper. Later he bought a dozen, then more and more as his business increased and his capital multiplied. Pockmarks' touch paper had never found a good market and now Ah Ji was buying up nearly a third of all his output. Pockmarks also let him stay for a while in the mill and tell him about the people and ways of Huluzhen, with all its complexities and wonderful happenings. And now he was able to go and see Chouchou on the sly.

Once Chouchou said, "You're less and less like you used to be, Ah Ji. Now you really have a way with words!"

"That's nothing," replied Ah Ji. "The people in Huluzhen are full of news and they really know how to talk!"

Chouchou said, "Huluzhen sounds really good!"

"Then will you go? I'll take you," Ah Ji asked.

But Chouchou replied, "No, I'm not going." Ah Ji took out a bottle of "Snowflake Lotion" and gave it to Chouchou, who smelt it and exclaimed, "What a beautiful fragrance!" but then returned the bottle to Ah Ji.

"Why don't you want it?" Ah Ji asked. "I bought it specially for you!" Then he pressed it into her hands and left.

Chouchou sat down and started pulling the bamboo out from the crusher again, but her heart was all in a flurry. She rubbed a little of the "Snowflake Lotion" on her face, but worried she wouldn't rub it in properly and her father would see it. When she went to look at herself in the channel water, she heard Ah Ji singing from out on the river.

*"From this mountain I look at how high that mountain is,
And see a tree bearing the luscious peaches of love.
Can't reach them with a long stick or short stick,
So taking off my shoes, I climb the tree to shake.
To the left I shake, to the right I shake,
Shake until the peaches roll all over the hill.
The young men who pass by take one to taste,
If they don't get lovesick they're bound to get T.B.!
A lovesick man is no matter for concern,
But a lovesick girl has put her life at risk."*

5

Ah Ji's touch paper stall became famous, and soon he moved it to the teahouse. If someone came to buy touch paper, he would go to the stall and sell it. If there were no customers, Ah Ji would help Erniang serve the boatmen. He never tired, always knew what to say, and could deal with anyone or anything, never overlooking a thing. When Erniang played the *pipa*, he would accompany her on the *xiao*. The boatmen would say, "Erniang, this disciple of yours is really smart!" She would reply, "He's my foster son!" Ah Ji was perfectly willing to accept his position as foster son, never hiding the fact from anyone. With time, he became even more astute and alert. At night Ah Ji still slept by the boiler. One night Erniang came down from upstairs and boiled a pot of tea. While she was drinking it she asked Ah Ji, "Three days ago when you went to the touch paper mill, did you reveal your heart to Chouchou?"

"Yes."

"What did she say?"

"She blushed and got embarrassed and then left."

"Didn't you look at her eyes? They should have spoken to you."

"I couldn't tell. She walked to the door of the room and all she said was, 'Aren't you afraid of my father?.'"

"Then she's just about agreed! Tell me, Ah Ji, did you hold her hand?"

"Why do you say that?"

"Ah Ji's still shy! You have to take her hand, and then when you're about to get married you won't be shy at all. I asked you that because I wanted to know how far things have progressed."

Ah Ji took note of what Sun Erniang said, as he really wanted to find out exactly what Chouchou's feelings towards him were. The next time he went to the touch paper mill, he was presented with a wonderful opportunity, as Pockmarks was out and Chouchou's deaf-mute uncle was working in the paper pulp room. Ah Ji was able to slip in from behind the water wheel without Dog, who was busy chewing on a bone, noticing him. Chouchou was both surprised and happy, and took Ah Ji over to the corner of the room to chat. There the bamboo crusher, now going up and down empty, hid the two of them from view and prevented them from being heard outside. Ah Ji asked Chouchou if she had thought about going with him to Huluzhen. She said her father didn't approve. "How could he not approve?" asked Ah Ji, since by now he bought almost all of Pockmarks' produce. Chouchou said, "My father says you're not to be trusted. The more you run about the countryside, the less honest and decent you become. Once your type of person gets money, one can never rely on them, and in the end you're left with nothing!"

Ah Ji said, "Your old man's such a stick-in-the-mud. Is he always going to look upon people like that?" Then he asked, "What do you think?" Chouchou did not answer. Ah Ji looked at Chouchou's pale face and a rush of blood went through him. He took Chouchou by the hand. She struggled to get her hand free, but Ah Ji had it held tight. Ah Ji became confused, Chouchou became confused, and almost unconsciously the two of them pressed together and became one.

When they regained their senses, both were perspiring profusely and frightened out of their wits. Chouchou began to cry loudly. Ah Ji went into a panic, and had not a clue what to do, until in the end he slapped himself on the face and begged Chouchou to forgive him. Chouchou stopped crying and said to him, "Dad said you were bad news, and he was damned well right! Get out of here!"

When Ah Ji heard Chouchou speak to him like this, his heart started pounding, and he stayed where he was and asked, "Chouchou, do you really think I'm bad news?"

"Get out!"

"Won't you forgive me? Won't you promise to marry me?"

"Now I have.... I can't do anything but marry you, can I? I told you to go, so go!"

A stone dropped to the ground, and Ah Ji left.

Back in Huluzhen, Ah Ji recalled what happened in the bamboo crushing room with alarm and fear, but after a while this turned to joy, and when Sun Erniang asked how things went, he told her that Chouchou had agreed, and said nothing more.

Time slipped by and soon half a month had passed. A boatman from Ziyangzhen came into the teahouse and said that thirty miles up the river at Ziyangzhen a new kind of mountain tea had gone into production. This tea cleaned one's blood, made one's eyes bright, prevented cancer and reduced blood pressure, and what's more it was cheap. Sun Erniang liked the sound of it, and wanted to take the boat up to Ziyangzhen to buy some. Ah Ji said, "You're not so strong, and a few days out there on the river, with its wind and waves, is bound to wear you out. It would be better if I went and bought it for you."

"So I know now that when I die I can do so in peace. And when I do meet my end, I can leave the teahouse to you without any qualms! But you haven't been around much, and you don't know anything about tea, so it's still best if I go. For the four or five days I'll be gone, you look after the teahouse properly. The life of a boatman is a tough one, and the fact that they come here shows they like us. So serve them well, and don't look down on these poor men, or our reputation will be ruined!"

Ah Ji reassured her, "Of course, don't worry!" At dawn the next day Sun Erniang boarded the boat. The river was enveloped in mist, but one could still see the ancient trees reaching for the skies, the vines hanging from them, the beautiful rocks and the clear springs along the banks. Somewhere a crow cawed noisily. After Erniang gave a few parting instructions to Ah Ji, the boat departed up the river.

Ah Ji ran the teahouse with great diligence, receiving the customers warmly, and doing all he could to please them. After five days Sun Erniang still had not returned. Every morning before dawn he opened up the teahouse, swept it clean, then looked out over the Han River, only to find a wide empty expanse of water lined with mountains on both sides. Its green-blue waters stretched out below the deep blue skies, in which hung a crescent moon that cast its pale light around Ah Ji. Suddenly he felt a chill run through him. He sneezed several times, then went back into the teahouse to start up the boiler and prepare tea. Soon customers began to arrive in twos and threes. The boatmen who got up early habitually had a cup of tea to start the day. That morning they asked, "Ah Ji, make it a bit stronger. If you drink a pot like this as soon as you get up, you won't get a headache all day! And hasn't Erniang come back yet?"

Ah Ji replied, "She's not back yet, but you never know, she could be back before you finish that cup of tea!" Just as he was saying that, Sun Erniang came back. However the Sun Erniang that came back wasn't a living one, but a dead body wrapped up in a mat! She had bought the three hundred pounds of tea and caught the same boat back. After a day and a night on the river, the wind suddenly picked up, the waves became rough, and the boatman lost control of his vessel. The boat was dragged onto huge rocks and it capsized. The boatman knew the waters, but his head was smashed in half. Sun Erniang could not swim, and after flailing about among the waves, a large wave dragged her to the river bed. When other boats in the distance saw the boat go over, and they knew that Sun Erniang was on it, they cried out and raced over to the scene, but no trace could be found of her. All the boats moored by the river bank and the boatmen dived in to look for her. They found her, but by the time they got to her and pulled her out of the water, she was dead.

All of Huluzhen was shocked at the news of Sun Erniang's death. The boatmen came to the teahouse to mourn her passing. They all chipped in to buy a top quality coffin and woollen burial attire for her. When they unwrapped the mat to put her body in the coffin, Ah Ji saw her eyes shut but her face still moist as if she were alive, and he broke into uncontrollable tears. Then he fainted by her coffin, and the boatmen brought him to by splashing water on him. They said to him, "Ah Ji, Erniang didn't have a relative in the whole town, not a husband nor a son, so don't cry yourself rotten, as you'll have to fill the role of the son and oversee the burial!" Those words brought Ah Ji to his senses, and in an instant he seemed to mature several years. He opened Sun Erniang's money box and told a few boatmen to go and prepare the grave, arrange a band to play funeral music, and buy rice and flour so they could invite mourners for a meal.

At noon the next day, the funeral procession began. Ah Ji wore white mourning dress, and tears streamed down his face as he performed the son's rituals before Sun Erniang's coffin. Eight men lifted the coffin on to their shoulders and they set out from the teahouse; over fifty boatmen from all over the river carrying wreaths lead the way, and they were followed by the funeral band blowing horns and beating drums and cymbals. Next came a boatman setting off fire crackers, then Ah Ji carrying a picture of Sun Erniang, followed by the coffin. Behind them were other boatmen and townsfolk of all ages and walks of life. The procession went up River Street and along the winding street that snaked its way around the town, firecrackers exploding and horns blowing. The boatmen carrying the coffin would take three steps forward, three to the left, three to the right, then one back, before proceeding forward three steps again, all in imitation of a boat rocking on the waves. Thus the procession went forward at a snail's pace, and all those watching were so deeply moved that they burst into tears. After they reached the top of the hill in the town, they took the steep, narrow path straight up the mountain behind Huluzhen. Carrying the coffin up this path was really hard work, so all present took turns to bear the coffin, which seemed to be standing almost vertical as it was carried up the steep slope above the white-capped procession. Thus Sun Erniang was buried way up on the mountain.

When Ah Ji had finished patting down the last shovelful of soil on the grave, he turned around to see that the hunchback from the temple gate had also come. He had bought touch paper from Ah Ji the day before and was now burning it before the grave. When he finished, he gave Ah Ji a length of cloth about six feet long, upon which he had written a funeral elegy. Ah Ji read it. It said:

"Although one can still find remains of the painted boats of old,
That fabled sea bird leaves without a trace.
There cannot be a boat passing by Huluzhen,
Whose captain will not stop here to pay respects."

Ah Ji took over the teahouse, which now was really just the teahouse building itself, sixty or seventy cane deck chairs, and all the teapots and teacups. All of Sun Erniang's savings that had not been spent on the three hundred pounds of Ziyangzhen tea, now on the bottom of the river, had been spent on the funeral. Ah Ji wanted to leave the place, but whenever he saw the boatmen coming to drink tea as they had always done, he could not bring himself to go, and so he stayed on. Although he was now the owner, the sign outside still said "Sun Erniang's Teahouse". Ah Ji wanted to make sure that the teahouse would always be a part of Huluzhen and that the boatmen would always come to it. He got up early and went to bed late, and learnt to play Sun Erniang's *pipa* and sing her songs. However, when he first performed before the boatmen, he broke into tears, and soon the boatmen were sobbing too. So Ah Ji stopped singing and said to those present, "When Sun Erniang was alive she sang songs to soothe you, but when I sing you weep. If Erniang knew, she would not stand for it. Since she's dead and can't come back to life, let's get on with living. So let's sing *Still in this world!*"

> "Still in this world, still in this world,
> Mulberries and willows shoot forth new leaves,
> Still in this world, still in this world.
> The dead have passed to the Underworld,
> But we remain in this world above.
> The dead return to the Underworld,
> We remain in the sunshine-filled world."

All the boatmen joined in the singing.

For the next three months, Ah Ji was busy improving the teahouse, so he did not have time to go to Seven Mile Flat to buy any touch paper from Pockmarks or see Chouchou in the bamboo crushing room.

6

After four months the teahouse was flourishing. All the boats from the Han River and all the rafts from the Xun River would stop at Huluzhen and come to the teahouse to drink tea. However Ah Ji found that the people around the town did not treat him with proper respect. When he met them on the street they would say, "Ah Ji, business is booming, eh!"

Ah Ji would laugh and say, "Only with everybody's help!"

Then the other person would say, "Now that Erniang is dead, you can look for a wife!"

Ah Ji still laughed, but immediately felt something was wrong, that the person meant something he did not yet understand, and so he asked, "What do you mean?".

"Well, you stuck with her right to the end. You're smart, and you've got foresight!"

Ah Ji became angry, and even by the time he got back to the teahouse he had still not regained his cool. He knew people in the town were jealous of him and spread ugly rumours about him and about Sun Erniang. But all Ah Ji did was clean and above board. His anger only made him want to improve the teahouse even more. He worked harder and harder at upgrading the running of the teahouse. He bought a new boiler, twenty new cane deck chairs, and began to sell cigarettes, candy and fruit. Business grew even more. He decided to hire a waitress, and found one in the daughter of an old lady who lived in River Street. This girl had a flattish face, but a pretty waist, and was good with her hands and soft and gentle by nature, besides which she had a good voice. However, after only a week had passed, rumours began flying wildly. It was said Ah Ji had an improper relationship with this new waitress, and that he'd done the same thing when Sun Erniang was alive. The waitress felt so humiliated that she left without giving notice. This gave the townspeople even more cause for gossip. When Ah Ji went out into the street he could feel people were talking about him behind his back. Thus the reputation of the teahouse declined. Ah Ji went and threw himself beside the portrait of Sun Erniang and howled in despair, hating himself for having brought so much trouble upon the teahouse.

Ah Ji closed down the teahouse for a while and went to the town government to have them investigate his case and clear his reputation. Officials went to interview the daughter of the old lady, who denied anything had ever happened between her and Ah Ji, even saying they could take her to the hospital and examine her if they wished. Then the officials interviewed the people who had been spreading the rumours only to find it was all based on hearsay. Thus the town government told Ah Ji not to worry as they were only rumours, and that he should go back and open his teahouse again. However, although he had been cleared, one hand cannot cover the mouths of thousands, and when he was really busy and offered good money for a new waitress, nobody responded. It was only at this juncture that Ah Ji understood what Pockmarks had said — that people's morals were on the decline and they were not as kind-hearted as they used to be. Ah Ji now hated these disgusting trends too, but at the same time Pockmarks still hated him. Ah Ji felt Chouchou was the only decent person in the world and he desperately wanted to see her. He wanted to think of a way to marry her and bring her back to Huluzhen, where they could manage the teahouse in peace and prosperity.

So the teahouse was closed again, and Ah Ji left Huluzhen, taking all his savings with him, and went to Seven Mile Flat. On arriving at the Seven Mile Flat crossing, Ah Ji jumped on to the stone bank, but to his surprise noticed the channel water flowed straight down. This was the channel that Pockmarks used to divert water from the stream to drive the water wheel, after which the water flowed down by the village into the Han River. Now the undiverted water ran all over the stones in front of the village. A doubt grew in Ah Ji's mind, and when he looked at the touch paper mill in the distance, he could see the buildings were still there but the water wheel and the crusher no longer made their awful racket. "Has Pockmarks given up the mill?" Ah Ji's heart raced. If the mill was no longer running, and Chouchou was not sitting there day after day working the bamboo crusher, it should be even easier for him to take her to Huluzhen!

In front of the mill, a deadly silent reigned. Ah Ji suddenly became afraid, as the silence somehow seemed eerie. Dog came running out of the mill and made straight for Ah Ji, but he neither bit nor barked. Ah Ji thought, "Could it be that in the four months I've been away, Dog has become docile?" He said to the dog, "Dog, where's Chouchou?" Suddenly, Dog became frightened and let out a long terrifying howl. Ah Ji was shocked out of his wits. Then he noticed Pockmarks and the mute old uncle sitting on a pile of stones outside the paper pulp room. They were sitting in silence tying up dried touch paper into bundles, and when they heard Dog's wild howl, they looked up and gazed woodenly at Ah Ji as he walked over, then looked down again and continued tying their bundles.

Ah Ji was used to Pockmarks' unfriendly ways, but sensed something was wrong when he did not greet Ah Ji with his usual venom and hatred!

"Why isn't the crusher crushing bamboo?" Ah Ji asked.

"Because it's not."

"And Chouchou?"

"Dead."

"Dead?!"

"Dead." Ah Ji was struck dumb, stood for a moment in a daze, then ran to the bamboo crushing room. The water trough had collapsed and the water wheel stood still, its paddles dry and split. The square crusher stood in its place, and below it lay a pile of half crushed bamboo. In a mad fit he rushed back and yelled at Pockmarks. "Chouchou's dead! How did she die?"

But Pockmarks raised his fist and landed a blow right in the pit of Ah Ji's stomach, sending Ah Ji sprawling on the ground. Then he went and sat still as before, and said to Ah Ji, "Calm down. Chouchou is really dead."

Ah Ji was brought to his senses. He sat on the ground sobbing, and asked how Chouchou died. Pockmarks sat there with his head lowered, tying his bundles of paper and telling the story, almost like he was telling a tale of ancient times.

Pockmarks had noticed for several days that Chouchou was not herself, and soon she began to avoid him, going off by herself to vomit in the grass hut that served as a toilet. Pockmarks thought she was ill and told her to go and see a doctor, but she wouldn't go. The next night Pockmarks heard Chouchou moaning in her room, but when he asked what was the matter, she said her stomach hurt a bit but it was nothing to worry about, and with that went off to the toilet. Pockmarks guessed she had diarrhoea, thought nothing more of it, and just went back to sleep. The next morning when he called Chouchou to go out and crush bamboo, there was no answer. He went into her room and found a bowl with a mixture made of crushed porcelain and glass at the top of her *kang*, most of which was now gone. Pockmarks panicked. He knew this mixture was for inducing abortions, so he ran to the grass hut, and in the doorway he found Chouchou lying dead, blood running from her mouth and from between her legs. When the story finished, Ah Ji broke into uncontrollable tears.

Pockmarks said, "I don't care about the loss of face in having Chouchou die, but tell me, which one of you sleazy characters seduced Chouchou and made her do such a disgusting thing? I should be blamed. Why did I start up the touch paper mill and let all those shady people come here? I didn't look after Chouchou properly!"

Ah Ji said, "You didn't look after Chouchou properly! You 'looked after' her to death!"

"Crap," Pockmarks said. "It was a good thing she died. If she hadn't, how would she have been able to face life? If she hadn't died I would never have realized that it was my just deserts for opening that mill. I'm never going to run it again. Once I've sold the last few hundred pounds of touch paper I'm not going to do anything! If anybody wants the water wheel or crusher they can have it for free!"

Ah Ji said, "I want it."

"Want what? You still want the touch paper?"

"I'll buy it."

"How much do you want?"

"All of it!"

He took several wads of money out from inside his jacket, threw them on the ground, then went inside and brought out piles and piles of touch paper, which he put by the channel. Then he took a broad axe and went into the bamboo crushing room. With a crack he smashed up the water wheel and then the crusher, and piled touch paper on top of it. Then he knelt down and put a match to it all. Although bamboo relied on water to grow, when it was made into paper it was really flammable, and once it caught fire it did not take long before black smoke started belching out and flames leapt up towards the heavens. Chouchou had sat there for years crushing bamboo, and that bamboo had become thousands and thousands of sheets of paper which people burnt for the souls of their dead. Who would have guessed that the last, and indeed the largest, pile of the paper would be burnt for her own soul.

Ah Ji's hair and eyebrows were singed, but still he knelt there like a pile of wood or stone. Pockmarks and the deaf-mute uncle were completely stunned. They watched the black ashes fly up into the sky, then fall again, blackening the ground and blackening them, until tears started cascading from their eyes.

Just then some rafts carrying piles of bamboo went past on the Han River. The rafts were manned by another group of young men, going to a new touch paper mill in another village to sell their bamboo. When they saw the smoke and flames at Seven Mile Flat, they struck up an ancient Han River work song:

Yo — ao — ao, he, ao — ai, hai —!
Yo — ai — yo —!
Ao — ai — hai — you —!
Ao — ai — hai — ai — ai— hai —
Ai—

Translated by David Pattinson

Hong Taitai

◉

—— **CHENG NAISHAN** ——

Cheng Naishan, a recently emerging woman writer, was born and brought up in Shanghai. After graduating from the Shanghai Teachers' College in 1956, she taught in a middle school. Since 1985 she has been a full-time writer. Stories such as "The Blue House", "The Poor Street", "The Clove Villa", "Daughters' Tribulations", "The Truly Great Men" and "The Bankers" depict the life and psychology of the Shanghai upper-class and their descendants. Her works have a strong local style.

EVERYBODY called her Hong Taitai.* Fifty years ago that name was celebrated throughout Shanghai society. A party marking a baby's first month of life, a wedding banquet or a birthday all fell short of perfection if Hong Taitai was not in attendance. There was a period after 1949 when the words "Hong Taitai" seemed redolent of mothballs, as if they had been shaken from a camphorwood chest. But within the circle of the few rich families in Shanghai, for example, they still carried a good deal of weight right up until the "great proletarian cultural revolution" of the 1960s. In Shanghai, one had one's own little circle of happiness. And no matter how the storms raged outside, as long as one had three meals a day and stuck to one's own affairs, and thanks to the government policy of buying out the bourgeoisie, one could rest assured of eating at the Park Hotel today, the "Maison Rouge" or Jade Buddha Temple tomorrow. No one would interfere. It was a very active period for Hong Taitai. The managers of both the public and private sections of the big restaurants and hotels all knew her; she was a very warm person. If Hong Taitai came forward to do the honours for a banquet on some special occasion, it would be

---

*Taitai is the traditional term for Mrs or wife, which fell into disuse after 1949 for being considered a very bourgeois title and was severely discouraged during the "cultural revolution". The Chinese term is retained here, rather than replaced with the English "Mrs" to call attention to this connotation which the term "Mrs" lacks.

reasonably priced, but ample. And the food would be something special, quite out of the ordinary.

My first impression of her dates from my tenth birthday.

I was the ninth child in the family, nicknamed "Jiujiu", or "Little Ninth". My parents were in America. When they left they had been afraid that I was too small to make such a long trip and would be in the way. Then the situation had changed, unexpectedly and so greatly, and I was left behind in Shanghai for good to live with my eldest brother and his wife. My brother was 21 years older than I and often joked that he could have fathered a child my age. He did spoil me as if I were his own daughter. Fatherliness in an eldest brother has always been the Chinese way.

The day of my tenth birthday they did things up a bit on my account, though it was nothing more than noodles and a few dishes. In those days my brother and sister-in-law were rather careful of appearances. They couldn't have competed with Hong Taitai at any rate; she was the wife of a bourgeois. Brother and his wife, no matter what, were subject to their work units, and they had to be careful. So they did no more than invite the brothers and sisters still in Shanghai over for an ordinary family dinner.

We had just sat down — we hadn't even got around to pouring the wine — when there was a knock at the door, and a voice, vivacious and sweet, was heard, "I've come to beg a bowl of birthday noodles."

"It's Hong Taitai!" My sister-in-law gasped, startled, and pushing back her chair she fled into her room to change her dress.

"That's how thoughtful she is." My brother hastened to open the door; sisters and sisters-in-law busied themselves getting an extra bowl and chopsticks, bustling and rushing about. Thinking back on it now, this Hong Taitai's entrance into my life was strangely like that of the domineering Wang Xifeng in *A Dream of Red Mansions* who always announced her arrival on to the scene with some arresting remark like: "So sorry I'm late welcoming visitors from afar!" The exact words were different, but the effect was the same. Her voice was so confident and hearty; she had an air of being completely at home.

"Hong Taitai!" The family stood to greet her.

"Ah, I made it on time." Hong Taitai said, removing her white kidskin gloves. She wore a square of checked wool on her head, the ends so long they fluttered with her every movement, adding immensely to her charm. When she took off her full-length cashmere coat, she was wearing a claret-coloured *qipao** underneath, a phoenix embroidered in gold thread down the front, dazzling in its brilliance. In the 1950s such elegance had become a rare sight for anyone, let alone a child such as myself who had

---

*Traditional high-necked, close-fitting Chinese dress.

as yet seen nothing of the world. This sudden manifestation of such a gorgeously-dressed beauty took my breath away.

She sat down next to me and pressed a red envelope into my hand. There was a shining golden character glued to the envelope — longevity — but because it was in the traditional, complicated form, it took me a moment to recognize it. At that time such red envelopes, used for giving presents of money to children on special occasions, were no longer on sale. Hong Taitai said she had glued it together herself of red paper; the character was also her own handiwork.

"Hong Taitai, really, you shouldn't put yourself out of pocket over Jiujiu's birthday. She's a child." My sister-in-law had changed and come back out, and though she was much younger than Hong Taitai, she looked faded beside her. The only thing one noticed in that whole room was that brilliant combination of red and gold: dazzling, but pleasingly so!

"Mr Hong and I are old friends of your parents. I went to see Jiujiu at the hospital the day she was born. She was so alert and bright-eyed, such personality, not like most babies. When the nurse brought you in you were as pink as a glutinous rice dumpling." She described it vividly, and I was enthralled.

"At first your parents planned to come for you after a while, but now look.... They must miss you terribly. I pity you that your mother isn't here. So though I pay no attention when one of your brothers or sisters has a birthday, Jiujiu is different; I have to come to celebrate your tenth birthday, to stand in for your mother and raise a glass to you, wishing you long life!" Her words warmed my heart.

After the meal, my brothers and sisters put on some music, *A Rose for You*, a Xinjiang folk song quite popular at the time and, the brothers and brothers-in-law all surged toward Hong Taitai. But she frowned, and with a graceful flick of the hand in which she held a cigarette, said, "Put on Bing Crosby. Us old folks like the old songs." When that bewitching voice was heard, she laid aside her cigarette and began, tripping lightly, to dance. As she danced, the side slits in that claret *qipao* rose and fell, now hiding, now revealing her graceful legs. I really hoped I might grow up a bit faster and be all that she was: full of life, charming, beautiful.

When all the guests had gone, I took out the red envelope she had given me and counted: forty yuan! Forty yuan in those days!

"A grand gesture. Mr Hong is the only one who could afford her," Sister-in-law said, pouting her lower lip. "What a memory she has. How could she remember Jiujiu's birthday, let alone that it was her tenth!"

"That's her stock-in-trade." Having said that, brother added sympathetically, "Her lot is a hard one, too. If she'd been born into a good family and got an education, she'd certainly have done well, an intelligent person like that."

Only later did I find out that Mr Hong was in the raw silk business and when Mrs Hong took up with him, he was already quite successful. He had a wife and family, but he rented a small house in the western district of Shanghai and lived there with Hong Taitai. She it was he took everywhere with him, thus in everybody's mind, she was "Hong Taitai". But there was talk, both out in the open and on the sly, some of it not very complimentary. As for the true facts of Hong Taitai's background, no one was able to find out. Even the Hong's housemaid, Ah Ju, knew only that one night, carrying a white leather bag, she had arrived with Mr Hong and had been there ever since. It was said that Hong Taitai was a good cook, and Mr Hong had grown pink and stout under her care. Almost overnight she became well-known; Mei Lanfang* and Zhou Xuan** both were guests in the Hong family parlour. For a time, the house was filled with important guests every day. It seemed that this Hong Taitai had "arrived" in society the same way — a white leather bag in hand. And with her arrival, Mr Hong's business expanded.

My second meeting with Hong Taitai occurred while I was in senior middle school, at Mr Hong's memorial service. Elder Brother was the natural representative of our family, he took me along on the strength of my having been the recipient of Mr Hong's forty-yuan birthday gift. The service was held at the International Funeral Home. There were leading comrades from both the Chinese People's Political Consultative Conference and the Association of Industry and Commerce present. As we entered, I saw Hong Taitai dressed in a black taffeta *qipao* with close-fitting sleeves, wearing a pair of the black leather pointed-toe shoes that were extremely popular in the sixties. Though there were indications that she was putting on weight, her graceful waist made her appear as lovely as ever. She walked composedly among those who had come to pay their condolences, greeting those who ought to be greeted, nodding to those who needed nodding to. The grief weighing on her made her seem even more dignified and noble. On the hairnet holding the thick tresses was a spray of pure white orchids, giving her a very refined air. As soon as her glance fell on us, she hurried to greet us.

"Jiujiu, you've become a young lady." Her gentle voice dispelled the dread I felt in this venue of eternal parting. "You're the next generation. Wear a yellow flower."*** Her soft white hand fastened the yellow bloom to my blouse. She began to speak of all Mr Hong's good qualities, and as she spoke she grew sad and dabbed at the tears in the corners of her eyes with a flaxen handkerchief. By comparison with the main wife, weeping and wailing to one side, she appeared to be more highly bred, more worthy of the title Mrs. Yet in the end it was mere similitude, for when the formalities began, she conscientiously peeled off to one side, a mourner

---
*A Beijing opera star.
**A popular film star.
***Flowers, real or artificial, are worn as symbols of mourning.

who knew her place.

"Hong Taitai will suffer now! This is really difficult for her!" The other mourners commented surreptitiously among themselves.

"Yes, Mr Hong was a man among men. But was he willing to entrust the family property to Hong Taitai? Naturally, it was safer with his wife. With him gone, Hong Taitai is left with nothing, not even a last word. It's hard for her."

Hearing such talk, looking at the lovely black-garbed Hong Taitai, I thought of Chen Bailu in Cao Yu's play, *Sunrise*.

Once Mr Hong died, we saw little of Hong Taitai. In the adults' eyes, she was, after all, a woman of uncertain past!

In a twinkling, I was twenty years old. The celebration was still a family affair. Recalling the gaiety of ten years ago, I couldn't help thinking of Hong Taitai. I accused Elder Brother of being a snob, but he said I was naive. As we locked horns, there was a soft knocking at the door. It was Hong Taitai's maid, Ah Ju, a woman about thirty years old from Shaoxing. She was carrying a red-lacquered tray which held a specially-prepared duck. Attached to the duck was a glittering gold *shou* character — longevity — exactly like the one I had received ten years before.

"Hong Taitai's indisposed, so she sent me to convey her best wishes to Jiujiu. She prepared the duck herself," Ah Ju rattled off as instructed. One could see she had learned it off by heart before she came. Everyone asked after Hong Taitai, and Ah Ju stammered, "The house has been let out. Hong Taitai has a second-floor room with a balcony and a room on the first floor for me and the kitchen. It's enough for the two of us; it's fine, just fine. Goodbye now." With that she made her escape.

Everybody began to inspect the duck. It lacked nothing in appearance, fragrance or flavour. It was then the three hard years of natural calamities. A duck such as this one would cost at least ten yuan on the black market. At the same time that we were saying what a crime it was to eat Hong Taitai's food, we were all scrutinizing the duck. It was lean. It was quite possible that it was one Ah Ju had stood in line all night to buy, in which case it wouldn't have cost much more than two yuan. Since it had been personally cooked and sent over specially, it seemed to be worth much more than that. But the gift was small after all, so she didn't appear in person. "She's a very capable woman!" everyone agreed.

Not long after, the tempest* blew up in 1966 and people could hardly fend for themselves, much less worry about Hong Taitai.

Two years passed and things became relatively quiet. I happened to be walking by Hong Taitai's one day, and looking up at her balcony without thinking, I suddenly discovered the old familiar curtain fabric. Spurred by this, I headed upstairs. A young man wearing a work overall

---

*The "cultural revolution".

with "work safely" printed on it barred my way and asked in a rough manner, "Who are you? Who are you looking for?" "I'm looking for Hong Taitai," I stammered out. I regretted that as soon as it was out. To call someone "taitai" in those days was to invite criticism.

Unexpectedly, he sang out, "Hong Taitai, someone to see you," and led me upstairs.

"Jiujiu!" Hong Taitai welcomed me with surprise and pleasure and wiped away tears, moved. How rare in those days, a genuine sigh and embrace. I leaned against her bosom and cried.

The room was still furnished with French-style furniture. The mirror was covered with pictures of leaders, the best method of protecting mirrors in those days. Ah Ju brought tea, and I had just said, "Thank you, Ah Ju," when Hong Taitai corrected me softly, "Call her Sister Ah Ju. I've adopted her." That guy on the stairs was Ah Ju's husband.

Hong Taitai was wearing a blue Chinese-style cotton jacket. With her hair cut short, in revolutionary fashion, she looked much like someone who would be principal of an elementary school.

"Thanks to their moving in with me, no one dares bother me. The house was ransacked till there was not even one yuan left and I was half-dead myself. As I was crying over it, Ah Ju came and said we should bring her man to live with us; he was a worker and no one would dare bully me then. I said I didn't want to involve them in my troubles, but she said, 'Anyway I'm a servant. Even if worst came to worst I'd still be a servant. I'm not afraid.' I'm so grateful to Ah Ju and her family!"

"Hong Taitai," Sister Ah Ju cut her short, embarrassed.

"I've told you before, don't call me Hong Taitai. Call me mother."

"Ah," Ah Ju laughed ingenuously. "I can't do it. I'm not used to it."

"I get only 18 yuan a month for living expenses, so I have to depend on the two of them to take care of me, and they have two children of their own." Hong Taitai sighed deeply. "Ai, how could I have come to this! If I had only gone out to work earlier on, I wouldn't have got into this predicament, no income at all!"

Hong Taitai kept me on to dinner. She hadn't been able to break that habit. With Ah Ju, her husband and their two lovely innocent daughters, plus Hong Taitai and myself, there were six gathered round the square table. It was a home-style meal of two dishes and a soup with an additional plate of scrambled eggs in my honour. The bluish glow of the 8-watt fluorescent tube shone gently on us. Hong Taitai now and again put some food into the children's bowls with her chopsticks, very grandmotherly. I thought I heard them call her "Nanna", and I found it very strange. "They mean mother's mother," Hong Taitai explained. "I like them to call me that." The children, seeing their opportunity, purposely raised a chorus of "Nanna", and Hong Taitai beamed. I sensed that she had never before laughed so contentedly. Her son-in-law stolidly scooped in his food without saying a word. But when I was taking my leave he dashed ahead turning on the stairway lights all the way down. "My son-in-law hasn't any education; he's a bit rough, but he's a very good man," Hong Taitai told me softly. "There's no need to be afraid of him."

When I got back and told my brother and sister-in-law what had happened, they expressed great admiration for Hong Taitai. "That Hong Taitai, she can take the bad with the good. What an incredibly capable woman!"

Later I got married. Tied down to housework and child, I hardly made the effort to see my brother and sister-in-law, let alone Hong Taitai.

In 1982, my parents made their first visit back to Shanghai from the US. All the old friends gathered, and of course Hong Taitai was invited as well. During the "cultural revolution" many of them had lost touch with each other, and they were glad to renew relationships, but though it grew quite late, Hong Taitai still didn't appear.

"Where's Hong Taitai? We're waiting for her reappearance in society."

"Ah, didn't you know, she's a famous slowpoke."

Just as we were really growing anxious, she arrived, accompanied by Ah Ju. She was wearing a downy mohair coat over a close-fitting black satin jacket, and though her hair was raven black, you could tell it had been dyed. Yes, she had aged some, but she was as graceful and refined as ever. The company rose to greet her, but she pushed Ah Ju forward, "My adopted daughter."

When it came time to eat, no place had been set for Ah Ju.

"Ah Ju, go out and have a bowl of noodles and come back for Hong Taitai in two hours," we suggested.

"Just squeeze together a bit," Hong Taitai pulled Ah Ju to the table and asked the waiter to bring another bowl and chopsticks. The others were rather startled; the atmosphere grew somewhat embarrassed. Though society as a whole had changed, such circles still clung to iron-clad rules. Before all the hot dishes had been served, Hong Taitai got up to leave, saying she had something to do.

The gathering fell to discussing her.

"How could she take a servant into the family? She must be crazy!"

"Well, it's not so surprising. Her own background is more or less the same."

"That's what happens when one lives with servants. You become petty and overlook etiquette."

These dreadful comments, served up with the food and drink, dropped airily from their mouths. I hastily gathered up my child and left.

A few days ago, a woman friend of mine moved by chance to a place in Hong Taitai's lane, and I dropped by to see her, since I was in the neighbourhood.

She welcomed me happily, "Jiujiu's come!" Her silver hair made her look kinder than ever. She said she no longer dyed it. "I'm getting old, and it doesn't turn out well anymore," she said, patting her hair. Sister Ah Ju politely brought tea and sweets for me.

"Jiujiu thinks of me. Of the old crowd, you're the only one who thinks of coming to see me. How big is your son now?"

"Ten." As I said it, I remembered my own tenth birthday and told her how struck I had been by her beauty.

She smiled wanly. "That's past."

She told me that in the beginning a few old friends still came to see her. Now everything was back to normal after the "cultural revolution". There were even mah-jongg parties and dancing, but she was done with it all because her stiff old legs couldn't manage it now.

"Actually it's all a waste of money and time. Ah Ju is so busy. I can't do much to help her, but I can knit a few sweaters, to thank her for being so good to me. They're extremely frugal themselves, but they know my delicate appetite, and there's always one dish especially for me at each meal. There aren't many daughters — even natural-born ones — like that." She touched my sleeve, speaking emotionally, while her hands never ceased their work on the small sweater she was knitting.

"Mother Hong, what are you making?" A passing neighbour stopped in.

"My granddaughter's having her baby any day now. I'm knitting it a little sweater."

"Well! The fourth generation! You're very lucky, Mother Hong!"

"Yes, I am," Hong Taitai replied contentedly, and she smiled.

Translated by Janice Wickeri

Marriage of the Dead

●

—— LI RUI ——

Li Rui was brought up in Beijing. After the "cultural revolution" started in 1966, he discontinued his studies and was sent to do manual labour in the countryside. He became an editor of Shanxi Literature *magazine in 1977 and began writing in 1974. He has published two collections of short stories, namely* The Red House *and* The Lost Lock Pendant. *The short story "Marriage of the Dead" won a national award.*

IN front of the courtyard gate, a worn spindle of jujube wood twirled swiftly in hoary hands, one strand of creamy linen after another wound on to it seemingly without end together with wisps of time. The afternoon sunlight, crumbled by the vast yellow land, spread itself kindly. One suddenly felt that the setting sun was declining not into the mountains in the west but into the old woman's weak eyes.

Not far away, several men were digging up the grave under her husband's direction. Spades and picks kept hitting bricks and stones and chill, metallic clanks crumbled into the gentleness of the sunset. He had been Party secretary of the village, and although that had been quite some time ago, the grave had remained a weight on his mind.

It had stood there alone for all of fourteen years, and the young Beijing woman in it had herself long turned to yellow soil.

"If the poor girl hadn't died, she'd have been up to her knees in kids by now."

A strand of woman's sympathy for women was spun into the hempen yarn tight around the spindle: it was a happy day for the young woman, for today she would be reburied with her man. The villagers had temporized and discussed, discussed and temporized and in the end got the money to buy a "man" as a helpmeet for her who had been alone in her grave for fourteen years. A fortune-teller had been hired and concluded that the horoscopes tallied.

Beside the grave rested two brightly-painted coffins, intended for skeletons and so not big, each with a red ribbon tied to it. The bones of the purchased dead man had been laid in one of the decorated caskets; the other was empty. When the men had opened the grave and taken the woman from her resting place of fourteen years, they would place her in it and bury them together, after which one person from every family was to go to the cave of the village head for buckwheat noodles with boiled mutton and carrots in thick gravy. Her loneliness made their hearts ache, with her parents far, far away in Beijing, her classmates gone without looking back and only she left here. She had passed through the land of the living all alone, so her marriage in the underworld should be celebrated elaborately and extravagantly.

As the spades and picks came up against the brick-and-mortar grave mound, the odd sparks shot into the dry air. Someone brought up the worrying subject of the harvest.

"If it doesn't rain now, we'll have a drought on our hands come autumn...."

A drought and its repercussions were as clear as could be, so no one responded over the random clanging.

"With a downpour like that year's we'd have nothing to worry about."

A man paused: "If it hadn't been so heavy, Yuxiang wouldn't have died."

They all stopped, old memories surfacing in their minds.

"Do you think it was the black snake sent the rain that year?"

"Superstition again!" said the ex-secretary with a frown.

"I don't mean to be superstitious, but the black serpent's quite an omen."

"It's superstition!" repeated the ex-secretary with a second frown.

The other was not convinced: "Then what's wrong with the kids in the school? Loads of them fall ill. Even the teacher's come down with it. I never wanted Yuxiang's memorial hall used as a school. There's no worse luck than a lonely ghost."

"Suppose we don't use the memorial hall; is anyone going to build a village school?"

"We would have had a school if we had made less of those terraced fields.... And Yuxiang probably wouldn't have been killed if she hadn't gone with you to make them!"

This retort was too cutting.

The ex-secretary was momentarily at a loss. As he pulled the burning cigarette from his mouth, a shimmering thread of saliva that extended from its butt was torn apart. Suddenly he burst into a fit of coughing which reddened his face. Long ago though it had been, the fact that he had been Party secretary was not a thing either the villagers or he himself could have forgotten.

Someone tried to smooth things over. "You can't say that. It's all a matter of fate whether you live or die. Nobody has any control over anybody. Without the black snake, Yuxiang would have been alive today. The black snake's a monster all right; it just crept up when the rope was tossed out...."

The topic had been gone over again and again for fourteen years, and no one around had the slightest interest in doing so yet again. The cold, metallic clangs started up again.

It had been a year when all the villagers and the high school graduates from Beijing worked hard under the Party secretary for a winter and a spring and raised three tidy, level terraced fields, for which they had won a red flag, though the first mountain torrents of summer had washed away two of the fields. At the second flood, the young graduates had taken the red flag from the home of the Party secretary to the field, stuck it at the edge and pledged to fight the flood and save the field. Like a raging bull, the waters had engulfed the field dam in the blink of an eye. The young graduates had jumped in hand in hand, like they did in the films. The old Party secretary had knelt down on the ground in the rain and kowtowed till his forehead bled, begging them to come out. By the time the others had been pulled from the water, the collapsing dam had dragged Yuxiang into the current. Men ran after her for several dozen metres with a rope. Now and then she appeared above the surface flailing her arms and had at last caught the rope that was tossed to her. But as the men pooled their strength to haul it in, all at once they had seen a thick black snake with its rear section coiled tightly around her waist as it crawled up the rope at lightning speed, its long forked tongue darting right and left from its up-raised head. Its dripping body had shimmered coldly, and in a blink, it had advanced three or four metres. The rope crew had shrieked and all let go, and the long, thick rope together with the snake had splashed into the water and disappeared beneath the waves. Only at the bend fifteen kilometres downstream had her corpse been washed on to the bank. The searchers had said the waters could strip the clothes off you, and Yuxiang had not had a stitch on her: a tender, white body such as they had never seen had been ringed at the waist by a livid bruise where the snake had wrapped itself around her.

Then she had got into the newspaper. Then the Party secretary of the county had held a thousand-strong rally. Then the memorial hall block had been built. Then there had been the grave and the stone in front of it, reading "An example to school leavers, a heroine of the Lüliang Mountains" on the front, with on the back, "Cheng Yuxiang, born in a railway worker's family in Beijing May 5, 1953; gradtued from Beijing No. 37 Middle School 1968; settled in Shenyu Village, Tuyao Brigade, Chashang Commune, Lüliang Mountain Region, January 1969; heroically gave her life fighting floods to save terraced fields August 17, 1972".

After this there had been no more news reports or meetings, but the thought of the lonely grave at the end of the village had disturbed the villagers:

"Shouldn't think the place could be clean with a lonely ghost left at the south end of the village."

But for fear of hurting the feelings of her schoolmates, and, more importantly, of flouting the decision of the County Party Committee, the grave still stood at the end of the village. Neither the newspaper nor the inscription had mentioned the black snake, but the villagers could not forget the daunting scene and always firmly believed that some sadness, however hard to put a finger on, gathered in the bricks and mortar of that grave. Fourteen years had slipped by. Her schoolmates had gone and would not be back; a number of people had filled the office of Party secretary of the county; none remembered the young woman as the green grass grew slowly out of the chinks of the brickwork.

After the brickwork had been removed, the spades worked much more freely in the soft yellow earth. Gradually the men sank into the pit, until only the silver tips of the spades hurling wet yellowness out of the pit glistened in the sun. A foot trod on nothing, and a spade fell deep into empty space. Expected though this was, the men's hearts still leapt.

"Reached it?"

"Yes."

"Steady on. Don't damage her."

"I know."

The ex-secretary handed down the waiting liquor bottle.

"A mouthful, all of you, against the damp down there."

All the men, drinkers or not, took a gulp. The strong smell of liquor wafted from the grave pit.

Made of bad wood, the coffin had rotted, and when the decayed lid was removed by hand, the complete skeleton shone whitely. The atmosphere in the pit once again froze with tension. This, too, was expected, but all were rooted to the spot with terror before the bones all the same. All those who had seen the delicate, pale flesh that had clothed the skeleton fourteen years before still remembered the talking, laughing woman supported by it. When the torrent had swallowed her up, her long pigtails had floated back to the surface of the water, and the red wool binding them had flashed back into view; yet now a gleaming skeleton lay in the yellow earth, and a still distinguishable smell of decay rose from the mud and the bones at the bottom of the grave.

The ex-secretary passed down the new coffin. "Quick, shift Yuxiang into this, head first."

They squatted down anyhow, and the hollow thump of bones on wood took over for a while. The bones and the sound led to an age-old yet peaceful topic.

"It all comes down to the same thing, for emperors and all."

"You can go at any age, but what gets me is, if she was going to die, why did she have to come all the way out here from Beijing to do it?"

"Won't the yellow earth there take burials?"

"Nothing like here. I bet they don't have such big memorial meetings when you die."

"I won't need one, just a son to carry my flag mourning and a band to play."

"That's feudal," said the ex-secretary, turning serious.

"Oh no, you aren't feudal," mocked someone. "When you die, you'll get burned up like a good civil servant, bit by bit over a slow flame. I'll drive you off in a cart when the time comes."

Laughter burst from the grave pit and was cut off abruptly as the ex-secretary coughed himself crimson in the face, while two tears spilled from his blood-red eye sockets. Suddenly there was a shout.

"Oh, look! That thing's still there!"

Four or five heads bunched together and a dozen eyes opened wide around a red plastic cover.

"It was Yuxiang's!"

"It's the *Quotations from Chairman Mao* she always used."

"Ah...."

"Oh...."

The mood within the walls of the grave wavered uncertainly among surprise, praise and fear. It was actually bloodcurdling to have the past dug up alive like that.

"What shall we do with it," asked someone hesitantly, "move it for her?"

The ex-secretary erupted.

"Why not?" he bawled at the men down in the pit. "You prefer to keep it yourself and make your bloody fortune? Move it! Every hair belongs to her. Move!"

The men were browbeaten into a cowed silence. The sound of their heavy panting rang out alone and loudly.

The quarrel must have been heard, for the spindle at the courtyard gate stopped and a hoary hand was raised to shade a brow.

"Is today the day to throw your weight about, you old codger?"

The dug grave was closed again, except for the original cover of brickwork. The new mound of yellow earth stood out plainly and looked peaceful and calm in the vast yellow land, and the kindly setting sun seemed as if it was truly appeased at last.

The ex-secretary tore open the last packet of cigarettes bought in the village and counted. Just enough for two more each. After he had passed them out, he shook the bottle and found there was still something at the bottom, so the lot of them sat on the ground before the grave and took a drink while they smoked. One round warmed everyone's spirits.

"What shall we do with the stone?" asked one, poking a cigarette at the grave.

"With what?"

"The stone. There was only Yuxiang buried there before, and the stone was just for her. But now there are two of them, and he has a name too. If it comes to that, he's the head of the family!"

It was a problem.

They brooded, puffs of smoke emerging above their heads. Through its veil, one person was looking at the ex-secretary. The old man swallowed a mouthful of liquor, the heat of which burned all the way down to the bottom of his heart.

"No need. Let him put up with it. Yuxiang earned that stone with her life. Never mind about anybody else. People in this village have to remember that!"

No one made a reply. More puffs of smoke emerged. The ex-secretary stood up and slapped the dust off his behind.

"Back for buckwheat noodles!"

At the sight of them dispersing from the grave, the twirling spindle stopped once more. She pulled off a strand of linen and put it into her mouth. As she slowly smoothed it with saliva, she pondered over the task entrusted to her by her husband. While the sinking of the late sun expanded the desolate mountain country, placid thoughts were drawn slowly from the thread in her mouth and melted in the thickening dusk.

After their noodles, the old couple sat up by the twirling spindle, till at midnight it stopped.

"Shall I go now?"

"Yes."

She handed him a basket that she had prepared.

"Everything's there, cigarettes, liquor, food and incense. Have a look."

"That's fine."

"Tell Yuxiang when you go that the lad was born in the year of the snake — couldn't be a better match. In the land of living we marry flesh and blood. In the underworld they do better and marry bones. Bones make a proper marriage!"

"More superstition!"

"If you aren't superstitious, why did you wait till midnight?"

"That's different!"

"How? Anyway I know she was a wretched girl. She lived in our cave for two years. She's as good as my own daughter...."

Her tears came faster than her words. Exasperated with them, he turned and went. It was very dark, with neither stars nor moon.

The russet spindle twirled again under the oil lamp, evenly taking strand after strand of linen. All at once a violent fit of coughing came from the graveside; she turned her head anxiously. The cough leapt from the dank depths of the black night as if from the hollow, decayed bole of an old tree, resembling both weeping and laughter.

Others were awakened in the caves of the village, their rigid forms buried deep in the darkness, their ears pricked up in apprehension.

Translated by Wu Jingchao

Ten Years Deducted

●

—— SHEN RONG ——

Shen Rong is a well-known woman writer. Brought up in Sichuan, she left junior middle school at the age of fifteen to be a salesgirl in a bookshop for workers. In 1952 she transferred to the Southwest Workers' Daily *and in 1954 went to study Russian in Beijing. After graduation she worked as a translator in the Central Radio Station. She published her first novel* Evergreen *in 1975 and another novel* The Bright and the Dark *in 1978. The novelette "At Middle Age", which won a national award in 1980, brought her wide recognition for its courageous depiction of the life and problems of middle-aged professionals.*

WORD wafted like a spring breeze through the whole office building. "They say a directive will be coming down, deducting ten years from everybody's age!"

"Wishful thinking," said a sceptic.

"Believe it or not," was the indignant retort. "The Chinese Age Research Association after two years' investigation and three months' discussion has drafted a proposal for the higher-ups. It's going to be ratified and issued any day now."

The sceptic remained dubious.

"Really? If so, that's the best news I ever heard!"

His informant explained:

"The age researchers agreed that the ten years of the 'cultural revolution, wasted ten years of everyone's precious time. This ten years debit should be cancelled out...."

That made sense. The sceptic was convinced.

"Deduct ten years and instead of sixty-one I'll be fifty-one — splendid!"

"And I'll be forty-eight, not fifty-eight — fine!"

"This is wonderful news!"

"Brilliant, great!"

The gentle spring breeze swelled up into a whirlwind engulfing everyone.

"Have you heard? Ten years deducted!"

"Ten years off, no doubt about it."

"Minus ten years!"

All dashed around to spread the news.

An hour before it was time to leave the whole building was deserted.

Ji Wenyao, now sixty-four, as soon as he got home, yelled towards the kitchen:

"Minghua, come here quick!"

"What's up?" At her husband's call Fang Minghua hurried out holding some spinach she was cleaning.

Ji was standing in the middle of the room, arms akimbo, his face lit up. Hearing his wife come in he turned his head, his eyes flashing, and said incisively:

"This room needs smartening up. Tomorrow go and order a set of Romanian furniture."

She stepped forward in surprise and asked quietly:

"Are you crazy, Old Ji? We've only those few thousand in the bank. If you squander them...."

"Bah, you don't understand." Face flushed, neck dilated, he cried, "Now we must start a new life!"

Their son and daughter as if by tacit consent hurried in from their different rooms not knowing what to make of their father's announcement. Was the old man off his rocker?

"Get out, this is none of your business." Old Ji shooed away the inquisitive young people.

He then closed the door and, quite out of character, leapt forward to throw his arms round his wife's plump shoulders. This display of affection, the first in dozens of years, alarmed her even more than his order to buy Romanian furniture. She wondered: What's wrong with him? He's been so down in the dumps about reaching retirement age, he's never demonstrative like this in the daytime, and even in bed he just sighs to himself as if I weren't there beside him. What's got into him today? A man in his sixties carrying on like those romantic characters in TV plays — she blushed for him. But Old Ji didn't notice, his eyes were blazing. Half hugging, half carrying her, he lugged his impassive wife to the wicker chair and sat her down, then whispered jubilantly into her ear:

"I'll tell you some top-secret news. A directive's coming down, we're all to have ten years deducted from our age."

"Ten — years — deducted?" Minghua let fall the spinach, her big eyes nearly popping out of her head. "Well I never! Is it true?"

"It's true. The directive will be arriving any minute."

"Oh my! Well I never!" She sprang to her feet to throw her arms round her husband's scrawny shoulders and peck at his high forehead. Then, shocked by her own behaviour, she felt as if carried back thirty years in time. Old Ji looked blank for a moment then took her hands and the two of them turned three circles in the middle of the room.

"Oh my. I'm dizzy." Not till Minghua pulled free and patted her stout chest did they stop whirling merrily round.

"Well, dear? Don't you think we ought to buy a set of Romanian furniture?" Ji looked confidently at his rejuvenated wife.

"We ought." Her big eyes were shining.

"Oughtn't we to make a fresh start?"

"We ought, we ought." Her voice was unsteady and there were tears in her eyes.

Old Ji plumped down on the armchair and closed his eyes while rosy dreams of the future flooded his mind. Abruptly opening his eyes he said resolutely:

"Of course our private lives are a minor matter, the main thing is we now have ten more years to work. This time I'm determined to make a go of it. Our bureau is so slack I must take a firm grip on things. On the back-up work too; the head of our general office is not a suitable choice at all. The airs our drivers give themselves, they need to be straightened out too...."

He flourished his arms, his slit eyes agleam with excitement.

"The question of the leading group will have to be reconsidered. I was forced to appoint the best of a bad lot. That Zhang Mingming is a bookworm with no experience of leadership. Ten years, give me ten years and I'll get together a good leading group, a young one with really new blood, chosen from today's college students. Graduates of twenty-three or twenty-four, I'll groom them myself for ten years and then...."

Minghua took little interest in the overhauling of the leading group, looking forward to the wonderful life ahead.

"I think I'll get another armchair too."

"Get a suite instead, more modern."

"And our bed, we'll get a soft one in its place." She reddened.

"Quite right. After sleeping hard all our lives we should get a soft bed to move with the times."

"The money...."

"What does money matter." Ji Wenyao took a long-term view, filled with pride and enthusiasm. "The main thing is getting another ten years, ah, that's something no money could buy."

"As they were talking excitedly, hitting it off so well, their daughter opened the door a crack to ask:

"Mum, what shall we have for supper?"

"Oh, cook whatever you want." Minghua had forgotten completely about the meal.

"No!" Old Ji raised one hand and announced, "We'll go out and eat roast duck, I'm standing treat. You and your brother go first to get a table, your mother and I will follow."

"Oh!" His daughter gaped at seeing her parents in such high spirits. Without asking the reason she went to call her brother.

Brother and sister hurried off to the roast duck restaurant, speculating on the way there. He said perhaps an exception had been made in the old man's case and he was being kept on. She thought that maybe he had been promoted or got a bonus. Of course neither of them could guess that the deduction of ten years was worth infinitely more than any promotion.

At home the old couple were still deep in conversation.

"Minghua, you should smarten yourself up too. Ten years off makes you just forty-eight."

"Me? Forty-eight?" she murmured as if dreaming. The vitality of her long-lost youth was animating her plump flabby figure, to her bewilderment.

"Tomorrow buy yourself a cream-coloured coat for spring and autumn." Old Ji looked critically at her tight grey uniform and said decisively, almost protestingly, "Why shouldn't we be in fashion? Just wait. After supper I'll buy myself an Italian-style jacket like Zhang Mingming's. He's forty-nine this year; if he can wear one, why shouldn't I?"

"Right!" Minghua smoothed her scruffy, lustreless grey hair. "I'll dye my hair too and treat myself to a visit to a first-rate beauty-parlour. Ha, the young folk call me a stick-in-the-mud, but put back the clock ten years and I'll show them how to live...."

Old Ji sprang to his feet and chimed in:

"That's it, we must know how to live. We'll travel. Go to Lushan, Huangshan, Jiuzhaigou. Even if we can't swim we'll go to have a look at the ocean. The fifties, that's the prime of life. Really, in the past we had no idea how to live!"

Not pausing to comment Minghua went on thinking aloud:

"If ten years are deducted and I'm just forty-nine, I can work another six years. I must go back and do a good job too."

"You...." Old Ji sounded dubious.

"Six years, six years, I can work for another six years," she exulted.

"You'd better not," Ji said. "Your health isn't up to it."

"My health's fine." In her eagerness to get back to work she really felt quite fit.

"If you take up your old job, who'll do all the housework?"

"We'll get a maid."

"But that lot of women from Anhui* are too irresponsible. You can't

---

*In recent years many young women from Anhui have come to work as housemaids in big cities like Beijing.

trust one of them to take over here."

Minghua began to waver.

"Besides, since you've already retired you don't want to make more trouble for the leadership, right? If all the old retired cadres asked to go back, well, that would mess things up." Ji shuddered at the thought.

"No, I've still six years in which I can work," she insisted. "If you won't take me back in the bureau, I can transfer somewhere else. I'll work as a Party secretary or deputy secretary in some firm — how about that?"

"Well ... those firms are a very mixed lot."

"All the more reason to strengthen their leadership. We old people are the ones to do ideological and political work."

"All right."

Ji nodded, pleasing her as much as if the head of the Organization Department had agreed. She chortled:

"That's fine then! Those researchers are really understanding. Ten years off, a fresh start — that's beyond my wildest dreams."

"Well, I dreamed of it." Quite carried away, Ji cried out vehemently, "The 'cultural revolution' robbed me of ten of my best years. Ten years, think what I could have done in that time. Ten wasted years, leaving me white-haired and decrepit. Who's to make good that loss? Why did I have to take such bitter medicine? Give me back my youth! Give me ten years back! Now this research association is giving me back that decade of my youth. Good for them, this should have been done long ago."

Not wanting her husband to recall painful memories, Minghua smiled and changed the subject.

"All right, let's go and eat roast duck."

Zhang Mingming, forty-nine that year, couldn't analyze his reaction. It seemed a mixture of pleasure and distress, of sweetness and bitterness.

Ten years off certainly pleased him. Working on scientific research he knew the value of time. Especially for him, a middle-aged intellectual approaching fifty, the recovery of ten years was a heaven-sent opportunity. Look at researchers overseas. A scientist in his twenties could win an international reputation by presenting a thesis at an international conference, then go on to head his field while in his thirties, his name known throughout the world — there were many such cases. Then look at him: a brilliant, most promising student in college with just as good a grounding as anyone else. But unluckily he had been born at the wrong time, and sent to do physical labour in the countryside. When he got down again to his interrupted studies the technical material was strange to him, his brain didn't function well and his hands trembled. Now with this extra ten years he could make a fresh start. If he went all out and research conditions improved, with less time wasted bickering over trifles, why, he could put twenty years' work into ten years and distinguish himself by scaling the heights of science.

He was pleased, just as pleased as everyone else, if not more so.

But a colleague slapped his back and asked:

"Old Zhang, what are you so happy about?"

"What do you mean?" Why shouldn't he be happy?

"Deducting ten years makes Ji Wenyao fifty-four. So he won't retire, you won't take over the bureau."

Quite true. That being the case Ji won't retire. He doesn't want to. He'll stick on as bureau head. And what about me? Of course I won't be promoted. I'll remain an engineer doing scientific research in the lab and library.... Yet two days ago the ministry sent for me to tell me that Old Ji would be retiring and they'd decided to put me in charge.... Does that still hold good?

He really didn't want an official post. The highest he had ever held was that of group head, and convening a group meeting was the height of his political experience. He had never expected an official title, least of all the imposing one of bureau head. He had always been a "bookworm". In the "cultural revolution" he had come under fire as "a reactionary revisionist set on becoming an expert". Since the overthrow of the "gang of four" he had spent all his time in his lab, not talking to a soul.

But somehow or other when it came to choosing a third-echelon leading group he had been chosen. In each public opinion poll his name headed the list, just as he had always come top in examinations. When he was summoned to the ministry it sounded as if the whole business had been settled. In that case he couldn't understand where or how he had shown any leading ability, to be favoured by the authorities and trusted by the rank and file. Thinking it over he felt most ashamed. He had never had any administrative ability, let alone any leadership qualities.

His wife Xue Minru, moderately good-looking and intelligent, was an admirable wife and mother. She took a keen interest in her husband's affairs and knew the disputes in his bureau very well. Her comment had been:

"It's because you're not leadership material that you've been chosen for a leading post."

Zhang Mingming was puzzled by this statement. What does that mean, he wondered. Then he thought: maybe there's some truth in it. Because I've no ability to lead or definite views of my own, and I've not jockeyed for position, no one need worry about me. Perhaps that's why I've been given this opening.

Of course there was also an "opposition party". It was said that at one Party meeting in the bureau his problem had been disputed all afternoon. What the dispute was about he wasn't clear. Nor what his problem was either. After that, though, he felt that he had become a "controversial figure". And this "controversy" wouldn't be resolved nor would his "problem" be cleared up till the day he became bureau head.

Gradually as these public opinion polls and arguments went on, Zhang Mingming became accustomed to his role as someone due to be promoted and a "controversial figure". Sometimes he even imagined that he might really make a good bureau head, though he had never held such a position.

"Better take the job," said Minru. "It's not as if you'd grabbed at it. When you're bureau chief at least you won't have to squeeze on to the bus to go to work."

But now he wouldn't get the job. Was he sorry? A little, not altogether. What it boiled down to was: his feelings were mixed.

He went home at a loss.

"Back? Good, the meal's just ready." Minru went into the kitchen to fetch one meat dish, one vegetable dish and a bowl of egg and pickles soup. The meat dish wasn't greasy and the green vegetables looked very tempting.

His wife was an excellent housekeeper, considerate, clever and deft. During the three hard years when their neighbours contracted hepatitis or dropsy, she kept their family fit by cooking coarse grain so that it tasted good, boiling bones to make soup and using melon rind in place of vegetables. Now farm products were plentiful but fish and meat had risen so much in price that everybody claimed they couldn't afford them. However, Minru knew how to cook tasty inexpensive meals. When Zhang saw the supper she had served he lost no time in washing his hands, sitting down at the table and picking up his chopsticks.

"What succulent celery," he remarked. "Is it expensive? The papers say celery keeps your blood pressure down."

Minru simply smiled.

"These pickles are good too, they give the soup a fine flavour."

Still she just smiled and said nothing.

"Bamboo shoots with pork...." He went on praising this simple meal as if he were a gourmet.

She laughed and cut him short to ask:

"What's got into you today? Has anything happened?"

"No, nothing." He made a show of surprise. "I was just admiring your cooking."

"You never do normally, so why today?" She was still smiling.

Feeling driven into a corner he retorted:

"It's because I don't normally that I'm saying this now."

"No, you're hiding something from me." She could see through him.

With a sigh he put down his chopsticks.

"I'm not hiding anything, but I don't know what to make of it myself or how to tell you."

Minru smiled complacently. Her husband might be an expert researcher, a top man in his own field, but when it came to psychoanalysis he was no match for her.

"Never mind, just tell me." She sounded like a teacher patiently encouraging a child.

"Today word came that a directive's coming down to deduct ten years from everybody's age."

"Impossible."

"It's true."

"Really?"

"Really and truly."

She thought this over and looked at him with big limpid eyes, then chuckled.

"So you won't be bureau head."

"That's right."

"Does that upset you?"

"No. I can't explain it, but I feel put out."

He took up his chopsticks again to fiddle with the rice in his bowl as he went on:

"To start with I'm not leadership material and I didn't want this job. But they've made such a mess of things these last few years, it seems I ought to take over. Still, this sudden change makes me feel a bit...." He was at a loss for words.

Minru said incisively:

"If you don't get the job so much the better. You think it's a cushy post?"

Zhang looked up at his wife, surprised by her decisive tone of voice. A few days ago when he'd told her about his impending promotion, she had shown genuine elation. She'd said, "Look at you — you didn't grab at the job and now these laurels have been put on your head." Now the laurels were lost she wasn't upset or angry, as if there had never been any talk of promotion.

"As bureau head, head of the bureau, you'd have been expected to solve every problem big or small — could you have stood it?" she asked. "Allocation of housing, finding jobs or kindergartens for people's children. How could you manage all that?"

True, no one could manage it all.

"Stick to your speciality. An extra ten years will make all the difference to what you can achieve...."

Yes, it would certainly make all the difference.

Zhang felt easier in his mind, with a sense of light-hearted well-being.

He went to bed expecting to sleep soundly. But he woke in the middle of the night with a feeling of faint regret and deprivation.

Thirty-nine-year-old Zheng Zhenhai shot out of the bureau and cycled swiftly home. There he took off his old grey jacket and tossed it on to a chair, conscious of inexhaustible energy. This deduction of ten years seemed to call for prompt action to solve many major problems.

"Hey!"

No one answered his call. His ten-year-old son was fooling about as usual in the alley, and where was his wife who usually responded? Out visiting? Hell! What sort of home was this?

His home-made armchair was so misproportioned that his spine didn't reach the back, while the low arms and high seat made sitting there positively tiring. All because she had to keep up with the neighbours and since they couldn't afford an armchair had insisted on his making a set himself. What a philistine! It was sickening the way every family had armchairs like this, as standard as a cadre's uniform. So philistine!

Whatever had made him choose her? Such a vulgar family with no interests in life except food, clothing, pay and perks. Family education was all-important. She was the spitting image of her mother: the same crude way of talking, and fat as a barrel since the birth of the boy, with no good looks, no figure, no character. Whatever had made him choose someone like her?

Hell! It came of being in too much of a hurry. A bachelor nearing thirty couldn't be choosy. Now with ten years off he was only twenty-nine! He must think over this problem seriously. Yesterday she'd squawked and flounced about because he'd bought a carton of good cigarettes, threatening to divorce him — they couldn't go on like this. Divorce? Go ahead! Twenty-nine was just the right age to find a wife, a slender college graduate of twenty-two or twenty-three with a refined, modern outlook. College students should marry other college students. She was half-baked, just from a technical school. He could kick himself for making such a mistake.

He must re-organize his life, not muddle along like this. Where the hell had she gone?

In fact, after work she'd bolted out of the bureau to head for a shop selling women's clothes.

The thought of ten years off had thrown Yuejuan into raptures and fired her imagination. A woman one year short of forty, she was suddenly restored to a girl of twenty-nine. For her this heaven-sent stroke of luck was a boon not all the money in the world could buy.

Twenty-nine — to be so young was glorious! She glanced down at her faded, drab, unprepossessing uniform with a stab of pained resentment. Hurrying into the shop she pounded up to the section displaying the latest fashions, her eyes scanning the dazzling costumes hanging there till a scarlet dress with a white gauze border struck her. She asked to try it on. The salesgirl looked her up and down, her impassive face cold and stony, her cold look implying contempt.

"Well? Aren't I fit to wear this?" Yuejuan fumed inwardly, as she often had in recent years when shopping for clothes, because whenever something took her fancy Zhenhai always ticked her off: "That makes you look like mutton dressed like lamb." What was wrong with that? Did she have to dress like an old woman? Generally she went home in a rage without buying anything, to squabble with him all night. How unlucky she was, landed for life with such a stick-in-the-mud.

Why stop to argue with the salesgirl? I'll pay for what I buy, you hand it over and mind your own bloody business! What did the silly fool know? Had she heard about the directive? This is just the dress for someone of twenty-nine. The Chinese are too conservative. In other countries, the older ladies are the more they prink themselves up. Eighty-year-olds wear green and red. What does it matter to you what I choose to wear? However you glare at me, I'm taking this.

Having paid up, Yuejuan went into the fitting room. In the long mirror the scarlet dress which hugged her plump figure so tightly seemed a rather outsize mass of fiery red, but really hot stuff, really smart. Well, she'd have to start slimming. Ten years could be deducted from her age by a directive from the higher-ups, but to deduct ten pounds from her weight she'd have to sweat blood. She'd long since stopped eating animal fat and ate only the minimum of starchy food, even cutting down on fruit. However was she to slim?

She huffed and puffed her way home, threw open the door and burst in like a ball of fire. Zheng leapt up in horror from his armchair to ask:

"What's come over you?"

"What do you mean?"

"Where on earth did you get that dress?"

"I bought it. So what?" She raised the hem of the dress and circled round like a model with a coquettish smile.

He at once poured cold water on her.

"Don't imagine that gaudy colours are beautiful — it depends on who's wearing them."

"Why shouldn't I wear them?"

"A dress like that is out of place on you; you're past the age for it. Just think of your age."

"I have thought; that's why I bought it. Twenty-nine! Just the right age to dress up."

"Twenty-nine?" Zheng was taken aback.

"That's right, twenty-nine. Minus ten years makes me twenty-nine, less one month. I insist on wearing reds and greens — so there!" She was gesticulating like an affectedly coy pop singer careering about the stage.

Confound the woman, at her age, so broad in the beam, what a sight she was carrying on like this because of ten years off! Zheng shut his eyes, then opened them abruptly to glare at her.

"The higher-ups are issuing this directive so as to give full play to cadres' youthful vitality and speed up modernization, not so that you'll dress up!"

"How does dressing up affect modernization?" She sprang to her feet. "Does the directive forbid us to dress up? Eh?"

"I mean you can't dress up without taking into account your appearance and figure...."

"What's wrong with my figure?" Touched on a sore spot she struck back. "I'll tell you a home truth. You think me fat; I think you scrawny, scrawny as a pullet, with deep lines like tramways on your forehead, and you can't walk three steps without wheezing. Bah! I wanted an intellectual for a husband. But with you, what better treatment have we had? You're nothing but an intellectual in name. No decent clothes, no decent place to live in. Well? Now I'm twenty-nine, still young, I can find a pedlar anywhere in the street who's better off than you, whether he sells peanuts or sugar-coated haws."

"Go ahead then and find one."

"It's easy. We'll divorce today, and tomorrow I'll register my new marriage."

"Let's divorce then."

With that the fat was in the fire. Normally Yuejuan kept talking of "divorce" while to Zheng the term was taboo. Now that devil was using it too. Of all the gall! This wouldn't do.

It was all the fault of those damn researchers. She butted her husband with her head and raged:

"Deducting ten years has sent you round the bend. Who are you to want a divorce? No way!"

"You think by deducting ten years you can have your way in everything — you're crazy!"

"Little Lin, there's a dance tomorrow at the Workers' Cultural Palace. Here's a ticket for you." Big Sister Li of the trade union beckoned to Lin Sufen.

Ignoring her, Sufen quickened her step and hurried out of the bureau.

Take off ten years and she was only nineteen. No one could call her an old maid any more. The trade union needn't worry about a slip of a girl. She didn't need help from the matchmakers' office either. Didn't need to attend dances organized to bring young people together. All that was done with!

Unmarried at twenty-nine she found it hard to bear the pitying, derisive, vigilant or suspicious glances that everyone cast at her. She was pitied for being single, all alone; scoffed at for missing the bus by being too choosy; guarded against as hyper-sensitive and easily hurt; suspected of being hysterical and warped. One noon when she went to the boiler room to poach herself two eggs in a bowl of instant noodles, she heard someone behind her comment:

"Knows how to cosset herself."

"Neurotic."

She swallowed back tears. If a girl of twenty-nine poached herself two eggs instead of having lunch in the canteen, did that make her neurotic? What theory of psychology was that?

Even her best friends kept urging her to find a man to share her life. As if to be single at twenty-nine were a crime, making her a target of public criticism, a natural object of gossip. The endless idle talk had destroyed her peace of mind. Was there nothing more important in the world, no more urgent business than finding yourself a husband? How wretched, hateful, maddening and ridiculous!

Now she had been liberated. I'm a girl of nineteen, so all of you shut up! She looked up at the clear blue sky flecked with small white clouds like handkerchiefs to gag those officious gossips. Wonderful! Throwing out her chest, glancing neither to right nor left, she hurried with a light step to the bicycle shed, found her "Pigeon" bicycle and flew off like a pigeon herself through the main gate.

It was the rush hour. The crowded streets were lined with state stores, collectively run or private shops. Pop music sounded on all sides. "I love you...." "You don't love me...." "I can't live without you...." "You've no place in your heart for me...." To hell with that rubbish!

Love was no longer old stock to be sold off fast. At nineteen she had plenty of time, plenty of chances. She must give top priority now to studying and improving herself. Real knowledge and ability could benefit society and create happiness for the people, thereby earning her respect, enriching her life and making it more significant. Then love would naturally seek her out and of course she wouldn't refuse it. But it should be a quiet, deep, half-hidden love.

She must get into college. Nineteen was just the age to go to college. There was no time to be wasted. If she did well in a television college or night school she could get a diploma. Still those weren't regular universities, not up to Beijing or Qinghua. Her life had been ruined by the interruption to her education. Strictly speaking she had reached only primary school standard, because in her fourth year in primary school the "cultural revolution" had started; but after skipping about in the alley for several years she counted as having finished her primary education. In middle school she felt as dizzy as if in a plane, unable to grasp nine-tenths of what they were taught, yet somehow or other she managed to graduate. Sent down to the country to steel herself by labour, she had forgotten the little she'd learned. When the "revolution" ended she went back to the city to wait for a job, but none materialized. She contrived to get into the service team under the bureau, though that was a collective, not state-run. Reckoning up like this, it seemed there was only one way for her to spend the rest of her life — find a husband, start a family, wash nappies, buy oil, salt, soya sauce, vinegar and grain, change the gas cylinder and squabble.

Was that all there was to life? It wasn't enough for Sufen. One should achieve something, leave something behind. But with her primary school level education, unable to grow rice or to mine coal, she was neither worker nor peasant, an "intellectual" with no education, a wretched ghost cut off from humankind.

She'd started from ABC. Spent practically all her spare time attending classes, and most of her pay on school fees and textbooks. Chinese, maths, English, drawing — she studied them all. But this method of catching up was too slow, too much of a strain. She wanted a crash course. Her age was against her. If she couldn't get quicker results, even if she ended up fully proficient it would be too late for her to win recognition.

She concentrated on English, hoping to make a breakthrough. Studied different textbooks, radio materials, TV classes and crash courses all at the same time. After a month she discovered that this breach was already besieged by countless others. All elderly bachelors or unmarried girls like her, trying to find a short cut to success. And this wasn't a short cut either. Even if you gained a good grasp of English what use would it be in China which is still backward as far as culture is concerned? Translate English into Chinese? Chinese into English? There were plenty of good translators among the graduates from foreign languages colleges. Who was going to look for new talents among young people waiting for employment?

She transferred to the "Correspondence College for Writers". Why not write stories or poems to disclose all the frustrations, uncertainties and aspirations of our generation? Let the reading public and youth of the twenty-first century know that for one brief phase in China the younger generation was unfairly treated and stupefied by history. Through no fault of their own they had lost all that should have been theirs by right and burdened with a heavy load they hadn't deserved. They would have to live out their lives weighed down by this crushing burden.

To talk of writing was easy. But how many works written by her age group made any appeal? When you picked up your pen you didn't know where to start. She'd torn off so many sheets from her pad that her family was desperately afraid that she was possessed. Apparently not everyone could be a writer.

Then what about studying accountancy? Accountants were in great demand....

She couldn't make up her mind. She vacillated, frustrated and unsure of herself, not knowing what she wanted or ought to do. Someone advised her, "Don't be senseless. At your age, just muddle along." Someone else said, "Once you're married you'll feel settled."

But that was the last thing she wanted.

Now this stupendous change: flowers were blooming, birds singing, the world had suddenly become infinitely beautiful. Subtract ten years and I'm just nineteen. To hell with all hesitation, frustration and wretchedness. Life hasn't abandoned me, the world belongs to me again. I must treasure every single moment and waste no time. Must set my life goals, not turn off the right track again. I mean to study, go to college and get myself a real education. This is my first objective.

Yes, starting today, as of now, I'll press towards this goal.

Cycling along and smiling all over her face, she headed for the textbook department of the Xinhua Bookstore.

The next morning the whole bureau seethed with excitement. Upstairs and down, inside and out, all was bustle, talk and laughter. Cardiac cases climbed up to the fifth floor without wheezing, changing colour or heart palpitations, as if nothing were wrong with them. Men of over sixty who normally talked slowly and indistinctly now raised their voices and spoke so incisively that they could be heard from one end of the corridor to the other. The doors of all the offices stood wide open and people wandered about as if at a fair to share their excitement, elation, dreams and illimitable plans.

At once everyone went into action. Some wrote slogans on banners, some made little green and red flags. The head of the recreation committee fetched out from the storeroom a drum the size of a round table and the red silk used for folk dances. In no time they all assembled in front of the bureau. Written in yellow characters on the red banners was the slogan, "Celebrate the return of youth." The small flags voiced their inmost feelings: "Support the brilliant decision of the Age Research Association", "Our new youth is devoted to modernization", "Long live youth!"

The big drum beat a rousing tattoo. Ji Wenyao felt his blood was boiling. Standing at the top of the steps he meant to say a few inspiring words before leading this grand parade, when suddenly he saw dozens of retired cadres rush in. Charging up to him they demanded:

"Why weren't we notified of this deduction of ten years?"

"You ... you've already retired," he said.

"No! That won't do!" the old men chorused.

Ji raised both hands and called from the top of the steps:

"Quiet, comrades. Please...."

They paid no attention, the roar of their voices rising to the sky.

"Ten years deducted applies to everyone. It's not fair to leave us out."

"We must carry out the directive, not just do as we please." Ji's voice had risen an octave.

"Where's the directive? Why hasn't it been relayed?"

"Snow us the directive!"

"Why don't you let us see it?"

Ji turned to the head of the general office.

"Where's the directive?"

The man answered bluntly:

"I don't know."

They were in this impasse when shouts went up from some newly recruited workers in their late teens:

"Ten years taken off — nothing doing!"

"Have we grown up for eighteen years and landed a job, just to be sent back to primary school — no way!"

The children of the bureau's kindergarten trooped up to Ji too like a flock of ducklings. Clinging to his legs and grabbing his hands they prattled:

"Ten years off, where can we go?"

"Mummy had to be cut open when I was born."

In desperation Ji called again to the head of the general office.

"The directive — hurry up and fetch the directive."

Seeing the man at a loss he thundered:

"Go and get it, quick, from the section for confidential documents."

The man rushed off to hunt through all the directives there, but failed to find it.

Well-meaning suggestions were made:

"Could it have been put in the archives?"

"Could it have been lent out?"

"Dammit! Suppose it's been thrown away!"

In all this confusion Ji kept a cool head. He ordered:

"Everybody's to make a search. Look carefully, all of you, in every corner."

"Shall we call off the parade?" asked the head of the general office.

"Why should we? First find that directive!"

Translated by Gladys Yang

中国优秀短篇小说选
(1949—1989)
熊猫丛书
*
中国文学出版社出版
(中国北京百万庄路24号)
中国国际图书贸易总公司发行
(中国国际书店)
外文印刷厂印刷
1989年第1版
ISBN 7-5071-0041-3／I.35
01950
10—E—2431 P